20th Annual Edition
KNIVES 2000

Edited by Ken Warner

KNIVES 2000 STAFF

Ken Warner, Editor

Ken Ramage, Editor
Firearms and DBI Books

Editorial Comments and Suggestions

We're always looking for feedback on our books. Please let us know what you like about this edition. If you have suggestions for articles you'd like to see in future editions, please contact

Ken Ramage/Knives
700 East State St.
Iola, WI 54990
email: ramagek@krause.com

THE COVER KNIVES

On our front cover we show just five specimens, five _grand_ knives. At upper right is a Joseph Szilaski folder of considerable complexity. Going clockwise, we have at lower right, a Moranesque hunter by Jay Hendricksen with impeccable — and not very simple — wire inlay. At center looms Daniel Stephan's deluxified push dagger, very heavily worked. Next is an improved version of L. A. McConnell's little claw knife. And finally, from Argentina, a magnificent _Facon_ and its sheath, all work by Mate Von Der Landken of Buenos Aires.

Ken Warner

© 1999
by Krause Publications
Printed in the United States of America.
All rights reserved.

Published by

krause publications

700 E. State Street • Iola, WI 54990-0001
Telephone: 715/445-2214
Web: www.krause.com

Please call or write for our free catalog.

Our toll-free number to place an order or obtain a free catalog is 800-258-0929 or please use our regular business telephone 715-445-2214 for editorial comment and further information.

Library of Congress Catalog Number: 80-67744

ISBN: 0-87341-770-4

INTRODUCTION

Change. Change. More change. As you look through this, the 20th of these annual publications, there's change on every hand. It's been happening all along, of course, but it is *so* visible now and here.

The very metals of which they make knives change before our eyes. At the beginning, there was O1, W2, 440C and maybe L6. That was that and we lived with it. Now it is bog iron and BG42, meteorites and cobalt alloy, patterned laminates and composite blades. New there are elaborations on the cobalt alloys and powdered metal technology and what-all to come.

Wood isn't even always wood anymore. Besides going out of favor with the smart money (because of a "negative result in the secondary market," whatever that means), wood is impregnated, dyed, transformed and, for all any observer knows, effloresced. And even if it weren't, there are about 200 species now commonly listed for knife handles. Just as a clue, please be advised pink ivory is now somewhat old hat.

And other grip materials fill those catalogs as well. There are at least two knives in this edition with giraffe bone grips. And what in the world is G-10?

There was once a choice of two colors of brass for fittings. Then came nickel silver and aluminum. Then stainless steel. Then Damascus. Then titanium. Now it's all those and blued steel and iron and bronze and mokume and precious metals, and the period makers have gone back to pewter, which you'll see some of here.

And the knives? Oh, what knives you can get these days! They're better, better-looking, stronger, lighter—everything positive, even the prices, if you consider workmanship, materials and inflation.

The whole thing is a lot more complex, even mechanically. There have nearly always been hundreds of patents every year on knives. At this moment, however, there are at least six new patented folding knife locks in the market, and two patented edge-switching devices, and new ways to fold and unfold to boot. Automatic knives apart, there are now semi-automatics, which is a concept to conjure late at night.

Twenty years, of course, is not really a long time. In terms of these annuals, they have gone by in a veritable blink. At the beginning, one had to search to find a custom knifemaker and a hardware store could show you all the knives there were in about eight square feet. This book now lists over 1500 individual makers and at least 50 commercial makers who weren't there then. So that is a big change.

Perhaps the most visible change is what you, the reader, can see. There are three major monthlies now, in glowing color, and all about knives. There are knife shows everywhere now and then we could not even have imagined a Blade Show. Cable TV offers knife lore somewhere every week, and the World Wide Web is free for the surfing to hundreds of sites for knife stuff.

Change everywhere in knives, exhilarating change...fun. And right here, too. It may be that some other hands will assemble this book for you next time. That, too, is just change, only that and nothing more.

Ken Warner

Knives 2000

CONTENTS

WOODEN SWORD AWARD: 2000

RICK DUNKERLEY

Your friendly reporter is about as surprised as Rick Dunkerley is going to be with this, but that probably makes sense -- Dunkerley makes a point of surprising. He shouldn't, but he did this time.

For instance, he's been at it a long time -- over 15 years. He still makes a straight knife now and again. Most of the time he is a sole authorship guy. But all of the time he pops out these startling and surprising knives.

So here with one flourish of an editorial Wooden Sword in the direction of Lincoln, Montana.

Ken Warner

GREAT BOWIE KNIVES

I have known...

...the real things.

by Bernard Levine

I FIRST GOT interested in knives—all types of knives—back in 1971. To me bowie knives are just another type of cutlery, neither more nor less attractive than military knives, pocketknives, or table knives.

Bowies are historically interesting, many are aesthetically appealing, and some are now worth a great deal of money. But for me these knives exert no romantic fascination, so I have not gotten bogged down in the bloody legends and preposterous lore with which generations of writers and collectors have swamped these straightforward artifacts of American cutlery history.

Everyone, or so it seems, has his own mental image of a what a bowie knife ought to look like. Each one of these images is right, and nearly every one of them is wrong.

These images are right in the sense that a "bowie knife" is pretty much anything you want it to be—and this has been true since James Bowie's name first came to be associated with knives back in the late 1820s. Bowie's exploits were recounted in

words, not in pictures, and men seeking or making "a knife like Bowie's" gave their imaginations free rein. Until a few years

Bernard Levine, whose Bowie experiences these are.

ago, only a handful of people had ever actually seen Bowie's original knife.

Bowie knife images are usually wrong in that both James Bowie's actual knife (given to him by his brother Rezin), and knives later made to order for Rezin Bowie (according to Rezin, James never wanted anything more to do with knives as weapons after the Vidalia Sandbar Fight), do not look much like the standard bowie designs popular in the 1840s-1870s period. They look even less like the bowie-style hunting knives of the 1880s-1930s period, and nothing at all like the so-called "classic bowie knives" dreamed up in the 1940s and 1950s.

Three years ago I went through my files of photographs, picking out pictures of counterfeit, fake, and fantasy bowie knives, for inclusion in Gerald Witcher's excellent book, *Counterfeiting Antique Cutlery*. Whenever I came to a picture of a real bowie, I reluctantly had to pass it by—after all, the book was only about counterfeits. But at the time I thought, "Gee, I have seen a lot of nice bowies over the years, and owned—or at least photographed—quite a few choice ones. Someday I should gather these pictures all together..."

Before I get to the bowies that I have photographed myself, I want to address the topic of the "original" bowie knife. A number of collectors believe they own the original bowie. All but one of them are wrong.

Since the mid-19th century it has been known that shortly after James Bowie used his brother's knife to kill Major Norris Wright during the Vidalia Sandbar Fight, September 19, 1827, Bowie gave a knife to Edwin Forrest. Forrest identified this knife as the actual "hunting knife" Bowie had used in the fatal affray.

Edwin Forrest (1806-1872), a dramatic actor, was America's first widely popular entertainment celebrity. At his New York City stage debut in 1820 he was barely 14. In 1826-27 Forrest made his first national tour. Everywhere that he performed he inspired mass hysteria, and at least two actual riots—imagine Lord Byron, Elvis Presley, and James Dean all rolled into one. James Bowie had seen Forrest perform in New Orleans on the actor's first tour, and had met him socially there, as well.

Even then, when he was just 21, Forrest's arms collection was already world-renowned. It included custom weapons made for his own use, over-sized stage weapons made for his performances, and famous weapons that had belonged to emperors, kings, and generals.

In later years Forrest displayed the supposed Bowie knife and its scabbard in his glass-fronted cabinet of arms. In 1873, the year after Forrest died, his mansion in Philadelphia was severely damaged by fire. Later historians and collectors who have been aware of Forrest's arms collection assumed that the cabinet and its contents had all been destroyed in the conflagration.

The late William R. Williamson, eminent bowie collector of California, had learned of Forrest's arms cabinet in the 1960s. Bill detested libraries and museums, but he was a bloodhound for research out in the real world. He returned over and over again to Philadelphia, not satisfied that Forrest's collection could have totally disappeared—some charred relics, at least, must have survived the fire.

Finally, in 1988, he learned that the cabinet of arms had not even been in the mansion when the house burned. Years earlier Forrest had had it moved to his even larger summer home, outside of Philadelphia. After Forrest died, he left that suburban house in trust, to serve as a home for indigent actors. The cabinet had been sealed while Forrest still lived, and remained so still in 1988. Inside were the guns, the swords, and the knife that was supposed to have been Bowie's.

At least James Bowie was supposed to have told Forrest it was the knife. He would have had no reason to lie about it. It was Rezin Bowie who was the knife fancier in the family, not James.

By 1988 Forrest's estate had fallen on hard times. His heirs had decided to liquidate the arms collection. Bill Williamson purchased the Bowie knife, another knife, several pistols, and the original cabinet itself.

Of course no one can prove that the knife in the cabinet was really the same one sent to Forrest by Bowie. Even if someone could, that would still not prove that Bowie had sent the actual knife he had used at Vidalia Sandbar.

Further clouding the issue is Mr. Williamson's penchant for intrigue. However, I knew Bill more than 20 years. And, after he brought home "The Knife", he spoke to me on the telephone for three hours, recounting in detail the trail he had followed to locate, identify, and acquire it. That story had the ring of truth, and

This is it; the knowledgeable, which includes this writer (and the editor), believe this is the knife of Bowie's Sandbar Fight; there is no other viable candidate.

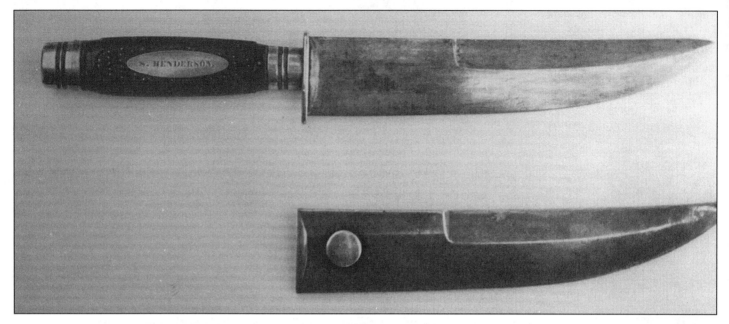

The classic Searles, commissioned of Searles by Rezin Bowie to give to Steven Henderson. It might have been the first thus commissioned.

some of its details I could confirm from other sources.

I am satisfied that this knife is probably the original bowie knife—or a knife as nearly like it as we ever are going to find. It is a large plain knife, without a guard. The handle slabs are checkered, and secured by three large rivets with silver burrs. Although its sheath is silver mounted, the knife does not look professionally made.

Rezin Bowie later wrote that he himself had made the knife which he had given to his brother James, prior to the Vidalia sandbar fight. Other Bowie family members claimed that "made" should not be taken literally—that Rezin in fact had commissioned the knife from a neighbor and sometime employee of the brothers named Jesse Clifft. If true, then Clifft would have forged the blade at his own blacksmith shop, located in Marksville, Louisiana, the seat of Avoyelles Parish where the Bowie brothers resided. A sheriff's inventory of that smithy still survives from 1830, when Clifft fled his debts in Louisiana to join Stephen Austin's colony in Texas.

While James Bowie supposedly did not relish the fame that his brother's knife

had brought him, Rezin evidently did. However Rezin graciously acknowledged that "The improvement in its [the bowie knife's] fabrication and the state of perfection which it has since acquired from experienced cutlers, was not brought about through my agency." However Rezin in fact did commission presentation knives from at least two such professional cutlers, examples of which survive in museum collections. And these are not the only surviving bowies by those particular makers.

Most likely the first cutler approached by Rezin Bowie was Daniel Searles (1782-1860). A native of Maryland, who subsequently plied his trades (gunsmith, cutler, and engraver) in Ohio, Indiana, and Louisiana, Searles had set up shop in Baton Rouge, the Louisiana state capital, in 1828—mere months after the sandbar fight. Many prominent citizens of Louisiana emulated Rezin Bowie, ordering bowie knives from Searles either for themselves or as gifts.

One recipient of a presentation Searles knife, about 1830, was a prominent New Orleans attorney named Steven Henderson, Jr. A decade ago Hend-

erson's great-great-great-grandson, also an attorney in New Orleans, sent me photos of the knife, which was then still in the family.

This foot-long knife has a straight-backed blade with a sharp false edge ground along both sides, and a minimal guard little wider than the blade. It has coin silver mounts, including silver pins inlaid in the checkered ebony handle, and a beautifully fitted silver scabbard. The recipient's name, S. HENDERSON, is engraved on a large, oval, silver escutcheon set into the reverse side of the handle (where it would show when the knife was worn). The maker's name, D. SEARLES, is engraved on a small, oval, gold escutcheon inlaid into the back edge of the blade. [This type of gold "back" used by Searles inspired the 1940s legends about bowie knives with "brass backs."]

The other cutler known to have made presentation knives for Rezin Bowie was Henry Schively, Jr. (worked c1810-1849), of Philadelphia. Up into the 1830s Philadelphia was the principal metropolis of the United States—eventually supplanted by New York City, once the Erie Canal (opened

This Schively Bowie, a fine specimen, is connected to Henry Clay and to the redoubtable Davy Crockett, who died with Bowie.

1825) provided inland water connection from New York to the Midwest. Around 1830 America's leading merchants, lawyers, and medical men all lived in Philadelphia. In 1832 Rezin Bowie was treated for an eye ailment by one of Philadelphia's leading physicians, Dr. William Pepper, Sr. Doctor Pepper was a neighbor and customer of Henry Schively, Jr.

Schively was the third of what were to be four generations of surgical instrument makers who worked in Philadelphia for about a century—from the late 18th century to about 1875. Surgical instruments were the most refined form of cutlery. The finest American bowie knives, and London hunting knives, too (see my article about these in *Knives '98*), were crafted by surgical instrument makers.

Schively bowies are as distinctive as Searles knives, and distinctively different, too. They have wider flatter handles than Searles's bowies, and Schively handles are shaped to fit the hand. They too are checkered, though I have never seen one with pique (pin-worked) checkering. Schively blades are wider, and less acutely pointed than Searles blades. They have a curved false edge ground only along one side of the straight back—the antecedent of later clip-point bowie blades. Schively used slightly larger cross-guards than Searles did—Forrest's "original" bowie knife has no guard at all.

The finest condition early bowie I have ever seen was a giant Schively with 16-inch blade, silver mounts, and checkered ivory handle. This lightweight elegant knife was in mint condition, with all of its original finish—the same distinctive bi-directional crocus polish used on long-bladed Liston amputation knives. Alas the day I saw that knife, in Southern California, I did not have a camera with me.

But James Taylor did have a camera along, when he visited the library in the town of Bedford, Massachusetts. There resides an unmarked Schively-style bowie, with a most remarkable provenance.

The knife was donated to the town by a descendant of Henry Clay, long-time leader of the Whig party, and its candidate for president in 1832 and 1844. In 1835 Clay, then a Senator from Kentucky, had been given the knife by a fellow Whig named David Crockett.

The previous November, Davy Crockett had failed to win re-election to a third term in the House from his district in Western Tennessee. After his defeat at the polls, Crockett embarked on a speaking tour of eastern cities, prior to leaving the United States for Texas.

Immensely popular as a humorist (much like Will Rogers a century later), Crockett was warmly received wherever

This Huber-made bowie from their Sheffield works in Philadelphia was found in Oregon.

The Huber knife was clearly marked and is unmistakable. So is the workmanship.

The crown end was turned and domed and checkered—the simplest way to dress it up.

John Ashmore was another Philadelphia cutler who made bowies like this, but did not, apparently, always mark them.

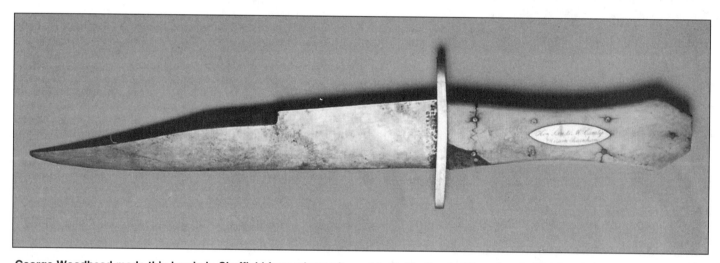

George Woodhead made this bowie in Sheffield from whence it went to Battle Creek, MI, and to California; and back to Battle Creek, getting a little damaged along the way.

he stopped. When he spoke in Philadelphia, a committee of citizens presented him with a "large hunting knife." Evidently he gave this knife to Clay the last time the two men met. The leather of its sheath is crudely inscribed *"Crocket"* with one T. A recurring theme in Crockett's humor was the absurdity of English spelling, and an example he used was the surplus T in his own name, a letter he usually omitted from his autograph.

A year later, in 1836, both Davy Crockett and James Bowie died at the Alamo, in Texas. If knives associated with famous people excite your imagination, this Schively bowie is hard to beat.

By the death of its eponym, James Bowie, in 1836, the bowie knife was already a well-established feature of American life. Cutlers and surgical instrument makers in major cities across the land cashed in on the fad.

One of the first firms to exploit this market was the leading cutlery and edge-tool manufacturer in Philadelphia. About 1826 Joseph English and brothers Henry and Frederick A. Huber had established their "Sheffield Works" in the Germantown section of the city. An 1840 insur-ance assay (three years after the firm's bankruptcy) describes a modest-sized complex of multi-story factory buildings, and a row of company-owned worker housing.

In a circa 1834 printed price list, the Sheffield Works offered tools for all

The presentation engraved on the Woodhead's es-cutcher tells a valid Michigan story.

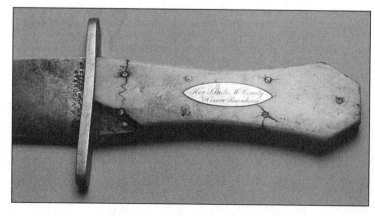

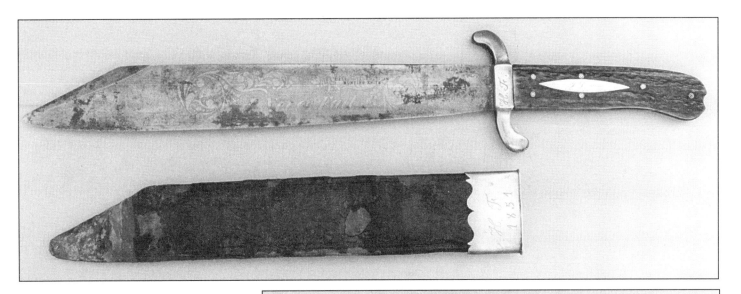

Levine, at right, has stood his ground behind many a knife show and flea market table to learn about knives.

Samuel C. Wragg of Sheffield made this big bowie. Below is the distinctive tapered tang and two-piece shell guard.

trades, as well as cutlery of all types, including:

Indian Tomahawks with Pipe and Spear,
Indian Knives,
Beaver Traps,
Bowie Knives,
Hunting Knives, Buck handle, $9.00/doz.
Hunting Knives, Leather Scabbard, Brass mounted, $36.00/doz.
Hunting Knives, Leather Scabbard, Ebony handle, Silver mounted, $72.00/doz.
Hunting Knives, Silver Scabbard, $96.00/doz.
Dirk Knives, Buck, Ivory, and Pearl Handles,
Pocket, Pen, and Desk Knives in (ditto). ...'

Silver-mounted bowie or "hunting" knives marked English & Hubers, Sheffield Works are well known to collectors today (a drawing of one is the logo of the Antique Bowie Knife Association). Joseph English left Philadelphia in 1837; Frederick Huber died in 1842; but after this, Henry Huber continued to make knives in Philadelphia. Five years ago I photographed one of his knives. It was reportedly found in the 1950s, in an abandoned cabin in eastern Oregon. (The present owner of this knife has argued that it was made in the late 1820s; I disagree.)

This knife's straight clip-point blade is saber-ground, with the flat slightly ta-

This is a Chevalier California knife, properly marked, with its original sheath. It turned up at a country auction in Illinois in 1999.

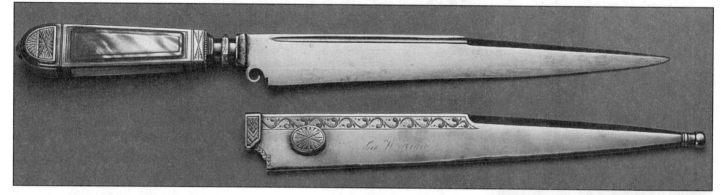

Samuel Bell made tough-looking delicately styled knives in Texas, mostly silver-mounted like this. (Weyer photo)

pered toward the back. It is similar in style to the blades of earlier, fancier, English & Hubers bowies. The ricasso is stamped, evidently with two separate stamps. The upper stamp says H. HUBER/ C. STEEL in two lines. The lower stamp says PHILAD. The abbreviations spelled out would be Henry Huber, Cast Steel, Philadelphia.

The cross guard is flat brass. In shape it is a long narrow oval, with the ends cut off in small concave half-circles. There is a leather cushion in front of the guard.

The handle is crown stag, secured by a single steel pin. The skull end of the crown was turned to form a raised round panel. The face of this panel is coarsely checkered, and is set with a raised brass pin in the center.

Another Philadelphia cutler whose bowies are well known today was John Ashmore. He was first listed in the city's 1832 directory as a "manufacturer of table knives, forks, razors, scissors, pen knives, carpenter's squares, &c. 82 North 6th." He relocated to 50 North 2nd Street in 1847. Evidently John Ashmore died about 1849, but the family business was carried on by his widow, Mary, until about 1858.

Ashmore bowies are large, stout, and plain. They have saber ground clip blades, brass mounts, and one-piece stag handles.

Actually, knives of this style were known to collectors long before their ori-

gin was discovered. Most examples are marked out on the blade with two generic stamps: WARRANTED and CAST STEEL. In 1992 I photographed a nearly identical example with a third crucial stamp—the name ASHMORE. From this Bill Williamson, who had spent a lot of time researching bowie knives in Philadelphia, filled in the blanks.

The great defining events in America of the 1840s were the Mexican War and the California Gold Rush. Both, especially the Gold Rush, fostered great demand for bowie knives. A steadily increasing proportion of this demand was met by the cutlers of Sheffield, England.

Since Colonial times Sheffield's cutlers had catered to American tastes. In 1828 they jumped on the bowie knife bandwagon, and by the 1830s were exporting a vast array of bowie knives both plain and fancy. By 1848 Sheffield cutlers had largely standardized their bowie knife styles, mounts, and blade etching.

One 1840s Sheffield-made style, with a nearly straight cutting edge, was depicted in period comic drawings of gold-seekers bound for California, as a vital part of the 49er's armamentarium. This style of bowie seems to have gone out of fashion soon after 1849, and examples are rare today. I photographed a nice one in 1995.

It is a large knife about 17 1/4-inches long, with an 11 3/4-inch forged blade. The blade has a distinctive flaring shape, with the back nearly straight for about

Levine's Michael Price dagger, the first of his California finds. He paid $3.98 cash money for it.

9 1/4-inches, and then terminating in a straight clip that runs down to the slightly convex full-length cutting edge. The clip, which is about 3 inches long, is sharpened like a skew chisel.

CELEBRATED AMERICAN/ HUNTING KNIFE is stamped in two lines out on the blade. Much of the mark side of the blade is covered with an elaborately etched design of leaf and scroll work, framing the words "I Never Fail". The blade shows no signs of re-sharpening, and the etching runs right down to the cutting edge.

The pistol grip handle is nearly 5 inches long. The two stag handle panels are secured to the tapered tang by six bullseye steel pins. A large pointed oval escutcheon is centered between the second pair of pins. There is a small half-round cutout at the butt, whose significance I cannot determine. The guard consists of two mirror-image nickel silver castings secured to either side of the ricasso, completely covering it. The guard's curved

flaring quillons are slightly rounded in cross-section.

The sheath is made of fancy stamped leather veneer over pasteboard. It has a fancy nickel silver throat, but the tip is missing.

I have seen only one other example of this style of knife; it is described and shown on pages 296-7 of *The Antique Bowie Knife Book* by Adams, Voyles, and Moss. That somewhat smaller knife has a similar shape and mounts. Its blade is stamped, out past the center, MADE FOR THE UNITED STATES BY SAMUEL C. WRAGG/ DIRK-KNIFE MAKER, 25 FURNACE HILL, SHEFFIELD.

The "dirk-knives" made by Samuel C. Wragg are the ornate folding bowies of the 1830s-1860s period, now well known to collectors. If Wragg indeed made one of these fixed blade knives, he probably made both; however it is also possible that they were both made on contract by some other cutler in Sheffield.

Another Sheffield bowie I have examined carried with it a poignant tale of the Gold Rush. Found in 1988 by knifemaker Tim Zowada in Battle Creek, Michigan, this plain knife has an oft-sharpened, flat-ground clip-point blade, and a coffin-shaped hilt. The handle scales are smooth bone, now badly cracked. The guard is flat nickel silver. The blade has no ricasso, but it is clearly marked down close to the guard: G. WOODHEAD. The next line, now obscured, was evidently George Woodhead's address: 36 Howard Street. Woodhead worked in Sheffield from about 1845 into the 1870s.

The knife's pointed oval escutcheon bears the following inscription: "*Hon. Sands McCamly / TO / Hiram Burnham.*" Zowada learned that Sands McCamly (1794-1864) had been the founder of Battle Creek back in 1835, on a site he had first seen in 1831.

Hiram Burnham, born in Vermont in 1798, was a surveyor who laid out many of the new towns in Wisconsin and Mich-

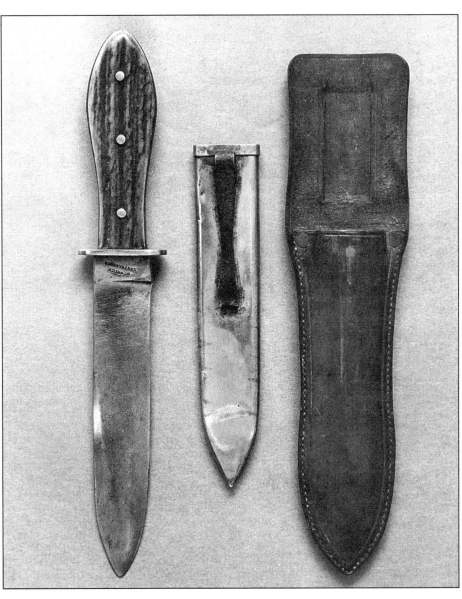

◀▲**Levine paid $12 for this complete Price hunter, with nickel silver scabbard and leather over-scabbard. He would pay $1200. for another.**

igan, probably including Battle Creek. Burnham's oldest son, named Dorr (born in 1825), married Sands McCamly's daughter, Harriet.

In 1852 Hiram Burnham, now a widower, decided to join the overland rush to California, accompanied by his daughter and his younger son, named Giles. Dorr and Harriet Burnham remained in Michigan. Evidently Harriet's father gave Hiram the bowie knife at this time, for self-defense on the westward trail.

In 1851, half of the overland emigrants to California died of cholera along the way. 1852 was not much better. Hiram Burnham contracted the debilitating disease on the last leg of the journey. He did live to reach California, but died soon afterwards, in September. His daughter died there in 1860, but she was buried at home in Michigan. Giles eventually returned to Battle Creek—probably with his father's bowie knife.

With thousands of Americans frantically equipping themselves for the arduous journey to the gold fields in 1849, American cutlers were not behindhand in catering to their demand. Perhaps the best known supplier of bowie knives to this trade was the leading dental instrument maker of New York City, John D. Chevalier (worked circa 1835-1866).

Chevalier made plain, stout, stag-handled, brass-mounted bowie knives, and proudly stamped their blades CHEVALIER'S CALIFORNIA KNIFE. Several examples are known, of various sizes. One of the most interesting turned up at a country auction in Illinois in the spring of 1999. It was photographed by the lucky buyer, who subsequently sent me the knife.

In addition to the usual three-part stamp, CHEVALIER'S CALIFORNIA KNIFE, the flat of the blade on this 12-1/4 inch knife is also stamped with his dental instrument mark: J.D.CHEVALIER/ NEW YORK. The frosting on the cake is the stamp on the ricasso: 184 BROADWAY.

Chevalier moved often, and for much of his career had two locations—one possibly managed by one of his sons. He first opened a shop on the fashionable part of Broadway, at number 182-1/2, in 1841 (listed in the 1842 directory, researched by Mark Indursky). In 1847, Chevalier moved (or the shop was re-numbered) to 184 Broadway. In 1849 he moved the shop across the street, to 193 Broadway.

This evidence seems to indicate that this "184 Broadway California Knife" was made in 1849, the first frantic year of the California Gold Rush. Though dark with the patina of age, the blade of this knife appears to have been no more than lightly honed. Alas the tip of its original red-leather brass-mounted sheath has been lost.

Samuel Bell (1798-1882) was a cutler, a cutlery importer, a silversmith, and the first mayor of Knoxville. Bankrupt in 1852, Bell left Tennessee for Texas, set-

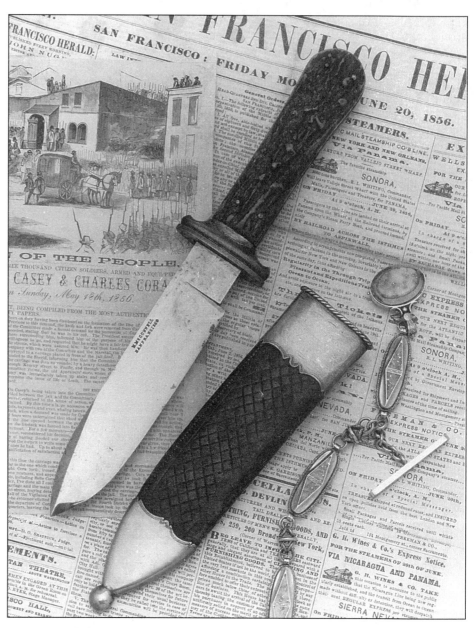

This seems to be the only surviving Bowie by Hugh McConnell, San Francisco's first recorded cutler.

tling in San Antonio. There (according to Bill Williamson) he made remarkably beautiful silver-mounted bowie knives, most of them unmarked.

At a 1989 knife show, a gentleman originally from Texas showed me an unmarked bowie knife that his father had won in a poker game, on a troop ship returning from Germany in 1945. I had no camera with me, but Jim Weyer was set up at the show, and he photographed the knife for me. It is similar in many details to some of the Bell knives shown by Williamson in a December 1987 *Blade Magazine* article.

This knife is 13 inches long overall, and is made in the style of a Mediterranean dagger. Its coin silver mounts are beautifully engraved. The raised handle panels are mother of pearl. The fitted silver sheath is engraved with an owner's name: Geo. W. Kelley.

I began my knife career in San Francisco, and took an early interest in the 19th century cutlers of the Golden City. My first book, *Knifemakers of Old San Francisco*, appeared in 1978 (for an autographed copy of the 1998 second edition, send $43.45 to Bernard Levine, PO Box 2404, Eugene OR 97402).

The first San Francisco bowie I found was in a showcase in a South of Market Goodwill Store about 1973. The price stamped on the silver-plated scabbard was $3.98, which I paid without haggling—even though the mark on the ricasso was barely legible. It looked to say N. FRICK/ S.F. CAL. I was halfway home before I realized that the letters in the stamp had been broken, and the name was actually M. PRICE.

Michael Price, I already knew, was the most influential and colorful of the California cutlers. Born in Limerick, Ireland, in 1833, Price arrived in San Francisco in the mid 1850s. Set up in his own shop by 1859, he enjoyed a thirty year career as the most famous, and possibly the highest paid, cutler in the United States. Price died in 1889.

I found my next Price bowie knife less than a year later, in a second-hand shop on Mission Street, for the considerably higher sum of $12. For the higher price, I did get the seller to throw in a nice pair of shears with it. This stag-handled knife came with both its nickel silver scabbard, and its original leather over-scabbard—the first of these I had seen.

Since then I have examined and photographed many California bowies. However the prices they change hands at these days seem to include an awful lot of 000s. For one Michael Price bowie that I sold on consignment, whose picture graces the cover of the 2nd edition of *Knifemakers of Old San Francisco*, I paid the owner 50% more than the cost of my house.

This knife came from an elderly lady in New Hampshire, whose father had been a doctor in San Francisco around the turn of the century. A patient without the money to pay for his treatment had left the knife as surety, but he had never returned to claim it. Mounted in abalone shell, silver, and gold, and tastefully engraved, this knife might have cost $150 when new—when gold traded at $16 an ounce.

▲Buck Bros. bowie. Without the guard, it might be a heavy butcher knife.

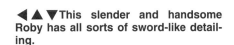

◀▲▼This slender and handsome Roby has all sorts of sword-like detailing.

However my favorite California bowie of all is one that got away. This knife surfaced in the early 1970s, in Oakland, but I learned about it a day too late to buy it. It vanished into a collection in Texas, where it remained until 1992—when it was sold at auction for more than $60,000.

Text cont'd page 19

As well made as any bowie, and larger than most of them, were the hunting knives made for explorers and sportsmen by the surgical instrument makers of London. Some similar knives were also made in Sheffield, and in several cities in India.

Not tools, like American hunting knives, these big blades were primarily weapons. They were used with a rapier-point bowie knife, and sold primarily in Latin America. With many variations in handle style and blade length, these knives remained in production until Collins went out of business in 1966.

In 1934 the U.S. Army Air Force adopted a shortened Model 18 for the tropical bail-out kit. Several other firms, including Case and Western, also made this pattern during World War II. After the war the introduction of reliable metal-cased pistol ammunition. In the 1880s, cutlery manufacturers in Sheffield introduced "hunting knives" made in a simplified bowie style. A defining feature of these fundamentally impractical knives is a straight-sided handle that tapers toward the butt; though awkward to wield, this shape is easy and cheap to fabricate. A later Sheffield executive attributed

THE NOT-QUITE BOWIES

▼The Shakespear knife by Wilkinson of London demonstrates the hunting style of a knife used to kill game animals.

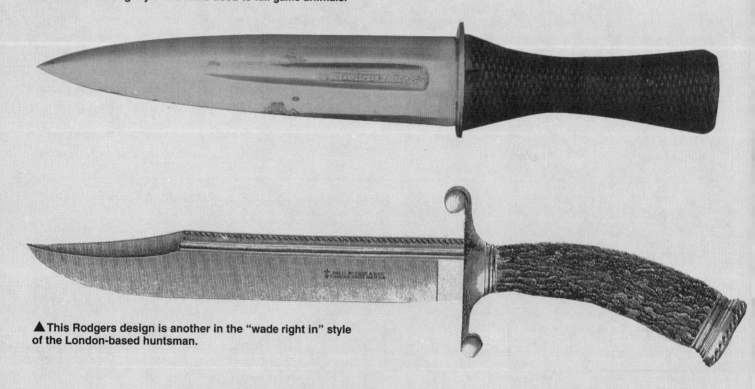

▲This Rodgers design is another in the "wade right in" style of the London-based huntsman.

like thrust for killing deer and hogs. See my story about London Hunting Knives in *Knives '98*.

In the late 1840s the Collins Company of Connecticut introduced its Model 17 and Model 18 *machetes pequenos*-small machetes made in the shape of a clip-similar knives continued in production, marketed as "bowie knives." Case kept the military-style black plastic handle, while Western went with hardwood or "plastic bone."

The bowie knife as sidearm began to decline in importance after 1872, with this design to William F. Cody, who supposedly used knives of this style as props in his "Wild West" show. Outdoor writers of the next two generations scorned the bowie-style hunter as a sure sign of a greenhorn—completely useless, save possibly as a hat-peg. ...

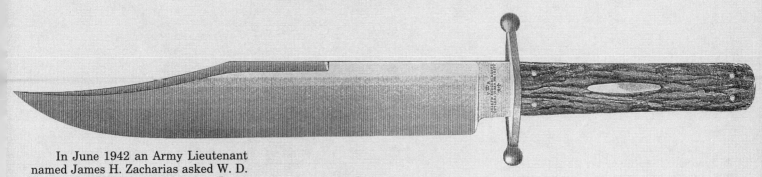

In June 1942 an Army Lieutenant named James H. Zacharias asked W. D. Randall of Florida to make him a "large bowie-type fighting knife." Randall talked him into a more practical design, which soon evolved into the Randall "All-Purpose Fighting Knife," and later the "Model 1." In profile this stout practical knife bears an uncanny resemblance to the earliest bowies made by Daniel Searles in Baton Rouge.

▲Later, this plain, easy-to-make bowie-shape—this is a Rodgers—flooded the late 19th century market.

▼Western was calling this the Bushman right after WWII; later it was the Bowie.

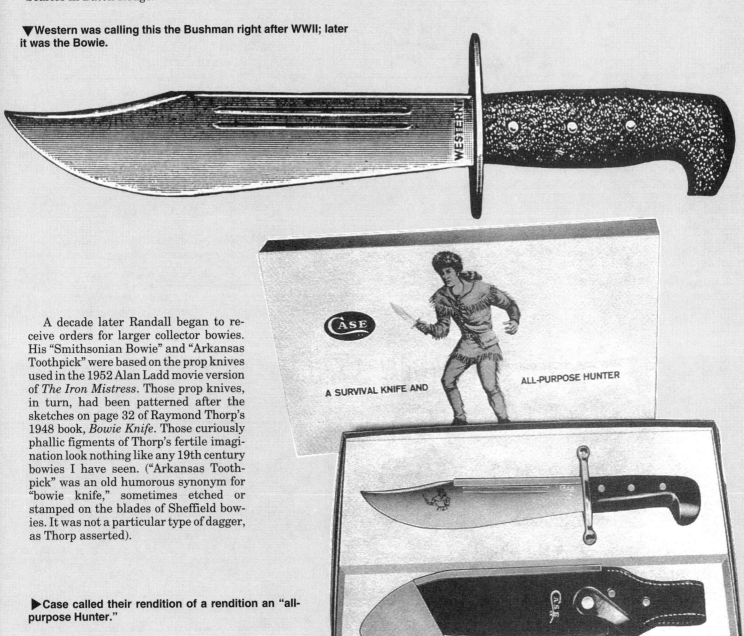

A decade later Randall began to receive orders for larger collector bowies. His "Smithsonian Bowie" and "Arkansas Toothpick" were based on the prop knives used in the 1952 Alan Ladd movie version of *The Iron Mistress*. Those prop knives, in turn, had been patterned after the sketches on page 32 of Raymond Thorp's 1948 book, *Bowie Knife*. Those curiously phallic figments of Thorp's fertile imagination look nothing like any 19th century bowies I have seen. ("Arkansas Toothpick" was an old humorous synonym for "bowie knife," sometimes etched or stamped on the blades of Sheffield bowies. It was not a particular type of dagger, as Thorp asserted).

▶Case called their rendition of a rendition an "all-purpose Hunter."

A SURVIVAL KNIFE AND   ALL-PURPOSE HUNTER

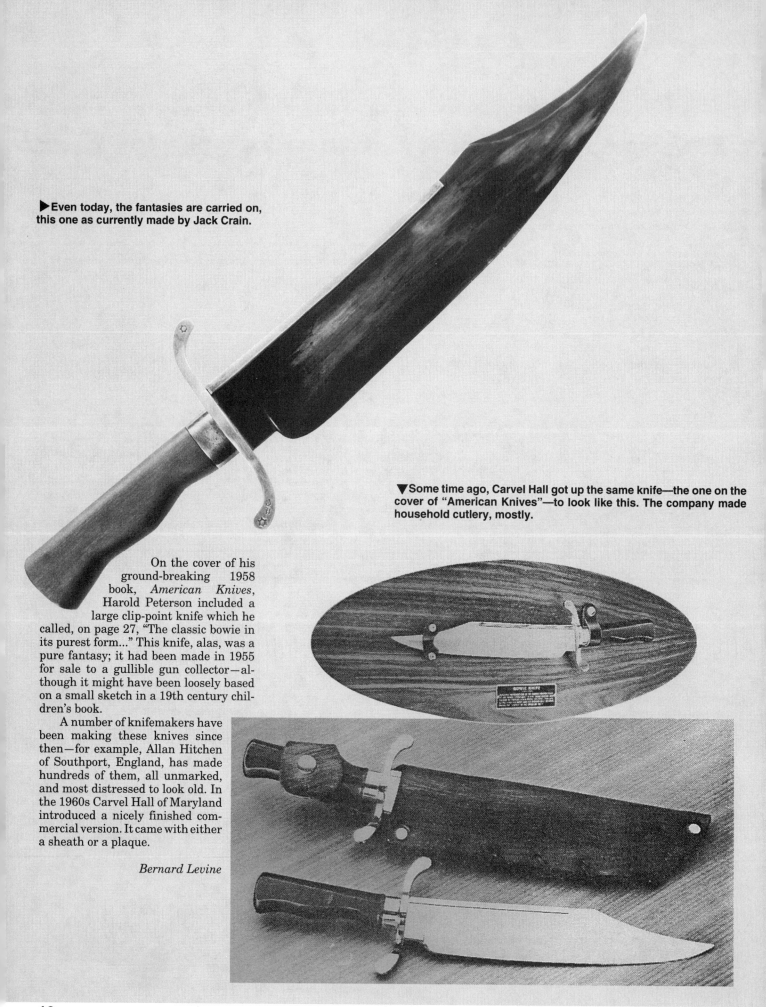

►Even today, the fantasies are carried on, this one as currently made by Jack Crain.

▼Some time ago, Carvel Hall got up the same knife—the one on the cover of "American Knives"—to look like this. The company made household cutlery, mostly.

On the cover of his ground-breaking 1958 book, *American Knives*, Harold Peterson included a large clip-point knife which he called, on page 27, "The classic bowie in its purest form..." This knife, alas, was a pure fantasy; it had been made in 1955 for sale to a gullible gun collector—although it might have been loosely based on a small sketch in a 19th century children's book.

A number of knifemakers have been making these knives since then—for example, Allan Hitchen of Southport, England, has made hundreds of them, all unmarked, and most distressed to look old. In the 1960s Carvel Hall of Maryland introduced a nicely finished commercial version. It came with either a sheath or a plaque.

Bernard Levine

Continued from page 15

This stag-handled silver-mounted knife is the only known surviving bowie by the first cutler recorded in San Francisco—Hugh McConnell. First listed in 1852, McConnell worked until his death in February 1863. He left the business to his employee and later partner, Frederick Will, who re-named the firm Will & Finck.

This superb knife has changed hands twice (at least) since 1992, at ever advancing prices. At this writing it is in the collection of Donald Littman of Oregon.

Much as the Gold Rush had inspired an abundance of bowie knives, the Civil War a decade later did much the same. Most wartime bowies were small, simple, and inexpensive.

Popular with troops on both sides were light-weight Sheffield bowies with fancy etched blades and hollow nickel silver handles—mis-named "cutlery handles" by today's collectors.

Levine has found, it appears, a tranquillity Bowie never did.

Bowie Knife Prices

As regards value, it is impossible to pin a precise market price on any antique bowie knife. While this market is presently very active, it is also both very narrow and very fickle.

There is a definite hierarchy of values, with the most expensive bowies being fine examples by early (pre-1836) southern U.S. makers, and by San Francisco makers. The second tier includes large, early, and exceptional Sheffield bowies. The third tier is bowies by early northeastern U.S. makers. The fourth tier embraces knives by later U.S. makers (such as Dufilho) or made for earlier U.S. retailers (such as F. C. Goergen of New Orleans), and also French makers. The fifth tier comprises later or plainer Sheffield bowies, U.S. factory bowies, plain Confederate bowies, fine early German bowies, and London hunting knives. The sixth tier encompasses bowie-style hunting knives made in England, America, or Germany, as well as older bowie-style knives made in India and Mexico.

Within these levels, both the original quality of a knife, and also its present condition, have important impact on both price and salability.

In the South cutlers, gunsmiths, and even some blacksmiths were prevailed upon to make large iron-mounted bowies, often with sword-like D-guards. Rebel troops found these big knives an impediment to marching and fighting, so usually they threw them away—or even buried them. For years the best place to find these knives was in Midwest G.A.R. halls; Union boys had sent them home as souvenirs. I found a nice one hanging on the wall of an old tool-making shop in San Francisco.

In the North, many firms with steel-working capability produced wartime bowie knives to arm local troops or militia. These included Buck Brothers, the chisel makers in Massachusetts; Rochus Heinisch, the pioneer scissors maker in New Jersey; and Andrew G. Hicks, a plane maker in Ohio. A few years back I sold a typical Buck Bros. bowie to a southern collector who specializes in this brand. Absent the large cross-guard, this knife might easily be mistaken for a butcher knife.

During the war, the Union's two leading sword firms, Ames and Roby, both made limited numbers of bowie knives. Often these knives have sword-like features, such as gilt brass mounts, or fancy etched blades (these are the only American-made bowies I know of with etched blades).

Ames Mfg. Co. had made bowies since at least the 1840s, most notably the Model 1849 Rifleman's knives for the U.S. Army. Roby, by contrast, had only made farm tools until the outbreak of war. Both firms, however, continued to make bowie knives after the war ended, in 1865.

In 1995 I sold a slender elegant Roby Mfg. Co. bowie that was made in West Chelmsford, Massachusetts, between 1867 and 1875. Like most Roby bowies, it had a tempered steel guard and patinated cast bronze mounts. Its handle was ebony. Both sides of its blade were fully etched, sword style, and the etching was highlighted with touches of engraving.

That's the list for now. This has been only a sampling—some of the more interesting antique bowie knives of the hundreds I have examined over the years. There are so many fakes, frauds, and fantasy knives out there that it is easy for the beginning collector to get discouraged. But fine authentic old bowie knives still come out of the woodwork, found by people prepared with the knowledge to recognize them. ●

HOW CAN A work knife made in the millions be almost totally unknown in the US?

This story starts about 1988 at a gun show when I ran across a ring-pull lock clasp knife with a flat, spine-mounted backspring. The knife was stamped "Okapi, Made In Germany" The blade also bore the likeness of an okapi and what looked to be Arabic characters. For those not familiar with okapis, they are African antelope related to the giraffe and first "discovered" in the early part of this century.

Once I owned this knife, I started noticing similar folders in various magazine and book photos taken of rural people in Africa. The ring pull lock system was very common on folding knives of the North American frontier during the 17th and 18th century but seems to

have faded out of the scene during the early part of the 19th. Carl Russell, author of "Firearms, Traps and Tools of the Mountain Man" points out in his book that this style of knife remained popular on the African continent.

I now assumed the knife was made for the African market, but I didn't know much more than that. Then I noticed a front-page article in the Wall Street Journal on, of all things, the Okapi Knife Company of South Africa. The main point of the article was that Okapi had proven it could compete with companies outside Africa for the machete market across the continent. Nothing on folding knives, but the article did tell me where they were and that they were still in business.

My next move was to give ex-South African knifemaker Chris Reeve a

phone call. As it turned out, he was very familiar with the brand, saying practically every rural black African carried one. He also mentioned that most South African soldiers, including himself, carried an Okapi folder. A cheap everyday working knife was his opinion. I didn't have a problem with that; I like genuine working knives no matter what their cost.

Finally, in May of 1999, my wife and I made a hunting and sight-seeing trip to South Africa. Naturally, I had a secondary goal of searching out more information on the Okapi company. This proved to be easier than I expected.

Okapi Knives was established in 1902 to supply inexpensive cutting tools to rural Africans who used them as everyday necessities. These are knives made to fit the budgets of peo-

Finding
OKAPI

by Steven Dick

On his first African trip, Steve Dick found good hunting and a new slant on knives—millions and millions of them.

ple whose annual income probably equals what the average American spends on fast food each month. The company's folders see use carving wood and soap stone, skinning game, working in the kitchen, harvesting crops and a hundred other everyday chores. Up until 1987, the knives were made on contract in Germany for the company. At that time production was moved to South Africa. Along with the simple one blade, exterior spring folding knives, the company offers a full line of cane knives, machetes, butcher knives, and inexpensive fixed blade hunters. Marketing director Renate Voss tells me the company produces 10,000 to 12,000 Model 907E locking folders per day or 3,500,000 a year! That doesn't even count their other folder and fixed blade production, just the 907E.

Along with the various African countries, Okapi sells their knives in the Middle East, Jamaica, South America, Indonesia, India, and Sri Lanka. The knives are so popular and well known in these regions that companies in China, Taiwan, and Pakistan have been known to counterfeit

Writer Dick couldn't get skinners to use his knives instead of their Okapis—they just went with what they knew.

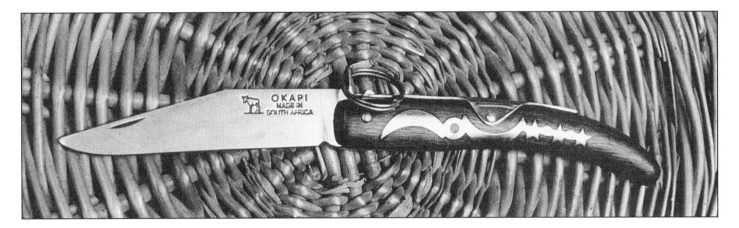

Tough enough and good enough for hard work—they make over 10,000 every day of this model alone. Handles are resin-impregnated wood; steel is 1055 carbon steel.

These two Okapis, one a locker, are on their way to being used hard.

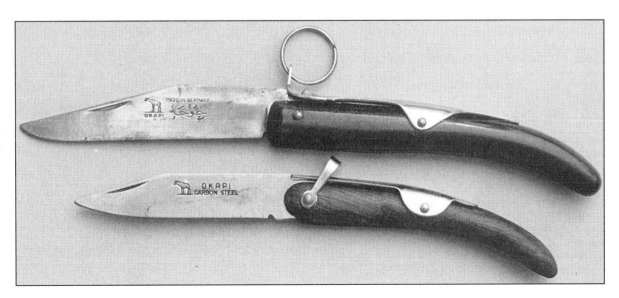

the brand, causing the real Okapi no end of problems. All genuine Okapi folders are made with high quality 1055 carbon steel blades and a resin-bonded wood-veneer handle. Many of the knock-offs are produced with soft stainless blades and plain wood handles.

Getting back to the hunting trip, as soon as we hung up a large waterbuck, one of the skinners produced a non-locking Okapi folder from his pocket.

being stupider than they looked! Needless to say, he sold his knife as did two other skinners. I was probably lucky that everyone in the local village didn't show up with their worn out folders looking for 20 Rand.

I'm not going to try and kid you about the "fine fit and finish" on these two-dollar knives. The ones I bought are more than a little rough. On the other hand, a few quick passes over a diamond hone had mine shaving sharp

and the lock seemed to hold the blade securely open. I suspect plain carbon steel makes more sense on a budget knife that some questionable grade of Far Eastern stainless. Compared to some of the bottom end Chinese and Pakistani folders one sees at discount stores and flea markets, Okapis are quite functional.

The knife I bought from the first skinner was made in Germany, so I asked how many big game animals he

Three African skinners do the job daily with $2 Okapis well-sharpened, might work up 50 animals a year and work such a knife for eight or ten years.

I offered to let him use one of the knives I had brought along for testing but he said, no, he was used to his Okapi. Every few minutes he would pick up a rough shaped chunk of sandstone to touch up his edge. Not only was this rock of very coarse grit, it totally lacked a flat surface for honing. He simply used a circular movement in a grove worn on one side of the stone. Crude, but it seemed to work for him.

The next day I stopped at a trading post a few miles from the Zimbabwe border and bought a dozen Model 907-E locking Okapis. Price, 12.90 Rand or about $2.10 each! The non-locking model, like our skinner was using, ran around 10.00 Rand each. Once I had a feel for what the knives retailed for, I offered the skinner 20.00 Rand for his used knife. This, of course, led to a round of comments about Americans

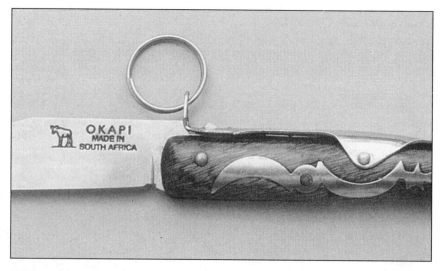

The ring-pull lock device has served as a using blade lock for centuries, goes on 3,500,000 Okapis a year.

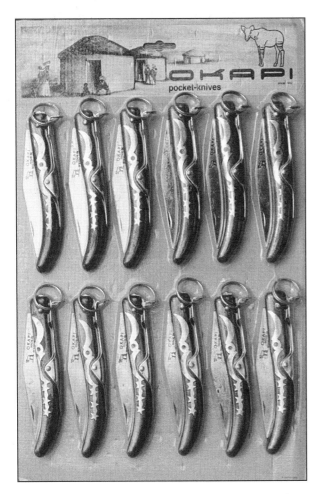

Okapis are sold off cards in working class commercial establishments all over the world.

Even in the game ranch meat shack, the Okapi works. Writer bought knives from two of these men.

had skinned with it. He said had never really kept count but thought it would have been around 40 or 50 per year. In any case, the blade was loose in the handle and sharpened down to the words "made in Germany". All three skinners' knives had seen the same kind of long hard use.

If there is a point to this story it is that there are still people around the world who need knives as everyday tools for wresting their subsistence from the land. While we convince ourselves a $300 hunter is mandatory to process our one deer a year, they do the same job daily with a $2.00 folding knife. That this knife, sold by the millions across Africa and Asia, is practically unknown in the US is astounding. •

**Okapi Knives
58/60 Green Street
Isithebe
Kwa Zulu-Natal
Republic of South Africa
Phone +27 32 4592883/4/5,
Fax 0324592934**

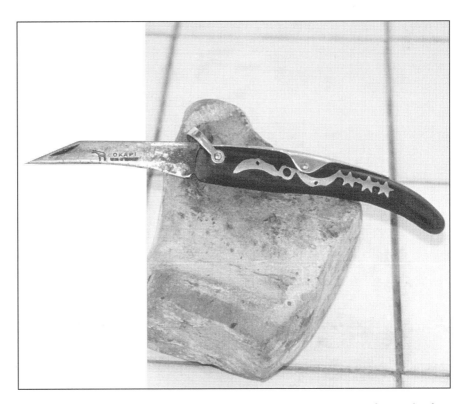

It just takes a sandy rock to keep the tough Okapi carbon steel blade going, and going, and going.

"I WANT TO know what this knife's worth," the tall and well-dressed gentleman told me as he laid a paper bag with a dark rusty blade extending from its depths down on the thin glass of my showcases. I had been discussing the trade of a Sheffield whittler in exchange for a small Bowie with the tableholder behind me, but I accepted the interruption and moved closer.

"They said over there," he motioned back over his shoulder, "that you wrote knife price guides and you would know what this is worth."

"Well, let's take a look at it," I commented, opening the bag and withdrawing four knives, the largest first, with its rusty blade, wood handle, unmarked. An 8-inch blade, closely resembling an old butcher knife.

"I think it's Confederate," he told me. "Why?"

"The guy I bought it from said it was, and I bought it in South Carolina. What can you tell me about it?"

"It looks to be an old butcher knife, I'd say it would sell most places around $5.00."

He was not too excited at my appraisal. "But it's Confederate," he argues.

THE MANY, MANY
PRICES OF KNIVES

Voyles often finds out about knives the hard way and this time it took sweating at a forge.

"OK, I'll give you that much. It's a Confederate butcher knife worth around $5.00."

With an obvious disdain for the value of my appraisal he snatched it from the table, snorted, and pushed it back into the bag.

The next knife was a 5-inch switchblade.

"This should be worth about a year and half in jail, or $15,000 dollars or so if you happen to be the test case from some ambitious headline-seeking assistant district attorney."

"But I'm a collector," he protested.

"There's no collector exemptions to any switchblade law I've seen, and it is a federal crime to carry a switchblade over a state line."

"But look around, there are some over there," he pointed to the left of the room, "and that fella had some." He pointed to three tables away.

"Yes, it does have value to those who want to flout the laws and take the risks. I'm not one of those."

The third knife gave more promise to our conversation. It was a handmade, wood-handled drop point hunter by a known maker.

"I bought that knife from him last year at this show," he beamed.

I tried to let him down easy: "You know that the aftermarket is not that good on wood-handled knives?"

"I paid $175.00 for that knife, last year, direct from the maker. He told me he had picked through two baskets of ironwood to get these handles."

"Did he go up?" I asked.

"What?"

"Has the maker gone up on his prices?"

"No, I don't think so," he said.

"Well the absolute top dollar for this knife is $175.00, but you can't sell it for that, because anyone with $175.00 is going right over to his table and buy one from him today. He's not backlogged on any orders. So to sell it you have to take less."

"Oh." His face took a grave cast.

"Do you know any collectors of wood-handled handmade knives?" I asked.

"No."

"Neither do I, which means you have to take even less."

We weren't doing too well. He pulled out a Boker Great American Story Knife: "This is 23 years old, I bought it when they first came out."

"Where'd you buy it?"

"At my hardware store. They held back one of each as they came in, but I'm only wanting to sell this one to get some of my money back."

"$10.00 to $15.00."

"But I paid $25.00 23 years ago."

"I know," I said, "but you have to understand that the normal discount was 50% off, meaning your hardware store bought it for $12.50. The hardware distributor who bought it paid 25% off of that, $9.37".

"It hasn't gone up?"

"A little," I added, "but you have to keep in mind they made 12,000 of each. In that year, some factory production runs for the entire year were 5,000. And a lot of them were traded for.

"But that's not all. During those same times some of the major Japanese importers had similar discounts, and if you had a distributorship with one importer you could trade for the Boker knives (or other knives you did not have a distributorship for). The importers of Japanese knives had a different price structure."

"What was that?"

"Well, you had the standard 50% less 25% like I mentioned, then you had another 10% if you were a big distributor, another 10% off if you were a really big distributor.'

My friend across the table was getting a bit incredulous, but I kept on. "And you got another 5% on the knives you bought in full cases. They traded for the Bokers from the 50% less 25% rate, so they ended up in the Boker knives pretty cheap."

"Let me get this straight now, 50% less 25% less 10% less another 10% and then still another 5% if you bought in case lots. No wonder these knives haven't gone up."

"Well there was also a 2% discount if you paid cash."

I continued, "So you see if you had been a distributor of Japanese imported knives and traded for one of these

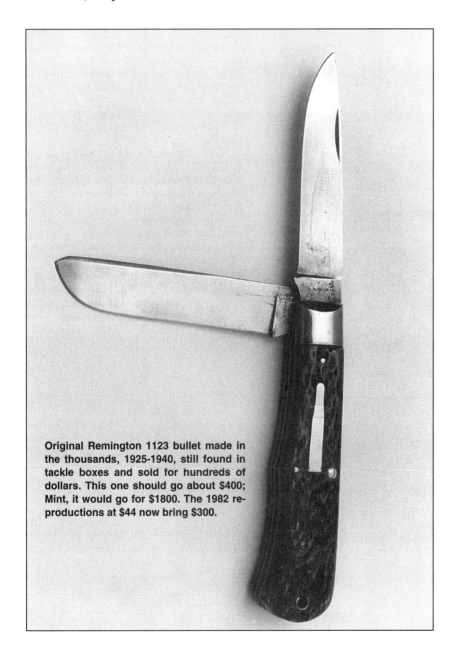

Original Remington 1123 bullet made in the thousands, 1925-1940, still found in tackle boxes and sold for hundreds of dollars. This one should go about $400; Mint, it would go for $1800. The 1982 reproductions at $44 now bring $300.

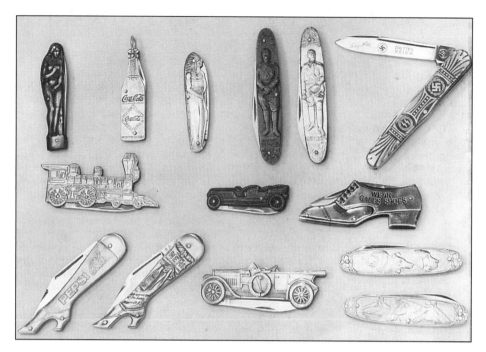

These nice figural knives are very collectible, or they would be if all these were not reproductions, some so good you can hardly tell.

Star Bicentennial Canoe in 1976 had a "retail" price of $30, but was bought and sold between $12 and $18. Now it can bring $20-$25.

Of course, his was the classic case of buying, holding, and closing your eyes.

If you walk into a knife purchase blind, don't be surprised if you bump into things.

Buying without checking what the market price is at that time, then never following up to see if they are going up or down, and believing every line of a promotional advertisement is begging for disappointment.

At the same time, there are a great many people who have made very good livings buying, selling, and even investing in knives. I've been lucky enough to provide a major part of my income, and at times all of my income, through the buying and selling of knives, most of them collector knives.

But to survive within that market requires the players pay close attention. There are the random treasure finds. In the past few years a Scagel was purchased from a gun dealer's table for $25.00 and resold later that same day for $10,000.00. A Michael Price knife was observed being taken to a church tag sale with a $25.00 tag on it when the owner's friend had the elderly lady take it out pending more research. That knife netted six figures within a few months. But for those that prosper and make long term gains in the knife game, it will most often be done buying a knife for $50.00 and selling it for $65.00.

Knowing whether the knife you are anticipating buying is worth $50.00 or $65.00 is knowing where it is along the pricing scale, and what factors are in play to affect that price.

Of course wearing the covers off a few dozen knife books and making knives the major subject of conversa-

▼ This Parker stag muskrat is a great example of a knife that could be bought at various discounts. And when the company filed Chapter 11 bankruptcy, prices went even lower.

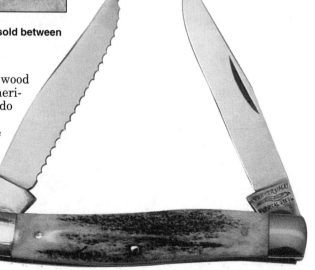

Boker knives, and put it on the shelf, you would have had just over $7.00 in it. If you sold today at the price between my estimates, you would have doubled your money."

I left out that if he had seen the knife was stalled and cashed out and put his money into a knife that was going up about 20 years earlier he would have had more money in his pocket today as well.

He shook his head, staring down on the table at the bagged Confederate butcher knife, the switchblade, the handmade hunter with wood handles, and the Great American Story Knife (Alamagordo model, I think).

"How does anyone make money in this business?" he asked.

"You have to like it," I replied.

He stared at me intently, knowing I wasn't joking and everything I had told him was true.

tion with everyone you meet doesn't hurt. Whether you like it or not, knives, are a knowledge game.

There are other factors though. Like the switchblade mentioned in the opening illustration, switchblades are bought and sold. There is demand. But the same can be said about dealing drugs as well. Both are illegal, both have a serious downside, and most of us choose to not be interested in items with serious downsides.

Dealing in legitimate collectible knives is a lot like playing poker. You don't have to win every hand, you just have to win the big ones or win more than you lose. For instance, I was once handed eight knives with matching patterns, different color celluloid handles, and the knives marked, "Simmons, Germany".

I had just got to the show and a dealer working the aisles came up with them.

"Look," he said, "these must have come off a card, and all are mint."

My mind clicked adding the tally: Swell end jack, $20.00, mint condition add $5.00, Good brand, Simmons $5.00, circa WWII or before name, add $10.00. I figured $40.00 each, maybe having to discount to $35.00, $30.00 each if the buyer took the set.

"How much do you want?" I asked.

"What will you give?"

Dealers who are buying never offer this free

This Case Cheetah came along in 1972, limited in a set. Since only 1,000 or so were made, the $75 price went to $150 and then to $210. In 1975, about 500 more were made. Today: roughly $250.

if we can help it. You know how much you have in your knives so we do not want to insult you with a low offer, and then again you might price it too cheap.

"I can price any knife on my table, and you are going to have to price yours." I say.

"Fifteen dollars each."

"Sold", I said, quickly peeling off the money.

As I walked the room later that day I walked by a German importer's table, and noticed a box of 24 each of the assorted knives I just bought. He noticed me looking, handing me one. "The trademark was expired, I've just brought these in from Germany, you need some? $6.00 each."

Sometimes just knowing the prices is not enough; you also have to know what is going on. In other words, pay very close attention.

The remedy to the above was not trying to rip someone off and get my money back. The next customer heard the facts and bought them from me at $6.00 each, and I spent the minutes after that trying

to turn my $48.00 return on my $120.00 investment into a $60.00 or $70.00 knife. I did. Then when I sold it, I took the $70.00 and looked for a $100.00 knife. By the end of the show, I was back to even, with a bit more knowledge on who I could trust in a knife deal.

In appraising knives there is always an initial question: "What kind of appraisal do you want?"

"What do you mean?" is always the comeback.

This Case Bicentennial folding hunter came with a glass-domed box in 1976 at a suggested retail of $150. Wholesale $75. Other discounts took it to $69. Current value, 23 years later and to a collector: $150-$165.

There are several different evaluations. All based on how I value the knives based on what I think I could get for them were I selling them.

There is the price a knife will bring in a single sale. If I take it today, put it on my table, I can get a price for it. That is the retail price. This is the price for insurance appraisals, because on a given day if your house burns, and you go to a show to replace your knives quickly, that is the price you will be paying.

If I price a knife for a quick sale, such as my scramble after buying the Simmons swell end reproductions, that is a sub-retail price.

Sometimes getting the lowdown is easier, such as at the Boker factory with designer Ditmar Pohl (r.).

But if I am looking at a knife and the collectors I know do not want that knife, or they already have it in their collections, that will have a negative effect on the price. If the knife is an unpopular pattern, or a handmade pattern that has fallen into unpopularity, such as a boot knife or tanto, that is going to have a negative effect on the price. If I know of no one who collects this style knife, that means I have to find the man who will buy the knife out there somewhere in the netherworld of collectors-not-yet-found, which means the price will be less than retail. This is a sub-retail price.

The reverse of that is if I have three collectors looking, for instance, for a Harvey McBurnette pearl folder, and I see one on the table, it is going to bring close to market.

If I spend a year trying to find that collector and cannot find him, then there is always the price-I-paid price, which sometimes is still too high, which means the next price is the "I-take-a-beating" price. Hanging onto a loser is just as bad as paying too much.

When a family brings me a collection to appraise I always

This new limited group from John Russell Cutlery Co., offered at $130 to $225, depending, ignores the earlier reissue which now sells around $50.

ask what their category is. If they want to piece each knife out, go to shows, pay the table, sit there and sell off the good knives, and end up closing out the dregs, that is one price and we're back to retail or less-than-retail as outlined above.

If they want me to auction the knives, or broker them to one of my contacts, the price they will receive will still be near retail, but less my commissions. I can work closer because my money isn't tied up in the inventory.

And still another price is if I hand them the cash right then.

Like everything else, when buying for resale, a dealer is probably buying at wholesale, which is close to 50% off market. The reason a dealer has to buy at 50% of market is when you sell no collector likes to pay market price (or book price).

If I try to sell a knife above book price I look like a thief or a fool. So I have to come down. I cut the price a percentage above what I originally valued it from my 50% discount. Then the buyer lays out a dozen knives, several thousand dollars worth, and wants a bit more discount. Do I give it? Usually.

Hopefully after the discounts from the volume buyers, the hagglers, and the friends who put me on the collection to start with, I have enough knives sold to end up paying my hotel bill, food, gasoline, airfare, and table rent. Hopefully.

At the bottom line the price of a knife is always what someone will pay you for it. I know of several instances when large collections were assembled and due to personal problems (usually divorce; sometimes a conflict with the court system) the knives had to be sold quickly. You know this story is not going to end well, don't you?

Telling your potential buyer of your problems is not likely to create a lot of sympathy. Rather there is something in that situation that causes the blood lust to arise in the more mercenary of our cutlery brethren. Where you really hang with your butt flapping in the wind is when you have this large collection, everyone knows you have to liquidate, and no one who really deals in the knives that you have assembled has enough money to hand you the cash. You then go outside your specialty to a general knife dealer. He may not know the finer points of your knives, but he has a good general knowledge, and will pay you what he feels is a price that keeps him from getting burned due to his lack of specific knowledge of your specialty of knives.

You get a price, but it's not your price.

With all this talk about different prices you may be confused, but that is normal, because pricing knives is confusing. Like it or not, if we own knives there comes a time when those knives will be sold. If by us as collectors, it helps if we know what price structure we are dealing with. No dealer is going to pay full book price for a knife. No collector is going to buy a complete collection of knives he doesn't collect. The custom maker who made your knife has a new generation of his handmade knives to sell, he's not interested in reselling yours. With the knowledge that you acquired by reading, paying attention, and with an understanding of how the price structure on knives works, you will enter the knife-selling game with at least realistic expectations.

There are many success stories littered among the failures. One reason I have the failures outnumbering the successes is to emphasize that if you do not pay attention, you can quickly go astray.

But one telling instance on how things can go right was a knife laying inside a showcase at a summer show in 1999, a small wood-handled hunter. The price was $1900.00. A tag was affixed to the sheath, reading "This knife purchased in April, 1979 from Bill Moran for $275.00."I bought it, and sold it for a profit the following week at a price slightly below market because it was such a quick turn. The collectors who bought it were well pleased.

Once you have laid your money down and picked up a knife, what you paid, what book price is, what retail is, means absolutely nothing. You can have it appraised, track other prices, but in the end someone has to pay you money for it for you to receive cash value. Once the ownership has been transferred, the only real price that will ever matter to you again will be the value the knife is worth on the day you receive money or goods for it.

Note: So you may ask how do I value and sell my knives? Do I leave a list of what I have paid for my heirs should something happen to me? No. My will has very specific instructions on how my wife is to gather the knives, the friends to contact, and the auction to be held. I wrote that first in 1990 in my first price guide, seven years before I entered the knife auction business. Neither my will nor my opinion has changed.

If you don't have a clue what you're doing, if you don't have the time, inclination, or desire to indulge in the learning curve to become knife and knife market knowledgeable, let someone who does handle it for you for a percentage.

The day you sell your knives can either be the best or worst day of your year, depending on your knowledge and your realistic expectations. This article is only a start on that. Good luck. ●

Harman's knife in its essence. It seems awfully simple, but perhaps is not.

The Invented Knife

by Ken Warner

IT STARTED AT a knife show with a fellow, a young and diffident fellow, who wanted to know what I thought of his knife design, his patented knife design. What was unusual here was that Wes—his name is Wes Harman—had applied for a patent on a blade shape. And, of all things, for a blade shape "useful in cleaning and dressing of game animals."

Wes Harman has applied for, and may very well receive, a patent for a hunting knife. His blade profile provides a generously S-shaped belly, extending back to the guard, and a straight and somewhat abrupt and steep false edge. Yes, this is a double-edge knife. The pictures tell the story of shape.

In Harman's patent application there are a number of "objects" of his invention—"an adaptable knife, a single continuous blade, an all-purpose

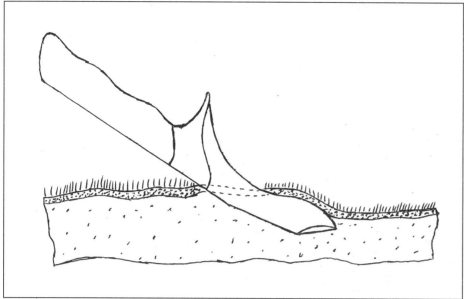

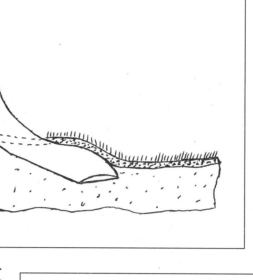

made his prototypes any which way he could, and got them tested by people who did hunt—a taxidermist, a biology teacher and his father. All have provided signed testimonials; all liked the knife; all had cogent and direct comments on its functioning.

So he found a firm of patent attorneys and is off to the races. He is now in the marketing phase (and can be reached at 540-574-3354 in Harrisonburg, VA) and that would seem to be that, except for what happened next.

What happened next was a phone call from a somewhat older man named Launce Barber who has also invented a knife. This one is more esoteric, a great deal more esoteric, and Barber's patent is pending as well. And he knows Wes Harman and claims him as a friend.

Barber is a hiker and camper and has worked in the outdoor retail field. He had come to understand the carabiner—

▲ ▶ These drawings accompanied Harman's patent application and seem pretty straightforward. It's the combination of features that makes the invention.

knife, a means to protect against puncturing organs, a knife that is singularly adept in dressing a game animal." All those can lead to claims.

Harman is not a knifemaker, nor has he done a great deal of hunting. Still, he

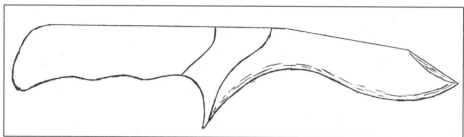

that locking metal loop like a giant key-ring the rockclimbers go nowhere without—and its uses and its appeal to outdoors activists. So he has built a folding knife based on the carabiner and you can see it here in pictures.

And, yes, Barber, too, is in the marketing phase (and he can be reached at 703-242-2660 in Vienna, VA) and is, as you might imagine, actively seeking a manufacturer.

The Barber pictures are interesting. His part is the carabiner; he has cheerfully cannibalized needed knife parts from existing models for his prototypes, although one seems to be all original and, not surprising, that one's the prettiest.

▲This "Tagalong" design seems the cleanest of Launce Barber's prototype carabiner knives, a knife that will be right there when needed.

▶ This is Barber's "Trekker" which provides an interesting combination of useful blades. Neither this nor the Tagalong model are on the market.

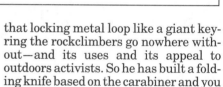

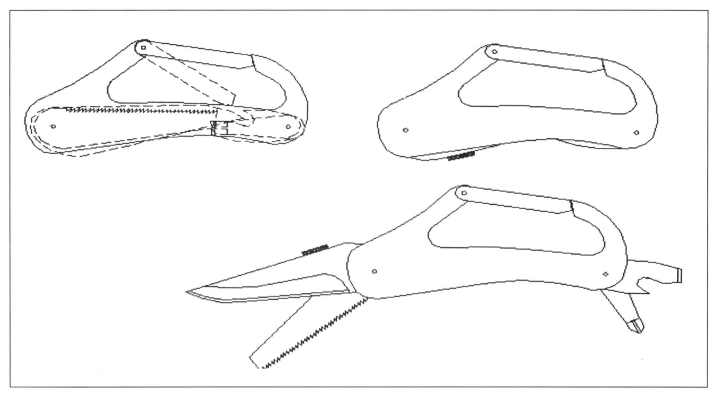

▲This drawing goes with Barber's presentation to potential partners and manufacturers. Altogether, a somewhat upscale approach when compared to the Wes Harman presentation.

mer/pick/mattock/whatever design. In its simplest form, shown here, it's a nice axe, a gorgeous axe, shaped and designed so the blade can turn 90 degrees and become a different tool entirely. It's only a short step from this pretty thing to a multi-tool with dozens of uses, of course, and Sigman is way ahead of you.

In fact, he is also off to the United States Patent Office, as well he should be.

And the point of this little presentation? Well, you're getting a look at these things before they actually happen, so to speak. Kind of fun. ●

OK. Two guys, two inventions, that's enough, right? Nope.

What happens next is none other than Corbet Sigman gets under the wire with his most handsome axe/hoe/froe/adze/ham-

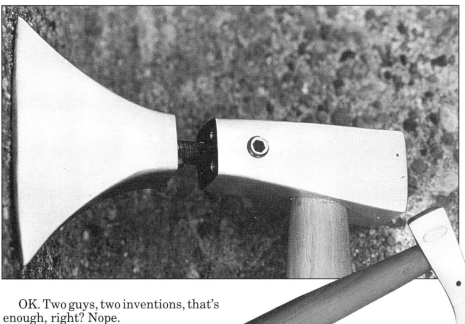

This is the wonderful Sigman axe/adze/hoe, a whole different kind of thing from the other two. And very good-looking.

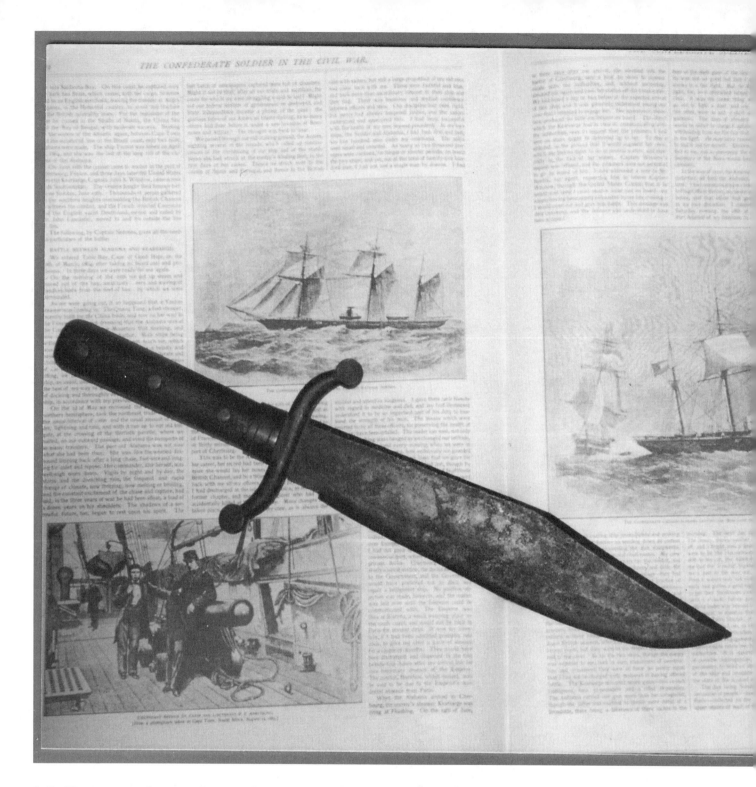

When in doubt, research!
That's what I did for....

MY $50

by Butch Winter

As the story goes, the Bowie was salvaged from the Confederate raider, *The Alabama*. *The Alabama* was sunk off the coast of France in 1864.

THE STORY BEGINS some twenty-five years ago. I was on my weekly pilgrimage to Dixie Gun Works, just looking for something to buy. In those days I was collecting U.S.-marked cartridge revolvers and supporting my wife's custom knife collection. I had this insane notion I was wealthy.

Turner Kirkland, founder of Dixie Gun Works, was in the habit of buying gun collections to obtain the antiques the collection might contain for the Antiques Arms Division of Dixie Gun Works. If there were "modern" guns in the collection, he was willing to part with them at what, to me at least, was the proverbial song. In those days, Turner just wasn't much interested in guns that fired metallic cartridges.

I bought, for instance, a near-mint, Type 94 Japanese Nambu, semi-automatic pistol (called the "surrender model" because the sear projected from the side and it could be fired by holding it by the slide and pressing the sear, even while holding it upside-down,) complete with holster and extra magazine for $22.50!

This particular day there was no bargain among the 500 or so guns on display, but there was this knife. I have to add that Turner Kirkland also liked to buy what he called "trinkets," items that interested him and things he thought he could make a couple of bucks on.

Well, being the knife person I am, the knife in the showcase aroused a great deal of interest. I asked to see it.

I was fascinated from the start. It was a Bowie knife, completely covered with patina. And it appeared to be unused, mint, whatever. Not a nick anywhere, just pits and corrosion and lots of both. But still mint. There was the clip-point blade, unsharpened, S-shaped iron (steel?) guard, ferrule behind the guard, wooden slab handles. And it felt good. Today, all those years later, it still feels good. What did I have here?

Turner came by while I was looking at the knife.

"You like that?, he asked.

When I nodded, he said, "It's probably a counterfeit. I was told it came off the wreck of the Confederate cruiser Alabama. A lot of things have been salvaged from the Alabama. I have a set of pistols that came from the wreck, but when I bought the knife the guy who sold it to me said it was probably a fake even though it is stamped "Murray and Gray'."

"Who is 'Murray and Gray'?" I asked.

"John Gray was supplier to the Confederacy, all kinds of edged weapons, swords, pikes and what all," Turner answered. "But I was told that for the knife to be authentic it needs to have 'Mole' stamped on it too."

"Who, or what, is Mole?"

"Robert Mole & Sons of Birmingham in England made swords and cutlasses for the Confederacy."

"So, you think it's a counterfeit?"

"Well, I don't really know all that much about knives. I just thought you should know if you're interested in buying it," Turner said.

I was intrigued. The price tag read $50. Well, since Rita had blown my $50 self-imposed limit on custom knives right after I gave her the collection, she couldn't complain about this expenditure on an interesting, really neat, probably not original, supposed to be counterfeit, which I wasn't going to tell her about anyway, might be real, had an interesting story, and I really, really, wanted, Bowie knife. Besides, as I said, I thought I was wealthy.

So I bought the knife. I displayed it among the Bowie knives in her collection some, carried it to gun shows, and saw one more almost like it. The second one had checkered hard rubber handles and, if I remember correctly, was marked "Mole" in addition to the Murray & Gray stamp.

Now and then, when I would see an antique Bowie knife expert I'd mention

COUNTERFEIT

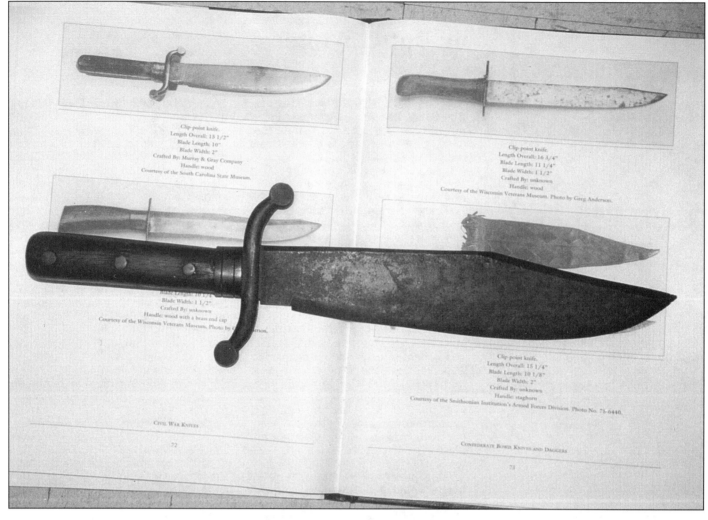

Note knife featured in upper left photo. The handle and guard are almost exactly the same as the $50 "counterfeit," however, the blade of the knife in the book appears to have been cleaned, or reground, except for the ricasso area.

my $50 find. Most of the time my question was met with gigantic disinterest, as in, "Oh, yeah, that's nice." And the subject was instantly changed.

Or, "Oh, yeah, I know about those, they're counterfeit." No more information, just, "They're counterfeit."

Well, it appears to me IF this, or these, since there is at least one more somewhere almost like it, is a counterfeit there should be more than two. And, if it is a counterfeit somebody should know who made it, and where the original-appearing stamp came from, and why there aren't any more floating around. What good does it do to counterfeit one knife? Why go to all this trouble to make one, or two, knives of this evident quality, and not capitalize further on the venture?

Suppose, just suppose, that this is not a counterfeit? Suppose that it, and its mate out there, were part of the shipment of knives for Murray & Gray headed for the Confederacy and the ship, maybe not the Alabama but a blockade runner since the Alabama

was a Confederate warship, was sunk? Suppose there was a shipment of Bowie knives made for Murray and Gray in England and these are the only two knives out of that shipment that were salvaged?

Or suppose they really did come from the Alabama and were part of the ship's complement of arms? The Alabama was purchased and fitted out in England and it's logical to assume that if there were Bowie knives destined for the Confederacy that were needed by the ship, they could have been obtained at that time.

Neither of these scenarios, however, would explain why this blade wasn't stamped "MOLE" and why there aren't more of them floating around. The circumstances explain why they got the reputation as counterfeits. If their origin can't be ascertained, then there is no provenance, and without provenance, there must be doubt.

Well, when in doubt, research. Confederate Edged Weapons lists Murray, John P. – 46 Broad St., Columbus,

Georgia. "Advertised as successor to Happolt & Murray in July, 1862. 'Maker and dealer in shotguns, rifles, pistols, dram flasks, knives, powder flasks, shot pouches, shot belts ... Murray had some connection with the firm of Greenwood & Gray ..."

John D. Gray, in the same source, of " ... Graysville and Columbus, Ga. ..." appears to have been a man far in advance of his time. Records concerning him are plentiful, but most confusing. Apparently he was engaged in making rifles, carbine, pikes, buckets, poleslides, canteens, tents, Bowie knives and sabers, along with various other sundries found necessary in the Confederate Army."

The Confederate Records of Georgia reflect that "... John D. Gray delivered 283 knives and 676 pikes to the State Arsenal and Armory at Milledgeville, Ga., on May 27, 1862, and an additional 317 knives and 769 Pikes on August 5."

Further, from Confederate Edged Weapons, "Supposedly John F. Murray was the superintendent for John D.

Note the stamp, "Murray & Gray Co" within a square, a much more difficult stamp to reproduce than "R. MOLE."

Gray and Greenwood & Gray (one of Gray's companies). No weapons have ever been found bearing the name of either 'Gray' or 'Greenwood & Gray'."

And further, "The Confederate Veteran of July, 1908 contains an article dealing with a visit by General Sherman to Georgia after the war. Upon reaching Graysville, Sherman, seeing a stone building by the Chicamauga River commented, 'In that house an Englishman made swords for the Confederacy'."

Then, after I had researched and written all of the above, I was given a new book by Marc Newman, Civil War Knives, to examine. Lo and behold, there, right in the frontispiece, is a picture of my knife. Well, not just exactly – there is a slight variation in the blade. But the guard is almost exactly the same; the ferrule is there and the wooden slabs show the same weathering, shrinkage, etc. that my $50 jewel does.

It is described as, "clip point knife, length overall: 15"; blade length, 10";

blade width, 2" (widest point), created by Murray & Gray Company; Handle, wood; Courtesy of the South Carolina State Museum."

The "Murray and Gray Co" within a square is stamped on the blade, not exactly in the same place and on the opposite side of the blade, (unless the negative was flopped), but it appears to be exactly the same stamp. Just above it is stamped "R. Mole", as near as I can tell by the photograph.

I was elated! Here is another knife almost exactly like my $50 counterfeit! And this one has the elusive "Mole" stamp. I am beginning to think that my knife is not a counterfeit at all. Consider all that has gone on before: the rumour that the knife is a counterfeit, but a very obscure counterfeit; the superb workmanship; the almost identical weathering, shrinkage, etc. of the knife in the museum in South Carolina with my knife; and finally, the questionable "Murray & Gray" stamp, a stamp not

known to appear on any edged weapons made for the Confederacy.

The collecting world is rife with unmarked, unstamped, mismarked, or mis-stamped items. In many cases the incorrect marking is what makes an item collectible: postage stamps printed upside-down come immediately to mind. Could my knife be one of these?

There has to be more. The lack of one stamp on the blade is not enough to make this knife a counterfeit. Anyone who can reproduce a stamp as complicated as "Murray & Gray" within a square can reproduce a stamp as simple as "R. Mole." Why go part way when the whole route is only a few steps more?

Frankly, I think my $50 counterfeit is just as authentic as the knife in the South Carolina museum. And, although I only gave $50 for it, I happen to think it's worth a whole lot more, maybe ten times more. What about 100 times more? ●

THE MODERN FIXED blade American hunting knife was quite literally invented by a fellow named Webster Marble. Prior to the introduction of the Marble hunting knives at the turn of the 20th century most American hunters used either their ever present pocket knife or a simple butcher knife for field dressing or skinning their game. About the only significant exceptions were the few that used imported English or German hunting knives or the even fewer that had custom knives made for them by specialty cutlers like those in San Francisco.

Webster Marble was an outdoorsman of considerable skill and experience who learned many of his outdoor skills as a cleaning solvents, and many more. However, they ultimately became best known for their excellent hunting and fishing knives.

Marble introduced his knife line in 1899 with the Ideal model. This knife has a fairly thick blade shaped somewhat like a miniature Bowie. Its most distinctive features are large fullers on both sides of the blade to lower the knife's weight. It was available in a blade lengths of 4.5, 5, 6, 7, and 8-inches with the vast majority in the three shorter lengths.

The Marble's Ideal was one of the most significant knives in American sporting history. It was extremely popular for decades among outdoorsmen of all types for most U. S.-made fixed blade hunting and combat knives, including even handmade knives. To this day the famous Randall knife line offers leather washer handles as standard for the majority of their models.

The Ideal was followed by many other knife models from a tiny all metal two-inch-bladed "Trout Knife" up to a ten-inch-bladed Trailmaker Bowie knife. The Ideal was intended to be an all-purpose utility knife but many hunting "authorities" criticized its relatively thick and sturdy blade as not suited to fine cutting. Marble countered with the "Expert" in 1906. The Expert had a very high shallow hollow grind with a much

THE NEW MARBLES:

Better knives and better designs

youth from his avid outdoorsman father. As a young man he worked as a timber cruiser and surveyor in some of the roughest wilderness in the lower forty-eight states. Being of an inventive turn of mind and having a family in the manufacturing business, he eventually turned to manufacturing his inventions in a small factory in Gladstone, Michigan. His earliest products included a waterproof match safe and the famous Marble's Safety Pocket Ax. The latter had a folding blade guard in its handle. The Marble's firm went on to make a wide variety of other products for outdoorsmen including: pin-on and pocket compasses, the Marble Game-Getter rifle/shotgun combination gun, takedown cleaning rod kits for all kinds of firearms, a clever gaff for landing fish, auxiliary cartridges, rifle sights, gun

and was copied by practically every U. S. fixed blade knife manufacturer as well as several in England and Germany. It was also the Ideal that served as the model for the millions of six-inch combat utility knives made for the U. S. military during WWII as well as the Marine Corps Fighting Utility Knife, the Navy Mark II combat knife, and the Navy and Air Force pilot's survival knife that is standard issue to this day.

Marble also introduced his patented leather washer handle with the Ideal. Prior to Marble's introduction of this handle the only use of leather washers as a knife handle in the U. S. that I am aware of was by Collins with some of their machetes and then they did not use Marble's threaded tang. Eventually, leather washer handles became the standard handle

by Chuck Karwan

thinner blade than the Ideal. It also had more belly in its curved edge for better skinning. While it is more fragile than the Ideal, the Marble's Expert with a five-inch blade is to my way of thinking one of the best all-around hunting knife designs ever fielded.

Shortly before WWI Marble's introduced their distinctive Woodcraft knife. The Woodcraft was based on the custom design of one of Marble's customers. Basically, it is shaped like a small sheep skinner with the top front of the blade clipped off resulting in a decent point. The result was a knife that was an excellent skinner with a fine enough point for caping and general utility use. Probably

Marble's also made a clever three-piece Folding Safety Fish knife and a similar Folding Safety Carver. There was also a line of conventional pocket knife models with the Marble's name on them available in the 1902-1908 period. It appears that with the exception of the folding fish and carver models, all of the Marble's folders were made for them by outside manufacturers, though Marble's may have supplied blades for the pre-WWI Folding Safety Hunter.

Up until WWII, the Marble's hunting knives were the premier line of commercial production fixed blade hunting knives available in the U. S. Marble's was too small to take on any large government con-

found that the booming sport of Sporting Clays was a natural outlet for their Poly-Choke line.

Craig Lauerman, the current president of Marble's, hooked up with Mike Stewart, the president of Blackjack Knives which was at the time probably the manufacturer of the highest quality production fixed-blade hunting-type knives in the country. To get Marble's into the knife business full-time, Lauerman contracted with Stewart to have Blackjack assemble several thousand Marble's Experts from existing blades and parts.

These "new" old Marble's knives were snapped up by several knife distributors

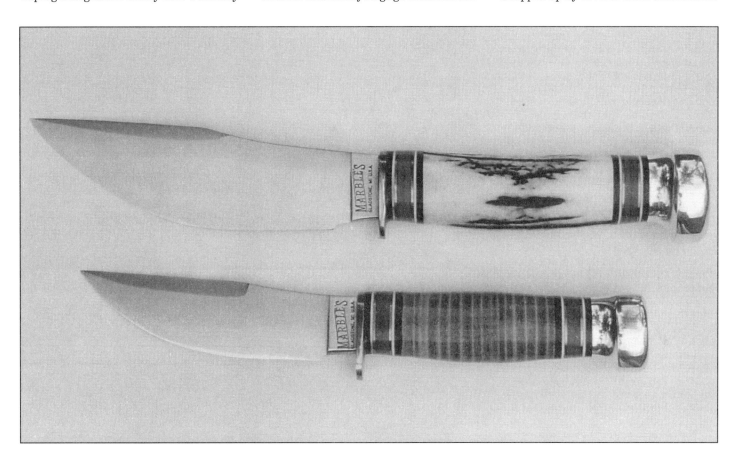

no other knife design is so strongly associated with Marble's than the Woodcraft.

The design of the Woodcraft was patented, but after the patent expired it was copied by just about everybody in the business. I have owned Woodcraft variations made in Sheffield, England; Solingen, Germany; and Sweden and have seen examples made in Finland, India, and Japan.

Marble's got involved with the folding knife business. The first was their Folding Safety Hunter. This unique knife had a blade longer than its handle which, when folded, fit into a folding handle extension. Blade lengths were 4.25 and 6.0 inches and the blade shape was the same as the Ideal. There was even a folding crossguard. After WWI the blade was changed into a flat ground clip type.

tracts during WWII, but their entire war-time knife production was purchased by various U. S. government agencies either for issue or resale to our servicemen at base and post exchanges and ship's stores.

After WWII, the market was flooded with surplus fixed blade hunting type knives like the Navy Mark I and II. It was impossible for manufacturers like Marble's to compete with the giveaway surplus prices so Marble's cut back their full-time knife production severely. Fortunately, their wide line of other products kept them in business where other knife makers like Pal, Cattaraugus, and others fell by the wayside.

Several years back the Lauerman family purchased Marble's with the intent of putting it back onto sound financial footing. They expanded the sight line and

While the new production brings back the Woodcraft (top) it also introduced a cute smaller version called the Fieldcraft that never existed before. It makes a great caping knife and an excellent all-around "trout and bird" or small game knife.

and many collectors with almost no advertising needed. These were primarily five-inch Experts, probably my personal favorite of the original Marble's line. There were several minor problems adjusting the heat treatment of these blades and dealing with pitting on the blade blanks but overall this project was a grand success. Stewart went on to help Marble's set up and train their own work force for knife production.

When Blackjack closed its doors through reasons that had little to do with the quality or quantity of its knife sales, Stewart took over the management of Marble's knife division. It was decided not only to produce various key Marble's knife models, but also to add some new ones. The revised traditional models were changed enough from the old production so they could not be confused. This was done for two reasons—the first was to protect the collectability and value of the old original Marble's knives; second, they wanted the new production Marble's knives to be better than the originals in performance by taking advantage of modern breakthroughs in blade steels and heat treatment such as the use of cryogenics.

The first of the totally new production Marble's knives, was appropriately, the Woodcraft 98. It has all of the classic lines of the original Woodcraft. However, the handle and the choil area have been lengthened 1/4 inch each. It is a simple fact that people are a lot bigger now than they were at the turn of the last century and most people will find this handle more comfortable than the original. The extra length in the blade balances off the handle extension and also allows a safe finger-forward choke-up grip.

The blade steel used is high carbon 52-100, one of the most popular steels with the custom blade forging community because of its toughness and superior edge holding ability. I believe Marble's is the very first production knife manufacturer to employ this steel in hunting knives. It is given sophisticated heat treatment enhanced by a sub-zero cryogenic stress relief process. The result is a blade with a 59-60 Rockwell C hardness that holds an edge to an incredible degree.

Some of the nostalgia types try to push the idea that the old Marble's knives are "better" than the new ones. Don't you believe it! Stewart says: "If put into a hydraulic press edge to edge the current knives are so much harder and tougher they would literally cut the old ones in half."

The factory edge on the new knives has to be tested to be appreciated. They have a convex polished edge I call bodaciously sharp. This is so sharp than when you put the knife up to the hair on your forearm you do not even have to touch the hairs—they will jump off in fright.

Along with the Woodcraft 98 came a cute smaller version called the Fieldcraft. It is basically a 2/3 scale version of the Woodcraft and is perfect for those that like a smaller fixed blade knife with all the excellent features of the Woodcraft. The Fieldcraft has been extremely popular with old and new Marble's customers and collectors.

A third knife was introduced about the same time that has no old-time Marble's heritage. It is called the Plainsman. This is a 4.25-inch bladed knife with a nice curved edge and a straight back. It is a great utility pattern that can do it all and has received an excellent response.

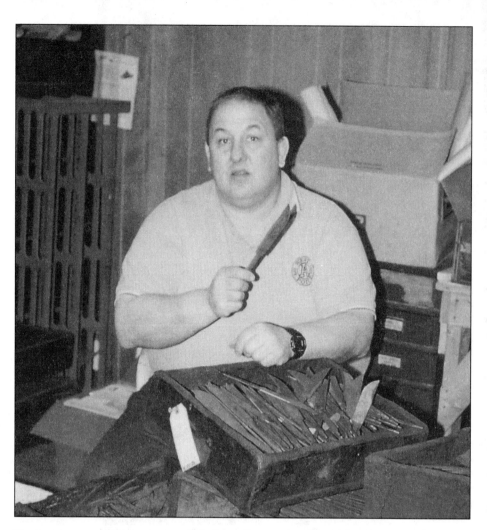

The author personally inspected hundreds of old blades that Marble's has on hand in the Marble's factory in Gladstone.

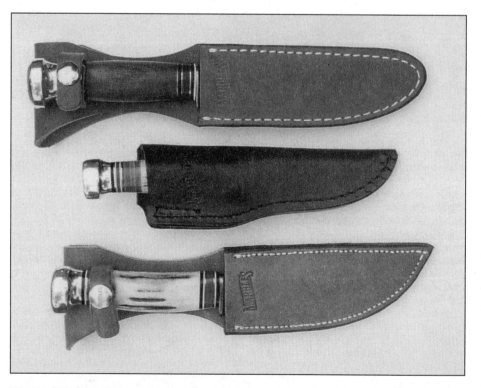

All of the Marble's knives come with extremely high quality leather scabbards. Most are traditional handle-strap models, but pouches are furnished with some models.

The fourth knife introduced was the Bison, another pattern that had no old Marble's heritage but at the same time is a terrific hunting knife of the upswept point type that many, including myself, prefer over the dropped point style for all-around use. This knife has a 4 5/8-inch blade and is reminiscent of the immortal Randall #3 in style and purpose. It is specifically designed to be easy to choke up on for fine work like caping.

All those new production Marble's have the same 52-100 steel and heat treatment as the Woodcraft 98. All come with leather scabbards of conventional style except the Fieldcraft and Plainsman have pouch sheaths which I would personally prefer for any of the knives.

ticularly in the bladesmith community, call such knives "camp knives" a term popularized by bladesmith Bill Moran who in turn got the name from a big old Sheffield pattern marked "Rio Grande Camp Knife."

Whether you call such a knife a bush knife, a trail knife, or a camp knife it is intended to be a replacement for a machete or a hatchet for light chopping while retaining the versatility of a knife for butchering, slicing, and carving. That is just how old Webster Marble marketed it, too.

Personally, I am very fond of these large field knives and the Trailmaker is a particular favorite. My friend, custom knife maker Wayne Goddard, once point-

However, there is a sort of reverse snobbery in many areas where small knives are thought to be the tools of the woods wise while large knives are strictly for the tenderfeet. That is true here in the Pacific Northwest where I reside. If you are seen afield here with a large knife, other than a machete, you will get comments like, "The size of a person's sexual organ is inversely proportional to the size of the knife he carries."

(EDITOR'S NOTE: Most of the early commentaries on the utility of small belt knives were made by men who went nowhere without an axe.)

I don't care, I like these large knives in general and the Trailmaker in partic-

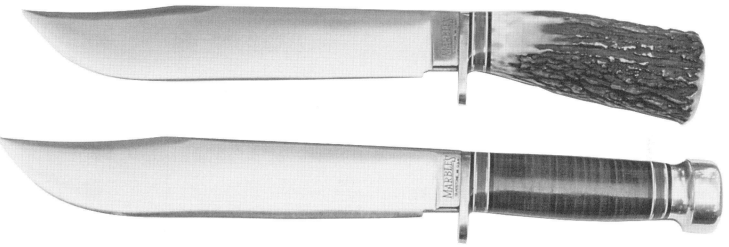

The Marble's Trailmaker was the first production bush knife made in this country. It is shown here with a leather washer or a stag handle. The ten-inch blade of this knife is one inch longer than most production Bowie knives from other makers and it is surprising how much difference that inch makes when chopping.

The Trailmaker is now available in a seven-inch version that was only available on special order in the old days. The black micarta version is only available from the Cutlery Shoppe.

The next knife that was added to the line was again a revival of an original Marble's pattern, the Trailmaker. This knife is being offered with the original ten-inch blade or a seven-inch blade, a length that could be had on special order in the old days. The original Trailmaker was probably the first commercial production trail or bush knife. Many, par-

ed out to me that if you look at the aboriginal and native peoples of the world that live and work close to the earth you will in most cases find that they all use some type of large knife on a daily basis. Wayne has turned his observance into Goddard's Law stating "The farther you are from a road the larger the knife you should have."

ular. They are extremely versatile and useful. I have noticed that when others in my hunting camp see how well a Trailmaker works for butchering and slicing or other chores, they often want to borrow it. However, you can save a lot of verbal grief if you carry your Trailmaker attached to your day pack rather than your belt.

Craig Lauerman, the president of Marble's, behind boxes of original Marble's knife blades many of which date back to the 1930s and '40s in manufacture. These blades will be assembled for collectors on a gradual basis, knife by knife.

Unlike the previously mentioned knives, the Trailmaker is made from 5160 spring steel with a hardness of 57-58 Rockwell C. This sacrifices some edge holding ability, but gains a great deal of toughness and shock resistance that are needed in a chopping tool.

Like the original Trailmakers, these new versions have a convex edge which, as old Webster Marble knew, is the best edge style for chopping that there is. I have chopped through five-inch thick logs with ease with my Trailmaker. A determined person could build a log cabin with one of these.

Marble's most recent addition to its knife line is something that old Webster Marble never had—a dropped point hunter called the Sport 99. The 3.5-inch 52-100 blade of this beauty looks like a Loveless dropped hunter in profile, but the rest of the knife is pure Marble's. It is attractively laser marked on the blade "R. W. Loveless -approved-W. L. Marble" in a football-shaped blade etching. This is the style of knife that many consider to be the best for the modern hunter for field dressing and skinning. Combining two great American knife making names on one knife is a masterpiece of marketing. Appropriately this little gem has a pouch-type sheath.

When production of the new blades began, they were originally marked with the original Marble's tang stamps. However, too many blades were cracked in the marking process so all blades are now laser engraved with the Marble's logo.

All models are available with the classic leather washer handle but most can also be had with handles of tigerwood,

The Marble's Expert, Woodcraft, Fieldcraft, Bison, and Plainsman. Note the figured hard Maple on the latter, a durable and good looking handle material available locally to Marbles, but never used in the past.

or fancy hard Michigan maple. Stag handles with an aluminum butt cap or stag butt cap can be had on special order. In addition many models can be had with a black micarta handle or a combination leather and stag handle exclusively from the Cutlery Shoppe. Similarly A. G. Rus-

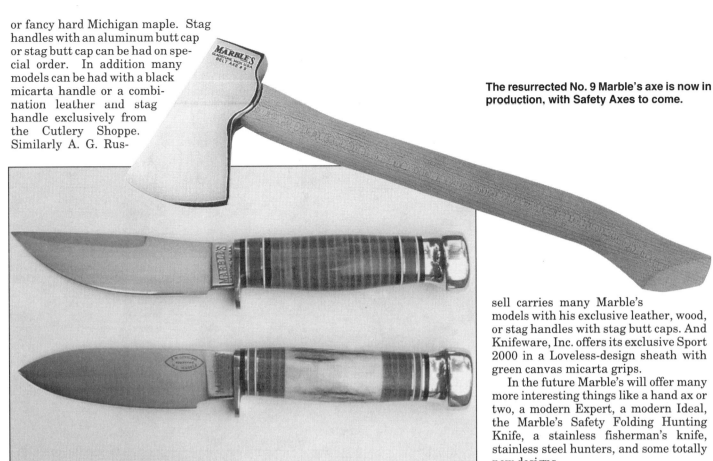

The resurrected No. 9 Marble's axe is now in production, with Safety Axes to come.

When the upswept point Fieldcraft was introduced into the Marble's line it begged for a dropped point counterpart like the Loveless-inspired Sport Model (bottom) shown here in the combination leather and stag handle exclusively available from the Cutlery Shoppe.

sell carries many Marble's models with his exclusive leather, wood, or stag handles with stag butt caps. And Knifeware, Inc. offers its exclusive Sport 2000 in a Loveless-design sheath with green canvas micarta grips.

In the future Marble's will offer many more interesting things like a hand ax or two, a modern Expert, a modern Ideal, the Marble's Safety Folding Hunting Knife, a stainless fisherman's knife, stainless steel hunters, and some totally new designs.

Many prefer the classic American fixed blade hunting knife for field work. What could be more appropriate than having the company that started it all making them for today's market?　　　　●

The Lauermans and a friend in front of Marbles's Gladstone plant on the Upper Penninsula of Michigan.

THIS FIGHTING KNIFE THING...

by Jack Collins

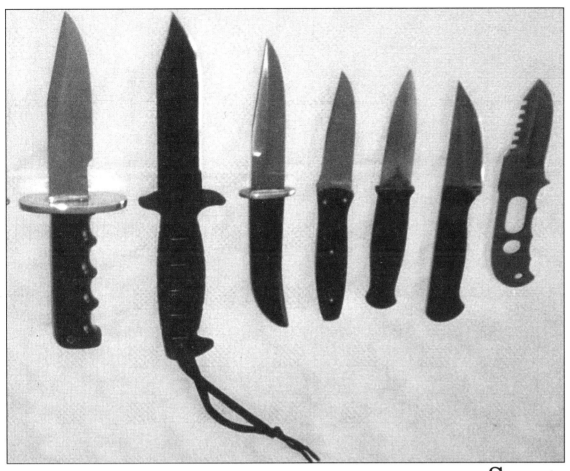

◀STRAIGHT FIGHTERS abound. From left, Randall Attack, Tim Britton Terminator, A. T. Barr Camp/Combat, Buck Nighthawk, Cold Steel Survival Rescue Knife (SRK), Randall No. 1 Fighting Knife, Randall Aircrew, Ontario Spec Plus Air Force Survival, Al Polkowski Boot Knife, Joel Chamblin Delta Boot Knife, Gerber Guardian, Bud Nealy Pesh Kabz, and Mike Franklin Hideout.

◀▼These are all folding fighters. From the left; Ontario Spec Plus Jump, Cold Steel Voyager, Colt Python (Ken Onion), Spyderco (Wayne Goddard), Benchmade Advanced Folding Combat Knife, Benchmade Ascent, Spyderco (Howard Viele), Benchmade Stryker (Alan Elishewitz), Benchmade Mini-AFCK, Benchmade #350 (Mel Pardue). Kershaw Talon. Parenthetical names are the designers, where known. Ontario and Colt models shown come with belt pouches. All others are furnished with pocket clips.

SUPPOSE THIS NATION were to be visited by an intelligent being from another world who tried to learn about our society by a study of our publications. And suppose this being got hold of any of our knife magazines, he (She? It?) would probably conclude that our major activity was fighting with knives. Should our civilization be studied by some far-distant-

From the 7-1/4-inch Gerber Guardian to the 15-5/8-inch Busse Combat Mistress, fighters come in all sizes, all useful for a variety of non-fighting tasks.

future survivors concerned with our demise and the reasons therefor, they might reasonably conclude that we had killed each other off with knives, knives we call "Fighting Knives".

Up until the close of the Second World War, we generally had only three knife labels for knives designed primarily for fighting: the Bowie, the Stiletto, and the Arkansas Toothpick. There were and are multiple variations on these themes. Some would add various large knives, like the Kurki made famous by the Ghurka fighting men of Nepal, and I cannot quibble over such, although it is my belief that most are agricultural implements adapted to less peaceful pursuits.

Of course, no one is suggesting that these are the original fighting knives, since one of the first uses for a sharpened stone was probably to eliminate competition for hunting territory or mating material. If you want a complete rundown on the history of fighting knives, check out the late M. H. Cole's series of books on the subject. I am going to discount bayonets which by definition are designed to be affixed to rifles. Since WWII, the Big One, there has been an expanding list of knives designed for fighting. In our '90s, this list could be described as "exploding".

Any knife publication has articles on "fighting knives". If that publication accepts advertising, it seems 50% of the advertising will concern itself with "fighting knives" or "survival knives". Why, for goodness sake, is this true? Have you ever gotten into a knife fight? Do you even know anyone who has ever been in a knife fight? Neither do I. I would be willing to stake a small wager that there are fewer than 500 people in this country who have engaged in knife fighting "for real."

For our purposes let's define knife fighting: two or more people, each armed with one or more knives, mutually attempting to kill, maim, or otherwise incapacitate each other, "mano a mano" (For those of you who've forgotten your high school Spanish, "mano a mano" means "hand to hand", not "man to man".) Now, how many knife fighters do you

know? We are not talking about the use of a knife as an expedient tool for self-defense or as a self-defense implement against an unarmed adversary, and the reason for excluding these is simple: any knife can serve in such a situation. A rusty tin can lid, a piece of broken glass, indeed the proverbial "sharp stick" can all be used to good advantage as a defensive tool. Our society has long since advanced (some might question this choice of words) beyond knives as primary weapons. The sword was born when? Who was the first person to fasten a knife on a stick and discover that it was possible to inflict damage on an opponent with less risk to one's own hide? Now gunpowder has obviated the blade in any forum as a primary tool for self-defense.

As a secondary, or back-up weapon, the knife has more validity, but not much. Few would argue there are not more effective back-up weapons available. Were we to argue cost effectiveness, the knife might rise to some level of acceptance. However, given the going rate for hand-made, or even "custom designed, factory made" fighting knives, this point becomes moot. One can buy good used small handguns for less than many of the advertised prices one sees in today's knife press.

What then has led to our apparent obsession with fighting knives? Is it the unceasing drumbeat of crime statistics from the media? Are we collectively paranoid? Is Armageddon upon us? Do we see ourselves as the local version of Bruce Willis or Wesley Snipes? Probably, yes. There is a Walter Mitty living in us all; living larger in some than in most, but there in all. And many still have faith in the Boy Scout maxim "Be Prepared". We live in affluent times, most of us. (Those who are not to some degree affluent are not reading this.) So if we want to spend our money to protect ourselves against some vague non-specific danger, whose business is it anyway? The knifemakers of the world, that's who.

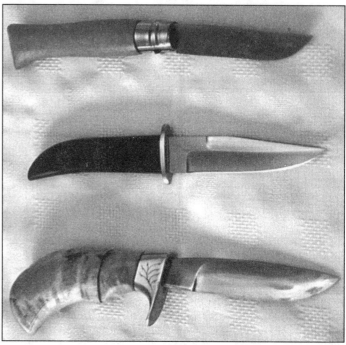

Does anyone seriously think he would be more severely cut with the Polkowski boot knife (center) than with the Ed Fowler Pronghorn (bottom) or the Opinel (top)?

I suggest, however, that the sky is not falling, Y2K notwithstanding. There is one overriding factor which makes fighting knives viable. THEY ARE USEFUL TOOLS! If one talks to veterans who carried the Marine Corps Fighting Knife (Ka-bar) they will to a man tell you that the knife was used almost exclusively as a utility tool. You may find one or two who actually used one to take out a sentry, or used one in some other sort of clandestine operation, but find anyone who used a "Ka-bar" in a knife fight as defined above, and lunch is on me.

Two things that make "fighting knives" fighting knives are the name and the carry mode! Examine any knife proffered as a fighting knife. You will find a commonality of characteristics which should be found in any knife for common use. These characteristics are not limited to those knives intended for combat, but may be emphasized more strongly than we are used to seeing in blades thought of for more mundane purposes. Common characteristics are:

1. The blade must be sharp. In many instances it is double-edged. While I don't personally care for double edges, having cut myself too many times already, there

is no denying that there can be twice as much edge length on a double-edged knife as on a single-edged one of equal length. So if one is careful, one may go twice as long without sharpening. Or, one can have two edges sharpened differently, for different purposes, e.g., cutting game and chopping wood. The fact that this same feature enables one to cut in two directions without turning the wrist, is gravy. But regardless of the specific shape of the blade; straight, curved, or recurved; or the technique used for forming the edge; stock removal or forging; or the geometry of the blade; straight, convex, or concave (hollow ground), the thing has got to be sharp.

▲ ▶ POCKET CLIP is a common feature on folders. In addition to making them easily accessible in a hurry, they make the knives handy in the garden or the workshop, without causing serious inconvenience. Dockers or Levis—the knives don't care.

2. The blade is pointed. The point may take any of several forms, the most popular now being the tanto, the clip, and the spear points.

Drop point knives are almost always for hunters. They don't have to be, of course, but that's the name usually applied. While this feature will certainly enable the insertion of the blade into an opponent, it has other, more benign uses. Ever try removing a splinter with a butter knife? Don't. Sorta like trying to teach a pig to sing—it wastes your time and annoys the pig. Just this morning, I removed an article from the newspaper using only the point of my pocket knife, a Benchmark Model 350, designed by Mel Pardue. Looks like a "fighter" to me, but is a great little everyday pocket knife.

3. There is a guard. Large or small, there is almost always at least the vestige of a guard. The nice thing about a guard is that it works in two directions. The same guard that prevents your opponent's blade from sliding down your blade to inflict cuts on your knife hand, also prevents your hand from slipping from the handle onto your own blade. Even that chef's knife in your kitchen shares that feature: protection for your knuckles. No, paring knives usually don't. Name me one knife used by people to cut themselves more than the common paring knife, and I'll buy lunch again.

Today's multitude of "fighting folders" has largely done away with guards in favor of some feature which stops the user's hand from slipping forward onto the blade, such as a finger groove for the index finger, a notched or grooved place to improve purchase for the thumb, or a slight flare of the handle or base of the blade. Does the same thing as a guard with less mass. We haven't placed a very high priority on parrying the opponent's thrust with our blades since we removed the brass strip from the back of the Bowie.

4. The handle is ergonomic and seldom made of natural materials. Shouldn't all handles be ergonomic? If we are going to hold on to something which has a sharp edge somewhere on it, doesn't it just make sense for it to be user friendly? A knife with a stag handle seems "sporting". Take the same knife and put a black micarta

or G-10 handle on it, and it immediately assumes sinister overtones. Part of this is simply hype. Black-handled knives look efficient, no-nonsense, business-like. The use of more modern materials allows the maker to style the handle to fit the user's perceived needs more easily than does the use of natural material.

5. Sheaths. Ah, yes, sheaths. A knife in a KYDEX sheath is a fighting knife. Take the same knife and house it in a leather sheath and it becomes a "hunting knife". Same knife, different sheath. Many fighting knives are provided with sheaths which are designed to be carried A.) Inside the belt or inside the pants, B.) Under the arm, C.) At the small of the back, D.) At the ankle or calf, or E.) Along the forearm. I have a knife made by Bud Nealy which came with his MCS, a multipurpose carry system. It embodies many of the above carry possibilities, yet

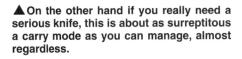

▲ On the other hand if you really need a serious knife, this is about as surreptitous a carry mode as you can manage, almost regardless.

the knife itself could easily be mistaken for a common kitchen knife. "Hunting" knives are worn on the hip and are acceptable.

Go figure.

Oh, yes, I have fighting knives. I love them. They are the most useful knives I own and I have never been in a knife fight, and will never be, unless I forget my gun, or am struck immobile. Most martial arts of which I am aware advise: attack the gun, run from the knife. Reason: you can outrun a knife but not a bullet. All of the knives pictured in this article are from my own rotating collection. Except for a few examples, such as sheepsfoot blades, most of my knives would qualify as "fighting knives". I make no apologies. I like them and use them as utility knives on a daily basis. And should I ever find myself in harm's way, in "the dark place", or "in the valley of the shadow of death", watch out Walter Mitty, here I come! ●

The New One-Hand Folders

The Camillus LEV-R-LOK has a relatively large lever on the side of the knife.

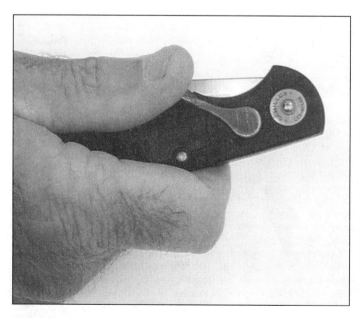

As the lever is pushed the blade opens.

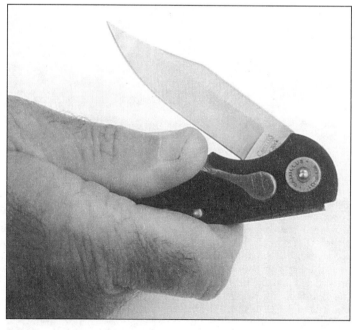

Push it and the blade snaps open.

A POPULAR FICTION writer of the post-WWII period, Donald Hamilton, wrote an extremely popular book series over a period of about forty years featuring a U. S. government secret agent named Matt Helm. Helm was sort of an American James Bond but a far more realistic and believable character than his English counterpart. Indeed I have known several people in my life like Helm but none like Bond. Hamilton's renditions of knife and gun usage in the Matt Helm books are, in my opinion, the most realistic and technically correct ever done in popular fiction. Please note that the Matt Helm movies starring Dean Martin were comedy farces that had little similarity to the books.

One of Helm's signature weapons in the books was a lockback folding knife that he opened one-handed. In the early books it was a German Solingen-made lockback which was eventually lost in combat, replaced by a similar specimen, and ultimately replaced in a later book by an example of the ubiquitous Buck 110 folder. I am convinced that the Matt Helm book series was a strong factor in the huge popularity of the Buck 110 and it also caused a great deal of interest in folders that could be quickly and easily opened with one hand.

The first phase involved working out one-hand opening methods for knives that were already available. The Buck 110 and the Gerber Folding Sportsman II lockbacks were particularly popular for this role. Early on, several outfits developed little levers and studs you could fit to your folder's blade to allow your thumb to open the knife in one motion. For a while there was also a great deal of interest in the Filipino balisong (butterfly) knives that could be opened one handed using a flashy twirling technique or by other more direct means. However, the balisong required more coordination for one-handed opening than many people had.

It was unquestionably the introduction of the Spyderco series of knives that caused the one-hand-opening revolution to take off. The Spyderco knives featured a hole in the blade that allowed the user's thumb to have enough purchase to easily thumb the knife open in one motion. Optionally, for models with enough weight in the handle, the user could hold the blade at the hole and snap the handle to the open position with a flick of the wrist. Interestingly, this was the same way Matt Helm opened his knives even though they did not have the Spyderco hole.

Spyderco also designed their knives to be easily unlocked and folded with one hand, a feature that is nearly as important as one-hand opening for many knife users. In addition, Spyderco introduced a pocket clip that allowed the knife to be carried securely but still where it is quickly accessible and easy to put away without a belt sheath.

To my way of thinking, the pocket clip was an extremely important aspect to the popularity of one-hand-opening knives. What is the point of being able to open a folding knife quickly with one hand if the knife cannot first be accessed easily and quickly? The quick access and fast opening of the Spyderco knives also rocketed them into prominence as viable defensive weapons beside being superb tools. Even though it has little to do with the topic of one-hand-opening folders, Spyderco also popularized serrated edges for folding knives though many, including your reporter, still prefer a conventional straight edge for most use.

Naturally, Spyderco's competitors followed suit with a variety of integral thumb studs, discs, slots, and holes to enable their knives to be easily opened with one hand along with a variety of pocket clips as well. I know at least three companies that pay a royalty to Spyderco for their use of holes of one shape or another on their blades.

Knife historians know that the obvious need for opening folding knives with one hand was addressed hundreds of years ago with the invention of the spring-blade knife. Such knives used a spring to push the blade open after a button or latch was pressed to release the blade. A number of examples are known that date back at least to the 1700's. In the mid-to-late 1800's such knives first saw mass production, primarily in Germany and Italy. In the late 1800's the Schrade family patented and began the production of inexpensive mass produced spring blade knives in the U. S. and such knives were eventually produced by practically all of the American folding knife manufacturers. Eventually these knives became known under a variety of names including: spring blade, switchblade, push-button, flick, and automatic knives.

Another type of one-hand-opening knife, the gravity knife, seems also to have been introduced in the U. S. in the late 1800's. With this type knife the

by Charles W. Karwan

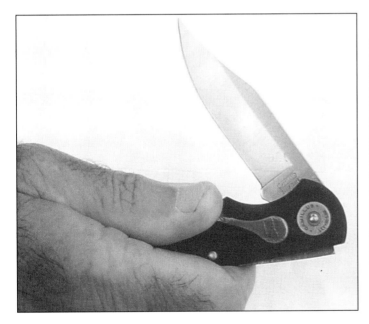

A hard push snaps the blade open.

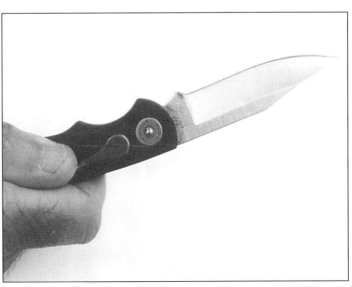

Once open, the blade is locked open.

blade was contained in a hollow handle. By pointing the knife downward and pressing a release the blade would fall into position by gravity where it would be locked in place. Pointing the knife upward and releasing the blade would allow it to fall back into the handle. However, gravity knives never caught on in this country probably because they tended to be bulky for their blade size, though they gained a following in Germany. Gravity knives eventually gained fame as the issue knife of the WWII German paratroopers while the American paratroopers of the same era were issued Schrade-type switchblades.

Switchblade knives had quite a broad following in the pre-WWII era. Small specimens were marketed to upper class women for cutting fruit and such with the selling point that they could be opened without risking breaking a manicured fingernail. Similarly models of switchblades were marketed to seamstresses for cutting thread one-handed if the other hand was occupied with the sewing machine. They were also promoted and popular with many fishermen who often do not have a spare hand available to help open a conventional folder when they are tying on a new fly or lure and need to trim the line. In certain western areas automatic opening knives were popular among cowboys because they usually had one hand occupied with reins.

In the early '50's the Italian stiletto style switchblade became popular among the street gangs in the U.S., apparently because they were featured in a number of movies involving gangs. Using the now all-too-familiar rhetoric that they were "the preferred weapon of the criminal", "they had only one purpose, to kill", and "no one needs a switchblade knife", and totally ignoring the fact that there were many valid uses for a one hand opening knife like a switchblade, the U.S. Congress passed a law in 1958 that made the interstate commerce in switchblade and gravity knives illegal in the U.S., with a few limited exceptions. This basically put all the U.S. knife manufacturers out of the automatic knife business except for a few military contracts.

In 1987, the late custom knife maker, Ron Miller of Largo, Florida, designed an extremely simple and clever switchblade knife mechanism. It used a simple cross button lock to lock the blade in both the closed and open positions and a coil torsion spring around the blade pivot to push the blade to the open position. His idea was to market this knife to the U.S. military special operations community which he eventually did. This was the now famous sterile (unmarked) Florida "Black Knife".

The design of this knife is a gem of engineering. The two-piece aluminum handle did away with the need for liners, bolsters, or handle scales. The use of Allen head screws to assemble the knife made it easy to disassemble for maintenance or repair. The simple push button locking system did away with the need for a separate blade locking mechanism. The use of a constant force torsion spring eliminated the problem of blade rebound present with

As the button of the Camillus CUDA is slid forward, the blade opens farther and farther.

many automatic knives that use a kicker spring. The entire knife was designed to have its major components produced on computer numerically controlled (CNC) machining centers. This also minimized hand work and maximized the ease of assembly.

Most of these original Black Knives were purchased by individual members of the military and law enforcement communities, though small lots of six to ten knives were purchased by military units including SEAL Teams, a Special Boat Unit, and Explosive Ordnance Demolitions (EOD) units.

Eventually some of these knives began to surface at gun and knife shows especially in the southeast. Since the knives were unmarked, rumors abounded that they were made for the CIA, Special Forces, SEALs, or even the KGB. They became in high demand among collectors and serious knife users. Since they were unmarked it was simple enough for anyone with access

to CNC machinery to make knockoffs and several people did.

Miller had never patented his design so there was no restriction keeping others from copying it. Eventually, quite a number of machine shops and cutlery manufacturers began to produce automatic knives under their own names using the same basic design as the Black Knife but changing the styling or size of the knife. Just a partial list of such manufacturers includes such names as Boker, Benchmade, Barrel Industries, Microtech, Paragon, Taylor Cutlery, JB Knives, and AutoTech.

At the same time there was a huge upsurge in interest in hand-made automatic knives. This has driven the state of the art in automatic opening knives to incredible heights with new mechanisms, the introduction of "double action" autos that can be opened manually or automatically, secret opening systems, and high art switchblades.

It was obvious that the knife buying public was extremely interested in automatic knives. However, the pesky Federal anti-switchblade law of 1958 was still on the books. Many switchblade manufacturers limited their sales to police and military personnel in an effort to stay within that law. Others limited their sales to individuals and dealers within their state since the Federal law only bans interstate commerce of these type knives. It was clear that there was a great deal of interest in knives like switchblades but many were uncomfortable about the legal restrictions on such knives.

Some of the more savvy observers came to the conclusion that the next generation of one hand opening knives should be more like switchblades in operation, but not actually fall in the switchblade category under the Federal law. To date there have been two different approaches taken to achieve this end.

The first was to design a knife that was manually opening with operation like a switchblade. That is, a button or mechanism is pressed or pushed in such a way that it manually opens the blade of the knife. In the past there has been a number of attempts along these

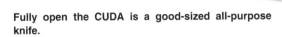

Fully open the CUDA is a good-sized all-purpose knife.

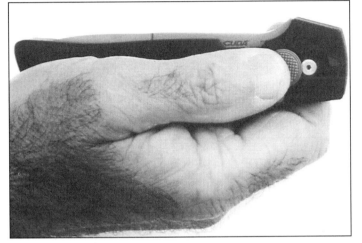

The thumb starts the CUDA blade.

As the button moves the blade moves.

A hard push gets a quick opening.

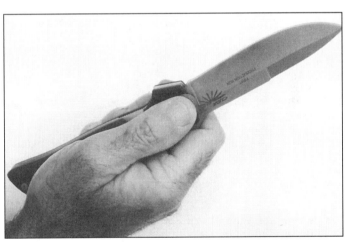

The blade movement is controlled entirely by the thumb.

lines but the knives were not particularly easy or quick to operate. The first manually opened knife that I am aware of that successfully approximated a switchblade in operation was the LEV-R-LOK now made by Camillus.

This clever little knife is a lockback with a blade just under three inches in length and an injection molded black Zytel handle. On the left side of the knife is a lever with a thumb pad not unlike that of an extended thumb safety on a semiautomatic pistol. Pressure on the lever moves the end of it about one inch in travel causing the blade to rotate and open to its full extent. If you press the lever slowly the blade opens slowly. If you press it smartly the blade snaps open with all the authority and speed of a switchblade. The design seems to work reliably and well.

The major complaint that I have heard about this knife is that the lever is too large and in the way when the knife is carried. I think that this perception is aggravated by the small size of the knife. While this knife has been reasonably popular, I believe that it would have been much more so if it was also offered in a larger version along the lines of the Buck 110 and with a pocket clip. The operating lever could stay the same size thereby being much more in proportion to the size of the knife than it is now. I should also note that the LEV-R-LOK is easily opened left handed using the second finger of the left hand.

While the LEV-R-LOC has been around a number of years the next knife I will cover has only been around about a year and a half as this is being written. Like the previous knife, it, too, is being made by Camillus and it is also a manually opening knife. However it is a much bigger knife with a blade length just under four inches. It is called the CUDA for Camillus Ultra Design Advantage.

The CUDA is large enough to be a serious weapon as well as a good general purpose utility knife. There are several different blade shapes offered. The blade of my specimen has an attractive dropped point profile with a 40% false edge on the top. Indeed, the blade and handle look very much like one of custom knife maker Bob Terzuola's tactical folders. The CUDA has a stainless steel blade, a liner locking mechanism, black G10 scales, and a pocket clip. There are other variations with and without serrations, different sizes, and with left handed buttons.

The CUDA's operating mechanism is just as clever as the LEV-R-LOK. It consists of a button on the forward left side of the handle that is pushed forward in a arch to open the blade. The button's travel is less than one inch going around the blade pivot in a track. There is also a track in the blade's pivot that the button's base rides in. The opening is wholly manual. If you slide the button forward slowly the blade opens slowly. If you slide it forward smartly the blade pops open with the same speed and authority as a switchblade.

My CUDA is difficult to operate left handed, but south-paws should not despair because Camillus offers a couple of CUDA variations set up specifically for lefties. I think that the CUDA has a great future ahead of it. At the 1998 Blade Show the CUDA was awarded the Most Innovative American Design of the year.

Both the CUDA and the LEV-R-LOK are totally manual opening knives that are not switchblades under the Federal law, but are capable of delivering the same snappy opening as a switchblade and have much of the same appeal.

Knife designer Blackie Collins took the one-hand-opening knife in a different direction with the Strut'N'Cut knife he designed for Meyerco. He says that he got the idea for the Strut'N'Cut's single strut opening mechanism from the suspension system on his Ducati motorcycle.

To the best of my knowledge the Strut'N'Cut was the world's first spring assisted manually opening knife, the second approach in the new generation of one hand opening knives. The way it works is that a spring-loaded strut inside the handle is attached to the blade in such a way that it pushes the blade into the handle. Rather than using a thumb stud, Blackie has serrated the pivot end of the blade to allow the index finger grip to pull the blade open. When the blade is manually opened more than half way the strut goes over top dead center and

then pushes the blade open. It snaps open sharply, again with the authority of an automatic opening knife.

Even though it uses a spring to assist or finish the opening of the blade it is not a switchblade under Federal law for several reasons. First it does not have a button or mechanism in the handle that is pressed to release the blade. Second the blade does not open "automatically" but rather must be manually opened about half way before the spring finishes the opening. However the blade does snap open in a most satisfying way similar to a switchblade and there is no question that this system is fast to use.

One thing you have to get used to with the Strut'N'Cut is that it closes with the same speed and authority as it opens so you must make sure there are no body parts in the blade's way when you are closing it or you will bleed. I speak from experience.

Since the Strut'N'Cut's introduction there has been a

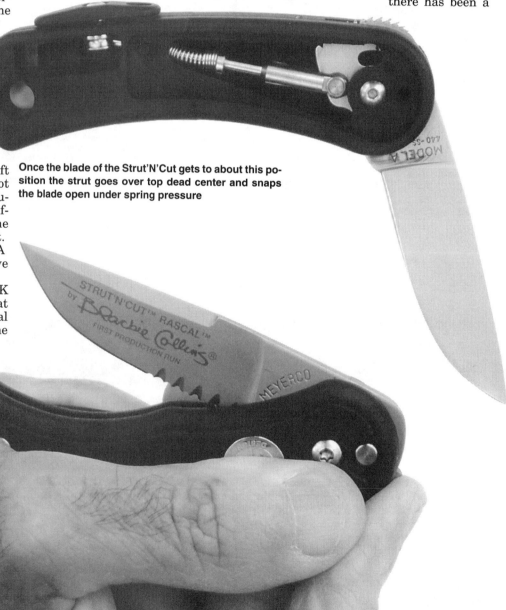

Once the blade of the Strut'N'Cut gets to about this position the strut goes over top dead center and snaps the blade open under spring pressure

This is how the Strut'N'Cut's blade is pulled open, generally by the thumb.

smaller version called the Rascal introduced as well as a new large version both with a more convenient locking system.

In some of my past writings I have used the term "semiautomatic" to describe this type knife. They are not automatic knives but do have some of the characteristics of an auto opener. Recently, during a chat with Blackie he said that he was using that term as well. It seems like a good way to describe this type knife.

More recently a talented custom knife maker in Hawaii named Ken Onion came up with yet another semiautomatic knife that uses a spring assist in its opening. In this case it uses a bent wire spring in a clever camming arrangement that holds the blade closed until the blade is opened about 30 degrees then the spring kicks the blade to the open position where it is locked by a liner type lock. Ken calls this system his "speed safe" mechanism using torsion bar technology for assisted opening. Ironically he got the idea for his opening system from the lobe on a cam in a Harley-Davidson motorcycle engine. I don't know what it is about these motorcycle guys but I find it interesting that the first two spring-assisted-opening knives to hit the market were inspired by motorcycle parts.

In the Ken Onion-designed Kershaw Ricochet, simply start the thumb peg out of the knife and it snaps open the rest of the way under spring pressure. Like the Strut'N'Cut, it does not fall under the Federal definition of a switchblade knife.

Ken went on to initiate a patent on his design and make a highly popular series of handmade folders using this system. They sold far quicker than he could make them. He then cut a deal with the Kershaw Knives company of Portland, Oregon where they would make production knives with this design.

The first Kershaw/Onion knife called the Random Task won the 1998 American-Made Knife of the Year from BLADE magazine and

their subsequent offerings of both smaller and larger knives using the Onion mechanism have been a huge hit.

I have the Kershaw model called the Model 1520 Ricochet. It is a dropped point utility knife with a 3.25 inch blade made from 440V, titanium alloy liners, polished G10 handle scales, and a pocket clip.

Butch Vallotton, one of this country's top custom makers of automatic knives, said when he saw it that my Kershaw/Onion was more of a custom quality knife than a production knife. I have to agree. This is one of the classiest production folders I have ever examined. Naturally this is not an inexpensive knife having a suggested retail of $175. Kershaw has also added several other knives using the Onion mechanism to their line that have injection molded polymer handles with a suggested retail of $60 to $90.

Opening this knife is simplicity itself. All you have to do is slide the back of your thumb nail under the opening peg on the blade starting the blade open about 30 degrees and the blade pops open the rest of the way by itself. It snaps open with most of the speed and authority of a switchblade. However, this knife is not a switchblade under the Federal law for precisely the same

reasons the Strut'n'Cut is not. Functionally, the major difference between the two is that with the Onion knife the blade has to be opened to a smaller degree manually than the Strut'N'Cut before the spring kicks over and assists the blade in opening. While the Strut'N'Cut's spring system assists the blade opening all the way to the open position the Onion system assists the blade until it is about halfway open and the rest of the opening is by inertia. The mechanics of these knives internally are totally different.

One should also note that even though these spring-assisted-opening knives are not switchblades under the federal law, they may be considered switchblades under state or local laws. California has a particularly draconian switchblade law that uses such terms as "similar type knife", "...is released automatically ..... by any other type mechanism whatsoever..." and other vague terms that no two lawyers or judges could agree on. So you should beware. Semi-automatic knives are likely to be illegal some places.

I know of at least one other major knife manufacturer that has yet another mechanically totally different spring assisted opening knife in the works that is extremely slick. I also know of yet another that is under consideration as well as at least three other extremely interesting and clever knife designs that are not switchblades legally but use springs in their opening. I think that it safe to say that, barring some new prohibitive legislation, the next generation of one-hand-opening knives is well on its way.

To be totally honest this new generation of one hand openers, whether they are totally mechanical or use spring assist mechanisms, offer little or no advantage in speed or ease of opening over a Spyderco type of one hand opener for most people. However, I have several friends and acquaintances that have arthritis, stiff joints, old injuries, or are not very coordinated that have trouble opening a Spyderco type one-handed. For those folks the new generation of one-hand-openers is a real boon. For the rest of us they are just real high in the neat category, and that is good enough for me! ●

At this position, the opening spring stops and lets the blade fly forward under inertia, different from the others.

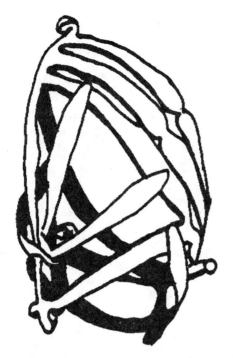

▲ Handguard skeleton is created by tangential winding strips reminiscent of ribbing. Iron-strips on the handguard of these schiavonas are connected by shrouds with guarding. The shape of pommel is simpler.

▼ Handguard skeleton is created by simple, double or triple tangential winding ladders reminiscent of grating. The shape of pommel is mostly "cat's head" with horn salients.

In Search of the

SCHIAVONA: IT'S A word known to those who know edged weapons, but not to many encyclopedias and dictionaries. Webster's Tenth Collegiate Dictionary doesn't have it. Nor do all those who sell antiques recognize it.

Schiavona were Venetian swords in the sixteenth to eighteenth centuries. Handsome they were and are, but somehow virtually unknown now. In their time, they were the arm of many

hired companies of the troops of the Doge of Venice in Dalmatia.

Earlier, in the fifteenth century, Slavonic mercenaries from the wild Balkans fought for Venice with exemplary fidelity. They were Slavs; Schiavona is the Italian word, derived from the Roman Sclavus, which meant war capture.

In the Blell collection in Tungea there is a schiavona inscribed "Soli deo gloria 1580." That solid datum marks

the rise of the Schiavana. Napoleon abolished the Republic of Venice in 1797, which is thus the absolute end.

The Schiavona has a straight blade and a characteristic basket hilt, a closed handguard protecting the sword hand. The blade is 32 to 40 inches long, double-edged, with one or two gutters or stiffeners.

Naturally, so widely used a design displays variations. There are Schia-

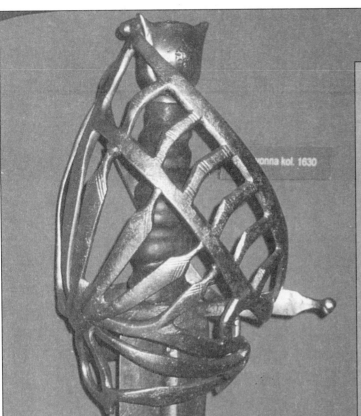

▲ From 1630 this schiavona clearly shows the ladder style of surround.

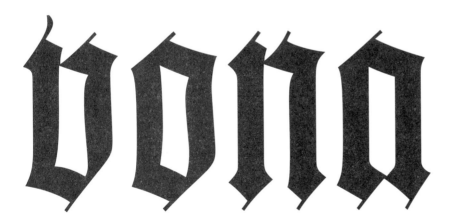

vona

vonas with single edges and five gutters, for instance.

Schiavona blades were made in Genoa, Milan, Toledo, Pasov, Solingen, Bellum, and in places unknown. Some are found made with parts of older swords.

One characteristic feature of the Schiavona is its angular pommel. This sometimes is formed as a "cats head" with horns. Centered in such pommels are buttons, or rosettes, with the sun or the lionhead motif. Pommels are generally brass or bronze; rarely silver, gold or iron.

Again, there are variations. Older Venetian swords show some. And there are authentic Schiavona with striped acorn pommels.

The typical Schiavona grips were wood, generally wound with wire and only sometimes covered with leather. Scabbards were leather-covered.

It's the handguard that virtually distinguishes the Schiavona. It's an elaborate construction of flat pieces of iron. As such, it makes a pretty massive sword grip.

by Karel Sutt

POSSIBLE EVOLUTION OF SCHIAVONA'S

Old Hungarian hilt.

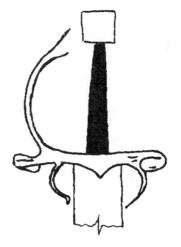

Medieval type of sword from a collection in Ermitage.

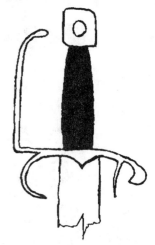

Sword from collection in Doge's palace in Venice.

POSSIBLE EVOLUTION OF SCHIAVONA'S

Hilt of landsknecht's sword; after 1540.

Two types of South-German swords.

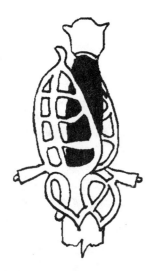

Similar sword with "cat's head" pommel.

Perhaps intermediate type between ribbing and grating handguard; about 1600. From a museum in Prague.

There are two basic types:

1. The shell is created by winding strips like ribbing connected to the guard-ring at the blade by iron shrouds. The pommel is simple.

2. The shell is created by ladder-like gratings, again connected to the guard-ring at the blade with shrouds, quite elaborately. The pommel is more complex.

The second type is quite popular with collectors. Often, the grating is decorated with small rosettes in relief. Production obviously was complex, and such Schiavonas come later in the world's history.

There is a small hook extension at the top of the Schiavona handguard, and its purpose unknown to us. Was it

HANDGUARD - RIBBING TYPE ━━━━━━━

Sword from collection of G. Bini, Rome; first half of 16th century.

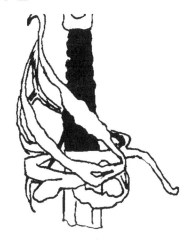

Sword dated 1570; Solingen blade.

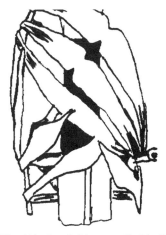

Hilt of Venice Schiavona; first half of 17th century.

HANDGUARD - GRATING TYPE ━━━━━━━

Sabre-mideuropean type; 16th-17th century.

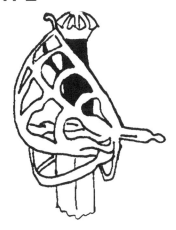

Sabre with pommel of landsknecht type and handguard of schiavona type; about 1600.

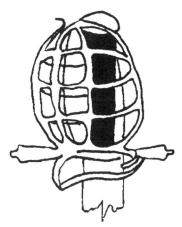

German hilt dated 1590-1610.

Typical grating handguards.

(left) Here's a ladder-style with fancy shrouding that forms yet another set of shapes.

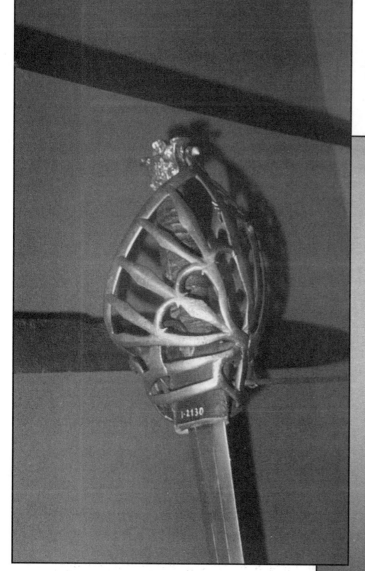

(left) Here's a ladder-style with fancy shrouding that forms yet another set of shapes.

(right) Schiavonas are worth some study. Apart from their violent history, they look so grand on display.

tactical and employed in swordplay, or just a hanger for a sword-knob? It's always there in a true Schiavona. That's all we know.

Any collection with one or several Schiavona looming among the others can be boasted. It is a special sword with its own mystery, as we have said.

As to that, there are more than 10 Schiavona in the collection of the Military Historical Museum in Prague. One has a most interesting handguard. It is the first type, with just a single traverse. It appears to be a

transition between the two types, a clue to how changes occured.

In my opinion, the first of ribbed handguards are older, carrying some features of the swords of the earlier German landsknechts. It seems normal to me to consider that the military population of Europe moved about and its ideas with it, just as we know religious and commercial groups did.

Thus, one finds other influences if one looks. There are earlier Venetian features to be found in some Schiavona and also some Balkan characteris-

tics. There are such questions as "Was one type for rankers and others for officers and gentlemen"?

We must learn about the Scottish question. The connection between the broadswords of the Scots and the Schiavona is obvious in a physical sense. It is not so easy to know when and how it happened.

Three centuries is a deep information abyss. At present, we can only study the swords. And the handsome Schiavona offers much to contemplate. ●

TRENDS

A Trend, in our terms, is something we notice is growing. And it might also be — not the same Trend — something that doesn't go away...like Bowie knives and daggers and miniatures.

One trend we see, and is plain here, is the upgrading...upgrading of talent, of effort, of material, of input, of result. And there is no very good way to measure that. One man uses river sand to create iron and charcoal to make it steel and folds and stretches it into a lovely katana blade and tempers it with care and creates a lovely temper line that promises a sword of excellence; the next figures out a nifty way to make a knife fold and unfold as no one ever did before; and the next combines craft and artistry of several kinds to create a knife that is beautiful in outline and texture and surface that may even tell, through its embellishment, a story all its own. Gauging one of these against the other, even if you used the prices, does not work. So some Trends are implicit, not explicit, and we don't separate them.

How do we locate the Trends we do report? Well, one guy looks at 3,000 new photos, all in one long look. In a good week, he sees a couple of trends.

That's what we list below, in our little table of contents — the trends that got noticed this year and the ones that are there every year.

Enjoy.

Ken Warner

THE BIG FOLDER

As MOST STUFF about modern folders does, this probably starts with the Grandaddy of them all—the Buck 110. It really made its mark and its market and . . . well, you all know that story. That knife taught us all.

One of the things the 110 taught me was that I liked a lighter and slimmer knife. And such came along pretty fast, probably starting with Al Mar. And I stayed right there for a long time. Oh, I gave the big guys a fair shake in print, and I tried 'em out as they came along, but I was into light and quick and all that stuff. And still am. Light and quick ain't bad.

And then last year an old buddy had some pretty big knives he makes on his table at a show somewhere or other. We

▶ **DICK ATKINSON: We're talking big here, nine inches long, just like the picture. It's a very comforting size in some circumstances.**

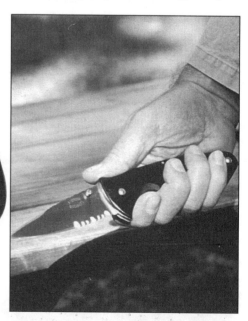

got to talking and I got to—well, there is no other word for it—fondling this big knife and the way that worked out is the knife went home with me. And home was colder than where I got the knife and I put on the old (three years) bomber jacket and dropped that big folder in the right-hand slash pocket and it was a marriage made in heaven. Except for on airplanes and such, that knife stayed right there for six months. It came out and got used a lot—on the mail, on ice on the windshield, on ropes and tangled dog hair and an occasional steak—and made a lot of sense.

It was Dick Atkinson's big folder and you can see it here. It led me to some other big guys, like Spyderco's Terzuola design.

And that led me to remember some hunting seasons when I was quite happy with those big European military folders with the sawblades.

Atkinson was right cooperative. He put a special edge on one for me, and serrated and put a pocket clip on another. A genuinely big folder needs a clip if you aren't wearing your old (three years) bomber jacket and for me that stops around May 1 most years. Turns out he sells a lot of those folders, those big ones. And I understand why … now.

It looks silly to say it on paper, but the great thing about a big folder is its size. There is quite a bit of handle—five inches,

about—and a blade approaching four inches, as thick and meaty as the maker wants it to be. The Atkinson is 1 1/4-inches wide across the ricasso, has a triangular blade just over 3 3/4-inches, and the point is in the middle. The curves of the generous handle provide a giant handguard, and when you take it out of the ol' bomber jacket pocket with gloves on, open it and start flailing away—well, perhaps not flailing—at ice on the windshield, that solid grip is mighty comforting.

Some others are about that big; most slimmer. Wimpff designs from Klotzli, for instance, are nice and long and much slimmer. That Terzuola Spyderco is way ample, too—it goes 1 1/4-inches across the ricasso; so was a Wayne Goddard design I have carried. Their newest toughie by J.D. Smith, though leaner and meaner, still offers the big guy sureties. And the Emerson headliners and the Benchmade line has them and … and … and … there's a good one there from everyone. And Buck still makes the Buck 110!

I looked for some other big custom folders and found a few and you can see them here. If knives like these handmades are a little too pricey or something, and you

DICK ATKINSON: You can get the big knife with these options—a Spyderco clip and hand-cut serrations.

DICK ATKINSON: In the hand, it's a handful. You can hang onto and lean into this properly made liner lock with its titanium liners under Micarta scales and ATS-34 blade.

have a nice old (three years or more) bomber jacket, find near about any ol' big folder. They fit good in bomber pockets.

Ken Warner

▶ **CHARLIE DAVIS:** This is made from a file under the Anza name. but it fills the bill for size and shape to be a big folder in the sense we're talking.

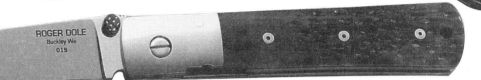

▶ **ROGER DOLE:** Nine inches overall, it goes, with Dole's integral bolster liner. The four-inch blade is ATS-34. (Point Seven photo)

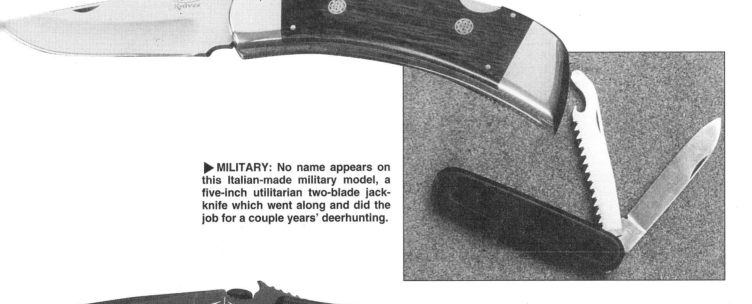

▲ **SPYDERCO:** This is Bob Terzuola's big liner lock as done in Golden, CO, in CPM440V. It's a cutting fool and plenty big enough.

▼ **PHIL CIARMITARO:** This one goes 8 3/4-inches as you see it, with a PAC Knives label, in brass and green Diamondwood. Blade is 3 3/4-inches.

▶ **MILITARY:** No name appears on this Italian-made military model, a five-inch utilitarian two-blade jackknife which went along and did the job for a couple years' deerhunting.

◀ **EMERSON:** This is a factory knife, the Commander, and it goes 8 3/4-inches open and provides withal plenty of hand grip and a lot of edge. (Weyer photo)

►ROGER DOLE: Big one in 440C and G-10, nearly nine inches long. Titanium liner is split. (Point Seven photo)

◄MIKE VAGNINO: Eager liner-lock with bright red bone scales over titanium and a Sandvik 12C27 blade. Neat.

THE TACTICAL KNIFE PHENOMENON

THERE ARE HUNDREDS, even thousands, of 1830-1860-era Bowie knives now in the hands of mostly American collectors. That's a stone fact. Your reporter has handled three hundred of them himself and he's no student. And it's a curious fact, as well. Regardless of what you read and how it is reported there were NOT thousands of knife fights or cutting scrapes or "rough medleys" or street affrays attended by people sufficiently affluent to pay Sheffield prices or higher for large knives to carry to such. There may have been a lot of violence back then, but like all violence everywhere, it was mostly carried out with what tools came to hand.

But someone bought all those knives back then, right? Have you ever wondered who?

There are two more curious facts, these of a contemporary nature.

New Curious Fact One: There are ten of thousands of what are called "tactical" knives sold every week in the 50 states. They are folders from three inches up, a few automatic knives, and a host of straight knives, large and small. Mostly they have black handles, often black blades, and a certain look. You know very well exactly what I am talking about.

New Curious Fact Two: There are not thousands of knife fights, street affrays, chance medleys at hand every week, or indeed, every month. There may be a lot of that stuff, but very little of it is accomplished by people who can afford to buy and to carry $169 quick-openers with ATS-34 blades, liner locks and carbon fiber handles.

So who is buying all the tactical knives?

There does not seem to be any major marketing problem in locating buyers. And they are buying perhaps the most sophisticated tools ever provided by a beneficient Nature for edged defense. All but a very few of those buyers have to be, in knife terms, all dressed up with no place to go.

I know. There is no answer, but it is a hell of a question. And they are some really swell knives, these knives of today with the tactical look. We follow here with photos of some of the best ever made. Enjoy.

Ken Warner

JOHN W. SMITH: Carbon fiber, Damascus, ATS-34—all the best stuff in slim, almost dressy defense items. (Point Seven photo)

◀ **PAT CRAWFORD:** The master's new big ones, the straight goods and the jazzed up model—nearly nine inches long. (Point Seven photo)

▶ **PAUL FOX:** The veteran sense of line and bright titanium color provide a no-nonsense pretty knife. (Point Seven photo)

▶ **CARL ZAKABI:** The Big Kahuna, they call it—goes over nine inches in ATS-34 and G-10 with titanium liners. (Weyer photo)

▶ **TI-KNIVES:** In a handmade kind of niche, this new company goes out there for the tactical look, the fencing grip, all of it.

▶ **GRANT HAWK:** Folder with D.O.G. (Deadbolt Over Grablatch) lock, done up in ATS-34 and 6061 aluminum and it stashes its lanyard.

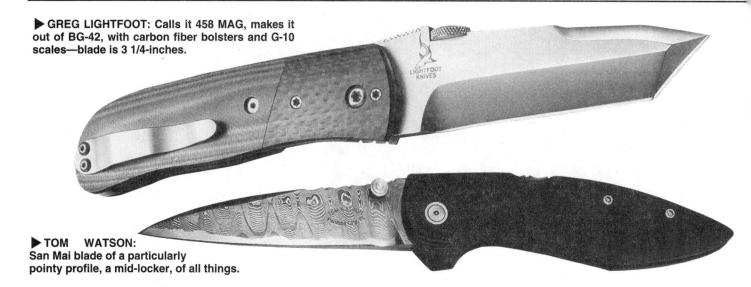

▶GREG LIGHTFOOT: Calls it 458 MAG, makes it out of BG-42, with carbon fiber bolsters and G-10 scales—blade is 3 1/4-inches.

▶TOM WATSON: San Mai blade of a particularly pointy profile, a mid-locker, of all things.

▲BRONKO GILJEVIC: Aussie offers 4 1/2-inch 440C blade, and take-apart screw-fastened scales.

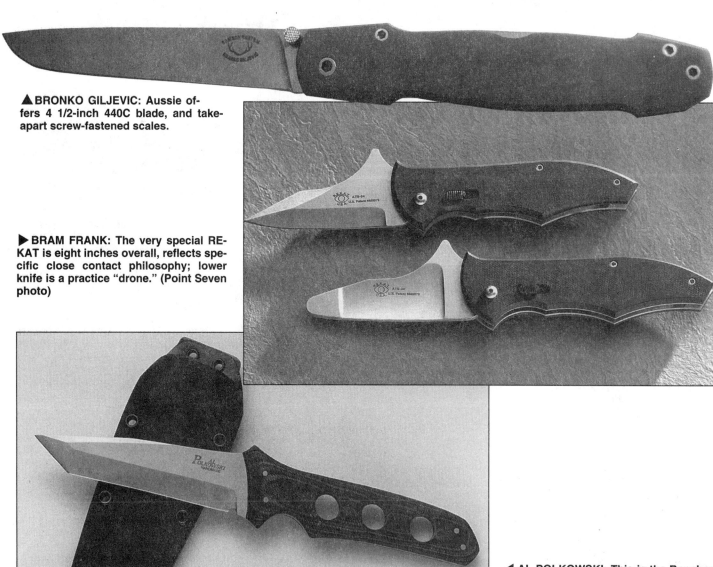

▶BRAM FRANK: The very special RE-KAT is eight inches overall, reflects specific close contact philosophy; lower knife is a practice "drone." (Point Seven photo)

◀AL POLKOWSKI: This is the Banshee with a four-inch blade in tanto profile, cutouts, G-10 scales. (Weyer photo)

◀ CHRIS HATIN: Chisel ground T.E.C. design; the scales on the upper knife are lignum vitae; knives are three-inches. (Weyer photo)

▶ JOHN GRECO: Moderately nasty personal knife in Greco's choice of nicely-coated high-carbon steel—tough knife. (Weyer photo)

▶ MICHAEL M. SANDERS: It's a drop hunter, but a tactical drop hunter—a four-incher with bead-blasted finish. (Embrey photo)

▶ JEFF ISGRO: His TEK Model 1 in glass-beaded D2 and green and black linen Micarta, full tanged at 8 1/2-inches.

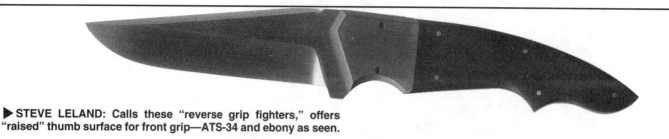

▶ **STEVE LELAND:** Calls these "reverse grip fighters," offers "raised" thumb surface for front grip—ATS-34 and ebony as seen.

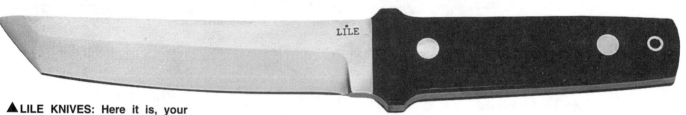

◀ **R.J. MARTIN:** A meld of the heavy steeply-ground edges, carbon fiber sheathing and grip liner with glassed silk wrap—very solid in the hand.

▲ **LILE KNIVES:** Here it is, your thoroughly American tanto, a no-nonsense defense tool with maximum blade strength for the profile.

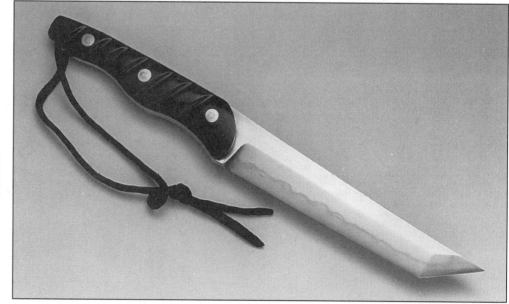

▶ **STEVE CORKUM:** Shaped black paper Micarta, with full-tanged and clay-tempered 1050, so there's a handsome temperline along the entire edge. (Weyer photo)

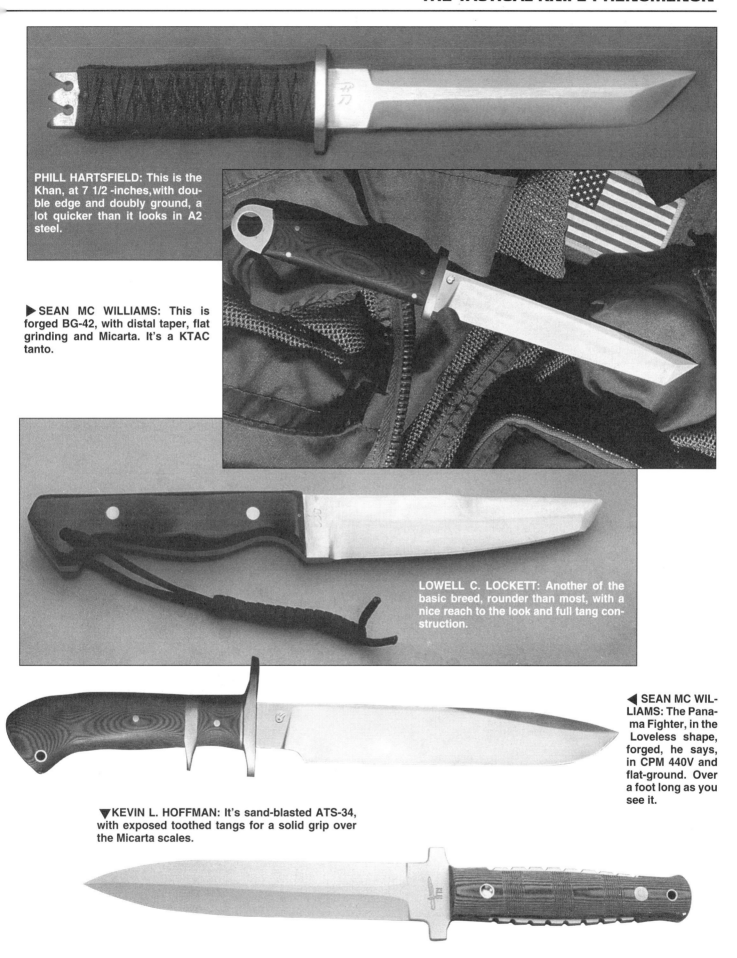

PHILL HARTSFIELD: This is the Khan, at 7 1/2 -inches, with double edge and doubly ground, a lot quicker than it looks in A2 steel.

►SEAN MC WILLIAMS: This is forged BG-42, with distal taper, flat grinding and Micarta. It's a KTAC tanto.

LOWELL C. LOCKETT: Another of the basic breed, rounder than most, with a nice reach to the look and full tang construction.

◄SEAN MC WILLIAMS: The Panama Fighter, in the Loveless shape, forged, he says, in CPM 440V and flat-ground. Over a foot long as you see it.

▼KEVIN L. HOFFMAN: It's sand-blasted ATS-34, with exposed toothed tangs for a solid grip over the Micarta scales.

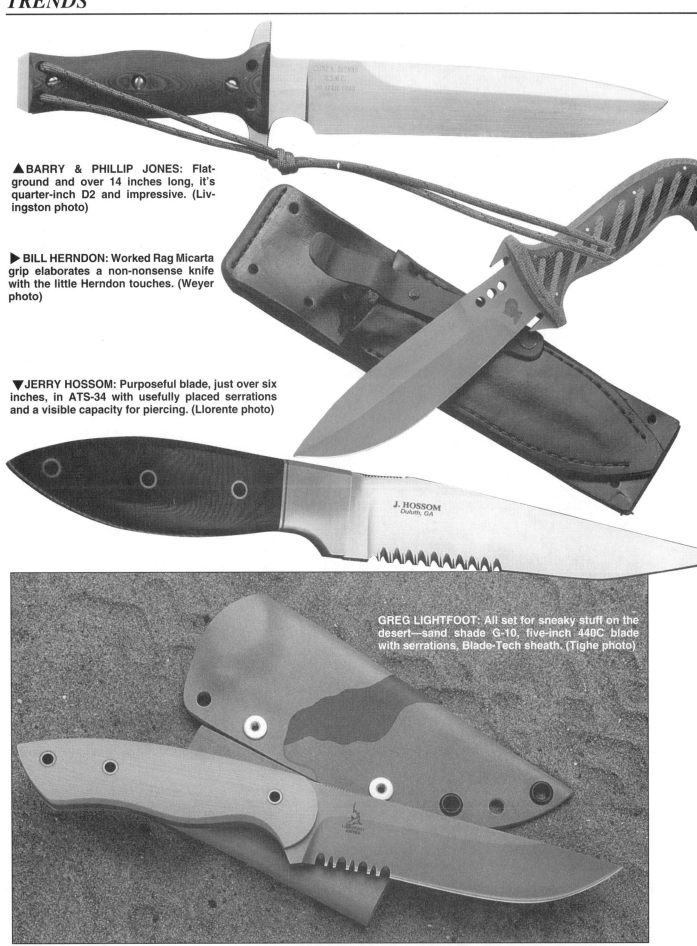

▲BARRY & PHILLIP JONES: Flat-ground and over 14 inches long, it's quarter-inch D2 and impressive. (Livingston photo)

▶BILL HERNDON: Worked Rag Micarta grip elaborates a non-nonsense knife with the little Herndon touches. (Weyer photo)

▼JERRY HOSSOM: Purposeful blade, just over six inches, in ATS-34 with usefully placed serrations and a visible capacity for piercing. (Llorente photo)

GREG LIGHTFOOT: All set for sneaky stuff on the desert—sand shade G-10, five-inch 440C blade with serrations, Blade-Tech sheath. (Tighe photo)

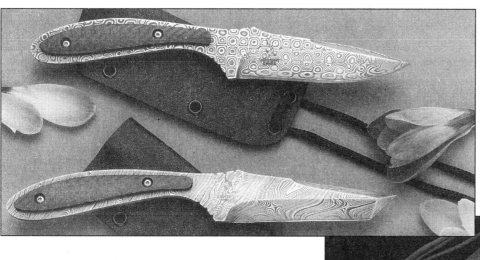

▶ GREG LIGHTFOOT: Little pretties he calls neck razors, here in a couple kinds of Damascus and two blade shapes, just over three inches. (Tighe photo)

▼ MORRIS C. WORRELL: High style in ATS-34 blades just under four inches, and a purposeful look to the exposed tangs.

▼ E.V. CHAVER: One's a folder, one not; both are ATS-34. He'll furnish either or a matched set. They're just over a slim eight inches. (Weyer photo)

▼ ED HALLIGAN: Cute little fellow he calls the City Slicker. The blade is ATS-34 at four inches; grip is left "toothy." (Weyer photo)

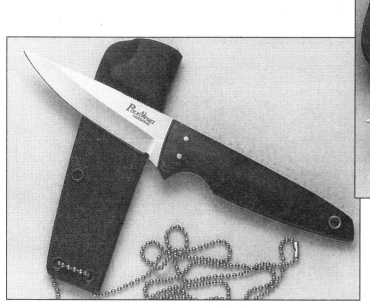

◀ AL POLKOWSKI: Another pretty big neck knife, called the Hang Tight, at just under eight inches with a classy profile. (Weyer photo)

The Year in Bowies

BETWEEN THE GULF of Mexico, the Pacific Ocean and the Atlantic, Bowie knives are not ever going to go missing. We speak often in oceanic terms of objects in the market—they " . . . ebb and flow . . . " for instance. Well, Bowies these days only flow; they haven't done any ebbing lately.

That is so in the handmade field and it is possibly even more so among the commercial guys. Ontario knives just unleashed a whole phalanx of Bowies after designs by Bill Bagwell, whose Bowieness is not contrived. They are going, we are told, very well indeed, and they really are Bowies, so what is next? More Bowies from other commercial cutlers, we bet.

The knives you will see right close here are not Bagwells, however, but the efforts of the year by scores of serious individual knifemakers. It seems they fall, here and now, into three categories—three successful categories. There is the simple and clean line, often executed without flourish, executed in the very best of materials; there is the interpreted replica of standout designs from the originals, many of them handsomely gorgeous; and

there are the 20th century styles, some of them "fantasies" as Bernard Levine terms them (See his report in this issue on page 6.), but honest knives and tools for all that.

If there's a trend in Bowies, it is the same trend as we see in other accepted knife designs—elaboration toward higher prices, more significant expressions of craft and talent. The Bowie, over the 170 years since a "rough medley" on a sandbar near Natchez, Mississippi, has often trended that way.

Ken Warner

▶TIM HANCOCK: Prizewinner and why not? It's 15 1/2-inches overall, in mastodon, nickel silver and Damascus, and it's gorgeous. (Point Seven photo)

▶STEPHEN J. RAPP: In 440C, it makes you wish the old Sheffield guys could see it and get jealous. Blade is ten inches. (Weyer photo)

▼JARRELL LAMBERT: Yet another rendition, this one at eight inches, and somewhat simplified in 52100 steel with a giraffe bone handle. (Point Seven photo)

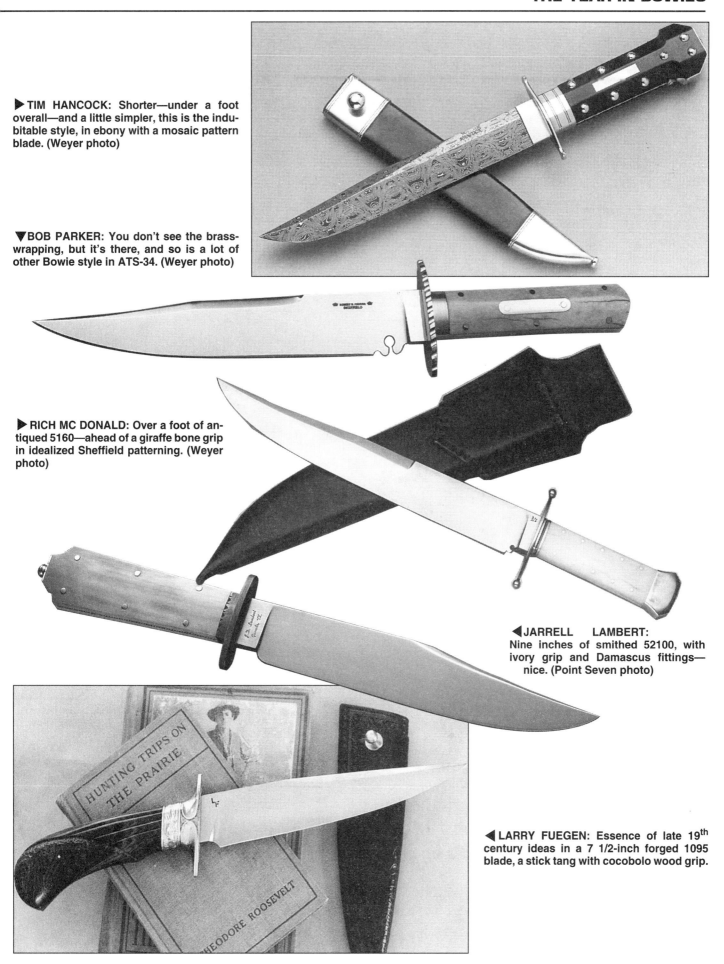

►TIM HANCOCK: Shorter—under a foot overall—and a little simpler, this is the indubitable style, in ebony with a mosaic pattern blade. (Weyer photo)

▼BOB PARKER: You don't see the brass-wrapping, but it's there, and so is a lot of other Bowie style in ATS-34. (Weyer photo)

►RICH MC DONALD: Over a foot of antiqued 5160—ahead of a giraffe bone grip in idealized Sheffield patterning. (Weyer photo)

◄JARRELL LAMBERT: Nine inches of smithed 52100, with ivory grip and Damascus fittings—nice. (Point Seven photo)

◄LARRY FUEGEN: Essence of late 19th century ideas in a 7 1/2-inch forged 1095 blade, a stick tang with cocobolo wood grip.

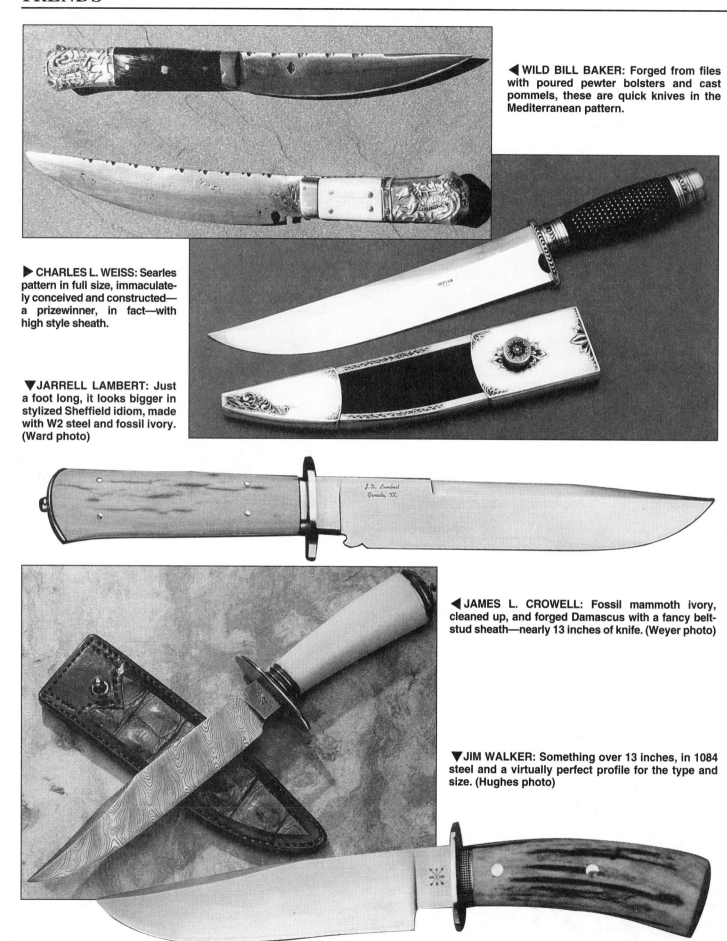

◀ **WILD BILL BAKER:** Forged from files with poured pewter bolsters and cast pommels, these are quick knives in the Mediterranean pattern.

▶ **CHARLES L. WEISS:** Searles pattern in full size, immaculately conceived and constructed— a prizewinner, in fact—with high style sheath.

▼ **JARRELL LAMBERT:** Just a foot long, it looks bigger in stylized Sheffield idiom, made with W2 steel and fossil ivory. (Ward photo)

◀ **JAMES L. CROWELL:** Fossil mammoth ivory, cleaned up, and forged Damascus with a fancy belt-stud sheath—nearly 13 inches of knife. (Weyer photo)

▼ **JIM WALKER:** Something over 13 inches, in 1084 steel and a virtually perfect profile for the type and size. (Hughes photo)

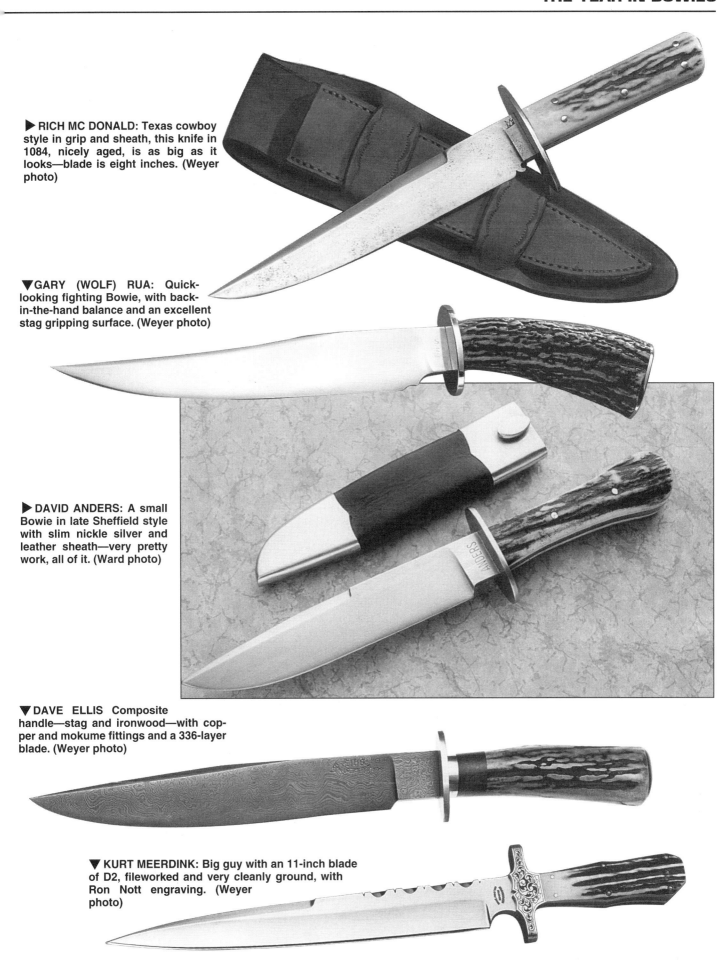

▶ RICH MC DONALD: Texas cowboy style in grip and sheath, this knife in 1084, nicely aged, is as big as it looks—blade is eight inches. (Weyer photo)

▼ GARY (WOLF) RUA: Quick-looking fighting Bowie, with back-in-the-hand balance and an excellent stag gripping surface. (Weyer photo)

▶ DAVID ANDERS: A small Bowie in late Sheffield style with slim nickle silver and leather sheath—very pretty work, all of it. (Ward photo)

▼ DAVE ELLIS Composite handle—stag and ironwood—with copper and mokume fittings and a 336-layer blade. (Weyer photo)

▼ KURT MEERDINK: Big guy with an 11-inch blade of D2, fileworked and very cleanly ground, with Ron Nott engraving. (Weyer photo)

▼MICHAEL ROBERTS: Big knife from a big file goes nearly 15 inches overall; grip is bone; sheath is copper and brass. (Point Seven photo)

▼JOE KEESLAR: The Mediterranean dirk with 10-inch blade in 52100, fitted in silver over desert ironwood, 15 inches overall. (Weyer photo)

▲FRANK CARLISLE: The Iron Mistress herself, just about, at 16 inches overall, flat ground in 440C with stainless fittings.

▲MIKE MANABE: The nearly patented Manabe triple temper line in 52100 at 11 inches, ironwood with ferrules and fittings in stainless, copper, mokume-gane. (Weyer photo)

◄RED ST. CYR: Differentially tempered L6 at 10 inches with wrought iron guard, copper and Damascus fittings with oosic. (Weyer photo)

▶JAY MAINES: The Bowie at seven inches and in the modern lingo—tough-looking 440C with kingwood.

◀BILL SNOW: Thoroughly modern, with long sharp false edge, dropped main edge, saber slope in the ergonomic grip. Blade is ATS-34.

▶GREG NEELY: Big guy won a big prize. It's over 16 inches; 12-inch blade is 01 and 1084; engraving by Terry Theis. (Weyer photo)

▲ED HALLIGAN: Very distinctive big Bowie with high style semi-coffin grip and a serious 12 1/2-inch blade in, of course, Damascus. (Weyer photo)

▲ALEX DANIELS: Fully engraved Bowie embellished by Christian Meyer and most handsome. Blade reads "*A Daniels me fecit*" as well it should. (Weyer photo)

▶KEITH KILBY: This one has both bells and whistles. Composite blade, high-style Damascus fittings and D-guard, fossil ivory at 17 1/2-inches overall. (Point Seven photo)

More and Better Slip-joints

HAVING FIRST DISCOVERED they could make credible slip-joint knives, makers who liked the idea then kind of sneaked in looking for the market, and now it is all there—the makers, the market and the knives. Kind of funny for an old-timer to walk up to a table full of fine-looking handmade knives and not a straight knife or even a liner-lock in the bunch—just those old-timey things with nail nicks and lots of blades, some of them.

Priced right up there with the big boys they are, too. And why not? They are no easier to make than the next thing. If you want to sell them, they have to be righ-

teously finished inside and out, they have to walk and talk, and they have to look first-cabin.

There is room for some adventure in an exaggerated line here or a remarkable handle material there in slip-joints, but mainly they evoke the times that were, only better. So you have your trappers and your congresses and senators and your toenails and sunfish. You get some whittlers and hunters. You don't get much that looks ordinary.

And, as one expert has said, these are as good as Sheffield ever made, and they are stainless, to boot. Judge for yourself—here are a bunch of them.

Ken Warner

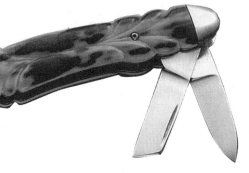

▲ **BAILEY P. BRADSHAW:** The blades are 52100, the master at three inches; scales are carved mastodon ivory; the whole is stupendous. (Point Seven photo)

▶ **D. RARDON:** The one below is an original Schatt & Morgan; the other is its twin in ATS-34, new-made. (Point Seven photo)

▶ **REESE BOSE:** Nifty spear-bladed small peanut with an elegant grind. (Busfield photo)

▶ **DAN BURKE:** Glorious Congress shape in stainless and matchless abalone. (Point Seven photo)

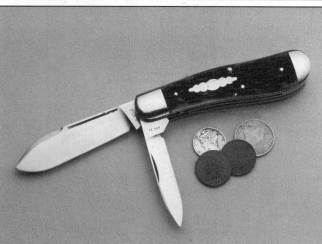

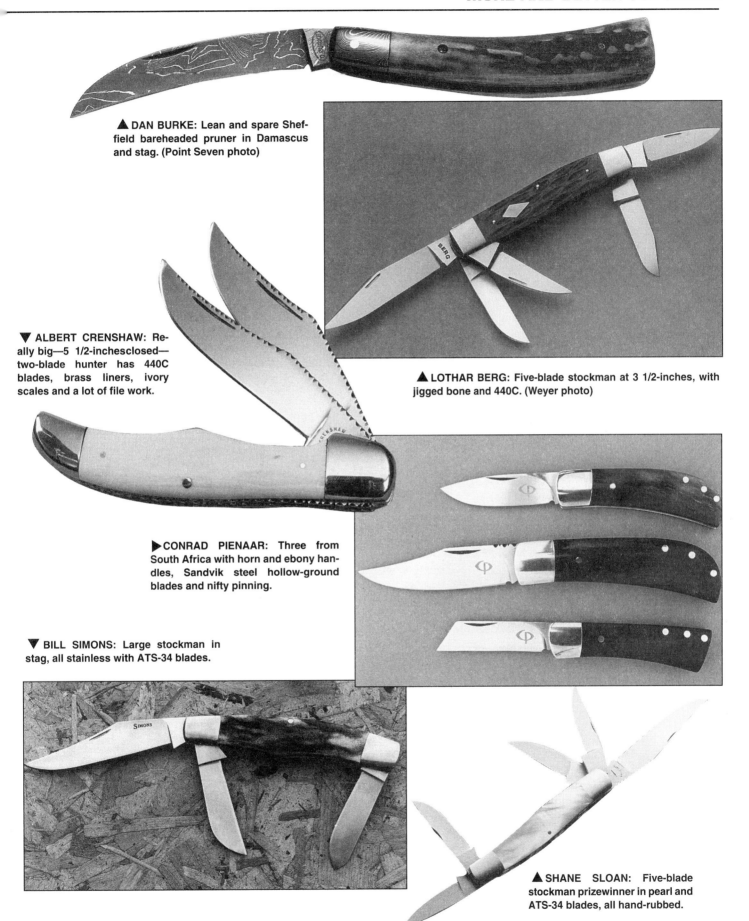

▲ DAN BURKE: Lean and spare Sheffield bareheaded pruner in Damascus and stag. (Point Seven photo)

▼ ALBERT CRENSHAW: Really big—5 1/2-inchesclosed—two-blade hunter has 440C blades, brass liners, ivory scales and a lot of file work.

▲ LOTHAR BERG: Five-blade stockman at 3 1/2-inches, with jigged bone and 440C. (Weyer photo)

▶CONRAD PIENAAR: Three from South Africa with horn and ebony handles, Sandvik steel hollow-ground blades and nifty pinning.

▼ BILL SIMONS: Large stockman in stag, all stainless with ATS-34 blades.

▲ SHANE SLOAN: Five-blade stockman prizewinner in pearl and ATS-34 blades, all hand-rubbed.

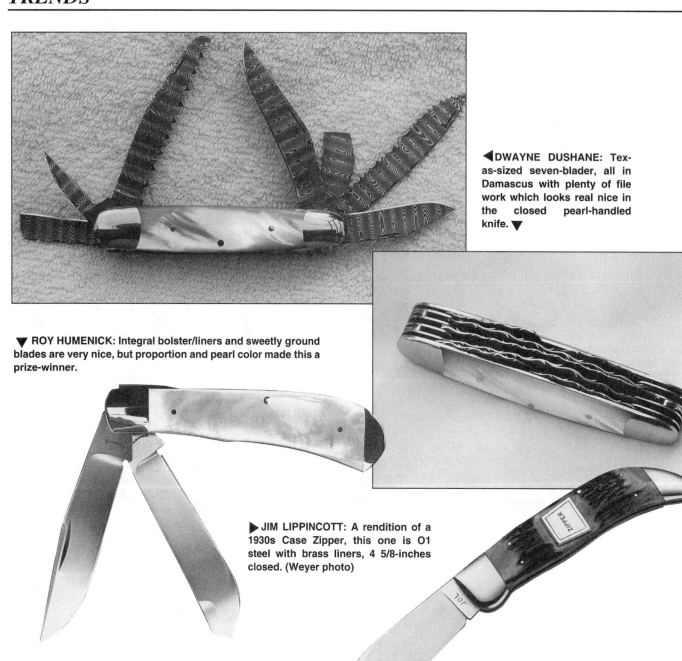

◄DWAYNE DUSHANE: Texas-sized seven-blader, all in Damascus with plenty of file work which looks real nice in the closed pearl-handled knife. ▼

▼ ROY HUMENICK: Integral bolster/liners and sweetly ground blades are very nice, but proportion and pearl color made this a prize-winner.

►JIM LIPPINCOTT: A rendition of a 1930s Case Zipper, this one is O1 steel with brass liners, 4 5/8-inches closed. (Weyer photo)

▼ P.J. TOMES: Four-inch serpentine muskrats in pearl or stag with CPM420 blades.

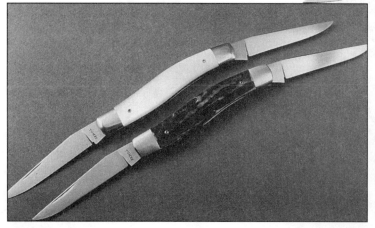

▼ BILL SIMONS: He calls this a saddle horn trapper, all stainless and stabilized walnut.

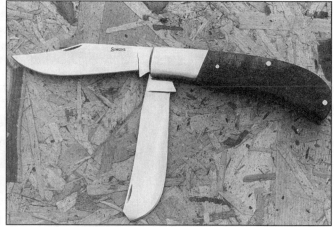

▶CLAY GAULT: Another carefully worked Gault special knife for the special hunter who likes a three-inch penknife in Vascowear and sheephorn.

▼BOB LEVINE: Stout fellow, his Model 2, in ivory, titanium and 440C.

◀DAN NEDVED: Old-time jack-knife with worked bolster, celluloid tortoiseshell and good looks.

◀EUGENE W. SHADLEY: Senator pen, just over six inches as you see it, in pearl and stainless steel.

◀PHILLIP BOOTH: Three-inch coke-bottle pattern jack, with raindrop Damascus, stainless steel fittings and stag. (Weyer photo)

▼GARY WINGO: Red bone scales, carefully jigged, set off stainless fittings and blades in a very traditional bareheaded trapper.

▲JOHN HOLLAND: Red bone whittler in stainless, including 440C blades. Knife is 8 1/2-inches long as you see it.

This Year In Swords

PRIMITIVES CALLED BRONZE and iron swords "long knives" when first they met them. Some who carried swords into new and strange lands were named "Long Knife" by people they met. And, surely, many a modern knifemaker comes a cropper when he essays a sword and creates a long knife.

Often a 12-inch-bladed knife, a good one, tilts the scale nearly as far as a good 30-inch sword. Swords are different. This reporter does not know how they are different, but he knows they are. And he does not know they are good things, but he know they are there and they are not going to go away.

We are privileged this year to bring, separately, but close at hand, the story of a righteous sword, perhaps a holy sword. It was built here and travelled to a shrine far away where it rests, we are told, honored and shining, and is likely to rest for centuries, right there.

And we are privileged to show you what knifemakers, and no doubt a swordmaker or two, have done with their craft this time. It appears the katana has been calling loudly these past months, and the Celts appear to be coming, but we no doubt have swords for everyone. Enjoy them.

Ken Warner

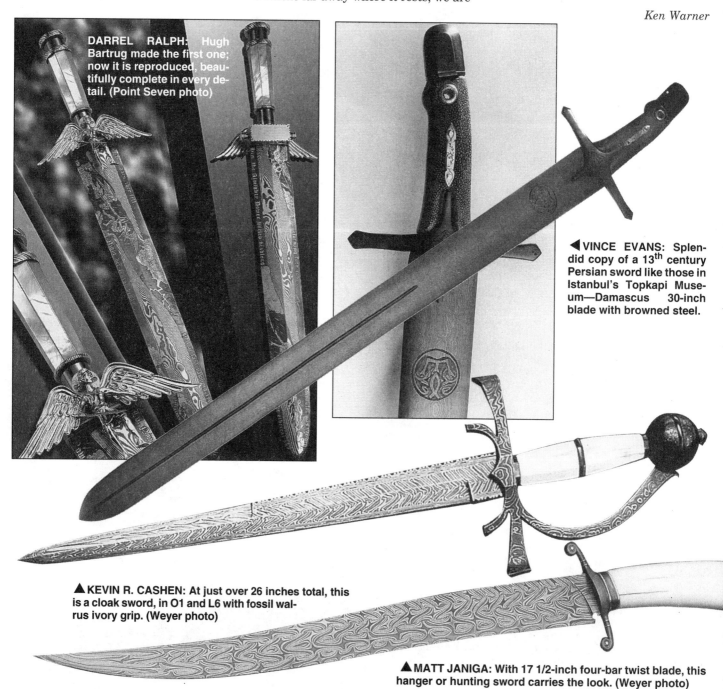

DARREL RALPH: Hugh Bartrug made the first one; now it is reproduced, beautifully complete in every detail. (Point Seven photo)

◄ VINCE EVANS: Splendid copy of a 13th century Persian sword like those in Istanbul's Topkapi Museum—Damascus 30-inch blade with browned steel.

▲ KEVIN R. CASHEN: At just over 26 inches total, this is a cloak sword, in O1 and L6 with fossil walrus ivory grip. (Weyer photo)

▲ MATT JANIGA: With 17 1/2-inch four-bar twist blade, this hanger or hunting sword carries the look. (Weyer photo)

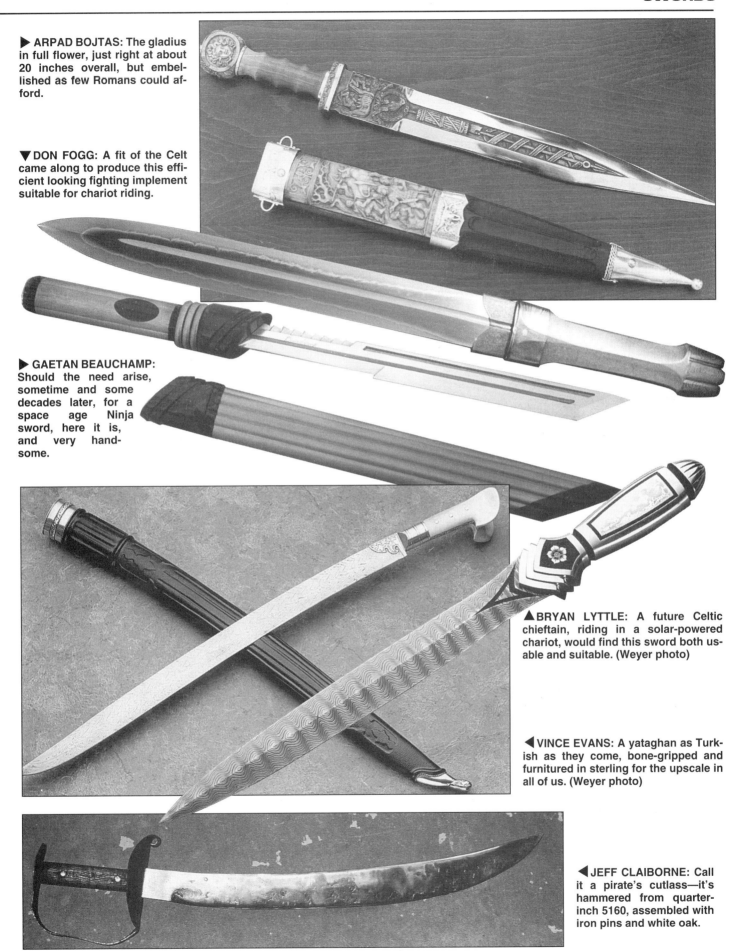

▶ **ARPAD BOJTAS:** The gladius in full flower, just right at about 20 inches overall, but embellished as few Romans could afford.

▼ **DON FOGG:** A fit of the Celt came along to produce this efficient looking fighting implement suitable for chariot riding.

▶ **GAETAN BEAUCHAMP:** Should the need arise, sometime and some decades later, for a space age Ninja sword, here it is, and very handsome.

▲ **BRYAN LYTTLE:** A future Celtic chieftain, riding in a solar-powered chariot, would find this sword both usable and suitable. (Weyer photo)

◀ **VINCE EVANS:** A yataghan as Turkish as they come, bone-gripped and furnitured in sterling for the upscale in all of us. (Weyer photo)

◀ **JEFF CLAIBORNE:** Call it a pirate's cutlass—it's hammered from quarter-inch 5160, assembled with iron pins and white oak.

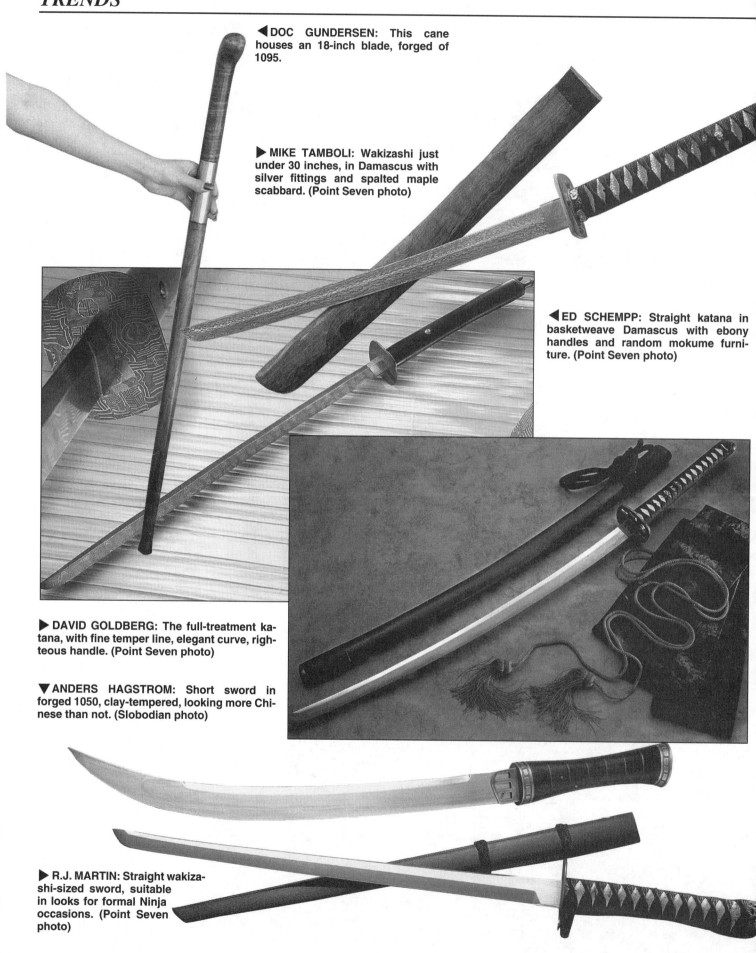

◄DOC GUNDERSEN: This cane houses an 18-inch blade, forged of 1095.

►MIKE TAMBOLI: Wakizashi just under 30 inches, in Damascus with silver fittings and spalted maple scabbard. (Point Seven photo)

◄ED SCHEMPP: Straight katana in basketweave Damascus with ebony handles and random mokume furniture. (Point Seven photo)

►DAVID GOLDBERG: The full-treatment katana, with fine temper line, elegant curve, righteous handle. (Point Seven photo)

▼ANDERS HAGSTROM: Short sword in forged 1050, clay-tempered, looking more Chinese than not. (Slobodian photo)

►R.J. MARTIN: Straight wakizashi-sized sword, suitable in looks for formal Ninja occasions. (Point Seven photo)

The Sword of Khalsa

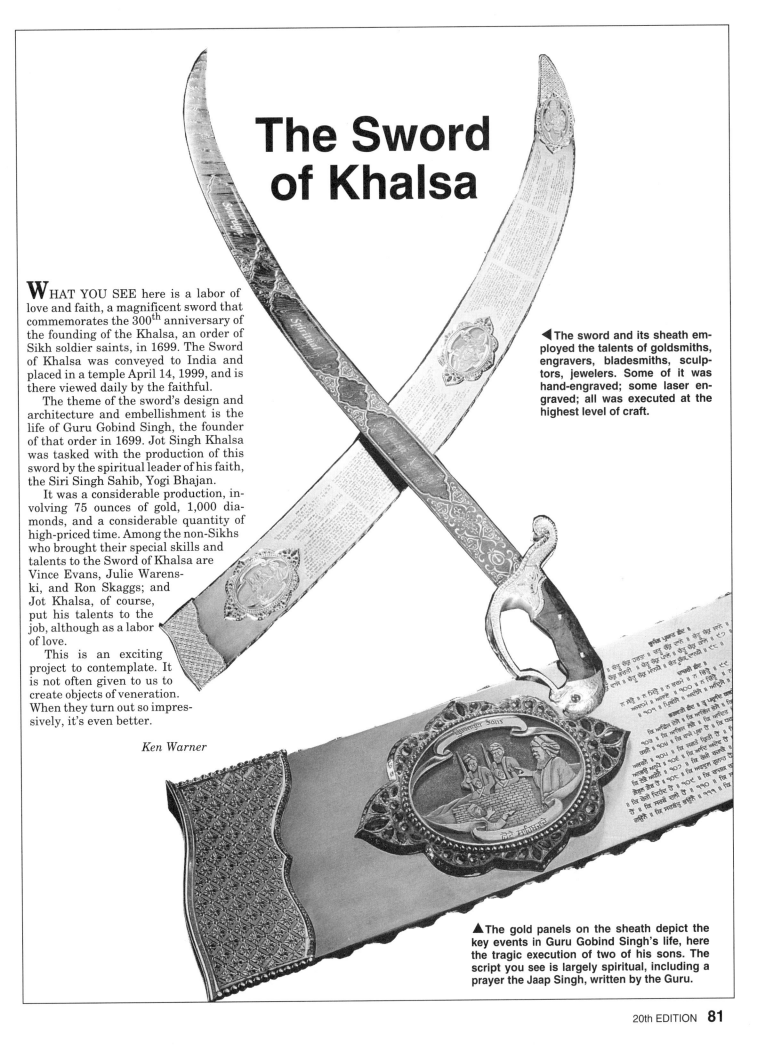

WHAT YOU SEE here is a labor of love and faith, a magnificent sword that commemorates the 300th anniversary of the founding of the Khalsa, an order of Sikh soldier saints, in 1699. The Sword of Khalsa was conveyed to India and placed in a temple April 14, 1999, and is there viewed daily by the faithful.

The theme of the sword's design and architecture and embellishment is the life of Guru Gobind Singh, the founder of that order in 1699. Jot Singh Khalsa was tasked with the production of this sword by the spiritual leader of his faith, the Siri Singh Sahib, Yogi Bhajan.

It was a considerable production, involving 75 ounces of gold, 1,000 diamonds, and a considerable quantity of high-priced time. Among the non-Sikhs who brought their special skills and talents to the Sword of Khalsa are Vince Evans, Julie Warenski, and Ron Skaggs; and Jot Khalsa, of course, put his talents to the job, although as a labor of love.

This is an exciting project to contemplate. It is not often given to us to create objects of veneration. When they turn out so impressively, it's even better.

Ken Warner

◀The sword and its sheath employed the talents of goldsmiths, engravers, bladesmiths, sculptors, jewelers. Some of it was hand-engraved; some laser engraved; all was executed at the highest level of craft.

▲The gold panels on the sheath depict the key events in Guru Gobind Singh's life, here the tragic execution of two of his sons. The script you see is largely spiritual, including a prayer the Jaap Singh, written by the Guru.

All Kinds of Plain Knives

PLAIN DOES NOT mean ordinary; plain by no means is ugly; plain is not the same as simple, either. Nor is it crude. Plain is not making a show for the show's sake. Plain is unembellished, not fancy.

Plain means straightforward; a lot of the time it means strong, visually strong for us since we are looking at photos; plain means what you see is what you get, most of the time.

Plain is a positive attribute. It comes easily to some; others have to strive. In knives, plain can be very beautiful.

Thus we are making a special effort to present a lot of plain knives here, mostly because they tend to get pushed aside, when it comes to public display both in this book and in other venues as well. They shouldn't, as you will see.

It is the nature of plain that there is no plain style. There are plain swords and plain penknives and plain tantos and even plain Scottish dirks. So we have winnowed out the plainest from our big pile of pictures and given them the very plainest arrangement—none at all—and we hope you like them.

Ken Warner

▼ **T. M. DOWELL:** Seriously simple and plain first-class drop-point hunter, actually, a decade old—it's ATS-34 or D2, maybe Vascowear. (Weyer photo)

▼ **WALLY HAYES:** You couldn't hardly get any simpler than this 13-inch blade in 52100, with maple grip. (Weyer photo)

▲ **PAOLO SCORDIA:** A good kitchen knife of 440C and cocobolo, flat ground with half tang and good-looking.

FRANK GAMBLE: Nothing flashy here but the natural surface of the stag, but it cuts a nice line. (Chan photo)

▼ **LILE KNIVES:** One of Jimmie's oldies—the right blade, two slabs and a couple of rivets. Profile is almost everything here.

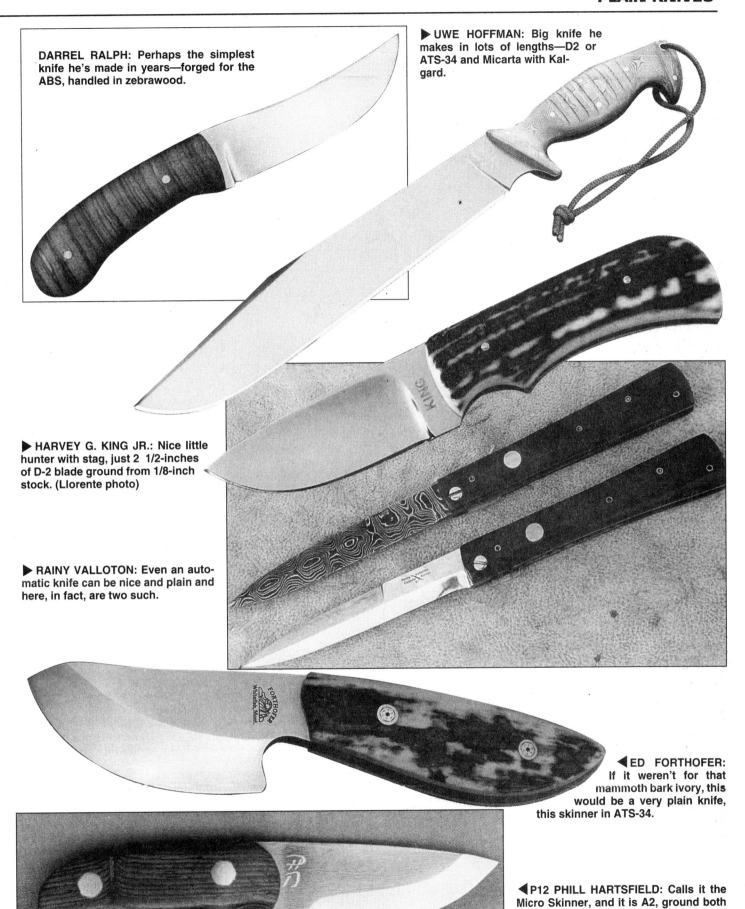

DARREL RALPH: Perhaps the simplest knife he's made in years—forged for the ABS, handled in zebrawood.

▶ **UWE HOFFMAN:** Big knife he makes in lots of lengths—D2 or ATS-34 and Micarta with Kalgard.

▶ **HARVEY G. KING JR.:** Nice little hunter with stag, just 2 1/2-inches of D-2 blade ground from 1/8-inch stock. (Llorente photo)

▶ **RAINY VALLOTON:** Even an automatic knife can be nice and plain and here, in fact, are two such.

◀ **ED FORTHOFER:** If it weren't for that mammoth bark ivory, this would be a very plain knife, this skinner in ATS-34.

◀ **P12 PHILL HARTSFIELD:** Calls it the Micro Skinner, and it is A2, ground both sides, with a cocobolo grip.

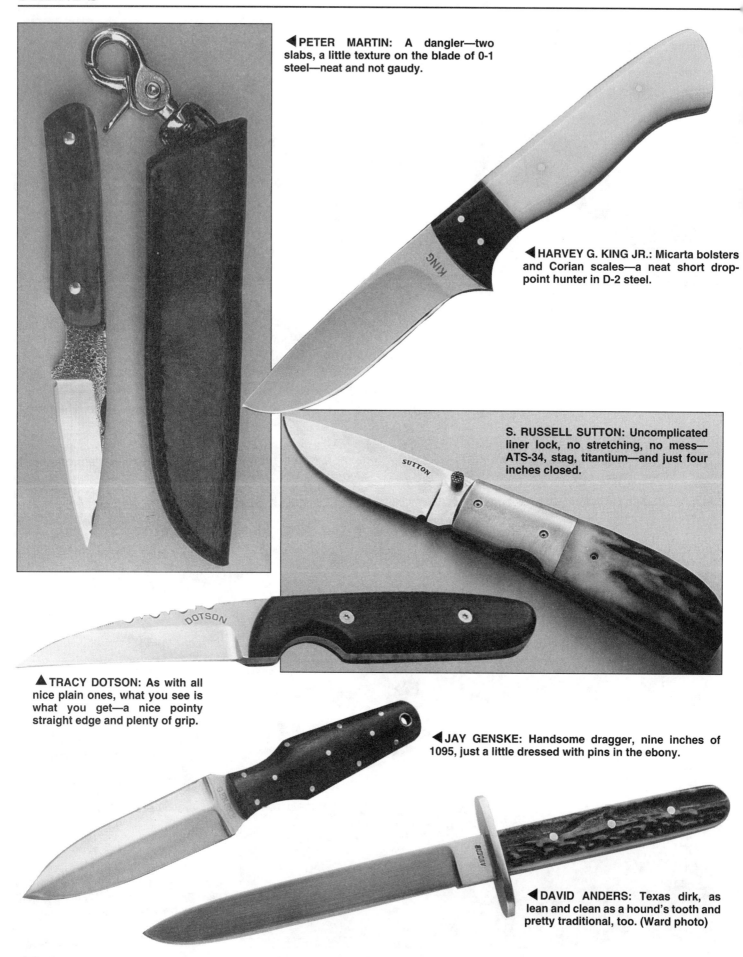

◀PETER MARTIN: A dangler—two slabs, a little texture on the blade of 0-1 steel—neat and not gaudy.

◀HARVEY G. KING JR.: Micarta bolsters and Corian scales—a neat short drop-point hunter in D-2 steel.

S. RUSSELL SUTTON: Uncomplicated liner lock, no stretching, no mess—ATS-34, stag, titantium—and just four inches closed.

▲TRACY DOTSON: As with all nice plain ones, what you see is what you get—a nice pointy straight edge and plenty of grip.

◀JAY GENSKE: Handsome dragger, nine inches of 1095, just a little dressed with pins in the ebony.

◀DAVID ANDERS: Texas dirk, as lean and clean as a hound's tooth and pretty traditional, too. (Ward photo)

▶ MORRIS C. WORRELL: Nice little personal knife, forged in 5160 with a hidden tang in the cocobolo handle, nickle silver bolsters.

◀ CHUCK ANDERSON: Eleven inches of efficient fillet knife, Micarta and Pakkawood scales. (Weyer photo)

DON MAXWELL: Nothing pushy here but the materials—ATS-34, brass and mastodon ivory—so he calls it a utility folder. (Chan photo)

▼ MIKE YURCO: Is California buckeye fancy if it's pinned with Micarta pins on a 440C blade? Probably not.

▶ V.J. MC CRACKIN: Clean drop point with a skinner sweep...just a real good-looking regular knife.

▶ CARL S. ZAKABI: Deeply hollow-ground 2 3/4-inch 440C blade and Diamondwood scales—handy-looking little guy. (Weyer photo)

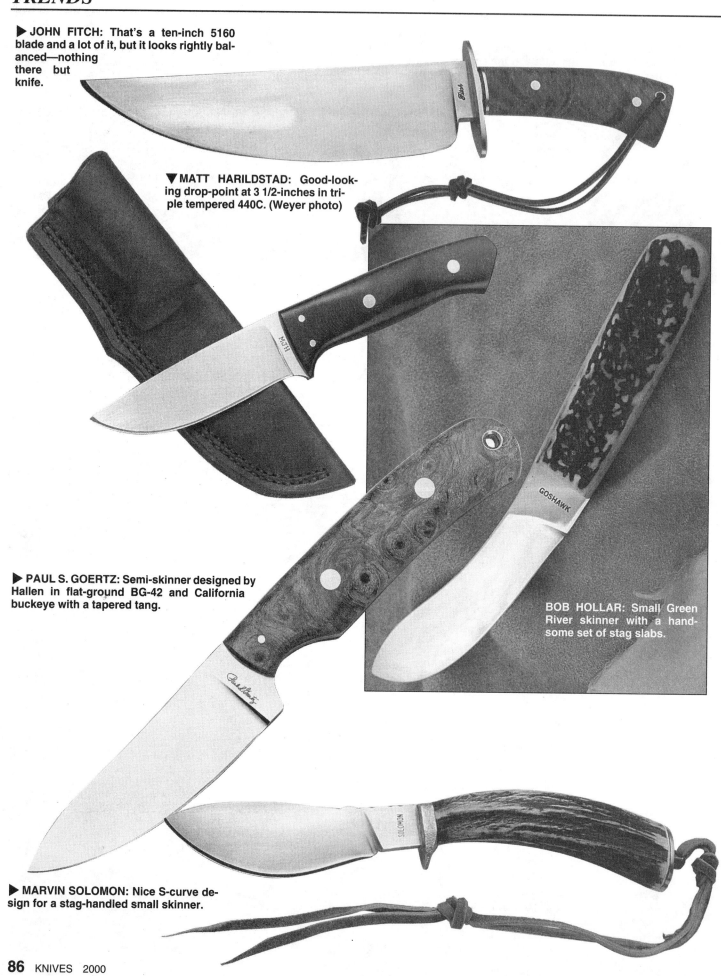

▶ JOHN FITCH: That's a ten-inch 5160 blade and a lot of it, but it looks rightly balanced—nothing there but knife.

▼ MATT HARILDSTAD: Good-looking drop-point at 3 1/2-inches in triple tempered 440C. (Weyer photo)

▶ PAUL S. GOERTZ: Semi-skinner designed by Hallen in flat-ground BG-42 and California buckeye with a tapered tang.

BOB HOLLAR: Small Green River skinner with a handsome set of stag slabs.

▶ MARVIN SOLOMON: Nice S-curve design for a stag-handled small skinner.

Knives of Stone

FOR PROBABLY A little longer than we have been what we are, we have been making use of knives of stone. In many out-of-the-way places on the planet, stone implements are still in use and still useful.

However, what you see here is made in shops full of steel implements. We do not need these knives. We do need, probably, the knowledge it takes to make them. Someone should be preserving it and these knifemakers, each for his own reason, have chosen to do so.

As you can learn elsewhere (Page 136 in State of the Art) stone edges are not bad edges. Stone knives take some special care, but down where the edge meets the meat, the flint can work just fine.

This is a little bit of the year's work in stone or flint or obsidian.

Ken Warner

▶ ERRETT CALLAHAN: The bison by Soodalter is from a drawing in the cavern of Niaux; the handle is mule deer; the assembly is with sinew and fish glue.

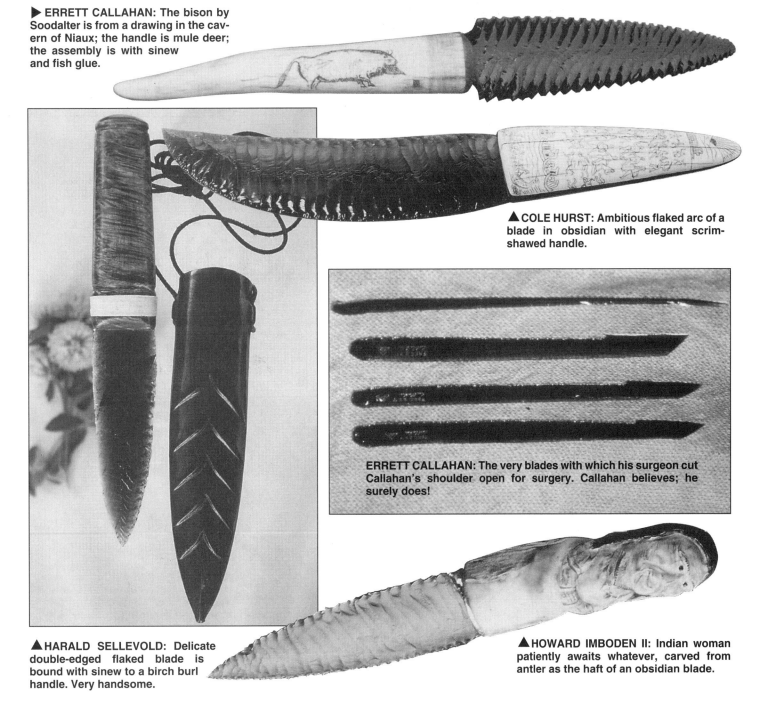

▲COLE HURST: Ambitious flaked arc of a blade in obsidian with elegant scrimshawed handle.

ERRETT CALLAHAN: The very blades with which his surgeon cut Callahan's shoulder open for surgery. Callahan believes; he surely does!

▲HARALD SELLEVOLD: Delicate double-edged flaked blade is bound with sinew to a birch burl handle. Very handsome.

▲HOWARD IMBODEN II: Indian woman patiently awaits whatever, carved from antler as the haft of an obsidian blade.

From Otherwhere, We Get . . .
Fantasies

SOME OF THEM are sculptors, some day-dreamers, some, no doubt, are lyric artists. What all those who create the sort of fantastic knife shapes and conceptions you see here have in common is different eyes from the rest of us.

That means that none of them can explain themselves. It would be like explaining traffic signals to a cat or table manners to a dog, so far as they are concerned. We would not, as the saying goes, get it.

What we do get however, are the knives. Such as these do not sell to everyone, but they sell very well indeed to some. Well, actually, knives that look a lot like the less outrageous of these sell big-time in the mail-order catalogs and collectibles market, but that is a whole different story.

Whatever your viewpoint on the propriety of these designs, it is obvious it requires more than average craft to pull them off.

In some cases it also takes a lot of Band-Aids. These are not forgiving profiles.

Whether it is a whole career, like the late William Cronk's or the present Virgil England's, or it's a sometime sport, the fantasy knife is a legitimate effort. And here are some of the best of late. Enjoy.

Ken Warner

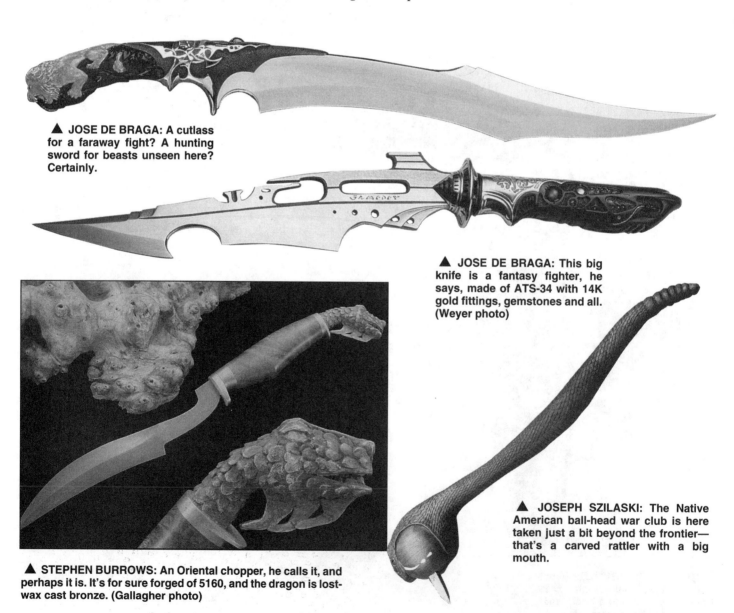

▲ JOSE DE BRAGA: A cutlass for a faraway fight? A hunting sword for beasts unseen here? Certainly.

▲ JOSE DE BRAGA: This big knife is a fantasy fighter, he says, made of ATS-34 with 14K gold fittings, gemstones and all. (Weyer photo)

▲ STEPHEN BURROWS: An Oriental chopper, he calls it, and perhaps it is. It's for sure forged of 5160, and the dragon is lost-wax cast bronze. (Gallagher photo)

▲ JOSEPH SZILASKI: The Native American ball-head war club is here taken just a bit beyond the frontier—that's a carved rattler with a big mouth.

▼ RON MYERS: With or without forged blades, these are Myers Sticks, and destined for the kits of free-fall fighters anywhere. (Point Seven photo)

▲ WOLFGANG LOERCHNER: A pair of small pretties destined for another kind of table setting somewhere way out there. But gorgeous! (Weyer photo)

▼ C. R. HUDSON: This is a 31-inch battle-axe with a few otherwordly touches, made of wrought iron with 13 inset steel edges. Wow.

▼ DANIEL STEPHAN: This is 16 inches long and the profile is sort of normal, but the sculpting is from otherwhere. Definitely. (Point Seven photo)

◄ GIL HIBBEN: Of course, and what else? It's called the Mantis, it's 19 inches long, and it is a Paul Ehlers design. (Weyer photo)

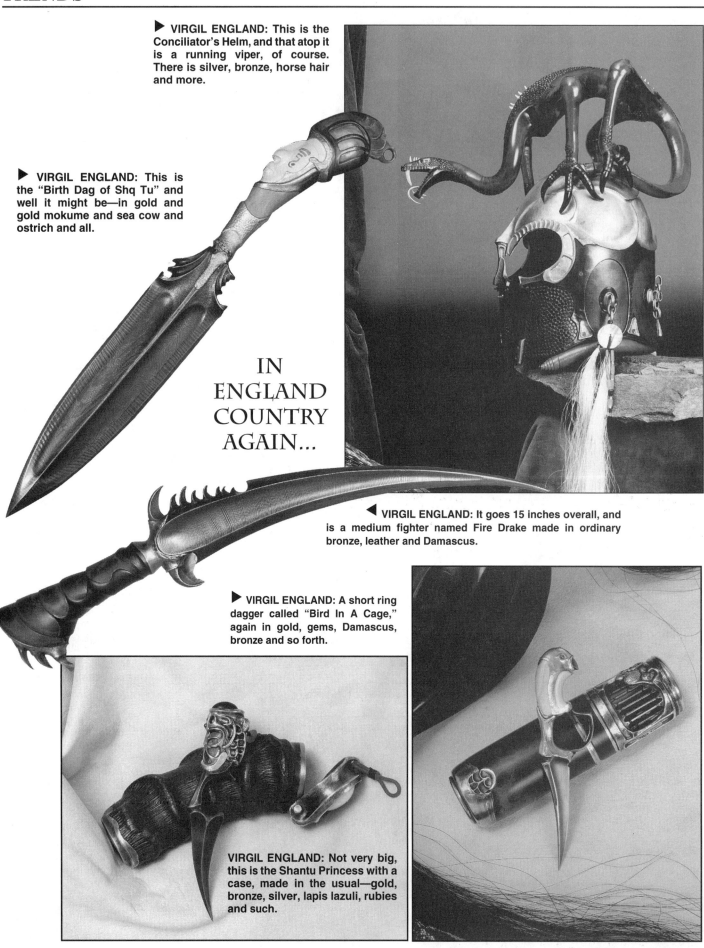

▶ VIRGIL ENGLAND: This is the Conciliator's Helm, and that atop it is a running viper, of course. There is silver, bronze, horse hair and more.

▶ VIRGIL ENGLAND: This is the "Birth Dag of Shq Tu" and well it might be—in gold and gold mokume and sea cow and ostrich and all.

IN
ENGLAND
COUNTRY
AGAIN...

◀ VIRGIL ENGLAND: It goes 15 inches overall, and is a medium fighter named Fire Drake made in ordinary bronze, leather and Damascus.

▶ VIRGIL ENGLAND: A short ring dagger called "Bird In A Cage," again in gold, gems, Damascus, bronze and so forth.

VIRGIL ENGLAND: Not very big, this is the Shantu Princess with a case, made in the usual—gold, bronze, silver, lapis lazuli, rubies and such.

Period Pieces

WE HAD THIS discussion last year. These are not frontier or buckskinner or primitive—they are period pieces. The period, more or less, is 1700-1850 and the place is North America. It is presumed other places and other times have their own period pieces, which we will leave to them.

You see here the obligatory big knife, the clasp knife, the penny knife and a raft of tomahawks and war clubs. You see them because this is the year for that stuff. Another year, and it could be rifle knives and mountain man scalpers or even dirk knives.

It's a special thing, this talent for re-creating the past physically, right in your hand. How close, line for line and ounce for ounce, these are to what actually was is not so important as their feel.

So that's what you are looking at here. You're seeing brand-new artifacts intended to reproduce sensations that are 100 to 200 years gone. It's not a lot stranger than science fiction. In fact, maybe it is science fiction, but awfully good-looking.

Ken Warner

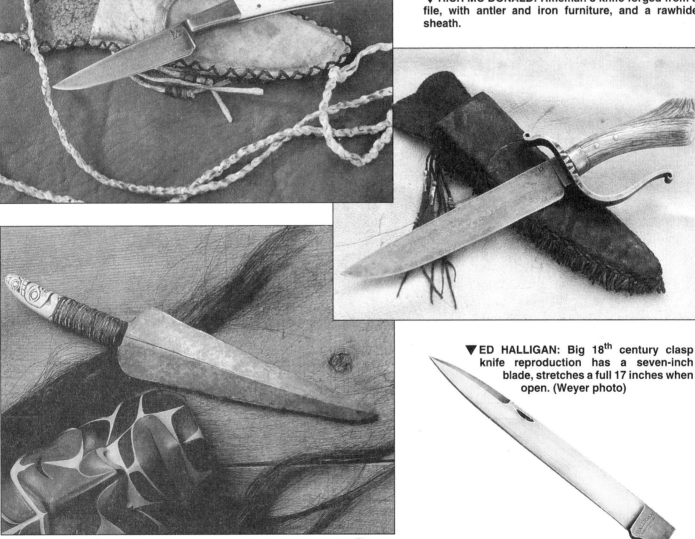

◄ RICH MC DONALD: Neck knife, forged and fitted with a bone handle and copper bolster. Blade is 3 3/4-inches.

▼ RICH MC DONALD: Rifleman's knife forged from a file, with antler and iron furniture, and a rawhide sheath.

▼ ED HALLIGAN: Big 18th century clasp knife reproduction has a seven-inch blade, stretches a full 17 inches when open. (Weyer photo)

▲ SCOTT SLOBODIAN: Nine inches of forged copper make this Pacific Northwest Indian dagger with whalebone grip, leather-wrapped.

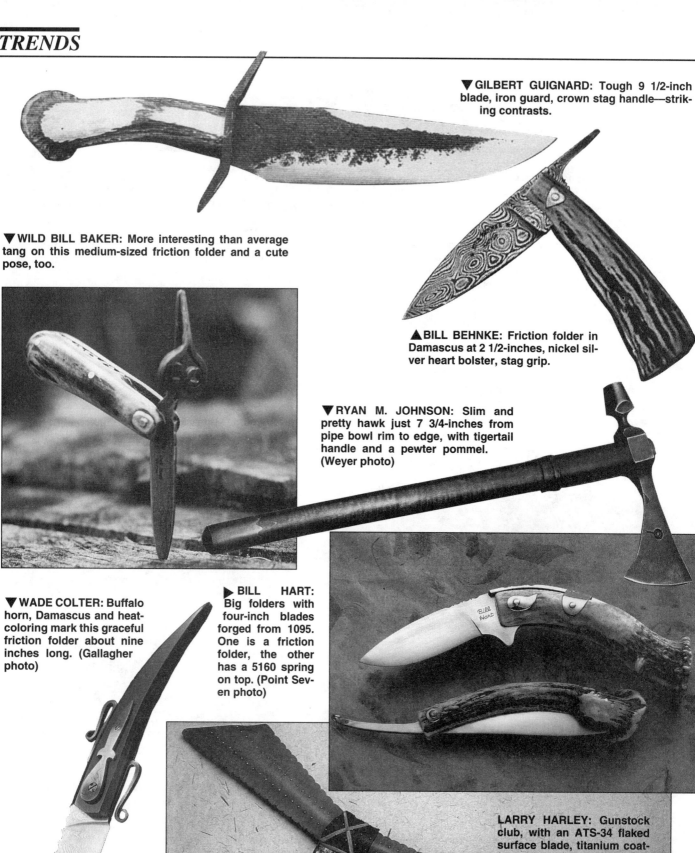

▼GILBERT GUIGNARD: Tough 9 1/2-inch blade, iron guard, crown stag handle—striking contrasts.

▼WILD BILL BAKER: More interesting than average tang on this medium-sized friction folder and a cute pose, too.

▲BILL BEHNKE: Friction folder in Damascus at 2 1/2-inches, nickel silver heart bolster, stag grip.

▼RYAN M. JOHNSON: Slim and pretty hawk just 7 3/4-inches from pipe bowl rim to edge, with tigertail handle and a pewter pommel. (Weyer photo)

▼WADE COLTER: Buffalo horn, Damascus and heat-coloring mark this graceful friction folder about nine inches long. (Gallagher photo)

▶BILL HART: Big folders with four-inch blades forged from 1095. One is a friction folder, the other has a 5160 spring on top. (Point Seven photo)

LARRY HARLEY: Gunstock club, with an ATS-34 flaked surface blade, titanium coated. Piece is 34 inches long. (Point Seven photo)

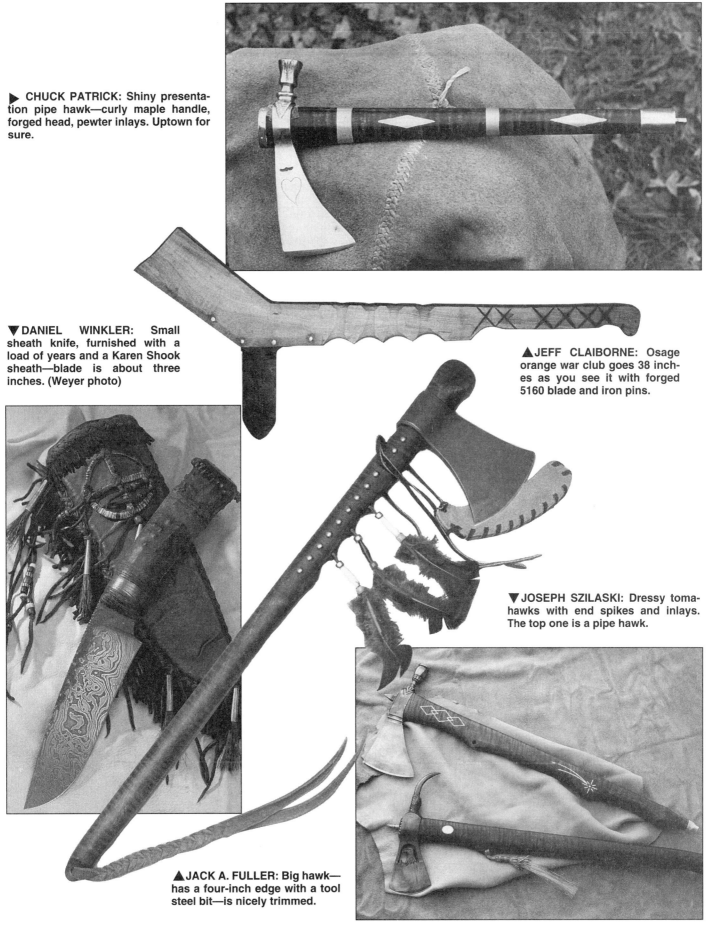

▶ **CHUCK PATRICK:** Shiny presentation pipe hawk—curly maple handle, forged head, pewter inlays. Uptown for sure.

▼ **DANIEL WINKLER:** Small sheath knife, furnished with a load of years and a Karen Shook sheath—blade is about three inches. (Weyer photo)

▲ **JEFF CLAIBORNE:** Osage orange war club goes 38 inches as you see it with forged 5160 blade and iron pins.

▼ **JOSEPH SZILASKI:** Dressy tomahawks with end spikes and inlays. The top one is a pipe hawk.

▲ **JACK A. FULLER:** Big hawk—has a four-inch edge with a tool steel bit—is nicely trimmed.

Flamboyant Folders

FLAMBOYANT IS DESCRIBED as "...strikingly elaborate or colorful display..." and all these knives certainly fill that bill one way or another. There are lots of ways for a knife to be flamboyant.

Some get there on the sheer exuberance of their profiles. They would be attention-getters if they were only silhouettes.

For others, it's the impact of the surfaces, either tactile or visual or—we have to face this—money-related. It is not that unusual to find sterling where others use nickle, gold instead of brass and rubies instead of garnets wherever a knifemaker or his customer want to make a splash.

And there is the fundamental material itself—a piece of falling star, for instance, in the blade, wood from a well-known tree, steel so worked and laminated as to spell out names or wave Old Glory. At least one famous knife in recent years was made of solid gold, although it was its workmanship that made the headlines.

If you'll look close at hand here, you'll see some of that, every one a folder. They're doing some lavish things with knives that fold these days.

Ken Warner

◄VAN BARNETT: Exercise in sole authorship, it's over eight inches long in deeply carved Damascus trimmed with 14KT gold and mammoth ivory.

►GLENN WATERS: Prodigious elaboration in gold and pearl and Damascus steel—rising sun and comets and a bug, to name three.

▲JOE KIOUS: One of those cases where the profile was plenty, but the embellishment ain't bad. It's Ray Cover engraving and inlays. (Point Seven photo)

◄HOWARD HITCHMOUGH: It's the surfaces here and the shape, with the gold mostly hidden along the spine. The blade is just over three inches. (Point Seven photo)

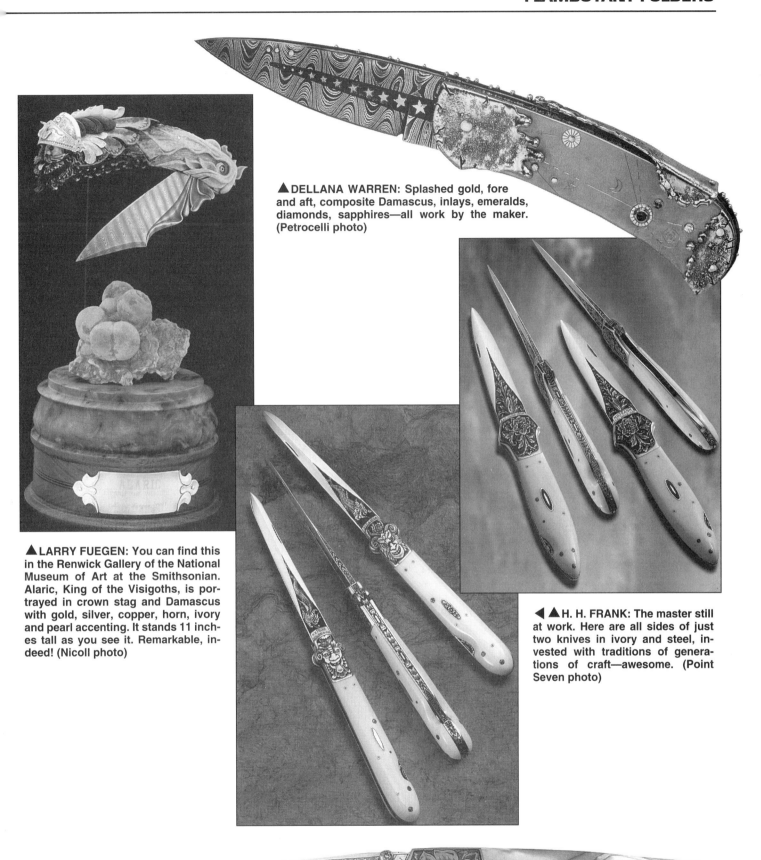

▲DELLANA WARREN: Splashed gold, fore and aft, composite Damascus, inlays, emeralds, diamonds, sapphires—all work by the maker. (Petrocelli photo)

▲LARRY FUEGEN: You can find this in the Renwick Gallery of the National Museum of Art at the Smithsonian. Alaric, King of the Visigoths, is portrayed in crown stag and Damascus with gold, silver, copper, horn, ivory and pearl accenting. It stands 11 inches tall as you see it. Remarkable, indeed! (Nicoll photo)

◄▲H. H. FRANK: The master still at work. Here are all sides of just two knives in ivory and steel, invested with traditions of generations of craft—awesome. (Point Seven photo)

►E. G. PETERSON: Simple, true, but very eye-catching—the pearl pattern and the flowers create a special knife.

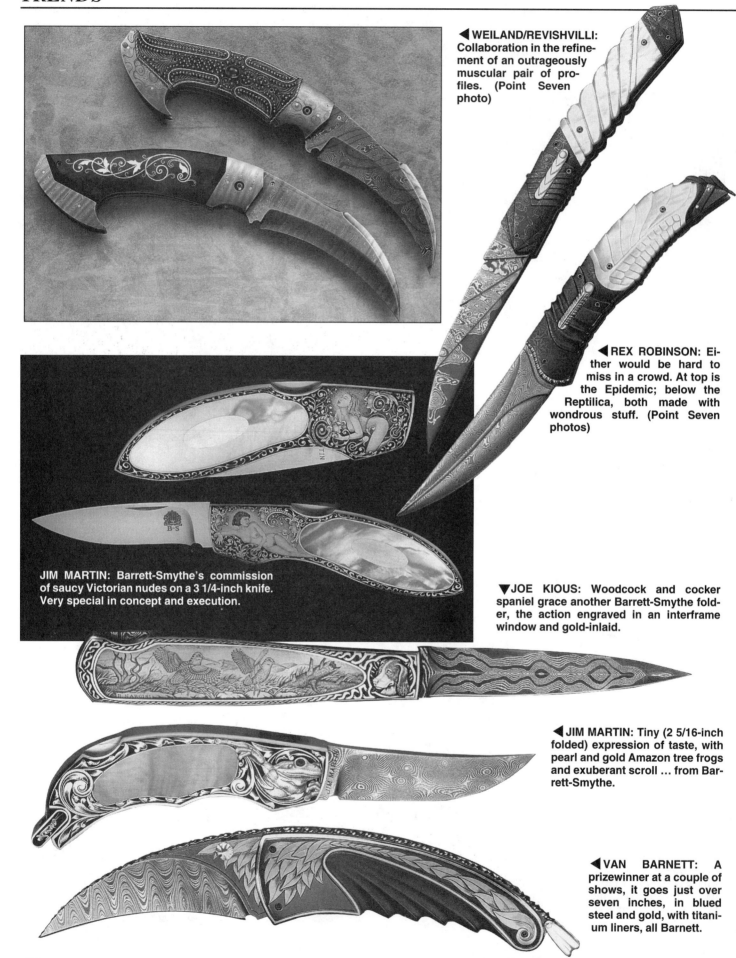

WEILAND/REVISHVILLI: Collaboration in the refinement of an outrageously muscular pair of profiles. (Point Seven photo)

REX ROBINSON: Either would be hard to miss in a crowd. At top is the Epidemic; below the Reptilica, both made with wondrous stuff. (Point Seven photos)

JIM MARTIN: Barrett-Smythe's commission of saucy Victorian nudes on a 3 1/4-inch knife. Very special in concept and execution.

JOE KIOUS: Woodcock and cocker spaniel grace another Barrett-Smythe folder, the action engraved in an interframe window and gold-inlaid.

JIM MARTIN: Tiny (2 5/16-inch folded) expression of taste, with pearl and gold Amazon tree frogs and exuberant scroll ... from Barrett-Smythe.

VAN BARNETT: A prizewinner at a couple of shows, it goes just over seven inches, in blued steel and gold, with titanium liners, all Barnett.

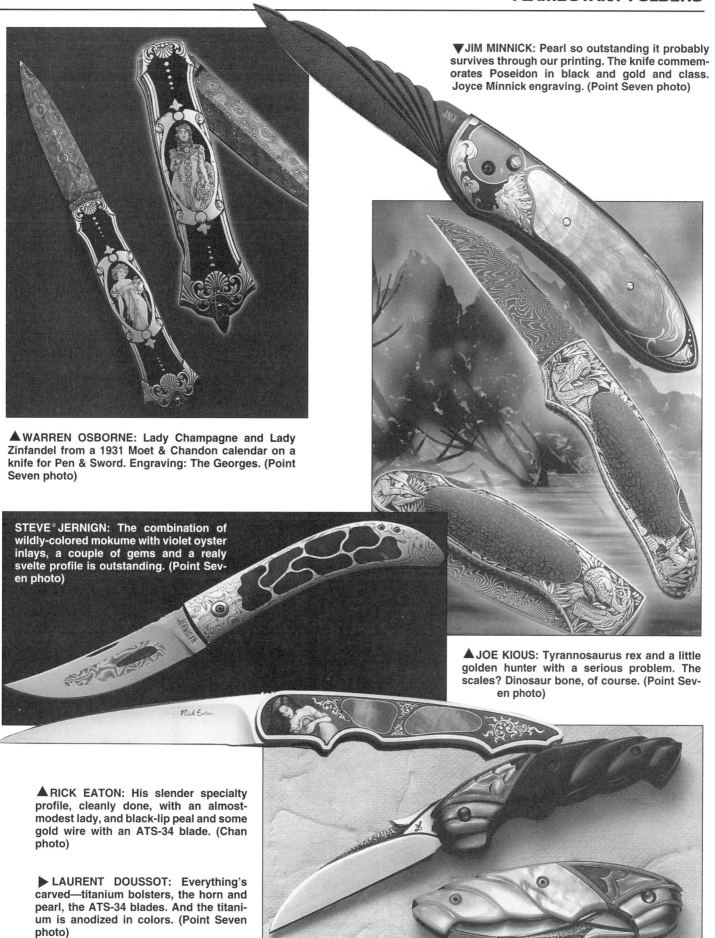

▼JIM MINNICK: Pearl so outstanding it probably survives through our printing. The knife commemorates Poseidon in black and gold and class. Joyce Minnick engraving. (Point Seven photo)

▲WARREN OSBORNE: Lady Champagne and Lady Zinfandel from a 1931 Moet & Chandon calendar on a knife for Pen & Sword. Engraving: The Georges. (Point Seven photo)

STEVE° JERNIGN: The combination of wildly-colored mokume with violet oyster inlays, a couple of gems and a realy svelte profile is outstanding. (Point Seven photo)

▲JOE KIOUS: Tyrannosaurus rex and a little golden hunter with a serious problem. The scales? Dinosaur bone, of course. (Point Seven photo)

▲RICK EATON: His slender specialty profile, cleanly done, with an almost-modest lady, and black-lip peal and some gold wire with an ATS-34 blade. (Chan photo)

▶ LAURENT DOUSSOT: Everything's carved—titanium bolsters, the horn and pearl, the ATS-34 blades. And the titanium is anodized in colors. (Point Seven photo)

Bodacious Straight Knives

SOME DICTIONARY SCHOLARS believe the thoroughly American word *bodacious* is simply a combination of the words *bold* and *audacious*. What that means to us is that we have exactly the word we need to describe this group of knives.

These are not necessarily the boldest or most audacious of the designs in this very edition of this book, but every one is anyway bodacious. That is, they are either big or surprising or forward or lavish—whatever they are is a little beyond expectations.

There's a lot of decoration, of painstaking effort, of almost outrageous conception. There is no rhyme nor reason nor continuity ... except they are every one, one way or another, fun. Most are pretty expensive, too, but that is the way of the whole world, not just this one.

Ken Warner

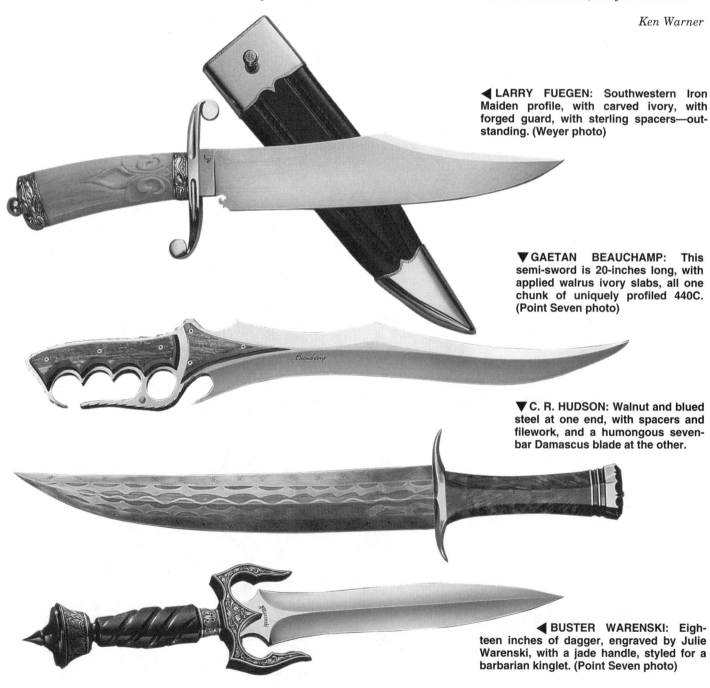

◀LARRY FUEGEN: Southwestern Iron Maiden profile, with carved ivory, with forged guard, with sterling spacers—outstanding. (Weyer photo)

▼GAETAN BEAUCHAMP: This semi-sword is 20-inches long, with applied walrus ivory slabs, all one chunk of uniquely profiled 440C. (Point Seven photo)

▼C. R. HUDSON: Walnut and blued steel at one end, with spacers and filework, and a humongous seven-bar Damascus blade at the other.

◀BUSTER WARENSKI: Eighteen inches of dagger, engraved by Julie Warenski, with a jade handle, styled for a barbarian kinglet. (Point Seven photo)

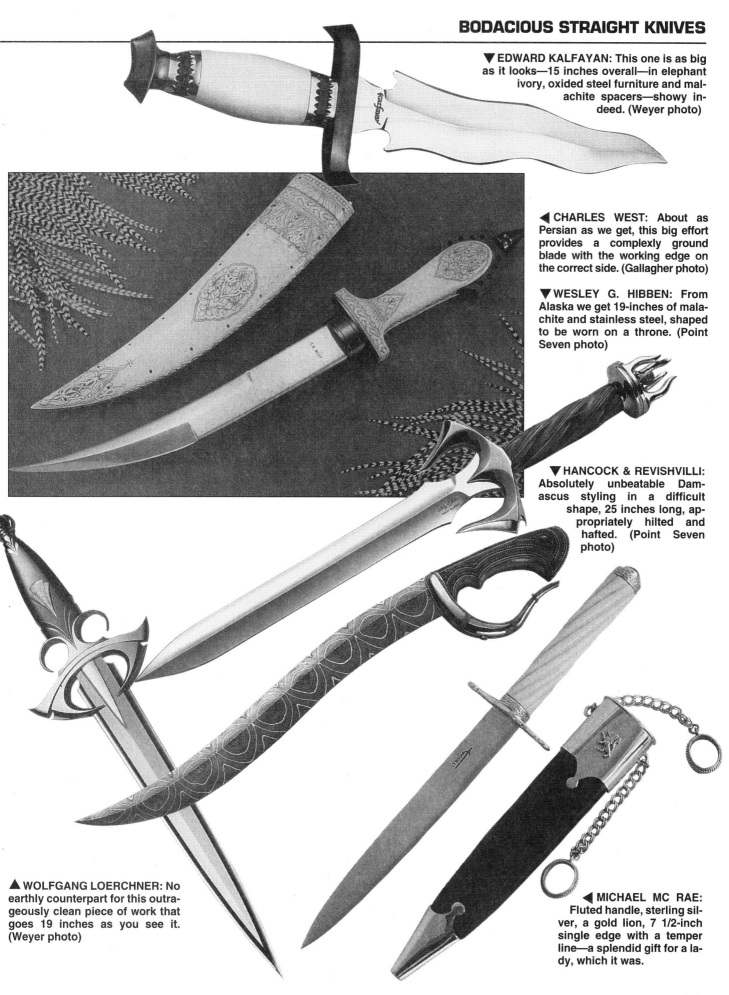

▼ EDWARD KALFAYAN: This one is as big as it looks—15 inches overall—in elephant ivory, oxided steel furniture and malachite spacers—showy indeed. (Weyer photo)

◀ CHARLES WEST: About as Persian as we get, this big effort provides a complexly ground blade with the working edge on the correct side. (Gallagher photo)

▼ WESLEY G. HIBBEN: From Alaska we get 19-inches of malachite and stainless steel, shaped to be worn on a throne. (Point Seven photo)

▼ HANCOCK & REVISHVILLI: Absolutely unbeatable Damascus styling in a difficult shape, 25 inches long, appropriately hilted and hafted. (Point Seven photo)

▲ WOLFGANG LOERCHNER: No earthly counterpart for this outrageously clean piece of work that goes 19 inches as you see it. (Weyer photo)

◀ MICHAEL MC RAE: Fluted handle, sterling silver, a gold lion, 7 1/2-inch single edge with a temper line—a splendid gift for a lady, which it was.

►GLENN WATERS: Outrageous decorative effects here—gold leaf over rayskin with silver leaf patches, gold and copper inlays and "sort-of-netsukes."

►ZAZA REVISHVILLI: All-out traditional silver work with garnets on a blade by Hibben from a Thomas billet—great collaboration. (Point Seven photo)

▲ARPAD BOJTAS: Tiger and snake duke it out in ATS-34 "semi-integral" dagger just under nine-inches overall—a new way to do it, looks like.

▲JERRY FISK: This Morning Star has a Damascus ball and pommel, iron spikes and handle—distinctly formidable at 28-inches overall. (Weyer photo)

◄RAYMOND B. RYBAR, JR.: Biblical significance etched along the blade of a splendid dagger, its quillons made of sterling silver horses.

▶JOSE DE BRAGA: A ton of idiosyncratically carved ATS-34 touched up with 14K gold and carved wood to match—prodigious. (Weyer photo)

▲DAL LECK: A really big dagger, with three-bar composite blade—this impressive piece is 18 inches long. (Box photo)

▲BILL FIORINI: Nothing here but perfect dark stag, chased silver, a little gold, a spiderweb Damascus blade—just your everyday deluxed dagger. (Point Seven photo)

JAY FISHER: What's there to say? You see ten 440C fish exploding in flight, comprising eight steak knives and a carving set, the whole weighing 17 pounds.

▶DAL LECK: The Lady of The Lake has a forged hand; she holds the big Dal Leck dagger above. Clever, these Lecks.

ALEX DANIELS: Small, but showy, an all-out engraved pearl dagger and sheath—just under seven inches. (Point Seven photo)

ETHNICITY

ELSEWHERE WE POINT out that ethnic and foreign sorts of knives are often made in the U.S., and sometimes made very well indeed. In contrast, that is, to the fact that not many makers overseas appear to make knives that look very American. (Of course, this may look quite the other way around to someone over there, in which case they should start a knife annual themselves and say so.)

Here on these pages are some of those ethnic sorts of knives. We have quite a run on Scots patterns, as well as the usual tries at Japanese and not-so Japanese. But that's not all—there are some other things happening.

Are these compliments to those other folks or not? Well, the people who make the knives you see here certainly intend them to be tributes to designs and styles

they personally admire enough to emulate. Are they entitled? Well, maybe not elsewhere, but they sure are in the U.S. because here if they don't do it well enough, they go broke.

This is how the ethnic trade looks this year. Check the swords out, too, and some of the tacticals. And enjoy.

Ken Warner

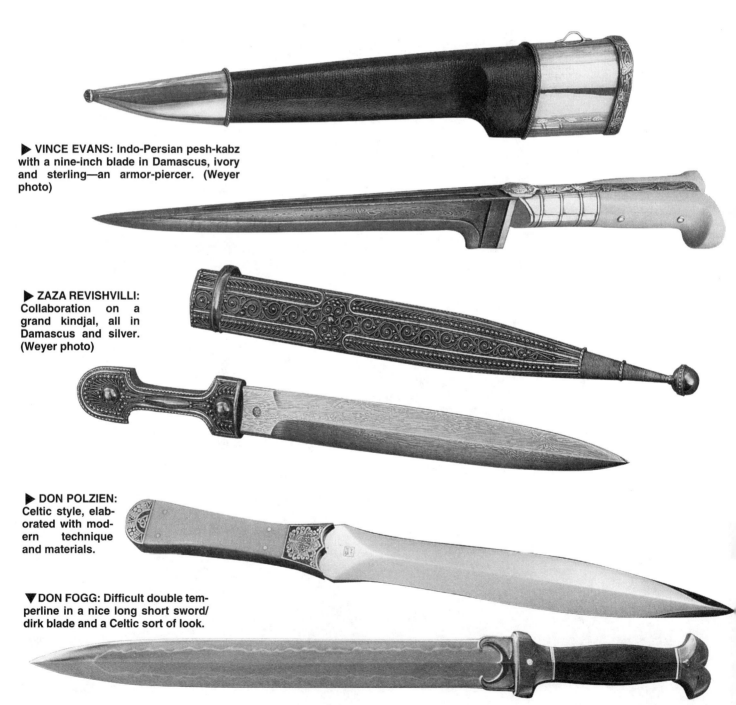

▶ VINCE EVANS: Indo-Persian pesh-kabz with a nine-inch blade in Damascus, ivory and sterling—an armor-piercer. (Weyer photo)

▶ ZAZA REVISHVILLI: Collaboration on a grand kindjal, all in Damascus and silver. (Weyer photo)

▶ DON POLZIEN: Celtic style, elaborated with modern technique and materials.

▼ DON FOGG: Difficult double temperline in a nice long short sword/dirk blade and a Celtic sort of look.

▶ PETER HENRY: Scots dirk and sgian dubh, the dirk of the 1745-1760 period, and all, including scabbards, pretty up-town stuff.

◀ VINCE EVANS: As with the old ones, there are very nearly never two alike in the Scots basket-hilt business and so it is here. (Weyer photo)

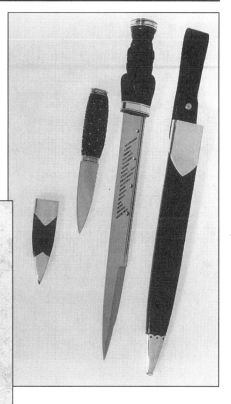

▶ JOE HUDDLESTON: The all-out dirk set in the very best of Victorian style, with a brooch to match the hilt—gorgeous Scots dandyism. (Weyer photo)

▼ MICK SEARS: Scottish sgian dubh, styled with a crown stag grip and nicely made—fit for any Scot stocking top.

BRYAN LYTTLE: The dirk and stocking knife set gone high-style in ways far more 20th century than 18th century.

◀ MICHAEL MC RAE: Replica, except for fancier furniture, of the dirk in the grip of the corpse of John MacRae on the field of Sherrifmuir, September, 1715. That's real.

MICHAEL MC RAE: The Damascus blade is differentially tempered and just over 3 1/2-inches; the rest is pretty fancy.

▲ WALLY HAYES: Matched dirks, one trimmed in sterling, the other in gold (to tell them apart, of course.) Carved grips are ebony. (Weyer photo)

◀STEPHEN LINDBERG: A small kwaiken for neckwear, chisel ground in ATS-34. Sheath is Kydex-lined.

◀SCOTT SLOBODIAN: Broad-bladed fighting weapon in the style of those originals made from polearm blades. Good looking. (Weyer photo)

▼STEPHEN LINDBERG: A simplified kwaiken or utility knife in apple coral, double ground of ATS-34—seven inches overall.

▼DON POLZIEN: Fancy tanto, all very dressy, but with a dead-serious fighting blade. Note the clouds on the temper line.

◀HEINZ LEBER: Simplified short tanto in Damascus with walrus ivory and North American full-tang construction.

▼WAYNE WATANABE: Modernized tanto with a wrapped full-tang and a little netsuke—businesslike.

▶ PHILL HARTSFIELD: It's his ETM 100, just under five inches long, chisel-ground in A2 steel, cord-wrapped.

▲ DAVID GOLDBERG: Dressy tanto with beautiful rayskin covering and gold touches. Includes the utility knife. (Point Seven photo)

▲ DON POLZIEN: Slotted blade, fully carved wooden sheath and grip—not your usual tanto, but good-looking.

▲ ANDERS HOGSTROM: It's a Persian bedside dagger in 1050 with copper, sterling, frogskin. (Slobodian photo)

▶ ERIC BERGLAND: Finnish camp knife in forged 1084 with madrone wood and caribou. Blade is just over six inches. (Weyer photo)

In The Style Of....

SOME OF US find suitable and agreeable designs in styles already accomplished by others. Thus, in their turns, significant knifemakers are joined in their design ideas by other makers. It happened to William Scagel and to W. D. Randall Jr. and to Robert W. Loveless and to William F. Moran Jr. and it hasn't stopped for any of those.

You'll see a small group labeled Rod Chappell here. It's been a while since there were a lot of these exuberant knives about. Chappell himself hasn't been active for a while. Yet, here are these new knives. So we'll look at them.

No telling who is next. We can be sure there will be someone, however, and he or she is probably represented elsewhere in this very book.

Ken Warner

LORA SUE BETHKE: Steel is 5160 at 3 1/2-inches and the composite grip — brass, fiber spacers, leather, antler is practically blueprint for Scagel style.

Scagel

▼ JAMES R. LUCIE: The very profile of the camp knives the master made, forged in 5160 steel and marked with his krisses.

▲ CHARLES HILLMAN: Nine different Scagel styles here, most of them close enough to make the grade.

► JAMES R. LUCIE: This Scagel hunter was made for singer Willie Nelson and Lucie says it is the best of this style he's made.

► FRANK GAMBLE: The steel here is ATS-34, but most of the handle was assembled with material Scagel himself left behind in his shop. (Chan photo)

◄ JAMES R. LUCIE: A little fish knife done up as Scagel did them—a lot of spacers and an antler tine.

Loveless

▶ WILLIAM MC DONALD: It's 440C, right at 8 1/2-inches as you see it, with a familiar shape to its logo, too.

▶ LILE KNIVES: A stag chute knife as it was designed to be built, Lovelessian in every line.

▶ BOB PARKER: Only minor proportional changes separate this profile from the Loveless sub-hilt fighter. It's ATS-34 and Micarta. (Weyer photo)

▶ T. W. DOWNING: The handle isn't too close, but the layout is righteous and Downing knows how.

▲ JAMES M. HAND: An unabashed Big Bear in Damascus and Wildwoods scales, nicely double-hollow-ground, which is de rigeur.

▶ RICARDO VELARDE: Minor departures here, but the source is clear. These are all in the style of ... (Point Seven photo)

◀WILLIAM F. MORAN JR.: He knows exactly how to get the Moran look, no matter what the knife style, but he is practiced. (Holter photo)

Moran

▶ MARK C. SENTZ: A presentation quillon dagger in the old style and with a splendid maple case.

▼WILLIAM R. HURT: Big quillon dagger in the most traditional of blade shapes and grip spiraling and wrapping—very in the style of ...

◀E. JAY HENDRICKSON: It's over 17 inches long, every inch in the correct tradition, but the finished embellishment out-models the mode. (Point Seven photo)

▶ BOB RUPERT: In 1095 steel with maple and silver wire, this skinner/flesher looks like Moran might have made it a while back.

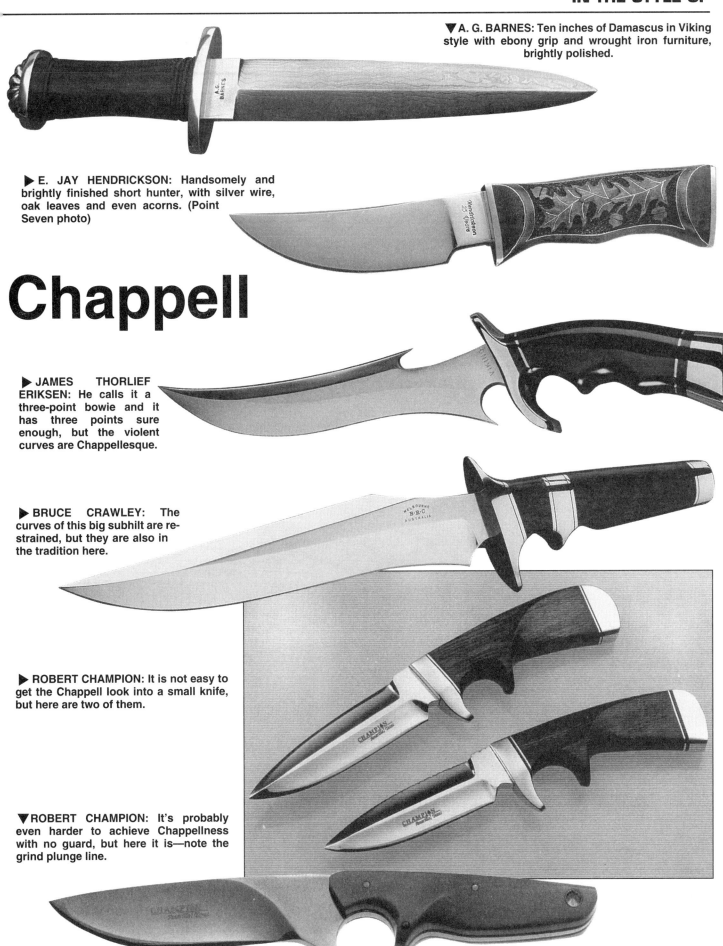

▼A. G. BARNES: Ten inches of Damascus in Viking style with ebony grip and wrought iron furniture, brightly polished.

▶E. JAY HENDRICKSON: Handsomely and brightly finished short hunter, with silver wire, oak leaves and even acorns. (Point Seven photo)

Chappell

▶JAMES THORLIEF ERIKSEN: He calls it a three-point bowie and it has three points sure enough, but the violent curves are Chappellesque.

▶BRUCE CRAWLEY: The curves of this big subhilt are restrained, but they are also in the tradition here.

▶ROBERT CHAMPION: It is not easy to get the Chappell look into a small knife, but here are two of them.

▼ROBERT CHAMPION: It's probably even harder to achieve Chappellness with no guard, but here it is—note the grind plunge line.

Kits & Sets

SOMETIMES THE IDEA calls for two or more pieces and then it is either a set or a kit and here are some to look at for this year.

The kitchen and the hunter get the most attention with this kind of thing. However, anybody can play.

This time, however, there's nothing exotic. Just some nice-looking stuff well worth looking at and we hope you enjoy it.

Ken Warner

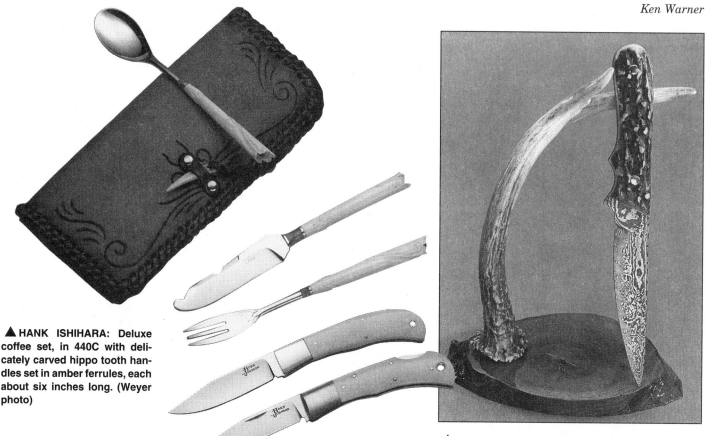

▲ HANK ISHIHARA: Deluxe coffee set, in 440C with delicately carved hippo tooth handles set in amber ferrules, each about six inches long. (Weyer photo)

▼ LLOYD PENDLETON: The Big Five, an absolutely splendiferous aggregation of clean and pretty design with gorgeous engraving. (Weyer photo)

▲ HORN & JOHNSON: A pair to draw to—one stiff, one folder—made in concert by two of the big names. (Weyer

▲ SCOTT S. DICKISON: Simple desk display mode for a simple hunter with dramatic texture—a conversation starter in any office. (Weyer photo)

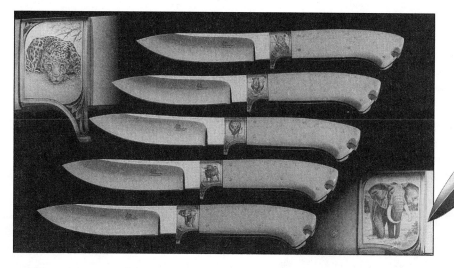

▲ RICARDO VELARDE: A pair in pearl, one for defense, one for work. The boot knife is just under eight inches long. (Point Seven photo)

▲ BILL COFFEE: A bear hunter pair, obviously, scrimmed by Linda Petree, and enough knives for the whole job. (Gallagher photo)

▶GEORGE TICHBOURNE: High end kitchen knives, a really full array all in 440C and black paper Micarta … serious stuff.

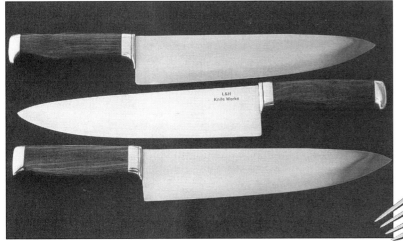

◀DOC GUNDERSEN: Ten inches of 440C with cocobolo handles in classic chef's shape—redoubtable knives.

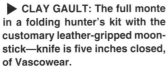

▲ FANIE LA GRANGE: Posies on a pair built for any table, any cuisine.

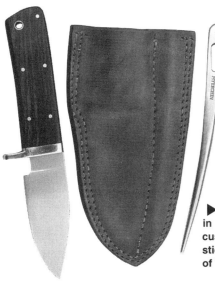

◀MILTON CHOATE: A boater's set, with a Choate utility hunter and a Meyerchin marlinspike.

▶ CLAY GAULT: The full monte in a folding hunter's kit with the customary leather-gripped moonstick—knife is five inches closed, of Vascowear.

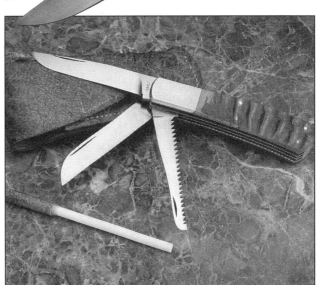

Knives With Style

THEY COME FROM everywhere, the knives that carry their own style. We don't show all of them here—you can see them throughout the book. However, these seem to be especially stylish to this writer.

There are familiar names here, old-timers, even. Some of those got to be old-timers by having their own style. And there are new names and obscure names. Some of those are dabblers; some we may see as old-timers a few years hence.

Looking for real style is one of the most enjoyable ways to tour a big knife show. But if you can't do that, here's a dose for now.

Ken Warner

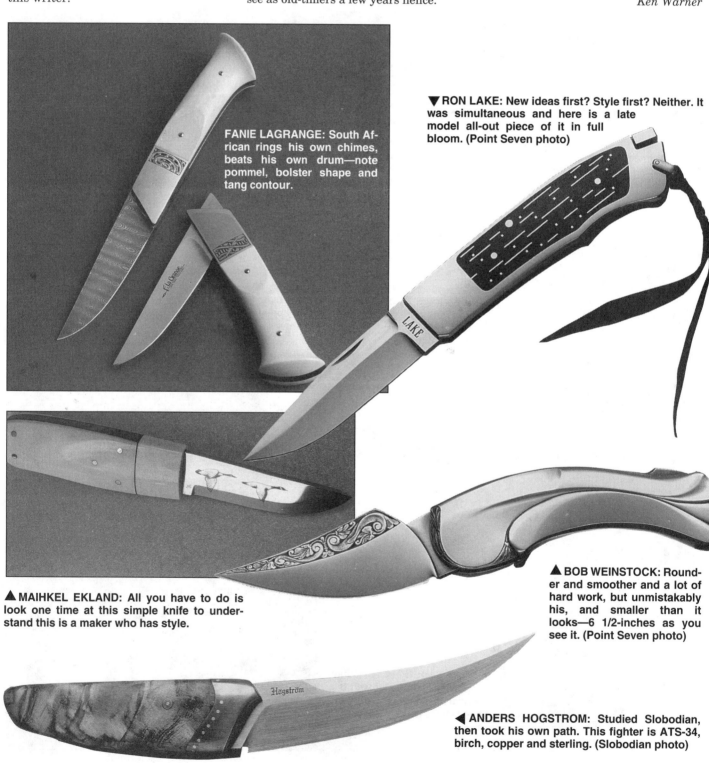

FANIE LAGRANGE: South African rings his own chimes, beats his own drum—note pommel, bolster shape and tang contour.

▼RON LAKE: New ideas first? Style first? Neither. It was simultaneous and here is a late model all-out piece of it in full bloom. (Point Seven photo)

▲MAIHKEL EKLAND: All you have to do is look one time at this simple knife to understand this is a maker who has style.

▲BOB WEINSTOCK: Rounder and smoother and a lot of hard work, but unmistakably his, and smaller than it looks—6 1/2-inches as you see it. (Point Seven photo)

◄ANDERS HOGSTROM: Studied Slobodian, then took his own path. This fighter is ATS-34, birch, copper and sterling. (Slobodian photo)

▼DALTON HOLDER: This is the new look; it grows from the old look, called "My Knife" for years. It's personal as hell and pretty Western, too. (Point Seven photo)

▲BARRY GALLAGHER: This is about as plain as this guy gets and still the style is there—blue smoothed, but not quite, bone with 52100 and gems.

▼TAKAO MAE: Idiosyncratically sculpted in his own idea, this maker's knives are his alone—striking profiles.

▼JIM CROWELL: Except for the somewhat wild pattern in the blade, this is as restrained as knife designs get, but so perfectly so it is high style indeed. (Weyer photo)

▲FRANCO BONASSI: Very, very simple—clean arcs at each end, a bolster length close to the Golden Mean—and very tough elegance.

▶MARDI MESHESHIAN: Under five inches closed, there is hardly anything to this little dagger except how neat it looks. Must be stylish. (Weyer photo)

Notable Folders

WE LIVE, WE handmade knife people, in a flood of folders. There is no way to pick one category to fit them all into, nice and neat. *Folders* doesn't work, for instance—way too broad. *Tactical* is much too narrow. You have to recognize *Fabulous* and we do. And then, all through the book, there they are. *Slip-joints* get their own slot, of course.

So you do all that and you still have this stack of real good pictures of real nice folding knives. There is also this giant stack of not so good photos or of not so good knives, and not a few duplicates from guys who send in a dozen photos, but they are already dealt with.

So you say, "OK. These are special or interesting or whatever, but what's the category?"

And there is none.

Since they belong in the book, you decide they are notable. And so right here, you can look at some notable folders.

Ken Warner

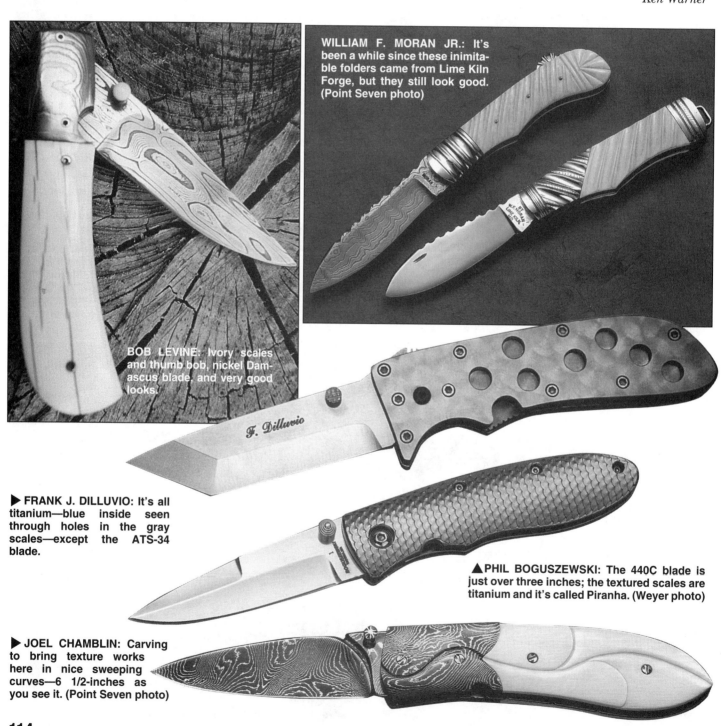

BOB LEVINE: Ivory scales and thumb bob, nickel Damascus blade, and very good looks.

WILLIAM F. MORAN JR.: It's been a while since these inimitable folders came from Lime Kiln Forge, but they still look good. (Point Seven photo)

▶ FRANK J. DILLUVIO: It's all titanium—blue inside seen through holes in the gray scales—except the ATS-34 blade.

▲PHIL BOGUSZEWSKI: The 440C blade is just over three inches; the textured scales are titanium and it's called Piranha. (Weyer photo)

▶ JOEL CHAMBLIN: Carving to bring texture works here in nice sweeping curves—6 1/2-inches as you see it. (Point Seven photo)

▶ **FRANK J. DILLUVIO:** In another part of his forest, this maker makes a tough looking little pearl liner lock.

BUDDY GAINES: ATS-34; four inches closed; pearl—and clean, clean lines with an interesting pivot pin cover. (Gallagher photo)

▶ **MICHAEL VAGNINO:** An extra-clean rendition of a working pocket knife—looks just about right in gold lip, titanium and ATS-34.

▲ **BARRY GALLAGHER:** Racy Wharncliffe one-blade, just over three inches closed, in Damascus and pearl.

▶ **ROD OLSON:** Gents folder in ATS-34 and pearl; one set up with stainless fittings; the other in 14K gold. (Weyer photo)

▲ **KURT B. SIMMONDS:** Aussie's folding dirk in 440C, sterling silver and ivory scales—very 19th century.

▶ **JACK LEVIN:** It goes ten inches in Damascus and titanium and ebony with a button release, but it is not a switchblade. (Weyer photo)

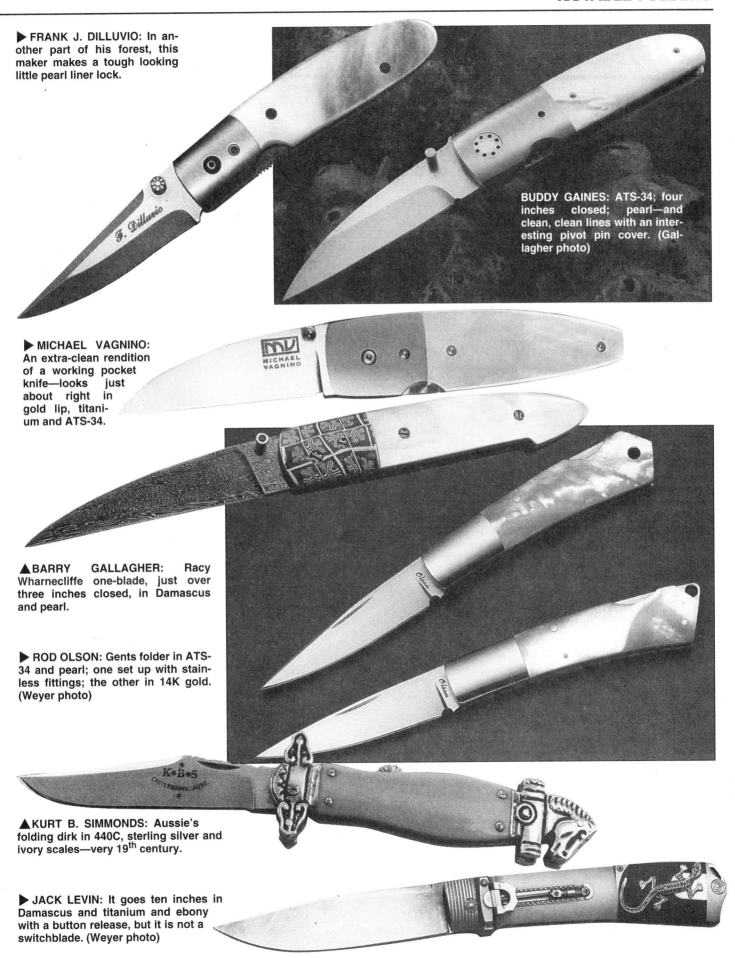

▶ FRANK LAMPSON: Neat squared-up little guy with a rear lock and great pearl scales.

▶ BRIAN TIGHE: Bilaterally symmetrical dagger has de Braga pearl carving and lots of class. (Weyer photo)

◀ SHAWN AND SHARLA HANSON: Very dressy daggers, very likely automatics, done up with upscale attention to detail. (Point Seven photo)

▶ WOLFGANG LOERCHNER: His very own vision of the folding dagger, delivered in stainless steel.

▲ GEORGE DAILEY: It's a big 'un—10 1/2-inches as you see it. It's all Damascus and pearl and texture and purpose. (Point Seven photo)

The Overseas Look

NORTH AMERICA REMAINS a melting pot, as the sociologists have said for eons, and therefore a lot of overseas-looking, even ethnic, knives are produced here. Paradoxically, not many knives are made overseas that look North American. That's what we are looking at in this grouping.

Please understand. This two dozen or so knives you're looking at here range from sound and sturdy to fantastically in-teresting. There is no dross. It's all good. All, however, have the overseas look.

It does not seem to matter which sea—Atlantic, South Atlantic, Pacific, Black seas, or the Mediterranean—knives from across any of them are different. Mostly, they are very nicely different, and especially these, else why would we bother here?

This is not an exercise in chauvinism. Fact is, most of these makers are quite successful, sooner or later, in finding an active market in the U.S. The knives are their own excuse, their own explanation. There is a difference.

As you can plainly see. Look and enjoy.
Ken Warner

FLY ME TO THE MOON series

HARUMI HIRAYAMA

◀ **HARUMI HIRAYAMA:** The lighthearted and happy knife is just right on this designer/knife-maker's New Year's card.

▶ **AAD VAN RIJSWIJK:** Seriously deluxe shaving outfit with ivory, ivory everywhere.

▶ **FRANCESCO PACHI:** Virile straight hunter has glowing fossil ivory around its pinned stick tang. The Damascus is by Knickmeyer.

▼ **FRANCO BONASSI:** Simpler liner locks far more complex than they look with fileworked titanium liners and bright scales.

TRENDS

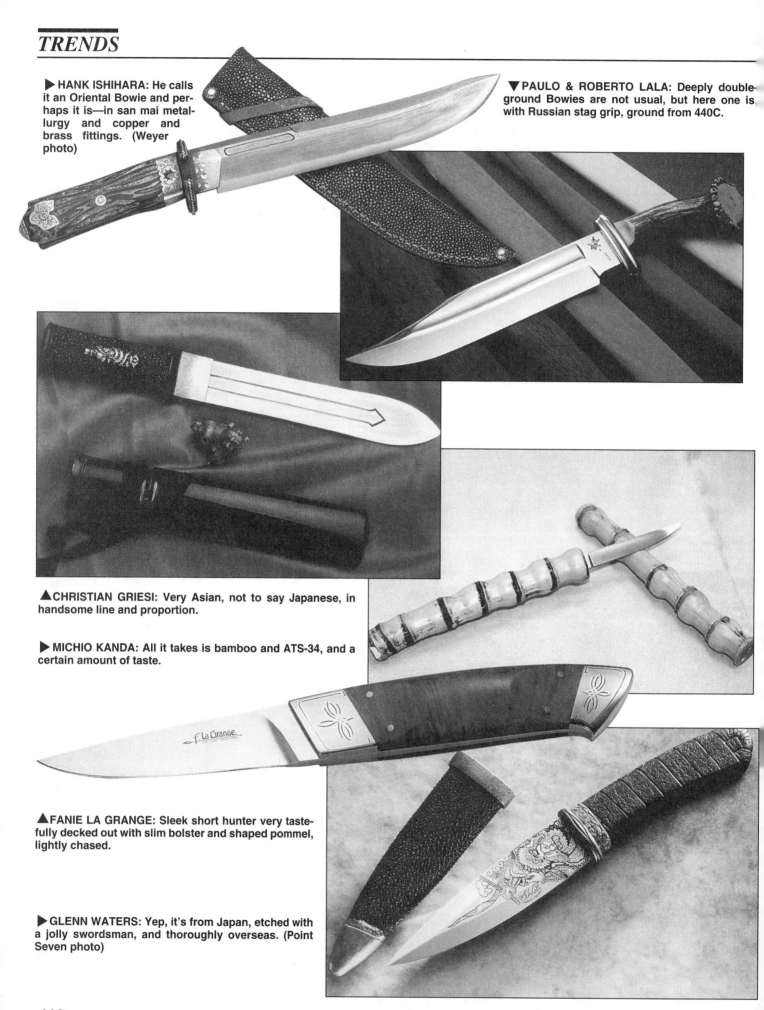

▶ **HANK ISHIHARA:** He calls it an Oriental Bowie and perhaps it is—in san mai metallurgy and copper and brass fittings. (Weyer photo)

▼ **PAULO & ROBERTO LALA:** Deeply double-ground Bowies are not usual, but here one is with Russian stag grip, ground from 440C.

▲ **CHRISTIAN GRIESI:** Very Asian, not to say Japanese, in handsome line and proportion.

▶ **MICHIO KANDA:** All it takes is bamboo and ATS-34, and a certain amount of taste.

▲ **FANIE LA GRANGE:** Sleek short hunter very tastefully decked out with slim bolster and shaped pommel, lightly chased.

▶ **GLENN WATERS:** Yep, it's from Japan, etched with a jolly swordsman, and thoroughly overseas. (Point Seven photo)

► KAI EMBRETSEN: Striking composite blade and striking proportion—10 inches overall. (Point Seven photo)

◄ GERT VAN DEN ELSEN: Celtic hunters, this Netherlander says, with three-inch blades and silver fittings over stag or blackwood. Could be.

▼ JOCKL GREISS: Very handsome straight hunter, trimmed in silver with Rados Damascus and a walrus tusk handle.

▼ REINHARD TSCHAGER: Striking fossil walrus grips, with gold ferrule and Denig Damascus blade 3 1/2-inches long.

◄ BERNARD BERTHOLUS: Sardinian dagger from a Caribbean perspective in buffalo horn and carbon steel.

▲LUDWIG FRUHMANN: Not quite Loveless integral drop po
with ivory scales and handsome bolster engraving.

▶BUNSHIDO KOYAMA: Liner lock
in a thoroughly modern idiom and
most handsome anodized titanium.

▶FRANCO BONAS-
SI: Simplicity again with very
complex surfaces.

PASCAL GRAVELINE: 19th century sticker
reproduced with Laguiole-style lockwork
in Sandvik steel and ivory, engraved by
Casetto.

▶KEIDOH SUGIHARA: Throughly modern
liner lock with a most engaging temper line.

▶ARIJ KOPLAAN: Folder that fools you with its straight knife look and proportion—it's just 6 1/2-inches long as you see it. (Weyer photo)

▶MARC CARLSSON: Runic serpent with a very fierce straight-edged tooth and screw construction.

▶JEAN PIERRE GANSTER: High style in a liner lock with stainless Damascus and walrus ivory handsomely shaped.

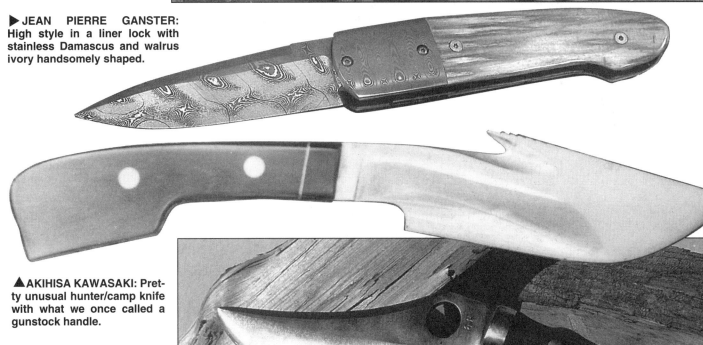

▲AKIHISA KAWASAKI: Pretty unusual hunter/camp knife with what we once called a gunstock handle.

▶MARIO EIRAS GARCIA: Big camp knife, ground to cut forever in the hands of a large person.

T.M. DOWELL: A Grandaddy knife, father to the idea. This one is an immaculate 1987 so-called "full" integral and handsome it is. (Weyer photo)

Integrality

WHEN WE SAY "integral" here, we mean a knife that is still all one piece, having been carved, ground, filed, perhaps even milled, from a single bar ... blade, tang, guard if there is one, pommel if there is one, even, in some cases, an interframe. As you might imagine, sometimes this gets interesting.

Somewhere, there is a wakizashi, a short sword after the Japanese style, fabricated by Edmund Davidson. It weighs about two pounds. It started as a 23-pound chunk of steel that itself cost several hundred dollars. I leave you to imagine the process—I certainly cannot.

No such shenanigan was in the mind of knifemaker's Guild co-founder and certified old-timer T.M. Dowell with his integral knives. The first of the moderns to make a point of integrality, Dowell sought

performance. He thought—and proved—that he could get the same knife lighter and maybe a little slicker if he did it the hard way.

That is a key point. Obviously, the integral idea is the simplest—you just cut away what you don't think looks like your knife. In practice, it's the most complex, as consideration of the Dowell integral we show here reveals. This knife was made about 1987. It has an integral guard and pommel and a tapered tang and quite elegant versions of what are inelegantly called handle slabs. Please look at it so you can in truth see that there is not a straight line anywhere in view, and yet both sides match. And then realize this is a full four-inch drop point hunting knife made of stainless steel and it only weighs a couple of ounces.

So that is what Ted Dowell was looking for and found. Others have sought and still seek other kinds of performance. Tom Johanning wants strength, and he wants it bad. For Davidson, it is more of a challenge in workmanship. He likes to be a little alone with his knives, and he can market these tough-to-make knives all over the world. A German, Richard K. Hehn, may make even more of a point of integrality than Davidson. He does some pretty complex things.

There are others, of course. And if we had pictures of their work at hand we would name them and discuss them. The integral idea stays alive, helped, no doubt, by the increasing availability of very, very clever machine tools. And because some people make some very good knives that way.

Ken Warner

EDMUND DAVIDSON: A recent ambitious integral hunter in 440 C and horn, with Jere Davidson gold lacing and engraving and some good looks. (Point Seven photo)

TOM JOHANNING: This is the point of integrality for this maker—he starts with a six-pound billet of A-8 Modified and can push the resulting knife through steel decking.

EDMUND DAVIDSON: This was some chunk of 440 C before the maker turned it into this 13-inch tanto-style integral. (Point Seven photo)

RICHARD K. HEHN: Graceful curving line in the handle belies the complexity of the effort in this most handsome integral hunter.

RICHARD K. HEHN: Profligate expenditure of machine time produces this remarkable integral hunter style with a very complex handle.

LARRY HARLEY: The ineffable Bristolian produced this all-metal Persian sort of thing in integral style from, no doubt, his own forging. (Point Seven photo)

The Automatic Quandary

THE THING HAS been going on pretty long, this *affaire du coeur* with the automatic knife, the switchblade, if you will. People collected the old ones pretty hard, and just about collected them out of public existence. And Lord knows the factories of Germany and Italy and Spain and other places tried to keep the pipelines full of new ones with the eager help of tourists and non-tourists and other smugglers.

This is a little strange for a pastime and circumstance that seems to do no harm and yet is all but fully illegal. It is not—the switchblade, that is—regarded as wrong and it probably is not wrong even if it is illegal. There were whole stretches of time when it was not illegal, any more than, say, the little radio

opened and deployed, and those are the manual one-handers. There is also a new breed, the semi-automatics (see Chuck Karwan's report, page 46) which assist manual opening, but do not fall within the legal definition of switchblades since they don't involve buttons or latches.

Observers of the scene, like this reporter, are left to wonder. With all these wonderful new designs, which are, like genuine automatics, great fun to operate, aside from the utility aspect, render the somewhat ridiculous switchblade prohibitions moot?

Will it finally dawn on the legislators or the administrators that this is ridiculous? Or will it go the other way? Will this seeming preoccupation with very quick folders bring some sort of official entanglement with all the one-hand folders? Is there some hero of big government competent to wrestle with this particular bucket of worms? And what will he do about the entirely respectable and

▲ STEVE SCHWARZER: Unaccustomed severity of line in this large folder. Not a piece of Damascus in sight either, but look at that nifty latch. (Point Seven photo)

thing you can open your car trunk with or the one you use to unlock and open the garage door. There were U.S. patents granted on switchblade knife designs in this century.

And now here we are faced with a world of knives that are as "fast" as automatic knives when it comes to being

▲ WILLIAM J. MC HENRY: A bow to the Italian influence in a liner-locked dagger with a button and a safety and very pretty Damascus.

wealthy automatic knife collector who might have $100,000 or so invested in his two dozen little miracles of design and workmanship and who decides to defend them with another $100,000 or so? Or the craftsman who can prove he never engaged in interstate commerce with a switchblade? Or

▲ RAINY D. VALLOTON: Nifty semi-coffin shape in a dagger of dainty dimension—the case is maybe four inches or a four and a little.

any of a half-dozen other categories of respectable citizen distinguishable from the rest of us only by the possession of some very interesting folding knives?

▲ A.D. RARDON: Yep, it's a double automatic, works both ways in titanium and pearl with a scale release. (Weyer photo)

There is this: Given a Federal officer who desires a scalp, a collector or dealer or maker who made a public mistake could quite easily find himself hapless in a world of hurt. The regulations are there. They are not plain and they are not simple, but they can get a person into a felony conviction. There is no doubt about it. Even a favorable verdict could cost the house and the child's college fund.

Those are the somewhat weighty matters that come to mind together with this writer's sense of wonder as he examines the marvelous mechanisms and wonderful elaboration of the modern handmade automatic knife. They are doing some great work out there. And here is some of it, quandary or no.

Ken Warner

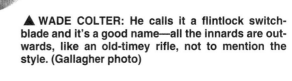

▲ WADE COLTER: He calls it a flintlock switch-blade and it's a good name—all the innards are outwards, like an old-timey rifle, not to mention the style. (Gallagher photo)

▼ JAMES B. LINCOLN: Bolster release completely belies the snappy nature of this biggish folder with Montgomery engraving, a lot of file work.

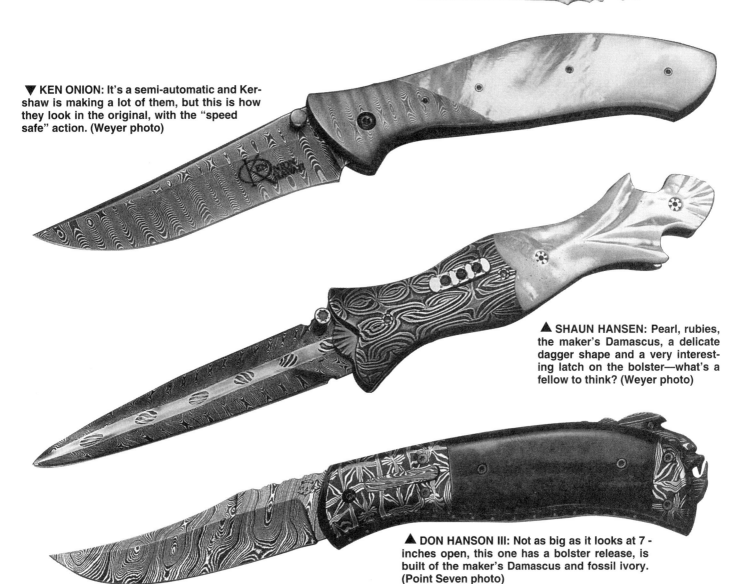

▼ KEN ONION: It's a semi-automatic and Kershaw is making a lot of them, but this is how they look in the original, with the "speed safe" action. (Weyer photo)

▲ SHAUN HANSEN: Pearl, rubies, the maker's Damascus, a delicate dagger shape and a very interesting latch on the bolster—what's a fellow to think? (Weyer photo)

▲ DON HANSON III: Not as big as it looks at 7 - inches open, this one has a bolster release, is built of the maker's Damascus and fossil ivory. (Point Seven photo)

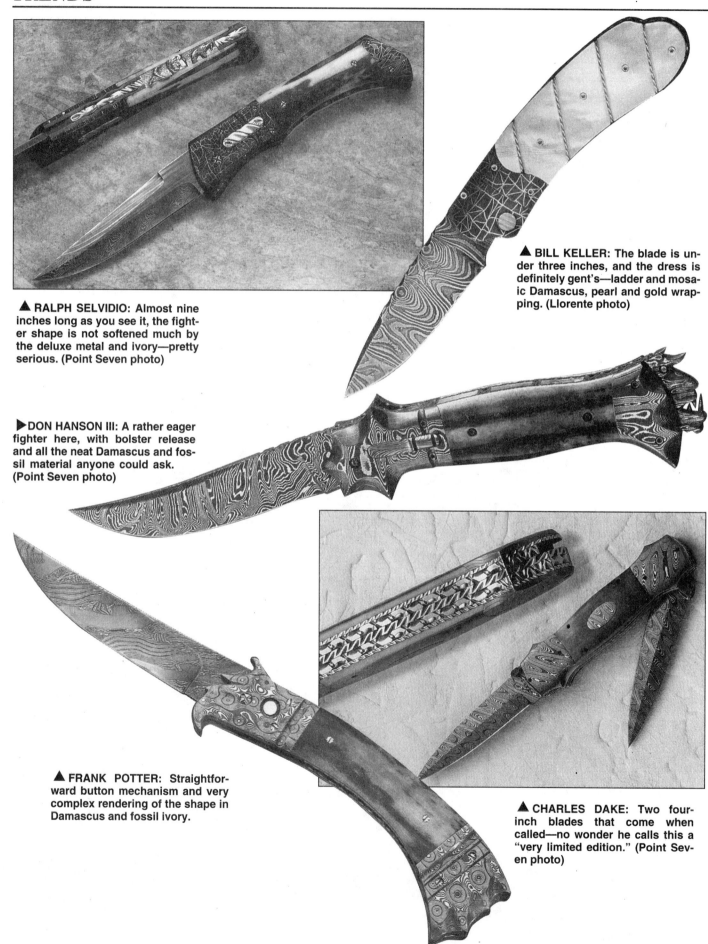

▲ RALPH SELVIDIO: Almost nine inches long as you see it, the fighter shape is not softened much by the deluxe metal and ivory—pretty serious. (Point Seven photo)

▶DON HANSON III: A rather eager fighter here, with bolster release and all the neat Damascus and fossil material anyone could ask. (Point Seven photo)

▲ FRANK POTTER: Straightforward button mechanism and very complex rendering of the shape in Damascus and fossil ivory.

▲ BILL KELLER: The blade is under three inches, and the dress is definitely gent's—ladder and mosaic Damascus, pearl and gold wrapping. (Llorente photo)

▲ CHARLES DAKE: Two four-inch blades that come when called—no wonder he calls this a "very limited edition." (Point Seven photo)

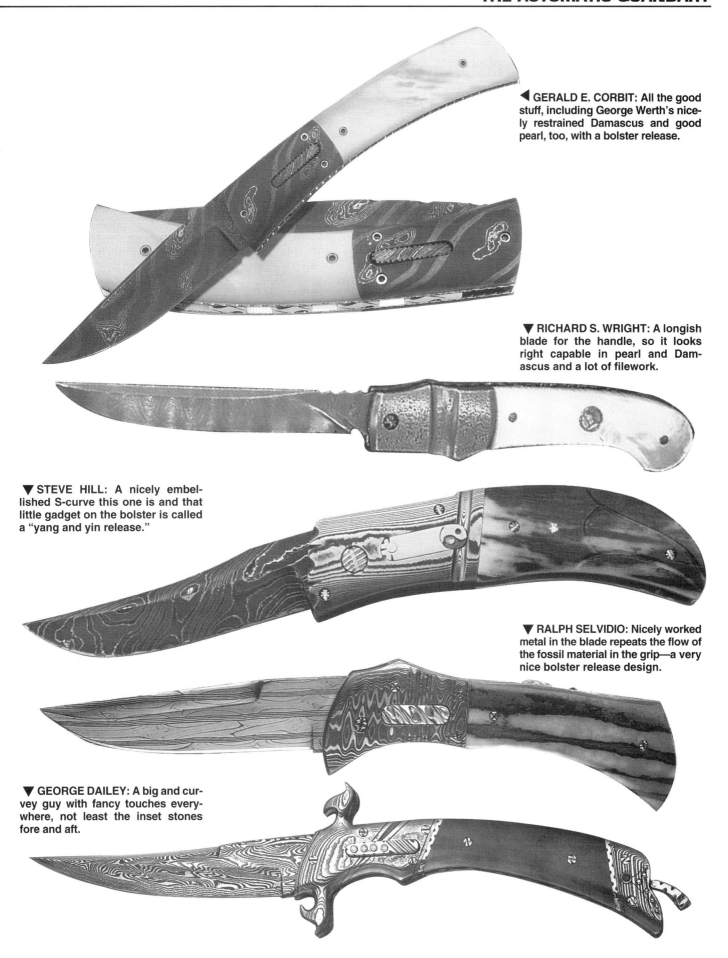

◀ GERALD E. CORBIT: All the good stuff, including George Werth's nicely restrained Damascus and good pearl, too, with a bolster release.

▼ RICHARD S. WRIGHT: A longish blade for the handle, so it looks right capable in pearl and Damascus and a lot of filework.

▼ STEVE HILL: A nicely embellished S-curve this one is and that little gadget on the bolster is called a "yang and yin release."

▼ RALPH SELVIDIO: Nicely worked metal in the blade repeats the flow of the fossil material in the grip—a very nice bolster release design.

▼ GEORGE DAILEY: A big and curvey guy with fancy touches everywhere, not least the inset stones fore and aft.

ONCE AGAIN WITH SMALL

EARLY ON, THERE were just a few brave souls giving miniature knives a shot, and then, in what we might call the middle years, it appeared everybody had to try one or two. There are collections of miniatures made by makers who don't make miniatures, in fact. You wouldn't believe the cajoling and persuading it sometimes took to get a knifemaker to make a miniature. And you also would not believe how difficult it was to get such a man to make a second miniature.

That couldn't last long, of course, as the word got out. And there was a doldrum for a bit. Then things started improving, and now there are more than a couple of spe-

cialists and they turn out a great deal of work, it appears to this reporter. How anyone, in a given span between shows, or from one year to the next, can make dozens of these little guys for sale passeth this reporter's understanding.

However, there they are. So there is no need to take any reporter's word in the matter. We have the little knives—and swords and axes and cutlasses and whatever—to look at. We sometimes see these little items in their little milieus. If it were as easy to make tiny little skeletons as apparently it is to make tiny little knives, there would be no limits—tiny pirate cutlasses thrust through tiny rib cag-

es, battlefields strewn with tiny skulls and tiny helmets with tiny spears and swords laying around.

And there is special casing as well, setting the miniature's scene in another way. It is also popular—well, it is at least fairly common—to make or display a big one and a little one, although this year we don't have such an example. It must be very difficult to make a red plastic-handled Swiss Army Knife just an inch or so long with five blades, but—and some of you will have to forgive me for this—when you do it very well, and several have, the result looks just as if those Swiss fellows at Victorinox or Wenger had sent their smallest workmen down into their tiniest workshop to do a day's work. That is probably a triumph, but it certainly is not one of your obvious triumphs, and a lot of effort to make a factory knife.

As it has been from the start, the test of a miniature is sufficient fidelity to detail and to scale that in a photo, without a ref-

▲ JIM MARTIN: The blade is 1 1/8-inch long and it pops out when you push the button and then the liner locks it. Fascinating.

Living on the Edge
Logos of the Loveless Legend
By Al Williams
Illustrated by Jim Weyer

erence, you cannot tell it is tiny. This reporter will not tell you where, but over the span of 20 years there has been more than one knife cited and captioned here as a big 'un when

▲ DON HUME: Here's Zorro's sword, with its 3 1/8-inch 440C blade, resting on a bench with his hat and gear in a corner of his casa. (Weyer photo)

◄ CHARLES A. WEISS: This rendition of a big and very collectable Loveless Delaware Maid knife must be OK—Loveless ordered one.

it wasn't. That leads to a guy smiling a secret smile and keeping his mouth shut, so there is not much harm done.

Enjoy what you see. There are lots more where these came from.

Ken Warner

▼DIANA CASTEEL: A cased shaving outfit, includes a one-inch razor, a strop, a mug and a brush, all the metal in Damascus. (Weyer photo)

▼JIM SORNBERGER: An all-out San Francisco dagger just barely big enough to open the mail, engraved and gold-inlaid to boot.

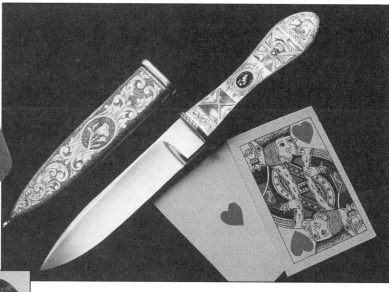

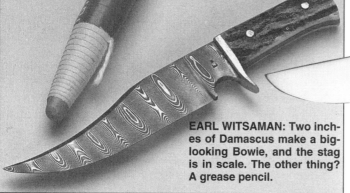

EARL WITSAMAN: Two inches of Damascus make a big-looking Bowie, and the stag is in scale. The other thing? A grease pencil.

▲EARL WITSAMAN: It's a limited edition of a Jimmy Lile knife, with Jimmy scrimmed thereon by Linda Karst—overall length is just under three inches. (Weyer photo)

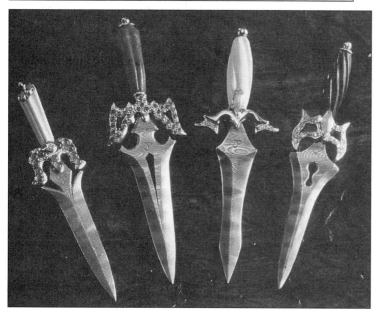

▲JEAN-PIERRE GANSTER: Stainless Damascus daggers way under three inches, with coral and such for handles, and gold and gems to boot.

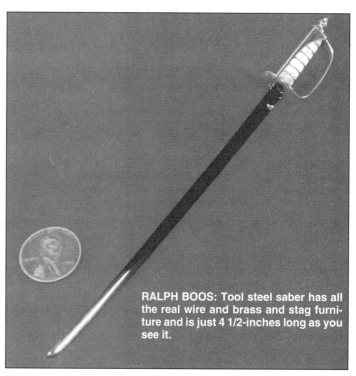

RALPH BOOS: Tool steel saber has all the real wire and brass and stag furniture and is just 4 1/2-inches long as you see it.

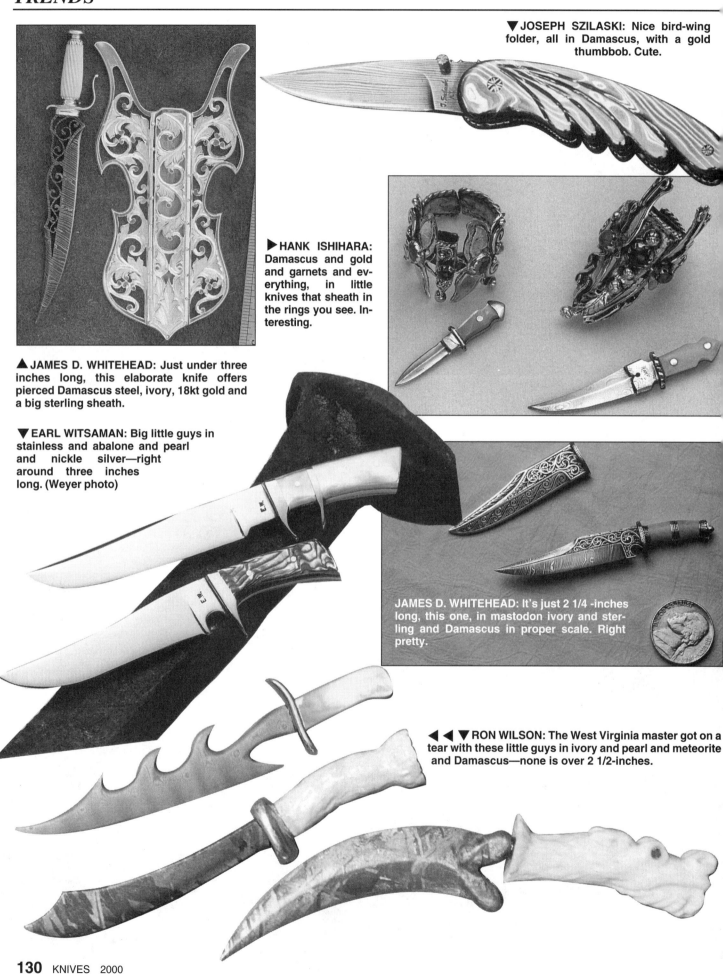

JOSEPH SZILASKI: Nice bird-wing folder, all in Damascus, with a gold thumbbob. Cute.

HANK ISHIHARA: Damascus and gold and garnets and everything, in little knives that sheath in the rings you see. Interesting.

JAMES D. WHITEHEAD: Just under three inches long, this elaborate knife offers pierced Damascus steel, ivory, 18kt gold and a big sterling sheath.

EARL WITSAMAN: Big little guys in stainless and abalone and pearl and nickle silver—right around three inches long. (Weyer photo)

JAMES D. WHITEHEAD: It's just 2 1/4 -inches long, this one, in mastodon ivory and sterling and Damascus in proper scale. Right pretty.

RON WILSON: The West Virginia master got on a tear with these little guys in ivory and pearl and meteorite and Damascus—none is over 2 1/2-inches.

This is the package that got the eight bucks. We were very easy.

Inside, the name was a shock—it was Shappu, not Ginsu.

Getting Ginsued

THERE THEY WERE, piled modestly on the corner of a table in a knife show, apparent relics of a TV war long ago fought. They were Ginsu Knives! And in, it said, the original TV package.

How would a writer about knives resist? Bang—there went eight bucks. In fact, there went sixteen bucks because we needed a set for photos. Wonderful lines of copy reeled through the mind as—at home—the package was opened.

We got Ginsued! Well, actually, we got Shappued big time and our family relationship with China may never recover. The knives were made in China!

These were not Ginsu knives, even if they were "The Original" and "Guaranteed for 50 Years" and "As Seen On TV" and even if the package did have wonderful color photos of the wondrous Ginsu blades of late-night TV song and story. The package shouted, "Hai!" But the knives were none of those things. There were ten knives and they were probably worth 80 cents each, but the disappointment was great.

It is likely the package was made from the original dies—they have a die-formed liner inside to hold the knives. But the big clue for us was the name on all of the 10 knives

in the Ginsu package—they plainly said "Shappu 2000," right there on the blades in big letters. And they did not fit in the little die-formed cavities very well either.

Later, and elsewhere, we found the same size box labelled "Shappu 2000." It

was four bucks. I have not had the heart to open it to see what the knives look like. The only way I'll heal is if they are marked "Ginsu" and, somehow, I don't think so.

Ken Warner

▶ Flying under truer colors, the same—approximately—knife set went just four bucks ... later.

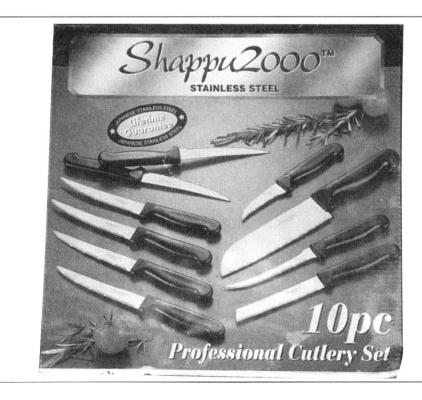

Miscellany

by Ken Warner

◄JAY MAINES: Fossil in a Bowie butt is 65,000,000 years old and from Morocco. Mighty interesting inlay, right?

▲ GLENN WATERS: Prize-winner has T. Rex hatching, its tail the blade. Silver with Damascus and very different.

▼ GLENN MARSHALL: An Astro-Gemini commemorative styled after the old Case, this one in D2 with an 8 1/2-inch blade.

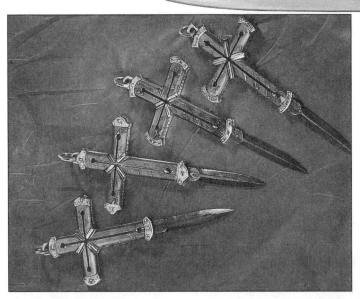

▲ JEAN PIERRE GANSTER: Not your average pendant crucifix, these three-inch Damascus pieces have slide-out two-inch Damascus blades.

►RUANA KNIFE WORKS: Their 60th Anniversary Knife sure seems collectible—it's a limited edition and a good looker.

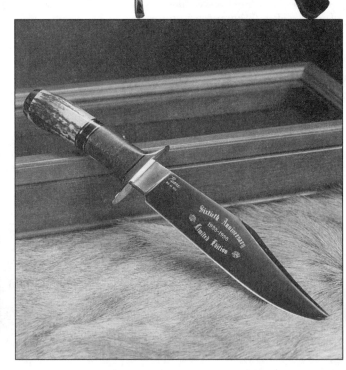

STATE
OF
THE ART

Here's where the new materials, the new techniques show up. And often really good examples of some of the old stuff, as well. Every year there is this kind of interesting material as the active minds keep searching for the magic.

And every year they continue the good old stunts, and they do them better and better and better. That's why we take fresh looks every year at the same things. It's usually worth the effort.

There is often quite technical material to review. This is not a tome for the guys who make knives; but to understand those guys, the user often has to know things. In this issue, for instance, there is a remarkable photographic inspection of knife edges.

The problem with the State of the Art is that it just is. You ought not manipulate it. So we don't. What you see is what you get.

Ken Warner

THE STUDY OF STEEL AND STUFF

▲STEVEN RAPP: Here's how it's done, in just 12 pieces at 9 1/2-inches overall. Engraving is Julie Warenski's. (Point Seven photo)

▼STEVE DUNN: Maximum use of a Damascus pattern called "thorns and thistles." Blade is just over 10-inches. (Point Seven photo)

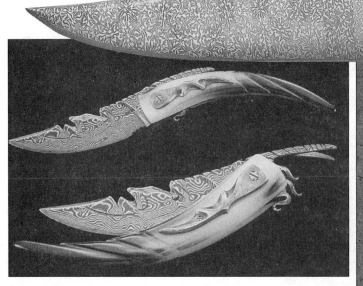

▲WADE COLTER: Back of blade is a face; handle is common old muskox horn. (Point Seven photo)

ROBERT WEINSTOCK: Steel carved like sculpture in clay in this remarkable gold-trimmed folder. (Point Seven photo)

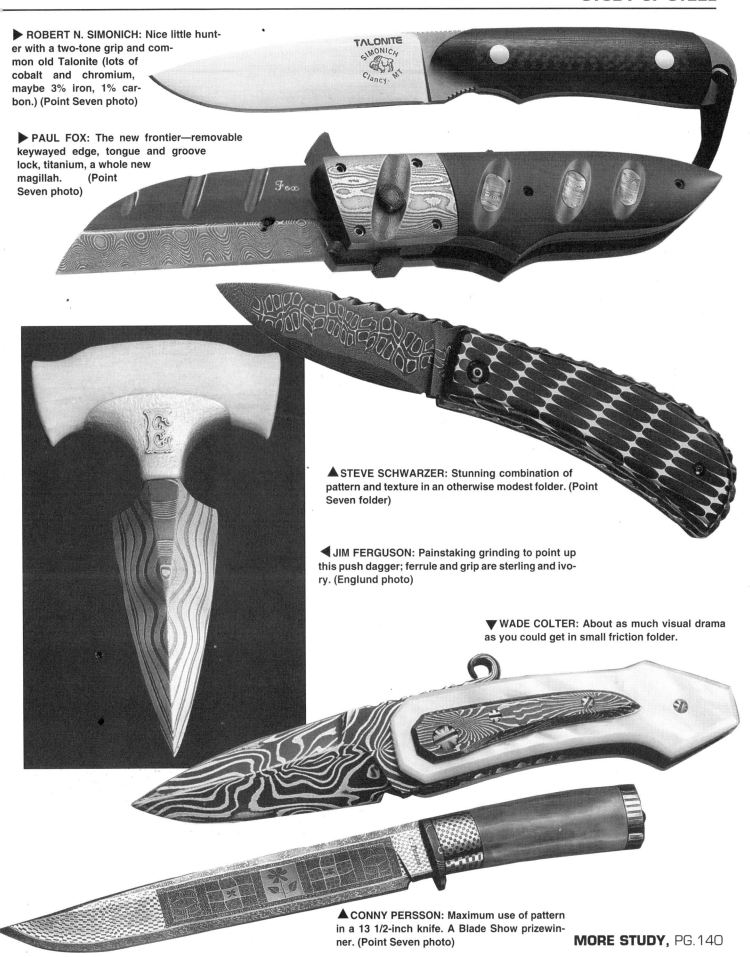

▶ ROBERT N. SIMONICH: Nice little hunter with a two-tone grip and common old Talonite (lots of cobalt and chromium, maybe 3% iron, 1% carbon.) (Point Seven photo)

▶ PAUL FOX: The new frontier—removable keywayed edge, tongue and groove lock, titanium, a whole new magillah. (Point Seven photo)

▲ STEVE SCHWARZER: Stunning combination of pattern and texture in an otherwise modest folder. (Point Seven folder)

◀ JIM FERGUSON: Painstaking grinding to point up this push dagger; ferrule and grip are sterling and ivory. (Englund photo)

▼ WADE COLTER: About as much visual drama as you could get in small friction folder.

▲ CONNY PERSSON: Maximum use of pattern in a 13 1/2-inch knife. A Blade Show prizewinner. (Point Seven photo)

MORE STUDY, PG. 140

The diagonal "bar" is one-half the ground edge of an Old Timer folder blade, lit from the right and shown at 575X.

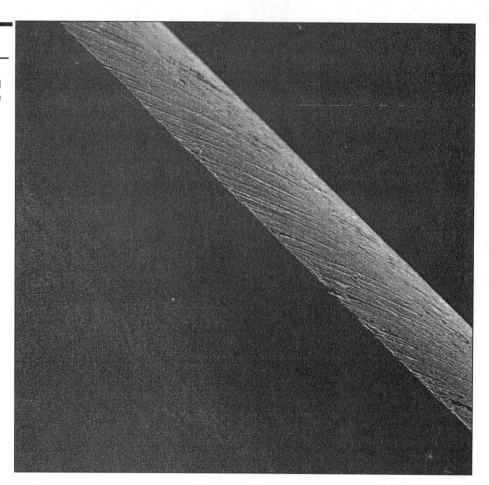

THESE REMARKABLE PHOTOS were acquired from Errett Callahan who has more than the ordinary interest in keen edges. He makes them in stone, in the first place, and has let himself be cut by them in the second. (That is a long story. It suffices to say it was all legitimate and medical—surgery on his personal shoulder.)

The photos were made by Roger Rothschild of Fairbanks, Alaska, in academic pursuit. Whatever it is he is pursuing, Mr. Rothschild pursues it most successfully, if we are to judge by these images. There are five of them.

They are, successively, the very edge of a Schrade 1080T pocketknife at 575X, then at 1000X, then at 1400X, and then 2500X. The last picture is of an obsidian blade—these things happen when Callahan is involved—in the same aspect at 3000X.

Obviously, the obsidian edge, essentially a controlled fracture in glass, is

Edges As The Camera Sees Them

sharp and clean way beyond what is doubtless a perfectly usable knife edge in steel. It is this difference which persuaded a surgeon to try and Callahan to permit obsidian scalpels to do the cutting on Callahan's rebuilt shoulder. It worked—clean cuts, minimum bleeding.

The other four pictures are more instructive for most of us, however. Certainly the steel pocketknife edge was cleanly ground and prepared. Even at 1000 times magnification, it is looking good. At 1400X, the surface is looking pretty rough; at 2800X, it becomes hard to believe that is a good cutting edge. And yet it was. It was not so keen, of course, as the flint edge, but perfectly useful.

This obsidian edge is shown lit from below and is not all that impressive, until you realize this image is that edge at 3000X magnification! We see a genuinely clean pair of surfaces, which explains the keen cutting such an edge accomplishes.

◀ Enlarged to 1000X, the steel blade edge, is starting to show a rough but regular surface, but was obviously cleanly ground or honed.

▶ Now closer, at 1400X magnification, the steel edge is starting to fray visually. Still quite regular in general, there are some visible gullies.

And what are we to learn here? First, that what the books say is correct: knife edges are sort of raggedy. Second, that being a little finicky yourself about your edges probably pays off. Third—the camera can show us things we never knew were there. And fourth, maybe obsidian really is really sharp.

Ken Warner

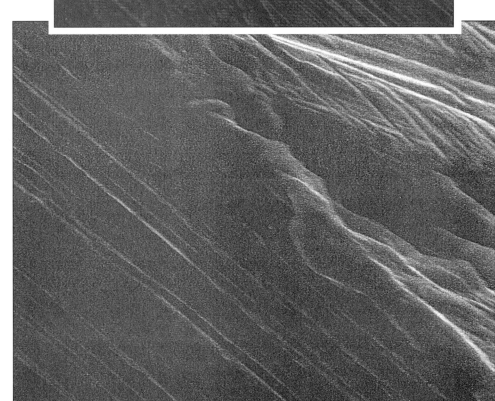

▶ Bumped up to very high magnification at 2800X, the steel edge is very lumpy, and while it is still an organized surface, it is obviously less so than one would expect.

George Young's 6K Passion

I HAVE MET others who made knives from Stellite 6K. Mike Franklin used to and I think I have one of those, and my old friend Harry Archer made two (in, of all places, Bob Loveless's shop) and I have one of those. I learned a lot about Stellite 6K from those knives, although not enough to tell you much about the material itself as material.

Franklin made enough of the knives, mostly little ones, that no old-timer is surprised by the fact. And the little hunter worked fine. Cute knife, too. And Harry said two was enough. Said the stuff didn't care how hot it got and the grinding took forever. But he persevered and made one for him and one for me. Little guys. Cute little guys.

So that was kind of it for me and Stellite knives. Lots of people tried, too. Mostly they made small and simple

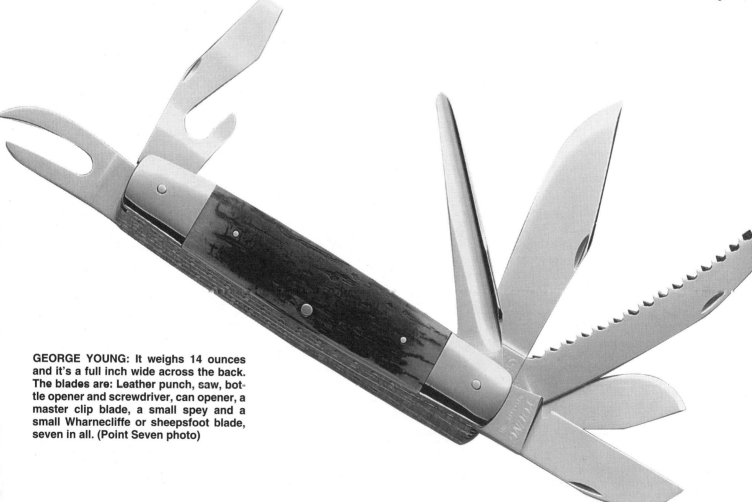

GEORGE YOUNG: It weighs 14 ounces and it's a full inch wide across the back. The blades are: Leather punch, saw, bottle opener and screwdriver, can opener, a master clip blade, a small spey and a small Wharncliffe or sheepsfoot blade, seven in all. (Point Seven photo)

GEORGE YOUNG: It's five inches long and an inch deep from this point of view, which shows us five rows of backsprings, four rows of liners and integral bolster-liners, together with the fossil ivory scales and a considerable number of unerring file cuts. (Point Seven photo)

knives. I suppose there are more than a couple flirting with Stellite 6K (and some new material, similar, and other such, no doubt) as I write this.

I guarantee you, however, this: Ain't nobody in a Stellite 6K class with George Young of Kokomo, Indiana. You know about the mind-set of the hog and chicken when it comes to a ham'n'eggs breakfast? The chicken, they say, is cooperating very well, but the hog—he's committed! Well, that's George Young about Stellite 6K—he's committed … big-time.

Your attention is directed to the amazing knife presented here. It is five inches long, closed; it has seven blades and fossil ivory scales; it is very nicely made; it nests and walks and talks and all of that good stuff. And it is all Stellite 6K. Any number of knifemakers who have seen it just shake their heads over it and those among them competent to make such a seven-blade folder shake their heads twice.

They all consider George Young a marvel.

He is pretty good, obviously, but mostly he is a little obsessed with Stellite. He makes Stellite hunting knives and other straight designs and by happy chance you can see one on the cover of this publication. And he makes Stellite kitchen knives—three-inch parers and five-inch utilities, and he'd make, I bet 18-inch steak cimiters if anyone asked (which I emphatically am not.)

You may hear more of Stellite. One smith was threatening to forge some whilst being told he had a 120-degree "window" and that was all. In its use for such industrial purposes as turbine blades in jet engines, it is forged, but when we talk about that we are talking maximum effort die sinking and controlled heating and 30,000-pound drop presses and a process that shakes the world for a quarter-mile while it is happening. I think our guy was talking about hitting it with a five-pound hammer on an anvil, or maybe a quick run through a Little Giant power hammer. So we'll see.

Regardless, what we know positively at this moment is that a lot of us have been wrong. Stellite 6K is NOT too tough to work with. Ask George Young and look at his knives. Like right here.

Ken Warner

GEORGE YOUNG: A variety of techniques are on display here. The small outside blades are nested by crimping (or grinding offset to suit); the central three blades each have dedicated space, which simplifies assembly considerably.

▲▶ PIERRE REVERDY: How it progresses in the Reverdy mode—pattern to parts to laminated image in a forged steel blade.

Pierre Reverdy At Work

◀▲ PIERRE REVERDY: This is called the Santa Claus knife, the blade forged and shaped with smooth subtlety; the same elements stacked in the handle slabs with elemental brutality.

▶ PIERRE REVERDY: This remarkable small folder looks somewhat ordinary, all things considered.

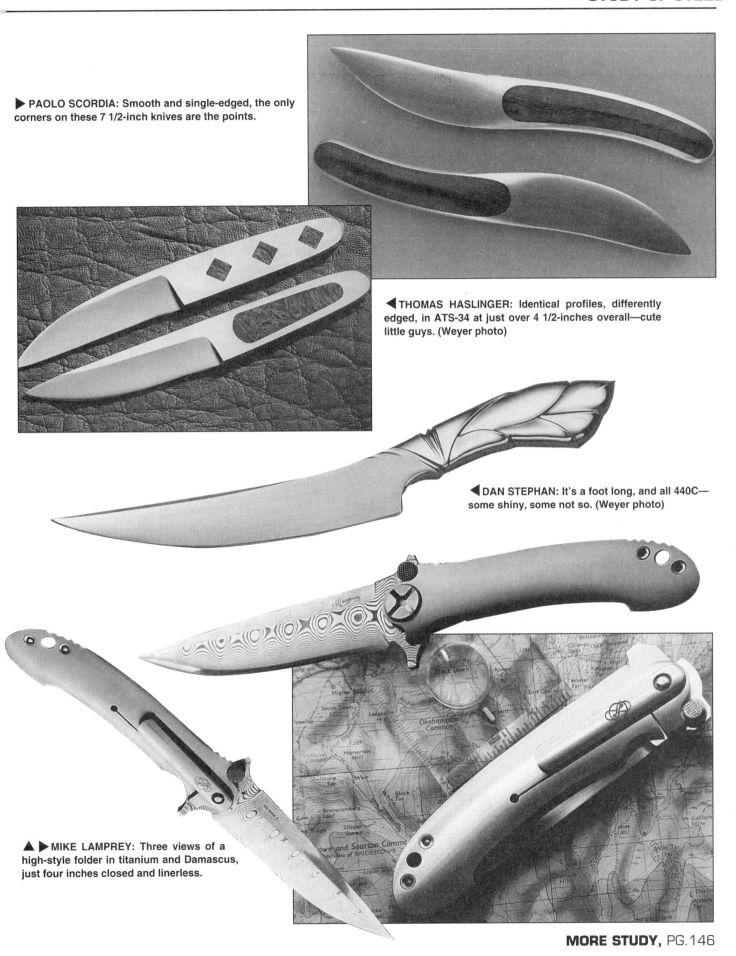

▶ **PAOLO SCORDIA:** Smooth and single-edged, the only corners on these 7 1/2-inch knives are the points.

◀**THOMAS HASLINGER:** Identical profiles, differently edged, in ATS-34 at just over 4 1/2-inches overall—cute little guys. (Weyer photo)

◀**DAN STEPHAN:** It's a foot long, and all 440C—some shiny, some not so. (Weyer photo)

▲ ▶**MIKE LAMPREY:** Three views of a high-style folder in titanium and Damascus, just four inches closed and linerless.

MORE STUDY, PG.146

Once More With Carter

Last year you saw this knife, absolutely the most-used, middle-of-the-road Japanese kitchen design, called a waba-cho done by Carter in a laminate with stainless steel.

YOU MET THIS guy's chef knife last year. He's a Canadian and a Caucasian and the Master Smith of a Japanese country knifesmithy, where they turn out, among other forged things, over 200 bladed tools every month. He got there, not long after high school in Halifax. More or less, he just walked in, fascinated, and stayed, and did, as they say, right well.

Obviously, Murray Carter has a way with steel. Country or no, Japanese smiths do not permit just anyone to make knives in their shops. Long-time, multi-generation businesses anywhere in the world do not surrender their fates to any but the most able of foreigners. And Murray Carter became the 17th head of the smithy, having learned from the 16th. So we can assume Carter can do it. And he thinks maybe he can do it over here and that is why he was at the Blade Show.

The big thing in the Carter tools—his name is on them in ideographs and in English—is the laminated blade. Most of them are laminates of soft—rather soft, at any rate—stainless steels around sturdy layers of Hitachi's high carbon blade steels. It is thus, Carter reasons,

he can achieve in his forge something as close to the best of both worlds as one can get.

Quite obviously, the meticulous care of an edge 3/8-inch wide is far easier than that same care on a whole blade. Also obviously, a nice thick blade provides fine geometry for long-term intensive cutting. Given a high chromium content, it is not so necessary to polish out the non-cutting portions of a blade and thus one can attain a distinctive, rough-and-ready look at no loss

▲ This is so serious a field worker's tool, this kama, one should be a farmer to own it. That's not a nick in the blade— it is biting the wood.

of utility and without incurring high finishing costs. So whether or not the best of both worlds is there, a great deal of both worlds is available to Carter's customers.

This is not an unreasoned approach, simply the way of a hands-on smith. Murray Carter knows just what he is doing scientifically and, indeed, philosophically. He outlines his belief in his methods and his knives very nicely in an essay you will find nearby.

There is also another name, and its reason for being you will also see in the essay. Blades which come from his forge with the name MUTEKI on them are not actually forged. They are shaped and tempered as the others, but not forged. You can see a MUTEKI hunter here, rather distinctively finished with textured flats. There are also traditional tools, Japanese carpenter knives and kitchen knives and the like, very smooth, with the MUTEKI name. Very sturdy, very sharp, and pretty good-looking, this MUTEKI line. And, as he says, they're less money.

It's a great story, Carter's is, and the knives are up to it. Which is why we show them—and him—here.

Ken Warner

▲ All-purpose woodworking knife, as clean and neat as a raindrop. It is marked MUTEKI.

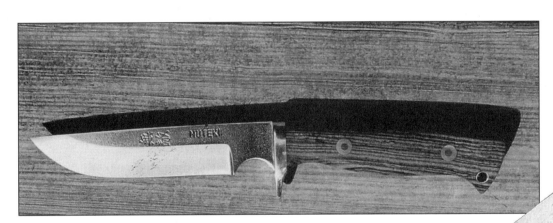

▲ This is Murray Carter's MUTEKI hunter, a very solid knife indeed. It is not forged, but it is some stout and plenty sharp.

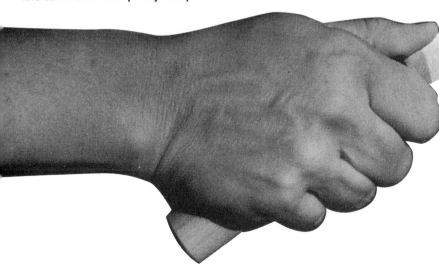

◀ Carter believes knives are cutting tools first, and that is how he builds them.

IN HIS OWN WORDS:

THE FOLLOWING IS a brief compilation of my thoughts regarding blades. This opinion is based on twelve years of practical bladesmithing experience.

The purpose of any blade is to cut. It is a tool that should cut keenly and consistently over a reasonable length of time. It is these practical cutting requirements that have led metallurgists to proclaim the superiority of carbon steel above all else as a "cutting" metal. This is supported by the fact that it is truly rare to find a professional in any tool-using environment who does not use a form of carbon steel for this purpose.

When worked appropriately, heat treated correctly, and given proper edge geometry, high quality cutlery grade carbon steel produces a combination of edge keenness, edge retention, flexibility, and ease of sharpening that is unparalleled by any other material.

I am often disappointed by the commercially available blades that I periodically examine. It seems to me that the blade "industry" has shifted the emphasis from products featuring true cutting ability to products that are "strong" and "tough". These products will cut adequately for a brief period of time, but are well below the potential of cutting performance offered by modern metallurgical technology.

I will take the liberty of defining "toughness" and "strength" in order to clarify my point, I define "toughness" as the ability of a steel to resist breaking. "Strength" I define as the capacity of a steel to sustain the application of force without yielding its structural integrity.

For example, a lead pipe can be abused extensively, it will deform, but it is difficult to chip or crack. The lead pipe illustrates my concept of "tough". "Strength" may be illustrated by clamping a piece of metal in a vise, and attempting to bend it. Its sustained unwillingness to yield and bend is "strength".

Modern marketing trends and techniques have led people to believe that a blade's value lies in its strength rather than in its traditional function; to be able to retain a keen edge over a practical period of usage, and be easy to re-sharpen.

The basic types of Japanese cutlery.

Wabōchō
Used for general cooking puroses

Nakiri−Bōchō
Used for slicing and dicing vegetables

Deba−Bōchō
Used for rough dressing fish

Yanagi−Ba
Used for delicate and artistic slicing of raw fish

The result of this is that we have a plethora of commercially available "butterknives" that may also be utilized as mini-crowbars, but a dearth of practical cutting instruments.

Within a piece of cutlery grade carbon steel there is a complex relationship between enduring keenness, toughness and strength. This relationship depends upon the hardness of the steel after heat treating. In the cutlery industry, hardness is measured by utilizing a point system which starts at 20 points and increases incrementally until it reaches 70 points.

This is known as the Rockwell "C" scale, commonly represented by the abbreviation "HRC". In general, the higher the HRC rating, the keener the steel is when sharpened. The lower the HRC rating, the tougher the steel is.

Steel is generally considered strong when it takes much force to bend it, and it can then spring back to its original dimensions. The problem with this situation is that the steel has been heat-treated like a spring (HRC 55) rather than a blade designed for cutting.

In my opinion, a steel blade heat-treated to HRC 63-64 would produce amazing keenness with enough toughness and strength to withstand repeated use. However, at this hardness, the slightest abuse would probably result in a broken blade. Personally, I believe that blades should not be made to withstand abuse, to the detriment of their cutting ability.

Enter the "laminated" blade.

With laminated blades, there doesn't have to be a trade-off between edge hardness and keenness and toughness. By utilizing a high carbon (over 1% carbon) cutlery steel core laminated between two layers of lower carbon steel, one can maintain an edge hardness of HRC 63 to 64 while achieving any level of toughness or strength desired by his choice of outer laminations.

For example, wrought iron laminated to a center core of cutlery steel will give the ultimate combination of toughness and hardness. 1035 steel laminated to a center core of cutlery steel will give a blade spring-like qualities without compromising edge hardness. And stainless steels may be used as the outer laminate, thereby almost elminating the historical drawback of carbon steel; RUST.

However, not all available laminations fully utilize this potential advantage. For example, some commercially available three-layer blades utilize a combination of an AUS 8 stainless steel core enveloped by two slabs of 420J2 stainless steel.

There are two inherent problems with this combination:

1. Commercially tempered AUS 8 stainless stell merely attains an HRC 59 approximate hardness. This is not nearly

The Laminated Blade: Superiorities and Shortcomings

enough to achieve excellent edge retention and keenness.

2. Commercially tempered 420J2 stainless steel reaches HRC 53 approximate hardness. This is, for all intents and purposes, way too hard to qualify as a "toughening" laminate.

I have seen similar blades snap cleanly in half under minor stresses.

At Tabaruzaka Smithy we produce two lines of cutlery:

1. Our traditional line of Japanese two-layer and three-layer hand-forged cutlery, and custom knives that blend the best of hand-forging and material technology.

2. Our "Muteki" brand of cutlery which is not hand forged but utilizes the same basic materials as our traditional line.

Muteki products are manufactured on a semi-custom basis, thus they are reasonably priced. They feature approximately 85% of the performance of my hand-forged products. This is performance that ranks well above and beyond similar commercially available products in the same price range.

Homogenous steel blades make for striking comparisons. For example, a "normal" homogenous steel blade will cut

through a fresh piece of bamboo twenty times. When slapped forcefully against the same bamboo it will either break or remain perfectly straight, depending upon its composition and manufacturing processes.

One of my typical three-layer laminated blades will cut the same bamboo two hundred times. When slapped forcefully against the bamboo it will bend somewhat, but not break. It can then be easily restraightened to cut the bamboo another two hundred times.

This is a knife, not a crowbar!

Murray M. Carter

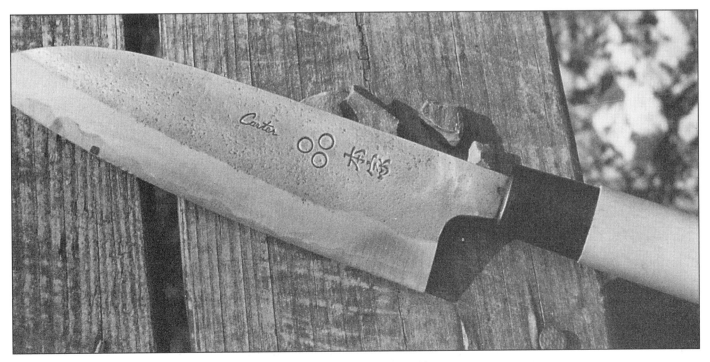

▲ The name Carter means it is forged in two-layer or three-layer traditional fashion, and the non-cutting layers may well be stainless steel.

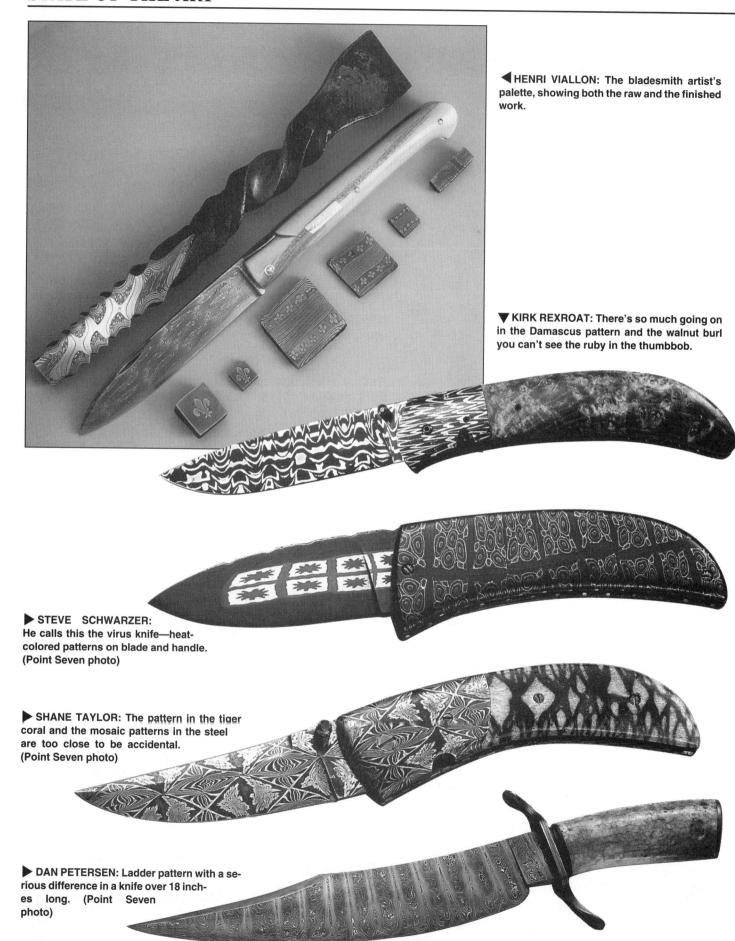

◄HENRI VIALLON: The bladesmith artist's palette, showing both the raw and the finished work.

▼KIRK REXROAT: There's so much going on in the Damascus pattern and the walnut burl you can't see the ruby in the thumbbob.

►STEVE SCHWARZER: He calls this the virus knife—heat-colored patterns on blade and handle. (Point Seven photo)

►SHANE TAYLOR: The pattern in the tiger coral and the mosaic patterns in the steel are too close to be accidental. (Point Seven photo)

►DAN PETERSEN: Ladder pattern with a serious difference in a knife over 18 inches long. (Point Seven photo)

▶ REVISHVILI/WEILAND: Melding two disparate textures isn't always easy, but It Is often good-looking. (Point Seven photo)

▶ JERRY T. DURAN: The old Harley Davidson primary chain trick again in a knife that goes over 8 inches. (Weyer photo)

▶ ED CAFFREY: Handsome handling of the mosaic idea in the Bowie idiom—11 1/2-inches of pattern. (Point Seven photo)

▼ ▶ RICK DUNKERLEY: These show the artist at play with laminated patterns forming the parts of folding knives, all about six inches long as you see them. They are not much less startling in person. (Point Seven photo)

KNIFE LEATHER

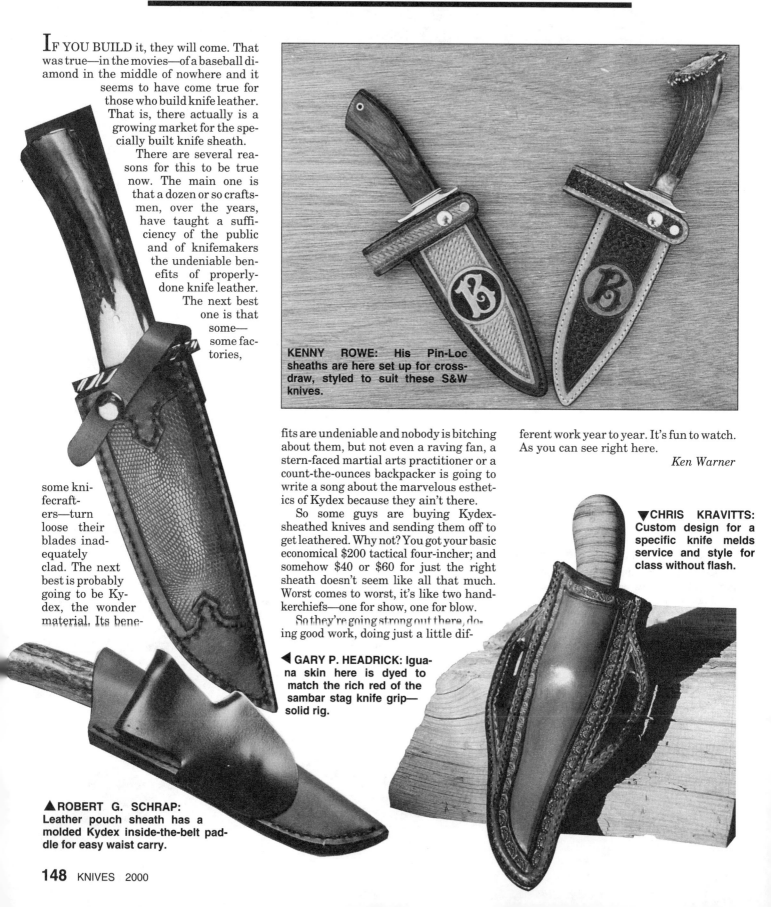

IF YOU BUILD it, they will come. That was true—in the movies—of a baseball diamond in the middle of nowhere and it seems to have come true for those who build knife leather. That is, there actually is a growing market for the specially built knife sheath.

There are several reasons for this to be true now. The main one is that a dozen or so craftsmen, over the years, have taught a sufficiency of the public and of knifemakers the undeniable benefits of properly-done knife leather. The next best one is that some—some factories, some knifecrafters—turn loose their blades inadequately clad. The next best is probably going to be Kydex, the wonder material. Its bene-

KENNY ROWE: His Pin-Loc sheaths are here set up for cross-draw, styled to suit these S&W knives.

fits are undeniable and nobody is bitching about them, but not even a raving fan, a stern-faced martial arts practitioner or a count-the-ounces backpacker is going to write a song about the marvelous esthetics of Kydex because they ain't there.

So some guys are buying Kydex-sheathed knives and sending them off to get leathered. Why not? You got your basic economical $200 tactical four-incher; and somehow $40 or $60 for just the right sheath doesn't seem like all that much. Worst comes to worst, it's like two hand-kerchiefs—one for show, one for blow.

So they're going strong out there, doing good work, doing just a little dif-ferent work year to year. It's fun to watch. As you can see right here.

Ken Warner

▼**CHRIS KRAVITTS:** Custom design for a specific knife melds service and style for class without flash.

◀ **GARY P. HEADRICK:** Iguana skin here is dyed to match the rich red of the sambar stag knife grip—solid rig.

▲**ROBERT G. SCHRAP:** Leather pouch sheath has a molded Kydex inside-the-belt paddle for easy waist carry.

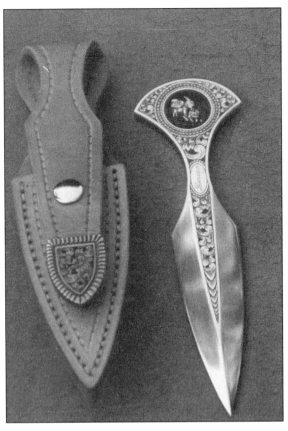

▼CHRIS KRAVITTS: Southwest motif carved into a cowhide sheath for a curvy hunter.

▲RICHARD LARSEN: Straightforward over-the-top clasp for a pretty dainty punch dagger.

►KENNY ROWE: The full monte—axe, big knife, little knife, other stuff—in a saddle-suitable shoulder bag.

▼YASUTAKA WADA: Slick snakeskin pocket protector for a nifty little push dagger.

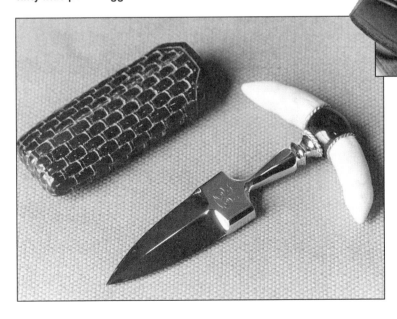

▲PEGGY PATRICK: Double sheath for Morrisey knives gets it all together.

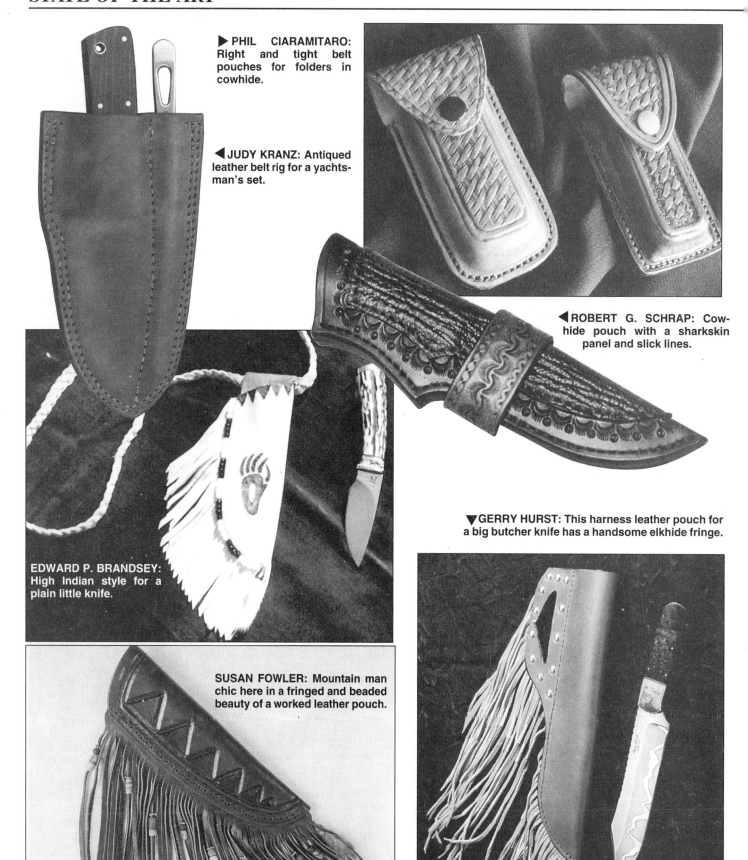

▶ PHIL CIARAMITARO: Right and tight belt pouches for folders in cowhide.

◀ JUDY KRANZ: Antiqued leather belt rig for a yachtsman's set.

◀ ROBERT G. SCHRAP: Cowhide pouch with a sharkskin panel and slick lines.

EDWARD P. BRANDSEY: High Indian style for a plain little knife.

▼ GERRY HURST: This harness leather pouch for a big butcher knife has a handsome elkhide fringe.

SUSAN FOWLER: Mountain man chic here in a fringed and beaded beauty of a worked leather pouch.

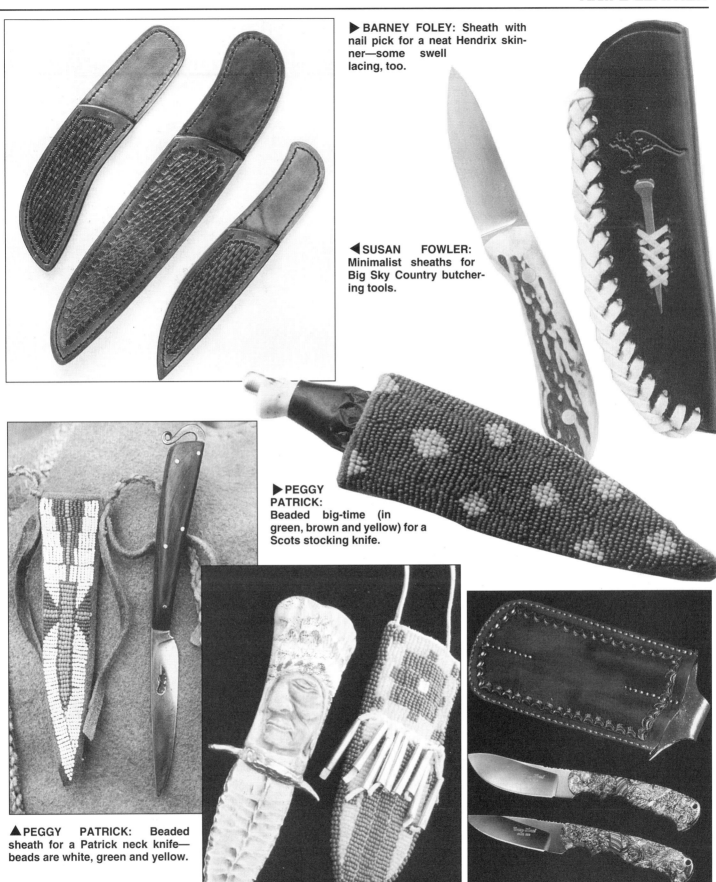

▶BARNEY FOLEY: Sheath with nail pick for a neat Hendrix skinner—some swell lacing, too.

◀SUSAN FOWLER: Minimalist sheaths for Big Sky Country butchering tools.

▶PEGGY PATRICK: Beaded big-time (in green, brown and yellow) for a Scots stocking knife.

▲PEGGY PATRICK: Beaded sheath for a Patrick neck knife—beads are white, green and yellow.

▶HOWARD IMBODEN II: Nicely beaded and bangled sheath for a broad neck knife.

▲GERRY HURST: Utilitarian belt carrier for a slim hunter set.

SCRIMSHAW

by Ken Warner

▲STEPHEN STUART: Antique-looking, all of it—Stuart scrim, Winkler knife, Shook fixings. (Point Seven photo)

▲VIVECA SAHLIN: Eyes of the eagle in white on black.

▲LYNN BENADE: Eyes of a lady on a Chamblee knife.

▲VIVECA SAHLIN: Eyes of a bigger eagle—disturbing.

▲ RONI DIETRICH: Eyes of the tiger, scrimmed on ivory.

◀ VIVECA SAHLIN: Native American eyes across the years.

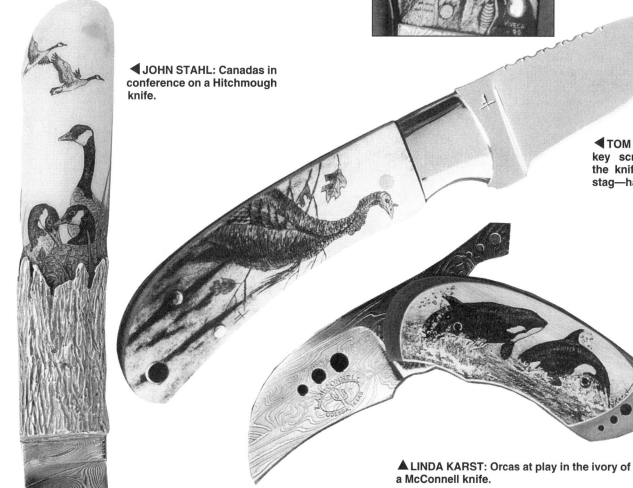

◀ JOHN STAHL: Canadas in conference on a Hitchmough knife.

◀ TOM HIGH: Turkey scrimmed by the knifemaker on stag—handsome.

▲ LINDA KARST: Orcas at play in the ivory of a McConnell knife.

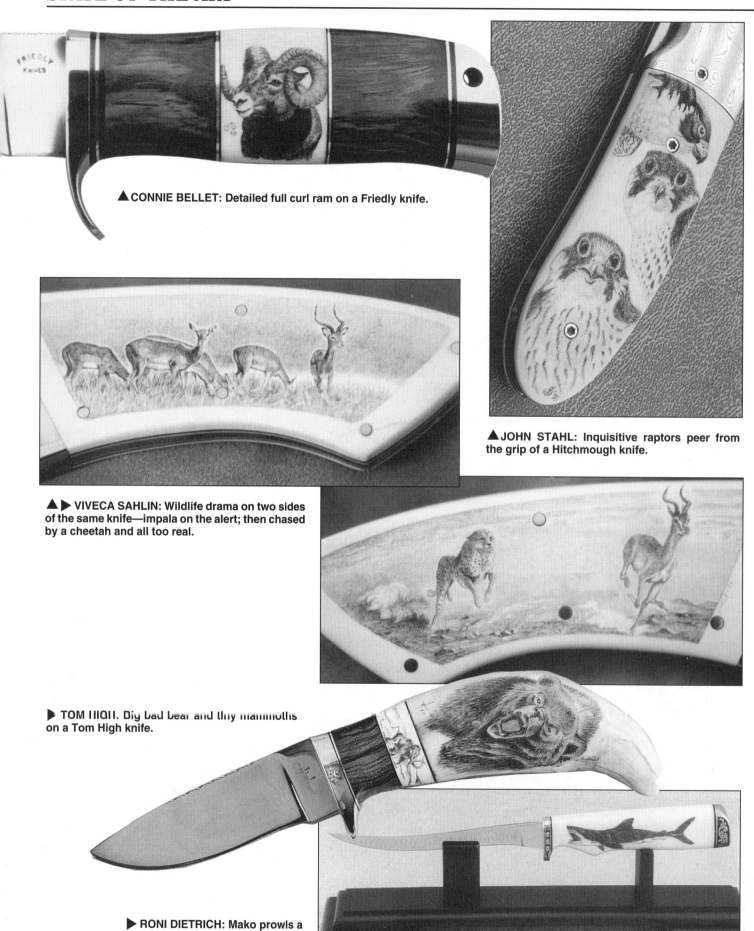

▲CONNIE BELLET: Detailed full curl ram on a Friedly knife.

▲JOHN STAHL: Inquisitive raptors peer from the grip of a Hitchmough knife.

▲▶ VIVECA SAHLIN: Wildlife drama on two sides of the same knife—impala on the alert; then chased by a cheetah and all too real.

▶ TOM HIGH: Big bad bear and tiny mammoths on a Tom High knife.

▶ RONI DIETRICH: Mako prowls a racked-up fillet knife.

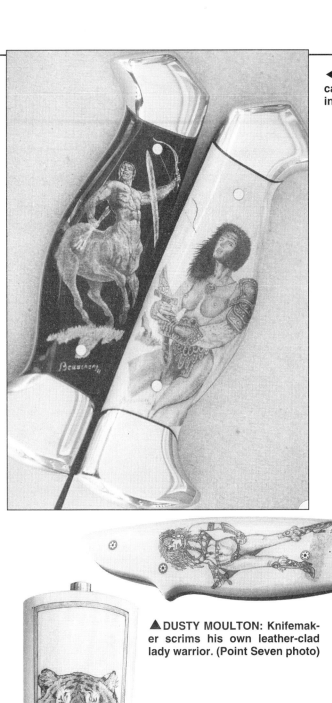

◀GAETAN BEAUCHAMP: Mythical? Prehistoric? Take your choice in black or white.

◀RONI DIETRICH: Casual blonde casually sketched in motion.

▲DUSTY MOULTON: Knifemaker scrims his own leather-clad lady warrior. (Point Seven photo)

◀LINDA KARST: Interested tiger on the grip of a Dennis Friedly knife.

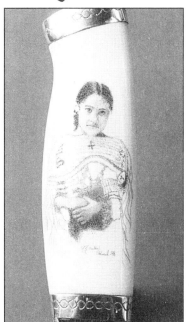

▲MAIHKEL EKLUND: Winsome ethnic lady on a Peenti Turinen knife.

▲RONI DIETRICH: Grim Masai in battle gear, but not painted yet.

ENGRAVING

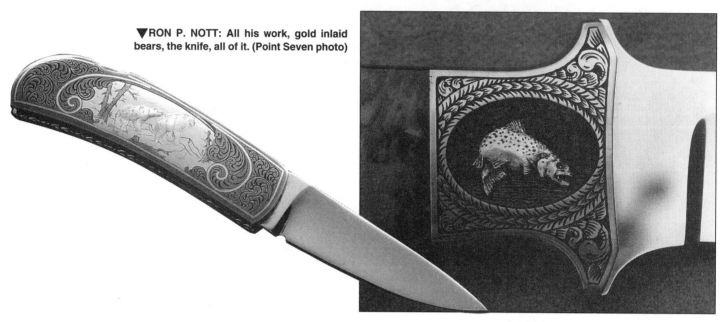

▼RON P. NOTT: All his work, gold inlaid bears, the knife, all of it. (Point Seven photo)

▲BRUCE SHAW: Big fish turns gracefully on a D'Holder knife.

▼BILLY BATES: Bold and different scroll on an A. T. Barr folder.

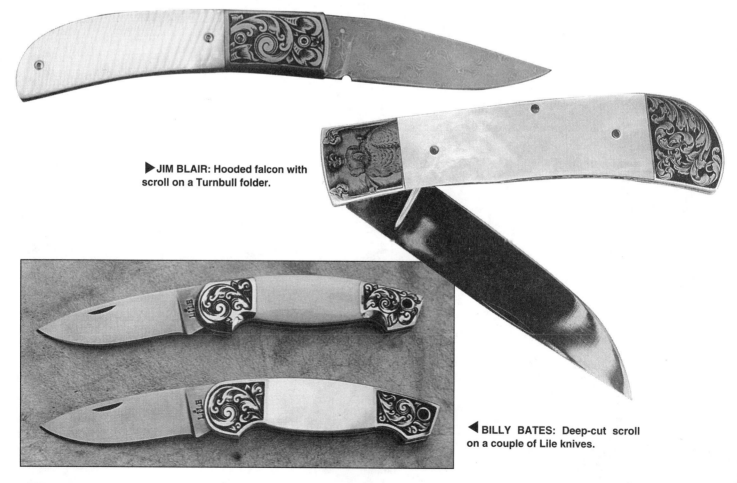

▶JIM BLAIR: Hooded falcon with scroll on a Turnbull folder.

◀BILLY BATES: Deep-cut scroll on a couple of Lile knives.

▶ BRIAN LYTTLE: High style in art deco-ish mode. (Weyer photo)

▶ JULIE WARENSKI: Heavy coverage fore and aft on a David Lang dagger. (Weyer photo)

▶ DON BELL: Gold work and chiseling in titanium, nicely anodized, on a Peter Wile knife. (Point Seven photo)

▶ PETE FORTHOFER: Cast silver sheep head on a dramatic bolster.

▶CHRIS MEYER: Angry lion in scroll on a Khalsa folder (Point Seven photo)

▲ TANYA VAN HOY: Enigmatic scrollwork on a Hossom hunter. (Llorente photo)

▶ SIMON LYTTON: Handsome layout on a Terzuola folder with accessory. (Point Seven photo)

◀ DON BELL: Bright titanium flowers on a pearl-handled Wile knife. (Point Seven photo)

▲ RON NOTT: Very conservative gray knife with illumination in gold (Point Seven photo)

▲ DAVID MORTON: Nicely designed scroll panel on a Lozier knife. (Weyer photo)

▲ E.G. PETERSON: A handsome skinner made more so with a gold sheep.

▲ RICK EATON: All his own work ...
lovely layout, lovely woman, nifty knife.
(Point Seven photo)

▲ JIM SORNBERGER:
Virile skull on a Michael
McClure knife.

▶ LISA TOMLIN: Bears both
sides of a Lozier boot knife –
nice design. (Weyer photo)

▲ JERE DAVIDSON: Bold scroll
pattern on a Forthofer hunter.

▲ TIM ADLAM: Very suitable scroll on
a Kohls knife.

CARVING AND ETCHING

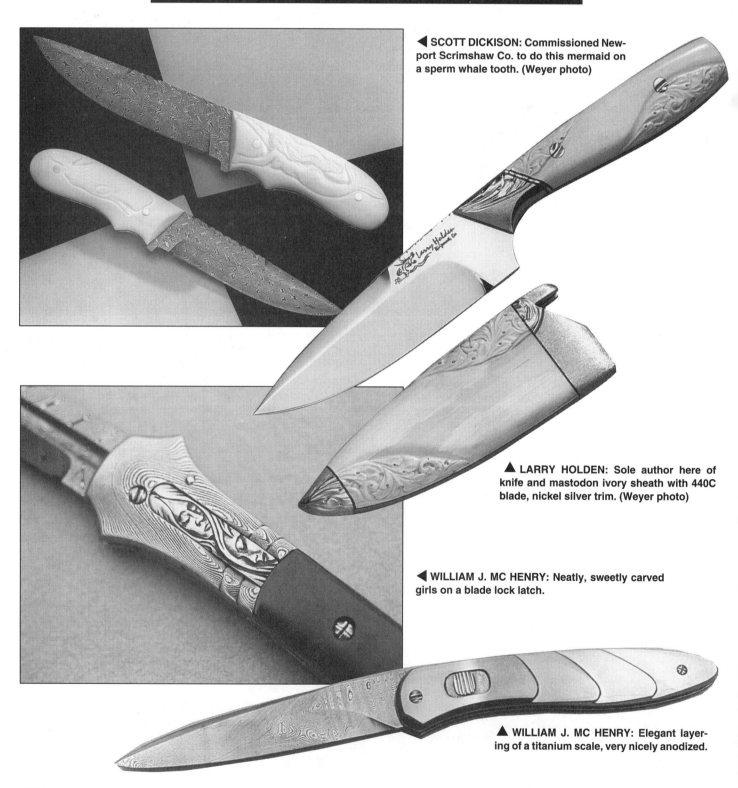

◀ SCOTT DICKISON: Commissioned Newport Scrimshaw Co. to do this mermaid on a sperm whale tooth. (Weyer photo)

▲ LARRY HOLDEN: Sole author here of knife and mastodon ivory sheath with 440C blade, nickel silver trim. (Weyer photo)

◀ WILLIAM J. MC HENRY: Neatly, sweetly carved girls on a blade lock latch.

▲ WILLIAM J. MC HENRY: Elegant layering of a titanium scale, very nicely anodized.

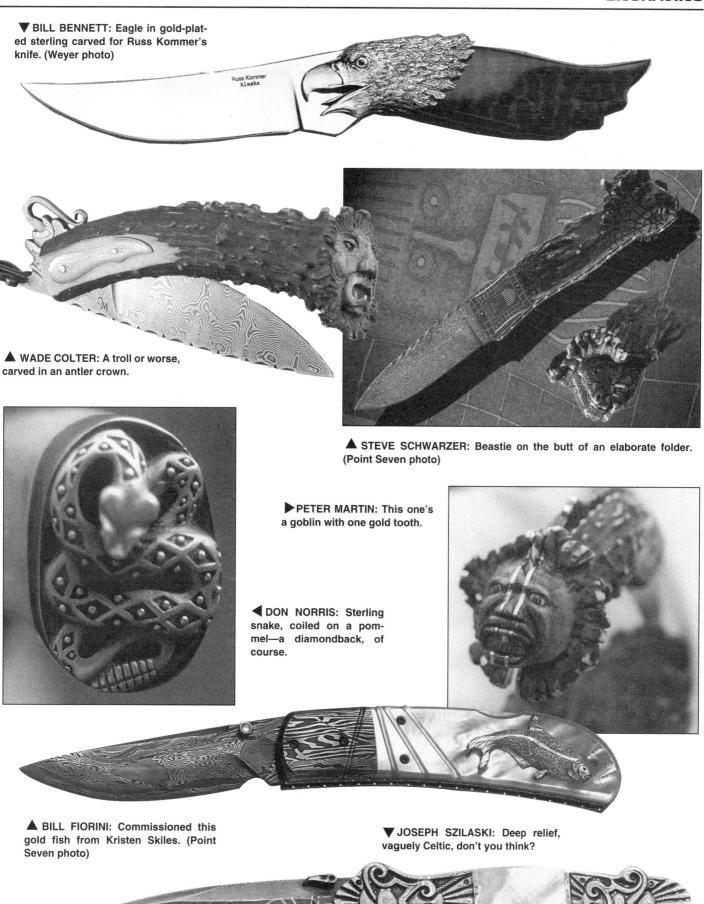

▼ BILL BENNETT: Eagle in gold-plated sterling carved for Russ Kommer's knife. (Weyer photo)

▲ WADE COLTER: A troll or worse, carved in an antler crown.

▲ STEVE SCHWARZER: Beastie on the butt of an elaborate folder. (Point Seven photo)

▶ PETER MARTIN: This one's a goblin with one gold tooth.

◀ DON NORRIS: Sterling snake, coiled on a pommel—a diamondback, of course.

▲ BILL FIORINI: Commissioned this gold fish from Kristen Skiles. (Point Seven photo)

▼ JOSEPH SZILASKI: Deep relief, vaguely Celtic, don't you think?

▶ **FRANCINE MARTIN:** Horses and riders on a Norris Bowie blade. (Weyer photo)

▲ **MAIHKEL EKLUND:** Splendid design—a feeding moose on a wide blade.

▲ **DAVID BOYE:** Handsome bird wing and traceries on a leaf-shaped blade. (Weyer photo)

▶ **CHARLES HILLMAN:** Big bear busts out of etched blade, work by maker.

▼ **LEONARD LEIBOWITZ:** The flag at Iwo Jima on a Nolen knife.

FACTORY TRENDS

We used to say commercial production knives tended toward the tried and true. That is not going to be factual for much longer.

We've got companies in major production of automatic knives for which they've found a legal law enforcement market; we've got sports knives from overseas that are very handcrafted, and some very, very high-tech.

There are companies turning to military-style knives—a wider range than ever, it would appear—and other companies shunning phosphate coatings and the dark look.

We only talk about the new ones—or ones we think you don't know about—here, but there will be nifty pictures to look at anyway.

Ken Warner

CUTLERY OFFSHOOTS

by Bernard Levine

IF YOU PUT a strawberry plant in your garden, you will soon have its offshoots sprouting up all over the place. The same seems to be true of some cutlery plants - factories, that is. Certain cutlery factories, beyond producing knives, have proven to be hotbeds for propagating new cutlery firms.

Gerber Legendary Blades of Portland, Oregon is a well-known modern example. In its earliest incarnation from 1939 to 1941, Gerber pooled the knifemaking skills of David Z. Murphy with the marketing savvy of Joseph R. Gerber. When America entered World War II, Murphy went off on his own, making Murphy Combat knives in large numbers for the war effort.

In 1945, Gerber resumed making carving sets, soon adding a few sport hunting and fishing knife models as a minor sideline (for more about the history of Gerber, see the new Levine's Guide to knives and Their Values, 4th Edition, also from DBI Books/Krause Publications). Two of Gerber's employees just after the war were brothers named Ed and Frank Barteaux, whose father was a knifemaker in rural Waldport, Oregon. With the encouragement of Francis "Ham" Gerber, Job's eldest son and then president of the family cutlery firm, the Barteaux brothers soon went off on their own to found Barteaux Machetes, Inc., in Portland.

Jump ahead now to 1966. Gerber Legendary Blades has just built a big new factory, its present facility on Southwest 72nd Avenue in Portland. The staff is expanding, and so are the product lines. A key new employee hired by president Joseph "Pete" Gerber Jr., Ham's younger half-brother, is a salesman named Pete Kershaw.

Five years later in 1971, Pete Gerber retains the Los Angeles industrial design firm of Zeirhut, Vedder & Shimano to help develop new packaging. Mr. Shimano brings with him to Portland his new assistant, a recent Art Center School of Design graduate named Al Mar. Pete Gerber likes Mar's style and proceeds to recruit him away from Shimano. The clincher is Gerber's sales pitch is that Mar, a native of Seattle, will feel more at home back in the Northwest, in Oregon, than he did in Southern California. Soon Al Mar is Gerber's resident designer.

Skip ahead three more years, to 1974. Pete Kershaw, now national sales manager at Gerber, arrives at a parting of the ways. He sees a rosy future in the sport knife market, but Gerber's main empha-

GERBER: These deluxe renditions of the Gerber Mark I (the little one) and the Gerber Mark II reflect the glory days of marketing to the military direct to the user through Post Exchanges everywhere. For some time the plain models packaged as "survival knives," and maybe that's what they were.

GERBER: Rare photo of the late Joseph Gerber in conference with his early mainstay knifemaker, the late David Z. Murphy. The Gerber firm is still with us, and Murphy's son, also David, keeps that name alive as well.

sis is still on its Legendary carving knife line. Kershaw decides to start his own company and arranges an alliance with Kai Cutlery of Seki City, Japan, the "Sheffield of the East." Kai is to manufacture sporting knives that Kershaw designs for the American market, and then Kershaw will market through his new firm, Kershaw Cutlery Co.

Another five years go by. It is 1979, and Al Mar is ready to set up his own enterprise, too. The structure of Al Mar Knives is similar to that of Kershaw: design and marketing in the U.S., production in Seki City. Many of Mar's designs have a more martial edge, reflecting Al's 1960s service in the U.S. Army Special Forces. Al Mar died in 1992, but the business is ably carried on by his wife and daughter.

Gerber, Kershaw, and Al Mar Knives are all in the Portland area, but the biggest cutlery firm there now is none of the above. It is the Leatherman Tool Group, pioneer in the modern revival of the folding plier knife. In 1982, Tim Leatherman approached Gerber with his two handmade prototypes. Gerber executives and engineers loved the product and were eager to take it on—all of them, that is, except the boss. Pete Gerber did not see it as part of the Gerber line and turned down the idea.

The rest is pliers history. Leatherman started his own firm in Portland, from scratch, and it now employs more people than Gerber. Pete Gerber is enjoying his retirement, having sold the firm to Fiskars of Finland (founded 1649) in 1987. And Gerber's best-selling product today is the Multi-Plier, the firm's belated but highly successful answer to the Leatherman Tool.

Skip ahead now to 1995. At the

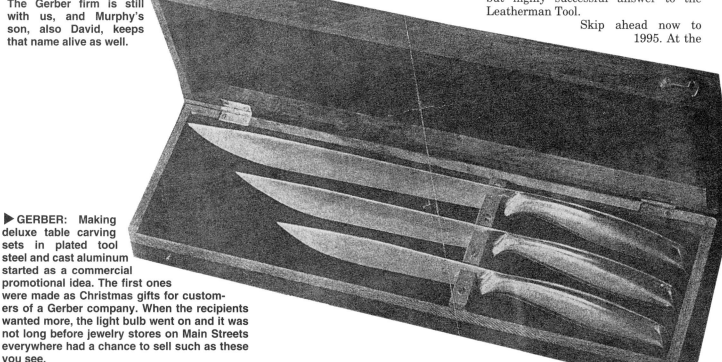

GERBER: Making deluxe table carving sets in plated tool steel and cast aluminum started as a commercial promotional idea. The first ones were made as Christmas gifts for customers of a Gerber company. When the recipients wanted more, the light bulb went on and it was not long before jewelry stores on Main Streets everywhere had a chance to sell such as these you see.

1995 winter SHOT Show in Las Vegas, a new Northwest cutlery firm exhibited for the first time. It is an offshoot of an offshoot. The Columbia River Knife & Tool Co. of Wilsonville, Oregon, was founded April 1, 1994, by two long-time employees of Kershaw. Paul Gillespie had worked ten years there, while Rod Bremer had worked eight. Columbia River has a partnership interest in a brand-new high-tech knife factory in Taiwan, where it manufactures a variety of sport knives, several of them designed by custom maker Jim Hammond of Alabama.

The proliferation of such offshoot companies from Gerber is not unique in American cutlery history, nor is it even all that unusual. An even more complex proliferation of firms can be traced back to the decision of a man named Charles Sherwood to build a little pocketknife factory in the village of Camillus, New York, twenty-five miles west of Syracuse, just over a century ago, in 1894.

Sherwood manufactured knives in Camillus for a couple of years, but could not make the operation pay. In 1896 he leased the plant to a jobber from Rochester, New York, named Millard F. Robeson. Robeson was a better marketer than Sherwood, and by 1898 he had outgrown the Camillus facility and built his own factory back in Rochester. Robeson Cutlery Co. grew to be a major player in the American cutlery industry, known both for technological innovation and for repeated brushes with bankruptcy. It ceased production in 1965 and went out of business in 1977.

While Robeson was at Camillus, the U.S. Congress passed the confiscatory Dingley Tariff act of 1897. With most imported knives now priced out of the market, American cutlery importers scrambled to find domestic sources of supply. After Robeson had returned to Rochester, a major New York City cutlery importer called Adolph Kastor & Bros. (founded 1876) stepped in and purchased Sherwood's factory in 1902, renaming it Camillus Cutlery Co.

Two decades later, in 1922, Kastor hired a teenager named Albert M. Baer as a salesman. Adolph Kastor retired in 1927 and was succeeded by his son Alfred. In 1938 Alfred Kastor and Albert M. Baer had a falling out, and Baer resigned, although by this time he had become a major shareholder in Camillus. In 1941, Baer purchased the Ulster Knife Co. in Ellenville, New York, itself an offshoot of the old Co-Operative Knife Co., which had failed in 1876. During World War II, Ulster formed a joint venture with Imperial Knife Co. of Rhode Island. Imperial was founded in 1916 by Michael and Felix Mirando, brothers who had learned the cutlery trade in Frosolone, Italy, and who had been working for the Empire Knife Co. in Con-

necticut (founded 1856). The joint venture was called Kingston Cutlery Co.

After the war, in 1946, Kingston purchased the Schrade Cutlery Co. of Walden, New York (founded 1904). The resulting triple combination was called Imperial Knife Associated Companies. Since 1984, it has been called Imperial Schrade Corporation, and it is the largest cutlery firm in the world. Its chairman and principal shareholder was the late Albert M. Baer.

The story of Camillus offshoots does not stop there. Back in 1915, Camillus employed a foreman named Carl Tillmanns. Tillmanns had emigrated from Solingen with a team of master cutlers who had been friends since childhood. Put out of work by the Dingley Tariff, they had gone to America to seek employment. Wherever Tillmanns went, the others followed.

In 1915, the World War in Europe was in its second year, but America was still officially neutral. Camillus, however, accepted subcontracts from Simmons Hardware Company of St. Louis, to make pocketknives for the French and Canadian navies. Tillmanns's team was assigned this work, but they refused to be parties to this violation of American neutrality, and quit en masse. After leaving Camillus, Tillmanns led his team down to Newark, New Jersey, where they went to

work for Boker, a firm which, like them, had close family ties in Germany.

After the war had ended, in November 1918, the Remington Arms Co. decided to convert its newly built ammunition plant in Bridgeport, Connecticut into the world's most modern cutlery factory. To head up this enterprise, they sought out an experienced and forward-looking master cutler. The man they chose was Carl Tillmanns. In 1919, Tillmanns and his whole crew, evidently complete with pattern books, decamped from Newark to the soggy shores of Bridgeport. For twenty years thereafter, Remington dominated the cutlery market of the United States. But then, in November 1940, the firm abruptly left the knife business, selling all its tools and patterns to the Pal Blade Co.

In 1982, with knife collecting growing apace, Remington once again began to market pocket and sheath knives. This time the knives are contract made, however, manufactured for Remington by an

◀ CAMILLUS: The company put its shoulder to the military wheel every time it was needed, witness this M3 knife from 1943 and this deluxe rendition of a wartime knife made for the Marine Corps in the Fairbairn-Sykes pattern.

▲ ROBESON/CASE: Related companies they were and both worked the military side of the street in concert with the rest of the industry. This is Robeson's USN MKII belt knife—universally called by the Marines, regardless of maker, the KA-BAR—and the much rarer Case dagger, also in the Fairbairn-Sykes pattern, made for the Special Service Force.

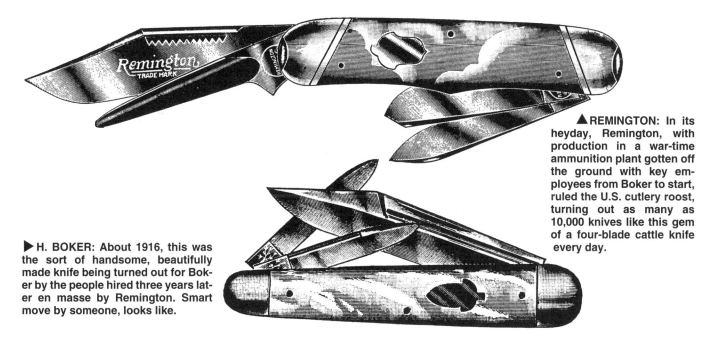

▲REMINGTON: In its heyday, Remington, with production in a war-time ammunition plant gotten off the ground with key employees from Boker to start, ruled the U.S. cutlery roost, turning out as many as 10,000 knives like this gem of a four-blade cattle knife every day.

▶H. BOKER: About 1916, this was the sort of handsome, beautifully made knife being turned out for Boker by the people hired three years later en masse by Remington. Smart move by someone, looks like.

old-line firm in upstate New York called Camillus Cutlery Co.

The history of the American cutlery industry is replete with such offshoot births. One of the most bizarre is the story of Walden Knife Co. It was formed in 1870 by a group of cutlers who had been working for New York Knife Co. of Walden, New York (founded 1852). These men were so incensed by New York Knife's restrictive policy toward employee baseball games that they quit en masse, and started their own rival firm.

Walden Knife's principal customer was the Simmons Hardware Company of St. Louis. In 1902 Simmons purchased the Walden plant, where its premium Keen Kutter line of knives was made. However, for special products (such as French and Canadian navy knives in 1915), Simmons contracted with whatever manufacturers had the skill and the available capacity (in that case, Camillus; see above).

After World War I, in 1922, Simmons hardware merged with Winchester Repeating Arms Co. of Connecticut, now embarked in the hardware business. Winchester had already converted part of its New Haven facility to cutlery produc-

tion, consolidating there the machinery and most of the personnel of Napanoch Knife Co. and Eagle Knife Co. In 1923, Walden Knife Co. was added to the mix. Both Winchester and Keen Kutter knives were made there until 1930; Winchester knives until 1942. Napanoch employees who had stayed behind in Napanoch, New York, meanwhile had formed their own offshoot firm, called Honk Falls Knife Co. It was active from 1921 to 1929.

In 1931, New York Knife Co., the parent plant of all these offshoots, went out of business through pure mismanagement. Its world-renowned Arm & Ham-

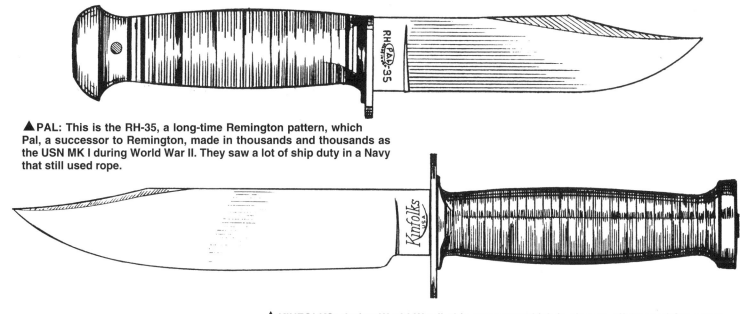

▲PAL: This is the RH-35, a long-time Remington pattern, which Pal, a successor to Remington, made in thousands and thousands as the USN MK I during World War II. They saw a lot of ship duty in a Navy that still used rope.

▲KINFOLKS: during World War II, this company which is also an offshoot of Case and was owned and run by people named Case, put together hunter blades like this one with a double guard and military grip and pommel, for sale to the insatiable market for gifts to servicemen, of whom we had well over 10,000,000.

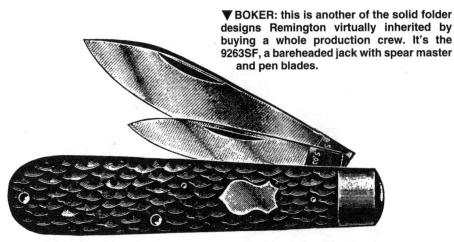

▼ BOKER: this is another of the solid folder designs Remington virtually inherited by buying a whole production crew. It's the 9263SF, a bareheaded jack with spear master and pen blades.

mer trademark (first used circa 1880) lay dormant for a time, but in 1936 it was acquired by Imperial Knife Co. for use on its machine-made Jack-master knives.

In 1984, the firm, called Western Cutlery Co. since 1956, was sold to Coleman and became Coleman-Western. It was sold twice more in 1990 and 1991, and is

same. Case then formed a joint venture with Cattaraugus Cutlery Co. of Little Valley, New York (founded 1886). They built a new factory there called Kinfolks, Inc., because the founder of Cattaraugus, J.B.F. Champlin, was married to another Case sister, Theresa. Her brother, Jean Case, ran Kinfolks until 1935, followed by his son, Dean J. Case. Kinfolks was an independent firm, which closed when Dean Case died in 1951.

In 1940, Robeson Cutlery Co. was on the verge of bankruptcy (not for the first time, nor for the last). New blood was needed at the top, so the directors recruited Emerson Case, nephew of Dean J. Case, to be president. He led Robeson to its period of greatest prosperity, which ended abruptly upon his death in 1965.

In 1941, Case joined with ALCOA (the Aluminum Company of America) in a joint

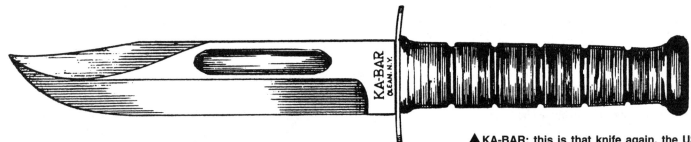

▲ KA-BAR: this is that knife again, the USN MK II, but this is the one the Marines first saw, a product of Union Cutlery, which was owned by brothers-in-law of the Cases. The sturdy knife is still in production with Ka-Bar and with other names on it.

Both to collectors and to consumers, W.R. Case & Sons of Bradford, Pennsylvania (founded 1902), is perhaps the best-known name in knives. When Case opened its own factory in 1905, knife production there was initially under the direction of Harvey N. Platts, who with his four brothers had apprenticed to their father, Charles W. Platts, a Sheffield emigrant who had advanced to superintendent of the Northfield Knife Co. of Northfield, Connecticut (founded 1858).

In 1911, Harvey N. Platts left Case and moved to Boulder, Colorado, for his health. There he started a jobbing business called Western States Cutlery Co. In 1920, Western States built its first factory.

now a subsidiary of Camillus, in upstate New York.

The next Case offshoot was in name only. In 1923, the Brown brothers, Wallace and Emerson, registered a new trademark for their Union Cutlery Co. of Olean, New York (founded circa 1890 in Pennsylvania). This mark was "Ka-Bar." Much later company publicists interpreted this brand as meaning "Kilt a B'ar" (killed a bear), but in actual fact it was a contraction of "Case Brothers." Wallace and Emerson's mother, Emma Case Brown, was a sister of W.R. Case and the four other Case brothers, and her boys were treated like part of the Case family. Union/Ka-Bar got into hunting knives in a big way in the early 1920s. In 1925, W.R. Case & Sons decided to do the

venture called Alcas (ALcoa + CASe) Cutlery Co., in Olean, New York. The firm's first product line was commercial cook and butcher knives, sold in conjunction with WearEver pots and pans. Soon added to the mix was the premium Cutco line of household cutlery, which were sold door-to-door like brushes and encyclopedias.

In 1984, Cutco-Alcas became an independent firm. By that time, it was also manufacturing limited-edition and sport knives both under its own name and under contract for such firms as Aurum Etchings. It also made combat knives on contract for its former Olean neighbor, KaBar Cutlery, which since 1966 had been a subsidiary of Cole National Corporation in Ohio. But then, in 1966, Alcas bought Ka-Bar from Cole, and brought it back home to Olean.

It is safe to assume that cutlery firm offshoots will continue to proliferate. As this is prepared for publication, there is one large bankruptcy happening, and at least six new firms have formed in the past two years, all with national selling plans, so continued change is the only certain outcome.   •

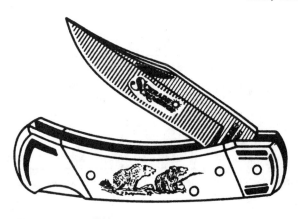

◄ IMPERIAL SCHRADE CORPORATION: This company makes many kinds of knives, this being a Schrade Scrimshaw Model in a lock-blade hunter pattern. Every Imperial Schrade knife made carries with it the names Ulster Knife Co., and, of course, Schrade Cutlery Co.

This is the whole family, and the resemblance one to the other is clear. They are the F1, A1, S1 and WM1 from Fallkniven AB in Sweden.

The Little

Swedish Family

The firstborn was a survival knife for the Swedish Royal Air Force, arriving in 1995, named F1. There was even a special model of this, titanium coated, 500 of them. Then came the A1, bigger and intended for heavier work.

And now there are two more, named, with typical Swedish abandon, the S1 and the WM 1. These two have convex-ground blades, the S1 Forest Knife at five inches; the WM1 Woman's Knife at

three inches. There are sheath options for these—the traditional sort of dangler and others.

It is indeed a family. All have the same VG10 steel, all have the soft-grip handles; all the same clean no-frills line. And none are made in Sweden.

There is probably eventually an end to this proliferation, since designer and boss Peter Hjortberger firmly believes that enough is enough. We may not be

there yet, however. He has four knives at 3, 4, 5 and 6 inch length and is seeing a growing interest in them both commercially and militarily—it's a nice little Swedish family, as it is. However, families sometime grow without advance planning, so the story may not be complete.

Ken Warner

NEW KNIVES IN PRODUCTION

► SPYDERCO: It's the Toad, designed, they say, by D'Alton Holder, who actually claims it. Truth is, it's a nice tool.

▲AL MAR: Nice old wooden sign backs up the new Havana Clipper, a marvelously named cigar tool.

◄SWISS-TECH: The one that got the mini-tool ball rolling is still around, still works.

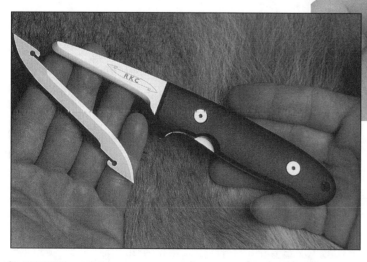

► RICKARD KNIFE CO.: It looks like a liner-lock folder, but instead, it offers dual edges which lock into a blade frame. Next is a folder, they say.

► WENGER: The roots are still there, in the Alpine Backpacker, a genuine pocket-knife with seven blades, nine functions and a host of uses.

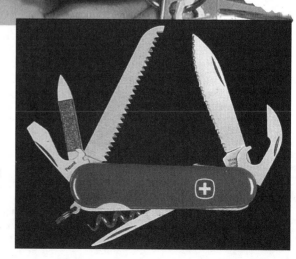

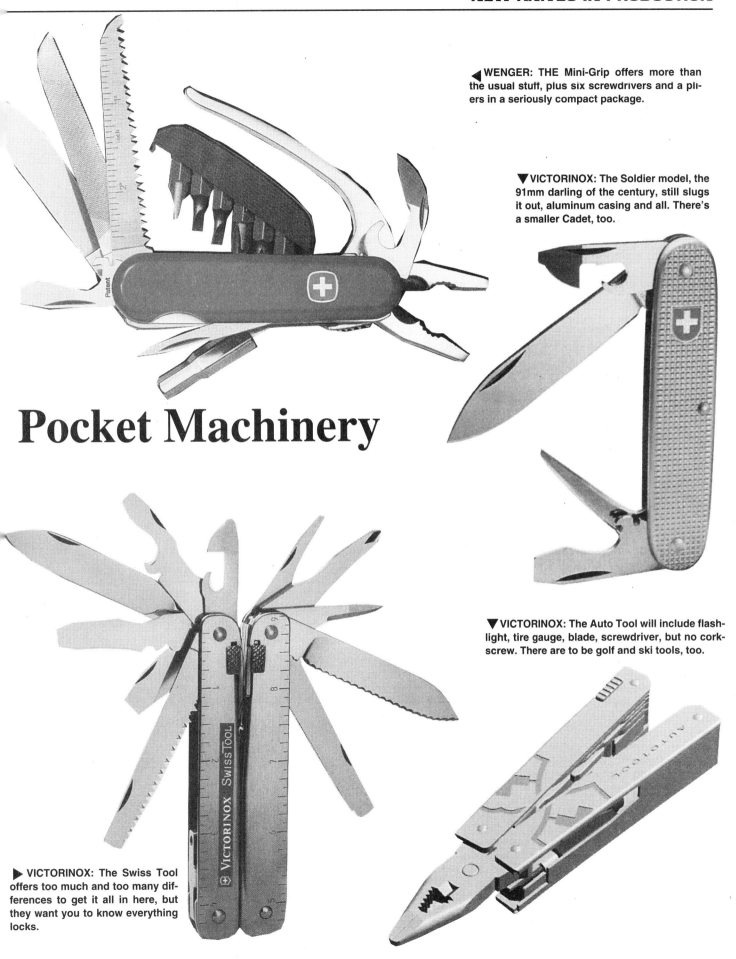

◄ WENGER: THE Mini-Grip offers more than the usual stuff, plus six screwdrivers and a pliers in a seriously compact package.

▼ VICTORINOX: The Soldier model, the 91mm darling of the century, still slugs it out, aluminum casing and all. There's a smaller Cadet, too.

Pocket Machinery

▼ VICTORINOX: The Auto Tool will include flashlight, tire gauge, blade, screwdriver, but no corkscrew. There are to be golf and ski tools, too.

► VICTORINOX: The Swiss Tool offers too much and too many differences to get it all in here, but they want you to know everything locks.

▲KABAR: This is the D2 Extreme—laser-cut blades, machined aluminum handles, 7 5/8-inches long as you see it.

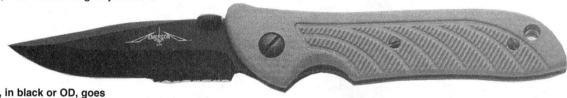

▶EMERSON: The Raven, in black or OD, goes 8 3/8-inches open, has 154CM blade, clipped or tanto, Kevlar-stuffed polymer grips.

Tacticals and Tools

◀S.O.G.: The AutoClip series provides all the usual in a small tactical type, plus the patented adjustable tension device on the clip—just dial what you want.

▲AL MAR KNIVES: The original and wonderful Hawks and Falcons now revisit us as lightweights—still the right shape and size.

▶BROWNING: This is the Barracuda family and they do indeed look pretty mouthy, and also tough.

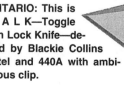

▶ONTARIO: This is the T A L K—Toggle Action Lock Knife—designed by Blackie Collins in Zytel and 440A with ambidextrous clip.

▲EDGE DESIGN INC.: The Genesis-1 is designed in ATS34 and G-10 to be a user's knife with a blade just under four inches.

▲GATCO/TIMBERLINE: This is the Special Services knife, all stainless steel, with clip and 3.4-inch blade—slim and very tough.

▶REMINGTON: This is the Rattler, a big guy in the new mode, designed for the heavy-duty cuts, serrations and all.

▼OUTDOOR EDGE: From the Designer Series, this is the Magna Kit Carson worked up, has AUS-8 blade at four inches, choice of aluminum or Zytel grip.

◀Boker: Another in Boker's forward-looking folders, set up, to our eyes, for a virtually certain American appeal. This one's the Gemini.

▶OUTDOOR EDGE: The Impulse was adapted from Darrel Ralph's personal designs, offers Sandvik steel and Kraton grips at 8 1/2 -inches overall.

Straight Stuff

▲**CAMILLUS:** The CUDA comes in several forms and this bad boy is one of the biggest. It's a full-service combat knife.

▶**MARBLE ARMS:** You can have the Trailmaker in these and more than a couple other variations—a nice range of new old-timers.

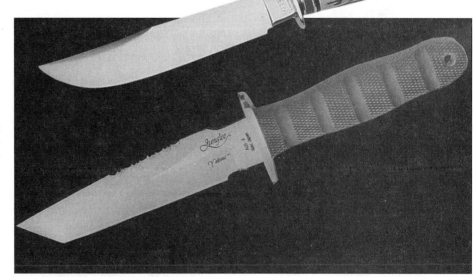

▶**GUTMANN CUTLERY:** This is the Junglee Yakusa, and yakusa is Japanese for naughty fellow and this Yakusa could be that way, too.

▶**BUSSE COMBAT KNIFE CO.:** This is the Collector Grade Battle Mistress, and goes 15 1/2-inches overall, weighs 19 ounces.

▶KNIFEWARE, INC.: This logo—and that convex edge—will be on tour big knives before the year is out.

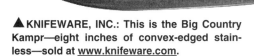

▲KNIFEWARE, INC.: This is the Big Country Kampr—eight inches of convex-edged stainless—sold at www.knifeware.com.

▶KNIFEWARE, INC.: Green canvas Micarta Loveless-approved Marble Sport 2000 in a Loveless-design sheath at www.lovelessknives.com.

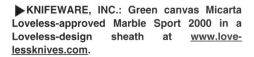

▼GATCO/TIMBERLINE: The Spec-War is still with us, and its high-tech sheath as well, including that startling geometry in both.

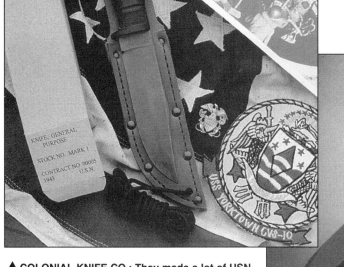

▲COLONIAL KNIFE CO.: They made a lot of USN Mark I knives in World War II and now they are making some more—in every detail like the veterans.

FACTORY

▶ GUTMANN CUTLERY: Handsome Hattori fighter is in Gutmann's Junglee line, one of the company's many imports.

◀ GROHMANN KNIVES LTD.: The D.H. Russell No. 1 in stainless is one of nine or more models made in Nova Scotia.

▲ ONTARIO KNIVES: Here is the line of four Bagwell Bowies, 14 5/8 to 16 3/4-inches long, with the quick look, the long edge.

▲ GATCO/TIMBERLINE: The Aviator puts all the Spec War geometry and good looks together in a different and smaller package.

▶ MARBLE ARMS: The drop-point Sport 2000 offers a short and stout convex ground hunter in a typical choice of handles.

▶BROWNING: This is the Kodiak FDT, which means Field Dressing Tool, and with those blades, it certainly is.

▲OUTDOOR EDGE: The Kodi-Pak capes, guts, skins, butchers and quarters with three tools, all sheathed together.

Game Management

▶GUTMANN CUTLERY: This is the Junglee Alaskan hook cleaver, with more than a few uses obvious to anyone who has seen a large dead animal.

▼REMINGTON: Every camp needs a hatchet and Remington aims to provide with this thoroughly modern number.

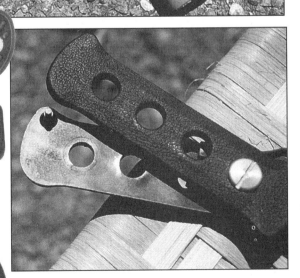

▲▲P.J. TURNER: The Uluchet packs like a pistol, works like a hatchet or a skinner—your choice. Handle latch is now bigger and beefier.

W.R. CASE & SONS: The Hobo is back and Case has him in more than a few finishes, this one the prettiest.

REMINGTON: The 1999 Bullet is a big sleeve-board two-blade jack with spear and pen blades and a long nail nick.

Traditions

REMINGTON: Another new Remington is an old friend, the scout or camp knife, a burly fellow with the correct four blades.

QUEEN CUTLERY: It's Queen steel and chipped bark Delrin for this nice hunter-size button lock folder.

THOMPSON CENTER: The T/C Knife No. 8 is this handsome Schatt & Morgan four-bladed scout knife—150 knives is all there are.

DIRECTORY

There are only a very few reasons a legitimate maker or manufacturer or importer or supply source is not listed herein. Chiefly, they are: We never heard of or from him or it, or we did, but something went wrong at our end, which happens. This is intended to be a complete directory for knife owners. If you know of someone or some firm who should be here and isn't, please write and tell us. And if you are that someone, do the same. Please.

This is not, of course, a catalog, so we can't tell you everything about any one entry. And there are, as we implied above, omissions, often the omitted guy's fault. We give everyone the same opportunity.

As the table of contents below tells you, the pages from here on are divided into lists, the biggest being the list of custom knife makers (because there are so many of them). We have made a few changes in this set of lists, here in the 20th edition, so if you are a long-time reader, review them.

We picked all these categories because they seemed to us to be the most useful for you. Over the years, it seems to have worked out that way.

Ken Warner

custom knifemakers

a

ABBOTT, WILLIAM M., Box 102A, RR #2, Chandlerville, IL, 62627/217-458-2325
Specialties: High-grade edged weapons. **Patterns:** Locking folders, Bowies, working straight knives, kitchen cutlery, minis. **Technical:** Grinds D2, ATS-34, 440C and commercial Damascus. Heat-treats; Rockwell tests. Prefers natural handle materials. **Prices:** $100 to $1,000. **Remarks:** Part-time maker; first knife sold in 1984. **Mark:** Name.

ABERNATHY, PAUL J., 3033 Park St., Eureka, CA, 95501/707-442-3593
Specialties: Period pieces and traditional straight knives of his design and in standard patterns. **Patterns:** Miniature daggers, fighters and swords. **Technical:** Forges and files SS, brass and sterling silver. **Prices:** $100 to $250; some to $500. **Remarks:** Part-time maker. Doing business as Abernathy's Miniatures. **Mark:** Stylized initials.

ADAMS, LES, 6413 NW 200 St., Hialeah, FL, 33015/305-625-1699
Specialties: Working straight knives of his design. **Patterns:** Fighters, hunters and fillet knives. **Technical:** Grinds ATS-34, 440C and D2. Offers scrimshawed handles. **Prices:** $100 to $200; some to $290. **Remarks:** Part-time maker; first knife sold in 1989. **Mark:** First initial, last name, Custom Knives.

ADAMS, WILLIAM D., 9318 Cole Creek Dr., Houston, TX, 77040/713-855-5643
Specialties: Hunter scalpels and utility knives of his design. **Patterns:** Hunters and utility/camp knives. **Technical:** Grinds 1095, 440C and 440V. Uses stabilized wood and other stabilized materials. **Prices:** $100 to $200. **Remarks:** Part-time maker; first knife sold in 1994. **Mark:** Last name in script.

AIDA, YOSHIHITO, 26-7 Narimasu 2-chome, Itabashi-ku, Tokyo 175, JAPAN, /81-3-3939-0052
Specialties: High-tech working straight knives and folders of his design. **Patterns:** Bowies, lockbacks, hunters, fighters, fishing knives, boots. **Technical:** Grinds CV-134, ATS-34; buys Damascus; works in traditional Japanese fashion for some handles and sheaths. **Prices:** $400 to $900; some higher. **Remarks:** Full-time maker; first knife sold in 1978. **Mark:** Initial logo and Riverside West.

ALBERICCI, EMILIO, 19 via Masone, 24100, Bergamo, ITALY, /01139-35-215120
Specialties: Folders and Bowies. **Patterns:** Collector knives. **Technical:** Uses stock removal with extreme lavoration accuracy; offers exotic and high-tech materials. **Prices:** Not currently selling. **Remarks:** Part-time maker. **Mark:** None.

ALDERMAN, ROBERT, 3388 Jewel Lake Rd., Sagle, ID, 83860/208-263-5996
Specialties: Classic and traditional working straight knives in standard patterns or to customer specs and his design; period pieces. **Patterns:** Bowies, fighters, hunters and utility/camp knives. **Technical:** Casts, forges and grinds 1084; forges and grinds L6 and O1. Prefers an old appearance. **Prices:** $100 to $350; some to $700. **Remarks:** Full-time maker; first knife sold in 1975. Doing business as Trackers Forge. **Mark:** Deer track.

ALEXANDER, DARREL, Box 381, Ten Sleep, WY, 82442/307-366-2699
Specialties: Traditional working straight knives. **Patterns:** Hunters, boots and fishing knives. **Technical:** Grinds D2, 440C, ATS-34 and 154CM. **Prices:** $75 to $120; some to $250. **Remarks:** Full-time maker; first knife sold in 1983. **Mark:** Name, city, state.

ALLEN, JOE, 120 W. Glendale St., Princeton, IN, 47670/812-386-7276
Specialties: Hunting and outdoor knives. **Patterns:** Bowies, working hunters, daggers and skinners. **Technical:** Grinds 440C and ATS-34. **Prices:** $125 to $400. **Remarks:** Part-time maker; first knife sold in 1976. **Mark:** Full name, year, city, state.

ALLEN, MIKE "WHISKERS", 12745 Fontenot Acres Rd., Malakoff, TX, 75148/903-489-1026
Specialties: Working and collector-quality lockbacks and automatic folders to customer specs. **Patterns:** Hunters, tantos, Bowies, swords and miniatures. **Technical:** Forges Damascus to shape; grinds 440C and ATS-34. Engraves. **Prices:** $150 and up. **Remarks:** Full-time maker; first knife sold in 1984. **Mark:** Whiskers and serial number.

ALLRED, ELVAN, 2403 Lansing Blvd., Wichita Falls, TX, 76309/817-691-9563
Specialties: Fancy, high-art straight knives and folders of his design. **Patterns:** Fighters, hunters and locking folders. **Technical:** Grinds ATS-34, 440C and D2. Most knives are engraved; many have custom-fitted cases or sheaths. **Prices:** $250 to $750; some to $1,500. **Remarks:** Full-time maker; first knife sold in 1992. Doing business as Allred and Sons. **Mark:** First initial, last name, city, state.

ALVERSON, TIM (R.V.), 1158 Maple St., Klamath Falls, OR, 97601/541-884-9119
Specialties: Fancy working knives to customer specs; other types on request. **Patterns:** Bowies, daggers, folders and miniatures. **Technical:** Grinds 440C, ATS-34; buys some Damascus. **Prices:** Start at $175. **Remarks:** Full-time maker; first knife sold in 1981. **Mark:** R.V.A. around rosebud.

AMERI, MAURO, Via Riaello No. 20, Trensasco St. Olcese, 16010 Genova, ITALY, /010-8357077
Specialties: Working and using knives of his design. **Patterns:** Hunters, Bowies and utility/camp knives. **Technical:** Grinds 440C, ATS-34 and 154CM. Handles in wood or Micarta; offers sheaths. **Prices:** $200 to $1,200. **Remarks:** Spare-time maker; first knife sold in 1982. **Mark:** Last name, city.

AMES, MICKEY L., 801 S Little, Ft Scott, KS, 66701/316-223-0285
Specialties: Traditional working and using straight knives of his design and to customer specs. **Patterns:** Bowies, hunters and utility/camp knives. **Technical:** Forges 5160, 1084, 1095 and makes own Damascus. Filework; silver wire inlay. **Prices:** Start at $100. **Remarks:** Part-time maker; first knife sold in 1990. Doing business as Ames Forge. **Mark:** Last name.

AMOR JR., MIGUEL, 485-H Judie Lane, Lancaster, PA, 17603/717-426-6355
Specialties: Working and fancy straight knives in standard patterns; some to customer specs. **Patterns:** Bowies, hunters, fighters and tantos. **Technical:** Grinds 440C, ATS-34, carbon steel and commercial Damascus; forges some in high carbon steels. **Prices:** $125 to $500; some to $1,500 and higher. **Remarks:** Part-time maker; first knife sold in 1983. **Mark:** Last name. On collectors' pieces: last name, city, state.

AMOUREUX, A.W., 3210 Woodland Pk. Dr., Anchorage, AK, 99517/907-248-4442
Specialties: Heavy-duty working straight knives. **Patterns:** Bowies, fighters, camp knives and hunters for Alaska use. **Technical:** Grinds 440C, ATS-34 and 154CM. **Prices:** $80 to $2,000. **Remarks:** Part-time maker; first knife sold in 1974. **Mark:** ALSTAR.

ANDERS, DAVID, 157 Barnes Dr., Center Ridge, AR, 72027/501-893-2294
Specialties: Working straight knives of his design. **Patterns:** Bowies, fighters and hunters. **Technical:** Forges 5160, 1080 and Damascus. **Prices:** $225 to $3200. **Remarks:** Part-time maker; first knife sold in 1988. Doing business as Anders Knives. **Mark:** Last name/MS.

ANDERSEN, HENRIK LEFOLII, Jagtvej 8, Groenholt, 3480, Fredensborg, DENMARK, /0011-45-48483026
Specialties: Hunters and matched pairs for the serious hunter. **Patterns:** Working folders for bowhunters. **Technical:** Grinds A2; uses materials native to Scandinavia. **Prices:** Start at $250. **Remarks:** Part-time maker; first knife sold in 1985. **Mark:** Initials with arrow.

ANDERSON, EDWIN, C/O Glen Cove Sport Shop, 189 Forest Ave., Glen Cove, NY, 11542/516-676-7120
Specialties: Hunters, fighters, boot knives and folders. **Patterns:** Standard patterns or customer designs. **Technical:** Grinds Stellite 6K, ATS-34, and 440C. Offers integral patterns. **Prices:** $200 to $500; some to $1,500. **Remarks:** Full-time gunsmith, part-time knifemaker; first knife sold in 1977. **Mark:** Name over state.

ANDERSON, GARY D., RD 2, Box 2399C, Spring Grove, PA, 17362-9802/717-229-2665
Specialties: Art-quality blades, folders and working knives. **Patterns:** Traditional and classic designs; customer patterns welcome. **Technical:** Forges Damascus and carbon steels. Offers silver inlay, mokume, file-

work, checkering. **Prices:** $250 to $750; some higher. **Remarks:** Full-time maker; first knife sold in 1985. **Mark:** GAND, MS.

ANDERSON, MEL, 1718 Lee Lane, Cedaredge, CO, 81413/970-856-6465
Specialties: Full-size, miniature and one-of-a-kind straight knives and folders of his design. **Patterns:** Bowies, daggers, fighters, hunters and pressure folders. **Technical:** Grinds 440C, 5160, D2, 1095 and Damascus; offers antler, ivory and wood carved handles. **Prices:** Start at $145. **Remarks:** Full-time maker; first knife sold in 1987. **Mark:** Scratchy Hand.

ANDERSON, TOM, 955 Canal Road Extd., Manchester, PA, 17345/717-266-6475
Specialties: High-tech one-hand folders designed on computer. **Patterns:** Fighters, utility, and dress knives. **Technical:** Grinds ATS-34, BG-42 and stainless damascus. Uses titanium, carbon fiber and select natural handle materials. **Prices:** Start at $275. **Remarks:** Doing business as Anderson Technologies; first knife sold in 1996. **Mark:** Stylized A over T logo with company name.

ANDRESS, RONNIE, 415 Audubon Dr. N., Satsuma, AL, 36572/334-675-7604
Specialties: Working straight knives in standard patterns. **Patterns:** Boots, Bowies, hunters, friction folders and camp knives. **Technical:** Forges 1095, 5160, O1 and his own Damascus. Offers filework and inlays. **Prices:** $125 to $500. **Remarks:** Part-time maker; first knife sold in 1983. Doing business as Andress Knives. **Mark:** Last name, J.S. Other: Jeweler, gold work, stone setter (dropped doing business as Andress Knives).

ANDREWS, ERIC, 132 Halbert Street, Grand Ledge, MI, 48837/517-627-7304
Specialties: Traditional working and using straight knives of his design. **Patterns:** Full-tang hunters, skinners and utility knives. **Technical:** Forges carbon steel; heat-treats. All knives come with sheath; most handles are of wood. **Prices:** $80 to $160. **Remarks:** Part-time maker; first knife sold in 1990. Doing business as The Tinkers Bench.

ANDREWS, DON, N. 5155 Ezy St., Coeur D'Alene, ID, 83814/208-765-8844
Specialties: Plain and fancy folders and straight knives. **Technical:** Grinds D2, 440C, ATS-34; does lost wax casting for guards and pommels. **Prices:** Moderate to upscale. **Remarks:** Full-time maker; first knife sold in 1983. **Mark:** Name.

ANKROM, W.E., 14 Marquette Dr., Cody, WY, 82414/307-587-3017
Specialties: Straight working knives and folders of his design. **Patterns:** Hunters, fighters, boots; lockbacks and liner locks. **Technical:** Grinds ATS-34 and commercial Damascus. **Prices:** $400 and up. **Remarks:** Full-time maker; first knife sold in 1975. **Mark:** Name, city, state.

ANSO, JENS, Spobjergvej 161, DK 8220 Brabrand, DENMARK, /+45 894 497 39
Specialties: Working knives of my own design. **Patterns:** Hunters and tacticals. Folders and straight blades. Tantoes, droppoint, Sheepfoot. **Technical:** Grinds Damasteel, ATS-34, BG-42, D2, 01. I use handrubbed finish on all blades except Damascus which are polished. **Price:** $100 to $400, some up to $500. **Remarks:** Part-time maker. First knife sold 1997. Doing business as ANSOKNIVES. **Mark:** ANSO.

ANTONIO JR., WILLIAM J., 6 Michigan State Dr, Newark, DE, 19713-1161/302-368-8211
Specialties: Fancy working straight knives of his design. **Patterns:** Hunting, survival and fishing knives. **Technical:** Grinds D2, 440C and 154CM; offers stainless Damascus. **Prices:** $125 to $395; some to $900. **Remarks:** Part-time maker; first knife sold in 1978. **Mark:** Last name, city, state.

AOUN, CHARLES, 69 Nahant St, Wakefield, MA, 01880/781-224-3353
Specialties: Classic and fancy straight knives of his design. **Patterns:** Fighters, hunters and personal knives. **Technical:** Grinds W2, 1095, ATS-34 and Damascus. Uses natural handle materials; embellishes with silver and semi-precious stones. **Prices:** Start at $290. **Remarks:** Part-time maker; first knife sold in 1995. Doing business as Galeb Knives. **Mark:** G stamped on ricasso or choil.

APPLETON, RAY, Box 325, Byers, CO, 80103/303-822-5866
Specialties: One-of-a-kind folding knives. **Patterns:** Unique folding multi-locks and high-tech patterns. **Technical:** All parts machined; D2,

S7, 440C, and 6a14v. **Prices:** Start at $8,500. **Remarks:** Spare-time maker; first knife sold in 1986. **Mark:** Initials within arrowhead, signed & dated.

ARCHER, RAY, PO Box 129, Medicine Bow, WY, 82329/307-379-2567
Specialties: Working straight knives and small one-of-a-kind. **Patterns:** Utility hunters/skinners. **Technical:** Flat grinds ATS 34, 440C, D2; buys Damascus. **Price:** $100 to $500. **Remarks:** Part-time maker; first knife sold 1994. **Mark:** Last name over city and state.

ARIZONA KNIFE SOURCE, 1219 E Glendale Ave #3, Phoenix, AZ, 85020/602-264-4020 Orders: Toll free 88-86-KNIFE. Retailer, Distributor, Mail-Order Sales, Appraiser.

ARNOLD, JOE, 47 Patience Cres., London, Ont., CANADA, N6E 2K7/519-686-2623
Specialties: Traditional working and using straight knives of his design and to customer specs. **Patterns:** Fighters, hunters and Bowies. **Technical:** Grinds 440C, ATS-34 and 5160. **Prices:** $75 to $500; some to $2,500. **Remarks:** Part-time maker; first knife sold in 1988. **Mark:** Last name, country.

ARROWOOD, DALE, 556 Lassetter Rd., Sharpsburg, GA, 30277/404-253-9672
Specialties: Fancy and traditional straight knives of his design and to customer specs. **Patterns:** Bowies, fighters and hunters. **Technical:** Grinds ATS-34 and 440C; forges high-carbon steel. Engraves and scrimshaws. **Prices:** $125 to $200; some $245. **Remarks:** Part-time maker; first knife sold in 1989. **Mark:** Anvil with an arrow through it; Old English "Arrowood Knives".

ASHBY, DOUGLAS, 10123 Deermont, Dallas, TX, 75243/214-238-7531
Specialties: Traditional and fancy straight knives of his design or to customer specs. **Patterns:** Hunters, fighters and utility/camp knives. **Technical:** Grinds 440C, ATS-34 and commercial Damascus. **Prices:** $75 to $200; some $500. **Remarks:** Part-time maker; first knife sold in 1990. **Mark:** Name, city.

ASHWORTH, BOYD, 3135 Barrett Ct., Powder Springs, GA, 30073/770-943-4963
Specialties: Fancy Damascus locking folders. **Patterns:** Fighters, hunters and gents. **Technical:** Forges own Damascus; offers filework; uses exotic handle materials. **Prices:** $500 to $2,500. **Remarks:** Part-time maker; first knife sold in 1993. **Mark:** Last name.

ATKINSON, DICK, General Delivery, Wausau, FL, 32463/850-638-8524
Specialties: Working straight knives and folders of his design; some fancy. **Patterns:** Hunters, fighters, boots; locking folders in interframes. **Technical:** Grinds A2, 440C and 154CM. Likes filework. **Prices:** $85 to $300; some exceptional knives. **Remarks:** Full-time maker; first knife sold in 1977. **Mark:** Name, city, state.

AYARRAGARAY, CRISTIAN L., Buenos Aires 250, (3100) Parana-Entre Rios, ARGENTINA, /043-231753
Specialties: Traditional working straight knives of his design. **Patterns:** Fishing and hunting knives. **Technical:** Grinds and forges carbon steel. Uses native Argentine woods and deer antler. **Prices:** $150 to $250; some to $400. **Remarks:** Full-time maker; first knife sold in 1980. **Mark:** Last name, signature.

b

BÜRGER, GÜNTER, Horststr. 55, 44581 Castrop-Rauxel, GERMANY, /02305-77145

BABCOCK, RAYMOND G., Rt. 1 Box 328A, Vincent, OH, 45784/614-678-2688
Specialties: Plain and fancy working straight knives. I will make knives to my design and to custom specifications. I also make folding knives of my design. **Patterns:** Hunting knives, bowies and folders. **Technical:** Hollow grinds L6. **Prices:** $95 to $500. **Remarks:** Part-time maker; first knife sold in 1973. **Mark:** First initial & last name; R. Babcock.

BACHE-WIIG, TOM, N-5966, Eivindvik, NORWAY, /4757784290
Specialties: High-art and working knives of his design. **Patterns:** Hunters, utility knives, hatchets, axes and art knives. **Technical:** Grinds Uddeholm Elmax, powder metallurgy tool stainless steel. Handles made of rear burls of Nordic woods stabilized with vacuum/high-pressure technique. **Prices:** $430 to $900; some to $2,300. **Remarks:** Part-time maker; first knife sold 1988. **Mark:** Etched name and eagle head.

custom knifemakers

BAILEY, JOSEPH D., 3213 Jonesboro Dr., Nashville, TN, 37214/615-889-3172 **Specialties:** Working and using straight knives; collector pieces. **Patterns:** Bowies, hunters, fillet knives and personal knives. **Technical:** 440C, ATS-34, Damascus and wire Damascus. Offers scrimshaw. **Prices:** $65 to $175; some to $500. **Remarks:** Part-time maker; first knife sold in 1988. **Mark:** First and middle initials, last name--Custom Made.

BAILEY, RYAN, 4185 S St Rt 605, Galena, OH, 43021/614-577-1040 **Specialties:** Fancy, high-art, high-tech, collectible straight knives and folders of his design and to customer specs; unique mechanisms, some disassemble. **Patterns:** Daggers, fighters and swords. **Technical:** Does own Damascus & forging from high carbon. Embellishes with file work & gold work. **Prices:** $200 to $2500. **Remarks:** Full-time maker; first knife sold in 1999. Doing business as Briar Knives. **Mark:** RLB.

BAILEY, KIRBY C., 2055 F.M. 2790 W., Lytle, TX, 78052/830-772-3376 **Specialties:** I do my own heat treating, file work. **Patterns:** Hunters, folders, fighters, bowies, miniatures. **Technical:** I do all my own work to the knives, kitchen, & steak knives. **Prices:** $150 to $1,000. **Remarks:** I build any kind of hand cutlery. **Mark:** K.C.B. & serial no.

BAKER, HERB, 326 S. Hamilton St., Eden, NC, 27288/910-627-0338

BAKER, WILD BILL, Box 361, Boiceville, NY, 12412/914-657-8646 **Specialties:** Primitive knives, buckskinners. **Patterns:** Skinners, camp knives and Bowies. **Technical:** Works with L6, files and rasps. **Prices:** $100 to $350. **Remarks:** Part-time maker; first knife sold in 1989. **Mark:** Wild Bill Baker, oak Leaf Forge, or both.

BAKER, VANCE, 574 Co. Rd. 675, Riceville, TN, 37370/423-745-9157 **Specialties:** Traditional working straight knives of his design and to customer specs. Prefers drop-point hunters and small Bowies. **Patterns:** Hunters, utility and kitchen knives. **Technical:** Forges Damascus, cable, L6 and 5160. **Prices:** $100 to $250; some to $500. **Remarks:** Part-time maker; first knife sold in 1985. **Mark:** Initials connected.

BAKER, RAY, P.O. Box 303, Sapulpa, OK, 74067/918-224-8013 **Specialties:** High-tech working straight knives. **Patterns:** Hunters, fighters, Bowies, skinners and boots of his design and to customer specs. **Technical:** Grinds 440C, 1095 spring steel or customer request; heat-treats. Custom-made scabbards for any knife. **Prices:** $125 to $500; some to $1,000. **Remarks:** Full-time maker; first knife sold in 1981. **Mark:** First initial, last name.

BALBACH, MARKUS, Friedrichstrasse 2, 35789 Weilmunster-Laubuseschbach/Ts., GERMANY, 06475-8911/ **Specialties:** High-art knives and working/using straight knives and folders of his design and to customer specs. **Patterns:** Hunters and daggers. **Technical:** Forges and grinds Damascus steel. **Prices:** $250 to $600; some to $2,000. **Remarks:** Full-time maker; first knife sold in 1984. Doing business as Kunst-und Damastschmiede M. Balbach. **Mark:** Initials stamped inside the handle.

BALDWIN, PHILLIP, P.O. Box 563, Snohomish, WA, 98290/425-334-5569 **Specialties:** One-of-a-kind elegant table cutlery; exotics. **Patterns:** Elegant or exotic knives. Likes the challenge of axes, spears and specialty tools. **Technical:** Forges W2, W1 and his own pattern welded steel and mokume-gane. **Prices:** Start at $1,000. **Remarks:** Full-time maker; first knife sold in 1973. **Mark:** Last initial marked with chisel.

BALL, ROBERT, 809 W. 7th Ave., Port Angeles, WA, 98362/360-457-0315 **Specialties:** Classic straight knives; working/using knives of all designs. **Patterns:** Bowies, hunters and fillets. **Technical:** Grinds ATS-34. Uses local Olympic hardwoods, stabilized woods, horn and antler. **Prices:** $225 to $1,700. **Remarks:** Part-time maker; first knife sold in 1990. Doing business as Olympic Knives. **Mark:** First initial, last name.

BALL, KEN, 127 Sundown Manor, Mooresville, IN, 46158/317-834-4803 **Specialties:** Classic working/using straight knives of his design and to customer specs. **Patterns:** Hunters and utility/camp knives. **Technical:** Flat-grinds ATS-34. Offers filework. **Prices:** $150 to $400. **Remarks:** Part-time maker; first knife sold in 1994. Doing business as Ball Custom Knives. **Mark:** Last name.

BALLESTRA, SANTINO, via D. Tempesta 11/17, 18039 Ventimiglia (IM), ITALY, 0184-215228/ **Specialties:** Using and collecting straight knives. **Patterns:** Hunting, fighting, skinners, Bowies, medieval daggers and knives. **Technical:** Forges ATS-34, D2, O2, 1060 and his own Damascus. Uses ivory and silver. **Prices:** $500 to $2,000; some higher. **Remarks:** Full-time maker; first knife sold in 1979. **Mark:** First initial, last name.

BALLEW, DALE, P.O. Box 1277, Bowling Green, VA, 22427/804-633-5701 **Specialties:** Miniatures only to customer specs. **Patterns:** Bowies, daggers and fighters. **Technical:** Files 440C stainless; uses ivory, abalone, exotic woods and some precious stones. **Prices:** $100 to $800. **Remarks:** Part-time maker; first knife sold in 1988. **Mark:** Initials and last name.

BANKS, DAVID L., 99 Blackfoot Ave.,#3, Riverton, WY, 82501/307-856-3154 **Specialties:** Heavy-duty working straight knives. **Patterns:** Hunters, Bowies and camp knives. **Technical:** Forges 5160, 52100 and his own Damascus; differential heat treat and tempers. Handles made of horn, antlers and exotic wood. Hand-stitched harness leather sheaths. **Prices:** $200 to $500; some higher. **Remarks:** Part-time maker. **Mark:** Initials connected.

BARBEE, JIM, RR 1, Box B, Ft. Stockton, TX, 79735/915-336-2882 **Specialties:** Texas-type hunter's knives. **Patterns:** Solid using patterns. **Technical:** Grinds 440C; likes stag, Micarta and ivory. **Prices:** $125 to $200; some to $500. **Remarks:** Full-time maker and heat-treater. First knife sold in the 60s. **Mark:** Name, city.

BARBER, ROBERT E., 1828 Franklin Dr., Charlottesville, VA, 22911-8513/804-295-4036 **Specialties:** Working straight knives and trapper pocketknives, some fancy with filework. **Patterns:** Hunters, skinners, combat knives/fighters and Bowies. **Technical:** Grinds ATS-34, 440C, D2 and A2. **Prices:** $35 to $800. **Remarks:** Part-time maker; first knife sold in 1984. **Mark:** Initials within rebel hat logo.

BARBOSA, R RUI, 913 PRESIDENTE, PRUDENTE-SP, BRAZIL, / **Specialties:** Straight knives. **Patterns:** Bowies, utilities and fighters. **Technical:** Grinds. **Prices:** $80 to $400. **Mark:** M R Boscoli.

BARDSLEY, NORMAN P., 197 Cottage St., Pawtucket, RI, 02860/401-725-9132 **Specialties:** Working and fantasy knives. **Patterns:** Fighters, tantos, boots in renaissance and fantasy fashion; upscale display and presentation pieces. **Technical:** Grinds 440C, ATS-34, O1 and Damascus. Uses exotic hides for sheaths. **Prices:** $100 to $15,000. **Remarks:** Full-time maker. **Mark:** Last name in script with logo.

BAREFOOT, JOE W., 117 Oakbrook Dr., Liberty, SC, 29657/ **Specialties:** Working straight knives of his design. **Patterns:** Hunters, fighters and boots; tantos and survival knives. **Technical:** Grinds D2, 440C and ATS-34. Mirror finishes. Uses ivory and stag on customer request only. **Prices:** $50 to $160; some to $500. **Remarks:** Part-time maker; first knife sold in 1980. **Mark:** Bare footprint.

BARKER, ROBERT G., 2311 Branch Rd., Bishop, GA, 30621/706-769-7827 **Specialties:** Traditional working/using straight knives of his design. **Patterns:** Bowies, hunters and utility knives, ABS Journeyman Smith.. **Technical:** Hand forged carbon & Damascus. Forges to shape high-carbon 5160, cable and chain. Differentially heat-treats. **Prices:** $200 to $500; some to $1,000. **Remarks:** Spare-time maker; first knife sold in 1987. **Mark:** BARKER/J.S.

BARNES, AUBREY G., 11341 Rock Hill Road, Hagerstown, MD, 21740/301-223-4587 **Specialties:** Classic working and using knives of his design, to customer specs and in standard patterns. **Patterns:** Bowies, hunters, fighters, daggers and utility/camping knives. **Technical:** Forges 5160, 1085, 06 and Damascus. Silver-wire inlays. **Prices:** $300 to $2,500. **Remarks:** Full-time maker; first knife sold in 1992. Doing business as Falling Waters Forge. **Mark:** First and middle initials, last name, M.S.

BARNES, GARY L., 305 Church St., Box 138, New Windsor, MD, 21776/410-635-6243 **Specialties:** Color anodized aluminum button-lock folders. **Patterns:** Folders only. **Technical:** Mostly forges his own Damascus; uses exotic handle materials; creates unique locking mechanisms. Most knives are embellished. **Prices:** Start at $250. **Remarks:** Full-time maker. First knife sold in 1976. **Mark:** Name or an ornate last initial with a dagger.

BARNES, JIM, 2909 Forest Trail, San Angelo, TX, 76904/915-944-2239 **Specialties:** Traditional and working straight and folder knives of all designs. **Patterns:** Hunters and locking folders. **Technical:** Grinds ATS-34, 440C and D2; heat-treats. All folders have filework. Offers hand-tooled sheaths with basket weave. Engraves some knife bolsters. **Prices:** $95 to $350; some to $1,000. **Remarks:** Full-time maker; first knife sold in 1984, no longer make automatics. Doing business as Jim Barnes Custom Knives. **Mark:** Logo with name, city, state.

BARNES, JACK, P.O. Box 1315, Whitefish, MT, 59937-1315/406-862-6078

BARNETT, VAN, 168 Riverbend Blvd., Saint Albans, WV, 25177/304-727-5512 **Specialties:** Collector grade one of a kind / embellished high art daggers and art folders. **Patterns:** Art daggers and folders. **Technical:** Forges and grinds own Damascus. **Prices:** Upscale. **Remarks:** Designs and makes one of a kind highly embellished art knives using high karat golds, diamonds and other gemstones, pearls, stone and fossil ivories, carved steel guards and blades, all knives are carved and or engraved, does own engraving, carving and other embellishments, sole authorship; full-time maker since 1981. **Mark:** V. H. Barnett or Van Barnett in script. Other: Does one high art collaboration a year with Dellana.

BARNGROVER, JERRY, RR #4, Box 1230, Afton, OK, 74331/918-257-5076

BARR, A.T., P.O. Box 828, Nicholasville, KY, 40340-0828/606-885-1042 **Specialties:** Working and collector grade liner lock folders. **Patterns:** Liner lock folders. **Technical:** Flat-grinds ATS-34, BG 42, Damascus, D2, A2 and O1; hand-rubbed finish. Satin finish. **Prices:** Start at $275. **Remarks:** Currently not taking orders. Part-time maker; first knife sold in 1979. **Mark:** Full name, city and state.

BARRETT, CECIL TERRY, 2514 Linda Lane, Colorado Springs, CO, 80909/719-473-8325 **Specialties:** Working and using straight knives and folders of his design, to customer specs and in standard patterns. **Patterns:** Bowies, hunters, kitchen knives, locking folders and slip-joint folders. **Technical:** Grinds 440C, D2 and ATS-34. Wood and leather sheaths. **Prices:** $65 to $500; some to $750. **Remarks:** Full-time maker. **Mark:** Stamped middle name.

BARRETT, R.W., P.O. Box 304, Madison, AL, 35758-0304/205-539-3439 **Specialties:** Traditional and fancy straight knives. Makes standard patterns and one of a kinds. **Patterns:** Hunters, fighters, skinners and art knives. **Technical:** Grinds 440C, ATS-34 and O1. Scrimshaws and offers photography. **Prices:** $150 to $250; some to $500. **Remarks:** Spare-time maker; first knife sold in 1989. **Mark:** First and middle initials, last name, city, state.

BARRON, BRIAN, 123 12th Ave., San Mateo, CA, 94402/650-341-2683 **Specialties:** Traditional straight knives. **Patterns:** Daggers, hunters and swords. **Technical:** Grinds 440C, ATS-34 and 1095. Sculpts bolsters using an S-curve. **Prices:** $130 to $270; some to $1,500. **Remarks:** Part-time maker; first knife sold in 1993. **Mark:** Diamond Drag "Barron".

BARRY III, JAMES J., 115 Flagler Promenade No, West Palm Beach, FL, 33405/561-832-4197 **Specialties:** High-art working straight knives of his design. **Patterns:** Hunters, daggers and fishing knives. **Technical:** Grinds 440C only. Prefers exotic materials for handles. Most knives embellished with filework, carving and scrimshaw. Many pieces designed to stand unassisted. **Prices:** $100 to $500; some to $5,000. **Remarks:** Part-time maker; first knife sold in 1975. **Mark:** Branded initials.

BARTLOW, JOHN, 111 Orchard Rd., Box 568, Norris, TN, 37828/423-494-9421 **Specialties:** New liner locks. **Patterns:** Working hunters, skinners, capers, bird and trout knives, saltwater fillets. **Technical:** Working on 6 new liner lock designs. **Prices:** $150 to $1,500. **Remarks:** Part-time maker; first knife sold in 1979. Field-tests knives. **Mark:** Last name.

BARTRUG, HUGH E., 2701 34th St. N., #142, St. Petersburg, FL, 33713/813-323-1136 **Specialties:** Inlaid straight knives and exotic folders; high-art knives and period pieces. **Patterns:** Hunters, Bowies and daggers; traditional patterns. **Technical:** Diffuses mokume. Forges 100 percent nickel, wrought iron, mosaic Damascus, shokeedo and O1 tool steel; grinds. **Prices:** $210 to $2,500; some to $5,000. **Remarks:** Retired maker; first knife sold in 1980. **Mark:** Ashley Forge or name.

BASKETT, LEE GENE, 427 Sutzer Ck. Rd., Eastview, KY, 42732/502-862-5019 **Specialties:** Fancy working knives and fantasy pieces, often set up in desk stands. **Patterns:** Fighters, Bowies and survival knives; locking folders, butterflies and traditional styles. **Technical:** Grinds O1, 440C; buys Damascus. Filework provided on most knives. **Prices:** Start at $95. **Remarks:** Part-time maker; first knife sold in 1980. **Mark:** Last name.

BATSON, JAMES, 176 Brentwood Lane, Madison, AL, 35758/205-971-6860 **Specialties:** Forged Damascus blades and fittings in collectible period pieces. **Patterns:** Integral art knives, Bowies, folders, American-styled blades and miniatures. **Technical:** Forges 52100, 5160 and his Damascus. **Prices:** $150 to $1,800; some to $4,500. **Remarks:** Full-time maker; first knife sold in 1978. **Mark:** Name, bladesmith with horse's head.

BATSON, RICHARD G., 6591 Waterford Rd., Rixeyville, VA, 22737/540-937-5932 **Specialties:** Military, utility and fighting knives in working and presentation grade. **Patterns:** Daggers, combat and utility knives. **Technical:** Grinds O1, 1095 and 440C. Etches and scrimshaws; offers polished, Parkerized finishes. **Prices:** $175 to $350; some to $900. **Remarks:** Full-time maker. First knife sold in 1958. **Mark:** Bat in circle, hand-signed and serial numbered.

BATTLE AXE, THE, 722 Greenwood, Wichita, KS, 67211/316-264-0171 **Specialties:** Fantasy. **Patterns:** Swords, battle axes. **Technical:** Forge and grind. **Remarks:** First knife sold in 1994.

BATTS, KEITH, Rt. 1, Box 266E, Hooks, TX, 75561/903-832-1140 **Specialties:** Working straight knives of his design or to customer specs. **Patterns:** Bowies, hunters, skinners, camp knives and others. **Technical:** Forges 5160 and his Damascus; offers filework. **Prices:** $245 to $895. **Remarks:** Part-time maker; first knife sold in 1988. **Mark:** Last name.

BAUCHOP, PETER, c/o Beck's Cutlery Specialties, 107 Edinburgh S, Cary, NC, 27511/919-460-0203 **Specialties:** Working straight knives and period pieces. **Patterns:** Fighters, swords and survival knives. **Technical:** Grinds O1, D2, G3, 440C and AST-34. Scrimshaws. **Prices:** $100 to $350; some to $1500. **Remarks:** Full-time maker; first knife sold in 1980. **Mark:** Bow and axe (BOW-CHOP).

BAUCHOP, ROBERT, P.O. Box 330, Munster, Kwazulu-Natal, 4278 SOUTH AFRICA, /+27 39 3192449 **Specialties:** Fantasy knives; working and using knives of his design and to customer specs. **Patterns:** Hunters, swords, utility/camp knives, diver's knives and large swords. **Technical:** Grinds Sandvick 12C27, D2, 440C. Uses South African hardwoods red ivory, wild olive, African blackwood, etc.--on handles. **Prices:** $200 to $800; some to $2,000. **Remarks:** Full-time maker; first knife sold in 1986. Doing business as Bauchop Custom Knives and swords. **Mark:** Viking helmet with Bauchop (bow and chopper) crest.

BEAM, JOHN R., 1310 Foothills Rd., Kalispell, MT, 59901/406-755-2593 **Specialties:** Classic, high-art and working straight knives of his design. **Patterns:** Bowies and hunters. **Technical:** Grinds 440C, Damascus and scrap. **Prices:** $175 to $600; some to $3,000. **Remarks:** Part-time maker; first knife sold in 1996. Doing business as Beam's Knives. **Mark:** Beam's Knives.

BEATTY, GORDON H., 121 Petty Rd., Seneca, SC, 29672/864-882-6278 **Specialties:** Working straight knives, some fancy. **Patterns:** Traditional patterns, mini-skinners and letter openers. **Technical:** Grinds 440C, D2 and ATS-34; makes knives one at a time. **Prices:** $75 to $450; some to $450. **Remarks:** Part-time maker; first knife sold in 1982. **Mark:** Name.

BEAUCHAMP, GAETAN, 125, de la Rivire, Stoneham, PQ, CANADA, G0A 4P0/418-848-1914
Specialties: Working knives and folders of his design and to customer specs. **Patterns:** Hunters, fighters, fantasy knives. **Technical:** Grinds ATS-34, 440C, Damascus. Scrimshaws on ivory; specializes in buffalo horn and black backgrounds. Offers a variety of handle materials. **Prices:** Start at $125. **Remarks:** Full-time maker; first knife sold in 1992. **Mark:** Signature etched on blade.

BEAVER, D. "BUTCH" AND JUDY, 48835 N. 25 Ave., Phoenix, AZ, 85027/602-465-7831
Specialties: Straight knives, daggers and "see-thru" titanium art folders. **Patterns:** No models or standard designs; prefer custom orders. **Technical:** Grind 440C and ATS-34. Most knives are embellished. **Prices:** $135 to $800; some much higher. **Remarks:** Full-time makers. First D. Beaver knife sold in 1979; first J. Beaver knife sold in 1984. **Mark:** Name, city, state with desert scene.

BECKER, FRANZ, AM Kreuzberg 2, 84533, Marktl/Inn, GERMANY, 08678-8020/
Specialties: Stainless steel knives in working sizes. **Patterns:** Semi- and full-integral knives; interframe folders. **Technical:** Grinds stainless steels; likes natural handle materials. **Prices:** $200 to $2,000. **Mark:** Name, country.

BECKETT, NORMAN L., 1501 N. Chaco Ave., Farmington, NM, 87401/505-325-4468
Specialties: Fancy, traditional and working straight knives of his design. **Patterns:** Bowies, fighters and hunters. **Technical:** Grinds ATS-34, 440C and Damascus. File works blades; hollow and flat grinds. Prefers mirror finishes. Uses exotic handle material and stabilized woods. Hand-tooled or inlaid sheaths. **Prices:** $150 to $900; some to $2,500 and up. **Remarks:** Full-time maker; first knife sold in 1993. Doing business as Norm Beckett Knives. **Mark:** First and last name, maker, city and state.

BEERS, RAY, 8 Manorbrook Rd., Monkton, MD, 21111/Summer 410-472-2229

BEERS, RAY, 2501 Lakefront Dr., Lake Wales, FL, 33853/Winter 941-696-3036

BEHNKE, WILLIAM, 931 W Sanborn Rd, Lake City, MI, 4965-7600/616-839-3342
Specialties: Hunters, belt knives and folders. **Patterns:** Traditional styling in moderate-sized straight and folding knives. **Technical:** Forges his own Damascus, cable, saw chain and 5160; likes brass and natural materials. **Prices:** $100 to $1,500. **Remarks:** Part-time maker. **Mark:** Name.

BELL, MICHAEL, Rt. 1, Box 1220, Coquille, OR, 97423/541-396-3605
Specialties: Full line of traditional Japanese swords. **Patterns:** Tantos and Katanas in various styles. **Technical:** Uses own special steel; all blades forge-welded. **Prices:** Knives from $300, cable swords $2,000 to $7,500, traditional swords $4,000 to $15,000. **Remarks:** Full-time maker; first knife sold in 1972. Served apprenticeship with Japanese swordmaker. Doing business as Dragonfly Forge. **Mark:** Kuni Mitsu or Dragonfly.

BELL, DONALD, 2 Division St., Bedford, Nova Scotia, CANADA, B4A 1Y8/902-835-2623
Specialties: Fancy knives; working/using straight knives and folders of his design. **Patterns:** Hunters, locking folders, jewelry knives. **Technical:** Grinds Damascus and ATS-34; forges and grinds O1; pierces and carves blades. **Prices:** $150 to $650; some to $1,200. **Remarks:** Spare-time maker; first knife sold in 1993. **Mark:** Bell symbol with first initial inside.

BENJAMIN JR., GEORGE, 3001 Foxy Lane, Kissimmee, FL, 34746/407-846-7259
Specialties: Fighters in various styles to include Persian, Moro and military. **Patterns:** Daggers, skinners and one-of-a-kind grinds. **Technical:** Forges O1, D2, A2, 5160 and Damascus. Favors Pakkawood, Micarta, and mirror or Parkerized finishes. Makes unique para-military leather sheaths. **Prices:** $150 to $600; some to $1,200. **Remarks:** Doing business as The Leather Box. **Mark:** Southern Pride Knives.

BENNETT, PETER, P.O. Box 143, Engadine N.S.W. 2233, AUSTRALIA, /02-520-4975 (home)
Specialties: Fancy and embellished working and using straight knives to customer specs and in standard patterns. **Patterns:** Fighters, hunters, bird/trout and fillet knives. **Technical:** Grinds 440C, ATS-34 and Damascus. Uses rare Australian desert timbers for handles. **Prices:** $90 to $500; some to $1,500. **Remarks:** Full-time maker; first knife sold in 1985. **Mark:** First and middle initials, last name; country.

BENSON, DON, 2505 Jackson St., #112, Escalon, CA, 95320/209-838-7921
Specialties: Working straight knives of his design. **Patterns:** Axes, Bowies, tantos and hunters. **Technical:** Grinds 440C. **Prices:** $100 to $150; some to $400. **Remarks:** Spare-time maker; first knife sold in 1980. **Mark:** Name.

BER, DAVE, 656 Miller Rd, San Juan Island, WA, 98250/206-378-7230
Specialties: Working straight and folding knives for the sportsman; welcomes customer designs. **Patterns:** Hunters, skinners, Bowies, kitchen and fishing knives. **Technical:** Forges and grinds saw blade steel, wire Damascus, O1, L6, 4160 and 440C. **Prices:** $100 to $500. **Remarks:** Full-time maker; first knife sold in 1985. **Mark:** Last Name.

BERGER, MAX A., 5716 John Richard Ct., Carmichael, CA, 95608/916-972-9229
Specialties: Fantasy and working/using straight knives of his design. **Patterns:** Fighters, hunters and utility/camp knives. **Technical:** Grinds ATS-34 and 440C. Offers fileworks and combinations of mirror polish and satin finish blades. **Prices:** $200 to $600; some to $2,500. **Remarks:** Part-time maker; first knife sold in 1992. **Mark:** Last name.

BERGH, ROGER, PL1137, 83070 NRA, SWEDEN, /+46 613 12046

BERTHOLUS, BERNARD, Atelier Du Brute, De Forge 21, rue Fersen 06600, Antibes, FRANCE, /04 93 34 95 90
Specialties: Traditional working and using straight knives of his design. **Patterns:** Bowies, daggers and hunters. **Technical:** Forges ATS-34, 440, D2 and carbon steels. **Prices:** $120 to $150; some to $400. **Remarks:** Full-time maker; first knife sold in 1990. **Mark:** City and last name.

BERTUZZI, ETTORE, Via Partigiani 3, 24068 Seriate (Bergamo), ITALY, /035-294262
Specialties: Classic straight knives and folders of his design, to customer specs and in standard patterns. **Patterns:** Bowies, hunters and locking folders. **Technical:** Grinds ATS-34, D3, D2 and various Damascus. **Prices:** $300 to $500. **Remarks:** Part-time maker; first knife sold in 1993. **Mark:** Name etched on ricasso.

BESEDICK, FRANK E., RR 2, Box 802, Ruffsdale, PA, 15679/412-696-3312
Specialties: Traditional working and using straight knives of his design. **Patterns:** Hunters, utility/camp knives and miniatures; buckskinner blades and tomahawks. **Technical:** Forges and grinds 5160, O1 and Damascus. Offers filework and scrimshaw. **Prices:** $75 to $300; some to $750. **Remarks:** Part-time maker; first knife sold in 1990. **Mark:** Name or initials.

BETHKE, LORA SUE, 13420 Lincoln St., Grand Haven, MI, 49417/616-842-8268
Specialties: Classic and traditional straight knives of her design. **Patterns:** Boots, Bowies and hunters. **Technical:** Forges 5160. **Prices:** Start at $250. **Remarks:** Part-time maker; first knife sold in 1997. **Mark:** Full name.

BEUKES, TINUS, 83 Henry St., Risiville, Vereeniging 1939, SOUTH AFRICA, /27 16 423 2053
Specialties: Working straight knives. **Patterns:** Hunters, skinners and kitchen knives. **Technical:** Grinds D2, 440C and chain, cable and stainless Damascus. **Prices:** $80 to $180. **Remarks:** Part-time maker; first knife sold in 1993. **Mark:** Full name, city, logo.

BEVERLY II, LARRY H., P.O. Box 741, Spotsylvania, VA, 22553/540-898-3951
Specialties: Working straight knives, slip-joints and liner locks. Welcomes customer designs. **Patterns:** Bowies, hunters, guardless fighters and miniatures. **Technical:** Grinds 440C, A2 and O1. **Prices:** $65 to $400. **Remarks:** Part-time maker; first knife sold in 1986. **Mark:** Initials or last name in script.

BEZUIDENHOUT, BUZZ, 30 Surlingham Ave., Malvern, Queensburgh, Natal 4093, SOUTH AFRICA, /031-444098
Specialties: Traditional working and using straight knives of his design and to customer specs. **Patterns:** boots, hunters, kitchen knives and utility/camp knives. **Technical:** Grinds 12C27, 440C and ATS-34. Uses local hardwoods, horn - kudu, impala, buffalo - giraffe bone and ivory for

handles. **Prices:** $150 to $200; some to $1500. **Remarks:** Spare-time maker, first knife sold in 1988. **Mark:** First name with a bee emblem.

BIGGERS, GARY, Ventura Knives, 1278 Colina Vista, Ventura, CA, 93003/805-658-6610
Specialties: Working straight knives of his design. **Patterns:** Hunters, boots/fighters, Bowies and utility knives. **Technical:** Grinds ATS-34 and commercial Damascus. Other steels available. Prefers natural handle materials. **Prices:** $100-$350. **Remarks:** Part-time maker: first knife sold in 1996. Doing business as Ventura Knives. **Mark:** First and last name, city and state.

BLACK, SCOTT, 570 Malcom Rd., Covington, GA, 30209/
Specialties: Working/using folders of his design. **Patterns:** Daggers, hunters, utility/camp knives and friction folders. **Technical:** Forges pattern welded, cable, 1095, O1 and 5160. **Prices:** $100 to $500. **Remarks:** Part-time maker; first knife sold in 1992. Doing business as Copperhead Forge. **Mark:** Hot mark on blade, copperhead snake.

BLACK, TOM, 921 Grecian NW, Albuquerque, NM, 87107/505-344-2549
Specialties: Working knives to fancy straight knives of his design. **Patterns:** Drop-point skinners, folders, using knives, Bowies and daggers. **Technical:** Grinds 440C, 154CM, ATS-34, A2, D2 and Damascus. Offers engraving and scrimshaw. **Prices:** $185 to $1,250; some over $7,500. **Remarks:** Full-time maker; first knife sold in 1970. **Mark:** Name, city, state.

BLACK, EARL, 3466 South, 700 East, Salt Lake City, UT, 84106/801-466-8395
Specialties: High-art straight knives and folders; period pieces. **Patterns:** Boots, Bowies and daggers; lockers and gents. **Technical:** Grinds 440C and 154CM. Buys some Damascus. Scrimshaws and engraves. **Prices:** $200 to $1,800; some to $2,500 and higher. **Remarks:** Full-time maker; first knife sold in 1980. **Mark:** Name, city, state.

BLACKTON, ANDREW E., 12521 Fifth Isle, Bayonet Point, FL, 34667/727-869-1406
Specialties: Straight and folding knives, some fancy. **Patterns:** Hunters, Bowies and daggers. **Technical:** Grinds D2, 440C and 154CM. Offers some embellishment. **Prices:** $125 to $450; some to $2,000. **Remarks:** Full-time maker. **Mark:** Last name in script.

BLANCHARD, G.R. (GARY), 3507 S Maryland Pkwy #E, Las Vegas, NV, 89109/702-733-8333
Specialties: Fancy folders and high-art straight knives of his design. **Patterns:** Boots, daggers and locking folders. **Technical:** Grinds 440C and ATS-34, O1 blueable. Engraves knives. **Prices:** $400 to $15,000; some to $18,000 or more. **Remarks:** Full-time maker; first knife sold in 1989. **Mark:** First and middle initials, last name.

BLASINGAME, ROBERT, 2906 Swanson Lane, Kilgore, TX, 75662/903-983-3546
Specialties: Classic working and using straight knives and folders of his design and to customer specs. **Patterns:** Bowies, daggers, fighters and hunters; one-of-a-kind historic reproductions. **Technical:** Hand-forges P.W. Damascus, cable Damascus and chain Damascus. **Prices:** $150 to $1,000; some to $2,000. **Remarks:** Full-time maker; first knife sold in 1968. **Mark:** Large knives--last name over anvil; folders--initials.

BLAUM, ROY, 319 N. Columbia St., Covington, LA, 70433/504-893-1060
Specialties: Working straight knives and folders of his design; lightweight easy-open folders. **Patterns:** Hunters, boots, fishing and woodcarving/whittling knives. **Technical:** Grinds A2, D2, O1, 154CM and ATS-34. Offers leatherwork. **Prices:** $40 to $800; some higher. **Remarks:** Full-time maker; first knife sold in 1976. **Mark:** Engraved signature or etched logo.

BLOMBERG, GREGG, Rt. 1, Box 1762, Lopez, WA, 98261/206-468-2103
Specialties: Edged tools for carvers and sculptors. **Patterns:** Crooked knives; straight utilities; adzes. **Technical:** Forges and grinds W2, D2, 1095 and ATS-34. **Prices:** Straight knives average $160. **Remarks:** Full-time maker; first knife sold in 1978. Doing business as Kestrel Tool. **Mark:** Kestrel with flying falcon logo.

BLOOMER, ALAN T., RR 1, Box 108, Maquon, IL, 61458/309-875-3583
Specialties: Working and using straight knives and folders of his design. **Patterns:** Lock-back folders and Damascus straight knives and folders. **Technical:** Grinds 440C, D2 and A2. Does own leatherwork. **Prices:** $85 to $450. **Remarks:** Part-time maker; first knife sold in 1986. **Mark:** Last name stamp.

BLUM, KENNETH, 1729 Burleson, Brenham, TX, 77833/409-836-9577
Specialties: Traditional working straight knives of his design. **Patterns:** Camp knives, Hunters and Bowies. **Technical:** Forges 5160; grinds 440C and D2. Uses exotic woods and Micarta for handles. **Prices:** $150 to $300. **Remarks:** Part-time maker; first knife sold in 1978. **Mark:** Last name on ricasso.

BLUM, CHUCK, 743 S. Brea Blvd., #10, Brea, CA, 92621/714-529-0484
Specialties: Art and investment daggers and Bowies. **Technical:** Flat-grinds; hollow-grinds 440C, ATS-34 on working knives. **Prices:** $125 to $8,500. **Remarks:** Part-time maker; first knife sold in 1985. **Mark:** First and middle initials and last name with sailboat logo.

BOARDMAN, GUY, 39 Mountain Ridge R., New Germany 3619, SOUTH AFRICA, /031-726-921
Specialties: American and South African styles. **Patterns:** Bowies, American and South African hunters, plus more. **Technical:** Grinds Bohler steels, some ATS-34. **Prices:** $100 to $600. **Remarks:** Part-time maker; first knife sold in 1986. **Mark:** Name, city, country.

BOATRIGHT, BASEL, 11 Timber Point, New Braunfels, TX, 78132/210-609-0807
Specialties: Working and using knives of his design. **Patterns:** Hunters, skinners and utility/camp knives. **Technical:** Grinds and hand-tempers 5160. **Prices:** $75 to $300. **Remarks:** Part-time maker. **Mark:** Stamped BBB.

BOCHMAN, BRUCE, 183 Howard Place, Grants Pass, OR, 97526/503-471-1985
Specialties: Working straight knives in standard patterns. **Patterns:** Bowies, hunters, fishing and bird knives. **Technical:** 440C; mirror or satin finish. **Prices:** $140 to $250; some to $750. **Remarks:** Part-time maker; first knife sold in 1977. **Mark:** Custom blades by B. Bochman.

BODEN, HARRY, Via Gellia Mill, Bonsall Matlock, Derbyshire DE4 2AJ, ENGLAND, /0629-825176
Specialties: Traditional working straight knives and folders of his design. **Patterns:** Hunters, locking folders and utility/camp knives. **Technical:** Grinds Sandvik 12C27, D2 and O1. **Prices:** £70 to £150; some to £300. **Remarks:** Full-time maker; first knife sold in 1986. **Mark:** Full name.

BODNER, GERALD "JERRY", 4102 Spyglass Ct., Louisville, KY, 40229/502-968-5946
Specialties: Fantasy straight knives in standard patterns. **Patterns:** Bowies, fighters, hunters and micro-miniature knives. **Technical:** Grinds Damascus, 440C and D2. Offers filework. **Prices:** $35 to $180. **Remarks:** Part-time maker; first knife sold in 1993. **Mark:** Last name in script and JAB in oval above knives.

BODOLAY, ANTAL, Rua Wilson Soares Fernandes #31, Planalto, Belo Horizonte MG-31730-700, BRAZIL, /031-494-1885
Specialties: Working folders and fixed blades of his design or to customer specs; some art daggers and period pieces. **Patterns:** Daggers, hunters, locking folders, utility knives and Khukris. **Technical:** Grinds D6, high carbon steels and 420 stainless. Forges files on request. **Prices:** $30 to $350. **Remarks:** Full-time maker; first knife sold in 1965. **Mark:** Last name in script.

BOEHLKE, GUENTER, Parkstrasse 2, 56412 Grossholbach, GERMANY, 2602-5440/
Specialties: Classic working/using straight knives of his design. **Patterns:** Hunters, utility/camp knives and ancient remakes. **Technical:** Grinds Damascus, CPM-T-440V and 440C. Inlays gemstones and ivory. **Prices:** $220 to $700; some to $2,000. **Remarks:** Spare-time maker; first knife sold in 1985. **Mark:** Name, address and bow and arrow.

BOGUSZEWSKI, PHIL, P.O. Box 99329, Tacoma, WA, 98499/253-581-7096
Specialties: Working folders--some fancy--mostly of his design. **Patterns:** Folders, slip-joints and lockers; also makes anodized titanium frame folders. **Technical:** Grinds 440C; offers filework. **Prices:** $300 to $1,500. **Remarks:** Full-time maker; first knife sold in 1979. **Mark:** Name, city and state.

custom knifemakers

BOHRMANN, BRUCE, 29 Portland St., Yarmouth, ME, 04096/207-846-3385
Specialties: Straight using sport knives. **Patterns:** Hunters, fishing, camp and steak knives. **Technical:** Grinds 154CM; likes wood handles. **Prices:** $350 to $450. **Remarks:** Full-time maker; first knife sold in 1976. **Mark:** Name, city and state.

BOJTOS, ÁRPÁD, Dobsinskeho 10, 98403 Lucenec, Slovakia, /00421-863- 9323214
Specialties: Fantasy and high-art knives. **Patterns:** Daggers, fighters and hunters. **Technical:** Grinds ATS-34. Carves on steel, handle materials and sheaths. **Prices:** $2,000 to $5,000; some to $8,000. **Remarks:** Full-time maker; first knife sold in 1990. **Mark:** Stylized initials.

BOLD, STU, 63 D'Andrea Tr., Sarnia, Ont., CANADA, N7S 6H3/519-383-7610
Specialties: Traditional working/using straight knives in standard patterns and to customer specs. **Patterns:** Boots, Bowies and hunters. **Technical:** Grinds ATS-34, 440C and Damascus; mosaic pins. Offers scrimshaw and hand-tooled leather sheaths. **Prices:** $140 to $500; some to $2,000. **Remarks:** Part-time maker; first knife sold in 1983. **Mark:** Name, city, province.

BOLEWARE, DAVID, P.O. Box 96, Carson, MS, 39427/601-943-5372
Specialties: Traditional and working/using straight knives of his design, to customer specs and in standard patterns. **Patterns:** Bowies, hunters and utility/camp knives. **Technical:** Grinds ATS-34, 440C and Damascus. **Prices:** $85 to $350; some to $600. **Remarks:** Part-time maker; first knife sold in 1989. **Mark:** First and last name, city, state.

BOLTON, CHARLES B., P.O. Box 6, Jonesburg, MO, 63351/314-488-5785
Specialties: Working straight knives in standard patterns. **Patterns:** Hunters, skinners, boots and fighters. **Technical:** Grinds 440C and ATS-34. **Prices:** $100 to $300; some to $600. **Remarks:** Full-time maker; first knife sold in 1973. **Mark:** Last name.

BONASSI, FRANCO, Via Superiore 14, Pordenone 33170, ITALY, /434-550821
Specialties: Fancy and working one-of-a-kind straight knives of his design. **Patterns:** Hunters, skinners, utility and liner locks. **Technical:** Grinds CPM, ATS-34, 154CM and commercial Damascus. Uses only titanium foreguards and pommels. **Prices:** Start at $250. **Remarks:** Spare-time maker; first knife sold in 1988. **Mark:** FRANK.

BOOCO, GORDON, 175 Ash St., P.O. Box 174, Hayden, CO, 81639/970-276-3195
Specialties: Fancy working straight knives of his design and to customer specs. **Patterns:** Hunters and Bowies. **Technical:** Grinds 440C, D2 and A2. Heat-treats. **Prices:** $150 to $350; some $600 and higher. **Remarks:** Part-time maker; first knife sold in 1984. **Mark:** Last name with push dagger artwork.

BOOS, RALPH, 5107 40 Ave., Edmonton, Alberta, CANADA, T6L 1B3/780-463-7094
Specialties: Classic, fancy and fantasy miniature knives and swords of his design or to customer specs. **Patterns:** Bowies, daggers and swords. **Technical:** Hand files O1, stainless and Damascus. Engraves and carves. Does heat bluing and acid etching. **Prices:** $125 to $350; some to $1,000. **Remarks:** Part-time maker; first knife sold in 1982. **Mark:** First and last initials back to back.

BOOTH, PHILIP W., 301 S. Jeffery Ave., Ithaca, MI, 48847/517-875-2844
Specialties: Folding knives, various mechanisms, maker of the "minnow" series small folding knife. **Patterns:** lock backs, liner locks, classic pattern multi-blades. **Technical:** Grinds ATS-34, 440C, 1095 and commercial Damascus. Prefers natural materials, offers file work and scrimshaw. **Prices:** $200 and up. **Remarks:** Full-time maker; first knife sold in 1991. **Mark:** Last name or name with city and map logo.

BORGER, WOLF, Benzstrasse 8, 76676 Graben-Neudorf, GERMANY, /07255-72303
Specialties: High-tech working and using straight knives and folders, many with corkscrews or other tools, of his design. **Patterns:** Hunters, Bowies and folders with various locking systems. **Technical:** Grinds 440C, ATS-34 and CPM. Uses stainless Damascus. **Prices:** $250 to $900; some to $1,500. **Remarks:** Full-time maker; first knife sold in 1975. **Mark:** Howling wolf and name; first name on Damascus blades.

BOSE, TONY, 7252 N. County Rd., 300 E., Shelburn, IN, 47879-9778/812-397-5114
Specialties: Traditional working and using knives in standard patterns; multi-blade folders. **Patterns:** Multi-blade slip-joints. **Technical:** Grinds commercial Damascus, ATS-34 and D2. **Prices:** $400 to $1200. **Remarks:** Full-time maker; first knife sold in 1975. **Mark:** First initial, last name, city, state.

BOSE, REESE, 9014 S. Co. Rd. 550W, Lewis, IN, 47858/812-495-6372
Specialties: Traditional working and using knives in standard patterns and multi-blade folders. **Patterns:** Multi-blade slip-joints. **Technical:** Grinds commercial Damascus, ATS-34 and D2. **Prices:** $200 to $1,500. **Remarks:** Full-time maker; first knife sold in 1992. Photos by Jack Busfield. **Mark:** First initial, last name. Started 1973.

BOSSAERTS, CARL, Rua Albert Einstein 906, 14051-110, Ribeirao Preto, S.P. BRAZIL, /016 633 7063
Specialties: Working and using straight knives of his design, to customer specs and in standard patterns. **Patterns:** Hunters, fighters and utility/camp knives. **Technical:** Grinds ATS-34, 440V and 440C; does filework. **Prices:** 60 to $400. **Remarks:** Part-time maker; first knife sold in 1992. **Mark:** Initials joined together.

BOSWORTH, DEAN, 329 Mahogany Dr., Key Largo, FL, 33037/305-451-1564
Specialties: Working/using straight knives of his design. **Patterns:** Fighters, hunters and utility/camp knives. **Technical:** Grinds 440C, ATS-34 and D2; some stock removal. Offers hand-rubbed satin finish; most sheaths are wet formed and hand stitched. **Prices:** $225 to $375; some to $500. **Remarks:** Part-time maker; first knife sold in 1985. **Mark:** BOZ stamped in block letters.

BOURBEAU, JEAN YVES, 15 Rue Remillard, Notre Dame, Ile Perrot, Quebec, CANADA, J7V 8M9/514-453-1069
Specialties: Fancy/embellished and fantasy folders of his design. **Patterns:** Bowies, fighters and locking folders. **Technical:** Grinds 440C, ATS-34 and Damascus. Carves precious wood for handles. **Prices:** $150 to $1000. **Remarks:** Part-time maker; first knife sold in 1994. **Mark:** Interlaced initials.

BOUSE, D. MICHAEL, 1010 Victoria Pl., Waldorf, MD, 20602/301-843-0449
Specialties: Traditional and working/using straight knives of his design. **Patterns:** Daggers, fighters and hunters. **Technical:** Forges 5160 and Damascus; grinds D2; differential hardened blades; decorative handle pins. **Prices:** $125 to $350. **Remarks:** Spare-time maker; first knife sold in 1992. Doing business as Michael's Handmade Knives. **Mark:** Etched last name.

BOWEN, TILTON, Rt. 1, Box 225A, Baker, WV, 26801/304-897-6159
Specialties: Straight, stout working knives. **Patterns:** Hunters, fighters and boots; also offers buckskinner and throwing knives. All my D2-blades since 1st of year, 1997 are Deep Cryogenic processed. **Technical:** Grinds D2 and 4140. **Prices:** $60 to $275. **Remarks:** Full-time maker; first knife sold in 1982-1983. Sells wholesale to dealers. **Mark:** Initials and BOWEN BLADES, WV.

BOYD, FRANCIS, 1811 Prince St., Berkeley, CA, 94703/510-841-7210
Specialties: Folders and kitchen knives; Japanese swords. **Patterns:** Push-button sturdy locking folders; San Francisco-style chef's knives. **Technical:** Forges and grinds, mostly uses high-carbon steels. **Prices:** Moderate to heavy. **Remarks:** Designer. **Mark:** Name.

BOYE, DAVID, P.O. Box 1238, Dolan Springs, AZ, 86441/520-767-4273
Specialties: Folders, hunting and kitchen knives. Forerunner in the use of dendritic steel and dendritic cobalt for blades. **Patterns:** Boye Basics sheath knives, lockback folders, kitchen knives and hunting knives. **Technical:** Casts blades in stainless 440Cand cobalt. **Prices:** From $79 to $500. **Remarks:** Full-time maker; author of *Step-by-Step Knifemaking*; **Mark:** Name.

BOYER, MARK, 10515 Woodinville Dr., #17, Bothell, WA, 98011/206-487-9370
Specialties: High-tech and working/using straight knives of his design. **Patterns:** Fighters and utility/camp knives. **Technical:** Grinds 1095 and D2. Offers Kydex sheaths; heat-treats. **Prices:** $45 to $120. **Remarks:** Part-time maker; first knife sold in 1994. Doing business as Boyer Blades. **Mark:** Eagle holding two swords with name.

BOYES, TOM, N81 W16140 Robin Hood Dr, Menomonee Falls, WI, 53051/
Specialties: Hunters, working knives. **Technical:** Grinds ATS134, 440C, Damascus. **Prices:** $75 to $250. **Remarks:** First knife sold in 1998.

BRACK, DOUGLAS D., 119 Camino Ruiz, #71, Camirillo, CA, 93012/ 805-987-0490
Specialties: Working straight knives of his design. **Patterns:** Heavy-duty skinners, fighters and boots. **Technical:** Grinds 440C, ATS-34 and 5160; forges cable. **Prices:** $90 to $180; some to $300. **Remarks:** Part-time maker; first knife sold in 1984. **Mark:** tat.

BRADBURN, GARY, 1714 Park Pl., Wichita, KS, 67203/316-269-4273
Specialties: Straight knives of his design and to customer specs. **Patterns:** Bowies, fighters, hunters and miniatures. **Technical:** Forges 5160 and his own Damascus; grinds D2. **Prices:** $50 to $350; some to $800. **Remarks:** Full-time maker; first knife sold 1991. **Mark:** Last name or last initial inside a shamrock.

BRADLEY, DENNIS, 2410 Bradley Acres Rd., Blairsville, GA, 30512/ 706-745-4364
Specialties: Working straight knives and folders, some high-art. **Patterns:** Hunters, boots and daggers; slip-joints and two-blades. **Technical:** Grinds ATS-34, D2, 440C and commercial Damascus. **Prices:** $100 to $500; some to $2,000. **Remarks:** Part-time maker; first knife sold in 1973. **Mark:** BRADLEY KNIVES in double heart logo.

BRADLEY, JOHN, P.O. Box 37, Pomona Park, FL, 32181/904-649-4739
Specialties: Fixed-blade using knives. **Patterns:** Skinners, bowies, camp knives and Sgian Dubhs. **Technical:** Hand forged from 52100, 1095 and own Damascus. **Prices:** $125 to $500; some higher. **Remarks:** Part-time maker; first knife sold in 1988. **Mark:** Last name.

BRANDSEY, EDWARD P., 1207 Portage Lane, Woodstock, IL, 60098/ 815-337-6010
Specialties: Working straight knives; period pieces and art knives. **Patterns:** Hunters, fighters, Bowies and daggers, some buckskinner styles. **Technical:** ATS-34, 440-C, 0-1, and some Damascus. **Prices:** $150 to $350; some to $2,500. **Remarks:** Part-time maker; first knife sold in 1973. **Mark:** Initials connected.

BRANTON, ROBERT, 4976 Seewee Rd., Awendaw, SC, 29429/843-928-3624
Specialties: Working straight knives of his design or to customer specs; throwing knives. **Patterns:** Hunters, fighters and some miniatures. **Technical:** Grinds ATS-34, A2 and 1050; forges 5160, O1. Offers hollow- or convex-grinds. **Prices:** $25 to $400. **Remarks:** Part-time maker; first knife sold in 1985. Doing business as Pro-Flyte, Inc. **Mark:** Last name; or first and last name, city, state.

BRAY JR., W. LOWELL, 6931 Manor Beach Rd., New Port Richey, FL, 34652/727-847-1428
Specialties: Traditional working and using straight knives and folders of his design. **Patterns:** Hunters, kitchen knives and utility knives. **Technical:** Grinds 440C & ATS34; forges high carbon. **Prices:** $70 to $300. **Remarks:** Spare-time maker; first knife sold in 1992. **Mark:** Lowell Bray Knives in shield.

BRAYTON, JIM, 713 Park St., Burkburnett, TX, 76354/817-569-4726
Specialties: Working knives and period pieces, some fancy. **Patterns:** Bowies, hunters, fighters. **Technical:** Grinds ATS-34, delivers it at 60 Rc. **Prices:** $55 to $500; some higher. **Remarks:** Full-time maker; first knife sold in 1970. **Mark:** Initials or name.

BREND, WALTER J., Rt. 7, Box 224, Walterboro, SC, 29488/803-538-8256
Specialties: Art and working knives. **Patterns:** Combat knives, survival knives, liner locks and Bowies. **Technical:** ATS-34. **Prices:** $425 to $1,100; some to $3,500. **Remarks:** Full-time maker; first knife sold in 1980. **Mark:** Confederate flag.

BRENNAN, JUDSON, P.O. Box 1165, Delta Junction, AK, 99737/907-895-5153
Specialties: Period pieces. **Patterns:** All kinds of Bowies, rifle knives, daggers. **Technical:** Forges miscellaneous steels. **Prices:** Upscale, good value. **Remarks:** Muzzle-loading gunsmith; first knife sold in 1978. **Mark:** Name.

BRESHEARS, CLINT, 1261 Keats, Manhattan Beach, CA, 90266/310-372-0739
Specialties: Working straight knives and folders. **Patterns:** Hunters, Bowies and survival knives. Folders are mostly hunters. **Technical:** Grinds 440C, 154CM and ATS-34; prefers mirror finishes. **Prices:** $125 to $200; some to $500. **Remarks:** Part-time maker; first knife sold in 1978. **Mark:** First name.

BREUER, LONNIE, P.O. Box 877384, Wasilla, AK, 99687-7384/
Specialties: Fancy working straight knives. **Patterns:** Hunters, camp knives and axes, folders and Bowies. **Technical:** Grinds 440C, AEB-L and D2; likes wire inlay, scrimshaw, decorative filing. **Prices:** $60 to $150; some to $300. **Remarks:** Part-time maker; first knife sold in 1977. **Mark:** Signature.

BRIDGES, JUSTIN W., Box 974, Fish Hatchery Rd., Dubois, WY, 82513/307-455-2769
Specialties: Working and using straight knives and folders in standard patterns. **Patterns:** Hunters, gent's knives and locking folders. **Technical:** Grinds 440C, 154CM and buys Damascus. **Prices:** $250 to $1,000; some to $3,000. **Remarks:** Full-time maker; first knife sold in 1988. Doing business as Wind River Knives. **Mark:** WRK connected; sometimes a circle with name, city and state.

BRIDWELL, RICHARD A., Rt. 2, Milford Ch. Rd., Taylors, SC, 29687/ 803-895-1715
Specialties: Working straight knives and folders. **Patterns:** Boot and fishing knives, fighters and hunters. **Technical:** Grinds stainless steels and D2. **Prices:** $85 to $165; some to $600. **Remarks:** Part-time maker; first knife sold in 1974. **Mark:** Last name logo.

BRIGHTWELL, MARK, 21104 Creekside Dr., Leander, TX, 78641/512-267-4110
Specialties: Fancy and plain folders of his design. **Patterns:** Fighters, hunters and gents, some traditional. **Technical:** Hollow- or flat- grinds ATS-34, D2, custom Damascus; elaborate filework; heat-treats. Extensive choice of natural handle materials; no synthetics. **Prices:** $300 to $1,500. **Remarks:** Full-time maker. **Mark:** Last name.

BRIGNARDELLO, E.D., 71 Village Woods Dr., Crete, IL, 60401/708-672-6687
Specialties: Working straight knives; some display pieces. **Patterns:** Hunters, fighters, boots and Bowies; some push knives. **Technical:** Grinds 440C, 154CM and ATS-34; likes mirror finishes. **Prices:** $130 to $250; some to $500. **Remarks:** Part-time maker; first knife sold in 1978. **Mark:** Name and city.

BRITTON, TIM, 2100 Wolf Lane, Kinston, NC, 28501/252-523-8631
Specialties: Small and simple working knives, sgian dubhs and special tactical designs. **Technical:** Forges and grinds stainless steel. **Prices:** $110-$600. **Remarks:** Veteran knifemaker. **Mark:** Etched signature.

BROADWELL, DAVID, P.O. Box 4314, Wichita Falls, TX, 76308/940-692-1727
Specialties: Sculpted high-art straight and folding knives. **Patterns:** Daggers, sub-hilted fighters, folders, sculpted art knives and some Bowies. **Technical:** Grinds mostly Damascus; carves; prefers natural handle materials, including stone. Some embellishment. **Prices:** $300 to $3,000; some higher. **Remarks:** Full-time maker; first knife sold in 1982. **Mark:** Stylized emblem bisecting "B"/with last name below.

BROCK, KENNETH L., P.O. Box 375, 207 N. Skinner Rd., Allenspark, CO, 80510/303-747-2547
Specialties: Full-tang working knives and button-lock folders of his design. **Patterns:** Hunters, miniatures and minis. **Technical:** Flat-grinds D2 and 440C; makes own sheaths; heat-treats. **Prices:** $50 to $500. **Remarks:** Part-time maker; first knife sold in 1978. **Mark:** Last name, city, state and serial number.

BROOKER, DENNIS, Rt. 1, Box 12A, Derby, IA, 50068/515-533-2103
Specialties: Fancy straight knives and folders of his design. **Patterns:** Hunters, folders and boots. **Technical:** Forges and grinds. Full-time engraver and designer; instruction available. **Prices:** Moderate to upscale. **Remarks:** Part-time maker. Takes no orders; sells only completed work. **Mark:** Name.

BROOKS, STEVE R., Box 105, Big Timber, MT, 59011/406-932-5114
Specialties: Working straight knives and folders; period pieces. **Patterns:** Hunters, Bowies and camp knives; folding lockers; axes, tomahawks and buckskinner knives; swords and stilettos. **Technical:** Forges

custom knifemakers

O1, Damascus and mosaic Damascus. Some knives come embellished. **Prices:** $150 to $2,000. **Remarks:** Full-time maker; first knife sold in 1982. **Mark:** Lazy initials.

BROOKS, MICHAEL, 4412 47th St, Lubbock, TX, 79414-3320/806-793-1635
Specialties: Working straight knives of his design or to customer specs. **Patterns:** Tantos, swords, Bowies, hunters, skinners and boots. **Technical:** Grinds 440C, D2 and ATS-34; offers wide variety of handle materials. **Prices:** $40 to $800. **Remarks:** Part-time maker; first knife sold in 1985. **Mark:** Initials.

BROOME, THOMAS A., 1212 E. Aliak Ave., Kenai, AK, 99611-8205/
Specialties: Traditional working straight knives and folders. **Patterns:** Full range of straight knives and a few folders. **Technical:** Grinds D2, 440C, 440V, ATS-34 and BG42. **Prices:** $75 to $175; some to $2,000. **Remarks:** Full-time maker; first knife sold in 1979. Doing business as Thom's Custom Knives. **Mark:** Full name, city, state in logo.

BROTHERS, ROBERT L., 989 Philpott Rd., Colville, WA, 99114/509-684-8922
Specialties: Traditional working and using straight knives and folders of his design and to customer specs. **Patterns:** Bowies, fighters and hunters. **Technical:** Grinds D2; forges Damascus. Makes own Damascus from saw steel, wire rope and chain; part-time goldsmith and stone-setter. **Prices:** $100 to $400; some higher. **Remarks:** Part-time maker; first knife sold in 1986. **Mark:** Initials and year made.

BROUGHTON, DON R., 4690 Edwardsville-Galena Rd., Floyd Knobs, IN, 47119/812-923-9222
Specialties: Period pieces and antique finish. **Patterns:** Bowies, tomahawks, rifleman's knives, patch knives and belt knives. **Technical:** Forges 1095, 5160, 52100 and own Damascus. Uses antique finish. **Prices:** $150 to $750; some to $1,500. **Remarks:** Full-time maker; first knife sold in 1987. **Mark:** Tomahawk head, M.S.

BROWER, MAX, 2016 Story St., Boone, IA, 50036/515-432-2938
Specialties: Working/using straight knives. **Patterns:** Bowies, hunters and boots. **Technical:** Grinds 440C. **Prices:** Start at $125. **Remarks:** Spare-time maker; first knife sold in 1981. **Mark:** Last name.

BROWN, HAROLD E., 3654 NW Hwy. 72, Arcadia, FL, 34266/941-494-7514
Specialties: Fancy and exotic working knives. **Patterns:** Hunters, folders and fillet knives. **Technical:** Grinds D2, 440C and ATS-34. Embellishment available. **Prices:** $100 to $750; some to $1,000. **Remarks:** Full-time maker; first knife sold in 1976. **Mark:** Name and city with logo.

BROWN, ROB E., P.O. Box 15107, Emerald Hill 6011, Port Elizabeth, SOUTH AFRICA, /27-41-3661086
Specialties: Contemporary-designed straight knives and period pieces. **Patterns:** Utility knives, hunters, boots, fighters and daggers. **Technical:** Grinds 440C, D2, ATS-34 and commercial Damascus. Knives mostly mirror finished; African handle materials. **Prices:** $100 to $1,500. **Remarks:** Full-time maker; first knife sold in 1985. **Mark:** Name and country.

BROWN, TED, 7621 Firestone Blvd., Suite 104, Downey, CA, 90241/213-869-9945
Specialties: Working straight knives in standard patterns. **Patterns:** Hunters, Bowies, fishing knives. **Technical:** Grinds stainless steel; some integral work. **Prices:** $100 to $350; some to $500. **Remarks:** Part-time maker; first knife sold in 1982. **Mark:** Name, address in snake logo.

BROWN, PETER, 10 Island View St., Emerald Beach 2456, AUSTRALIA, /02-809-0265
Specialties: Heavy-duty working knives. **Patterns:** Swords, fighters, tantos, hunting and fishing knives. **Technical:** Grinds 440C, 420 and ATS-34; makes his own Damascus steel. Heat-treats; scrimshaws. **Prices:** $135 to $500; some to $800. **Remarks:** Spare-time maker; first knife sold in 1978. **Mark:** Interlacing initials.

BROWN, TROY L., HC 73, Box 526, Park Hill, OK, 74451/918-457-4128
Specialties: Working and using straight knives and folders. **Patterns:** Bowies, hunters and locking folders. **Technical:** Grinds 440C and D2; forges 5160. Prefers stag, wood and Micarta for handles. Offers engraved bolsters and guards. **Prices:** $75 to $500. **Remarks:** Full-time maker; first knife sold in 1994. Doing business as Troy Brown Custom Knives. **Mark:** First and last name.

BROWN, JIM, 1097 Fernleigh Cove, Little Rock, AR, 72210/

BROWNE, RICK, 980 West 13th St., Upland, CA, 91786/909-985-1728
Specialties: High-tech integral working straight knives of his design. **Patterns:** Hunters, fighters and daggers. No heavy-duty knives. **Technical:** Grinds D2, 440C and ATS-34. **Prices:** Start at $200. **Remarks:** Part-time maker; first knife sold in 1975. **Mark:** Name, city, state.

BRUNCKHORST, LYLE, Country Village, 23706 Bothell-Everett Hwy., Bothell, WA, 98021/425-402-3484
Specialties: Traditional working and using straight knives and folders of his design. **Patterns:** Bowies, hunters and locking folders. **Technical:** Grinds ATS-34; forges 5160 and his own Damascus. Iridescent RR spike knives. Offers scrimshaw, inlays and animal carvings in horn handles. **Prices:** $225 to $750; some to $3,750. **Remarks:** Full-time maker; first knife sold in 1976. Doing business as Bronk's Knifeworks. **Mark:** Bucking horse.

BRUNETTA, DAVID, P.O. Box 4972, Laguna Beach, CA, 92652/714-497-9611
Specialties: Straights and folders and art knives. **Patterns:** Bowies, camp/hunting, folders, fighters. **Technical:** Grinds ATS-34, D2, BG42. forges O1, 52100, 5160, 1095, makes own Damascus. **Prices:** $300 to $9000. **Mark:** Circle DB logo with last name straight or curved.

BUCHMAN, BILL, 63312 South Rd., Bend, OR, 97701/503-382-8851
Specialties: Working straight knives. **Patterns:** Hunters, Bowies, fighters, kitchen cutlery, carving sets and boots. Makes some saddlemaker knives. **Technical:** Forges 440C and Sandvik 15N20. Prefers 440C for saltwater. **Prices:** $95 to $400. **Remarks:** Part-time maker; first knife sold in 1982. **Mark:** Initials or last name.

BUCHNER, BILL, P.O. Box 73, Idleyld Park, OR, 97447/541-498-2247
Specialties: Working straight knives, kitchen knives and high-art knives of his design. **Technical:** Uses W1, L6 and his own Damascus. Invented "spectrum metal" for letter openers, folder handles and jewelry. Likes sculpturing and carving in Damascus. **Prices:** $40 to $3,000; some higher. **Remarks:** Full-time maker; first knife sold in 1978. **Mark:** Signature.

BUCHOLZ, MARK A., 9197 West Parkview Terrace Loop, Eagle River, AK, 99577/907-694-1037
Specialties: Liner lock folders. **Patterns:** Hunters and fighters. **Technical:** Grinds ATS-34. **Prices:** Upscale. **Remarks:** Full-time maker; first knife sold in 1976. **Mark:** Name, city and state in buffalo skull logo or signature.

BUCKBEE, DONALD M., 243 South Jackson Trail, Grayling, MI, 49738/517-348-1386
Specialties: Working straight knives, some fancy, in standard patterns; concentrating on kitchen knives. **Patterns:** Kitchen knives, hunters, Bowies. **Technical:** Grinds D2, 440C, ATS-34. Makes ultra-lights in hunter patterns. **Prices:** $100 to $250; some to $350. **Remarks:** Part-time maker; first knife sold in 1984. **Mark:** Antlered bee--a buck bee.

BUCKNER, JIMMIE H., P.O. Box 162, Putney, GA, 31782/912-436-4182
Specialties: Camp knives, Bowies (1 of a kind), liner lock folders, tomahawks, lamp axs, neck knives for law enforcement and hide out knives for body guards and professional people. **Patterns:** Hunters camp knives, Bowies. **Technical:** Forges 1084, 5160 and Damascus (own), own heat treats. **Prices:** $195 to $795 and up. **Remarks:** Full-time maker; first knife sold in 1980, ABS Mastersmith. **Mark:** Name over spade.

BUEBENDORF, ROBERT E., 108 Lazybrooke Rd., Monroe, CT, 06468/203-452-1769
Specialties: Traditional and fancy straight knives of his design. **Patterns:** Hand-makes and embellishes belt buckle knives. **Technical:** Forges and grinds 440C, O1, W2, 1095, his own Damascus and 154CM. **Prices:** $200 to $500. **Remarks:** Full-time maker; first knife sold in 1978. **Mark:** First and middle initials, last name and MAKER.

BUGDEN, JOHN, Rt. #6, Box 7, Murray, KY, 42071/502-753-0305
Specialties: Working straight knives; period pieces. **Patterns:** Hunters, boots and survival knives. **Technical:** Grinds O1, 440C; buys Damascus. Offers filework. **Prices:** $125 to $500. **Remarks:** Full-time maker; first knife sold in 1975. **Mark:** Initials.

BULLARD, TOM, Rt. 1, Box 127-B, Comfort, TX, 78013/210-860-2159
Specialties: Armadillo handle material on hunter and folders. **Patterns:** Bowies, hunters, lockback folders. **Technical:** Grinds 440-C, ATS-34,

commercial Damascus. **Prices:** $150 to $500. **Remarks:**Offers filework and engraving. **Mark:** Tbullard, city, state.

BULLARD, RANDALL, 7 Mesa Dr., Canyon, TX, 79015/806-655-0590
Specialties: Working/using straight knives and folders of his design or to customer specs. **Patterns:** Hunters, locking folders and slip-joint folders. **Technical:** Grinds O1, ATS-34 and 440C. Does file work. **Prices:** $125 to $300; some to $500. **Remarks:** Part-time maker; first knife sold in 1993. Doing business as Bullard Custom Knives. **Mark:** First and middle initials, last name, maker, city and state.

BULLARD, BILL, Rt. 5, Box 35, Andalusia, AL, 36420/334-222-9003
Specialties: Traditional working and using straight knives and folders of his design. **Patterns:** Hunters, slip-joint folders and utility/camp knives and folders to customer specs; armadillo tail handles on sheath knives. **Technical:** Forges Damascus, cable and carbon steels. Offers filework. **Prices:** $100 to $500; some to $1,500. **Remarks:** Part-time maker; first knife sold in 1974. Doing business as Five Runs Forge. **Mark:** Last name stamped on ricasso. Other: I do not use armadillo tails for handles!

BURAK, CHET, KNIFE SERVICES PHOTOGRAPHER, PO BOX 14383, E PROVIDENCE, RI, 02914/401-431-0625

BURDEN, JAMES, 405 Kelly St., Burkburnett, TX, 76354/

BURGER, FRED, Box 436, Munster 4278, Kwa-Zulu Natal, SOUTH AFRICA, /
Specialties: Straight knives of his design. **Patterns:** Gentlemen's sword canes in various designs. **Technical:** Carbon steel and 440C blades. **Prices:** Range of handles; $200 to $600. **Remarks:** Full-time maker with son, Barry, since 1987. **Mark:** Last name in oval pierced by a dagger.

BURGER, PON, 12 Glenwood Ave., Woodlands, Bulawayo, Zimbabwe, AFRICA, 75514/
Specialties: Collectors items. **Patterns:** Fighters, locking folders of traditional styles, buckles. **Technical:** Scrimshaws 440C blade. Uses polished buffalo horn with brass fittings. Cased in buffalo hide book. **Prices:** $450 to $1100. **Remarks:** Full-time maker; first knife sold in 1973. Doing business as Burger Products. **Mark:** Spirit of Africa.

BURKE, DAN, 22001 Ole Barn Rd., Edmond, OK, 73034/405-341-3406
Specialties: Traditional folders of his design and in standard patterns. **Patterns:** Slip-joint folders and traditional folders. **Technical:** Grinds D2 and BG-42. Prefers natural handle materials; heat-treats. **Prices:** $280 to $800. **Remarks:** Full-time maker; first knife sold in 1976. **Mark:** First and last name.

BURNETT, MAX, 537 Old Dug Mtn. Rd., Paris, AR, 72855/501-963-2767
Specialties: Fixed blade hunters, fillet, kitchen knives, hand tools. **Patterns:** Conventional, no frills. **Technical:** Stock removal process; oxy-acetylene heat treat of high carbon steel. **Prices:** Starting prices; fixed hunters $75, fillet $25, kitchen $20 & up. **Remarks:** Price depends on materials used. Spare-time maker; first knife sold in 1964. **Mark:** M.OGG & SN#.

BURROWS, STEPHEN R., 3532 Michigan, Kansas City, MO, 64109/816-921-1573
Specialties: Fantasy straight knives of his design, to customer specs and in standard patterns; period pieces. **Patterns:** Fantasy, bird and trout knives, daggers, fighters and hunters. **Technical:** Forges 5160 and 1095 high-carbon steel, O1 and his Damascus. Offers lost wax casting in bronze or silver of crossguards and pommels. **Prices:** $65 to $600; some to $2,000. **Remarks:** Full-time maker; first knife sold in 1983. Doing business as Gypsy Silk. **Mark:** Etched name.

BUSFIELD, JOHN, 153 Devonshire Circle, Roanoke Rapids, NC, 27870/252-537-3949
Specialties: Investor-grade folders; high-grade working straight knives. **Patterns:** Original price-style and trailing-point interframe and sculpted-frame folders, drop-point hunters and semi-skinners. **Technical:** Grinds 154CM and ATS-34. Offers interframes, gold frames and inlays; uses jade, agate and lapis. **Prices:** $275 to $2,000. **Remarks:** Full-time maker; first knife sold in 1979. **Mark:** Last name and address.

BUSSE, JERRY, 11651 Co. Rd. 12, Wauseon, OH, 43567/419-923-6471
Specialties: Working straight knives. **Patterns:** Heavy combat knives and camp knives. **Technical:** Grinds D2, A2, ATS-34 and 440C; hollow-grinds most blades. **Prices:** $1,100 to $3,500. **Remarks:** Full-time maker; first knife sold in 1983. **Mark:** Last name in logo.

BYBEE, BARRY J., 795 Lock Rd. E., Cadiz, KY, 42211-8615/
Specialties: Working straight knives of his design. **Patterns:** Hunters, fighters, boot knives, tantos and Bowies. **Technical:** Grinds ATS-34, 440C. Likes stag and Micarta for handle materials. **Prices:** $125 to $200; some to $1,000. **Remarks:** Part-time maker; first knife sold in 1968. **Mark:** Arrowhead logo with name, city and state.

CAFFREY, EDWARD J., 2608 Central Ave. West, Great Falls, MT, 59404/406-727-9102
Specialties: Working/using knives and collector pieces; will accept customer designs. **Patterns:** Hunters, fighters, camp/utility, folders, hawks and hatchets. **Technical:** Forges 5160, 52100, his Damascus, cable and chain Damascus. **Prices:** Start at $125. **Remarks:** Part-time maker; first knife sold in 1989. **Mark:** Last name or engraved initials.

CALDWELL, BILL, 255 Rebecca, West Monroe, LA, 71292/318-323-3025
Specialties: Straight knives and folders with machined bolsters and liners. **Patterns:** Fighters, Bowies, survival knives, tomahawks, razors and push knives. **Technical:** Owns and operates a very large, well-equipped blacksmith and bladesmith shop extant with six large forges and eight power hammers. **Prices:** $400 to $3,500; some to $10,000. **Remarks:** Full-time maker and self-styled blacksmith; first knife sold in 1962. **Mark:** Wild Bill & Sons.

CALLAHAN, ERRETT, 2 Fredonia, Lynchburg, VA, 24503/
Specialties: Obsidian knives. **Patterns:** Modern styles and Stone Age replicas. **Technical:** Flakes and knaps to order. **Prices:** $100 to $3,400. **Remarks:** Part-time maker; first flint blades sold in 1974. **Mark:** Blade--engraved name, year and arrow; handle--signed edition, year and unit number.

CALLAHAN, F. TERRY, P.O. Box 880, Boerne, TX, 78006/210-981-8274
Specialties: Custom hand-forged edged knives, collectible and functional. **Patterns:** Bowies, folders, daggers, hunters, camp knives and swords. **Technical:** Forges 5160, 1095 and his own Damascus. Offers filework and handmade sheaths. **Prices:** $125 to $2,000. **Remarks:** First knife sold in 1990. **Mark:** Initials inside a keystone symbol.

CAMERON, RON G., P.O. Box 183, Logandale, NV, 89021/702-398-3356
Specialties: Fancy and embellished working/using straight knives and folders of his design. **Patterns:** Bowies, hunters and utility/camp knives. **Technical:** Grinds ATS-34, 440C and Devin Thomas Damascus. Does filework, fancy pins, mokume fittings. Uses exotic hardwoods, stag and Micarta for handles. **Prices:** $100 to $300; some to $600. **Remarks:** Part-time maker; first knife sold in 1994. Doing business as Cameron Handmade Knives. **Mark:** Last name, town, state or last name.

CAMP, JEFF, 1621 Hwy 563, Dubach, LA, 71235/318-777-8571
Specialties: Fancy working and using straight knives of his design and to customer specs. **Patterns:** Bowies, hunters, utility/camp knives and folders. **Technical:** Forges 5168, L6 and his Damascus. Offers filework; makes mokume. **Prices:** $260 to $1,000. **Remarks:** Part-time maker; first knife sold in 1991. **Mark:** Initials in script and JS.

CAMPBELL, DICK, 20000 Silver Ranch Rd., Conifer, CO, 80433/303-697-0150
Specialties: Fancy working straight knives and folders; period pieces. **Patterns:** Bowies, fighters, miniatures and titanium folders. **Technical:** Grinds 440C; uses titanium. Prefers natural materials. **Prices:** $130 to $750; some to $1,200. **Remarks:** Part-time maker; first knife sold in 1975. **Mark:** Name.

CANDRELLA, JOE, 1219 Barness Dr., Warminster, PA, 18974/215-675-0143
Specialties: Working straight knives, some fancy. **Patterns:** Daggers, boots, Bowies. **Technical:** Grinds 440C and 154CM. **Prices:** $100 to $200; some to $1,000. **Remarks:** Part-time maker; first knife sold in 1985. Does business as Franjo. **Mark:** FRANJO with knife as J.

CANDADY, DANIEL L.,
Box 301, Allendale, SC, 29810/803-584-2813
Specialties: Working straight knives and folders in standard patterns. **Patterns:** Drop-point hunters, Bowies, skinners, fishing knives with con-

custom knifemakers

cave grind, steak knives and kitchen cutlery. **Technical:** Grinds D2, 440C and ATS-34. **Prices:** $65 to $325; some to $500. **Remarks:** Full-time maker; first knife sold in 1980. **Mark:** Last name.

CANNON, RAYMOND W., P.O. Box 1412, Homer, AK, 99603/907-235-7779
Specialties: Fancy working knives, folders and swords of his design or to customer specs; many one-of-a-kind pieces. **Patterns:** Bowies, daggers and skinners. **Technical:** Forges and grinds O1, A6, 52100, 5160, his combinations for his own Damascus. **Remarks:** First knife sold in 1984. **Mark:** Cannon Alaska or "Handforged by Wes Cannon".

CANTER, RONALD E., 96 Bon Air Circle, Jackson, TN, 38305/901-668-1780
Specialties: Traditional working knives to customer specs. **Patterns:** Beavertail skinners, Bowies, hand axes and folding lockers. **Technical:** Grinds A1, 440C and 154CM. **Prices:** $65 to $250; some $500 and higher. **Remarks:** Spare-time maker; first knife sold in 1973. **Mark:** Three last initials intertwined.

CAPDEPON, ROBERT, 829 Vatican Rd., Carencro, LA, 70520/318-896-8753
Specialties: Traditional straight knives and folders of his design. **Patterns:** Boots, hunters and locking folders. **Technical:** Grinds ATS-34, 440C and D2. Hand-rubbed finish on blades. Likes natural horn materials for handles, including ivory. Offers engraving. **Prices:** $250 to $750. **Remarks:** Full-time maker; first knife made in 1992. **Mark:** Last name.

CAPDEPON, RANDY, 553 Joli Rd., Carencro, LA, 70520/318-896-4113
Specialties: Straight knives and folders of his design. **Patterns:** Hunters and locking folders. **Technical:** Grinds ATS-34, 440C and D2. **Prices:** $200 to $600. **Remarks:** Part-time maker; first knife made in 1992. Doing business as Capdepon Knives. **Mark:** Last name.

CAREY JR., CHARLES W., 1003 Minter Rd., Griffin, GA, 30223/770-228-8994
Specialties: Working and using knives of his design and to customer specs; period pieces. **Patterns:** Fighters, hunters, utility/camp knives and forged-to-shape miniatures. **Technical:** Forges 5160, old files and cable. Offers filework; ages some of his knives. **Prices:** $35 to $400. **Remarks:** Part-time maker; first knife sold in 1991. **Mark:** Knife logo.

CARGILL, BOB, RR 1, Box 383, Ocoee, TN, 37361/615-338-8418
Specialties: Unique multi-blade folders of his design. **Patterns:** Adaptations of traditional pocketknives in many styles. **Technical:** Grinds 1095, 440, ATS-34 and Damascus. **Prices:** Start at $500; some to $10,000. **Remarks:** Full-time maker; first knife sold in 1974. **Mark:** Cargill Knives.

CARLISLE, FRANK, 5930 Hereford, Detroit, MI, 48224/313-882-8349
Specialties: Fancy/embellished and fantasy folders of his design. **Patterns:** Hunters, locking folders and swords. **Technical:** Grinds Damascus and stainless. **Prices:** $80 to $300. **Remarks:** Full-time maker; first knife sold in 1993. Doing business as Carlisle Cutlery. **Mark:** Last name.

CARLSSON, MARC BJORN, Pileatraede 42, 1112 Copenhagen K, DENMARK, /+45 33 91 15 99
Specialties: High-tech knives and folders. **Patterns:** Skinners, tantos, swords, folders and art knives. **Technical:** Grinds ATS-34, Elmax and D2. **Prices:** Start at $250. **Remarks:** Doing business as "Mememto Mori", Professional jeweler and knifemaker. Doing business as Metal Point. **Mark:** First name in runic letters within Viking ship.

CAROLINA CUSTOM KNIVES, (SEE TOMMY McNABB)

CARSON, HAROLD J. "KIT", 1076 Brizendine Lane, Vine Grove, KY, 40175/270 877-6300
Specialties: Military fixed blades and folders; art pieces. **Patterns:** Fighters, D handles, daggers, combat folders and Crosslock styles. **Technical:** Grinds 440C, ATS-34, D2, O1 and Damascus. **Prices:** $400 to $750; some to $5,000. **Remarks:** Full-time maker; first knife sold in 1973. **Mark:** Name stamped or engraved.

CARTER, MURRAY M, 2506 Toyo Oka, Uek Kamoto, Kumamoto, JAPAN 861-0163, /81-96-272-6759
Specialties: Traditional Japanese cutlery, utilizing Son soh ko (3 layer) or Kata-ha (two layer) blade construction. **Patterns:** Works from over 200 standard Japanese and North American designs. **Technical:** Forges or grinds Hitachi white steel #1, Hitachi blue super steel or Hitachi ZDP247

stainless steel exclusively. Forges own Damascus. **Prices:** $30 to $300. **Remarks:** Full-time maker. First knife sold in 1989. Owner & designer of "Muteki" brand knives. **Mark:** Name with Japanese character on forged pieces. "Muteki" with Japanese characters on stock-removal blades.

CARTER, FRED, 5219 Deer Creek Rd., Wichita Falls, TX, 76302/817-723-4020
Specialties: High-art investor-class straight knives; some working hunters and fighters. **Patterns:** Classic daggers, Bowies; interframe, stainless and blued steel folders with gold inlay. **Technical:** Grinds a variety of steels. Uses no glue or solder. Engraves and inlays. **Prices:** Generally upscale. **Remarks:** Full-time maker. **Mark:** Signature in oval logo.

CASHEN, KEVIN R., 5615 Tyler St., Hubbardston, MI, 48845/517-981-6780
Specialties: Working straight knives, high art pattern welded swords, traditional renaissance and ethnic pieces. **Patterns:** Hunters, bowies, utility knives, swords, daggers. **Technical:** Forges 1095, 1084 and his own O1/L6 Damascus. **Prices:** $100 to $4,000+. **Remarks:** Full-time maker; first knife sold in 1985. Doing business as Matherton Forge. **Mark:** Black letter Old English initials and mastersmith stamp.

CASTEEL, DIANNA, P.O. Box 63, Monteagle, TN, 37356/931-723-0851
Specialties: Small, delicate daggers and miniatures; most knives one of a kind. **Patterns:** Daggers, boot knives, fighters and miniatures. **Technical:** Grinds 440C; makes her own Damascus. **Prices:** Start at $350; miniatures start at $250. **Remarks:** Full-time maker. **Mark:** Di in script.

CASTEEL, DOUGLAS, P.O. Box 63, Monteagle, TN, 37356/931-723-0851
Specialties: One-of-a-kind collector-class period pieces. **Patterns:** Daggers, Bowies, swords and folders. **Technical:** Grinds 440C; makes his own Damascus. Offers gold and silver castings. **Prices:** Upscale. **Remarks:** Full-time maker; first knife sold in 1982. **Mark:** Last name.

CATOE, DAVID R, 4024 Heutte Dr, Norfolk, VA, 23518/757-480-3191
Technical: Does own forging, Damascus and heat treatments. **Price:** $200 to $500; some higher. **Remarks:** Part-time maker; trained by Dan Maragni 1985-1988; first knife sold 1989. **Mark:** Leaf of a camillia.

CAUDELL, RICHARD M., P.O. Box 602, Lawrenceville, IL, 62439/618-943-5278
Specialties: Classic working/using straight knives in standard patterns. **Patterns:** Boots, fighters, combat fighters and utility/camp knives. **Technical:** Hollow-grinds 440C, ATS-34 and A2. **Prices:** $115 to $600; some to $1,200. **Remarks:** First knife sold in 1994. Doing business as Caudell's Custom Knives. **Mark:** Last name.

CENTOFANTE, FRANK AND TONY, P.O. Box 928, Madisonville, TN, 37354-0928/423-442-5767
Specialties: Fancy working folders. **Patterns:** Lockers and liner locks. **Technical:** Grinds ATS-34; hand-rubbed satin finish on blades. **Prices:** $300 to $900. **Remarks:** Full-time maker; first knife sold in 1968. **Mark:** Name, city, state.

CHAFFEE, JEFF L., 14314 N Washington St., P.O. Box 1, Morris, IN, 47033/812-934-6350
Specialties: Fnacy working and utility folders and straight knives. **Patterns:** Fighters, dagger, hunter and locking folders. **Technical:** Grinds commercial Damascus, 440C, ATS-34, D2 and O1. Prefers natural handle materials. **Prices:** $350 to $2,000. **Remarks:** Part-time maker; first knife sold in 1988. **Mark:** Last name.

CHAMBERLAIN, JOHN B., 1621 Angela St., Wenatchee, WA, 98801/509-663-6720
Specialties: Fancy working and using straight knives mainly to customer specs, though starting to make some standard patterns. **Patterns:** Hunters, Bowies and daggers. **Technical:** Grinds D2, ATS-34, M2, M4 and L6. **Prices:** $60 to $190; some to $2,500. **Remarks:** Full-time maker; first knife sold in 1943. **Mark:** Name, city, state.

CHAMBERLAIN, JON A., 15 S. Lombard, E. Wenatchee, WA, 98802/509-884-6591
Specialties: Working and kitchen knives to customer specs; exotics on special order. **Patterns:** Over 100 patterns in stock. **Technical:** Prefers ATS-34, D2, L6 and Damascus. **Prices:** Start at $50. **Remarks:** First knife sold in 1986. Doing business as Johnny Custom Knifemakers. **Mark:** Name in oval with city and state enclosing.

CHAMBERLAIN, CHARLES R., P.O. Box 156, Barren Springs, VA, 24313-0156/703-381-5137

CHAMBERLIN, JOHN A., 11535 Our Rd., Anchorage, AK, 99516/907-346-1524
Specialties: Art and working knives. **Patterns:** Daggers and hunters; some folders. **Technical:** Grinds ATS-34, 440C, A2, D2 and Damascus. Uses Alaskan handle materials such as oosic, jade, whale jawbone, fossil ivory. **Prices:** Start at $100. **Remarks:** Does own heat treating and cryogenic deep freeze. Full-time maker; first knife sold in 1984. **Mark:** Name over English shield and dagger.

CHAMBLIN, JOEL, 296 New Hebron Church Rd., Concord, GA, 30206/770-884-9055
Specialties: Traditional folders. **Patterns:** Multiblades, utility and fancy locking folders. **Technical:** Grinds ATS-34 and commercial Damascus. Offers filework. **Prices:** Start at $250. **Remarks:** Full-time maker; first knife sold in 1989. **Mark:** Last name.

CHAMPAGNE, PAUL, 48 Brightman Rd., Mechanicville, NY, 12118/518-664-4179
Specialties: Rugged, ornate straight knives in the Japanese tradition. **Patterns:** Katanas, wakizashis, tantos and some European daggers. **Technical:** Forges and hand-finishes carbon steels and his own Damascus. Makes Tamahagane for use in traditional blades; uses traditional heat-treating techniques. **Prices:** Start at $750. **Remarks:** Has passed all traditional Japanese cutting tests. Doing business as Twilight Forge. **Mark:** Three diamonds over a stylized crown.

CHAMPION, ROBERT, 1806 Plateau Ln, Amarillo, TX, 79106/806-359-0446
Specialties: Traditional working straight knives and folders. **Patterns:** Hunters, locking and slip-joint folders; some sub-hilt fighters. **Technical:** Grinds A2, 440C, D2. **Prices:** $100 to $600. **Remarks:** Part-time maker; first knife sold in 1979. **Mark:** Last name with dagger logo, city and state.

CHAPO, WILLIAM G., 45 Wildridge Rd., Wilton, CT, 06897/203-544-9424
Specialties: Classic straight knives and folders of his design and to customer specs; period pieces. **Patterns:** Boots, Bowies and locking folders. **Technical:** Forges stainless Damascus. Offers filework. **Prices:** $350 to $950; some to $2,200. **Remarks:** Full-time maker; first knife sold in 1989. **Mark:** First and middle initials, last name, city, state.

CHARD, GORDON R., 104 S. Holiday Lane, Iola, KS, 66749/316-365-2311
Specialties: High-tech locking folders. **Patterns:** Titanium sidelock folders, push-button locking folders, interframe lockbacks and some art knives. **Technical:** Flat- and hollow-grinds mostly ATS-34, some Damascus; hand-finishes blades. **Prices:** $135 to $2,500. **Remarks:** Full-time maker; first knife sold in 1983. **Mark:** Name, city and state in wheat logo.

CHASE, JOHN E., P.O. Drawer H, Aledo, TX, 76008/817-441-8331
Specialties: Straight high-tech working knives in standard patterns or to customer specs. **Patterns:** Hunters, fighters, daggers and Bowies. **Technical:** Grinds D2, 440C; offers mostly satin finishes. **Prices:** Start at $195. **Remarks:** Part-time maker; first knife sold in 1974. **Mark:** Last name in logo.

CHASE, ALEX, 101 S. Sheridan Ave., DeLand, FL, 32720/904-734-9918
Specialties: Historical steels, classic and traditional straight knives of his design and to customer specs. **Patterns:** Art, fighters and hunters. **Technical:** Forges O1-L6 Damascus, meteoric Damascus, 52100, 5160; uses fossil walrus & mastadon ivory etc. **Prices:** $150 to $1,000; some to $3,500. **Remarks:** Part-time maker; first knife sold in 1990. Doing business as Confederate Forge. **Mark:** Stylized initials-A.C.

CHASTAIN, WADE, Rt. 2, Box 137-A, Horse Shoe, NC, 28742/704-891-4803
Specialties: Fancy fantasy and high-art straight knives of his design; period pieces. Known for unique mounts. **Patterns:** Bowies, daggers and fighters. **Technical:** Grinds 440C, ATS-34 and O1. Engraves; offers jeweling. **Prices:** $400 to $1,200; some to $2,000. **Remarks:** Full-time maker; first knife sold in 1984. Doing business as The Iron Master. **Mark:** Engraved last name.

CHAUVIN, JOHN, 200 Anna St., Scott, LA, 70583/318-237-6138
Specialties: Traditional working and using straight knives of his design, to customer specs and in standard patterns. **Patterns:** Bowies, fighters, and hunters. **Technical:** Grinds ATS-34, 440C and O1 high carbon. Paul Bos heat treating. Uses ivory, stag, oosic and stabilized Louisiana swamp maple for handle materials. Makes sheaths using alligator and ostrich. **Prices:** $125 to $200; Bowies start at $500. **Remarks:** Part-time maker; first knife sold in 1995. **Mark:** Full name, city, state.

CHEATHAM, BILL, P.O. Box 636, Laveen, AZ, 85339/602-237-2786
Specialties: Working straight knives and folders. **Patterns:** Hunters, fighters, boots and axes; locking folders. **Technical:** Grinds 440C. **Prices:** $150 to $350; exceptional knives to $600. **Remarks:** Full-time maker; first knife sold in 1976. **Mark:** Name, city, state.

CHELQUIST, CLIFF, P.O. Box 91, Arroyo Grande, CA, 93421/805-489-8095
Specialties: Highly polished sportsman's knives. **Patterns:** Bird knives to Bowies. **Technical:** Grinds D2 and ATS-34. **Prices:** $75 to $150; some to $400. **Remarks:** Spare-time maker; first knife sold in 1983. **Mark:** Last initial.

CHOATE, MILTON, 1665 W County 17-1/2, Somerton, AZ, 85350/520-627-7251
Specialties: Classic working and using straight knives of his design, to customer specs and in standard patterns. **Patterns:** Bowies, hunters and utility/camp knives. **Technical:** Grinds 440C; grinds and forges 1095 and 5160. Does filework on top and guards on request. **Prices:** $85 to $600. **Remarks:** Part-time maker; first knife made in 1990. All knives come with handmade sheaths by Judy Kranz. **Mark:** JK.

CHURCHMAN, T.W., 7402 Tall Cedar, San Antonio, TX, 78249/210-690-8641
Specialties: Fancy and traditional straight knives and bird/trout knives of his design and to customer specs. **Patterns:** Bird/trout knives, Bowies, daggers, fighters and boot knives, some single blade folders. **Technical:** Grinds 440C and D2. Offers fancy filework, lined sheaths, exotic and stabilized woods, and twisted silver wire on fluted handles. **Prices:** $75 to $300; some to $1,500. **Remarks:** Part-time maker; first knife sold in 1981. Doing business as Custom Knives Churchman Made. **Mark:** Last name, dagger.

CLAIBORNE, RON, 2918 Ellistown Rd., Knox, TN, 37924/615-524-2054
Specialties: Working and using straight knives; period pieces. **Patterns:** Hunters, Bowies and daggers. **Technical:** Forges his own Damascus; grinds 440C, O1, W2 and 1095. Prefers bone and natural handle materials; some exotic woods. **Prices:** $125 to $300; some to $900. **Remarks:** Part-time maker; first knife sold in 1979. Doing business as Thunder Mountain Forge Claiborne Knives. **Mark:** Last name.

CLAIBORNE, JEFF, 1470 Roberts Rd, Franklin, IN, 46131/317-736-7443
Specialties: All one of a kind by hand--no jigs or fixtures-- swords, straight knives, period pieces, multi-blade folders. Handle--uses ivory, stag, pearl, oosic, bone or exotic wood. **Technical:** Forges cable Damascus, grinds O1, D2, 1095, 5160, 52100. **Prices:** $100 and up. **Remarks:** Part-time maker; first knife sold in 1989. **Mark:** Stylized initials in an oval.

CLARK, W.R., 13009 Los Nietos Rd., Bldg. G., Santa Fe Springs, CA, 90670/310-906-0233

CLARK, ROGER, Rt. 1, Box 538, Rockdale, TX, 76567/512-446-3388
Specialties: Traditional working and using straight knives of his design or to customer specs. **Patterns:** Hunters, Bowies and camp knives; primitive styles for blackpowder hunters. **Technical:** Forges 1084, O1 and Damascus. Sheaths are extra. **Prices:** Primitive styles start at $100; shiny blades start at $150; Damascus start at $250. **Remarks:** Full-time maker; first knife sold in 1989. **Mark:** First initial, last name.

CLARK, HOWARD F., 115 35th Pl., Runnells, IA, 50237/515-966-2126
Specialties: Damascus knives of all kinds; folders and straight knives. **Patterns:** Most anything. **Technical:** Forges 1086, L6, 52100 and his own all tool steel Damascus; bar stock; forged blanks. **Prices:** $500 to $3,000. **Remarks:** Full-time maker; first knife sold in 1979. Doing business as Morgan Valley Forge. **Mark:** Block letters and serial number on folders; anvil/initials logo on straight knives.

CLARK, D.E. (LUCKY), 126 Woodland St., Mineral Point, PA, 15942/814-322-4725
Specialties: Working straight knives and folders to customer specs. **Patterns:** Customer designs. **Technical:** Grinds D2, 440C, 154CM. **Prices:**

custom knifemakers

$100 to $200; some higher. **Remarks:** Part-time maker; first knife sold in 1975. **Mark:** Name on one side; "Lucky" on other.

CLARK, DAVE, P.O. Box 597, Andrews, NC, 28901/828-321-8067
Specialties: Folders to customer specs. **Patterns:** Locking folders. **Technical:** Grinds 440C, D2 and stainless Damascus. **Prices:** $400 to $1,500. **Remarks:** Full-time maker; first knife sold in 1988. **Mark:** Name.

CLASSIC CUTLERY, 336 College Hill Rd, Hopkinton, NH, 03229/603-746-2413

CLAY, WAYNE, Box 474B, Pelham, TN, 37366/615-467-3472
Specialties: Working straight knives and folders in standard patterns. **Patterns:** Hunters, fighters and kitchen knives; gents and hunter patterns. **Technical:** Grinds 154CM and ATS-34. **Prices:** $125 to $250; some to $1,000. **Remarks:** Full-time maker; first knife sold in 1978. **Mark:** Name.

CLAY, J.D., 5050 Hall Rd., Greenup, KY, 41144/606-473-6769
Specialties: Veteran knife maker--specializing in collector quality working knives. **Patterns:** Practical hunters and locking folders. **Technical:** Grinds 440C and ATS-34. **Prices:** Start at $150. **Remarks:** Full-time maker; first knife sold in 1972. **Mark:** Name stamp in script on blade.

CLICK, JOE, U-344 Rd. 2, Liberty Center, OH, 43532/419-875-6199
Specialties: Fancy/embellished and traditional working/using straight knives of his design, to customer specs and in standard patterns. **Patterns:** Bowies, hunters and utility/camp knives. **Technical:** Grinds and forges A2, D2, 5160 and Damascus. Does fancy filework; triple temper. Uses ivory for handle material. **Prices:** $75 to $300; some to $700. **Remarks:** Doing business as Click Custom Knives. **Mark:** Full name.

COATS, ELDON, P.O. Box 201, Bonanza, OR, 97623/503-545-6960
Specialties: Plain to fancy working knives of his design or to customer specs. Will work with collectors. **Patterns:** Hunters, skinners, fighters, survival knives, Bowies, boots, fillet knives, axes and miniatures. **Technical:** Flat-grinds mostly by hand 440C, D2, 5160. Uses exotic hardwoods, Micarta and ivory for handles. Bead blasts; uses commercial heat-treater. Makes own sheaths. Scrimshaws and engraves. **Prices:** $50 to $250; miniatures start at $35; collector pieces to $1,200. **Remarks:** Full-time maker; first knife sold in 1987. **Mark:** Name, with dagger in T.

COBB, LOWELL D., 823 Julia St., Daytona Beach, FL, 32114/904-252-3514
Specialties: Working straight knives of his design or to customer specs. **Patterns:** Fighters, hunters, skinners, fillet knives and Bowies. **Technical:** Grinds 440C; embellishments available. **Prices:** $100 to $500. **Remarks:** Part-time maker; first knife sold in 1986. **Mark:** Name.

COFER, RON, 188 Ozora Road, Loganville, GA, 30052/
Specialties: Fancy working and using straight knives of his design. **Patterns:** Hunters, Bowies and fighters. **Technical:** Grinds 440C and ATS-34. Heat-treats. Some knives have carved stag handles or scrimshaw. Makes leather sheath for each knife and walnut and deer antler display stands for art knives. **Prices:** $125 to $250; some to $600. **Remarks:** Spare-time maker; first knife sold in 1991. **Mark:** Name, serial number.

COFFMAN, DANNY, 505 Angel Dr. S., Jacksonville, AL, 36265/205-435-5848
Specialties: Straight knives and folders of his design. **Patterns:** Hunters, locking and slip-joint folders. **Technical:** Grinds Damascus, 440C and D2. Offers filework and engraving. **Prices:** $100 to $400; some to $800. **Remarks:** Spare-time maker; first knife sold in 1992. Doing business as Customs by Coffman. **Mark:** Last name stamped or engraved.

COHEN, N.J. (NORM), 2408 Sugarcone Rd., Baltimore, MD, 21209/410-484-3841
Specialties: Working class knives. **Patterns:** Hunters, skinners, bird knives, push daggers, boots, kitchen and practical customer designs. **Technical:** Stock removal 440C, ATS-34. Uses Micarta, Corian. Some woods in handles. **Prices:** $50 to $250. **Remarks:** Part-time maker; first knife sold in 1982. **Mark:** Etched initials or NJC MAKER.

COHEN, TERRY A., P.O. Box 406, Laytonville, CA, 95454/
Specialties: Working straight knives and folders. **Patterns:** Bowies to boot knives and locking folders; mini-boot knives. **Technical:** Grinds stainless; hand rubs; tries for good balance. **Prices:** $85 to $150; some to $325. **Remarks:** Part-time maker; first knife sold in 1983. **Mark:** TERRY KNIVES, city and state.

COIL, JIMMIE J., 2936 Asbury Pl., Owensboro, KY, 42302/502-684-7827
Specialties: Traditional working and using straight knives of his design. **Patterns:** Hunters, Bowies and fighters. **Technical:** Grinds 440C, ATS-34 and D2. Blades are flat-ground with brush finish; most have tapered tang. Offers filework. **Prices:** $65 to $250; some to $750. **Remarks:** Spare-time maker; first knife sold in 1974. **Mark:** Name.

COLE, WELBORN I., 3284 Inman Dr. NE, Atlanta, GA, 30319/404-261-3977
Specialties: Traditional straight knives of his design. **Patterns:** Hunters. **Technical:** Grinds 440C, ATS-34 and D2. Good wood scales. **Prices:** NA. **Remarks:** Full-time maker; first knife sold in 1983. **Mark:** Script initials.

COLEMAN, KEITH E., 5001 Starfire Pl NW, Albuquerque, NM, 87120-2010/505-899-3783
Specialties: Affordable collector-grade straight knives and folders; some fancy. **Patterns:** Fighters, tantos, combat folders, gents folders and boots. **Technical:** Grinds ATS-34 and Damascus. Prefers specialty woods; offers filework. **Prices:** $150 to $700; some to $1,500. **Remarks:** Full-time maker; first knife sold in 1980. **Mark:** Name, city and state.

COLLINS, A.J., 9651 Elon Ave., Arleta, CA, 91331/818-762-7728
Specialties: Working dress knives of his design. **Patterns:** Street survival knives, swords, axes. **Technical:** Grinds O1, 440C, 154CM. **Prices:** Start at $100. **Remarks:** Full-time maker; first knife sold in 1972. Doing business as Kustom Krafted Knives--KKK. **Mark:** Name.

COLLINS, LYNN M., 138 Berkley Dr., Elyria, OH, 44035/440-366-7101
Specialties: Working straight knives. **Patterns:** Field knives, boots and fighters. **Technical:** Grinds D2, 154CM and 440C. **Prices:** Start at $150. **Remarks:** Spare-time maker; first knife sold in 1980. **Mark:** Initials, asterisks.

COLLINS, HAROLD, 503 First St., West Union, OH, 45693/513-544-2982
Specialties: Traditional using straight knives and folders of his design or to customer specs. **Patterns:** Hunters, Bowies and locking folders. **Technical:** Forges and grinds 440C, ATS-34, D2, O1 and 5160. Flat-grinds standard; filework available. **Prices:** $75 to $300. **Remarks:** Full-time maker; first knife sold in 1989. **Mark:** First initial, last name, Maker.

COLTER, WADE, P.O. Box 2340, Colstrip, MT, 59323/406-748-4573
Specialties: Fancy and embellished straight knives, folders and swords of his design; historical and period pieces. **Patterns:** Bowies, swords and folders. **Technical:** Hand forges 52100 ball bearing steel and L6, 1090, cable and chain Damascus from 5N20 & 1084. Carves and makes sheaths. **Prices:** $250 to $3500. **Remarks:** Part-time maker; first knife sold in 1990. Doing business as "Colter's Hell" Forge. **Mark:** Initials on left side ricasso.

COMPTON, WILLIAM E., 106 N. Sequoia Ct., Sterling, VA, 20164/703-430-2129
Specialties: Working straight knives of his design or to customer specs; some fancy knives. **Patterns:** Hunters, camp knives, Bowies and some kitchen knives. **Technical:** Also forges 5160, 1095 and make my own Damascus and do silverwire inlay. **Prices:** $100 to $600; some to $1,200. **Remarks:** Part-time maker; first knife sold in 1994. Doing business as Comptons Custom Knives. **Mark:** First and middle initials, last name, city & state.

CONABLE, MATT, P.O. Box 1329, 26 North Rd. One West, Chino Valley, AZ, 86323/520-636-2402

CONKEY, TOM, 9122 Keyser Rd., Nokesville, VA, 22123/703-791-3867
Specialties: Classic straight knives and folders of his design and to customer specs. **Patterns:** Boots, hunters and locking folders. **Technical:** Grinds ATS-34, O1 and commercial Damascus. Lockbacks have jeweled scales and locking bars with dovetailed bolsters. Folders utilize unique 2-piece bushing of his design and manufacture. Sheaths are handmade. Presentation boxes made upon request. **Prices:** $100 to $500. **Remarks:** Part-time maker; first knife sold in 1991. Collaborates with Dan Thomas. **Mark:** Last name with "handcrafted" underneath.

CONKLIN, GEORGE L., Box 902, Ft. Benton, MT, 59442/406-622-3268
Specialties: Designer and manufacturer of the "Brisket Breaker." **Patterns:** Hunters, utility/camp knives and hatchets. **Technical:** Grinds 440C, ATS-34, D2, 1095, 154CM and 5160. Offers some forging and heat-treats for others. Offers some jeweling. **Prices:** $65 to $200; some

to $1,000. **Remarks:** Full-time maker. Doing business as Rocky Mountain Knives. **Mark:** Last name in script.

CONLEY, BOB, 1013 Creasy Rd., Jonesboro, TN, 37659/423-753-3302
Specialties: Working straight knives and folders. **Patterns:** Lockers, two-blades, gents, hunters, traditional styles, straight hunters. **Technical:** Grinds 440C, 154CM and ATS-34. Engraves. **Prices:** $250 to $450; some to $600. **Remarks:** Full-time maker; first knife sold in 1979. **Mark:** Full name, city, state.

CONN JR., C.T., 206 Highland Ave., Attalla, AL, 35954/205-538-7688
Specialties: Working folders, some fancy. **Patterns:** Full range of folding knives. **Technical:** Grinds O2, 440C and 154CM. **Prices:** $125 to $300; some to $600. **Remarks:** Part-time maker; first knife sold in 1982. **Mark:** Name.

CONNELL, STEVE, 217 VALLEY ST, ADAMSVILLE, AL, 35005-1852/205-674-0440

CONNOLLY, JAMES, 2486 Oro-Quincy Hwy., Oroville, CA, 95966/916-534-5363
Specialties: Classic working and using knives of his design. **Patterns:** Boots, Bowies and daggers. **Technical:** Grinds ATS-34; forges 5160; forges and grinds O1. **Prices:** $100 to $500; some to $1,500. **Remarks:** Full-time maker; first knife sold in 1980. Doing business as Gold Rush Designs. **Mark:** First initial, last name, Handmade.

CONNOR, MICHAEL, Box 502, Winters, TX, 79567/915-754-5602
Specialties: High-art straight knives and folders. **Patterns:** Hunters to camp knives to traditional locking folders. **Technical:** Forges 5160, O1 and his own Damascus. **Prices:** $275 to $3,000. **Remarks:** Part-time maker; first knife sold in 1974. **Mark:** Last name, M.S.

CONTI, JEFFREY D., 4629 Feigley Rd. W., Port Orchard, WA, 98366/206-405-0075
Specialties: Working straight knives. **Patterns:** Fighters and survival knives; hunters, camp knives and fishing knives. **Technical:** Grinds D2, 154CM and O1. Engraves. **Prices:** Start at $80. **Remarks:** Part-time maker; first knife sold in 1980. **Mark:** Initials, year, steel type, name and number of knife.

COOGAN, ROBERT, 1560 Craft Center Dr., Smithville, TN, 37166/615-597-6801
Specialties: One-of-a-kind knives. **Patterns:** Unique items like ooloo-style Appalachian herb knives. **Technical:** Forges; his Damascus is made from nickel steel and W1. **Prices:** Start at $100. **Remarks:** Part-time maker; first knife sold in 1979. **Mark:** Initials.

COOK, MIKE A., 10927 Shilton Rd., Portland, MI, 48875/517-647-2518
Specialties: Fancy/embellished and period pieces of his design. **Patterns:** Daggers, fighters and hunters. **Technical:** Stone bladed knives in agate, obsidian and jasper. Scrimshaws; opal inlays. **Prices:** $60 to $300; some to $800. **Remarks:** Part-time maker; first knife sold in 1988. Doing business as Art of Ishi. **Mark:** Initials and year.

COOK, LOUISE, 475 Robinson Ln., Ozark, IL, 62972/618-777-2932
Specialties: Working and using straight knives of her design and to customer specs; period pieces. **Patterns:** Bowies, hunters and utility/camp knives. **Technical:** Forges 5160. Filework; pin work; silver wire inlay. **Prices:** Start at $50/inch. **Remarks:** Part-time maker; first knife sold in 1990. Doing business as Panther Creek Forge. **Mark:** First name and journeyman stamp on one side; panther head on the other.

COOK, JAMES R., 3611 Hwy. 26 W., Nashville, AR, 71852/870 845 5173
Specialties: Working straight knives and folders of his design or to customer specs. **Patterns:** Bowies, hunters and camp knives. **Technical:** Forges 5160, O1 and Damascus from O1 and 1018. **Prices:** $195 to $5,500. **Remarks:** Part-time maker; first knife sold in 1986. **Mark:** First and middle initials, last name.

COOK, MIKE, 475 Robinson Ln, Ozark, IL, 62972/618-777-2932
Specialties: Traditional working and using straight knives of his design and to customer specs. **Patterns:** Bowies, hunters and utility/camp knives. **Technical:** Forges 5160. Filework; pin work. **Prices:** Start at $50/inch. **Remarks:** Spare-time maker; first knife sold in 1991. **Mark:** First initial, last name and journeyman stamp on one side; panther head on the other.

COOMBS JR., LAMONT, RFD #1, Box 1412, Bucksport, ME, 04416/207-469-3057
Specialties: Classic fancy and embellished straight knives; traditional working and using straight knives. Knives of his design and to customer specs. **Patterns:** Hunters, folders and utility/camp knives. **Technical:** Hollow- and flat-grinds ATS-34, 440C, A2, D2 and O1; grinds Damascus from other makers. **Prices:** With sheaths--$65 to $500; some to $1,500. **Remarks:** Part-time maker; first knife sold in 1988. **Mark:** Last name on banner, handmade underneath.

COON, RAYMOND C., 21135 SE Tillstrom Rd., Gresham, OR, 97080/503-658-2252
Specialties: Working straight knives in standard patterns. **Patterns:** Hunters, Bowies, boots and axes. **Technical:** Forges high carbon steel and Damascus; grinds stainless. **Prices:** Start at $100. **Remarks:** Part-time maker; first knife sold in 1995. **Mark:** First initial, last name.

COPELAND, GEORGE STEVE, 220 Pat Carr Lane, Alpine, TN, 38543/615-823-5214
Specialties: Traditional and fancy working straight knives and folders. **Patterns:** Friction folders, Congress two- and four-blade folders, button locks and one- and two-blade automatics. **Technical:** Stock removal of 440C, ATS-34 and A2; heat-treats. **Prices:** $180 to $950; some higher. **Remarks:** Full-time maker; first knife sold in 1979. Doing business as Alpine Mountain Knives. **Mark:** G.S. Copeland (HANDMADE); some with four-leaf clover stamp.

CORBIT, GERALD E., 1701 St. John Rd., Elizabethtown, KY, 42701/502-765-7728
Specialties: Fancy and working liner lock folders and automatic knives. **Patterns:** Automatics and liner lock folders. **Technical:** Grinds 440C, ATS-34 and commercial Damascus. Heat-treats; offers scrimshaw, engraving and filework on blades and liners. Finishes include polished, satin and bead blasted. **Prices:** $350 to $2,000. **Remarks:** Part-time makers; first knife sold in 1991. Doing business as Corbit Custom Knives. **Mark:** Last name in script, town and state.

CORBY, HAROLD, 218 Brandonwood Dr., Johnson City, TN, 37604/615-926-9781
Specialties: Large fighters and Bowies; self-protection knives; art knives. Along with art knives and combat knives, Corby now has a all new automatic MO.PB1, also sidelock MO LL-1 with titanium linners G-10 handles. **Patterns:** Sub-hilt fighters and hunters. **Technical:** Grinds 154CM, ATS-34 and 440C. **Prices:** $200 to $6,000. **Remarks:** Full-time maker; first knife sold in 1969. Doing business as Knives by Corby. **Mark:** Last name.

CORDOVA, JOSEPH G., P.O. Box 977, Peralta, NM, 87042/505-869-3912
Specialties: One-of-a-kind designs, some to customer specs. **Patterns:** Fighter called the 'Gladiator', hunters, boots and cutlery. **Technical:** Forges 1095, 5160; grinds ATS-34, 440C and 154CM. **Prices:** Moderate to upscale. **Remarks:** Full-time maker; first knife sold in 1953. **Mark:** Cordova made.

CORRADO, JIM, 2915 Cavitt Creek Rd., Glide, OR, 97443/503-496-3951
Specialties: High-tech, high-art folding knives. **Patterns:** Makes early European single and multi-blade designs. **Technical:** Forges mostly L6 and his own Damascus. Uses natural handle material; stag, pearl, ivory, and imitation tortoise shell. **Prices:** Start at $250. **Remarks:** Full-time maker; first knife sold in 1974. **Mark:** Name, date and state with shield logo.

CORWIN, DON, 9325 Avedon Dr., Saline, MI, 48176/734-429-0820
Specialties: Traditional-style knives to customer specs. **Patterns:** One- to five-blade folders, slip-joints, lockers and miniatures. **Technical:** Grinds 440C, ATS-34, 154CM and Damascus; makes own mokume. **Prices:** $200 to $600. **Remarks:** Part-time maker; first knife sold in 1987. **Mark:** Last name in arrowhead logo and year.

COSBY, E. BLANTON, 2954 Pierpont Ave., Columbus, GA, 31904/706-323-0327
Specialties: Traditional working and using straight knives and folders of his design or to customer specs. **Patterns:** Hunters, Bowies, boots and switchblades. **Technical:** Grinds 440C, 12C27, ATS-34 and commercial Damascus. **Prices:** $125 to $350; some to $700. **Remarks:** Full-time maker; first knife sold in 1988. **Mark:** Engraved initials and year.

custom knifemakers

COSGROVE, CHARLES G., 2112 Briarwood Dr., Amarillo, TX, 79124/806-352-0334
Specialties: Traditional fixed or locking blade working knives. **Patterns:** Hunters, Bowies and locking folders. **Technical:** Stock removal using 440C, ATS-34 and D2; heat-treats. Makes heavy, hand-stitched sheaths. **Prices:** $250 to $2,500. **Remarks:** Full-time maker; first knife sold in 1968. No longer accepting customer designs. **Mark:** First initial, last name, or full name over city and state.

COSTA, SCOTT, 409 Coventry Rd, Spicewood, TX, 78669/830-693-3431
Specialties: Working straight knives. **Patterns:** Hunters, skinners, axes, trophy sets, custom boxed steak sets, carving sets and bar sets. **Technical:** Grinds D2, ATS-34, 440 and Damascus. Heat-treats. **Prices:** $225 to $2,000. **Remarks:** Full-time maker; first knife sold in 1985. **Mark:** Initials connected.

COTTRILL, JAMES I., 1776 Ransburg Ave., Columbus, OH, 43223/614-274-0020
Specialties: Working straight knives of his design. **Patterns:** Caters to the boating and hunting crowd; cutlery. **Technical:** Grinds O1, D2 and 440C. Likes filework. **Prices:** $95 to $250; some to $500. **Remarks:** Full-time maker; first knife sold in 1977. **Mark:** Name, city, state, in oval logo.

COUGHLIN, MICHAEL M., 1690 S Fulton Way, #311, Denver, CO, 80231/303-283-0302
Specialties: Edged weapons, fighters, folders and special weapons. **Patterns:** Bowies, fighters, tomahawks, utility/camp knives, concealment knives, duty knives for police/fire rescue and swords. **Technical:** Grinds O1, D2, ATS-34 and Damascus. Offers filework. **Prices:** $300 to $750. **Remarks:** Part-time maker; first knife sold in 1985. **Mark:** Last name and model.

COURTNEY, ELDON, 2718 Bullinger, Wichita, KS, 67204/316-838-4053
Specialties: Working straight knives of his design. **Patterns:** Hunters, fighters and one of a kinds. **Technical:** Grinds and tempers L6, 440C and spring steel. **Prices:** $100 to $500; some to $1,500. **Remarks:** Full-time maker; first knife sold in 1977. **Mark:** Full name, city and state.

COURTOIS, BRYAN, 3 Lawn Avenue, Saco, ME, 04072/
Specialties: Working straight knives; prefers customer designs, no standard patterns. **Patterns:** Functional hunters; everyday knives. **Technical:** Grinds S7, O1, 440C or customer request. Hollow-grinds with a variety of finishes. Specializes in granite handles and custom skeleton knives. **Prices:** Start at $75. **Remarks:** Part-time maker; first knife sold in 1988. Doing business as Castle Knives. **Mark:** A rook chess piece machined into blade using electrical discharge process.

COUSINO, GEORGE, 7818 Norfolk, Onsted, MI, 49265/Phone: 517-467-4911
Specialties: Working straight knives. **Patterns:** Hunters, Bowies, buckskinners, folders and daggers. **Technical:** Grinds D2, 440C. **Prices:** $85 to $125; some to $600. **Remarks:** Part-time maker; first knife sold in 1981. **Mark:** Last name.

COVER, RAYMOND A., Rt. 1, Box 194, Mineral Point, MO, 63660/314-749-3783
Specialties: High-tech working straight knives and folders in standard patterns. **Patterns:** Bowies and boots; two-bladed folders. **Technical:** Grinds D2, 440C and 154CM. **Prices:** $135 to $250; some to $400. **Remarks:** Part-time maker; first knife sold in 1974. **Mark:** Name.

COWLES, DON, 1026 Lawndale Dr., Royal Oak, MI, 48067/248-541-4619
Specialties: Traditional and working/using straight knives of his design. **Patterns:** Hunters, kitchen knives and utility/camp knives. **Technical:** Grinds ATS-34, CPM440V, CPM 420V. Scrimshaws; pearl inlays in some handles. **Prices:** $150 to $600; some to $1,000. **Remarks:** Full-time maker; first knife sold in 1994. **Mark:** Full name with oak leaf.

COX, SAM, 1756 Love Springs Rd., Gaffney, SC, 29341/864-489-1892
Specialties: Classic high-art working straight knives of his design. Duck knives copyrighted. **Patterns:** Diverse. **Technical:** Grinds 440C, ATS-34 and Damascus. **Prices:** $200 to $1,400. **Remarks:** Full-time maker; first knife sold in 1983. **Mark:** Cox Call and name.

COX, COLIN J., 107 N. Oxford Dr., Raymore, MO, 64083/816-322-1977
Specialties: Working straight knives and folders of his design; period pieces. **Patterns:** Hunters, fighters and survival knives. Folders, two-blades, gents and hunters. **Technical:** Grinds D2, 440C, 154CM and ATS-34. **Prices:** $125 to $750; some to $4,000. **Remarks:** Full-time maker; first knife sold in 1981. **Mark:** Full name, city and state.

CRAFT, RICHARD C., 3045 Longwood Dr., Jackson, MS, 39212/601-373-4046
Specialties: Fancy working knives. **Patterns:** Offers chopping knife and block for kitchen, bird knives and steak knives with presentation case. **Technical:** Grinds O1, L6 and 440C. Cases made of cherry or mahogany. **Prices:** $275 and up. **Remarks:** Part-time maker; first knife sold in 1985. **Mark:** Last name.

CRAFT III, JOHN M., Lockett Springs Ranch, P.O. Box 682, Williams, AZ, 86046/602-635-2190
Specialties: High-art straight knives to customer specs; period pieces. **Patterns:** Daggers, swords and utility/camp knives. **Technical:** Forges his own Damascus; 440C and ATS-34 by stock removal. **Prices:** $95 to $450; some to $2,500. **Remarks:** Full-time maker; first knife sold in 1985. **Mark:** Runic "M" in pommel or near butt.

CRAIG, ROGER L., 3451 SW Burlingame A201, Topeka, KS, 66611/785-266-6902
Specialties: Working and camp knives, some fantasy; all his design. **Patterns:** Fighters, hunters and locking folders. **Technical:** Grinds 1095 and 5160. Most knives have file work. **Prices:** $50 to $250. **Remarks:** Part-time maker; first knife sold in 1991. Doing business as Craig Knives. **Mark:** Last name-Craig.

CRAIN, JACK W., PO Box 212, Granbury, TX, 76048/817-599-6414
Specialties: Fantasy and period knives; combat and survival knives. **Patterns:** One-of-a-kind art or fantasy daggers, swords and Bowies; survival knives. **Technical:** Forges Damascus; grinds stainless steel. Carves. **Prices:** $350 to $2,500; some to $20,000. **Remarks:** Full-time maker; first knife sold in 1969. Designer and maker of the knives seen in the films *Executive Decision, Demolition Man, Predator I* and *II, Commando, Die Hard I* and *II, Road House, Ford Fairlane* and *Action Jackson,* and television shows *War of the Worlds, Air Wolf, Kung Fu: The Legend Cont.* and *Tales of the Crypt.* **Mark:** Annual change of registered trademark--stylized crane.

CRAIN, FRANK, 1127 W. Dalke, Spokane, WA, 99205/509-325-1596

CRAWFORD, PAT, 205 N. Center, West Memphis, AR, 72301/501-735-4632
Specialties: High-tech working straight knives--self-defense and combat types--and folders. **Patterns:** Folding patent locks, interframes, fighters and boots. **Technical:** Grinds 440C, ATS-34, D2 and 154CM. **Prices:** $125 to $2,000. **Remarks:** Full-time maker; first knife sold in 1973. **Mark:** Last name.

CRAWLEY, BRUCE R., 16 Binbrook Dr., Croydon 3136, Victoria, AUSTRALIA/
Specialties: Folders. **Patterns:** Hunters, lockback folders and Bowies. **Technical:** Grinds 440C, ATS-34 and commercial Damascus. Offers filework and mirror polish. **Prices:** $160 to $3500. **Remarks:** Part-time maker; first knife sold in 1990. **Mark:** Initials.

CRENSHAW, AL, Rt. 1, Box 717, Eufaula, OK, 74432/918-452-2128
Specialties: Folders of his design and in standard patterns. **Patterns:** Hunters, locking folders, slip-joint folders, multi blade folders. **Technical:** Grinds 440C, D2 and ATS-34. Does filework on backsprings and blades; offers scrimshaw on some handles. **Prices:** $150 to $300; some higher. **Remarks:** Full-time maker; first knife sold in 1981. Doing business as A. Crenshaw Knives. **Mark:** First initial, last name, Lake Efaula, state stamped; first initial last name in rainbow; Lake Efaula across bottom with Okla. in middle.

CROCKFORD, JACK, 1859 Harts Mill Rd., Chamblee, GA, 30341/770-457-4680
Specialties: Lockback folders. **Patterns:** Hunters, fishing and camp knives, traditional folders. **Technical:** Grinds A2, D2, ATS-34 and 440C. Engraves and scrimshaws. **Prices:** Start at $175. **Remarks:** Part-time maker; first knife sold in 1975. **Mark:** Name.

CROSS, ROBERT, RMB 200B, Manilla Rd., Tamworth 2340, NSW, AUSTRALIA/067-618385

CROSS, JOHN M., Rt. 1, Box 351, Bryceville, FL, 32009/904-266-9092 **Specialties:** Traditional working and using straight knives of his design. **Patterns:** Hunters, Bowies, utility/camp knives. **Technical:** Forges his own Damascus, O1 and 1095. Prefers natural handle materials, especially buffalo bone. **Prices:** $150 to $350; some up to $750. **Remarks:** Full-time maker; first knife sold in 1985. **Mark:** A cross.

CROWDER, ROBERT, Box 1374, Thompson Falls, MT, 59873/406-827-4754 **Specialties:** Traditional working knives to customer specs. **Patterns:** Hunters, Bowies, fighters and fillets. **Technical:** Grinds ATS-34, 154CM, 440C, Vascowear and commercial Damascus. **Prices:** $160 to $250; some to $2,500. **Remarks:** Part-time maker; first knife sold in 1985. **Mark:** First initial, last name.

CROWELL, JAMES L., H.C. 74, Box 368, Mtn. View, AR, 72560/870-269-4215 **Specialties:** Fancy period pieces and working knives to customer specs. **Patterns:** Hunters to daggers, war hammers to tantos; locking folders and slip-joints. **Technical:** Forges W2, O1, 5160, 1095 and his own Damascus. **Prices:** $325 to $2,500; some to $6,000. **Remarks:** Part-time maker; first knife sold in 1980. Earned ABS Masterblade Smith in 1986. **Mark:** A shooting star.

CULPEPPER, JOHN, 2102 Spencer Ave., Monroe, LA, 71201/318-323-3636 **Specialties:** Working straight knives. **Patterns:** Hunters, Bowies and camp knives in heavy-duty patterns. **Technical:** Grinds O1, D2 and 440C; hollow-grinds. **Prices:** $75 to $200; some $300. **Remarks:** Part-time maker; first knife sold in 1970. Doing business as Pepper Knives. **Mark:** Pepper.

CULVER, STEVE, 6002 162nd St, Valley Falls, KS, 66088/785-945-6227 **Specialties:** Edged tools and weapons, collectable and functionsl. **Patterns:** Bowies, daggers, swords, hunters, folders and edged tools. **Technical:** Forges carbon steels and his own pattern welded steels. Fancy filework available. **Prices:** $200 to $500; some to $4,000. **Remarks:** Part-time maker; first knife sold in 1989. **Mark:** Last name, J.S.

CULVER, GLORIA, 6002 162ND, VALLEY FALLS, KS, 66088/785-945-6227 **Specialties:** Knives of my own design. **Patterns:** Campers, hunters. **Technical:** Forges 5160. **Prices:** $75 to $300. **Remarks:** Full-time; first knife sold 1998. **Mark:** GC over a heart.

CUMMING, R.J., American Embassy Tunis, U.S. Dept. of State, Washington, D.C., 20521-6360/Int'l. direct dial 216-1-741-314 **Specialties:** Custom designs. **Patterns:** Hunters, fighters, Bowies and one-of-a-kind straight knives. Diver's tool knife. **Technical:** Grinds D2, 440C and 154CM. **Prices:** $175 to $550; some to $2,000. **Remarks:** Part-time maker; first knife sold in 1978. **Mark:** Last name.

CUTCHIN, ROY D., 960 Hwy. 169 S., Seale, AL, 36875/334-855-3080 **Specialties:** Fancy and working folders of his design. **Patterns:** Locking folders. **Technical:** Grinds ATS-34 and commercial Damascus; uses anodized titanium. **Prices:** Start at $250. **Remarks:** Part-time maker. **Mark:** First initial, last name, city and state, number.

CUTE, THOMAS, State Rt. 90-7071, Cortland, NY, 13045/607-749-4055 **Specialties:** Working straight knives. **Patterns:** Hunters, Bowies and fighters. **Technical:** Grinds O1, 440C and ATS-34. **Prices:** $100 to $1,000. **Remarks:** Full-time maker; first knife sold in 1974. **Mark:** Full name.

d

D'ANDREA, JOHN, 77 Pinecrest Terrace, Wayne, NJ, 07470/973-839-4559 **Specialties:** Fancy working straight knives and folders with filework and distinctive leatherwork. **Patterns:** Hunters, fighters, daggers, folders and an occasional sword. **Technical:** Grinds ATS-34, 154CM, 440C and D2. **Prices:** $180 to $600; some to $1,000. **Remarks:** Part-time maker; first knife sold in 1986. **Mark:** First name, last initial imposed on samurai sword.

D'ANGELO, LAURENCE, 14703 NE 17th Ave., Vancouver, WA, 98686/360-573-0546 **Specialties:** Straight knives of his design. **Patterns:** Bowies, hunters and locking folders. **Technical:** Grinds D2, ATS-34 and 440C. Handmakes all sheaths. **Prices:** $100 to $200. **Remarks:** Full-time maker; first knife sold in 1987. **Mark:** Football logo--first and middle initials, last name, city, state, Maker.

DACONCEICAO, JOHN M., 138 Perryville Rd., Rehoboth, MA, 02769/508-252-9686 **Specialties:** One-of-a-kind straight knives of his design and to customer specs. **Patterns:** Boots, fighters and folders. **Technical:** Grinds O1, 1095 and commercial Damascus. All knives come with leather sheath; cross-draw and shoulder harnesses available. **Prices:** $90 to $200; some to $500. **Remarks:** Part-time maker; first knife sold in 1993. **Mark:** JMD Blades.

DAHL, CHRIS W., Rt. 4, Box 558, Lake Geneva, WI, 53147/414-248-2464 **Specialties:** Period pieces and high-art display knives. **Patterns:** Daggers, fighters and hunters. **Technical:** Grinds 440C and stainless steel Damascus. Works exclusively with gemstone handles on all daggers. **Prices:** $500 to $5,000; some to $10,000. **Remarks:** Full-time maker. **Mark:** Full name--maker.

DAILEY, G.E., 577 Lincoln St., Seekonk, MA, 02771/508-336-5088 **Specialties:** One-of-a-kind exotic designed edged weapons. **Patterns:** Folders, daggers and swords. **Technical:** Reforges and grinds Damascus; prefers hollow-grinding. Engraves, carves, offers filework and sets stones and uses exotic gems and gold. **Prices:** Start at $1100. **Remarks:** Full-time maker. First knife sold in 1982. **Mark:** Last name or stylized initialed logo.

DAKE, C.M., 19759 Chef Menteur Hwy., New Orleans, LA, 70129-9602/504-254-0357 **Specialties:** Fancy working folders. **Patterns:** Front-lock lockbacks, button-lock folders. **Technical:** Grinds ATS-34 and Damascus. **Prices:** $500 to $2500; some higher. **Remarks:** Full-time maker; first knife sold in 1988. Doing business as Bayou Custom Cutlery. **Mark:** Last name.

DAMLOVAC, SAVA, 10292 Bradbury Dr., Indianapolis, IN, 46231/317-839-4952 **Specialties:** Period pieces, Fantasy, Viking, Moran type all Damascus daggers. **Patterns:** Bowies, fighters, daggers, Persian style knives. **Technical:** Uses own Damascus, some stainless, mostly hand forges. **Prices:** $150 to $2,500; some higher. **Remarks:** Full-time maker; first knife sold in 1993. **Mark:** "Sava' stamped in Damascus or etched in stainless. **Other:** Specialty, Bill Moran all Damascus dagger sets, in Moran style wood case.

DANIEL, TRAVIS E., 4015 Brownsboro Rd., Winston-Salem, NC, 27106/336-759-0640 **Specialties:** Traditional working straight knives of his design or to customer specs. **Patterns:** Hunters, fighters and utility/camp knives. **Technical:** Forges and grinds ATS-34 and his own Damascus. **Prices:** $90 to $1,250; some to $2,000. **Remarks:** Full-time maker; first knife sold in 1976. **Mark:** Carolina Custom Knives.

DANIELS, ALEX, 1416 County Rd. 415, Town Creek, AL, 35672/205-685-0943 **Specialties:** Working and using straight knives and folders; period pieces, reproduction Bowies. **Patterns:** Mostly reproduction Bowies but offer full line of knives. **Technical:** Now also using BG-42 along with 440C and ATS-34. **Prices:** $200 to $2,500. **Remarks:** Full-time maker; first knife sold in 1963. **Mark:** First and middle initials, last name, city and state.

DARBY, JED, 7878 E. Co. Rd. 50 N., Greensburg, IN, 47240/812-663-2696 **Specialties:** Traditional working/using straight knives of his design and to customer specs. **Patterns:** Bowies, hunters and utility/camp knives. **Technical:** Grinds 440C, ATS-34 and Damascus. **Prices:** $70 to $550; some to $1,000. **Remarks:** Full-time maker; first knife sold in 1992. Doing business as Darby Knives. **Mark:** Last name and year.

DARBY, RICK, 4026 Shelbourne, Youngstown, OH, 44511/216-793-3805 **Specialties:** Working straight knives. **Patterns:** Boots, fighters and hunters with mirror finish. **Technical:** Grinds 440C and CPM440V. **Prices:**

custom knifemakers

$125 to $300. **Remarks:** Part-time maker; first knife sold in 1974. **Mark:** First and middle initials, last name.

DAVENPORT, JACK, 36842 W. Center Ave., Dade City, FL, 33525/352-521-4088
Specialties: Titanium linerlock, button-lock and release. **Patterns:** Boots and double-ground fighters. **Technical:** Grinds ATS-34, 12C27 SS and Damascus; liquid nitrogen quench; heat-treats. **Prices:** $250 to $5,000. **Remarks:** Full-time maker; first knife sold in 1986. **Mark:** Last name.

DAVIDSON, EDMUND, 3345 Virginia Ave, Goshen, VA, 24439/540-997-5651
Specialties: Working straight knives; many integral patterns and upgraded models. **Patterns:** Heavy-duty skinners and camp knives. **Technical:** Grinds A2, ATS-34, BG-42, S7, 440C, CPM-T-440V. **Prices:** $75 to $1,500. **Remarks:** Full-time maker; first knife sold in 1986. **Mark:** Name in deerhead or motorcycle logo.

DAVIS, VERNON M., 1006 Lewis St., Waco, TX, 76705/817-799-7671
Specialties: Presentation-grade straight knives. **Patterns:** Bowies, daggers, boots, fighers, hunters and utility knives. **Technical:** Hollow-grinds 440C, ATS-34 and D2. Grinds an aesthetic grind line near choil. **Prices:** $125 to $550; some to $5,000. **Remarks:** Part-time maker; first knife sold in 1980. **Mark:** Last name and city inside outline of state.

DAVIS, W.C., 19300 S. School Rd., Raymore, MO, 64083/816-331-4491
Specialties: Fancy working straight knives and folders. **Patterns:** Folding lockers and slip-joints; straight hunters, fighters and Bowies. **Technical:** Grinds 440C, A2, ATS-34. **Prices:** $100 to $300; some to $1,000. **Remarks:** Full-time maker; first knife sold in 1972. **Mark:** Name.

DAVIS, K.M. TWIG, P.O. Box 267, Monroe, WA, 98272/206-794-7274
Specialties: Fancy working straight knives. **Patterns:** Hunters, boots, fishing knives, Bowies and daggers. **Technical:** Grinds ATS-34, D2, 440C. **Prices:** $150 to $450; some to $600. **Remarks:** Part-time maker; first knife sold in 1979. **Mark:** Twig.

DAVIS, TERRY, Box 111, Sumpter, OR, 97877/541-894-2307
Specialties: Traditional and contemporary folders. **Patterns:** Multi-blade folders, whittlers and interframe multiblades; sunfish patterns. **Technical:** Flat-grinds ATS-34. **Prices:** $400 to $1,000; some higher. **Remarks:** Full-time maker; first knife sold in 1985. **Mark:** Name in logo.

DAVIS, STEVE, 3370 Chatsworth Way, Powder Springs, GA, 30073/770-427-5740
Specialties: Traditional fancy folders and automatics of his design and to customer specs. **Patterns:** Automatics, locking folders and slip-joint folders. **Technical:** Grinds ATS-34, 440C and Damascus. Offers filework; prefers hand-rubbed finishes and natural handle materials. Uses pearl, ivory, stag and exotic woods. **Prices:** $150 to $500; some to $1,200. **Remarks:** Part-time maker; first knife sold in 1988. Doing business as Custom Knives by Steve Davis. **Mark:** Name engraved on blade. Snapdragon engraved on blades of automatics.

DAVIS, JESSE W., 7398A Hwy. 3, Sarah, MS, 38665/601-382-7332
Specialties: Working straight knives and folders in standard patterns and to customer specs. **Patterns:** Tantos, Bowies, locking folders, hunters and miniatures. **Technical:** Grinds O1, A2, D2, 440C and commercial Damascus. **Prices:** $125 to $300. **Remarks:** Part-time maker; first knife sold in 1977. **Mark:** Name or initials.

DAVIS, BARRY L., 4262 U.S. 20, Castleton, NY, 12033/518-477-5036
Specialties: Collector-quality and Damascus interframe folders. **Patterns:** Traditional gentlemen's folders. **Technical:** Makes Damascus; uses only natural handle materials. **Prices:** $1,000 to $2,500; some to $6,000. **Remarks:** Part-time maker; first knife sold in 1980. **Mark:** Initials.

DAVIS, CHARLIE, P.O. Box 710806, Santee, CA, 92072/619-561-9445
Specialties: Fancy and embellished working straight knives of his design. **Patterns:** Hunters, camp and utility knives. **Technical:** Grinds high-carbon files. **Prices:** $20 to $185 - custom depends. **Remarks:** Full-time maker; first knife sold in 1980. **Mark:** ANZA U.S.A. Other: we now offer custom and a folder.

DAVIS, DIXIE, Rt. 3, Clinton, SC, 29325/803-833-4964
Specialties: Working straight knives; fantasy pieces. **Patterns:** Hunters, fighters and boots. **Technical:** Grinds 440C, 154CM and ATS-34 with mirror finish. **Prices:** $85 to $140; some to $200. **Remarks:** Part-time maker; first knife sold in 1981. **Mark:** First name.

DAVIS, DON, 8415 Coyote Run, Loveland, CO, 80537-9665/970-669-9016
Specialties: Working straight knives in standard patterns or to customer specs. **Patterns:** Hunters, utility knives, skinners and survival knives. **Technical:** Grinds 440C, ATS-34. **Prices:** $75 to $250. **Remarks:** Full-time maker; first knife sold in 1985. **Mark:** Signature, city and state.

DAVIS, GREG, PO Box 272, Fillmore, UT, 84631/435-896-7410

DAVIS, JOHN, 235 Lampe Road, Selah, WA, 98942/509-697-3845
Specialties: Working and using straight knives of his own design, to customer specs and in standard patterns. **Patterns:** Boots, hunters, kitchen and utility/camp knives. **Technical:** Grinds ATS-34, 440C and commercial Damascus; makes own Damascus and mosaic Damascus. Embellishes with stabilized wood, mokume and nickel-silver. **Prices:** Start at $150. **Remarks:** Part-time maker; first knife sold in 1996. **Mark:** Name city and state on Damascus stamp initials.

DAWKINS, DUDLEY L., 221 NW Broadmoor Ave., Topeka, KS, 66606-1254/
Specialties: Stylized old or "Dawkins Forged" with anvil in center. New Tang Stamps. **Patterns:** Straight knives. **Technical:** Mostly carbon steel; some Damascus-all knives forged. **Prices:** $125 and up. **Remarks:** All knives supplied with wood-lined sheaths. **Other:** ABS Member - sole authorship.

DAWSON, BARRY, 10A Town Plaza, Suite 303, Durango, CO, 81301/500-288-7584
Specialties: Samurai swords, combat knives, collector daggers, folding knives and hunting knives. **Patterns:** Offers over 60 different models. **Technical:** Grinds 440C; heat-treats. **Prices:** $75 to $1,500; some to $5,000. **Remarks:** Full-time maker; first knife sold in 1975. **Mark:** Last name, USA in print or last name in script.

DE VILLIERS, ANDRE & KIRSTEN, PO Box 11366, Dorpspruit, Pietermantzburg 3206, SOUTH AFRICA, /0325 7851213

DEAN, HARVEY J., Rt. 2, Box 137, Rockdale, TX, 76567/512-446-3111
Specialties: Collectible, functional knives. **Patterns:** Bowies, hunters, folders, daggers, swords, battle axes, camp and combat knives. **Technical:** Forges 1095, O1 and his Damascus. **Prices:** $195 to $4,000. **Remarks:** Full-time maker; first knife sold in 1981. **Mark:** Last name and MS.

DEARING, JOHN, 1569 Flucom Rd., DeSoto, MO, 63020/314-586-1772
Specialties: Traditional working and using straight knives of his design; period pieces and fancy/embellished straight knives. **Patterns:** Hunters, Bowies, fighters, skinners, utility/camp knives and buckskinner blades. **Technical:** Forges and grinds 5160, 154CM and his own Damascus. Prefers natural handle materials. **Prices:** $85 to $350. **Remarks:** Part-time maker; first knife sold in 1985. Doing business as Arc Mountain Forge. **Mark:** Initials stylized into a deer hoofprint.

DEBRAGA, JOSE C., 1519 Du Grand Bourg, Val Belair, Queb., CANADA, G3J 1K4/418-847-7855
Specialties: Art knives, fantasy pieces and working knives of his design or to customer specs. **Patterns:** Knives with sculptured or carved handles, from miniatures to full-size working knives. **Technical:** Grinds and hand-files 440C and ATS-34. A variety of steels and handle materials available. Offers lost wax casting. **Prices:** Start at $300. **Remarks:** Full-time maker; wax modeler, sculptor and knifemaker; first knife sold in 1984. **Mark:** Initials in stylized script and serial number.

DEES, JAY, Rt. 1, Box 17C, Collins, MS, 39428/601-765-1846
Specialties: Traditional working/using straight knives of his design and to customer specs. **Patterns:** Bowies, skinners, hatchets, hunters and utility/camp knives. **Technical:** Grinds ATS-34, 440C and CPM440V. **Prices:** $75 to $200; some to $500. **Remarks:** Spare-time maker; first knife sold in 1995. **Mark:** Full name, city and state.

DEFEO, ROBERT A., 403 Lost Trail Dr., Henderson, NV, 89014/702-434-3717
Specialties: Working straight knives and period pieces. **Patterns:** Hunters, fighters, daggers and Bowies. **Technical:** Grinds D2, 440C and ATS-34. **Prices:** $150 to $500; some higher. **Remarks:** Part-time maker; first knife sold in 1982. **Mark:** Last name.

DEFREEST, WILLIAM G., P.O. Box 573, Barnwell, SC, 29812/803-259-7883
Specialties: Working straight knives and folders. **Patterns:** Fighters, hunters and boots; locking folders and slip-joints. **Technical:** Grinds 440C, 154CM and ATS-34; clean lines and mirror finishes. **Prices:** $100 to $700. **Remarks:** Full-time maker; first knife sold in 1974. **Mark:** GORDON.

DEGRAEVE, RICHARD, 329 Valencia St., Sebastian, FL, 32958/407-589-9005
Specialties: Working straight knives of his design or to customer specs. **Patterns:** Hunters and skinners with or without gut hooks, fillets, fighters, folders, skeleton knives, mini and art knives. **Technical:** Forges and grinds 440C, ATS-34, O1, high carbon steels; scrimshaws; enjoys filework. **Prices:** $55 to $400. **Remarks:** Full-time maker; first knife sold in 1985. **Mark:** Rich

DEL RASO, PETER, 28 Mayfield Dr, Mt. Waverly, Victoria, 3149, AUSTRALIA, /613-9807 6771
Specialties: Fixed Blades, some folders, art knives. **Patterns:** Daggers, Bowies, tactical, boot, personal and working knives. **Technical:** Grinds ATS-34, commercial Damascus and any other type of steel on request. **Prices:** $100 to $1500. **Remarks:** part time maker, first show in 1993. **Mark:** Makers surname stamped.

DELL, WOLFGANG, Am Alten Berg 9, D-73277 Owen-Teck, GERMANY, /49-7021-81802
Specialties: Fancy high-art straight of his design and to customer specs. **Patterns:** Fighters, hunters, bowies and utility/camp knives. **Technical:** Grinds ATS-34, 440B and 440C. Offers high gloss finish and engraving. **Prices:** $500 to $1,000; some to $1,600. **Remarks:** Full-time maker; first knife sold in 1992. **Mark:** Hopi hand of peace.

DELLANA, 168 Riverbend Blvd, St Albans, WV, 25177/304-727-5512
Specialties: Collector grade fancy/embellished high art folders and art daggers. **Patterns:** Locking folders and art daggers. **Technical:** Forges her own Damascus and W-2. Engraves, does stone setting, filework, carving and gold/platinum fabrication. Prefers exotic, high karat golds, platinum, silver, gemstone and mother of pearl handle materials. **Price:** Upscale. **Remarks:** Sole authorship, full-time maker, first knife sold in 1994. **Mark:** First name. On folders: hand engraved on inside liner with DELLANA, knife # (consecutively), name of knife, date completed, karat gold. **Other:** Also does one high art collaboration a year with Van Barnett.

DELONG, DICK, 17561 E. Ohio Circle, Aurora, CO, 80017/303-745-2652
Specialties: Fancy working knives and fantasy pieces. **Patterns:** Hunters and small skinners. **Technical:** Grinds and files O1, D2, 440C and Damascus. Offers cocobolo and osage orange for handles. **Prices:** Start at $50. **Remarks:** Part-time maker. **Mark:** Last name; some unmarked.

DEMPSEY, GORDON S., P.O. Box 7497, N. Kenai, AK, 99635/907-776-8425
Specialties: Working straight knives. **Patterns:** Hunters. **Technical:** Forges O1, pattern welded Damascus and carbon steel. **Prices:** $80 to $250. **Remarks:** Part-time maker; first knife sold in 1974. **Mark:** Name.

DENNEHY, JOHN D., P.O. Box 431, 3926 Hayes, Wellington, CO, 80549/970-568-9055
Specialties: Leatherworkers' knives to presentation Bowies. **Patterns:** Bowies, fighters, hunters, utilities, throwers. **Technical:** Uses 440C and O1; heat treats. **Remarks:** Part-time maker; first knife sold in 1989. Doing business as John-D Custom Leatherworks and Handmade Knives. **Mark:** John-D and shamrock.

DENNEHY, DAN, P.O. Box 2F, Del Norte, CO, 81132/719-657-2545
Specialties: Working knives, fighting and military knives, throwing knives. **Patterns:** Full range of straight knives, tomahawks, buckle knives. **Technical:** Forges and grinds A2, O1 and D2. **Prices:** $200 to $500. **Remarks:** Full-time maker; first knife sold in 1942. **Mark:** First name and last initial, city, state and shamrock.

DENT, DOUGLAS M., 1208 Chestnut St., S. Charleston, WV, 25309/304-768-3308
Specialties: Straight and folding sportsman's knives. **Patterns:** Hunters, boots and Bowies, interframe folders. **Technical:** Forges and grinds D2, 440C, 154CM and plain tool steels. **Prices:** $70 to $300; exceptional knives to $800. **Remarks:** Part-time maker; first knife sold in 1969. **Mark:** Last name.

DERINGER, CHRISTOPH, 1559 St. Louis #4, Sherbrooke, Quebec, CANADA, J1H 4P7/819-565-4260
Specialties: Traditional working/using straight knives and folders of his design and to customer specs. **Patterns:** Boots, hunters, folders, art knives, kitchen knives and utility/camp knives. **Technical:** Forges 5160, O1 and Damascus. Offers a variety of filework. **Prices:** Start at $250. **Remarks:** Full-time maker; first knife sold in 1989. **Mark:** Last name stamped/engraved.

DERR, HERBERT, P.O. Box 972, Clendenin, WV, 25045/304-548-5755
Specialties: Damascus one of a kind knives, carbon steels also. **Patterns:** Birdseye, Ladderback, Mosaics. **Technical:** All styles functional as well as artisticly pleasing. **Prices:** $90 to $175 carbon, $175 to $600 Damascus. **Remarks:** All Damascus made by maker. **Mark:** H. Derr

DES JARDINS, DENNIS, P.O. Box 1103, Plains, MT, 59859/406-826-3981
Specialties: Classic working/using straight knives of his design and to customer specs. **Patterns:** Bowies, hunters and utility/camp knives. **Technical:** Forges 5160 and L6, 5160, 203E and 1095 Damascus; fancy file work on all knives. **Prices:** $100 to $500; some to $1,000. **Remarks:** Full-time maker; first knife was sold in 1985. **Mark:** Initials, city and state.

DETMER, PHILLIP, 14140 Bluff Rd., Breese, IL, 62230/618-526-4834
Specialties: Working knives. **Patterns:** Bowies, daggers and hunters. **Technical:** Grinds ATS-34 and D2. **Prices:** $60 to $400. **Remarks:** Part-time maker; first knife sold in 1977. **Mark:** Last name with dagger.

DEYONG, CLARENCE, 1448 Glen Haven Dr, Fort Collins, CO, 80526/970-266-0959
Specialties: Working and using straight knives of his design and to customer specs. **Patterns:** Hunters, fighters and boots. **Technical:** Grinds 440C, D2, ATS-34. **Prices:** $75 to $150; some to $400. **Remarks:** Part-time maker; first knife sold in 1981. **Mark:** Last name and serial number.

DI MARZO, RICHARD, 2357 Center Pl., Birmingham, AL, 35205/205-252-3331

DICKERSON, GAVIN, P.O. Box 7672, Petit 1512, SOUTH AFRICA, /+27 011-965-0988
Specialties: Straight knives of his design or to customer specs. **Patterns:** Hunters, skinners, fighters and Bowies. **Technical:** Hollow-grinds D2, 440C, ATS-34, 12C27 and Damascus upon request. Prefers natural handle materials; offers synthetic handle materials. **Prices:** $190 to $2,500. **Remarks:** Part-time maker; first knife sold in 1982. **Mark:** Name in full.

DICKISON, SCOTT S., P.O. Box 357, Narragansett, RI, 02882/401-847-5893
Specialties: Working and using straight knives and locking folders of his design and automatics. **Patterns:** Trout knives, fishing and hunting knives. **Technical:** Forges and grinds commercial Damascus and D2, O1. Uses natural handle materials. **Prices:** $400 to $750; some higher. **Remarks:** Part-time maker; first knife sold in 1989. **Mark:** Stylized initials.

DIETZ, HOWARD, 421 Range Rd., New Braunfels, TX, 78132/830-885-4662
Specialties: Lock back folders, working straight knives. **Patterns:** Folding hunters, high grade pocket knives. ATS-34, 440C, CPM 440V, D2 and stainless Damascus. **Prices:** $300 to $1,000. **Remarks:** Full-time gun & knife maker; first knife sold in 1995. **Mark:** Name, city, and state.

DIETZEL, BILL, P.O. Box 1613, Middleburg, FL, 32068/904-282-1091
Specialties: Forged straight knives and folders. **Patterns:** His interpretations. **Technical:** Forges his Damascus and other steels. **Prices:** Middle ranges. **Remarks:** Likes natural materials; uses titanium in folder liners. **Mark:** Name.

DIGANGI, JOSEPH M., Box 225, Santa Cruz, NM, 87567/505-753-6414
Specialties: Kitchen and table cutlery. **Patterns:** French chef's knives, carving sets, steak knife sets, some camp knives and hunters. Holds patents and trademarks for "System II" kitchen cutlery set. **Technical:** Grinds 440C; buys Damascus. **Prices:** $150 to $450; some to $1,000. **Remarks:** Full-time maker; first knife sold in 1983. **Mark:** Last name.

DILL, ROBERT, 1812 Van Buren, Loveland, CO, 80538/970-667-5144
Specialties: Fancy and working knives of his design. **Patterns:** Hunters, Bowies and fighters. **Technical:** Grinds 440C and D2. **Prices:** $100 to $800. **Remarks:** Full-time maker; first knife sold in 1984. **Mark:** Logo stamped into blade.

custom knifemakers

DILL, DAVE, 7404 NW 30th St., Bethany, OK, 73008/405-789-0750
Specialties: Folders of his design. **Patterns:** Various patterns. **Technical:** Hand-grinds 440C, ATS-34. Offers engraving and filework on all folders. **Prices:** Starting at $450. **Remarks:** Full-time maker; first knife sold in 1987. **Mark:** First initial, last name.

DILLON, EARL E., 8908 Stanwin Ave., Arleta, CA, 91331/
Specialties: Fancy straight knives and folders. **Patterns:** Contemporary interpretations. **Technical:** Grinds 440C and AEB. **Prices:** $250 to $350; some over $500. **Remarks:** Part-time maker; first knife sold in 1984. Collaborates with Chuck Stapel. **Mark:** STAPEL-DILLON.

DILLUVIO, FRANK J., 13611 Joyce Dr., Warren, MI, 48093/810-775-1216
Specialties: Traditional working straight knives, some high-tech. **Patterns:** Hunters, Bowies, fishing knives, sub-hilts, liner lock™ folders and miniatures. **Technical:** Grinds D2, 440C, CPM; works for precision fits--no solder. **Prices:** $95 to $450; some to $800. **Remarks:** Full-time maker; first knife sold in 1984. **Mark:** Name and state.

DINGMAN, SCOTT, 4298 Parkers Lake Rd., NE, Bemidji, MN, 56601/218-751-6908
Specialties: Fancy working knives of his design. **Patterns:** Hunters, daggers, boots and camp knives. **Technical:** Forges O1, L6 and wire Damascus. Provides lost wax casting and hard cast bronze. Prefers exotic woods and high mirror finishes. **Prices:** $150 to $225; some to $500. **Remarks:** Full-time maker; first knife sold in 1983. **Mark:** Last name.

DION, GREG, 3032 S. Jackson St., Oxnard, CA, 93033/805-483-1781
Specialties: Working straight knives, some fancy. Welcomes special orders. **Patterns:** Hunters, fighters, camp knives, Bowies and tantos. **Technical:** Grinds ATS-34, 154CM and 440C. **Prices:** $85 to $300; some to $600. **Remarks:** Part-time maker; first knife sold in 1985. **Mark:** Name.

DIPPOLD, A.W., 90 Damascus Ln., Perryville, MO, 63775/573-547-1119
Specialties: Fancy one-of-a-kind locking folders. **Patterns:** Locking folders. **Technical:** Forges and grinds mosaic and pattern welded Damascus. Offers filework on all folders. **Prices:** $500 to $2,500; some higher. **Remarks:** Full-time maker; first knife sold in 1980. **Mark:** Last name in logo inside of liner.

DIXON JR., IRA E., P.O. Box 2581, Ventura, CA, 93002-2581/805-659-5867
Specialties: Utilitarian straight knives of his design. **Patterns:** Camp, hunters, boot, fighters. **Technical:** Grinds ATS-34, 440C, D2, 5160. **Prices:** $150 to $400. **Remarks:** Part-time maker; first knife sold in 1993. **Mark:** First name, Handmade.

DOLAN, ROBERT L., 220--B Naalae Road, Kula, HI, 96790/808-878-6406
Specialties: Working straight knives in standard patterns, his designs or to customer specs. **Patterns:** Fixed blades and potter's tools, ceramic saws. **Technical:** Grinds O1, D2, 440C and ATS-34. Heat-treats and engraves. **Prices:** Start at $75. **Remarks:** Full-time tool and knifemaker; first knife sold in 1985. **Mark:** Last name, USA.

DOMINY, CHUCK, P.O. Box 593, Colleyville, TX, 76034/817-498-4527
Specialties: Titanium liner lock folders. **Patterns:** Hunters, utility/camp knives and liner lock folders. **Technical:** Grinds 440C and ATS-34. **Prices:** $250 to $3,000. **Remarks:** Full-time maker; first knife sold in 1976. **Mark:** Last name.

DONOVAN, PATRICK, 1770 Hudson Dr., San Jose, CA, 95124/408-267-9825
Specialties: Working straight knives and folders; period pieces. **Patterns:** Hunters, boots and daggers; lockers and slip-joints. **Technical:** Grinds 440C. Embellishes. **Prices:** $75 to $475; some to $1,200. **Remarks:** Full-time maker; first knife sold in 1980. **Mark:** First name.

DOOLITTLE, MIKE, 13 Denise Ct., Novato, CA, 94947/415-897-3246
Specialties: Working straight knives in standard patterns. **Patterns:** Hunters and fishing knives. **Technical:** Grinds 440C, 154CM and ATS-34. **Prices:** $125 to $200; some to $750. **Remarks:** Part-time maker; first knife sold in 1981. **Mark:** Name, city and state.

DOTSON, TRACY, 1280 Hwy. C-4A, Baker, FL, 32531/850-537-2407
Specialties: Folding fighters and small folders. **Patterns:** Liner lock and lockback folders. **Technical:** Hollow-grinds ATS-34 and commercial Damascus. **Prices:** Start at $250. **Remarks:** Part-time maker; first knife sold in 1995. **Mark:** Last name.

DOUGLAS, JOHN J., 506 Powell Rd, Lynch Station, VA, 24571/804-369-7196
Specialties: Fancy and traditional straight knives and folders of his design and to customer specs. **Patterns:** Locking folders, swords and sgian dubhs. **Technical:** Grinds 440C stainless, ATS-34 stainless and customer's choice. Offers newly designed non-pivot uni-lock folders. Prefers highly polished finish. **Prices:** $160 to $1,400. **Remarks:** Full-time maker; first knife sold in 1975. Doing business as Douglas Keltic. **Mark:** Stylized initial. Folders are numbered; customs are dated.

DOURSIN, GERARD, Chemin des Croutoules, F 84210, Pernes les Fontaines, FRANCE, /
Specialties: Period pieces. **Patterns:** Liner locks and daggers. **Technical:** Forges mosaic Damascus. **Prices:** $600 to $4,000. **Remarks:** First knife sold in 1983. **Mark:** First initial, last name and I stop the lion.

DOUSSOT, LAURENT, 6262 De La Roche, Montreal, Quebec, CANADA, H2H 1W9/516-270-6992
Specialties: Fancy and embellished folders and fantasy knives. **Patterns:** Fighters and locking folders. **Technical:** Grinds ATS-34 and commercial Damascus. Scale carvings on all knives; most bolsters are carved titanium. **Prices:** $350 to $3,000. **Remarks:** Part-time maker; first knife was sold in 1992. **Mark:** Stylized initials inside circle.

DOWELL, T.M., 139 NW St. Helen's Pl., Bend, OR, 97701/541-382-8924
Specialties: Integral construction in hunting knives and period pieces. Famous "Funny" folders. **Patterns:** Hunters to sword canes, Price-style daggers to axes. **Technical:** Grinds BG42, D2, 154CM and Vasco Wear. Grinds BG42, D2, and 154CM. Makes his own Damascus. **Prices:** $185 and up. **Remarks:** Full-time maker; first knife sold in 1967. **Mark:** Initials logo.

DOWNIE, JAMES T., 10076 Estate Dr, Port Franks, Ont., CANADA, NOM 2LO/519-243-2290
Specialties: Serviceable straight knives and folders; period pieces. **Patterns:** Hunters, Bowies, camp knives and miniatures. **Technical:** Grinds D2, 440C and ATS-34, Damasteel, stainless steel Damascus. **Prices:** $100 to $500; some higher. **Remarks:** Full-time maker, supplier; first knife sold in 1978. **Mark:** Signature of first and middle initials, last name. Other: Canadian supplier, free catalogue.

DOWNING, TOM, 129 S. Bank St., Cortland, OH, 44410/330-637-0623
Specialties: Working straight knives; period pieces. **Patterns:** Hunters, fighters and tantos. **Technical:** Grinds 440C, ATs-34 and CPM-T-440V. Prefers natural handle materials. **Prices:** $150 to $900, some to $1500. **Remarks:** Part-time maker; first knife sold in 1979. **Mark:** First and middle initials, last name.

DOWNING, LARRY, 12268 Hwy. 181N, Bremen, KY, 42325/270-525-3523
Specialties: Working straight knives and folders. **Patterns:** From mini-knives to daggers, folding lockers to interframes. **Technical:** Forges and grinds 154CM, ATS-34 and his own Damascus. **Prices:** $150 to $750; some higher. **Remarks:** Part-time maker; first knife sold in 1979. **Mark:** Name in arrowhead.

DOWNS, JAMES F., 35 Sunset Rd., Londonderry, OH, 45647/614-887-2099
Specialties: Working straight knives of his design or to customer specs. **Patterns:** Folders, bowies, boot, hunters, utility. **Technical:** Grinds 440C. Prefers stag, jigged bone, Micarta and stabilized woods. **Prices:** $75 to $1,200. **Remarks:** Part-time maker; first knife sold in 1981. Brochures $2.00. **Mark:** Last name.

DOZIER, BOB, P.O. Box 1941, Springdale, AR, 72765/501-756-0023
Specialties: Using knives (fixed blades and folders). **Patterns:** Some fine collector-grade knives. **Technical:** Uses D2. Prefers Micarta handle material. **Prices:** Using knives: $95 to $595. **Remarks:** Full-time maker; first knife sold in 1965. **Mark:** State, made, last name in a circle.

DRAPER, AUDRA, #10 Creek Dr, Riverton, WY, 82501/307-856-6807 **Specialties:** One of a kind straight and folders. **Patterns:** Design custom knives, using, Bowies, and mini's. **Technical:** Forge 52100 and Damascus; I heat-treat all my knives. **Prices:** Start at $60 for key chain knives; up to $3000 for art knives. **Remarks:** Full-time maker; first knife sold in 1995. **Mark:** Audra

DRAPER, MIKE, #10 Creek Drive, Riverton, WY, 82501/307-856-6807 **Specialties:** Handforged working straight knives. **Patterns:** Hunters, bowies and camp knives. **Technical:** Forges 52100 and Damascus. **Prices:** Starting at $150. **Remarks:** Part-time maker; first knife sold in 1996. **Mark:** Initials M.J.D. or Name, city and state.

DRISCOLL, MARK, 4115 Avoyer Pl., La Mesa, CA, 91941/619-670-0695 **Specialties:** High-art, period pieces and working/using knives of his design or to customer specs; some fancy. **Patterns:** Swords, Bowies, Fighters, daggers, hunters and primitive (mountain man type styles). **Technical:** Forges 52100, 5160, O1, L6, 1095, and maker his own Damascus and mokume; also does nultiple quench heat treating. Uses exotic hardwoods, ivory and horn, offers fancy file work, carving, scrimshaws. **Prices:** $150 to $550; some to $1,500. **Remarks:** Part-time maker; first knife sold in 1986. Doing business as Mountain Man Knives. **Mark:** Double "M".

DRISKILL, BERYL, P.O. Box 187, Braggadocio, MO, 63826/573-757-6262 **Specialties:** Fancy working knives. **Patterns:** Hunting knives, fighters, Bowies, boots, daggers and lockback folders. **Technical:** Grinds ATS-34. **Prices:** Start at $200. **Remarks:** Part-time maker; first knife sold in 1984. **Mark:** Name.

DROST, MICHAEL B., Rt. 2, Box 49, French Creek, WV, 26218/304-472-7901 **Specialties:** Working/using straight knives and folders of all designs. **Patterns:** Hunters, locking folders and utility/camp knives. **Technical:** Grinds ATS-34, D2 and CPM-T-440V. Offers dove-tailed bolsters and spacers, filework and scrimshaw. **Prices:** $125 to $400; some to $740. **Remarks:** Full-time maker; first knife sold in 1990. Doing business as Drost Custom Knives. **Mark:** Name, city and state.

DROST, JASON D., Rt. 2 Box 49, French Creek, WV, 26218/304-472-7901 **Specialties:** Working/using straight knives of his design. **Patterns:** Hunters and utility/camp knives. **Technical:** Grinds 154 CM and D2. **Prices:** $125 to $5,000. **Remarks:** Spare-time maker; first knife sold in 1995. **Mark:** First and middle initials, last name, maker, city and state.

DUBE, PAUL, P.O. Box 122, Chaska, MN, 55318/612-361-0930 **Specialties:** Traditional working and using straight knives, high-art knives and period pieces of his design and to customer specs. **Patterns:** Fighters, Bowies, daggers, utility knives. **Technical:** Forges A2, 1050, 1095, S5, ATS-34; stock removal O1, S7 and Vascowear. **Prices:** $80 to $1,500; some to $6,000. **Remarks:** Full-time maker; first knife sold in 1988. Doing business as Troll Hammer Forge. **Mark:** Varies.

DUBLIN, DENNIS, 708 Stanley St., Box 986, Enderby, BC, CANADA, V0E 1V0/604-838-6753 **Specialties:** Working straight knives and folders, plain or fancy. **Patterns:** Hunters and Bowies, locking hunters, combination knives/axes. **Technical:** Forges and grinds high carbon steels. **Prices:** $100 to $400; some higher. **Remarks:** Full-time maker; first knife sold in 1970. **Mark:** Name.

DUFF, BILL, P.O. Box 694, Virginia City, NV, 89440/702-847-0566 **Specialties:** Working straight knives and folders. **Patterns:** Hunters and Bowies; locking folders and interframes. **Technical:** Grinds D2, 440C and 154CM. **Prices:** $175 to $3,500. **Remarks:** Part-time maker; first knife sold in 1976. **Mark:** Name, city, state and date.

DUFOUR, ARTHUR J., 8120 De Armoun Rd., Anchorage, AK, 99516/907-345-1701 **Specialties:** Working straight knives from standard patterns. **Patterns:** Hunters, Bowies, camp and fishing knives--grinded thin and pointed. **Technical:** Grinds 440C, ATS-34, AEB-L. Tempers 57-58R; hollow-grinds. **Prices:** $135; some to $250. **Remarks:** Part-time maker; first knife sold in 1970. **Mark:** Prospector logo.

DUGGER, DAVE, 2504 West 51, Westwood, KS, 66205/913-831-2382 **Specialties:** Working straight knives; fantasy pieces. **Patterns:** Hunters, boots and daggers in one of a kind styles. **Technical:** Grinds D2, 440C and 154CM. **Prices:** $75 to $350; some to $1,200. **Remarks:** Part-time maker; first knife sold in 1979. Not currently accepting orders. Doing business as Dog Knives. **Mark:** DOG.

DUNGY, LAWRENCE, 8 Southmont Dr., Little Rock, AR, 72209/501-568-2769 **Specialties:** Working straight knives and folders. **Patterns:** Bowies, skinners, hunters, boots, bird and trout knives. **Technical:** Grinds stainless and plain steels. **Prices:** $65 to $800. **Remarks:** Part-time maker; first knife sold in 1983. **Mark:** Dungy Handcrafted.

DUNKERLEY, RICK, Box 111, Lincoln, MT, 59639/406-362-3097 **Specialties:** Mosaic damascus folders and carbon steel utility knives. **Patterns:** One of a kind folders, standard hunters and utility designs. **Technical:** Forges 52100, Damascus and mosaic Damascus. Prefers natural handle materials. **Prices:** $200 and up. **Remarks:** Full-time maker; first knife sold in 1984. Doing business as Dunkerley Custom Knives. **Mark:** Dunkerley, MS.

DUNN, CHARLES K., 17740 GA Hwy. 116, Shiloh, GA, 31826/706-846-2666 **Specialties:** Fancy and working straight knives and folders of his design and to customer specs. **Patterns:** Bowies, hunters and locking folders. **Technical:** Grinds 440C and ATS-34. Engraves; filework offered. **Prices:** $75 to $300. **Remarks:** Part-time maker; first knife sold in 1988. **Mark:** First initial, last name, city, state.

DUNN, STEVE, 376 Biggerstaff Rd., Smiths Grove, KY, 42171/270-563-9830 **Specialties:** Working and using straight knives of his design; period pieces. **Patterns:** Hunters, skinners, Bowies, fighters, camp knives, folders, swords and battle axes. **Technical:** Forges his Damascus, O1, 5160, L6 and 1095. **Prices:** Moderate to upscale. **Remarks:** Full-time maker; first knife sold in 1990. **Mark:** Last name and MS.

DUNN, MELVIN T., 5830 NW Carlson Rd., Rossville, KS, 66533/785-584-6856 **Specialties:** Traditional working straight knives and folders. **Patterns:** Locking folders, straight hunters, fishing and kitchen knives. **Technical:** D2, 440V, 420V & 440C. **Prices:** $60 to $500. **Remarks:** Full-time maker; first knife sold in 1972. **Mark:** Name in script with address & year of mfg.

DURAN, JERRY T., P.O. Box 80692, Albuquerque, NM, 87198-0692/505-873-4676 **Specialties:** Liner locks & other folders. **Patterns:** Folders, Bowies, Hunters & Tactical Knives. **Technical:** Forges ATS34 & BG42 and carbon steel; makes own Damascus. **Prices:** Moderate to upscale. **Remarks:** Full-time maker; first knife sold in 1986. **Mark:** Name and name and city

DURIO, FRED, 289 Gulino St., Opelousas, LA, 70570/318-948-4831 **Specialties:** Working straight knives and folders; period pieces. **Patterns:** Bowies, camp knives, small hunters, folders, fancy period pieces, miniatures. **Technical:** Forges and grinds W2, 5160, 1095 and O1. Makes own Damascus and forge-welds cable Damascus. Offers filework and tapered tangs; prefers exotic and natural materials. **Prices:** $100 to $350; some to $1,000. **Remarks:** Part-time maker; first knife sold in 1986. **Mark:** Last name and J.S.

DUVALL, FRED, 10715 Hwy. 190, Benton, AR, 72015/501-778-9360 **Specialties:** Working straight knives and folders. **Patterns:** Locking folders, slip joints, hunters, fighters and Bowies. **Technical:** Grinds D2 and CPM440V; forges 5160. **Prices:** $100 to $400; some to $800. **Remarks:** Part-time maker; first knife sold in 1973. **Mark:** Last name.

DUVALL, LARRY E., Rt. 3, Gallatin, MO, 64640/816-663-2742 **Specialties:** Fancy working straight knives and folders. **Patterns:** Hunters to swords, minis to Bowies; locking folders. **Technical:** Grinds D2, 440C and 154CM. **Prices:** $150 to $350; some to $2,000. **Remarks:** Part-time maker; first knife sold in 1980. **Mark:** Name and address in logo.

DYESS, EDDIE, 1005 Hamilton, Roswell, NM, 88201/505-623-5599 **Specialties:** Working and using straight knives in standard patterns. **Patterns:** Hunters and fighters. **Technical:** Grinds 440C, 154CM and D2 on request. **Prices:** $85 to $135; some to $250. **Remarks:** Spare-time maker; first knife sold in 1980. **Mark:** Last name.

DYRNOE, PER, Sydskraenten 10, Tulstrup, DK 3400 Hilleroed, DENMARK, /+45 42287041
Specialties: Hand-crafted knives with zirconia ceramic blades. **Patterns:** Hunters, skinners, Norwegian-style tollekniives, most in animal-like ergonomic shapes. **Technical:** Handles of exotic hardwood, horn, fossile ivory, etc. Norwegian-style sheaths. **Prices:** Start at $500. **Remarks:** Part-time maker in cooperation with Hans J. Henriksen; first knife sold in 1993. **Mark:** Initial logo.

e

EAKER, ALLEN L., 416 Clinton Ave., Dept KI, Paris, IL, 61944/217-466-5160
Specialties: Traditional straight knives and folders of his design. **Patterns:** Hunters, locking folders and slip-joint folders. **Technical:** Grinds 440C; inlays. **Prices:** $125 to $325; some to $500. **Remarks:** Spare-time maker; first knife sold in 1994. **Mark:** Initials in tankard logo stamped on tang, serial number on back side.

EASLER, PAULA, P.O. Box 301-1025, Cross Anchor Rd., Woodruff, SC, 29388/864-476-7830
Specialties: Traditional fancy and embellished straight knives of her design. **Patterns:** Miniatures only--hunters, fighters, tantos, razors and mini-replicas. **Technical:** Grinds ATS-34, commercial Damascus. Stainless steel pins and bolsters. Heat-treats blades, many have file-worked tapered tangs; hand-rubbed satin finish standard; natural handle materials and gems. **Prices:** $85 to $400; some to $1,000. **Remarks:** Spare-time maker; first knife sold in 1989. **Mark:** First initial, last name in block letters.

EASLER JR., RUSSELL O., P.O. Box 301, Woodruff, SC, 29388/864-476-7830
Specialties: Working straight knives and folders. **Patterns:** Hunters, tantos and boots; locking folders and interframes. **Technical:** Grinds 440C, 154CM and ATS-34. **Prices:** $85 to $250; some to $600. **Remarks:** Part-time maker; first knife sold in 1973. **Mark:** Name or name with bear logo.

EATON, RICK, 9944 McCranie St, Shepherd, MT, 59079 3126/
Specialties: Interframe folders and one hand opening sidelocks. **Patterns:** Bowies, daggers, fighters and folders. **Technical:** Grinds 154CM, ATS-34, 440C and other maker's Damascus. Offers high-quality hand engraving, Bulino and gold inlay. **Prices:** Upscale. **Remarks:** Full-time maker; first knife sold in 1982. **Mark:** Full name or full name and address.

EATON, AL, P.O. Box 43, Clayton, CA, 94517/925-672-5351
Specialties: One-of-a-kind high-art knives and fantasy knives of his design, full size and miniature. **Patterns:** Hunters, fighters, daggers. **Technical:** Grinds 440C, 154CM and ATS-34; ivory and metal carving. **Prices:** $125 to $3,000; some to $5,000. **Remarks:** Full-time maker; first knife sold in 1977. **Mark:** Full name, city and state.

ECK, LARRY A., P.O. Box 665, Terrebonne, OR, 97760/503-548-7599
Specialties: Traditional working and using straight knives of his design, to customer specs and in standard patterns. **Patterns:** Boots, Bowies, fighters, hunters, fillets and tantos. **Technical:** Grinds ATS-34, D2, 440C and commercial Damascus. Prefers natural handle materials. Offers mirror and hand-rubbed finishes. **Prices:** $175 to $400; some to $750. **Remarks:** Part-time maker; first knife sold in 1991. **Mark:** First and middle initials, last name and state in logo.

ECKERSON, CHARLEY, 1117 Horseshoe Dr., Pueblo, CO, 81001/719-542-1734
Specialties: Traditional working/using straight knives. **Patterns:** Hunters, skinners, fishing, Bowies, military and SWAT. **Technical:** Grinds ATS-34, 440C, 440V, and A2. Likes Micarta, stag and woods. **Prices:** $160 to $400; and up. **Remarks:** Part-time maker; first knife sold in 1984. **Mark:** Stamped last name.

EDGE, TOMMY, P.O. Box 156, Cash, AR, 72421/501-477-5210
Specialties: Fancy/embellished working knives of his design. **Patterns:** Bowies, hunters and utility/camping knives. **Technical:** Grinds 440C, ATS-34 and D2. Makes own cable Damascus; offers filework. **Prices:** $70 to $250; some to $1,500. **Remarks:** Part-time maker; first knife sold in 1993. **Mark:** Stamped first initial, last name and stenciled name, city and state in oval shape.

EDWARDS, LYNN, Rt. 2, Box 614, W. Columbia, TX, 77486/409-345-4080
Specialties: Traditional working and using straight knives of his design and to customer specs. **Patterns:** Bowies, hunters and utility/camp knives. **Technical:** Forges 5168 and O1; forges and grinds D2. Triple-hardens on request; offers silver wire inlay, stone inlays and spacers, filework. **Prices:** $100 to $395; some to $800. **Remarks:** Part-time maker; first knife sold in 1988. Doing business as E&E Emporium. **Mark:** Last name in script.

EDWARDS, FAIN E., P.O. Box 280, Topton, NC, 28781/828-321-3127

EK, GARY WHITNEY, 1580 NE 125th St., North Miami, FL, 33161/305-891-2283
Specialties: Working straight knives of his design and to customer specs; period pieces. **Patterns:** Bowies, fighters and special-effect knives and swords. **Technical:** Grinds D2, Sandvik 13C26; forges and grinds 43-40 Ni Crm Moly. Offers custom refinishing and sharpening. **Prices:** $150 to $450; some to $1,200. **Remarks:** Full-time maker; first knife sold in 1971. **Mark:** Name or EKNIVES, city.

EKLUND, MAIHKEL, Föne 1155, S-82041 Frila, SWEDEN, /1111 82041 Farila
Specialties: Collector-grade working straight knives. **Patterns:** Hunters, Bowies and fighters. **Technical:** Grinds ATS-34, Uddeholm and Dama steel. Engraves and scrimshaws. **Prices:** $150 to $700. **Remarks:** Full-time maker; first knife sold in 1983. **Mark:** Initials or name.

ELDRIDGE, ALLAN, 7731 Four Winds Dr, Ft Worth, TX, 76133/817-370-7778
Specialties: Fancy classic straight knives in standard patterns. **Patterns:** Hunters, Bowies, fighters, folders and miniatures. **Technical:** Grinds O1 and Damascus. Engraves silver-wire inlays, pearl inlays, scrimshaws and offers filework. **Prices:** $50 to $500; some to $1,200. **Remarks:** Spare-time maker; first knife sold in 1965. **Mark:** Initials.

ELISHEWITZ, ALLEN, 17194 Preston Rd., Suite 123, #227, Dallas, TX, 75248-1203/972-380-4304
Specialties: Collectible high-tech working straight knives and folders of his design. **Patterns:** Fighters, combat knives and utility/camp knives. **Technical:** Grinds ATS-34, D2, A2 and Vascowear. All designs drafted and field-tested. **Prices:** $400 to $600. **Remarks:** Full-time maker; first knife sold in 1989. **Mark:** Last name with a Japanese crane.

ELKINS, R. VAN, P.O. Box 156, Bonita, LA, 71223/318-823-2124
Specialties: High-art Bowies, fighters, folders and period daggers; all one-of-a-kind pieces. **Patterns:** Welcomes customer designs. **Technical:** Forges his own Damascus in several patterns, O1 and 5160. **Prices:** $250 to $2,800. **Remarks:** First knife sold in 1984. **Mark:** Last name.

ELLEFSON, JOEL, P.O. Box 1016, 310 S. 1st St., Manhattan, MT, 59741/406-284-3111
Specialties: Working straight knives, fancy daggers and one-of-a-kinds. **Patterns:** Hunters, daggers and some folders. **Technical:** Grinds A2, 440C and ATS-34. Makes own mokume in bronze, brass, silver and shibuishi; makes brass/steel blades. **Prices:** $75 to $500; some to $2,000. **Remarks:** Part-time maker; first knife sold in 1978. **Mark:** Stylized last initial.

ELLERBE, W.B., 3871 Osceola Rd., Geneva, FL, 32732/407-349-5818
Specialties: Period and primitive knives and sheaths. **Patterns:** Bowies to patch knives, some tomahawks. **Technical:** Grinds Sheffield O1 and files. **Prices:** Start at $35. **Remarks:** Full-time maker; first knife sold in 1971. Doing business as Cypress Bend Custom Knives. **Mark:** Last name or initials.

ELLIOTT, MARCUS, Pen Dinas, Wyddfydd Rd., Great Orme, Llandudno Gwynedd, GREAT BRITAIN, LL30 2QL/01492-872747
Specialties: Fancy working knives. **Patterns:** Boots and small hunters. **Technical:** Grinds O1, 440C and ATS-34. **Prices:** $160 to $250. **Remarks:** Spare-time maker; first knife sold in 1981. Makes only a few knives each year. **Mark:** Last name.

ELLIOTT, J.P., 4507 Kanawha Ave., Charleston, WV, 25304/304-925-5045
Specialties: Classic and traditional straight knives and folders of his design and to customer specs. **Patterns:** Hunters, locking folders and Bowies. **Technical:** Grinds ATS-34, 154CM, O1, D2 and T-440-V. All guards silver-soldered; bolsters are pinned on straight knives, spot-welded on folders. **Prices:** $80 to $265; some to $1,000. **Remarks:** Full-

time maker; first knife sold in 1972. **Mark:** First and middle initials, last name, knifemaker, city, state.

ELLIS, WILLIAM DEAN, 8875 N. Barton, Fresno, CA, 93720/209-299-0303
Specialties: Classic and fancy knives of his design. **Patterns:** Boots, fighters and utility knives. **Technical:** Grinds ATS-34, D2 and Damascus. Offers tapered tangs and six patterns of filework; tooled multi-colored sheaths. **Prices:** $180 to $350; some to $1,300. **Remarks:** Part-time maker; first knife sold in 1991. Doing business as Billy's Blades. **Mark:** "B" in a five-point star next to "Billy," city and state within a rounded-corner rectangle.

ELLIS, DAVID, 3505 Camino Del Rio S., #334, San Diego, CA, 92108/619-285-1305 days
Specialties: Fighters and Bowies. **Patterns:** Utility knives. **Technical:** Forges and grinds 5160, O1, 1095; now working with pattern-welded Damascus. Most knives have hand-rubbed finish and single and double temper lines. Most knives are double or triple hardened and triple drawn. Prefers natural handle materials. **Prices:** $300 to $2,000; some to $5,000. **Remarks:** Part-time maker; first knife sold in 1988. **Mark:** Last name with dagger and rose below & M.S. mark.

EMBRETSEN, KAJ, FALUVAGEN 67, S-82821 Edsbyn, SWEDEN, /46-271-21057
Specialties: High quality folders. **Patterns:** Scandinavian style knives. **Technical:** Forges Damascus. Uses only his blades; natural materials. **Prices:** Upscale. **Remarks:** Full-time maker. **Mark:** Name.

EMBRY, BRAD, 4802 Bruton Road, Plant City, FL, 33565/813-752-8143
Specialties: High-tech and high-art folders and automatics. **Patterns:** Bowies and locking folders. **Technical:** Grinds ATS-34, 440C and Sanvik 12C27; integral frame inlays. **Prices:** $300 to $750; some to $1,000. **Remarks:** Full-time maker; first knife sold in 1974. Doing business as Embry Custom Knives.

EMERSON, ERNEST R., PO Box 4325, Redondo Beach, CA, 90278-8525/310-542-3050
Specialties: High-tech folders and combat fighters. **Patterns:** Fighters, linerlock combat folders and SPECWAR combat knives. **Technical:** Grinds ATS-34 and D2. Makes folders with titanium fittings, liners and locks. Chisel grind specialist. **Prices:** $275 to $475; some to $3,000. **Remarks:** Full-time maker; first knife sold in 1983. **Mark:** Last name and Specwar knives.

ENCE, JIM, 145 S. 200 East, Richfield, UT, 84701/801-896-6206
Specialties: High-art period pieces. **Patterns:** Daggers, art folders, fancy boot knives, fighters, Bowies and occasional hunters. **Technical:** Grinds 440C; makes his own and buys Damascus. **Prices:** $300 to $5,000; some higher. **Remarks:** Full-time maker; first knife sold in 1977. **Mark:** Name, city, state.

ENDERS, ROBERT, 3028 White Rd., Cement City, MI, 49233/517-529-9667
Specialties: Pocketknives and working straight knives. **Patterns:** Traditional folders with natural materials. **Technical:** Grinds D2, O1, 440C and ATS-34. **Prices:** $200 to $3,000. **Remarks:** Full-time maker; first knife sold in 1981. **Mark:** Name in state map logo.

ENEBOE, JAMES, 2860 Rosendale Rd., Schenectady, NY, 12309/518-370-0101
Specialties: Fantasy high-art straight knives, folders and automatics of his design. **Patterns:** Daggers and locking folders. **Technical:** Forges high-carbon steel; grinds W2-203E pattern welded, 52100 and 203E. Offers filework, stone inlays and sterling silver handle material. **Prices:** $1,000 to $5,000. **Remarks:** Full-time maker. **Mark:** Last name.

ENGLAND, VIRGIL, 629 W. 15th Ave., Anchorage, AK, 99501/907-274-9494
Specialties: Edged weapons and equipage, one of a kind only. **Patterns:** Axes, swords, lances and body armor. **Technical:** Forges and grinds as pieces dictate. Offers stainless and Damascus. **Prices:** Upscale. **Remarks:** A veteran knifemaker. No commissions. **Mark:** Stylized initials.

ENGLE, WILLIAM, 16608 Oak Ridge Rd., Boonville, MO, 65233/816-882-6277
Specialties: Traditional working and using straight knives of his design. **Patterns:** Hunters, Bowies and fighters. **Technical:** Grinds 440C, ATS-34 and 154 CM. **Prices:** $250 to $500; some higher. **Remarks:** Part-time

maker; first knife sold in 1982. All knives come with certificate of authenticity. **Mark:** Last name in block lettering.

ENGLEBRETSON, GEORGE, 1209 NW 49th St., Oklahoma City, OK, 73118/405-840-4784
Specialties: Working straight knives. **Patterns:** Hunters and Bowies. **Technical:** Grinds A2, D2, 440C and ATS-34. **Prices:** Start at $150. **Remarks:** Full-time maker; first knife sold in 1967. **Mark:** "By George," name and city.

ENGLISH, JIM, 14586 Olive Vista Dr., Jamul, CA, 91935/619-669-0833
Specialties: Traditional working straight knives to customer specs. **Patterns:** Hunters, Bowies, fighters, tantos, daggers, boot and utility/camp knives. **Technical:** Grinds 440C, ATS-34, commercial Damascus and customer choice. **Prices:** $130 to $350. **Remarks:** Part-time maker; first knife sold in 1985. In addition to custom line, also does business as Mountain Home Knives. **Mark:** Double "A," Double "J" logo.

ENOS III, THOMAS M., 12302 State Rd. 535, Orlando, FL, 32836/407-239-6205
Specialties: Heavy-duty working straight knives to customer specs; unusual designs. **Patterns:** Machetes, saltwater sport knives, carvers. **Technical:** Grinds 440C, D2, 154CM. **Prices:** $75 to $1,000. **Remarks:** Full-time maker; first knife sold in 1972. **Mark:** Name in knife logo and date, type of steel and serial number.

ERICKSON, CURT, 449 Washington Blvd., Ogden, UT, 84404/801-782-1184
Specialties: Daggers and large knives of integral construction. **Patterns:** Period pieces; Bowies and hunting knives. **Technical:** Grinds 440C and commercial Damascus steel; sculpts and carves components. **Prices:** $240 to $1,500; some to $3,000. **Remarks:** Full-time maker; first knife sold in 1982. **Mark:** Name, state.

ERICKSON, L.M., P.O. Box 132, Liberty, UT, 84310/801-745-2026
Specialties: Straight knives; period pieces. **Patterns:** Bowies, fighters, boots and hunters. **Technical:** Grinds 440C, 154CM and commercial Damascus. **Prices:** $200 to $900; some to $5,000. **Remarks:** Part-time maker; first knife sold in 1981. **Mark:** Name, city, state.

ERICKSON, WALTER E., 23883 Ada St., Warren, MI, 48091/313-759-1105
Specialties: Unusual survival knives and high-tech working knives. **Patterns:** Butterflies, hunters, tantos. **Technical:** Grinds ATS-34 or customer choice. **Prices:** $150 to $500; some to $1,500. **Remarks:** Full-time maker; first knife sold in 1981. **Mark:** ERIC or last name.

ERIKSEN, JAMES THORLIEF, dba Viking Knives, 3830 Dividend Dr, Garland, TX, 75042/972-494-3667
Specialties: Heavy-duty working and using straight knives and folders utilizing traditional, Viking original and customer specification patterns. Some high-tech and fancy/embellished knives available. **Patterns:** Bowies, hunters, skinners, boot and belt knives, utility/camp knives, fighters, daggers, locking folders, slip-joint folders and kitchen knives. **Technical:** Hollow-grinds 440C, D2, ASP-23, ATS-34, 154CM, Vascowear. **Prices:** $150 to $300; some to $600. **Remarks:** Full-time maker; first knife sold in 1985. Doing business as Viking Knives. For a color catalog showing 50 different models, mail $5 to above address. **Mark:** VIKING or VIKING USA for export.

ESSEGIAN, RICHARD, 7387 E. Tulare St., Fresno, CA, 93727/309-255-5950
Specialties: Fancy working knives of his design; art knives. **Patterns:** Bowies and some small hunters. **Technical:** Grinds A2, D2, 440C and 154CM. Engraves and inlays. **Prices:** Start at $600. **Remarks:** Part-time maker; first knife sold in 1986. **Mark:** Last name, city and state.

ETZLER, JOHN, 11200 N. Island, Grafton, OH, 44044/216-748-2460
Specialties: High-art and fantasy straight knives and folders of his design and to customer specs. **Patterns:** Folders, Daggers, fighters, utility knives. **Technical:** Forges and grinds nickel Damascus and tool steel; grinds stainless steels. Prefers exotic, natural materials. **Prices:** $250 to $1200; some to $6,500. **Remarks:** Full-time maker; first knife sold in 1992. **Mark:** Name or initials.

EVANS, VINCENT K. & GRACE, 6301 Apache Trail, Show Low, AZ, 85901/520-537-9123
Specialties: Working straight knives; period pieces; swords. **Patterns:** Scottish and central Asian patterns; bowies, hunters, folders. **Technical:** Forges 5160 and his own Damascus. **Prices:** $100 to $600; some to

custom knifemakers

$3,000. **Remarks:** Full-time maker; first knife sold in 1983. **Mark:** Last initial with fish logo.

EWING, JOHN H., 3276 Dutch Valley Rd., Clinton, TN, 37716/615-457-5757
Specialties: Working straight knives, hunters, camp knives. **Patterns:** Hunters. **Technical:** Grinds 440, Forges 5160 52100; prefers forging. **Prices:** $150 to $2,000. **Remarks:** Part-time maker; first knife sold in 1985. **Mark:** First initial, last name, some embellishing done on knives.

f

FANNIN, DAVID A., 2050 Idle Hour Center, #191, Lexington, KY, 40502/
Specialties: High-tech classic straight knives; period pieces; traditional working knives. **Patterns:** Hunters, fighters and swords. **Technical:** Draws wire from Damascus billets for wire Damascus. High-density, migrationless and hand-smelted Sagami school Damascus steel. Offers Hamon tempering; makes mokume. **Prices:** $200 to $1,200. **Remarks:** Full-time maker; first knife sold in 1985. Doing business as Athens Forge. **Mark:** None.

FARID, 8 SIDNEY CLOSE, Tunbridge Wells, Kent, ENGLAND, TN2 5QQ/01892-520345
Specialties: High-tech fighters and folders. **Patterns:** Fighters and integral locking folders. **Technical:** Grinds 440C, CPM-T-440V and tool steel D7. **Prices:** $275 to $1,200; some to $5,000. **Remarks:** Full-time maker; first knife sold in 1991. Accepts orders on Alpha-Beta alloy titanium integral locking folders only. **Mark:** First name and country.

FARR, DAN, 285 Glen Ellyn Way, Rochester, NY, 14618/

FARRIS, CAL, Box 41, Altoona, FL, 32702/904-669-9427
Specialties: Embellished working and using straight knives of his design. **Patterns:** Bowies, hunters and utility-camp knives. **Technical:** Grinds 440C and ATS-34; forges his own Damascus. Inlays with natural materials; uses sterling silver. Offers filework and heavy spacer work. **Prices:** $175 to $600; some to $1,000. **Remarks:** Full-time maker; first knife sold in 1976. **Mark:** Last name.

FASSIO, MELVIN G., 4585 Twin Cr. Rd., Bonner, MT, 59823/406-244-5208
Specialties: Working folders to customer specs. **Patterns:** Locking folders, hunters and traditional-style knives. **Technical:** Grinds 440C. **Prices:** $100 to $250. **Remarks:** Part-time maker; first knife sold in 1975. **Mark:** Name and city, dove logo.

FAUCHEAUX, HOWARD J., P.O. Box 206, Loreauville, LA, 70552/318-229-6467
Specialties: Working straight knives and folders; period pieces. Also a hatchet with caping knife in the handle. **Patterns:** Traditional locking folders, hunters, fighters and Bowies. **Technical:** Forges W2, 1095 and his own Damascus; stock removal D2. **Prices:** Start at $200. **Remarks:** Full-time maker; first knife sold in 1969. **Mark:** Last name.

FAUST, DICK, 624 Kings Hwy N, Rochester, NY, 14617/716-544-1948
Specialties: High performance working straight knives. **Patterns:** Hunters and utility/camp knives. **Technical:** Hollow grinds ATS-34, full tang. Exotic woods, stag and Micarta handles. Provides a custom leather sheath with each knife. **Prices:** From $100 to $500, some higher. **Remarks:** Full-time maker. **Mark:** Signature.

FAUST, JOACHIM, Kirchgasse 10, 95497 Goldkronach, GERMANY, /

FECAS, STEPHEN J., 1312 Shadow Lane, Anderson, SC, 29625/803-287-4834
Specialties: Working straight knives in standard patterns; some period pieces. **Patterns:** Hunters to claws, folding slip-joints to buckskinners. **Technical:** Grinds D2, 440C and 154CM; most knives hand-finished to 600 grit. **Prices:** $140 to $400; some to $750. **Remarks:** Part-time maker; first knife sold in 1977. **Mark:** Last name.

FERDINAND, DON, P.O. Box 1564, Shady Cove, OR, 97539-1564/503-560-3355
Specialties: One-of-a-kind working knives and period pieces; all tool steel Damascus. **Patterns:** Bowies, push knives and fishing knives. **Technical:** Forges high-carbon alloy steels L6, D2; makes his own Damascus. Exotic handle materials offered. **Prices:** $100 to $500. **Remarks:** Full-time maker since 1980. Does business as Wyvern. **Mark:** Initials connected.

FERGUSON, JIM, P.O. Box 764, San Angelo, TX, 76902/915-651-6656
Specialties: Straight working knives and folders. **Patterns:** Working belt knives, hunters, Bowies and some folders. **Technical:** Grinds ATS-34, D2 and Vascowear. Flat-grinds hunting knives. **Prices:** $200 to $600; some to $1,000. **Remarks:** Full-time maker; first knife sold in 1987. **Mark:** First and middle initials, last name.

FERGUSON, JIM, 32131 Via Bande, Temecula, CA, 92592/909-302-0267
Specialties: Nickel Damascus - Bowies - Daggers - Push Blades. **Patterns:** All styles. **Technical:** Forges Damascus & sells in US and Canada. **Prices:** $120 to $5,000. **Remarks:** 1200 Sq. Ft. commercial shop - 75 ton press. **Mark:** Jim Ferguson over push blade. Also make swords, battle axes & utilities.

FERGUSON, LEE, Rt. 2, Box 109, Hindsville, AR, 72738/501-443-0084
Specialties: Straight working knives and folders, some fancy. **Patterns:** Hunters, daggers, swords, locking folders and slip-joints. **Technical:** Grinds D2, 440C and ATS-34; heat-treats. **Prices:** $50 to $600; some to $4,000. **Remarks:** Part-time maker; first knife sold in 1977. **Mark:** Last name.

FERRARA, THOMAS, 122 Madison Dr., Naples, FL, 33942/813-597-3363
Specialties: High-art, traditional and working straight knives and folders of all designs. **Patterns:** Boots, Bowies, daggers, fighters and hunters. **Technical:** Grinds 440C, D2 and ATS-34; heat-treats. **Prices:** $100 to $700; osme to $1300. **Remarks:** Part-time maker; first knife sold in 1983. **Mark:** Last name.

FIELDER, WILLIAM V., 8406 Knowland Circle, Richmond, VA, 23229/804-750-1198
Specialties: Fancy working straight knives and folders of his design. **Patterns:** Hunters, boots and daggers; locking folders, interframes and traditional-style knives. **Technical:** Forges W2, O1 and his own Damascus; likes wire inlay. **Prices:** $25 to $500; some to $1000. **Remarks:** Full-time maker; first knife sold in 1982. **Mark:** Last name.

FIKES, JIMMY L., P.O. Box 3457, Jasper, AL, 35502/205-387-9302
Specialties: High-art working knives; artifact knives; using knives with cord-wrapped handles; swords nad combat weapons. **Patterns:** Axes to buckskinners, camp knives to miniatures, tantos to tomahawks; springless folders. **Technical:** Forges W2, O1 and his own Damascus. **Prices:** $135 to $3000; exceptional knives to $7000. **Remarks:** Full-time maker. **Mark:** Stylized initials.

FINCH, RICKY D., HC 68 Box 311-C, West Liberty, KY, 41472/606-743-7151
Specialties: Traditional working/using straight knives of his design or to customer spec. **Patterns:** Hunters, skinners & utility/camp knives. **Technical:** Grinds 440C & ATS-34, hand rubbed stain finish, use Micorta, stag, stabilized wood - natural & exotic. **Prices:** $55 to $175; some $250. **Remarks:** Part-time maker, first knife made 1994. Doing business as Finch Knives. **Mark:** Last name inside outline of state of Kentucky.

FIORINI, BILL, 390 North St, PO Box 237, Dakota, MN, 55925-0237/507-643-7946
Specialties: Fancy working knives and lockbacks. **Patterns:** Hunters, boots, Japanese-style knives and kitchen/utility knives. **Technical:** Forges own Damascus. **Prices:** Full range. **Remarks:** Full-time metal-smith researching pattern materials. **Mark:** Orchid crest with name KOKA in Japanese.

FISCHER, CLYDE E., HCR 40, Box 133, Nixon, TX, 78140-9400/830-582-1353
Specialties: Working knives for serious and professional hunters. **Patterns:** Heavy-duty hunters and survival blades; camp knives and buckskinner knives. **Technical:** Forges and grinds L6, O1 and his own Damascus. **Prices:** $100 to $250; some to $800. **Remarks:** Full-time maker; first knife sold in 1957. **Mark:** Fish.

FISHER, JAY, 104 S. Main St., P.O. Box 267, Magdalena, NM, 87825/
Specialties: High-art, ancient and exact working and using straight knives of his design. **Patterns:** Hunters, daggers and high-art sculptures. **Technical:** Grinds 440C, ATS-34 and D2. Prolific maker of stone-handled knives. **Prices:** $65 to $50,000; some higher. **Remarks:** Part-time maker; first knife sold in 1984. **Mark:** Very fine--JaFisher--Quality Custom Knives.

FISHER, THEO (TED), 8115 Modoc Lane, Montague, CA, 96064/916-459-3804
Specialties: High-art, ancient and exact working and using straight knives of his design. **Patterns:** Hunters, daggers and high-art sculptures. **Technical:** Grinds 440C, ATS-34 and D2. Prolific maker of stone-handled knives. **Prices:** $65 to $50,000; some higher. **Remarks:** Part-time maker; first knife sold in 1984. **Mark:** Very fine--JaFisher--Quality Custom Knives.

FISK, JERRY, 145 N Park Ave, Lockesburg, AR, 71846/870-289-3240
Specialties: Edged weapons, collectible and functional. **Patterns:** Bowies, daggers, swords, hunters, camp knives and others. Technical: Forges carbon steels and his own pattern welded steels. **Prices:** $250 to $15,000. **Remarks:** National living treasure. **Mark:** Name, MS.

FISTER, JIM, 5067 Fisherville Rd., Simpsonville, KY, 40067/502-834-7841
Specialties: One of a kind collectibles and period pieces.. **Patterns:** Bowies, camp knives, hunters, buckskinners, and daggers. **Technical:** Forges, 1085, 5160, 52100, his own Damascus, pattern and turkish. **Prices:** $150 to $2,500. **Remarks:** Part-time maker; first knife sold in 1982. **Mark:** Name & MS.

FITZGERALD, DENNIS M., 4219 Alverado Dr., Fort Wayne, IN, 46816-2847/219-447-1081
Specialties: Straight working knives. **Patterns:** Skinners, fighters, camp and utility knives; period pieces. **Technical:** Forges W2, O1, billet and cable-wire Damascus. Likes integral guards, bolsters and pommels. **Prices:** $100 to $500. **Remarks:** Part-time maker; first knife sold in 1985. Doing business as The Ringing Circle. **Mark:** Name and circle logo.

FLOURNOY, JOE, 5750 Lisbon Rd., El Dorado, AR, 71730/870-863-7208
Specialties: Working straight knives and folders. **Patterns:** Hunters, Bowies, camp knives, folders and daggers. **Technical:** Forges only high-carbon steel, steel cable and his own Damascus. **Prices:** $250 to $4,000. **Remarks:** First knife sold in 1977. **Mark:** Last name and MS in script.

FLYNN, BRUCE, 8139 W. County Rd. 650 S, Knightstown, IN, 46148-9348/317-779-4034

FOGARIZZU, BOITEDDU, via Crispi, 6, 07016 Pattada, ITALY, /
Specialties: Traditional Italian straight knives and folders. **Patterns:** Collectible folders. **Technical:** forges and grinds 12C27, ATS-34 and his Damascus. **Prices:** $200 to $3,000. **Remarks:** Full-time maker; first knife sold in 1958. **Mark:** Full name and registered logo.

FOGG, DON, 40 Alma Road, Jasper, AL, 35501-8813/205-483-0822
Specialties: Swords, daggers, Bowies and hunting knives. **Patterns:** Collectible folders. **Technical:** Hand forged high carbon & Damascus steel. **Prices:** $200 to $5,000. **Remarks:** Full-time maker; first knife sold in 1976. **Mark:** 24K gold cherry blossom.

FOLEY, BARNEY, 3M Reler Lane, Somerset, NJ, 08873/908-297-1880

FORD, ALLEN, 3927 Plumcrest Rd., Smyrna, GA, 30080/404-432-5061
Specialties: Art knives of his design. **Patterns:** Bowies, daggers and hunters. **Technical:** Hand finishes every knife. Scrimshaws. **Mark:** First initial, last name in script.

FORSTALL, AL, 38379 Aunt Massey Rd, Pearl River, LA, 70452/504-863-2930
Specialties: Traditional working and using straight knives of his design or to customer specs. **Patterns:** Fighters, hunters and utility/camp knives. **Technical:** Ginds ATS-34, 440C, commercial Damascus and others upon request. **Prices:** $75 to $250. **Remarks:** Spare-time maker; first knife sold in 1991. **Mark:** Fleur Di Lis with name.

FORTHOFER, PETE, 5535 Hwy. 93S, Whitefish, MT, 59937/406-862-2674
Specialties: Interframes with checkered wood inlays; working straight knives. **Patterns:** Interframe folders and traditional-style knives; hunters, fighters and Bowies. **Technical:** Grinds D2, 440C, 154CM and ATS-34. **Prices:** $350 to $2,500; some to $1,500. **Remarks:** Part-time maker; full-time gunsmith. First knife sold in 1979. **Mark:** Name and logo.

FORTUNE PRODUCTS, INC., 205 Hickory Creek Rd, Marble Falls, TX, 78654/830-693-6111
Specialties: Knife sharpeners.

FOSTER, R.L. (BOB), 745 Glendale Blvd., Mansfield, OH, 44907/

FOSTER, AL, 118 Woodway Dr, Magnolia, TX, 77355/409-372-9297
Specialties: Straight knives and folders. **Patterns:** Hunting, fishing, folders & bowies. **Technical:** Grinds 440-C, ATS-34 & D2. **Prices:** $100 to $1,000. **Remarks:** Full time maker; first knife sold in 1981. **Mark:** Scorpion logo & name.

FOWLER, ED A., Willow Bow Ranch, P.O. Box 1519, Riverton, WY, 82501/307-856-9815
Specialties: Heavy-duty working and using straight knives. **Patterns:** Hunters, camp, bird and trout knives, Bowies. **Technical:** Forges 52100, chainsaw Damascus; multiple-quench heat-treats. Engraves all knives. All handles are aged domestic sheephorn, Makes pouch-type sheaths. **Prices:** $450 to $3,000. **Remarks:** Full-time maker; first knife sold in 1962. **Mark:** Initials connected.

FOWLER, JERRY, 610 FM 1660 N., Hutto, TX, 78634/512-846-2860
Specialties: Using straight knives of his design. **Patterns:** A variety of hunting and camp knives, combat knives. Custom designs considered. **Technical:** Forges 5160, his own Damascus and cable Damascus. Makes sheaths. Prefers natural handle materials. **Prices:** Start at $150. **Remarks:** Part-time maker; first knife sold in 1986. Doing business as Fowler Forge Knifeworks. **Mark:** First initial, last name, date and J.S.

FOWLER, RICKY, 288 Jones McLain Rd, Richton, MS, 39476/601-989-2553
Specialties: Traditional working/using straight knives and folders of his design or to customer specifications. **Patterns:** Skinners, fighters, folders, Tantos, Bowies and utility/camp knives. **Technical:** Grinds O1, ATS-34, 440C, D2, A2 & commercial damascus. Forges 5160, Damascus, & other steels. **Prices:** Start at $135. **Remarks:** Full-time maker; first knife sold in 1994. Doing business as Fowler Custom Knives. **Mark:** Last name tang stamped & serial numbered.

FOWLER, CHARLES R., Rt. 2, Box 1446 A, Ft. McCoy, FL, 32134/904-467-3215
Specialties: Fancy high-art straight knives and traditional working straight knives of his design. **Patterns:** Boots, Bowies, daggers, fighters, hunters and utility knives. **Technical:** Forges L6, W2 and 5160. **Prices:** $300 to $1,200. **Remarks:** Part-time maker; first knife sold in 1986. Doing business as Falcon Crest Forge. **Mark:** Circle with falcon bust, name, bladesmith.

FOX, WENDELL, 4080 S. 39th, Springfield, OR, 97478/541-747-2126
Specialties: Large camping knives and friction folders of his design and to customer specs. **Patterns:** Hunters, locking folders, slip-joint folders and utility/camp knives. **Technical:** Forges high-carbon steel, cable, 52100, Damascus and his own timbers steel. All carbon cable blades are differentially tempered; all sheaths are wet-moulded. Offers fancy filework. **Prices:** Start at $200. **Remarks:** Full-time maker; first knife sold in 1952. **Mark:** Stamped name or logo.

FOX, JACK L., 7085 Canelo Hills Dr., Citrus Heights, CA, 95610/916-723-8647
Specialties: Traditional working/using straight knives of all designs. **Patterns:** Hunters, utility/camp knives and bird/fish knives. **Technical:** Grinds ATS-34, 440C and D2. **Prices:** $125 to $225; some to $350. **Remarks:** Spart-time maker; first knife sold in 1985. Doing business as Fox Knives. **Mark:** Stylized fox head.

FOX, PAUL, 4721 Rock Barn Road, Claremont, NC, 28610/704-459-2000
Specialties: Traditional working/using straight knives of all designs. **Patterns:** Hunters, utility/camp knives and bird/fish knives. **Technical:** Grinds ATS-34, 440C and D2. **Prices:** $125 to $225; some to $350. **Remarks:** Spart-time maker; first knife sold in 1985. Doing business as Fox Knives. **Mark:** Stylized fox head.

FRALEY, DEREK, P.O. Box 141, Dixon, CA, 95620/707-678-0393
Specialties: Traditional working/using straight knives and folders of his design and in standard patterns. **Patterns:** Fighters, hunters, utility/camp knives. **Technical:** Grinds ATS-34. Offers hand-stiched sheaths. **Prices:** Start at $100. **Remarks:** Part-time maker; first knife sold in 1990. **Mark:** First and middle initials, last name over buffalo.

custom knifemakers

FRANCE, DAN, Box 218, Cawood, KY, 40815/606-573-6104
Specialties: Traditional working and using straight knives of his design.
Patterns: Hunters, Bowies and utility/camp knives. **Technical:** forges
and grinds O1, 5160 and L6. **Prices:** $35 to $125; some to $350.
Remarks: Spare-time maker; first knife sold in 1985. **Mark:** First name.

FRANCIS, VANCE, 2612 Alpine Blvd., Alpine, CA, 91901/619-445-0979
Specialties: Working straight knives. **Patterns:** Bowies and utility knives.
Technical: Uses ATS-34, A2, D2 and Damascus; differentially tempers
large blades. **Prices:** $175 to $600. **Remarks:** Part-time maker. **Mark:**
First name, last name, city and state under feather in oval.

FRANK, HEINRICH H., 13868 NW Keleka Pl., Seal Rock, OR, 97376/
541-563-3041
Specialties: High-art investor-class folders, handmade and engraved.
Patterns: Folding daggers, hunter-size folders and gents. **Technical:**
Grinds 07 and O1. **Prices:** $4,800 to $16,000. **Remarks:** Full-time
maker; first knife sold in 1965. Doing business as H.H. Frank Knives.
Mark: Name, address and date.

FRANKLAND, ANDREW, P.O. Box 256, Wilderness 6560, SOUTH
AFRICA, /044-877-0260
Specialties: Classic working and using straight knives and folders of his
design and to customer specs. **Patterns:** Daggers, fighters, hunters and
utility/camp knives. **Technical:** Grinds 440C, D2 and ATS-34. All double-
edge knives have broad spine. **Prices:** $250 to $400; some to $1,500.
Remarks: full-time maker; first knife sold in 1979. **Mark:** Last name sur-
rounded by mountain, lake, forest scene.

FRANKLIN, MIKE, 9878 Big Run Rd., Aberdeen, OH, 45101/937-549-
2598
Specialties: High-tech tactical folders. **Patterns:** Tactical folders. **Technical:** Grinds CPM-T-440V, 440-C, ATS-34; titanium liners and bolsters;
carbon fiber scales. Uses radical grinds and severe serrations. **Prices:**
$275 to $600. **Remarks:** Full-time maker; first knife sold in 1969. **Mark:**
Stylized boar with HAWG.

FRASER, GRANT, RR2, Foresters Falls, Ont., CANADA, K0J 1V0/613-
582-3582
Specialties: Fancy and working straight knives of his design and to customer specs. **Patterns:** Bowies, daggers and hunters. **Technical:** Forges
and grinds O1 and 5160; grinds ATS-34. **Prices:** $125 to $255; some to
$1,200. **Remarks:** Full-time maker; first knife sold in 1983. **Mark:** Initial
tang stamp.

FRAZIER, RON, 2107 Urbine Rd., Powhatan, VA, 23139/804-794-8561
Specialties: Classy working knives of his design; some high-art straight
knives. **Patterns:** Wide assortment of straight knives, including miniatures and push knives. **Technical:** Grinds 440C; offers satin, mirror or
sand finishes. **Prices:** $85 to $700; some to $3,000. **Remarks:** Full-time
maker; first knife sold in 1976. **Mark:** Name in arch logo.

FRED, REED WYLE, 3149 X Street, Sacramento, CA, 95817/916-739-
0237
Specialties: Working using straight knives of his design. **Patterns:** Hunting and camp knives. **Technical:** Forges any 10 series, old files and carbon steels. Offers initialing upon request; prefers natural handle
materials. **Prices:** $30 to $300; some to $300. **Remarks:** Part-time
maker; first knife sold in 1994. Doing business as R.W. Fred Knifemaker.
Mark: Engraved first and last initials.

FREEMAN, JOHN, 160 Concession St., Cambridge, Ont., CANADA,
N1R 2I7/519-740-2707
Specialties: Working straight knives. **Patterns:** Hunters, skinners, utili-
ties, backpackers. **Technical:** Grinds A2, 440C and ATS-34. **Prices:**
Start at $125. **Remarks:** Full-time maker; first knife sold in 1985. **Mark:**
Full name, city, state, Handmade.

FREER, RALPH, P.O. Box 3482, Seal Beach, CA, 90740/562-493-4925
Specialties: Folders, fancy fixed blades, bowies. **Patterns:** All original.
Technical: ATS-34, 440C, stainless Damascus, titanium. **Prices:** $200
to $1500. **Remarks:** Lots of exotic woods, stag, bone & ivory, fancy file-
work. **Mark:** Freer. **Other:** Unique combinations of materials and steels,
lots of coloring.

FREILING, ALBERT J., 3700 Niner Rd., Finksburg, MD, 21048/301-
795-2880
Specialties: Working straight knives and folders; some period pieces.
Patterns: Boots, Bowies, survival knives and tomahawks in 4130 and
440C; some locking folders and interframes; ball-bearing folders. **Techni-**

cal: Grinds O1, 440C and 154CM. **Prices:** $100 to $300; some to $500.
Remarks: Part-time maker; first knife sold in 1966. **Mark:** Initials connected.

FREY JR., W. FREDERICK, 305 Walnut St., Milton, PA, 17847/570-
742-9576
Specialties: Working straight knives and folders, some fancy. **Patterns:**
Wide range--boot knives to tomahawks. **Technical:** Grinds A2, O1 and
D2; hand finishes only. **Prices:** $55 to $170; some to $600. **Remarks:**
Spare-time maker; first knife sold in 1983. **Mark:** Last name in script.

FRIEDLY, DENNIS E., 12 Cottontail Ln. - E, Cody, WY, 82414/307-527-
6811
Specialties: Fancy working straight knives and daggers, lock back folders and liner locks. **Patterns:** Hunters, fighters, short swords, minis and
miniatures; new line of full-tang hunters/boots. **Technical:** Grinds 440C,
commercial Damascus, mosaic damascus and ATS-34 blades; prefers
hidden tangs. **Prices:** $135 to $900; some to $2,500. **Remarks:** Full-time
maker; first knife sold in 1972. **Mark:** Name, city, state.

FRITZ, JESSE, P.O. Box 241, Slaton, TX, 79364/806-828-6190
Specialties: Working and using straight knives in standard patterns. **Patterns:** Hunters, utility/camp knives and skinners with gut hook. **Technical:** Grinds 440C, O1 and 1095. Fline-napped steel design, blued blades,
filework and machine jeweling. Inlays handles with turquoise, coral and
mother-of-pearl. Makes sheaths. **Prices:** $85 to $275; some to $500.
Mark: Crossed half ovals: handmade on top, last name in middle, city
and state on bottom.

FRIZZELL, TED, 14056 Low Gap Rd., West Fork, AR, 72774/501-839-
2516
Specialties: Swords, axes and self defense weapons. **Patterns:** Small
skeleton knives to large swords. **Technical:** Grinds 5160 almost exclu-
sively--1/4" to 1/2"-- bars some O1 and A2 on request. All knives come
with Kydex sheaths. **Prices:** $45 to $1,200. **Remarks:** Full-time maker;
first knife sold in 1984. Doing business as Mineral Mountain Hatchet
Works. **Mark:** A circle with line in the middle; MM and HW within the circle.

FRUHMANN, LUDWIG, Stegerwaldstr 8, 84489 Burghausen, GER-
MANY, /
Specialties: High-tech and working straight knives of his design. **Patterns:** Hunters, fighters and boots. **Technical:** Grinds ATS-34, CPM-T-
440V and Schneider Damascus. Prefers natural handle materials.
Prices: $200 to $1,500. **Remarks:** Spare-time maker; first knife sold in
1990. **Mark:** First initial and last name.

FUEGEN, LARRY, 108 Alna Rd, Wiscasset, ME, 04578/207-882-6391
Specialties: High-art folders and classic and working straight knives.
Patterns: Forged scroll folders, lockback folders and classic straight
knives. **Technical:** Forges 5160, 1095 and his own Damascus. Works in
exotic leather; offers elaborate filework and carving; likes natural handle
materials. **Prices:** $400 to $5,200. **Remarks:** Full-time maker; first knife
sold in 1975. **Mark:** Initials connected.

FUJIKAWA, SHUN, Sawa 1157 Kaizuka, Osaka 597, JAPAN, /81-724-
23-4032
Specialties: Folders of his design and to customer specs. **Patterns:**
Locking folders. **Technical:** Grinds his own steel. **Prices:** $450 to
$2,500; some to $3,000. **Remarks:** Part-time maker.

FUJISAKA, STANLEY, 45-004 Holowai St., Kaneohe, HI, 96744/808-
247-0017
Specialties: Fancy working straight knives and folders. **Patterns:** Hunters, boots, personal knives, daggers, collectible art knives. **Technical:**
Grinds 440C, 154CM and ATS-34; clean lines, inlays. **Prices:** $150 to
$1,200; some to $3,000. **Remarks:** Full-time maker; first knife sold in
1984. **Mark:** Name, city, state.

FUKUTA, TAK, 38-Umeagae-cho, Seki-City, Gifu-Pref, JAPAN, /0575-
22-0264
Specialties: Bench-made fancy straight knives and folders. **Patterns:**
Sheffield-type folders, Bowies and fighters. **Technical:** Grinds commer-
cial Damascus. **Prices:** Start at $300. **Remarks:** Full-time maker. **Mark:**
Name in knife logo.

FULLER, JOHN W., 6156 Ridge Way, Douglasville, GA, 30135/770-
942-1155
Specialties: Fancy working straight knives and folders in standard patterns. **Patterns:** Straight and folding hunters, gents, fighters. **Technical:**

Grinds ATS-34, 440C and commercial Damascus. **Prices:** $75 to $300. **Remarks:** Part-time maker; first knife sold in 1978. **Mark:** Name, city, state.

FULLER, BRUCE A., 1305 Airhart Dr., Baytown, TX, 77520/713-427-1848
Specialties: One-of-a-kind working/using straight knives and folders of his designs. **Patterns:** Bowies, hunters, folders, and utility/camp knives. **Technical:** Forges high-carbon steel and his own Damascus. prefers El Solo Mesquite and natural materials. Offers filework. **Prices:** $200 to $500; some to $1,800. **Remarks:** Spare-time maker; first knife sold in 1991. Doing business as Fullco Forge. **Mark:** Fullco, M.S.

FULLER, JACK A., 7103 Stretch Ct., New Market, MD, 21774/301-865-6886
Specialties: Straight working knives of his design and to customer specs. **Patterns:** Fighters, camp knives, hunters, tomahawks and art knives. **Technical:** Forges 5160, O1, W2 and his own Damascus. Does silver wire inlay and own leather work, wood lined sheaths for big camp knives. **Prices:** $300 to $850. **Remarks:** Part-time maker. First knife sold in 1979. **Mark:** Fuller's Forge, MS.

FULTON, MICKEY, 406 S Shasta St, Willows, CA, 95988/530-934-5780
Specialties: Working straight knives and folders of his design. **Patterns:** Hunters, Bowies, lockback folders and steak knife sets. **Technical:** Hand-filed, sanded, buffed ATS-34, 440C and A2. **Prices:** $65 to $600; some to $1,200. **Remarks:** Full-time maker; first knife sold in 1979. **Mark:** Signature.

g

GADDY, GARY LEE, 205 Ridgewood Lane, Washington, NC, 27889/919-946-4359
Specialties: Working/using straight knives of his design; period pieces. **Patterns:** Bowies, hunters, utility/camp knives. **Technical:** Grinds ATS-34, D2 and O1. Offers filework. **Prices:** $100 to $225; some to $400. **Remarks:** Spare-time maker; first knife sold in 1991. **Mark:** Etched name and quarter moon logo.

GAETA, ANGELO, R. Saldanha Marinho, 1295 Centro Jau, SP-17201-310, BRAZIL, /0146-224543
Specialties: Straight using knives to customer specs. **Pattersn:** Hunters, kitchen and utility knives. **Technical:** Grinds D6, ATS-34 and 440C stainless. titanium nitride golden finish upon request. **Prices:** $60 to $170. **Remarks:** Full-time maker; first knife sold in 1992. **Mark:** First initial, last name.

GAETA, ROBERTO, Rua Shikazu Myai 80, 05351 Sao Paulo, S.P., BRAZIL, /11-268-4626
Specialties: Wide range of using knives. **Patterns:** Brazilian and North American hunting and fighting knives. **Technical:** Grinds stainless steel; likes natural handle materials. **Prices:** $100 to $250; some to $500. **Remarks:** Full-time maker; first knife sold in 1979. **Mark:** BOB'G.

GAINEY, HAL, 904 Bucklevel Rd., Greenwood, SC, 29649/864-223-0225
Specialties: Traditional working and using straight knives and folders. **Patterns:** Hunters, slip-joint folders and utility/camp knives. **Technical:** Hollow-grinds ATS-34 and D2; makes sheaths. **Prices:** $95 to $145; some to $500. **Remarks:** Full-time maker; first knife sold in 1975. **Mark:** Eagle head and last name.

GALLAGHER, BARRY, 714 8th Ave. N., Lewistown, MT, 59457/406-538-7056
Specialties: One of a kind Damascus folders. **Patterns:** Folders - utility to high art, some straight knives - hunter, Bowies, and art pieces. **Technical:** Forges own mosaic Damascus and carbon steel, some stainless. **Prices:** $400 to $5,000+. **Remarks:** Full-time maker; first knife sold in 1993. Doing business as Gallagher Custom Knives. **Mark:** Last name.

GAMBLE, ROGER, 2801 65 Way N., St. Petersburg, FL, 33710/727-384-1470
Specialties: Traditional working/using straight knives and folders of his design. **Patterns:** Liner locks & hunters. **Technical:** Grinds ATS-34 and Damascus. **Prices:** $100 to $1000. **Remarks:** Part-time maker; first knife sold in 1982. Doing business as Gamble Knives. **Mark:** First name in a fan of cards over last name.

GAMBLE, FRANK, 3872 Dunbar Pl., Fremont, CA, 94536/510-797-7970
Specialties: Fantasy and high-art straight knives and folders of his design. **Patterns:** Daggers, fighters, hunters and special locking folders. **Technical:** Grinds 440C and ATS-34; forges Damascus. Inlays; offers jeweling. Prices $150 to $10,000. **Remarks:** Full-time maker; first knife sold in 1976. **Mark:** First initial, last name.

GANSTER, JEAN-PIERRE, 18, Rue du Vieil Hopital, F-67000 Strasbourg, FRANCE, /(0033) 388 32 65 61
Specialties: Fancy and high-art miniatures of his design and to customer specs. **patterns:** Bowies, daggers, fighters, hunters, locking folders and miniatures. **Technical:** Forges and grinds stainless Damascus, ATS-34, gold and silver. **Prices:** $100 to $380; some to $2,500. **Remarks:** Part-time maker; first knife sold in 1972. **Mark:** Stylized first initials.

GARBE, BOB, 33176 Klein, Fraser, MI, 48026/810-293-3664
Specialties: Folders and straight knives. **Patterns:** Hunters, locking folders and slip-joint folders. **Technical:** Grinds ATS-34. Offers filework. **Prices:** $100 to $1,000. **Remarks:** Full-time maker; first knife sold in 1991. **Mark:** Last name.

GARCIA, TONY, 134 Gregory Place, West Palm Beach, FL, 33405/561-582-1291
Specialties: Traditional working/using straight knives of his design and to customer specs. **Patterns:** Bowies, hunters, fillet and utility/camp knives. **Technical:** Grinds 440C, 440V and ATS-34. **Prices:** $125 to $250. **Remarks:** Part-time maker; first knife sold in 1992. **Mark:** Name, city, state; logo of fishing hook with arrow across it.

GARCIA, MARIO EIRAS, R. Edmundo Scanapieco, 300 Caxingui, Sao Paulo SP-05516-070, BRAZIL, /
Specialties: Fantasy knives of his design; one of a kind only. **Patterns:** Fighters, daggers, boots and two-bladed knives. **Technical:** Forges car leaf springs. Uses only natural handle material. **Prices:** $100 to $200. **Remarks:** Part-time maker; first knife sold in 1976. **Mark:** Two "B"s, one opposite the other.

GARDNER, ROB, 387 Mustang Blvd., Port Aransas, TX, 78373/361-749-3597
Specialties: High-art working and using knives of his design and to customer specs. **Patterns:** Daggers, hunters and ethnic-patterned knives. **Technical:** Forges Damascus, L6 and 10-series steels. Engraves and inlays. Handles and fittings may be carved. **Prices:** $175 to $500; some to $2,500. **Remarks:** Spare-time maker; first knife sold in 1987. **Mark:** Engraved initials.

GARNER JR., WILLIAM O., 2803 East DeSoto St., Pensacola, FL, 32503/850-438-2009
Specialties: Working straight and art knives. **Patterns:** Hunters and folders. **Technical:** Grinds 440C and ATS-34 steels. **Prices:** $235 to $600. **Remarks:** Full-time maker; first knife sold in 1985. **Mark:** First and last name in oval logo or last name.

GASTON, RON, 330 Gaston Dr., Woodruff, SC, 29388/803-433-0807
Specialties: Working period pieces. **Patterns:** Hunters, fighters, tantos, boots and a variety of other straight knives; single-blade slip-joint folders. **Technical:** Grinds ATS-34. Hand-rubbed satin finish is standard. **Prices:** $100 to $350; some to $1,000. **Remarks:** Full-time maker; first knife sold in 1980. **Mark:** Name.

GASTON, BERT, P.O. Box 9047, North Little Rock, AR, 72119/501-372-4747
Specialties: Traditional working and using straight knives of his design. **Patterns:** Hunters, Bowies and fighters. **Technical:** Forges his Damascus, 5168 and L6. Only uses natural handle materials. **Prices:** $200 to $500; some to $1,500. **Remarks:** Part-time maker; first knife sold in 1989. **Mark:** Stylized last initial and M.S.

GAUDETTE, LINDEN L., 5 Hitchcock Rd., Wilbraham, MA, 01095/413-596-4896
Specialties: Traditional working knives in standard patterns. **Patterns:** Broad-bladed hunters, Bowies and camp knives; wood carver knives; locking folders. **Technical:** Grinds ATS-34, 440C and 154CM. **Prices:** $150 to $400; some higher. **Remarks:** Full-time maker; first knife sold in 1975. **Mark:** Last name in Gothic logo; used to be initials in circle.

GAULT, CLAY, Rt. 1, Box 287, Lexington, TX, 78947/512-273-2873
Specialties: Classic straight and folding hunting knives and multi-blade folders of his design. **Patterns:** Folders and hunting knives. **Technical:**

Grinds BX-NSM 174 steel, custom rolled from billets to his specifications. Uses exotic leathers for sheaths, and natural materials for the multi-blade folders. **Prices:** $325 to $600; some higher. **Remarks:** Full-time maker; first knife sold in 1970. **Mark:** Name or name with cattle brand.

GEISLER, GARY R., P.O. Box 294, Clarksville, OH, 45113/937-383-4055
Specialties: Light and smooth working straight knives to customer specs. **Patterns:** Working knives. **Technical:** Grinds ATS-34, 440C and A2. Prefers mirror finishes. **Prices:** Start at $95. **Remarks:** Part-time maker; first knife sold in 1982. **Mark:** First and middle initials, last name and Maker in script.

GENGE, ROY E., P.O. Box 57, Eastlake, CO, 80614/303-451-7991
Specialties: High-tech working knives. **Patterns:** Bowies, hatchets, hunters, survival knives, buckskinners, kukris and others. **Technical:** Forges and grinds L6, S7, W1, W2, O1, Vascowear, 154CM, ATS-34 and commercial Damascus. **Prices:** $100 to $1,200. **Remarks:** Part-time maker; first knife sold in 1968. **Mark:** Name, city, state.

GENSKE, JAY, 262 1/2 Elm St., Fond du Lac, WI, 54935/414-921-6505
Specialties: Working/using knives and period peices of his design and to customer specs. **Patterns:** Bowies, fighters, hunters. **Technical:** Grinds ATS-34 and 440C; forges and grinds Damascus and cable. Offers custom-tooled sheaths, scabbards and hand carved handles. **Prices:** $95 to $500; some to $1,000. **Remarks:** Full-time maker; first knife sold in 1985. Doing business as Genske Knives. **Mark:** Stamped or engraved last name.

GEORGE, HARRY, 3137 Old Camp Long Rd., Aiken, SC, 29805/803-649-1963
Specialties: Working straight knives of his design or to customer specs. **Patterns:** Hunters, skinners and utility knives. **Technical:** Grinds ATS-34. Prefers natural handle materials, hollow-grinds and mirror finishes. **Prices:** Start at $70. **Remarks:** Part-time maker; first knife sold in 1985. Trained under George Herron. Member SCAK. Member Knifemakers Guild. **Mark:** Name, city, state.

GEORGE, TOM, P.O. Box 1298, Magalia, CA, 95954/916-873-3306
Specialties: Working straight knives, display knives and folders of his design. **Patterns:** Hunters, Bowies, daggers and buckskinners and folders. **Technical:** Uses D2, 440C, ATS-34 and 154CM. **Prices:** $175 to $4,500. **Remarks:** First knife sold in 1981. Custom orders accepted. **Mark:** Name.

GEORGE, LES, 1703 Payne, Wichita, KS, 67203/316-267-0736
Specialties: Classic, traditional and working/using straight knives of his design and to customer specs. **Patterns:** Fighters, hunters, swords and miniatures. **Technical:** Grinds D2; forges 5160 and Damascus. Uses mosaic handle pins and his own mokume-gane. **Prices:** $35 to $200; some to $800. **Remarks:** No orders taken at this time due to enlistment in the US Marine Corps.; first knife sold in 1992. Doing business as George Custom Knives. **Mark:** Last name or initials stacked.

GEPNER, DON, 2615 E. Tecumseh, Norman, OK, 73071/405-364-2750
Specialties: Traditional working and using straight knives of his design. **Patterns:** Bowies and daggers. **Technical:** Forges his Damascus, 1095 and 5160. **Prices:** $100 to $400; some to $1,000. **Remarks:** Spare-time maker; first knife sold in 1991. Has been forging since 1954; **Mark:** Last initial.

GERUS, GERRY, P.O. Box 2295, G.P.O. Cairns, Qld. 4870, AUSTRA-LIA, 070-341451/019 617935
Specialties: Fancy working and using straight knives of his design. **Patterns:** Hunters, Bowies and fighters. **Technical:** Uses 440C, ATS-34 and commercial Damascus. **Prices:** $275 to $600; some to $1,200. **Remarks:** Part-time maker; first knife sold in 1988. **Mark:** Last name; or last name, Hand Made, city, country.

GEVEDON, HANNERS (HANK), 1410 John Cash Rd., Crab Orchard, KY, 40419-9770/
Specialties: Traditional working and using straight knives. **Patterns:** Hunters, swords, utility and camp knives. **Technical:** Forges and grinds his own Damascus, 5160 and L6. Cast aluminum handles. **Prices:** $50 to $250; some to $400. **Remarks:** Part-time maker; first knife sold in 1983. **Mark:** Initials and LBF tang stamp.

GIAGU, SALVATORE AND DEROMA MARIA ROSARIA, Via V. Emanuele 64, 07016 Pattada (SS), ITALY, /079-755918
Specialties: Using and collecting traditional and new folders from Sardegna. **Patterns:** Folding, hunting, utility, skinners and kitchen knives. **Technical:** Forges ATS-34, 440, D2 and Damascus. **Prices:** $200 to $2,000; some higher. **Mark:** First inital, last name and name of town and muflon's head.

GIBSON, JAMES HOOT, RR1, Box 177F, Bunnell, FL, 32110/904-437-4383
Patterns: Bowies, daggers and hunters. **Technical:** Grinds ATS-34, 440C and Damascus. **Prices:** $150 to $1,200; some to $2,500. **Remarks:** Part-time maker; first knife sold in 1965. Doing business as Hoot's Handmade Knives. **Mark:** Hoot.

GILBERT, CHANTAL, 1421 Chemin de la Rive Sud, St Romuald, Quebec CANADA, G6W 2MX/418-839-8746

GILBREATH, RANDALL, 55 Crauswell Rd., Dora, AL, 35062/205-648-3902
Specialties: Damascus folders and fighters. **Patterns:** Folders and fixed blades. **Technical:** Forges Damascus and & high carbon; stock removal stainless steel. **Prices:** $300 to $1,500. **Remarks:** Full-time maker; first knife sold in 1979. **Mark:** Name in ribbon.

GILJEVIC, BRANKO, 35 Hayley Cresent, Queanbeyan 2620, N.S.W., AUSTRALIA, 0262977613/
Specialties: Classic working straight knives and folders of his design. **Patterns:** Hunters, Bowies, skinners and locking folders. **Technical:** Grinds 440C. Offers acid etching, scrimshaw and leather carving. **Prices:** $150 to $1,500. **Remarks:** Part-time maker; first knife sold in 1987. Doing business as Sambar Custom Knives. **Mark:** Company name in logo.

GILPIN, DAVID, 902 Falling Star Ln., Alabaster, AL, 35007/205-664-4777
Specialties: Classic, fancy and traditional knives of his design. **Patterns:** Japanese style swords. **Technical:** Grinds 440C, forges and grinds Damascus stainless, 1010, 1095 and 1084. Offers metal casting, electroplate and inlay. **Prices:** $500 to $5000; some to $12,000. **Remarks:** Full-time maker; first knife sold in 1994. **Mark:** First name in Japanese/Chinese characters.

GLASER, KEN, Rt. #1 Box 148, Purdy, MO, 65734/417-442-3371
Specialties: Working straight knives in standard patterns. **Patterns:** Hunters, bird and trout knives, boots. **Technical:** Hollow-grinds O1, D2 and 440C. **Prices:** $75 to $125; some to $250. **Remarks:** Part-time maker; first knife sold in 1983. **Mark:** Initials.

GLOVER, RON, 7702 Misty Springs Ct, Mason, OH, 45040/513-398-7857
Specialties: High-tech working straight knives and folders. **Patterns:** Hunters to Bowies; some interchangeable blade models; unique locking mechanisms. **Technical:** Grinds 440C, 154CM; buys Damascus. **Prices:** $70 to $500; some to $800. **Remarks:** Part-time maker; first knife sold in 1981. **Mark:** Name in script.

GODDARD, WAYNE, 473 Durham Ave., Eugene, OR, 97404/541-689-8098
Specialties: Working/using straight knives and folders. **Patterns:** Hunters and folders. **Technical:** Works exclusively with wire Damascus and his own-pattern welded material. **Prices:** $250 to $4000. **Remarks:** Full-time maker; first knife sold in 1963. Three-year backlog on orders. **Mark:** Blocked initials on forged blades; regular capital initials on stock removal.

GOERS, BRUCE, 3423 Royal Ct. S., Lakeland, FL, 33813/941-646-0984
Specialties: Fancy working and using straight knives of his design and to customer specs. **Patterns:** Hunters, fighters, Bowies and fantasy knives. **Technical:** Grinds ATS-34, some Damascus. **Prices:** $195 to $600; some to $1,300. **Remarks:** Part-time maker; first knife sold in 1990. Doing business as Vulture Cutlery. **Mark:** Buzzard with initials.

GOERTZ, PAUL S., 201 Union Ave. SE, #207, Renton, WA, 98059/425-228-9501
Specialties: Working straight knives of his design and to customer specs. **Patterns:** Hunters, skinners, camp, bird and fish knives, camp axes, some Bowies, fighters and boots. **Technical:** Grinds ATS-34, BG42, & CPM420V. **Prices:** $75 to $500. **Remarks:** Full-time maker; first knife sold in 1985. **Mark:** Signature.

custom knifemakers

GOFOURTH, JIM, 3776 Aliso Cyn. Rd., Santa Paula, CA, 93060/805-659-3814
Specialties: Period pieces and working knives. **Patterns:** Bowies, locking folders, patent lockers and others. **Technical:** Grinds A2 and 154CM. **Prices:** Moderate. **Remarks:** Spare-time maker. **Mark:** Initials interconnected.

GOGUEN, SCOTT, 166 Goguen Rd., Newport, NC, 28570/252-393-6013
Specialties: Classic and traditional straight knives; working/using knives of all designs. **Patterns:** Boots, Bowies, fighters, hunters, kitchen knives, utility/camp knives, straight knives and swords. **Technical:** Forges high carbon steel and own Damascus. Offers clay tempering and cord wrapped handles. **Prices:** $85 to $1,500. **Remarks:** Spare-time maker; first knife sold in1988. **Mark:** Last name.

GOLDBERG, DAVID, 1120 Blyth Ct., Blue Bell, PA, 19422/215-654-7117
Specialties: Japanese style designs. **Patterns:** Kozuka to dai-sho. **Technical:** Forges his own Damascus; hand-rubbed finish. Uses traditional materials, carves fittings, handles and scabbards. **Remarks:** Full-time maker; first knife sold in 1987. **Mark:** Last name in English and Japanese.

GOLDBERG, METALSMITH, DAVID, 1120 Blyth Ct, Blue Bell, PA, 19422/215-654-7117
Specialties: Japanese style swords and fittings. **Patterns:** Kozuka to Dai-Sho, Naginata, Yari and sword canes. **Technical:** Forges and heat treats his own Damascus, cable Damascus, meteorite, and handmade steel from carburized iron, straw ash and clay. Uses traditional materials, carves fittings, handles and cases. Sole author. **Prices:** Upon request. **Remarks:** Full-time maker; first knife sold in 1987. **Mark:** Last name in Japanese Kanju - "Kinzan".

GOLDING, ROBIN, P.O. Box 267, Lathrop, CA, 95330/209-982-0839
Specialties: Working straight knives of his design. **Patterns:** Survival knives, Bowie extractions, camp knives, dive knives and skinners. **Technical:** Grinds 440C, 154CM and ATS-34. **Prices:** $95 to $250; some to $500. **Remarks:** Full-time maker; first knife sold in 1985. Up to 1-1/2 year waiting period on orders. **Mark:** Signature of last name.

GOLTZ, WARREN L., 802 4th Ave. E., Ada, MN, 56510/218-784-7721
Specialties: Fancy working knives in standard patterns. **Patterns:** Hunters, Bowies and camp knives. **Technical:** Grinds 440C and ATS-34. **Prices:** $120 to $595; some $950. **Remarks:** Part-time maker; first knife sold in 1984. **Mark:** Last name.

GONZALEZ, LEONARDO WILLIAMS, Ituzaingo 473, Maldonado, CP 20000 URUGUAY, /598 42 21617
Specialties: Classic high-art and fantasy straight knives; traditional working and using knives of his design, in standard patterns or to customer specs. **Patterns:** Hunters, Bowies, daggers, fighters, boots, swords and utility/camp knives. **Technical:** Forges and grinds high carbon and stainless Bohler steels. **Prices:** $100 to $900. **Remarks:** Full-time maker; first knife sold in 1985. **Mark:** Willy, whale, R.O.U.

GOO, TAI, 3225 N. Winstel Blvd., Tucson, AZ, 85716/520-325-8095
Specialties: High-art, neo-tribal and fantasy knives. **Patterns:** Fighters, daggers, Bowies, buckskinners, edged fetishes and sculptures. **Technical:** Forges and grinds A6, 440C and his own Damascus with iron meteorites. **Prices:** $150 to $500; some to $10,000. **Remarks:** Full-time maker; first knife sold in 1978. **Mark:** Chiseled signature; mark in spacer and tang.

GOODE, BEAR, P.O. Box 6474, Navajo Dam, NM, 87419/505-632-8184
Specialties: Working/using straight knives of his design and in standard patterns. **Patterns:** Bowies, hunters and utility/camp knives. **Technical:** Grinds 440C, ATS-34, 154-CM; forges and grinds 1095, 5160 and other steels on request; uses Damascus. **Prices:** $60 to $225; some to $500 and up. **Remarks:** Part-time maker; first knife sold in 1993. Doing business as Bear Knives. **Mark:** First and last name with a three-toed paw print.

GORENFLO, JAMES T. (JT), 9145 Sullivan Rd., Baton Rouge, LA, 70818/504-261-5868
Specialties: Traditional working and using straight knives of his design. **Patterns:** Bowies, hunters and utility/camp knives. **Technical:** Forges 5160, 1095, 52100 and his own Damascus. **Prices:** Start at $125. **Remarks:** Part-time maker; first knife sold in 1992. **Mark:** Last name or initials, J.S. on reverse.

GOTTAGE, DANTE, 43227 Brooks Drive, Clinton Twp., MI, 48038-5323/810-286-7275
Specialties: Working knives of his design or to customer specs. **Patterns:** Large and small skinners, fighters, Bowies and fillet knives. **Technical:** Grinds O1, 440C and 154CM and ATS-34. **Prices:** $150 to $600. **Remarks:** Part-time maker; first knife sold in 1975. **Mark:** Full name in script letters.

GOTTAGE, JUDY, 43227 Brooks Drive., Clinton Twp., MI, 48038-5323/810-286-7275
Specialties: Custom folders of her design or to customer specs. **Patterns:** Interframes or integral. **Technical:** Stock removal. **Prices:** $300 to $3,000. **Remarks:** Full-time maker; first knife sold in 1980. **Mark:** Full name, maker in script.

GOTTSCHALK, GREGORY J., 12 First St. (Ft. Pitt), Carnegie, PA, 15106/412-279-6692
Specialties: Fancy working straight knives and folders to customer specs. **Patterns:** Hunters to tantos, locking folders to minis. **Technical:** Grinds 440C, 154CM, ATS-34. Now making own Damascus. Most knives have mirror finishes. **Prices:** Start at $75. **Remarks:** Part-time maker; first knife sold in 1977. **Mark:** Full name in crescent.

GOUKER, GARY B., P.O. Box 955, Sitka, AK, 99835/907-747-3476
Specialties: Hunting knives for hard use. **Patterns:** Skinners, semi-skinners, and such. **Technical:** Likes natural materials, inlays, stainless steel. **Prices:** Moderate. **Remarks:** New Alaskan maker. **Mark:** Name.

GRAFFEO, ANTHONY I., 100 Riess Place, Chalmette, LA, 70043/504-277-1428
Specialties: Traditional working and using straight knives of his design, to customer specs and in standard patterns. **Patterns:** Hunters, utility/camp knives and fishing knives. **Technical:** Hollow- and flat-grinds ATS-34, 440C and 154CM. Handle materials include Pakkawood, Micarta and sambar stag. **Prices:** $65 to $100; some to $250. **Remarks:** Part-time maker; first knife sold in 1991. Doing business as Knives by: Graf. **Mark:** First and middle initials, last name city, state, Maker.

GRAHAM, RANDAL, 926 Elm St SE, Medicine Hat, AB, T1A 1C1, CANADA, /403-528-4281
Specialties: High performance working knives and swords. Art swords. **Patterns:** Artistic variations on classic patterns of European and Japanese swords. **Technical:** Forges simple and high alloy carbon steels. Forges his own damascus and casts bronze. Prefers natural handle materials. **Prices:** $120 to $750 (US); some higher. **Remarks:** Full-time maker; first knife sold in 1975. **Mark:** Quatra-foil (logo).

GRAVELINE, PASCAL AND ISABELLE, 38, rue de Kerbrezillic, 29350 Moelan-sur-Mer, FRANCE, /33 2 98 39 73 33
Specialties: French replicas from the 17th, 18th and 19th centuries. **Patterns:** Traditional folders and multi-blade pocket knives; traveling knives, fruit knives and fork sets; puzzle knives and friend's knives; rivetless knives. **Technical:** Grind 12C27, ATS-34, Damascus and carbon steel. **Prices:** $200 to $1,500; some to $2,000. **Remarks:** Full-time makers; first knife sold in 1992. **Mark:** Last name over head of ram.

GRAY, DANIEL, GRAY KNIVES, RR 1 Box 6900 Rt 11, Brownville, ME, 04414/207-965-2191
Specialties: Straight knives, Fantasy, folders, automatics and traditional of my own design. **Patterns:** Automatics, fighters, hunters. **Technical:** Grind 01, 154CM & D2. **Prices:** From $155 to $750. **Remarks:** Part-time maker; first knife sold in 1974. **Mark:** Gray Knives.

GRAY, BOB, 8206 N. Lucia Court, Spokane, WA, 99208/509-468-3924
Specialties: Straight working knives of his own design or to customer specs. **Patterns:** Hunter, fillet and carving knives. **Technical:** Forges 5160, L6 and some 52100; grinds 440C. **Prices:** $100 to $600. **Remarks:** Part-time knife maker; first knife sold in 1991. Doing business as Hi-Land Knives. **Mark:** HI-L.

custom knifemakers

GREBE, GORDON S., P.O. Box 296, Anchor Point, AK, 99556-0296/907-235-8242
Specialties: Working straight knives and folders, some fancy. **Patterns:** Tantos, Bowies, boot fighter sets, locking folders. **Technical:** Grinds stainless steels; likes 1/4" inch stock and glass-bead finishes. **Prices:** $75 to $250; some to $2,000. **Remarks:** Full-time maker; first knife sold in 1968. **Mark:** Initials in lightning logo.

GRECO, JOHN & SHERRY, 100 Mattie Jones Road, Greensburg, KY, 42743/270-932-3335
Specialties: One-of-a-kind limited edition knives. **Patterns:** Fighters, daggers, camp knives. **Technical:** Forges and stock removes carbon steel. **Prices:** Moderate. **Remarks:** Full-time maker; first knife sold in 1986. **Mark:** Last name.

GREEN, ROGER M., 4640 Co. Rd. 1022, Joshua, TX, 76058/817-641-5057
Specialties: 19th century period pieces. **Patterns:** Investor-grade Sheffield Bowies and dirks, fighters and hunters. **Technical:** Grinds 440C and tool steels; forges Damascus and occasionally carbon steel. Prefers flat grinds and hand-rubbed finishes. **Prices:** $350 to $3,500. **Remarks:** Full-time maker; first knife sold in 1984. **Mark:** First and middle initials, last name.

GREEN, WILLIAM (BILL), 46 Warren Rd., View Bank AUSTRALIA, Vic., 3084/
Specialties: Traditional high-tech straight knives and folders. **Patterns:** Japanese-influenced designs, hunters, Bowies, folders and miniatures. **Technical:** Forges O1, D2 and his own Damascus. Offers lost wax castings for bolsters and pommels. Likes natural handle materials, gems, silver and gold. **Prices:** $400 to $750; some to $1,200. **Remarks:** Full-time maker. **Mark:** Initials.

GREEN, BILL, 706 Bradfield, Garland, TX, 75042/972-272-4748
Specialties: High-art and working straight knives and folders of his design and to customer specs. **Patterns:** Bowies, hunters, kitchen knives and locking folders. **Technical:** Grinds ATS-34, D2 and 440V. Hand-tooled custom sheaths. **Prices:** $70 to $350; some to $750. **Remarks:** Part-time maker; first knife sold in 1990. **Mark:** Last name.

GREENE, DAVID, 570 Malcom Rd., Covington, GA, 30209/770-784-0657
Specialties: Straight working using knives. **Patterns:** Hunters. **Technical:** Forges mosaic and twist Damascus. Prefers stag and desert ironwood for handle material.

GREENE, CHRIS, 707 Cherry Lane, Shelby, NC, 28150/704-434-5620

GREENFIELD, G.O., 2605 15th St. #522, Everett, WA, 98201/206-259-1672
Specialties: High-tech and working straight knives and folders of his design. **Patterns:** Boots, daggers, hunters and one of a kinds. **Technical:** Grinds ATS-34, D2, 440C and T-440V. Makes sheaths for each knife. **Prices:** $100 to $800; some to $10,000. **Remarks:** Part-time maker; first knife sold in 1978. **Mark:** Springfield®, serial number.

GREGORY, MICHAEL, 211 Calhoun Rd., Belton, SC, 29627/803-338-8898
Specialties: Working straight knives and folders. **Patterns:** Hunters, tantos, locking folders and slip-joints, boots and fighters. **Technical:** Grinds 440C, 154CM and ATS-34; mirror finishes. **Prices:** $95 to $200; some to $1,000. **Remarks:** Part-time maker; first knife sold in 1980. **Mark:** Name, city in logo.

GREINER, RICHARD, 1073 E. County Rd. 32, Green Springs, OH, 44836/

GREISS, JOCKL, obere Muhlstr. 5, 73252, Gutenberg, GERMANY, 07026-3224/
Specialties: Classic and working using straight knives of his design. **Patterns:** Bowies, daggers and hunters. **Technical:** Uses only Jerry Rados Damascus, D2 and ATS-34. All knives are one of a kind made by hand; no machines are used. **Prices:** $700 to $2000; some to $3000. **Remarks:** Full-time maker; first knife sold in 1984. **Mark:** An "X" with a long vertical line through it.

GRENIER, ROGER, 540 Chemin De La Dague, Saint Jovite, Que., CANADA, J0T 2H0/819-425-8893
Specialties: Working straight knives. **Patterns:** Heavy-duty Bowies, fighters, hunters, swords and miniatures. **Technical:** Grinds O1, D2 and

440C. **Prices:** $70 to $225; some to $800. **Remarks:** Full-time maker; first knife sold in 1981. **Mark:** Last name on blade.

GREY, PIET, P.O. Box 1493, Silverton 0127, SOUTH AFRICA, /012-803-8206
Specialties: Fancy working and using straight knives of his design. **Patterns:** Fighters, hunters and utility/camp knives. **Technical:** Grinds ATS-34 and AEB-L; forges and grinds Damascus. Solderless fitting of guards. Engraves and scrimshaws. **Prices:** $125 to $750; some to $1,500. **Remarks:** Full-time maker; first knife sold in 1970. **Mark:** Last name.

GRIESI, CHRISTIAN, 4122 S 'E' ST, SPRINGFIELD, OR, 97478/541-998-4991
SPECIALTIES: Traditional Japanese swords. **Patterns:** Tantos to Katanas, western-style hunting and fighting knives. **Technical:** 1050 steel, stock removal for swords, ATS 34 stainless for western knives. **Prices:** $500 to $3000. **Remarks:** Part-time maker apprenticed to Michael Bell, first knife sold in 1994. **Mark:** Takemitsu or last name.

GRIFFIN, THOMAS J., 591 Quevli Ave., Windom, MN, 56101/507-831-1089
Specialties: Period pieces and fantasy straight knives of his design. **Patterns:** Daggers and swords. **Technical:** Forges 1095, 52100 and L6. Most blades are his own Damascus; turned fittings and wire-wrapped grips. **Prices:** $250 to $800; some to $2,000. **Remarks:** Full-time maker; first knife sold in 1991. Doing business as Griffin Knives. **Mark:** Last name etched.

GRIFFIN, RENDON AND MARK, 9706 Cedardale, Houston, TX, 77055/713-468-0436
Specialties: Working folders and automatics of their designs. **Patterns:** Standard lockers and slip-joints. **Technical:** Most blade steels; stock removal. **Prices:** Start at $350. **Remarks:** Part-time makers; Rendon's first knife sold in 1966; Mark's in 1974. **Mark:** Last name logo.

GRIFFIN JR., HOWARD A., 14299 SW 31st Ct., Davie, FL, 33330/305-474-5406
Specialties: Working straight knives and folders. **Patterns:** Hunters, Bowies, locking folders with his own push-button lock design. **Technical:** Grinds 440C. **Prices:** $100 to $200; some to $500. **Remarks:** Part-time maker; first knife sold in 1983. **Mark:** Initials.

GRIGSBY, BEN, The Bluff Dweller House, P.O. Box 2096, 318 E. Main, Mt. View, AR, 72560/501-269-3337
Specialties: Period pieces in steel or flint. **Patterns:** Arkansas toothpicks, Bowies and flint blades of late archaic period. **Technical:** Grinds O1, D2, 440C and knappes flint of Ozark Hills. **Prices:** $150 to $500; some to $1,500. **Remarks:** Full-time maker; first knife sold in 1976. Doing business as Ben Grigsby Edged Tools and Weapons. **Mark:** Initials with cache river arrowhead logo.

GROSS, W.W., 325 Sherbrook Dr., High Point, NC, 27260/
Specialties: Working knives. **Patterns:** Hunters, boots, fighters. **Technical:** Grinds. **Prices:** Moderate. **Remarks:** Full-time maker. **Mark:** Name.

GROSSMAN, STEWART, 24 Water St., #419, Clinton, MA, 01510/508-365-2291; 800-mysword
Specialties: Miniatures and full-size knives and swords. **Patterns:** One of a kind miniatures--jewelry, replicas--and wire-wrapped figures. Full-size art, fantasy and combat knives, daggers and modular systems. **Technical:** Forges and grinds most metals and Damascus. Uses gems, crystals, electronics and motorized mechanisms. **Prices:** $20 to $300; some to $4,500 and higher. **Remarks:** Full-time maker; first knife sold in 1985. **Mark:** G1.

GRUBB, RICHARD E., 2759 Maplewood Dr., Columbus, OH, 43231/614-882-1530
Specialties: Miniatures to Bowies. **Patterns:** Bowies, skinners, hunters and miniatures. **Technical:** Grinds 440C and 440V; offers exotic handle materials. **Prices:** $100 to $2,000. **Remarks:** Part-time maker; first knife sold in 1989. **Mark:** Name.

GRUSSENMEYER, PAUL G., 101 S. White Horse Pike, Lindenwold, NJ, 08021-2304/856-435-1500
Specialties: Assembling fancy and fantasy straight knives with his own carved handles. **Patterns:** Bowies, daggers, folders, swords, hunters and miniatures. **Technical:** Uses forged steel and Damascus, stock removal and knapped obsidian blades. **Prices:** $250 to $2,500; some to $12,000. **Remarks:** Part-time maker; first knife sold in 1991. **Mark:** First and last initial hooked together on handle.

GUESS, RAYMOND L., 7214 Salineville Rd. NE, Mechanicstown, OH, 44651/330-738-2793
Specialties: Working straight knives and folders of his design or to customer specs. **Patterns:** Hunters, Bowies, fillet knives, steak and paring knife sets. **Technical:** Grinds 440C. Offers silver inlay work and mirror finishes. Custom-made leather sheath for each knife. **Prices:** $65 to $850; some to $700. **Remarks:** Spare-time maker; first knife sold in 1985. **Mark:** First initial, last name.

GUIGNARD, GIB, Box 3413, Quartzsite, AZ, 85359/520-927-4831
Specialties: Rustic finish on primitive bowies with stag or ironwood handles & turquois inlay. **Patterns:** Very large in 5160 & ATS-34 - Small & med. size hunting knives in ATS-34. **Technical:** Forges 5160 and grind ATS-34. **Prices:** $100 to $500. **Remarks:** Full-time maker; first knife sold in 1989. Doing business as Cactus Forge. **Mark:** Last name or G+ on period pieces and primitive.

GUNDERSEN, D.F. "DOC", 5811 South Siesta Lane, Tempe, AZ, 85283/
Specialties: Small and medium belt knives, sword canes/staffs, kitchen cutlery, slip joint folders, throwers. **Patterns:** Utility, hunters, fighters and sailors' knives. **Technical:** Both forged and stock removalknives available in a variety of steels. Unique carvings available on many items. **Prices:** $65 to $250. **Remarks:** Full-time maker; first knife sold in 1988. Doing business as L & H Knife Works. **Mark:** L&H Knife Works.

GUNN, NELSON L., 77 Blake Road, Epping, NH, 03042/603-679-5119
Specialties: Classic and working/using straight knives of his design. **Patterns:** Bowies, fighters and hunters. **Technical:** Ginds O1 and 440C. Carved stag handles with turquoise inlays. **Prices:** $125 to $300; some to $700. **Remarks:** Part-time maker; first knife sold in 1996. Doing business as Nelson's Custom Knives. **Mark:** First and last initial.

GUNTER, BRAD, 13 Imnaha Road, Tijeras, NM, 87059/505-281-8080

GURGANUS, CAROL, 2553 N.C. 45 South, Colerain, NC, 27924/252-356-4831
Specialties: Working and using straight knives. **Patterns:** Fighters, hunters and kitchen knives. **Technical:** Grinds D2, ATS-34 and Damascus steel. Uses stag, and exotic wood handles. **Prices:** $100 to $300. **Remarks:** Full-time maker; first knife sold in 1992. **Mark:** Female symbol, last name, city, state.

GURGANUS, MELVIN H., 2553 N.C. 45 South, Colerain, NC, 27924/252-356-4831
Specialties: High-tech working folders. **Patterns:** Leaf-lock and back-lock designs, bolstered and interframe. **Technical:** D2 and 440C; makes mokume. Wife Carol scrimshaws. Heat-treats, carves and offers lost wax casting. **Prices:** $300 to $3,000. **Remarks:** Part-time maker; first knife sold in 1983. **Mark:** First initial, last name and maker.

GUTH, KENNETH, 8 S. Michigan, 32nd Floor, Chicago, IL, 60603/312-346-1760
Specialties: One-of-a-kind ornate straight knives and folders. **Patterns:** Flemish, Japanese and African-styled knives. Also makes a few forged Damascus miniature knives with fossil ivory handles and 18K gold fittings and rivets. **Technical:** Forges and grinds high-carbon and 440C. Offers brass and steel laminations, goldsmithing. **Prices:** Upscale. **Remarks:** Full-time goldsmith and knifemaker. **Mark:** Last name.

GUTHRIE, GEORGE B., 1912 Puett Chapel Rd., Bassemer City, NC, 28016/704-629-3031
Specialties: Working knives of his design or to customer specs. **Patterns:** Hunters, boots, fighters, locking folders and slip-joints in traditional styles. **Technical:** Grinds D2, 440C and 154CM. **Prices:** $105 to $300; some to $450. **Remarks:** Part-time maker; first knife sold in 1978. **Mark:** Name in state.

GWOZDZ, BOB, 71 Starr Ln., Attleboro, MA, 02703/508-226-7475
Specialties: Fancy working straight knives. **Patterns:** Fighters, tantos and hunters. **Technical:** Grinds 440C. **Prices:** $150 to $400; some $500 and higher. **Remarks:** Part-time maker; first knife sold in 1983. Now attending law school. Will accept phone orders during summer months only. **Mark:** Name and serial number.

h

HAGEN, PHILIP L., P.O. Box 58, Pelican Rapids, MN, 56572/218-863-8503
Specialties: High-tech working straight knives and folders. **Patterns:** Defense-related straight knives; wide variety of folders. **Technical:** Forges and grinds 440C and his own Damascus; Uddeholm UHB. **Prices:** $100 to $800; some to $3,000. **Remarks:** Part-time maker; first knife sold in 1975. **Mark:** DOC HAGEN in shield, knife, banner logo; or DOC.

HAGGERTY, GEORGE S., P.O. Box 88, Jacksonville, VT, 05342/802-368-7437
Specialties: Working straight knives and folders. **Patterns:** Hunters, claws, camp and fishing knives, locking folders and backpackers. **Technical:** Forges and grinds W2, 440C and 154CM. **Prices:** $85 to $300. **Remarks:** Part-time maker; first knife sold in 1981. **Mark:** Initials or last name.

HAGUE, GEOFF, The Malt House, Hollow Ln., Wilton Marlborough, Wiltshire, ENGLAND, SN8 3SR/01672-870212
Specialties: Working knives to his design or to customer specs. **Patterns:** Hunters, skinners and fillet knives. **Technical:** Grinds ATS-34, D2, O1 and Damascus. **Prices:** Start at $200. **Remarks:** Full-time maker. **Mark:** Last name.

HAJOVSKY, ROBERT J., P.O. Box 77, Scotland, TX, 76379/817-541-2219
Specialties: Working straight knives; sub-hilted fighters. **Patterns:** Variety of straight knives. **Technical:** Grinds ATS-34 and others on request. **Prices:** $150 to $700. **Remarks:** Part-time maker; first knife sold in 1973. **Mark:** Bob-Sky Knives and name, city, state.

HALLIGAN, ED, 14 Meadow Way, Sharpsburg, GA, 30277/770-251-7720
Specialties: Working straight knives and folders, some fancy. **Patterns:** Linerlocks, hunters, skinners, boots, fighters and swords. **Technical:** Grinds ATS-34; forges 5160; makes cable and pattern Damascus. **Prices:** $160 to $2,500. **Remarks:** Full-time maker; first knife sold in 1985. Doing business as Halligan Knives. **Mark:** Last name, city, state and USA.

HAMLET JR., JOHNNY, 300 Billington, Clute, TX, 77531/409-265-6929
Specialties: Working straight knives and folders. **Patterns:** Hunters, fighters, fillet and kitchen knives, locking folders. Likes upswept knives and trailing-points. **Technical:** Grinds 440C, D2, ATS-34. Makes sheaths. **Prices:** $55 to $225; some to $500. **Remarks:** Part-time maker; first knife sold in 1988. **Mark:** Hamlet's Handmades in script.

HAMMOND, JIM, P.O. Box 486, Arab, AL, 35016/205-586-4151
Specialties: High-tech fighters and folders. **Patterns:** Proven-design fighters. **Technical:** Grinds 440C and ATS-34. **Prices:** $385 to $1,200; some to $8,500. **Remarks:** Full-time maker; first knife sold in 1977. Designer for Columbia River Knife & Tool. **Mark:** Full name, city, state in shield logo.

HANCOCK, TIM, 10805 N. 83rd St., Scottsdale, AZ, 85260/480-998-8849
Specialties: High-art and working straight knives and folders of his design and to customer specs. **Patterns:** Bowies, fighters, daggers, tantos, swords, folders. **Technical:** Forges Damascus and 52100; grinds ATS-34. Makes Damascus. Silver-wire inlays; offers carved fittings. **Prices:** $225 to $10,000; some to $5,000. **Remarks:** Full-time maker; first knife sold in 1988. **Mark:** Last name or heart.

HAND, BILL, P.O. Box 773, 1103 W. 7th St., Spearman, TX, 79081/806-659-2967
Specialties: Traditional working and using straight knives and folders of his design or to customer specs. **Patterns:** Hunters, Bowies and fighters. **Technical:** Forges 5160, 52100 and Damascus. **Prices:** Start at $150. **Remarks:** Part-time maker; Journeyman Smith. Current delivery time twelve to sixteen months. **Mark:** Stylized initials.

HAND M.D., JAMES E., 1001 Mockingbird Ln., Gloster, MS, 39638/601-225-4197
Specialties: All types of straight knives. **Patterns:** Hunters, fighters, boots and collector knives. **Technical:** Grinds ATS-34 and commercial Damascus. All knives are handmade. **Prices:** $125 to $850; some to

custom knifemakers

$1,200. **Remarks:** Full-time maker; first knife sold in 1985. **Mark:** Name and city.

HANSEN, ROBERT W., 35701 University Ave. N.E., Cambridge, MN, 55008/612-689-3242
Specialties: Working straight knives, folders and integrals.. **Patterns:** From hunters to minis, camp knives to miniatures; folding lockers and slip-joints in original styles. **Technical:** Grinds O1, 440C and 154CM; likes filework. **Prices:** $75 to $175; some to $550. **Remarks:** Part-time maker; first knife sold in 1983. **Mark:** Fish with last initial inside.

HANSON, TRAVIS, 651 Rangeline Rd., Mosinee, WI, 54455/715-693-3940
Specialties: Straight knives of his design and in standard patterns. **Patterns:** Hunters and miniatures. **Technical:** Grinds D2, 440C and Damascus. Offers scrimshaw and filework. **Prices:** $50 to $300; some to $550. **Remarks:** First knife sold in 1993. **Mark:** Name in script.

HARA, KOUJI, 292-2 Ohsugi, Seki-City, Gifu-Pref. 501-32, JAPAN, / 0575-24-7569
Specialties: High-tech and working straight knives of his design; some folders. **Patterns:** Hunters, locking folders and utility/camp knives. **Technical:** Grinds Cowry X, Cowry Y and ATS-34. Prefers high mirror polish; pearl handle inlay. **Prices:** $80 to $500; some to $1,000. **Remarks:** Full-time maker; first knife sold in 1980. Doing business as Knife House "Hara". **Mark:** First initial, last name in fish.

HARDY, SCOTT, 639 Myrtle Ave., Placerville, CA, 95667/916-622-5780
Specialties: Traditional working and using straight knives of his design. **Patterns:** Bowies, hunters and utility knives. **Technical:** Forges O1 and W2. Offers mirror finish; differentially tempers. **Prices:** $76 to $350; some to $1,000. **Remarks:** Part-time maker; first knife sold in 1982. **Mark:** First initial, last name and Handmade with bird logo.

HARILDSTAD, MATT, 18627 68 Ave, Edmonton, AB, T5T 2M8, CANADA, /780-481-3165
Specialties: Working knives, fancy fighting knives, kitchen cutlery, letter openers. **Patterns:** Full range of straight knives in classic patterns. **Technical:** Grinds ATS-34, 440C, commercial damascus and some high carbon. **Prices:** $120 to $500 (US). **Remarks:** Part-time maker, first knife sold in 1997. **Mark:** Name, city province.

HARKINS, J.A., P.O. Box 218, Conner, MT, 59827/406-821-1060
Specialties: Investment grade knives. **Patterns:** flush buttons, lockers. **Technical:** Grinds ATS-34 . Engraves; offers gem work. **Prices:** Start at $550. **Remarks:** Full-time maker and engraver; first knife sold in 1988. **Mark:** First and middle initials, last name. **Other:** Semi-retired; no longer accepts orders - "in stock" sales only.

HARLESS, WALT, P.O. Box 845, Stoneville, NC, 27048-0845/336-573-9768
Specialties: Traditional working straight knives. **Patterns:** Hunters, utility, combat and specialty knives; one of a kind historical interpretations. **Technical:** Grinds ATS-34 and 440C. **Prices:** $90 to $350; some to $1,200. **Remarks:** Full-time maker; first knife sold in 1978. Doing business as Arrow Forge. **Mark:** "A" with arrow; name, city, state.

HARLEY, LARRY W., 348 Deerfield Dr., Bristol, TN, 37620/423-878-5368 (shop)
Specialties: Working knives; period pieces. **Patterns:** Full range of straight knives, tomahawks, razors, buckskinners and hog spears. **Technical:** Forges and grinds ATS-34, D2, 440, O1, L6 and his own Damascus. **Prices:** $65 to $6,500. **Remarks:** Full-time maker; first knife sold in 1983. Guides (knife only) wild boar hunts. Doing business as Lonesome Pine Knives. **Mark:** Name, city and state in pine logo.

HARMON, JAY, 462 Victoria Rd., Woodstock, GA, 30189/770-928-2734
Specialties: Working straight knives and folders of his design or to customer specs; collector-grade pieces. **Patterns:** Bowies, daggers, fighters, boots, hunters and folders. **Technical:** Grinds 440C, 440V, ATS-34, D2 1095 and Damascus; heat-treats; makes own mokume. **Prices:** Start at $185. **Remarks:** Part-time maker; first knife sold in 1984. **Mark:** Last name.

HARRIS, RALPH DEWEY, 2607 Bell Shoals Rd., Brandon, FL, 33511/813-681-5293
Specialties: Collectible and working interframe locking folders. **Patterns:** High tech utility and gentleman's folders. **Technical:** Grinds 440C, ATS-34 and some commercial Damascus. Uses jeweled and color anodized titanium and 416SS for frames. Offers file work and engraving. **Prices:** $300 to $2,000. **Remarks:** Full-time maker; first knife sold in 1978. **Mark:** Last name, or name and city.

HARRIS, JAY, 991 Johnson St., Redwood City, CA, 94061/415-366-6077
Specialties: Traditional high-tech straight knives and folders of his design. **Patterns:** Daggers, fighters and locking folders. **Technical:** Uses 440C, ATS-34 and CPM. **Prices:** $250 to $850. **Remarks:** Spare-time maker; first knife sold in 1980.

HARSEY, WILLIAM H., 82710 N. Howe Ln., Creswell, OR, 97426/503-895-4941
Specialties: High-tech kitchen and outdoor knives. **Patterns:** Folding hunters, trout and bird folders; straight hunters, camp knives and axes. **Technical:** Grinds; etches. **Prices:** $125 to $300; some to $1,500. Folders start at $350. **Remarks:** Full-time maker; first knife sold in 1979. **Mark:** Full name, state, U.S.A.

HART, BILL, 647 Cedar Dr., Pasadena, MD, 21122/410-255-4981
Specialties: Fur-trade era working straight knives and folders. **Patterns:** Springback folders, skinners, Bowies and patch knives. **Technical:** Forges and stock removes 1095 and 5160 wire Damascus. **Prices:** $100 to $600. **Remarks:** Part-time maker; first knife sold in 1986. **Mark:** Name.

HARTMAN, ARLAN (LANNY), 340 Ruddiman, N. Muskegon, MI, 49445/616-744-3635
Specialties: Working straight knives and folders. **Patterns:** Drop-point hunters, coil spring lockers, slip-joints. **Technical:** Flat-grinds D2, 440C and ATS-34. **Prices:** $200 to $2,000. **Remarks:** Part-time maker; first knife sold in 1982. **Mark:** Last name.

HARTMANN, BRUCE JAMES, 961 Waterloo, Port Elgin, Ontario, CANADA, N0H 2C0/

HARTSFIELD, PHILL, P.O. Box 1637, Newport Beach, CA, 92659-0637/949-722-9792
Specialties: Heavy-duty working and using straight knives. **Patterns:** Fighters, swords and survival knives, most in Japanese profile. **Technical:** Grinds A2 and M2. **Prices:** $350 to $20,000. **Remarks:** Full-time maker; first knife sold about 1966. Doing business as A Cut Above. **Mark:** Initials, chiseled character plus register mark.

HARVEY, MAX, 14 Bass Rd., Bull Creek, Perth 6155, WESTERN AUSTRALIA, /09-332-7585
Specialties: Daggers, Bowies, fighters and fantasy knives. **Patterns:** Hunters, Bowies, tantos and skinners. **Technical:** Hollow- and flat-grinds 440C, ATS-34, 154CM and Damascus. Offers gem work. **Prices:** $250 to $4,000. **Remarks:** Part-time maker; first knife sold in 1981. **Mark:** First and middle initials, last name.

HARVEY, KEVIN, KEVIN'S CUSTOM KNIVES, PRIVATE BAG 1890, GOLD REEF CITY 2159, JOHANNESBURG, S AFRICA, /+27 11 496 1600
Specialties: Large knives of presentation quality and creative art knives. **Patterns:** Fixed blades of Bowie, dagger and fighter styles. Carving and cutlery sets. My design or customized. **Technical:** Stock removal forge carbon steel and my own Damascus. Indigenous African handle materials preferred. Stacked handles and file work often used. Shell mosaic and inlay. Own Scrimshaw. Ostrich, bullfrog, fish, crocodile and snake leathers used on unique sheaths. Surface texturing and heat coloring of materials. Work closely with jeweler, sculptor, engraver and case maker. **prices:** $500 to $9,000. **Remarks:** Full-time maker. First knife sold 1984. Work in living museum depicting the times of early gold mining in Johannesburg. **Mark:** First name in calligraphy, South Africa.

HATCH, KEN, RR 1 Box 83-A-5, Kooskia, ID, 83539/
Specialties: Indian & early trade knives. **Patterns:** Buckskinners and period Bowies. **Technical:** Forges and grinds 1095, O1, W2, ATS-34. Prefers natural handle materials. **Prices:** $85 to $400. **Remarks:** Part-time maker, custom leather & bead work; first knife sold in 1977. **Mark:** Last name or dragonfly stamp.

HAWK, JACK L., Rt. 1, Box 771, Ceres, VA, 24318/703-624-3878
Specialties: Fancy and embellished working and using straight knives of his design or to customer specs. **Patterns:** Hunters, Bowies and daggers. **Technical:** Hollow-grinds 440C, ATS-34 and D2; likes bone and ivory handles. **Prices:** $75 to $1,200. **Remarks:** Full-time maker; first knife sold in 1982. **Mark:** Full name and initials.

HAWK, GRANT, Box 401, Idaho City, ID, 83631/208-392-4911
Specialties: Cowboy fixed blades with horse hoof handles and rawhide laced sheaths; large folders with unique ambidextrous lock system. **Patterns:** Hunter/utility and tactical folders. **Technical:** Grinds ATS-34, zigzag finish, folder handles of 6061 aluminum or titanium. Handle overlays; horse hoof, exotic woods or other. Checkering of handle overlays available. **Prices:** Start at $325. **Remarks:** Full time maker, first knife sold in 1995. **Mark:** First initials and last name.

HAWK, GAVIN, Box 401, Idaho City, ID, 83631/208-392-4911
Specialties: Working straight knives with rawhide laced sheaths. **Patterns:** Hunter/utility. **Technical:** Grinds ATS-34 zigzag finish on blade flats; handle material horse hoof in combination with exotic wood or antler. **Prices:** Start at $175. **Remarks:** Part-time maker, 17 years old. Sold first knife in 1996. **Mark:** First and last name on butt cap.

HAWK, JOEY K., Rt. 1, Box 196, Ceres, VA, 24318/703-624-3282
Specialties: Working straight knives, some fancy. Welcomes customer designs. **Patterns:** Hunters, fighters, daggers, Bowies and miniatures. **Technical:** Grinds 440C or customer preference. Offers some knives with jeweling. **Prices:** $100 to $250; some to $500. **Remarks:** Part-time maker; first knife sold in 1983. **Mark:** First and middle initials, last name stamped.

HAWK, JOE, Rt. 1, Box 196, Ceres, VA, 24318/703-624-3282
Specialties: Fancy working knives of his design or to customer specs. **Patterns:** Hunters, combat knives, Bowies and fighters. **Technical:** Grinds mostly ATS-34, 154CM and 440C. Scrimshaws, carves, engraves and silver inlays. **Prices:** $150 to $2,100. **Remarks:** Full-time maker; first knife sold in 1958. **Mark:** Name with tomahawk logo.

HAWKINS, RADE, 110 Buckeye Rd., Fayetteville, GA, 30214/770-964-1177
Specialties: Exotic steels, custom designs, one-of-a-kind knives. **Patterns:** All styles. **Technical:** Grinds CPM10V, CPM440V, Vascomax C-350, Stelite K6 and Damascus. **Prices:** Start at $190. **Remarks:** Full-time maker; first knife sold in 1972. **Mark:** Full name, city, state; some last name only.

HAYES, DOLORES, P.O. Box 41405, Los Angeles, CA, 90041/213-258-9923
Specialties: High-art working and using straight knives of her design. **Patterns:** Art knives and miniatures. **Technical:** Grinds 440C, stainless AEB, commercial Damascus and ATS-34. **Prices:** $50 to $500; some to $2,000. **Remarks:** Spare-time maker; first knife sold in 1978. **Mark:** Last name.

HAYES, WALLY, 1024 Queen St., Orleans, Ont., CANADA, K4A-3N2/613-824-9520
Specialties: Classic and fancy straight knives and folders. **Patterns:** Daggers, Bowies, fighters, tantos. **Technical:** Forges own Damascus and O1; engraves. **Prices:** $250 to $1,500; some to $4,500. **Mark:** Last name, M.S. and serial number.

HAYNES, CHAP, RR #4, Tatamagouche, NS, CANADA, B0K 1V0/
Specialties: Ergonomic tools. **Patterns:** Hunters, Bowies, fised blade, working knives, tomahawks, swords and miniatures. **Technical:** Forges carbon steel, meteorite and his own Damascus. **Prices:** Start at $400. **Remarks:** Part-time maker; first knife sold in 1985. **Mark:** Smith at anvil logo with HAYNES GREAT BLADES.

HAYNIE, CHARLES, 125 Cherry Lane, Toccoa, GA, 30577/706-886-8665

HAYS, MARK, Hays Handmade Knives, 1034 Terry Way, Carrollton, TX, 75006/972-242-5197
Specialties: Working straight knives and folders. Patterns inspired by Randall & Stone. **Patterns:** Bowies, hunters and slip-joint folders. **Technical:** 440C stock removal. Repairs and restores Stone knives. **Prices:** Start at $150. **Remarks:** Part-time maker, brochure available, with Stone knives 1974-1983, 1990-1991; first knife sold in 1984. Employed by G.W. Stone 11 years. **Mark:** First initial, last name, state and serial number. **Other:** Relocating to Austin, TX summer '99.

HEASMAN, H.G., 28 St. Mary's Rd., Llandudno, N. Wales U.K., LL302UB/(UK)0492-876351
Specialties: Miniatures only. **Patterns:** Bowies, daggers and swords. **Technical:** Files from stock high-carbon and stainless steel. **Prices:**

$400 to $600. **Remarks:** Part-time maker; first knife sold in 1975. Doing business as Reduced Reality. **Mark:** NA.

HEDRICK, DON, 131 Beechwood Hills, Newport News, VA, 23608/757-877-8100
Specialties: Working straight knives; period pieces and fantasy knives. **Patterns:** Hunters, boots, Bowies and miniatures. **Technical:** Grinds 440C and commercial Damascus. **Prices:** $150 to $550; some to $1,200. **Remarks:** Part-time maker; first knife sold in 1982. **Mark:** First initial, last name in oval logo.

HEGWALD, J.L., 1106 Charles, Humboldt, KS, 66748/316-473-3523
Specialties: Working straight knives, some fancy. **Patterns:** Makes Bowies, miniatures. **Technical:** Forges or grinds O1, L6, 440C; mixes materials in handles. **Prices:** $35 to $200; some higher. **Remarks:** Part-time maker; first knife sold in 1983. **Mark:** First and middle initials.

HEGWOOD, JOEL, Rt. 4, Box 229, Summerville, GA, 30747/404-397-8187
Specialties: High-tech working knives of his design. **Patterns:** Hunters, boots and survival knives; locking folders, slip-joints and interframes. **Technical:** Grinds A2, O1 and D2; uses 7075 aluminum in lightweight folder frames. **Prices:** $65 to $125; some to $200. **Remarks:** Part-time maker; first knife sold in 1979. **Mark:** Last name.

HEHN, RICHARD KARL, Lehnmuehler Str. 1, 55444 Dorrebach, GERMANY, /06724 3152
Specialties: High-tech, full integral working knives. **Patterns:** Hunters, fighters & daggers. **Technical:** Grinds CPM T-440V, CPM T-420V, forges his own stainless Damascus. **Prices:** $350 to $4,500; some to $10,000. **Remarks:** Full-time maker; first knife sold in 1963. **Mark:** Runic last initial in logo.

HEITLER, HENRY, P.O. Box 15025, Tampa, FL, 33684-5025/813-933-1645
Specialties: Traditional working and using straight knives of his design and to customer specs. **Patterns:** Fighters, hunters, utility/camp knives and fillet knives. **Technical:** Flat-grinds ATS-34; offers tapered tangs. **Prices:** $135 to $450; some to $600. **Remarks:** Part-time maker; first knife sold in 1990. **Mark:** First initial, last name, city, state circling double "H"s.

HELTON, ROY, 5650 District Blvd., #128, Bakersfield, CA, 93313/805-833-2795
Specialties: Tactical and fancy lockback and liner lock folders. **Patterns:** Lockback and liner lock folders. **Technical:** Grinds ATS-34; commercial A2 and Damascus. Likes filework; anodizes. Mosly Ti frames. Uses mostly natural handle materials. **Prices:** Start at $300. **Remarks:** Full-time maker; first knife sold in 1975. **Mark:** Name, city, state.

HEMPHILL, JESSE, 896 Big Hill Rd., Berea, KY, 40403/
Specialties: Period pieces, folders and Scagel reproductions. **Patterns:** Hawks, Bowies sets, fighters and utility knives. **Technical:** Forges his own Damascus, D2, 5160 and 52100. **Prices:** $50 to $300; some to $500. **Remarks:** Full-time maker; first knife sold in 1986. **Mark:** Initials or a turtle.

HENDRICKS, SAMUEL J., 2162 Van Buren Rd., Maurertown, VA, 22644/703-436-3305
Specialties: Integral hunters and skinners of thin design. **Patterns:** Boots, hunters and locking folders. **Technical:** Grinds ATS-34, 440C and D2. Integral liners and bolsters of N-S and 7075 T6 aircraft aluminimum. Does leatherwork. **Prices:** $50 to $250; some to $500. **Remarks:** Full-time maker; first knife sold in 1992. **Mark:** First and middle initials, last name, city and state in football-style logo.

HENDRICKSON, E. JAY, 4204 Ballenger Creek Pike, Frederick, MD, 21703/301-663-6923
Specialties: Classic collectors and working straight knives of his design. **Patterns:** Bowies, Kukri's, camp, hunters, and fighters. **Technical:** Forges 06, 1084, 5160, 52100, D2, L6 and W2; makes Damascus; offers silver wire inlay and Moran styles. **Prices:** $300 to $4,000. **Remarks:** Full-time maker; first knife sold in 1975. **Mark:** Last name, M.S.

HENDRIX, WAYNE, 5210 Burtons Ferry Hwy, Allendale, SC, 29810/803-584-3825
Specialties: Working/using knives of his design. **Patterns:** Hunters and fillet knives. **Technical:** Grinds ATS-34, D2 and 440C. **Prices:** $55 to $300. **Remarks:** Full-time maker; first knife sold in 1985. **Mark:** Last name.

HENNON, ROBERT, 940 Vincent Lane, Ft. Walton Beach, FL, 32547/ 904-862-9734

HENRIKSEN, HANS J., Birkegaardsvej 24, DK 3200 Helsinge, DENMARK, / **Specialties:** Zirconia ceramic blades. **Patterns:** Customer designs. **Technical:** Slip-cast zirconia-water mix in plaster mould; offers hidden or full tang. **Prices:** White blades start at $10cm; colored +50 percent. **Remarks:** Part-time maker; first ceramic blade sold in 1989. **Mark:** Initial logo.

HENRY & SON, PETER, 332 Nine Mile Ride, Wokingham, Berkshire, ENGLAND, RG11 3NJ/0118-9734475 **Specialties:** Period pieces. **Patterns:** Period pieces only--Scottish dirks, sgian dubhs and Bowies, modern hunters. **Technical:** Grinds O1. **Prices:** £50 to £250 or $80 to $400. **Remarks:** Full-time maker; first knife sold in 1974. **Mark:** P. Henry & Son.

HENSLEY, WAYNE, P.O. Box 904, Conyers, GA, 30012/770-483-8938 **Specialties:** Period pieces and fancy working knives. **Patterns:** Boots to Bowies, locking folders to miniatures. Large variety of straight knives. **Technical:** Grinds D2, 440C, 154CM and commerical Damascus. **Prices:** $85 and up. **Remarks:** Full-time maker; first knife sold in 1974. **Mark:** Last name.

HERBST, PETER, Komotauer Strasse 26, 91207 Lauf a.d. Pegn., GERMANY, /09123-13315 **Specialties:** Working/using knives and folders of his design. **Patterns:** Hunters, fighters and daggers; interframe and integral. **Technical:** Grinds CPM-T-440V, UHB-Elmax, ATS-34 and stainless Damascus. **Prices:** $300 to $3,000; some to $8,000. **Remarks:** Full-time maker; first knife sold in 1981. **Mark:** First initial, last name.

HERGERT, BOB, 12 Geer Circle, Port Orford, OR, 97465/541-332-3010

HERMAN, TIM, 7721 Foster, Overland Park, KS, 66204/913-649-3860 **Specialties:** Investment-grade folders of his design; interframes and bolster frames. **Patterns:** Boots, Bowies, daggers and push knives; high-quality folders and interframes. **Technical:** Grinds ATS-34 and A.J. Hubbard Damascus. Engraves and gold inlays with pearl, jade, lapis and Australian opal. **Prices:** $1,000 to $15,000. **Remarks:** Full-time maker; first knife sold in 1978. **Mark:** Etched signature.

HERMES, DANA E., 39594 Kona Ct., Fremont, CA, 94538/415-490-0393 **Specialties:** Fancy and embellished classic straight knives of his design. **Patterns:** Hunters and Bowies. **Technical:** Grinds 440C and D2. **Prices:** $200 to $600; some to $1,000. **Remarks:** Spare-time maker; first knife sold in 1985. **Mark:** Last name.

HERNDON, WM. R. "BILL", 32520 Michigan St., Acton, CA, 93510/ 805-269-5860 **Specialties:** Straight knives, plain and fancy. **Technical:** Carbon steel (white and blued), Damascus, stainless steels. **Prices:** Start at $120. **Remarks:** Full-time maker; first knife sold in 1981. **Mark:** Signature and/ or helm logo.

HERRON, GEORGE, 474 Antonio Way, Springfield, SC, 29146/803-258-3914 / **Specialties:** High-tech working and using straight knives; some folders. **Patterns:** Hunters, fighters, boots in personal styles. **Technical:** Grinds 154CM, ATS-34. **Prices:** $75 to $500; some to $750. **Remarks:** Full-time maker; first knife sold in 1963. About 12 year back log. Not excepting orders. No catalog. **Mark:** Last name in script.

HESSER, DAVID, P.O. Box 1079, Dripping Springs, TX, 78620/512-894-0100 **Specialties:** High-art daggers and fantasy knives of his design; court weapons of the Renaissance. **Patterns:** Daggers, swords, axes, miniatures and sheath knives. **Technical:** Forges 1065, 1095, O1, D2 and recycled tool steel. Offers custom lapidary work and stone-setting, stone handles and custom hardwood scabbards. **Prices:** $95 to $500; some to $6,000. **Remarks:** Full-time maker; first knife sold in 1989. Doing business as Exotic Blades. **Mark:** Last name, year.

HETHCOAT, DON, Box 1764, Clovis, NM, 88101/505-762-5721 **Specialties:** Liner lock, working straight knives and folders. **Patterns:** Hunters, Bowies, locking and liner lock. **Technical:** Grinds stainless; forges Damascus. **Prices:** $300 to $5,000. **Remarks:** Part-time maker; first knife sold in 1969. **Mark:** Last name on all.

HETMANSKI, THOMAS S., 494 Orchard Dr., Mansfield, OH, 44903-9471/419-774-0165 **Specialties:** Working knives, replicas, military-style knives and miniatures. **Patterns:** Hunters, boots, miniatures and some folders. **Technical:** Grinds A2, 440C, ATS-34 and commercial Damascus. **Prices:** $150 to $400; some higher. **Remarks:** Part-time maker; first knife sold in 1982. **Mark:** Initials in monogram.

HIBBEN, GIL, P.O. Box 13, LaGrange, KY, 40031/502-222-1397 **Specialties:** Working knives and fantasy pieces to customer specs. **Patterns:** Full range of straight knives, including swords, axes and miniatures; some locking folders. **Technical:** Grinds D2, 440C and 154CM. **Prices:** $300 to $2,000; some to $10,000. **Remarks:** Full-time maker; first knife sold in 1957. Maker and designer of *Rambo III* knife; made swords for movie *Marked for Death* and throwing knife for movie *Under Seige*; made belt buckle knife and knives for movie *Perfect Weapon*; made knives featured in movie *Star Trek the Next Generation*; designer for United Cutlery. **Mark:** Hibben Knives. city and state, or signature.

HIBBEN, JOLEEN, P.O. Box 172, LaGrange, KY, 40031/502-222-0983 **Specialties:** Miniature straight knives of her design; period pieces. **Patterns:** Hunters, axes and fantasy knives. **Technical:** Grinds Damascus, 1095 tool steel and stainless 440C or ATS-34. Uses wood, ivory, bone, feathers and claws on/for handles. **Prices:** $60 to $200. **Remarks:** Spare-time maker; first knife sold in 1991. **Mark:** Initials or first name.

HIBBEN, WESTLEY G., 14101 Sunview Dr., Anchorage, AK, 99515/ **Specialties:** Working straight knives of his design or to customer specs. **Patterns:** Hunters, fighters, daggers, combat knives and some fantasy pieces. **Technical:** Grinds 440C mostly. Filework available. **prices:** $200 to $400; some to $3,000. **Remarks:** Part-time maker; first knife sold in 1988. **Mark:** Signature.

HIBBEN, DARYL, P.O. Box 172, 1331 Dawkins Rd., LaGrange, KY, 40031-0172/502-222-0983 **Specialties:** Working straight knives, some fancy to customer specs. **Patterns:** Hunters, fighters, Bowies, short sword, art and fantasy. **Technical:** Grinds 440C, ATS-34, 154CM, Damascus; prefers hollow-grinds. **Prices:** $175 to $3,000. **Remarks:** Full-time maker; first knife sold in 1979. **Mark:** Etched full name in script.

HIELSCHER, GUY, HC34, P.O. Box 992, Alliance, NE, 69301/308-762-4318 **Specialties:** Traditional and working straight knives of his design, to customer specs and in standard patterns. **Patterns:** Bowies, fighters, skinners, daggers and hunters. **Technical:** Forges his own Damascus from O1 and 1018 steel. **Prices:** $150 to $225; some to $850. **Remarks:** Part-time maker; first knife sold in 1988. Doing business as G.H. Knives. **Mark:** Initials in arrowhead.

HIGH, TOM, 5474 S. 112.8 Rd., Alamosa, CO, 81101/719-589-2108 **Specialties:** Hunters, some fancy. **Patterns:** Drop-points in several shapes; some semi-skinners. Knives designed by and for top outfitters and guides. **Technical:** Grinds ATS-34; likes hollow-grinds, mirror finishes; prefers scrimmable handles. **Prices:** $175 to $8,000. **Remarks:** Full-time maker; first knife sold in 1965. Limited edition wildlife series knives. **Mark:** Initials connected; arrow through last name on fancy knives.

HILKER, THOMAS N., P.O. Box 409, Williams, OR, 97544/541-846-6461 **Specialties:** Traditional working straight knives and folders. **Patterns:** Folding skinner in two sizes, Bowies, fork and knife sets, camp knives and interchangeables. **Technical:** Grinds D2, 440C and ATS-34. Heat-treats. **Prices:** $50 to $350; some to $400. Doing business as Thunderbolt Artisans. Only limited production models available; not currently taking orders. **Remarks:** Full-time maker; first knife sold in 1983. **Mark:** Last name.

HILL, HOWARD E., 111 Mission Lane, Polson, MT, 59860/406-883-3405 **Specialties:** Button lock, liner lock & the new slip lock folder. **Patterns:** Bowies, daggers, skinners and lockback folders. **Technical:** Grinds 440C; uses micro and satin finish. **Prices:** $150 to $1,000. **Remarks:** Full-time maker; first knife sold in 1981. **Mark:** Persuader.

HILL, RICK, 20 Nassau, Maryville, IL, 62062-5618/618-288-4370 **Specialties:** Working knives and period pieces to customer specs. **Patterns:** Hunters, locking folders, fighters and daggers. **Technical:** Grinds

D2, 440C and 154CM; forges his own Damascus. **Prices:** $75 to $500; some to $3,000. **Remarks:** Part-time maker; first knife sold in 1983. **Mark:** Full name in hill shape logo.

HILL, STEVEN E., 7814 Toucan Dr. (Nov-May), Nov-May, Orlando, FL, 32822/407-277-3549
Specialties: Fancy liner lock folders; some exotic mechanisms, some working grade. **Patterns:** Classic to cool. **Technical:** Grinds 440C, D2, and Damascus. Prefers natural handle materials; offers elaborate file-work, carving, and inlays. **Prices:** $375 to $4,000; some higher. **Remarks:** Full-time maker; first knife sold in 1978. **Mark:** First initial, last name and handmade. Other: June-Oct adr: 40 Rand Pond Rd, Goshen NH 03752 (603) 863-4762.

HILLMAN, CHARLES, 225 Waldoboro Rd, Friendship, ME, 04547/207-832-4634
Specialties: Working knives of my own or custom design. Heavy Scagel influence. **Patterns:** Hunters, fishing, camp and general utility. Occasional folders. **Technical:** Grinds D2 and 440C. File work, blade and handle carving, engraving. Natural handle materials-antler, bone, leather, wood, horn. Sheaths made to order. **Prices:** $60 to $500. **Remarks:** Part-time maker; first knive sold 1986. **Mark:** Last name in oak leaf.

HINDERER, RICK, 5423 Kister Rd., Wooster, OH, 44691/216-263-0962
Specialties: Working knives to one-of-a-kind Damascus straight knives and folders. **Patterns:** All. **Technical:** Grinds ATS-34 and D2; forges O1, W2 and his own nickel Damascus steel. **Prices:** $50 to $3,200. **Remarks:** Part-time maker; first knife sold in 1988. Doing business as Mustang Forge. **Mark:** Initials or first initial, last name.

HINK III, LES, 1599 Aptos Lane, Stockton, CA, 95206/209-547-1292
Specialties: Working straight knives and traditional folders in standard patterns or to customer specs. **Patterns:** Hunting and utility/camp knives; others on request. **Technical:** Grinds carbon and stainless steels. **Prices:** $80 to $200; some higher. **Remarks:** Part-time maker; first knife sold in 1980. Mark : Last name, or last name 3.

HINSON AND SON, R., 2419 Edgewood Rd., Columbus, GA, 31906/706-327-6801
Specialties: Working straight knives and folders. **Patterns:** Locking folders, liner locks, combat knives and swords. **Technical:** Grinds 440C and commercial Damascus. **Prices:** $100 to $350; some to $1,500. **Remarks:** Part-time maker; first knife sold in 1983. Son Bob is co-worker. **Mark:** HINSON, city and state.

HINTZ, GERALD M., 5402 Sahara Ct., Helena, MT, 59602/406-458-5412
Specialties: Fancy, high-art, working/using knives of his design. **Patterns:** Bowies, hunters, daggers, fish fillet and utility/camp knives. **Technical:** Forges ATS-34, 440C and D2. Animal art in horn handles or in the blade. **Prices:** $75 to $400; some to $1,000. **Remarks:** Part-time maker; first knife sold in 1980. Doing business as Big Joe's Custom Knives. Will take custom orders. **Mark:** F.S. or W.S. with first and middle initials and last name.

HIRAYAMA, HARUMI, 4-5-13 Kitamachi, Warabi City, Saitama Pref., JAPAN 335-0001, /048-443-2248
Specialties: High-tech working knives of her design. **Patterns:** Locking folders, interframes, straight gents and slip-joints. **Technical:** Grinds 440C or equivalent; uses natural handle materials and gold. **Prices:** Start at $700. **Remarks:** Part-time maker; first knife sold in 1985. **Mark:** First initial, last name.

HITCHMOUGH, HOWARD, 95 Old Street Road, Peterborough, NH, 03458-1637/603-924-4265
Specialties: High class folding knives. **Patterns:** Locking folders, pocketknives, liner locks, hunters and boots. **Technical:** Uses ATS-34, stainless Damascus and titanium. Prefers hand-rubbed finishes and natural handle materials. **Prices:** $250 to $1,500; some to $4,000. **Remarks:** Full-time maker; first knife sold in 1967. **Mark:** Last name.

HOCKENSMITH, DAN, P.O. Box E, Drake, CO, 80515/970-669-5404
Specialties: Traditional working and using straight knives of his design. **Patterns:** Hunters, Bowies, folders and utility/camp knives. **Technical:** Uses his Damascus, 5160, carbon steel. Hand forged. **Prices:** $150 to $600; some to $1,000. **Remarks:** full-time maker; first knife sold in 1987. **Mark:** Name, town & state, anvil.

HODGE, J.B., 1100 Woodmont Ave. SE, Huntsville, AL, 35801/205-536-8388
Specialties: Fancy working folders. **Patterns:** Slip-joints. **Technical:** Grinds 154CM and ATS-34. **Prices:** Start at $175. **Remarks:** Part-time maker; first knife sold in 1978. Not currently taking orders. **Mark:** Name, city and state.

HODGE III, JOHN, 422 S. 15th St., Palatka, FL, 32177/904-328-3897
Specialties: Fancy straight knives and folders. **Patterns:** Various. **Technical:** Pattern-welded Damascus--"Southern-style." **Prices:** To $1,000. **Remarks:** Part-time maker; first knife sold in 1981. **Mark:** JH3 logo.

HODGSON, RICHARD J., 9081 Tahoe Lane, Boulder, CO, 80301/303-666-9460
Specialties: Straight knives and folders in standard patterns. **Patterns:** High-tech knives in various patterns. **Technical:** Grinds 440C, AEB-L and CPM. **Prices:** $850 to $2,200. **Remarks:** Part-time maker. **Mark:** None.

HOEL, STEVE, P.O. Box 283, Pine, AZ, 85544/602-476-4278
Specialties: Investor-class folders, straight knives and period pieces of his design. **Patterns:** Folding interframes lockers and slip-joints; straight Bowies, boots and daggers. **Technical:** Grinds 154CM, ATS-34 and commercial Damascus. **Prices:** $600 to $1,200; some to $7,500. **Remarks:** Full-time maker. **Mark:** Initial logo with name and address.

HOFFMAN, KEVIN L., P.O. Box 5107, Winter Park, FL, 32793/407-678-3124
Specialties: High-tech working knives. **Patterns:** Frame lock folders, fighters, concealment rigs. **Technical:** Grinds ATS-34, 440C and Damascus; titanium folders. Makes Kydex sheaths. **Prices:** $150 to $2,000. **Remarks:** Full-time maker; first knife sold in 1981. **Mark:** Initials.

HOFFMANN, UWE H., P.O. Box 60114, Vancouver, BC, CANADA, V5W 4B5/604-572-7320 (after 5 p.m.)
Specialties: High-tech working knives, folders and fantasy knives of his design or to customer specs. **Patterns:** Hunters, fishing knives, combat and survival knives, folders and diver's knives. **Technical:** Grinds 440C, ATS-34, D2 and commercial Damascus. **Prices:** $95 to $900; some to $2,000 and higher. **Remarks:** Full-time maker; first knife sold in 1985. **Mark:** Hoffmann Handmade Knives.

HOGSTROM, ANDERS T., 2130 Valerga Dr #8, Belmont, CA, 94002/650-592-2989
Specialties: Short Dirks of own design. **Patterns:** Dirks, Daggers, Fighters, and an occasional Sword. **Technical:** Grinds 1050 High Carbon, ATS-34, 440C and occasional damascus. Does clay tempering and uses exotic hardwoods. **Prices:** Start at $200. **Marks:** Last name in various typefaces.

HOKE, THOMAS M., 3103 Smith Ln, Lagrange, KY, 40031/502-222-0350
Specialties: Working/using knives, straight knives. Own designs and customer specs. **Patterns:** Daggers, Bowies, Hunters. **Technical:** Grind 440C, Damascus and ATS-34. F ilework on all knives. Tooling on sheaths (custom fit on all knives). Any handle material - mostly exotic. **Prices:** $100 to $700; some to $1500. **Remarks:** Full-time maker, first knife sold in 1986. **Mark:** Dragon on banner which says T.M. Hoke.

HOLBROOK, H.L., Rt. #3, Box 585, Olive Hill, KY, 41164/606-738-6542/606-738-6842 Shop
Specialties: Traditional working using straight knives and folders of his design, to customer specs and in standard patterns. **Patterns:** Hunters, folders. **Technical:** Grinds 440C, ATS-34 and D2. Blades have hand-rubbed satin finish. Uses exotic woods, stag and Micarta. Hand sewn sheath with each straight knife. **Prices:** $90 to $270; some to $400. **Remarks:** Part-time maker; first knife sold in 1983. Doing business as Holbrook knives. **Mark:** Name, city, state.

HOLDER, D'ALTON, 7148 W. Country Gables Dr., Peoria, AZ, 85381/623-878-3064
Specialties: Deluxe working knives and high-art hunters. **Patterns:** Drop-point hunters, fighters, Bowies, miniatures and locking folders. **Technical:** Grinds 440C and 154CM; uses amber and other materials in combination on stick tangs. **Prices:** $150 to $350; some to $1,000. **Remarks:** Full-time maker; first knife sold in 1970. **Mark:** D'HOLDER, city and state.

HOLLAND, JOHN H., 143 Green Meadow Lane, Calhoun, GA, 30701/ 706-629-9622
Specialties: Traditional and fancy working/using straight knives and folders of his design, to customer specs and in standard patterns. **Patterns:** Hunters, and slip-joint folders. **Technical:** Grinds 440V and 440C. Offers engraving. **Prices:** $200 to $500; some to $1,000. **Remarks:** Part-time maker; first knife sold in 1988. doing business as Holland Knives. **Mark:** First and last name, city, state.

HOLLAR, BOB, 701 2nd Ave SW, Great Falls, MT, 59404/406-268-8252
Specialties: Working/using straight knives and folders of his design and to customer specs; period pieces. **Patterns:** Fighters, hunter, liner & back lock folders + axis type lock. **Technical:** Forges 52100, 5160, CPM 3V, 15N20 & 1084 (Damascus)*. **Prices:** $225 to $650; some to $1,500. **Remarks:** Full-time maker. doing business as Goshawk Knives. **Mark:** Hoshawk stamped or etched on left. Other: Burled woods, stag, ivory; all stabilized material for handles.

HOLLOWAY, PAUL, 714 Burksdale Rd., Norfolk, VA, 23518/804-588-7071
Specialties: Working straight knives and folders to customer specs. **Patterns:** Lockers and slip-joints; fighters and boots; fishing and push knives, from swords to miniatures. **Technical:** Grinds A2, D2, 154CM, 440C and ATS-34. **Prices:** $125 to $400; some to $1,200. **Remarks:** Part-time maker; first knife sold in 1981. **Mark:** Last name, or last name and city in logo.

HOLMES, ROBERT, 1431 S Eugene St, Baton Rouge, LA, 70808-1043/ 504-291-4864
Specialties: Using straight knives and folders of his design or to customer specs. **Patterns:** Bowies, utility hunters, camp knives, skinners, slip-joint and lock-back folders. **Technical:** Forges 1065, 1095 and L6. Makes his own Damascus and cable Damascus. Offers clay tempering. **Prices:** $150 to $1,500. **Remarks:** Part-time maker; first knife sold in 1988. **Mark:** DOC HOLMES, or anvil logo with last initial inside.

HOLUM, MORTEN, Bolerskrenten 28, 0691, Oslo, NORWAY, /011-47-22-27-69-96
Specialties: Working straight knives. **Patterns:** Traditional Norwegian knives, hunters, fighters, axes. **Technical:** Forges Damascus. Uses his own blades. **Prices:** $200 to $800; some to $1,500. **Remarks:** Part-time maker; first knife sold in 1986. **Mark:** Last name.

HORN, JESS, 87481 Rhodowood Dr., Florence, OR, 97439/541-997-2593
Specialties: Investor-class working folders; period pieces; collectibles. **Patterns:** High-tech design and finish in folders; liner locks, traditional slip-joints and featherweight models. **Technical:** Grinds ATS-34, 154CM. **Prices:** Start at $600. **Remarks:** Full-time maker; first knife sold in 1968. **Mark:** Full name or last name.

HORTON, SCOT, P.O. Box 451, Buhl, ID, 83316/208-543-4222
Specialties: Traditional working stiff knives and folders. **Patterns:** Hunters, skinners, utility and show knives. **Technical:** Grinds ATS-34. Uses stag, abalone and exotic woods. **Prices:** $200 to $1,200. **Remarks:** First knife sold in 1990. **Mark:** Full name in arch underlined with arrow, city, state.

HOWARD, DURVYN M., 4220 McLain St. S., Hokes Bluff, AL, 35903/ 205-492-5720
Specialties: Collectible upscale folders; multiple patents. **Patterns:** Fine gentlemen's folders. **Technical:** Uses natural and exotic materials, precious metals and gemstones. **Prices:** $5,000 to $20,000. **Remarks:** Full-time maker; now accepting orders--purchase through Barrett-Smythe Gallery, New York, NY, exclusive agent. **Mark:** Last name etched on tang; opposite side marked Barrett-Smythe.

HOWELL, ROBERT L., Box 1617, Kilgore, TX, 75663/903-986-4364
Specialties: Straight knives and folders of his design. **Patterns:** Hunters and locking folders. **Technical:** Grinds D2 and ATS-34; forges and grinds Damascus. **Prices:** $75 to $200; some to $2,500. **Remarks:** Part-time maker; first knife sold in 1978. Doing business as Howell Knives. **Mark:** Last name.

HOWELL, LEN, 550 Lee Rd. 169, Opelika, AL, 36804/334-749-1942
Specialties: Traditional and working knives of his design and to customer specs. **Patterns:** Buckskinner, hunters and utility/camp knives.

Technical: Forges cable Damascus, 1085 and 5160; makes own Damascus. **Mark:** Engraved last name.

HOWELL, TED, 1294 Wilson Rd., Wetumpka, AL, 36092/205-569-2281
Specialties: Working/using straight knives and folders of his design; period pieces. **Patterns:** Bowies, fighters, hunters. **Technical:** Forges 5160, 1085 and cable. Offers light engraving and scrimshaw; filework. **Prices:** $75 to $250; some to $450. **Remarks:** Part-time maker; first knife sold in 1991. Doing business as Howell Co. **Mark:** Last name, Slapout AL.

HOWSER, JOHN C., 54 Bell Ln., Frankfort, KY, 40601/502-875-3678
Specialties: Practical working knives. **Patterns:** Hunters, fighters, locking folders, fillet knives, slip-joint folders, liner locks. **Technical:** Grinds D2 and ATS-34; hand-rubbed satin finish; natural materials. **Prices:** $85 to $350; some to $500. **Remarks:** Part-time maker; first knife sold in 1974. **Mark:** Signature or stamp.

HOY, KEN, 54744 Pinchot Dr., North Fork, CA, 93643/209-877-7805

HRISOULAS, JIM, 330 S. Decatur Ave., Suite 109, Las Vegas, NV, 89107/702-566-8551
Specialties: Working straight knives; period pieces. **Patterns:** Swords, daggers and sgian dubhs. **Technical:** Double-edged differential heat treating. **Prices:** $85 to $175; some to $600 and higher. **Remarks:** Full-time maker; first knife sold in 1973. Author of *The Complete Bladesmith*, *The Pattern Welded Blade* and *The Master Bladesmith*. Doing business as Salamander Armoury. **Mark:** 8R logo and sword and salamander.

HUBBARD, ARTHUR J., 574 Cutlers Farm Road, Monroe, CT, 06468/ 203-268-3998
Specialties: Folders in locking liner designs in his own stainless steel damascus. Inlay work in some, multi-bar blades in S.S.D.; non-knife objects in S.S.D. **Technical:**The first in the USA to make Damascus in all-stainless steel. Mokume of copper and stainless steel, copper, brass and nickel-silver, copper and brass. **Prices:** Start at $350. **Remarks:** Full-time maker; first knife sold in 1976. **Mark:** Name, city and state; first and middle initials, last name, stainless; P.E.D. stainless.

HUDDLESTON, JOE D., 14129 93rd Ave. SE, Yelm, WA, 98597-9459/ 360-458-2361
Specialties: Period pieces, fancy straight knives of his design. **Patterns:** Daggers and Scottish dirks. **Technical:** Grinds ATS-34. Hand-carved knotwork handles, wooden or wood lined sheaths; uses gemstones and sterling silver mounts. **Prices:** $550 to $1,850; some to $5,000. **Remarks:** Full-time maker; first knife sold in 1993. Doing business as BladeCatcher Knives. **Mark:** BladeCatcher over a Spanish notch.

HUDSON, C. ROBBIN, 22280 Frazier Rd., Rock Hall, MD, 21661/410-639-7273
Specialties: High-art working knives. **Patterns:** Hunters, Bowies, fighters and kitchen knives. **Technical:** Forges W2, nickel steel, pure nickel steel, composite and mosaic Damascus; makes knives one at a time. **Prices:** 500 to $1200; some to $5,000. **Remarks:** Full-time maker; first knife sold in 1970. **Mark:** Last name and MS.

HUDSON, ROBERT, 3802 Black Cricket Ct., Humble, TX, 77396/713-454-7207
Specialties: Working straight knives of his design. **Patterns:** Bowies, hunters, skinners, fighters and utility knives. **Technical:** Grinds D2, 440C, 154CM and commercial Damascus. **Prices:** $85 to $350; some to $1,500. **Remarks:** Part-time maker; first knife sold in 1980. **Mark:** Full name, handmade, city and state.

HUEY, STEVE, 5060 W Port St, Eugene, OR, 97402/541-484-7344
Specialties: Working straight knives, some one-of-a-kind. **Patterns:** Folders, fixed hunting, fighters, kitchen knives, some one of a kind. **Technical:** D2 and ATS-34 carbon on request.. **Prices:** $75 to $600. **Remarks:**Part-time maker; first knife sold in 1981. **Mark:** Last name in rectangle.

HUGHES, DAN, 13743 Persimmon Blvd., West Palm Beach, FL, 33411/
Specialties: Working straight knives to customer specs. **Patterns:** Hunters, fighters, fillet knives. **Technical:** Grinds 440C and ATS-34. **Prices:** $55 to $175; some to $300. **Remarks:** Part-time maker; first knife sold in 1984. **Mark:** Initials.

HUGHES, DARYLE, 10979 Leonard, Nunica, MI, 49448/616-837-6623
Specialties: Working knives. **Patterns:** Buckskinners, hunters, camp knives, kitchen and fishing knives. **Technical:** Forges and grinds W2, O1

and D2. **Prices:** $40 to $100; some to $400. **Remarks:** Part-time maker; first knife sold in 1979. **Mark:** Name and city in logo.

HUGHES, ED, 280 1/2 Holly Lane, Grand Junction, CO, 81503/970-243-8547
Specialties: Working and art folders. **Patterns:** Folders. **Technical:** Grinds stainless steels. Engraves. **Prices:** $75 to $250; some to $600. **Remarks:** Full-time maker; first knife sold in 1978. **Mark:** Name or initials.

HUGHES, LAWRENCE, 207 W. Crestway, Plainview, TX, 79072/806-293-5406
Specialties: Working and display knives. **Patterns:** Bowies, daggers, hunters, buckskinners. **Technical:** Grinds D2, 440C and 154CM. **Prices:** $125 to $300; some to $2,000. **Remarks:** Full-time maker; first knife sold in 1979. **Mark:** Name with buffalo skull in center.

HULETT, STEVE, 115 Yellowstone Ave, West Yellowstone, MT, 59758/888-735-0634
Specialties: Classic, working/using knives, straight knives, folders. Your design, custom specs. **Patterns:** Utility/camp knives, hunters, and liner lock folders. **Technical:** Grinds 440C stainless steel, O1 Carbon, 1095. Shop is retail and knife shop--people watch their knives being made. We do everything in house--"all but smelt the ore, or tan the hide." **Prices:** $125 to $7,000. **Remarks:** Full-time maker; first knife sold in 1994.

HULL, MICHAEL J., 1330 Hermits Circle, Cottonwood, AZ, 86326/520-634-2871
Specialties: Period pieces and working knives; will work to customer specs. **Patterns:** Hunters, fighters, Bowies, camp and Mediterranean knives, etc. **Technical:** Grinds 440C, ATS-34 and BG42. **Prices:** $145 to $500; some to $1000. **Remarks:** Full-time maker; first knife sold in 1983. **Mark:** Name, city, state.

HULSEY, HOYT, 5699 Pope Ave., Steele, AL, 35987/205-538-6765
Specialties: Traditional working straight knives and folders of his design. **Patterns:** Hunters and utility/camp knives. **Technical:** Grinds 440C, ATS-34, O1 and A2. **Prices:** $75 to $150. **Remarks:** Part-time maker; first knife sold in 1989. **Mark:** Full name, city and state.

HUME, DON, 3511 Camino De La Cumbre, Sherman Oaks, CA, 91423/818-783-5486
Specialties: Medieval theme, straight blade working and collector designed pieces. **Patterns:** Hunters, daggers and Bowies. **Technical:** Grinds Damascus, 440C, 154CM with exotic handle material. **Prices:** $180 to $1600. **Remarks:** Part-time maker; first knife sold in 1987. **Mark:** Curved first and middle initials and last name; first of a series or one of a kinds also marked with the Fiera Madonna.

HUMENICK, ROY, P.O. Box 55, Rescue, CA, 95672/
Specialties: Traditional working knives and multi-blade folders of his design. **Patterns:** Traditional folders as well as hunters & fighters. **Technical:** Grinds ATS-34, works in Damascus. **Prices:** $200 to $600; some to $1,500. **Remarks:** First knife sold in 1984. **Mark:** Last name in ARC.

HUMPHREYS, JOEL, 3260 Palmer Rd, Bowling Green, FL, 33834-9801/941-773-0439
Specialties: Traditional working/using straight knives and folders of his design and in standard patterns. **Patterns:** Hunters, folders and utilitiy/camp knives. **Technical:** Grinds ATS-34, D2, 440C. All knives have tapered tangs, mitered bolster/handle joints, handles of horn or bone fitted sheaths. **Prices:** $135 to $225; some to $350. **Remarks:** Part-time maker; first knife sold in 1990. Doing business as Sovereign Knives. **Mark:** First name or "H" pierced by arrow.

HUNTER, HYRUM, 285 N. 300 W., P.O. Box 179, Aurora, UT, 84620/435-529-7244
Specialties: Working straight knives of my design or to customer specs. **Patterns:** Drop and clip, fighters dagger, some folders. **Technical:** Forged from two piece Damascus. **Prices:** Prices are adjusted according to size, complexity and material used. **Remarks:** I will consider any design you have. Part-time maker; first knife sold in 1990. **Mark:** Initials incircled with first initial and last name and city, then state. Some patterns are numbered.

HURST, GERARD, 6205 Loftus Ave NE, Albuquerque, NM, 87109/505-830-0956
Specialties: Fancy working straight knives and folders. Damascus bowies and art knives. Welcomes custom orders. **Technical:** Grinds D2,

ATS-34, 440-C, RWL 34. **Prices:** Start at $200, some to $800. **Remarks:** Part-time maker, first knife sold in 1997. **Mark:** Last name inside of logo.

HURST, COLE, 1583 Tedford, E. Wenatchee, WA, 98802/509-884-9206
Specialties: Fantasy, high-art and traditional straight knives. **Patterns:** Bowies, daggers and hunters. **Technical:** Blades are made of stone; handles are made of stone, wood or ivory and embellished with fancy woods, ivory or antlers. **Prices:** $100 to $300; some to $2,000. **Remarks:** Spare-time maker; first knife sold in 1985. **Mark:** Name and year.

HURST, JEFF, P.O. Box 247, Rutledge, TN, 37861/423-828-5729
Specialties: Working straight knives and folders of his design. **Patterns:** Tomahawks, hunters, boots, folders and fighters. **Technical:** Forges W2, O1 and his own Damascus. Makes mokume. **Prices:** $175 to $350; some to $500. **Remarks:** Full-time maker; first knife sold in 1984. Doing business as Buzzard's Knob Forge. **Mark:** Last name; partnered knives are marked with Newman L. Smith, handle artisan, and SH in script.

HURT, WILLIAM R., 9222 Oak Tree Cir., Frederick, MD, 21701/301-898-7143
Specialties: Traditional and working/using straight knives. **Patterns:** Bowies, hunters, fighters and utility knives. **Technical:** Forges 5160, O1 and O6; makes own Damascus. Offers silver wire inlay. **Prices:** $200 to $600; some higher. **Remarks:** Full-time maker; first knife osld in 1989. **Mark:** First and middle initials, last name.

HUSIAK, MYRON, P.O. Box 238, Altona 3018, Victoria, AUSTRALIA, /03-315-6752
Specialties: Straight knives and folders of his design or to customer specs. **Patterns:** Hunters, fighters, lock-back folders, skinners and boots. **Technical:** forges and grinds his own Damascus, 440C and ATS-34. **Prices:** $200 to $900. **Remarks:** Part-time maker; first knife sold in 1974. **Mark:** First initial, last name in logo and serial number.

HYDE, JIMMY, 5094 Stagecoach Rd., Ellenwood, GA, 30049/404-968-1951
Specialties: Working straight knives of any design; period pieces. **Patterns:** Bowies, hunters and utility knives. **Technical:** Grinds 440C and 5160; forges O1. Makes his own Damascus and cable Damascus. **Prices:** $75 to $200; some to $400. **Remarks:** Part-time maker; first knife sold in 1978. **Mark:** First initial, last name.

HYTOVICK, JOE"HY", 14872 SW 111th St., Dunnellon, FL, 34432/800-749-5339
Specialties: Straight, Folder & Miniature. **Technical:** Blades from Wootz, Damascus and Alloy steel. **Prices:** To $5,000. **Mark:** HY

I

IKOMA, FLAVIO YUJI, R. MANOEL R. TEIXEIRA, 108, 108, Centro Presidente Prudente, SP-19031-220, BRAZIL, /0182-22-0115
Specialties: Straight knives and folders of all designs. **Patterns:** Fighters, hunters, Bowies, swords, folders, skinners, utility and defense knives. **Technical:** Grinds and forges D6, 440C, high-carbon steels and Damascus. **Prices:** $60 to $350; some to $3,300. **Remarks:** Full-time maker; first knife sold in 1991. All stainless steel blades are ultra sub-zero quenched. **Mark:** Ikoma Knives beside eagle.

IMBODEN II, HOWARD L., 620 Deauville Dr., Dayton, OH, 45429/513-439-1536
Specialties: One-of-a-kind hunting, flint, steel and art knives. **Technical:** Forges and grinds stainless, high-carbon and Damascus. Uses obsidian, cast sterling silver, 14K and 18K gold guards. Carves ivory animals and more. **Prices:** $65 to $25,000. **Remarks:** Full-time maker; first knife sold in 1986. Doing business as Hill Originals. **Mark:** First and last initials, II.

IMEL, BILLY MACE, 1616 Bundy Ave., New Castle, IN, 47362/765-529-1651
Specialties: High-art working knives, period pieces and personal cutlery. **Patterns:** Daggers, fighters, hunters; locking folders and slip-joints with interframes. **Technical:** Grinds D2, 440C and 154CM. **Prices:** $200 to $2,000; some to $6,000. **Remarks:** Part-time maker; first knife sold in 1973. **Mark:** Name in monogram.

custom knifemakers

IRIE (SEE WOOD, BARRY B & IRIE) MICHAEL L, MICHAEL L, dba WOOD, IRIE & CO

IRON WOLF FORGE, SEE NELSON, KEN

ISGRO, JEFFERY, 1516 First St, West Babylon, NY, 11704/516-587-7516
Specialties: Tactica use knives - Bowies, Skinners, Capers and Hunters. **Technical:** ATS 34, 440 & D2. File work and glass beading available. Price: $120 to $400. **Remarks:** Part-time maker. **Mark:** First name, last name, Long Island, NY.

ISHIHARA, HANK, 86-18 Motomachi, Sakura City, Chiba Pref., JAPAN, /043-485-3208
Specialties: Fantasy working straight knives and folders of his design. **Patterns:** Boots, Bowies, daggers, fighters, hunters, fishing, locking folders and utility camp knives. **Technical:** Grinds ATS-34, 440C, D2, 440V, CV-134, COS25 and Damascus. Engraves. **Prices:** $250 to $1,000; some to $10,000. **Remarks:** Full-time maker; first knife sold in 1987. **Mark:** HANK.

j

JACKS, JIM, 344 S. Hollenbeck Ave., Covina, CA, 91723-2513/818-331-5665
Specialties: Working straight knives in standard patterns. **Patterns:** Bowies, hunters, fighters, fishing and camp knives, miniatures. **Technical:** Grinds Stellite 6K, 440C and ATS-34. **Prices:** Start at $100. **Remarks:** Spare-time maker; first knife sold in 1980. **Mark:** Initials in diamond logo.

JACKSON, JIM, 10 Chantry Close, Windsor, Berkshire SL4 5EP, ENGLAND, /01753-858729
Specialties: Working straight knives of his designs. **Patterns:** Large Bowies and hunters. **Technical:** Forges O1, 5160 and occasionally Damascus. Offers leatherwork. **Prices:** NA. **Remarks:** Part-time maker. **Mark:** Kentucky Dreamer around last initial, J.S..

JAMES, PETER, 2549 W. Golf Rd., #290, Hoffman Estates, IL, 60194/708-310-9113
Specialties: Working/using straight knives of his design and in standard patterns. **Patterns:** Bowies, daggers and urban companion knives. **Technical:** Grinds 440C and soligen tool. Makes a variety of sheaths for urban companion series. **Prices:** $48 to $250. **Remarks:** Part-time maker; first knife sold in 1986. doing business as Peter James & Sons. **Mark:** Initials overlapped.

JANIGA, MATTHEW A., 15950 Xenia St. NW, Andover, MN, 55304-2346/612-427-2510
Specialties: Period pieces, swords, daggers. **Patterns:** Daggers, fighters and swords. **Technical:** Forges 5160, Damascus and 52100. Does own heat treating. Forges own pattern-welded steel. **Prices:** $100 - $1000; some to $5,000. **Remarks:** Spare-time maker; first knife sold in 1991. **Mark:** Interwoven initials..

JARVIS, PAUL M., 30 Chalk St., Cambridge, MA, 02139/617-491-2900
Specialties: High-art knives and period pieces of his design. **Patterns:** Japanese and Mid-Eastern knives. **Technical:** Grinds Myer Damascus, ATS-34, D2 and O1. Specializes in height-relief Japanese-style carving. Works with silver, gold and gems. **Prices:** $200 to $17,000. **Remarks:** Part-time maker; first knife sold in 1978.

JEAN, GERRY, 25B Cliffside Dr., Manchester, CT, 06040/203 649 6449
Specialties: Historic replicas. **Patterns:** Survival and camp knives. **Technical:** Grinds A2, 440C and 154CM. Handle slabs applied in unique tongue-and-groove method. **Prices:** $125 to $250; some to $1,000. **Remarks:** Spare-time maker; first knife sold in 1973. **Mark:** Initials and serial number.

JJEFFRIES, ROBERT W., Route 2, Box 227, Red House, WV, 25168/304-586-9780
Specialties: Straight knives and folders. **Patterns:** Hunters, skinners and folders. **Technical:** Uses 440C, ATS-34; makes his own Damascus. **Prices:** Moderate. **Remarks:** Part-time maker; first knife sold in 1988. **Mark:** NA.

JENSEN, JOHN LEWIS, 138 Medway St., 2nd Floor, Providence, RI, 02906/PH: 401-351-5838
Specialties: One-of-a-kind exotic and fantasy edged weapons of his design. **Patterns:** Daggers, fighters, swords, axes, folders, war hammers

and maces. **Technical:** Hollow-grinds; reforges commercial Damascus, uses gold, gemstones, titanium, walrus ivory etc. **Prices:** $1,000 to $10,000. **Remarks:** Doing business as Magnus Design Studio. **Mark:** Logo.

JENSEN JR., CARL A., 8957 Country Road P-35, Blair, NE, 68008/402-426-3353
Specialties: Working knives of his design; some customer designs. **Patterns:** Hunters, fighters, boots and Bowies. **Technical:** Grinds A2, D2, O1, 440C, 5160 and ATS-34; recycles old files, leaf springs; heat-treats. **Prices:** $35 to $350. **Remarks:** Part-time maker; first knife sold in 1980. **Mark:** Stamp "BEAR'S CUTLERY" or etch of letters "BEAR" forming silhouette of a Bear.

JERNIGAN, STEVE, 3082 Tunnel Rd., Milton, FL, 32571/850-994-0802
Specialties: Investor-class folders and various theme pieces. **Patterns:** Array of models and sizes in sideplate locking interframes and conventional liner construction. **Technical:** Grinds ATS-34, CPM-T-440V and Damascus. Inlays mokume (and minerals) in blades and sculpts marble cases. **Prices:** $650 to $1,800; some to $6,000. **Remarks:** Full-time maker; first knife sold in 1982. Takes orders for folders only. **Mark:** Last name.

JETTON, CAY, P.O. Box 315, Winnsboro, TX, 75494/903-342-3317

JOBIN, JACQUES, 46 St. Dominique, Levis Quebec, CANADA, G6V 2M7/418-833-0283
Specialties: Fancy and working straight knives and folders; miniatures. **Patterns:** Minis, fantasy knives, fighters and some hunters. **Technical:** ATS-34, some Damascus and titanium. Likes native snakewood. Heat-treats. **Prices:** Start at $250. **Remarks:** Full-time maker; first knife sold in 1986. **Mark:** Signature on blade.

JOEHNK, BERND, Posadowskystrasse 22, 24148 Kiel, GERMANY, /0431-7297705
Specialties: One of a kind fancy/embellished and traditional straight knives of his design and to customer specs. **Patterns:** Daggers, fighters, hunters and letter openers. **Technical:** Grinds 440C, ATS-34, commercial Damascus and various stainless and corrosion-resistant steels. Likes filework. Leather sheaths. Offers engraving. **Prices:** Start at $300. **Remarks:** Part-time maker; first knife sold in1990. **Mark:** Full name and city.

JOHANSSON, ANDERS, LOVHAGSGATAN 39, S-724 71 Västerås, SWEDEN, /+46 21 358778
Specialties: Scandinavian traditional and modern straight knives. **Patterns:** Hunters, fighters and fantasy knives. **Technical:** Grinds stainless steel and makes own Damascus. Prefers Scandinavian wood, reindeer, water buffalo and mammoth for handle material. **Prices:** Start at $100. **Remarks:** Spare-time maker; first knife sold in 1994. **Mark:** Stylized initials.

JOHNS, ROB, 1423 S. Second, Enid, OK, 73701/405-242-2707
Specialties: Classic and fantasy straight knives of his design or to customer specs; fighters for use at Medieval fairs. **Patterns:** Bowies, daggers and swords. **Technical:** Forges and grinds 440C, D2 and 5160. Handles of nylon, walnut or wire-wrap. **Prices:** $150 to $350; some to $2,500. **Remarks:** Full-time maker; first knife sold in 1980. **Mark:** Medieval Customs, initials.

JOHNSON, HAROLD "HARRY" C., 307 Penn St, Trion, GA, 30753-1519/
Specialties: Working straight knives. **Patterns:** Mostly hunters and large Bowies. **Technical:** Grinds popular steels. Offers heat treating, leatherwork, sheaths and cases; keeps large assortment of woods in stock. **Prices:** $125 to $2,000; some higher. **Remarks:** Part-time maker; first knife sold in 1973. **Mark:** First initial, last name, city, state in oval logo.

JOHNSON, STEVEN R., 202 E. 200 N., P.O. Box 5, Manti, UT, 84642/801-835-7941
Specialties: Investor-class working knives. **Patterns:** Hunters, fighters and boots in clean-lined contemporary patterns. **Technical:** Grinds ATS-34. **Prices:** $450 to $4,500. **Remarks:** Full-time maker; first knife sold in 1972. **Mark:** Name, city, state.

JOHNSON, RYAN M., 7320 Foster Hixson Cemetery Rd., Hixson, TN, 37343/615-842-9323
Specialties: Working and using straight knives of his design and to customer specs. **Patterns:** Bowies, hunters and utiltiy/camp knives. **Technical:** Forges 5160, Damascus and files. Prices; $70 to $400; some to

$800. **Remarks:** Full-time maker; first knife sold in 1986. **Mark:** Sledge-hammer with halo.

JOHNSON, RUFFIN, 215 LaFonda Dr., Houston, TX, 77060/281-448-4407
Specialties: Working straight knives and folders. **Patterns:** Hunters, fighters and locking folders. **Technical:** Grinds 440C and 154CM; hidden tangs and fancy handles. **Prices:** $200 to $400; some to $1,095. **Remarks:** Full-time maker; first knife sold in 1972. **Mark:** Wolf head logo and signature.

JOHNSON, R.B., Box 11, Clearwater, MN, 55320/320-558-6128
Specialties: Liner Locks with Titanium - Mosaic Damascus. **Patterns:** Linerlock folders - skeleton hunters - frontier bowies. **Technical:** Damascus - Mosaic Damascus - A-2, O-1, 1095. **Prices:** $200 and up. **Remarks:** Full-time maker since 1973. Not accepting orders. **Mark:** Signature.

JOHNSON, KENNETH R., W3565 Lockington, Mindoro, WI, 54644/608-857-3035
Specialties: Hunters, clip-points, special orders. **Patterns:** Hunters, utility/camp knives and kitchen knives. **Technical:** Grinds 440C, D2 and O1. Makes sheaths. **prices:** $65 to $500. **Remarks:** Full-time maker; first knife sold in 1990. doing business as Corken Knives. **Mark:** CORKEN.

JOHNSON, GORDEN W., 5426 Sweetbriar, Houston, TX, 77017/713-645-8990
Specialties: Working knives and period pieces. **Patterns:** Hunters, boots and Bowies. **Technical:** Flat-grinds 440C; most knives have narrow tang. **Prices:** $90 to $450. **Remarks:** Full-time maker; first knife sold in 1974. **Mark:** Name, city, state.

JOHNSON, DURRELL CARMON, P.O. Box 594, Sparr, FL, 32192/352-622-5498
Specialties: Old-fashioned working straight knives and folders of his design or to customer specs. **Patterns:** Bowies, hunters, fighters, daggers, camp knives and Damascus miniatures. **Technical:** Forges 5160, his own Damascus, W2, wrought iron, nickel and horseshoe rasps. Offers filework. **Prices:** $100 to $2,000. **Remarks:** Full-time maker and blacksmith; first knife sold in 1957. **Mark:** Middle name.

JOHNSON, DAVID L., P.O. Box 222, Talkeetna, AK, 99676/907-733-2777
Specialties: Traditional working and using straight knives. **Patterns:** Bowies, fighters and hunters; outdoor knives. **Technical:** Grinds ATS-34, D2 and 440C. **Prices:** $100 to $200; some to $450. **Remarks:** Full-time maker; first knife sold in 1979. **Mark:** Name, city and state in banner.

JOHNSON, RANDY, 2575 E. Canal Dr., Turlock, CA, 95380/209-632-5401
Specialties: Straight knives and folders. **Patterns:** Locking folders. **Technical:** Grinds Damascus. **Prices:** $200 to $300. **Remarks:** Spare-time maker; first knife sold in 1989. Doing business as Puedo Knifeworks. **Mark:** PUEDO

JOHNSON, C.E. GENE, 5648 Redwood Ave., Portage, IN, 46368/219-762-5461
Specialties: Lock-back folders and springers of his design or to customer specs. **Patterns:** Hunters, Bowies, survival lock-back folders. **Technical:** Grinds D2, 440C, A18, O1, Damascus; likes filework. **Prices:** $100 to $2,000. **Remarks:** Full-time maker; first knife sold in 1975. **Mark:** "Gene" city, state and serial number.

JOKERST, CHARLES, 9312 Spaulding, Omaha, NE, 68134/402-571-2536
Specialties: Working knives in standard patterns. **Patterns:** Hunters, fighters and pocketknives. **Technical:** Grinds 440C, ATS-34. **Prices:** $90 to $170. **Remarks:** Spare-time maker; first knife sold in 1984. **Mark:** Early work marked RCJ; current work marked with last name and city.

JONES, JOHN, 12 Schooner Circuit, Manly West, QLD 4179, AUSTRALIA, /07-339-33390
Specialties: Straight knives and folders. **Patterns:** Working hunters, folding lockbacks, fancy daggers and miniatures. **Technical:** Grinds 440C, O1 and L6. **Prices:** $180 to $1200; some to $2,000. **Remarks:** Part-time maker; first knife sold in 1986. **Mark:** Jones

JONES, ENOCH, 7278 Moss Ln., Warrenton, VA, 20187/540-341-0292
Specialties: Fancy working straight knives. **Patterns:** Hunters, fighters, boots and Bowies. **Technical:** Forges and grinds O1, W2, 440C and

Damascus. **Prices:** $100 to $350; some to $1,000. **Remarks:** Part-time maker; first knife sold in 1982. **Mark:** First name.

JONES, CURTIS J., 39909 176th St. E., Palmdale, CA, 93591/805-264-2753
Specialties: Big Bowies, daggers, his own style of hunters. **Patterns:** Bowies, daggers, hunters, swords, boots and miniatures. **Technical:** Grinds 440C, ATS-34 and D2. Fitted guards only; does not solder. Heat-treats. Custom sheaths-hand-tooled and stiched. **Prices:** $125 to $1,500; some to $3,000. **Remarks:** Part-time maker; first knife sold in 1975. Not taking mail orders. **Mark:** Stylized initials on either side of three triangles interconnected.

JONES, CHARLES ANTHONY, 36 Broadgate Close, Bellaire Barnstaple, No. Devon E31 4AL, ENGLAND, /0271-75328
Specialties: Working straight knives. **Patterns:** Simple hunters, fighters and utility knives. **Technical:** Grinds 440C, O1 and D2; filework offered. Engraves. **Prices:** $100 to $500; engraving higher. **Remarks:** Spare-time maker; first knife sold in 1987. **Mark:** Tony, engraved.

JONES, BARRY M. AND PHILLIP G., 221 North Ave., Danville, VA, 24540/804-793-5282
Specialties: Working and using straight knives and folders of their design and to customer specs; combat and self-defense knives. **Patterns:** Bowies, fighters, daggers, swords, hunters and liner lock folders. **Technical:** Grinds 440C, ATS-34 and D2; flat-grinds only. All blades hand polished. **Prices:** $100 to $1000, some higher. **Remarks:** Part-time makers; first knife sold in 1989. **Mark:** Jones Knives, city, state.

JONES, FRANKLIN (FRANK) W., 6030 Old Dominion Rd, Columbus, GA, 31909/706-563-6051
Specialties: Traditional/working/tactical straight knives of his design. **Patterns:** Hunters, skinners, Bowies, fighters, kitchen, utility/camp knives. **Technical:** Forges cable damascus, 1085, 1095 and 5160. **Prices:** $100 to $550. **Remarks:** Full-time maker; Doing business as F.W. Jones Knives. **Mark:** F.W. Jones, Columbus, GA with year made.

JONES, BOB, 6219 Aztec NE, Albuquerque, NM, 87110/505-881-4472
Specialties: Fancy working knives of his design. **Patterns:** Mountain-man/buckskinner-type knives; multi-blade folders, locking folders, and slip-joints. **Technical:** Grinds A2, O1, 1095 and commerical Damascus; uses no stainless steel. Engraves. **Prices:** $100 to $500; some to $1,500. **Remarks:** full-time maker; first knife sold in 1960. **Mark:** Initials on fixed blades; initials encircled on folders.

JORGENSEN, GERD, Jernbanegata 8, N-3262 Larvik, NORWAY, /(+47) 33 18 66 06
Specialties: Scandinavian styles hunters, working/using straight knives of my design, flint knives. **Patterns:** Mild modifications of traditional Scandinavian patterns, hunters, camp knives and fighters/tactical. **Technical:** Grinds Sandvik 12C27, forges own blades collaborates with other Scandinavian blacksmiths. Buys Damascus blades. **Prices:** $150 to $400. **Remarks:** Part-time maker; first knife sold in 1990. **Mark:** First name or initials.

JOSÈ ALBERTO, PASCHOARELLI, (no address avilable)
Specialties: Bowies and large knives of his designs. **Technical:** Grinds 440C or K-100, forges 5160. Uses mostly natural materials for handles. Full-time maker since 1995. **Prices:** Small knives start at $120. Large knives start at $260. Stamp JAP Handmade.

k

K B S, KNIVES, RSD 181, North Castlemaine, Vic 3450, AUSTRALIA, /0011 61 3 54 705864
Specialties: Bowiers, daggers and miniatures. **Patterns:** Art daggers, traditional Bowies, fancy folders and miniatures. **Technical:** Hollow or flat grind, most steels. **Prices:** $200 to $600+. **Remarks:** Full-time maker; first knife sold in 1983. **Mark:** Initials and address in Southern Cross motif.

KACZOR, TOM, 375 Wharncliffe Rd. N., Upper London, Ont., CANADA, N6G 1E4/519-645-7640

KAGAWA, KOICHI, 1556 Horiyamashita, Hatano-Shi, Kanagawa, JAPAN, /
Specialties: Fancy high-tech straight knives and folders to customer specs. **Patterns:** Hunters, locking folders and slip-joints. **Technical:** Uses 440C and ATS-34. **Prices:** $500 to $2,000; some to $20,000.

custom knifemakers

Remarks: Part-time maker; first knife sold in 1986. **Mark:** First initial, last name-YOKOHAMA.

KALFAYAN, EDWARD N., 410 Channing, Ferndale, MI, 48220/248-548-4882
Specialties: Working straight knives and lockback folders; some art and fantasy pieces. **Patterns:** Bowies, toothpicks, fighters, daggers, swords and hunters. **Technical:** Grinds ATS-34, 440C, O1, 5160 and Damascus. **Prices:** $100 to $2,000. **Remarks:** Part-time maker; first knife sold in 1973. **Mark:** Last name.

KALUZA, WERNER, Lochnerstr. 32, 90441 Nurnberg, GERMANY, / 0911 666047
Specialties: Fancy high-art straight knives of his design. **Patterns:** Boots and ladies knives. **Technical:** Grinds ATS-34, CPM-T-440V and Schneider Damascus. Engraving available. **Prices:** NA. **Remarks:** Part-time maker. **Mark:** First initial and last name.

KANDA, MICHIO, 7-32-5 Shinzutumi-cho, Shinnanyo-shi, Yamaguchi 746, JAPAN, /0834-62-1910
Specialties: Fantasy knives of his design. **Patterns:** Animal knives. **Technical:** Grinds ATS-34. **Prices:** $300 to $3,000. **Remarks:** Full-time maker; first knife sold in 1985. Doing business as Shusui Kanda. **Mark:** Last name inside "M".

KARP, BOB, P.O. Box 47304, Phoenix, AZ, 85068/

KATO, KIYOSHI, 4-6-4 Himonya Meguro-ku, Tokyo 152, JAPAN, /
Specialties: Swords, Damascus knives, working knives and paper knives. **Patterns:** Traditional swords, hunters, Bowies and daggers. **Technical:** Forges his own Damascus and carbon steel. Grinds ATS-34. **Prices:** $260 to $700; some to $4,000. **Remarks:** Full-time maker. **Mark:** First initial, last name.

KAUFFMAN, DAVE, 120 Clark Creek Loop, Montana City, MT, 59634/ 406-442-9328
Specialties: Mosaic Damascus folders and fancy straight hunters. **Patterns:** Fighters, Bowies and drop-point hunters. **Technical:** Uses ATS-34 and his own mosaic Damascus. **Prices:** $300 to $1,200. **Remarks:** Full-time maker; first knife sold in 1989. On the cover of Knives '94. **Mark:** First and last name, city and state.

KAUFMAN, SCOTT, 302 Green Meadows Cr., Anderson, SC, 29624/ 864-231-9201
Specialties: Classic and working/using straight knives in standard patterns. **Patterns:** Fighters, hunters and utility/camp knives. Technical Grinds ATS-34, 440C, O1. **Prices:** $100 to $500. **Remarks:** Part-time maker; first knife sold in 1987. **Mark:** Kaufman Knives with Bible in middle.

KAWASAKI, AKIHISA, 11-8-9 Chome Minamiamachi, Suzurandai Kita-Ku, Kobe, JAPAN, /078-593-0418
Specialties: Working/using knives of his design. **Patterns:** Hunters, kit camp knives. **Technical:** Forges and grinds Molybdenum Panadium. Grinds ATS-34 and stainless steel. Uses Chinese Quince wood, desert ironwood and cow leather. **Prices:** $300 to $800; some to $1,200. **Remarks:** Full-time maker. **Mark:** Last name, first name.

KAY, J. WALLACE, 332 Slab Bridge Rd., Liberty, SC, 29657/

KEESLAR, JOSEPH F., 391 Radio Rd., Almo, KY, 42020/502-753-7919
Specialties: Classic Bowie reproductions and contemporary Bowies. **Patterns:** Period pieces, combat knives, hunters, daggers. **Technical:** Forges 5160 and his own Damascus. Decorative filework, engraving and custom leather sheaths available. **Prices:** $200 to $3,000. **Remarks:** Full-time maker; first knife sold in 1976. **Mark:** First and middle initials, last name in hammer, knife and anvil logo, M.S.

KEESLAR, STEVEN C., 115 Lane 216, Hamilton, IN, 46742/219-488-3161
Specialties: Traditional working/using straight knives of his design and to customer specs. **Patterns:** Bowies, hunters, utility/camp knives. **Technical:** Forges 5160, files 52100. **Prices:** $100 to $600; some to $1500. **Remarks:** Part-time maker; first knife sold in 1976. **Mark:** First initial, last name.

KEETON, WILLIAM L., 6095 Rehobeth Rd. SE, Laconia, IN, 47135-9550/812-969-2836
Specialties: Plain and fancy working knives. **Patterns:** Hunters and fighters; locking folders and slip-joints. Names patterns after Kentucky Derby winners. **Technical:** Grinds D2, ATS-34, 440C, 440V and 154CM; mirror and satin finishes. **Prices:** $95 to $2,000. **Remarks:** Full-time maker; first knife sold in 1971. **Mark:** Logo of key.

KEHIAYAN, ALFREDO, Cuzco 1455, Ing. Maschwitz, CP 1623 Buenos Aires, ARGENTINA, /03488-4-42212
Specialties: Functional straight knives. **Patterns:** Utility knives, skinners, hunters and boots. **Technical:** Forges and grinds SAE 52.100, SAE 6180, SAE 9260, SAE 5160, 440C and ATS-34, titanium with nitride. All blades mirror-polished; makes leather sheath and wood cases. **Prices:** $300 to $500; some to $6000. **Remarks:** Full-time maker; first knife sold in 1983. **Mark:** Name.

KEIDEL, GENE W. AND SCOTT J., 4661 105th Ave. SW, Dickinson, ND, 58601/
Specialties: Fancy/embellished and working/using straight knives of his design. **Patterns:** Bowies, hunters and miniatures. **Technical:** Gring 440C and O1 tool steel. Offer scrimshaw and filework. **Prices:** $95 to $500. **Remarks:** Full-time makers; first knife sold in1990. Doing business as Keidel Knives. **Mark:** Last name.

KELLEY, GARY, 17485 SW Pheasant Lane, Aloha, OR, 97006/503-848-9313
Specialties: Primitive knives and blades. **Patterns:** Fur trade era rifleman's knives, patch and throwing knives. **Technical:** Hand-forges and precision investment casts. **Prices:** $25 to $250. **Remarks:** Part-time maker. Staff photographer/writer for *Tactical Knives* magazine; does illustrative knife photography. Doing business as Reproduction Blades. **Mark:** Full name or initials.

KELLOGG, BRIAN R., 19048 Smith Creek Rd, New Market, VA, 22844/ 540-740-4292
Specialties: Fancy and working straight knives of his design and to customer specs. **Patterns:** Fighters, hunters and utility/camp knives. **Technical:** Grinds 440C, D2 and A2. Offers filework and fancy pin and cable pin work. Prefers natural handle materials. **Prices:** $75 to $225; some to $350. **Remarks:** Part-time maker; first knife sold in 1983. **Mark:** Last name.

KELLY, LANCE, 1723 Willow Oak Dr., Edgewater, FL, 32132/904-423-4933
Specialties: Investor-class straight knives and folders. **Patterns:** Kelly style in contemporary outlines. **Technical:** Grinds O1, D2 and 440C; engraves; inlays gold and silver. **Prices:** $600 to $3,500. **Remarks:** Full-time engraver and knifemaker; first knife sold in 1975. **Mark:** Last name.

KELSO, JIM, 577 Collar Hill Rd, Worcester, VT, 05682/802-229-4254
Specialties: Fancy high-art straight knives and folders that mix Eastern and Western influences. Only uses own designs, but accepts suggestions for themes. **Patterns:** Daggers, swords and locking folders. **Technical:** Grinds only custom Damascus. Works with top Damascus bladesmiths. **Prices:** $3,000 to $8,000; some to $15,000. **Remarks:** Full-time maker; first knife sold in 1980. **Mark:** Stylized initials.

KENNEDY, KELLY S., 9894 A.W. University, Odessa, TX, 79764/915-381-6165
Specialties: Traditional working and using straight knives of his design and to customer specs. **Patterns:** Bowies, hunters and utility/camp knives. **Technical:** Forges 5160, W2 and own Damascus. **Prices:** Moderate to upscale. **Remarks:** Full-time maker; first knife sold in 1991. Doing business as Noble House Armourers. **Mark:** Last name in script, J.S., A.B.S.

KENNEDY JR., BILL, P.O. Box 850431, Yukon, OK, 73085/405-354-9150
Specialties: Working straight knives. **Patterns:** Hunters, fighters, minis and fishing knives. **Technical:** Grinds D2, 440C and Damascus. **Prices:** $80 and higher. **Remarks:** Part-time maker; first knife sold in 1980. **Mark:** Last name and year made.

KENNELLEY, J.C., 1114 N. C St., Arkansas City, KS, 67005/316-442-0848
Specialties: Working straight knives; some fantasy pieces. **Patterns:** Hunters, fighters, skinners and fillet knives. **Technical:** Grinds D2 and 440C. **Prices:** $75 to $200; some to $500. **Remarks:** Part-time maker; first knife sold in 1982. **Mark:** Name logo.

KERLEY, TASMAN, PO Box 659, Belgrave Victoria, 3160, AUS-TRAILIA, /613-9754 6740
Specialties: Small personal knives, working patterns and liner lock folders. **Patterns:** Drop point hunters, boot knives, Sheffield style bowies and knives to customers design. **Technical:** Grinds ATS-34, 440c, O1 and D2, some forging. All types of handle material from basic woods and syn-

thetics to exotics and all leather work. **Prices:** $100 to $800 and higher. **Rremarks:** First knife sold in 1992; sometimes trades as Silk Edge Handmade Knives. **Mark:** Makers Initials orSilk Edge.

KERSTEN, MICHAEL, Borkzeile 17, 13583 Berlin, GERMANY, / **Specialties:** Working/using straight knives and folders of his design and camp knives. **Technical:** Grinds O1, D2, 440C, 440V and Damascus. Handle materials include brass, hardwood and bone. **Prices:** $250 to $1,000. **Remarks:** Spare-time maker; first knife sold in 1993. **Mark:** Last initial.

KESSLER, RALPH A., P.O. Box 357, 345 Sherwood Rd., Marietta, SC, 29661/864-836-7944 **Specialties:** Traditional-style knives. **Patterns:** Folders, hunters, fighters, Bowies and kitchen knives. **Technical:** Grinds D2, O1, A2 and ATS-34. Forges 1090 and 1095. **Prices:** $100 to $500. **Remarks:** Part-time maker; first knife sold in 1982. **Mark:** Last name or initials with last name.

KEYES, DAN, 6688 King St., Chino, CA, 91710/909-628-8329

KHALSA, JOT SINGH, 368 Village St., Millis, MA, 02054/508-376-8162 **Specialties:** Liner locks, straight knives and one-of-a-kind daggers of his design. **Patterns:** Classic with contemporary flair. Has line of knife jewelry sold through stores and dealers. **Technical:** Forges own Damascus, grinds stainless steels. Uses natural handle materials frequently minerals. Grinds ATS-34. Offers embellishment on folders & daggers. **Prices:** Start at $225. **Remarks:** Full-time maker; first knife sold in 1978. **Mark:** An Adi Skakti symbol.

KHARLAMOV, YURI, Oboronnay 46, 2, Tula, 300007, RUSSIA, / **Specialties:** Classic, fancy and traditional knives of his design. **Patterns:** Daggers and hunters. **Technical:** Forges only Damascus with nickel. Uses natural handle materials; engraves on metal, carves on nut-tree; silver and pearl inlays. **Prices:** $600 to $2380; some to $4000. **Remarks:** Full-time maker; first knife sold in 1988. **Mark:** Initials.

KI, SHIVA, 5222 Ritterman Ave., Baton Rouge, LA, 70805/225-356-7274 **Specialties:** Fancy working straight knives and folders to customer specs. **Patterns:** Emphasis on personal defense knives, martial arts weapons. **Technical:** Forges and grinds; makes own Damascus; prefers natural handle materials. **Prices:** $135 to $850; some to $1,800. **Remarks:** Full-time maker; first knife sold in 1981. **Mark:** Name with logo.

KIEFER, TONY, 112 Chateaugay Dr., Pataskala, OH, 43062/614-927-6910 **Specialties:** Traditional working and using straight knives in standard patterns. **Patterns:** Bowies, fighters and hunters. **Technical:** Grinds 440C and D2; forges D2. Flat-grinds Bowies; hollow-grinds drop-point and trailing-point hunters. **Prices:** $95 to $140; some to $200. **Remarks:** Spare-time maker; first knife sold in 1988. **Mark:** Last name.

KILBY, KEITH, 402 Jackson Trail Rd., Jefferson, GA, 30549/706-367-9997 **Specialties:** Works with all designs. **Patterns:** Mostly Bowies, camp knives and hunters of his design. **Technical:** Forges 52100, 5160, 1095, Damascus and mosaic Damascus. **Prices:** $100 to $3,500. **Remarks:** Part-time maker; first knife sold in 1974. Doing business as Foxwood Forge. **Mark:** Name or fox logo.

KIMSEY, KEVIN, 198 Cass White Rd. N.W., Cartersville, GA, 30121/ 770-387-0779 & 770-655-8879 **Specialties:** Tactical fixed blades & folders. **Patterns:** Fighters, folders, hunters and utility knives. **Technical:** Grinds 440C, ATS-34 and D2 carbon. **Prices:** $100 to $400; some to $600. **Remarks:** Three-time "Blade" award winner, Knifemaker since 1983. **Mark:** Rafter and stylized KK.

KING, BILL, 14830 Shaw Road, Tampa, FL, 33625/813-961-3455 **Specialties:** Folders, lockbacks, liner locks and stud openers. **Patterns:** Wide varieties; folders and dive knives. **Technical:** Sandvik 12-C-27, ATS-34 and some Damascus; single and double grinds. Offers filework and jewel embellishment; nickel-silver Damacus and mokume bolsters. **Prices:** $135 to $425; some to $650. **Remarks:** Full-time maker; first knife sold in 1976. All titanium fitting on liner-locks; screw construction on lock-backs. Automatic, large & small, available to Florida addresses only. **Mark:** Last name in crown.

KING, FRED, 430 Grassdale Rd, Cartersville, GA, 30120/770-382-8478 **Specialties:** Fancy and embellished working straight knives and folders. **Patterns:** Hunters, Bowies and fighters. **Technical:** Grinds ATS-34 and D2: forges 5160, L6, 52100, 203E and Damascus. Offers filework. **Prices:** $45 to $2500. **Remarks:** Spare-time maker; first knife sold in 1984. **Mark:** Kings Edge.

KING JR., HARVEY G., Box 184, Eskridge, KS, 66423-0184/785-449-2487 **Specialties:** Traditional working and using straight knives of his design and to customer specs. **Patterns:** Hunters, Bowies and fillet knives. **Technical:** Grinds O1, A2 and D2. Prefers natural handle materials; offers leatherwork. **Prices:** Start at $70. **Remarks:** 3/4 time maker; first knife sold in 1988. **Mark:** Name and serial number based on steel used, year made and number of knives made that year.

KINKADE, JACOB, 197 Rd. 154, Carpenter, WY, 82054/307-649-2446 **Specialties:** Working/using knives of his design or to customer specs; some miniature swords, daggers and battle axes. **Patterns:** Hunters, daggers, boots; some miniatures. **Technical:** Grinds carbon and stainless and commercial Damascus. Prefers natural handle material. **Prices:** Start at $30. **Remarks:** Part-time maker; first knife sold in 1990. **Mark:** Connected initials or none.

KINKER, MIKE, 8755 E County Rd 50 N, Greensburg, IN, 47240/812-663-5277 **Specialties:** Working/using knives, Straight knives. Your design. **Patterns:** Boots, daggers, hunters. **Technical:** Grind 440C, Damascus, Dovetail Bolsters, Jewelled Blade. **Prices:** $125 to 375; some to $1,000. **Remarks:** Part-time maker; first knife sold in 1991. Doing business as Kinker Knives. **Mark:** Kinker and Kinker plus year.

KINNIKIN, TODD, Eureka Forge, 8356 John McKeever Rd., House Springs, MO, 63051/314-938-6248 **Specialties:** Mosaic Damascus. **Patterns:** Hunters, fighters, folders and automatics. **Technical:** Forges own mosaic Damascus with tool steel Damascus edge. Prefers natural, fossil and artifact handle materials. **Prices:** $400 to $2,400. **Remarks:** Full-time maker; first knife sold in 1994. **Mark:** Initials connected.

KIOUS, JOE, 1015 Ridge Pointe Rd., Kerrville, TX, 78028/830-367-2277 **Specialties:** Investment-quality interframe folders. **Patterns:** Hunters, fighters, Bowies and miniatures; traditional folders. **Technical:** Grinds D2, 440C, CPM440V, 154CM and stainless Damascus. **Prices:** $175 to $1,000; some to $5,000. **Remarks:** Full-time maker; first knife sold in 1969. **Mark:** Last name, city and state.

KITSMILLER, JERRY, 67277 Las Vegas Dr., Montrose, CO, 81401/ 970-249-4290 **Specialties:** Working straight knives in standard patterns. **Patterns:** Hunters, boots and locking folders. **Technical:** Grinds ATS-34 and 440C only. **Prices:** $75 to $200; some to $300. **Remarks:** Spare-time maker; first knife sold in 1984. **Mark:** J&S Knives.

KNICKMEYER, HANK, 6300 Crosscreek, Cedar Hill, MO, 63016/314-285-3210 **Specialties:** Complex mosaic Damascus constructions. **Patterns:** Fixed blades, swords, folders and automatics. **Technical:** Mosaic Damascus with all tool steel Damascus edges. **Prices:** $500 to $2,000; some $3,000 and higher. **Remarks:** Part-time maker; first knife sold in 1989. Doing business as Dutch Creek Forge & Foundry. **Mark:** Initials connected.

KNIPSCHIELD, TERRY, 808 12th Ave. NE, Rochester, MN, 55906/507-288-7829 **Specialties:** Working straight and some folding knives in standard patterns. **Patterns:** Lockback and slip-joint knives. **Technical:** Grinds ATS-34. **Prices:** $55 to $350; some to $600. **Remarks:** Part-time maker; first knife sold in 1986. Doing business as Knip Custom Knives. **Mark:** KNIP in Old English with shield logo.

KNIPSTEIN, R.C. (JOE), 731 N. Fielder, Arlington, TX, 76012/817-265-2021 **Specialties:** Traditional pattern folders along with custom designs. **Patterns:** Hunters, Bowies, folders, fighters, utility knives. **Technical:** Grinds 440C, D2, 154CM and ATS-34. Natural handle materials and full tangs are standard. **Prices:** Start at $200. **Remarks:** Part-time maker; first knife sold in 1989. **Mark:** Last name.

KNUTH, JOSEPH E., 3307 Lookout Dr., Rockford, IL, 61109/815-874-9597
Specialties: High-art working straight knives of his design or to customer specs. **Patterns:** Daggers, fighters and swords. **Technical:** Grinds 440C, ATS-34 and D2. **Prices:** $150 to $1,500; some to $15,000. **Remarks:** Full-time maker; first knife sold in 1989. **Mark:** Initials on bolster face.

KOHLS, JERRY, W4737 State Rd 23 & 73, Princeton, WI, 54968/920-295-6597
Specialties: Working knives & period pieces. **Patterns:** Hunters-boots & bowies - your designs or mine. **Technical:** Grinds, ATS 34 440c 154CM & 1095 & commercial Damascus. **Remarks:** Part-time maker. **Mark:** Last Name.

KOJETIN, W., 20 Bapaume Rd., Delville, Germiston 1401, SOUTH AFRICA, /011 825 6680
Specialties: High-art and working straight knives of all designs. **Patterns:** Daggers, hunters and his own Manhunter Bowie. **Technical:** Grinds D2 and ATS-34; forges and grinds 440B/C. Offers "wrap-around" pava and abalone handles, scrolled wood or ivory, stacked filework and setting of faceted semi-precious stones. **Prices:** $185 to $600; some to $11,000. **Remarks:** Spare-time maker; first knife sold in 1962. **Mark:** Billy K.

KOLITZ, ROBERT, W9342 Canary Rd., Beaver Dam, WI, 53916/920-887-1287
Specialties: Working straight knives to customer specs. **Patterns:** Bowies, hunters, bird and trout knives, boots. **Technical:** Grinds O1, 440C; commercial Damascus. **Prices:** $50 to $100; some to $500. **Remarks:** Spare-time maker; first knife sold in 1979. **Mark:** Last initial.

KOMMER, RUSS, 9211 Abbott Loop Rd., Anchorage, AK, 99507/907-346-3339
Specialties: Working straight knives with the outdoorsman in mind. **Patterns:** Hunters, semi-skinners, fighters, folders and utility knives, art knives. **Technical:** Hollow-grinds ATS-34, 440C and 440V. **Prices:** $125 to $850; some to $3,000. **Remarks:** Full-time maker; first knife sold in 1995. **Mark:** Bear paw--full name, city and state or full name and state.

KOPP, TODD M., P.O. Box 3474, Apache Jct., AZ, 85217/602-983-6143
Specialties: Classic and traditional straight knives. **Patterns:** Bowies, boots, daggers, fighters and hunters. **Technical:** Grinds M1, ATS-34 and 4160. Some engraving and filework. **Prices:** $125 to $400; some to $800. **Remarks:** Part-time maker; first knife sold in 1989. **Mark:** Name, city and state.

KOUTSOPOULOS, GEORGE, 41491 Biggs Rd., LaGrange, OH, 44050/216-355-5013
Specialties: Heavy-duty working straight knives and folders. **Patterns:** Traditional hunters and skinners; lockbacks. **Technical:** Grinds 440C, 154CM, ATS-34. **Prices:** $75 to $275; some higher. **Remarks:** Spare-time maker; first knife sold in 1976. **Mark:** Initials in diamond logo.

KOVAL, MICHAEL T., 5819 Zarley St., New Albany, OH, 43054/614-855-0777
Specialties: Working straight knives of his design; period pieces. **Patterns:** Bowies, boots and daggers. **Technical:** Grinds D2, 440C and ATS34. **Prices:** $95 to $195; some to $495. **Remarks:** Full-time knife-maker supply house; spare-time knifemaker. **Mark:** Last name.

KOVAR, EUGENE, 2626 W. 98th St., Evergreen Park, IL, 60642/708-636-3724
Specialties: One-of-a-kind miniature knives only. **Patterns:** Fancy to fantasy miniature knives; knife pendants and tie tacks. **Technical:** Files and grinds nails, nickel-silver and sterling silver. **Prices:** $5 to $35; some to $100. **Mark:** GK.

KOYAMA, CAPTAIN BUNSHICHI, 3-23 Shirako-cho, Nakamura-ku, Nagoya City, 453-0817 JAPAN, /052-461-7070
Specialties: Innovative folding knife. **Patterns:** General purpose one hand. **Technical:** Grinds ATS-34 and Damascus. **Prices:** $400 to $900; some to $1,500. **Remarks:** Part-time maker; first knife sold in 1994. **Mark:** Captain B. Koyama and the shoulder straps of CAPTAIN.

KRAFT, ELMER, 1358 Meadowlark Lane, Big Arm, MT, 59910/406-849-5086
Specialties: Traditional working/using straight knives of all designs. **Patterns:** Fighters, hunters, utility/camp knives. **Technical:** Grinds 440C, D2. Custom makes sheaths. **Prices:** $125 to $350; some to $500. **Remarks:** Part-time maker; first knife sold in 1984. **Mark:** Last name.

KRAFT, STEVE, 315 S.E. 6th, Abilene, KS, 67410/913-263-2198
Specialties: Motorcycle chain Damascus with foot peg handle. **Patterns:** Hunters, boot knives and fighters. **Technical:** Forges chain Damascus and stock removal; grinds ATS-34. **Prices:** $150 to $1,000. **Remarks:** Part-time maker; first knife sold in 1984. **Mark:** Last name.

KRAMER, BOB, 1028 1st Ave. S., Seattle, WA, 98134/206-623-1088
Specialties: Traditional and working/using straight knives in standard patterns. **Patterns:** Bowies, daggers and kitchen knives. **Technical:** Forges 52100, 5160 and Damascus 1095 and L6. Triple quench, triple temper, nitro quench. **Prices:** $300 to $800; some to $3,000. **Remarks:** Full-time maker; first knife sold in 1992. Doing business as Bladesmith's Inc. **Mark:** Kramer M.S.

KRANNING, TERRY L., 1900 West Quinn, #153, Pocatello, ID, 83202/208-237-9047
Specialties: Miniature and full-size fantasy and working knives of his design. **Patterns:** Miniatures and some mini straight knives including razors, tomahawks, hunters, Bowies and fighters. **Technical:** Grinds 1095, 440C, commercial Damascus and nickel-silver. Uses exotic materials like meteorite. **Prices:** $40 to $150. **Remarks:** Part-time maker; first knife sold in 1978. **Mark:** Last initial or full initials in eagle head logo.

KRAPP, DENNY, 1826 Windsor Oak Dr., Apopka, FL, 32703/407-880-7115
Specialties: Fantasy and working straight knives of his design. **Patterns:** Hunters, fighters and utility/camp knives. **Technical:** Grinds ATS-34 and 440C. **Prices:** $85 to $300; some to $800. **Remarks:** Spare-time maker; first knife sold in 1988. **Mark:** Last name.

KRAUSE, ROY W., 22412 Corteville, St. Clair Shores, MI, 48081/810-296-3995
Specialties: Military and law enforcement/Japanese-style knives and swords. **Patterns:** Combat and back-up, Bowies, fighters, boot knives, daggers, tantos, wakazashis and katanas. **Technical:** Grinds ATS-34, A2, D2, 1045, O1 and commercial Damascus; differentially hardened Japanese-style blades. **Prices:** Moderate to upscale. **Remarks:** Full-time maker. **Mark:** Last name on traditional knives; initials in Japanese characters on Japanese-style knives.

KRAVITT, CHRIS, Treestump Leather, HC 31, Box 6484, Ellsworth, ME, 04605-9320/207-584-3000

KREIBICH, DONALD L., 6082 Boyd Ct., San Jose, CA, 95123/408-225-8354
Specialties: Working straight knives in standard patterns. **Patterns:** Bowies, boots and daggers; camp and fishing knives. **Technical:** Grinds 440C, 154CM and ATS-34; likes integrals. **Prices:** $100 to $200; some to $500. **Remarks:** Part-time maker; first knife sold in 1980. **Mark:** First and middle initials, last name.

KREMZNER, RAYMOND L., P.O. Box 31, Stevenson, MD, 21153/410-329-5226
Specialties: Working straight knives in standard patterns, some fancy. **Patterns:** Hunters, fighters, Bowies and camp knives. **Technical:** Forges 5160, 9260, W2 and his own Damascus. Offers wire inlay. **Prices:** $200 to $700; some higher. **Remarks:** Part-time maker; first knife sold in 1987. Mark Last name, JS.

KRESSLER, D.F., Schloss Odetzhausen, Schlossberg 1-85235, Odetzhausen, GERMANY, /08134-7758
Specialties: High-tech working knives. **Patterns:** Hunters, fighters, daggers. **Technical:** Grinds new state-of-the-art steels; prefers natural handle materials. **Prices:** Upscale. **Mark:** Name in logo.

KRETSINGER JR., PHILIP W., 17536 Bakersville Rd., Boonsboro, MD, 21713/301-432-6771
Specialties: Fancy and traditional period pieces. **Patterns:** Hunters, Bowies, camp knives, daggers, carvers, fighters. **Technical:** Forges W2, 5160 and his own Damascus. **Prices:** Start at $200. **Remarks:** Full-time knifemaker. **Mark:** Name.

KRUSE, MARTIN, P.O. Box 487, Reseda, CA, 91335/818-713-0172
Specialties: Fighters and working straight knives. **Patterns:** Full line of straight knives, swords, fighters, axes, kitchen cutlery. **Technical:** Forges and grinds O1, 1095, 5160 and Damascus; differential tempering. **Prices:** $85 to $700; some to $2,000. **Remarks:** Full-time maker; first knife sold in 1964. **Mark:** Initials.

KUBAIKO, HANK, PO Box 191, Winesburg, OH, 44690-0191/
Specialties: Distal tapering and clay zone tempering. **Patterns:** Bowies, fighters, fishing knives, kitchen cutlery, lockers, slip-joints, camp knives, axes and miniatures. Also makes American, European and traditional samurai swords and daggers. **Technical:** Grinds 440C, ATS-34 and D2; will use CPM-T-440V at extra cost. **Prices:** Moderate. **Remarks:** Full-time maker; first knife sold in 1982. Allow three months for sword order fulfillment. **Mark:** Alaskan Maid and name.

KUBASEK, JOHN A., 74 Northhampton St., Easthampton, MA, 01027/413-527-7917
Specialties: Left- and right-handed liner lock folders of his design or to customer specs. **Patterns:** Fighters, tantos, drop points and survival knives. **Technical:** Grinds ATS-34 and Damascus. **Prices:** $175 to $750. **Remarks:** Part-time maker; first knife sold in 1985. **Mark:** Name and address etched.

L

LA GRANGE, FANIE, 22 Sturke Rd., Selborne, Bellville 7530, SOUTH AFRICA, /27-021-9134199
Specialties: Fancy high-tech straight knives and folders of his design and to customer specs. **Patterns:** Daggers, hunters and locking folders. **Technical:** Grinds Sandvik 12C27 and ATS-34; forges and grinds Damascus. Engraves, enamels and anodizes bolsters. Uses rare and natural handle materials. **Prices:** $250 to $500; some higher. **Remarks:** Full-time maker; first knife sold in 1987. **Mark:** Name, town, country under Table Mountain.

LADD, JIM S., 1120 Helen, Deer Park, TX, 77536/713-479-7286
Specialties: Working knives and period pieces. **Patterns:** Hunters, boots and Bowies plus other straight knives. **Technical:** Grinds D2, 440C and 154CM. **Prices:** $125 to $225; some to $550. **Remarks:** Part-time maker; first knife sold in 1965. Doing business as The Tinker. **Mark:** First and middle initials, last name.

LADD, JIMMIE LEE, 1120 Helen, Deer Park, TX, 77536/713-479-7186
Specialties: Working straight knives. **Patterns:** Hunters, skinners and utility knives. **Technical:** Grinds 440C and D2. **Prices:** $75 to $225. **Remarks:** First knife sold in 1979. **Mark:** First and middle initials, last name.

LAGRANGE, FANNIE, 12 Canary Crescent, Table View 7441, South Africa, /27 21 55 76 805
Specialties: African influenced styles in folders & fixed blades. **Patterns:** All original patterns with many one-ofs. **Technical:** Mostly stock removal in 12c27, ATS34 , stainless Damascus. **Prices:** $350-$3000. **Remarks:** Professional maker. S A Guild Member 12 years. **Mark:** Name over spear.

LAINSON, TONY, 114 Park Ave., Council Bluffs, IA, 51503/712-322-5222
Specialties: Working straight knives, locking folders, straight razors, Bowies and tantos. **Technical:** Grinds ATS-34 and 440C. Prefers mirror finishes; handle materials include Micarta, Pakkawood and bone. **Prices:** $45 to $280; some to $450. **Remarks:** Part-time maker; first knife sold in 1987; not currently taking orders. **Mark:** Name and state.

LAKE, RON, 3360 Bendix Ave., Eugene, OR, 97401/503-484-2683
Specialties: High-tech working knives; inventor of the modern interframe folder. **Patterns:** Hunters, boots, etc.; locking folders. **Technical:** Grinds 154CM and ATS-34. Patented interframe with special lock release tab. **Prices:** $2,200 to $3,000; some higher. **Remarks:** Full-time maker; first knife sold in 1966. **Mark:** Last name.

LALA, PAULO RICARDO P. AND LALA, ROBERTO P., R. Daniel Martins, 636, Centro, Presidente Prudente, SP-19031-260, BRAZIL, /0182-210125
Specialties: Straight knives and folders of all designs to customer specs. **Patterns:** Bowies, daggers fighters, hunters and utility knives. **Technical:** Grinds and forges D6, 440C, high-carbon steels and Damascus. **Prices:** $60 to $400; some higher. **Remarks:** Full-time makers; first knife sold in 1991. All stainless steel blades are ultra sub-zero quenched. **Mark:** Sword carved on top of anvil under KORTH.

LAMBERT, JARRELL D., 2321 FM 2982, Granado, TX, 77962/512-771-3744
Specialties: Traditional working and using straight knives of his design and to customer specs. **Patterns:** Bowies, hunters, tantos and utility/camp knives. **Technical:** Grinds ATS-34; forges W2 and his own Damascus. Makes own sheaths. **Prices:** $80 to $600; some to $1000. **Remarks:** Part-time maker; first knife sold in 1982. **Mark:** Etched first and middle initials, last name; or stamped last name.

LAMBERT, RONALD S., 24 Vermont St., Johnston, RI, 02919/401-831-5427
Specialties: Traditional working and using straight knives of his design. **Patterns:** Boots, Bowies and hunters. **Technical:** Grinds O1 and 440C; forges 1070. Offers exotic wood handles; sheaths have exotic skin overlay. **Prices:** $100 to $500; some to $850. **Remarks:** Part-time maker; first knife sold in 1991. Doing business as RL Custom Knives. **Mark:** Initials; each knife is numbered.

LAMPREY, MIKE, 32 Pathfield, Great Torrington, Devon EX38 7BX, ENGLAND, /01805 601331
Specialties: High-tech locking folders of his design. **Patterns:** Sidelock folders. **Technical:** Grinds ATS-34, Dendritic 440C, PM stainless Damascus and Stellite 6K. Linerless handle shells in titanium. Belt clips in ATS-34. **Prices:** $300 to $750; some to $1,000. **Remarks:** Part-time maker; first knife sold in 1982. **Mark:** Signature or Celtic knot.

LAMPSON, FRANK G., Po Box 607, Rimrock, AZ, 86335/520-567-7395
Specialties: Working folders; one of a kinds. **Patterns:** Folders, hunters, utility knives, fillet knives and Bowies. **Technical:** Grinds ATS-34, 440C and 154CM. **Prices:** $100 to $750; some to $3,500. **Remarks:** Full-time maker; first knife sold in 1971. **Mark:** Name in fish logo.

LANCASTER, C.G., No 2 Schoonwinkel, St Parys, Par 45 Free State, SOUTH AFRICA, /0568112090
Specialties: High-tech working and using knives of his design and to customer specs. **Patterns:** Hunters, locking folders and utility/camp knives. **Technical:** Grinds Sandvik 12C27, 440C and D2. Offers anodized titanium bolsters. **Prices:** $450 to $750; some to $1,500. **Remarks:** Part-time maker; first knife sold in 1990. **Mark:** Etched logo.

LANCE, BILL, P.O. Box 4427, Eagle River, AK, 99577/907-694-1487
Specialties: Ooloos and working straight knives; limited issue sets. **Patterns:** Several ooloo patterns, drop-point skinners. **Technical:** Uses ATS-34, Vascomax 350; ivory, horn and high-class wood handles. **Prices:** $85 to $300; art sets to $3,000. **Remarks:** First knife sold in 1981. **Mark:** Last name over a lance.

LANDERS, JOHN, 758 Welcome Rd., Newnan, GA, 30263/404-253-5719
Specialties: High-art working straight knives and folders of his design. **Patterns:** hunters, fighters and slip-joint folders. **Technical:** Grinds 440C, ATS-34, 154CM and commerical Damascus. **Prices:** $85 to $250; some to $500. **Remarks:** Part-time maker; first knife sold in 1989. **Mark:** Last name.

LANDRUM, LEONARD "LEN", 979 Gumpond-Beall Rd., Lumberton, MS, 39455/601-796-4380
Specialties: Traditional working and using straight knives of his design and to customer specs. **Patterns:** Boots, Bowies, daggers, fighters, hunters, kitchen knives and utility/camp knives. **Technical:** Side lock folder with D2 & 52100 blades as well as Damascus. **Prices:** $100 to $500; some to $1,000. **Remarks:** Part-time maker; first knife sold in 1987. **Mark:** Handmade by Landrum.

LANE, BEN, 4802 Massie St., North Little Rock, AR, 72218/501-753-8238
Specialties: Fancy straight knives of his design and to customer specs; period pieces. **Patterns:** Bowies, hunters, utility/camp knives. **Technical:** Grinds D2 and 154CM; forges and grinds 1095. Offers intricate handle work including inlays and spacers. **Prices:** $120 to $450; some to $5,000. **Remarks:** Part-time maker; first knife sold in 1989. **Mark:** Full name, city, state.

LANG, KURT, 4908 S. Wildwood Dr., McHenry, IL, 60050/708-516-4649
Specialties: High-art working knives. **Patterns:** Bowies, utilitarian-type knives with rough finishes. **Technical:** Forges welded steel in European and Japanese styles. **Prices:** Moderate to upscale. **Remarks:** Part-time maker. **Mark:** "Crazy Eye" logo.

custom knifemakers

LANGE, DONALD G., Rt. 1, Box 66, Pelican Rapids, MN, 56572/ **Specialties:** High-quality Damascus hunters; welcomes customer designs. **Patterns:** Hunters, fighters and Bowies. **Technical:** Forges 5160, W2, L6 and his own Damascus. **Prices:** Moderate. **Remarks:** Full-time maker; first knife sold in 1969. **Mark:** Last name, M.S.

LANGLEY, GENE H., 1022 N. Price Rd., Florence, SC, 29506/843-669-3150 **Specialties:** Working knives in standard patterns. **Patterns:** Hunters, boots, fighters, locking folders and slip-joints. **Technical:** Grinds 440C, 154CM and ATS-34. **Prices:** $125 to $450; some to $1000. **Remarks:** Part-time maker; first knife sold in 1979. **Mark:** Name.

LANGSTON, BENNIE E., 2061 Pennington Gap, Memphis, TN, 38134/ 901-381-4443 **Specialties:** Traditional working straight knives and folders of his design. **Patterns:** Hunters, daggers and locking folders. **Technical:** Grinds 440C. Filework; mirror-finishes. **Prices:** $75 to $200. **Remarks:** Part-time maker; first knife sold in 1970. **Mark:** Last name and outline of state.

LANKTON, SCOTT, 8065 Jackson Rd. R-11, Ann Arbor, MI, 48103/ 313-426-3735 **Specialties:** Pattern welded swords, krisses and Viking period pieces. **Patterns:** One of a kind. **Technical:** Forges W2, L6 nickel and other steels. **Prices:** $600 to $12,000. **Remarks:** Part-time bladesmith, full-time smith; first knife sold in 1976. **Mark:** Last name logo.

LAPEN, CHARLES, Box 529, W. Brookfield, MA, 01585/ **Specialties:** Fancy working straight knives. **Patterns:** camp knives, Japanese-style swords and wood working tools, hunters, Bowies and feudal European knives. **Technical:** Forges 1075, car spring and his own Damascus. Favors narrow and Japanese tangs. **Prices:** $200 to $400; some to $2,000. **Remarks:** Part-time maker; first knife sold in 1972. **Mark:** Last name.

LAPLANTE, BRETT, 110 Dove Creek, McKinney, TX, 75069/972-837-4603 **Specialties:** Working straight knives and folders to customer specs. **Patterns:** Survival knives, Bowies, skinners, hunters. **Technical:** Grinds D2 and 440C. Heat-treats. **Prices:** $150 to $3,000. **Remarks:** Part-time maker; first knife sold in 1987. **Mark:** Last name in Canadian maple leaf logo.

LARSON, RICHARD, 549 E. Hawkeye Ave., Turlock, CA, 95380/209-668-1615 **Specialties:** Traditional working/using straight knives in standard patterns. **Patterns:** Bowies, hunters and utility/camp knives. **Technical:** Grinds ATS-34, 440C, and 154CM. Engraves and srimshaws holsters and handles. Hand-sews sheaths with tooling. **Prices:** $150 to $300; some to $1,000. **Remarks:** Part-time maker; first knife sold in 1986. Doing business as Larson Knives. **Mark:** Knife logo spelling last name.

LARY, ED, 651 Rangeline Rd., Mosinee, WI, 54455/715-693-3940 **Specialties:** Entry level to embellished investment grade. **Patterns:** Hunters, interframe folders, fighters and one-of-a-kind. **Technical:** Grinds D2, 440C, ATS-34 and Damascus; prefers natural handle material. Does fancy filework and fabricated sheaths. **Prices:** Moderate to upscale. **Remarks:** First knife sold in 1974. **Mark:** Name in script.

LAUGHLIN, DON, 190 Laughlin Dr., Vidor, TX, 77662/409-769-3390 **Specialties:** Straight knives and folders of his design. **Patterns:** Hunters, spring-back folders, drop points and trailing points. **Technical:** Grinds D2, 440C and 154CM; stock removal; makes his own Damascus. **Prices:** $175 to $250 for stock removal blades; $250 to $800 for Damascus blades. **Remarks:** Full-time maker; first knife sold in 1973. **Mark:** DEER or full name.

LAURENT, KERMIT, 1812 Acadia Dr., LaPlace, LA, 70068/504-652-5629 **Specialties:** Traditional and working straight knives and folders of his design. **Patterns:** Bowies, hunters and utility knives. **Technical:** Forges his own patterned and wire Damascus and most tool steels. Specializes in altering cable patterns. Uses stabilized handle materials, especially select exotic woods. **Prices:** $100 to $500; some to $50,000. **Remarks:** Full-time maker; first knife sold in 1982. Doing business as Kermit's Knife Works. **Mark:** First name.

LAWLER, TIM, Sabersmith, 11073 S Hartel, Grand Ledge, ME, 48837/ 517-281-8327

LAWLESS, CHARLES, 611 Haynes Rd. N.E., Arab, AL, 35016/205-586-4862 **Specialties:** Classic and traditional straight knives of his design or to customer specs. **Patterns:** Bowies, fighters and hunters. **Technical:** Forges 5160, O1 and 1095. Uses tapered tangs, dovetailed bolsters and mortised handle frames. Mostly natural materials. **Prices:** $50 to $400; some to $1,200. **Remarks:** Part-time maker; first knife sold in 1991. Doing business as Lawless Blades. **Mark:** Full name, bladesmith, city and state.

LAWRENCE, ALTON, 205 W. Stillwell, De Queen, AR, 71832/870-642-7643 **Specialties:** Classic straight knives and folders to customer specs. **Patterns:** Bowies, hunters, folders and utility/camp knives. **Technical:** Forges 5160, 1095, 1084, Damascus and railroad spikes. **Prices:** Start at $100. **Remarks:** Part-time maker; first knife sold in 1988. **Mark:** Last name inside fish symbol.

LAY, L.J., 602 Mimosa Dr., Burkburnett, TX, 76354/817-569-1329 **Specialties:** Working straight knives in standard patterns; some period pieces. **Patterns:** Drop-point hunters, Bowies and fighters. **Technical:** Grinds ATS-34 to mirror finish; likes Micarta handles. **Prices:** Moderate. **Remarks:** Full-time maker; first knife sold in 1985. **Mark:** Name or name with ram head and city or stamp L J Lay.

LAY, R.J. (BOB), Box 2781, Vanderhoof, B.C., CANADA, V0J 3A0/250-567-3856 **Specialties:** Traditional and working/using straight knives of his design. **Patterns:** Bowies, fighters and hunters. **Technical:** Grinds 440C; forges and grinds tool steels. Uses exotic handle and spacer material. File cut; prefers narrow tang. Sheaths available. **Prices:** $150 to $450; some to $1,100. (Can.) **Remarks:** Full-time maker; first knife sold in 1976. Doing business as Lay's Custom Knives. **Mark:** Signature acid etched.

LAZO, ROBERT T., 11850 SW 181 St., Miami, FL, 33177/305-232-1569 **Specialties:** Traditional working and using straight knives and folders in standard patterns. **Patterns:** Utility/camp knives, locking folders, fillet knives and some miniatures. **Technical:** Grinds 440C, ATS-34 and O1. All knives come with hand-tooled leather sheaths, some with fancy inlays. **Prices:** $90 to $250; some to $500. **Remarks:** Spare-time maker; first knife sold in 1990. **Mark:** Engraved or stamped name.

LEACH, MIKE J., 5377 W. Grand Blanc Rd., Swartz Creek, MI, 48473/ 810-655-4850 **Specialties:** Fancy working knives. **Patterns:** Hunters, fighters, Bowies and heavy-duty knives; slip-joint folders and integral straight patterns. **Technical:** Grinds D2, 440C and 154CM; buys Damascus. **Prices:** Start at $150. **Remarks:** Full-time maker; first knife sold in 1952. **Mark:** First initial, last name.

LEAVITT JR., EARL F., Pleasant Cove Rd., Box 306, E. Boothbay, ME, 04544/207-633-3210 **Specialties:** 1500-1870 working straight knives and fighters; pole arms. **Patterns:** Historically significant knives, classic/modern custom designs. **Technical:** Flat-grinds O1; heat-treats. Filework available. **Prices:** $90 to $350; some to $1000. **Remarks:** Full-time maker; first knife sold in 1981. Doing business as Old Colony Manufactory. **Mark:** Initials in oval.

LEBATARD, PAUL M., 14700 Old River Rd., Vancleave, MS, 39565/ 228-826-4137 **Specialties:** Sound working knives; lightweight folders. **Patterns:** Hunters, fillets, camp and kitchen knives, combat/survival utility knives, Bowies, toothpicks and one- or two-blade folders. **Technical:** Grinds ATS-34, A-2, D-2, 440-C; forges 52100 & 5160. Machines folder frames from aircraft aluminum. **Prices:** $50 to $550. **Remarks:** Part-time maker; first knife sold in 1974. Offers knife repair, restoration and sharpening. **Mark:** Last name.

LEBER, HEINZ, Box 446, Hudson's Hope, BC, CANADA, V0C 1V0/250-783-5304 **Specialties:** Working straight knives of his design. **Patterns:** 20 models, form capers to Bowies. **Technical:** Hollow-ginds D2 and M2 steel; mirror-finishes and full tang only. Likes moose, elk, stone sheep for handles. **Prices:** $175 to $1,000. **Remarks:** Full-time maker; first knife sold in 1975. **Mark:** Initials connected.

LEBLANC, JOHN, Rt. 2, Box 22950, Winnsboro, TX, 75494/903-629-7745

LECK, DAL, Box 1054, Hayden, CO, 81639/970-276-3663
Specialties: Classic, traditional and working knives of his design and in standard patterns; period pieces. **Patterns:** Boots, daggers, fighters, hunters and push daggers. **Technical:** Forges O1 and 5160; makes his own Damascus. **Prices:** $175 to $700; some to $1,500. **Remarks:** Part-time maker; first knife sold in 1990. Doing business as The Moonlight Smithy. **Mark:** Stamped: hammer & anvil with initials.

LEDBETTER, RANDY R., P.O. Box 897, Payette, Idaho, 83661/208-642-9833
Specialties: Fixed blade, working and art knives to customer specs. **Patterns:** Daggers, skinners, fighters, utility, Bowies, patch knives and letter openers. **Technical:** Stock removal; grinds Damascus, ATS-34, 440C, A2, planer and saw blades. **Prices:** $149 to $269. Sheaths are extra. **Remarks:** Part-time maker; first knife sold in 1991. **Mark:** Superimposed initials or first and middle initials and last name.

LEDFORD, BRACY R., 3670 N. Sherman Dr., Indianapolis, IN, 46218/317-546-6176
Specialties: Art knives and fantasy knives; working knives upon request. **Patterns:** Bowies, locking folders and hunters; coil spring action folders. **Technical:** Files and sandpapers 440C by hand; other steels available upon request; likes exotic handle materials. **Prices:** Folders start at $350; fixed blades $225. **Remarks:** Full-time maker; first knife sold in 1983. **Mark:** First and middle initials, last name, city and state.

LEE, TOMMY, P.O. Box 527, Taylors, SC, 29687/864-989-1271
Specialties: Working knives and period pieces. **Patterns:** Daggers, boots, fighters and folders. **Technical:** Forges and grinds 440C, ATS-34 and his own and commercial Damascus. **Prices:** $200 to $500; some to $2,000. **Remarks:** Full-time maker; first knife sold in 1974. **Mark:** Last name in capital block letters.

LEE, RANDY, P.O. Box 1873, St. Johns, AZ, 85936/520-337-2594
Specialties: Traditional working and using straight knives of his design. **Patterns:** Bowies, fighters, hunters, daggers and professional throwing knives. **Technical:** Grinds ATS-34, 440C and D2. Offers sheaths. **Prices:** $175 to $500; some to $800. **Remarks:** Part-time maker; first knife sold in 1979. **Mark:** Full name, city, state.

LEET, LARRY W., 14417 2nd Ave. S.W., Burien, WA, 98166-1505/
Specialties: Heavy-duty working knives. **Patterns:** Hunters, tantos, camp knives and Bowies. **Technical:** Grinds stainless steels; likes filework. **Remarks:** Full-time maker; first knife sold in 1970. **Mark:** Stylized initials.

LELAND, STEVE, 2300 Sirfrancis Drake Blvd., Fairfax, CA, 94930-1118/415-457-0318
Specialties: Traditional and working straight knives and folders of his design and to customer specs. Makes straight & locking folder sets. **Patterns:** Boots, hunters, fighters, Bowies. **Technical:** Grinds O1, ATS-34 and 440C. Does own heat treat. Makes nickel silver sheaths. **Prices:** $150 to $550; some to $1,500. **Remarks:** Part-time maker; first knife sold in 1987. Doing business as Leland Handmade Knives. **Mark:** Last name.

LEMAIRE, DENIS, 534 Verendrye St., Boucherville, P.Q., CANADA, J4B 2Y1/

LEONE, NICK, 9 Georgetown, Pontoon Beach, IL, 62040/618-797-1179
Specialties: Working straight knives and art daggers. **Patterns:** Bowies, skinners, hunters, camp/utility, fighters, daggers and primitive knives. **Technical:** Forges 5160, W2, O1, 1098, 52100 and his own Damascus. **Prices:** t$100 to $1,000; some to $3,500. **Remarks:** Full-time maker; first knife sold in 1987. Doing business as Anvil Head Forge. **Mark:** Last name, NL, AHF.

LEPORE, MICHAEL J., 66 Woodcutters Dr., Bethany, CT, 06524/203-393-3823
Specialties: One of a kind designs to customer specs; mostly handmade. **Patterns:** Fancy working straight knives and folders. **Technical:** Forges and grinds W2, W1 and O1; prefers natural handle materials. **Prices:** Start at $350. **Remarks:** Spare-time maker; first knife sold in 1984. **Mark:** Last name.

LERCH, MATTHEW, N88 W23462 North Lisbon Road, Sussex, WI, 53089/414-246-6362
Specialties: Gentlemen's working and investment-grade folders. **Patterns:** Interframe and integral folders; lock backs, slip-joints, side locks, button locks. **Technical:** Grinds ATS-34, 1095, 440 and Damascus. Offers filework and embellished bolsters. **Prices:** $400 to $1,000; some to $3,000. **Remarks:** Part-time maker; first knife sold in 1995. **Mark:** Last name.

LETCHER, BILLY, 200 Milkyway, Fort Collins, CO, 80525/970-223-9689
Specialties: Traditional working and using straight knives; fancy knives. **Patterns:** Boots, Bowies, daggers, fighters, hunters, letter openers. **Technical:** Grinds 440C, ATS-34 and D2. Maker does own engraving. **Prices:** $100 and up. **Remarks:** Part-time maker; first knife sold in 1983. **Mark:** Last name.

LEVENGOOD, BILL, 15011 Otto Rd., Tampa, FL, 33624/813-961-5688
Specialties: Working straight knives and folders. **Patterns:** Hunters, Bowies, folders and collector pieces. **Technical:** Grinds ATS-34, BG-42 and Damascus. **Prices:** $175 to $1,500. **Remarks:** Part-time maker; first knife sold in 1983. **Mark:** Last name, city, state.

LEVERETT, KEN, P.O. Box 696, Lithia, FL, 33547/813-689-8578
Specialties: High-tech and working straight knives and folders of his design and to customer specs. **Patterns:** Bowies, hunters and locking folders. **Technical:** Grinds ATS-34, Damascus. **Prices:** $100 to $350; some to $1,500. **Remarks:** Part-time maker; first knife sold in 1991. **Mark:** Name, city, state.

LEVIN, JACK, 72-16 Bay Pkwy., Brooklyn, NY, 11204/718-232-8574

LEVINE, BOB, 101 Westwood Dr., Tullahoma, TN, 37388/615-454-9943
Specialties: Working left- and right-handed Liner Lock® folders. **Patterns:** Hunters and folders. **Technical:** Grinds ATS-34, 440C, D2, O1 and some Damascus; hollow and some flat grinds. Uses sheephorn, fossil ivory, Micarta and exotic woods. Provides custom leather sheath with each knife. **Prices:** $105 to $500; some higher. **Remarks:** Full-time maker; first knife sold in 1984. **Mark:** Name and logo.

LEWIS, STEVE, PO Box 9056, Woodland Park, CO, 80866/719-686-1120 or 888-685-2322
Specialties: Buy, sell, trade and consign custom-made knives. Mail order and major shows.

LEWIS, MIKE, 111 W. Central Ave., Tracy, CA, 95376/209-836-5753
Specialties: Traditional straight knives. **Patterns:** Swords and daggers. **Technical:** Grinds 440C, ATS-34 and 5160. Frequently uses cast bronze and cast nickel guards and pommels. **Prices:** $100 to $750. **Remarks:** Part-time maker; first knife sold in 1988. **Mark:** Dragon Steel and serial number.

LEWIS, TOM R., 1613 Standpipe Rd., Carlsbad, NM, 88220/505-885-3616
Specialties: Traditional working straight knives and pocketknives. **Patterns:** Outdoor knives, hunting knives and Bowies and pocketknives. **Technical:** Grinds ATS-34 and CPM-T-440V; forges 52100. Makes wire, pattern welded and chainsaw Damascus. **Prices:** $75 to $650. **Remarks:** Part-time maker; first knife sold in 1980. Doing business as TR Lewis Handmade Knives. **Mark:** Lewis family crest.

LEWIS, K.J., 374 Cook Rd., Lugoff, SC, 29078/803-438-4343

LICATA, STEVEN, 116 Front St., Mineola, NY, 11501/516-248-8633
Specialties: Fantasy and high-art knives. **Patterns:** Daggers, fighters, axes and swords. **Technical:** Forges O1, 440C and Damascus. **Prices:** $200 to $5,000. **Remarks:** Full-time maker; first knife sold in 1989. **Mark:** Stylized initials.

LIEBENBERG, ANDRE, 8 Hilma Rd., Bordeauxrandburg 2196, SOUTH AFRICA, /011-787-2303
Specialties: High-art straight knives of his design. **Patterns:** Daggers, fighters and swords. **Technical:** Grinds 440C and 12C27. **Prices:** $250 to $500; some $4,000 and higher. Giraffe bone handles with semi-precious stones. **Remarks:** Spare-time maker; first knife sold in 1990. **Mark:** Initials.

LIEGEY, KENNETH R., 132 Carney Dr., Millwood, WV, 25262/304-273-9545
Specialties: Traditional working/using straight knives of his design and to customer specs. **Patterns:** Hunters, utility/camp knives, miniatures. **Technical:** Grinds 440C. **Prices:** $75 to $150; some to $300. **Remarks:** Spare-time maker; first knife sold in 1977. **Mark:** First and middle initials, last name.

custom knifemakers

LIGHTFOOT, GREG, 5502-45 Street, Lloydminster, AB, CANADA, T9V 0C2/403-875-0789
Specialties: Stainless steel Damascus folders and fixed blades. **Patterns:** Boots, fighters and locking folders. **Technical:** Grinds ATS-34, 440C and D2. Kydex or leather sheaths on fixed blades; titanium, G-10, Micarta and carbon fiber on folders. Offers engraving. **Prices:** $250 to $500; some to $850. **Remarks:** Full-time maker; first knife sold in 1988. Doing business as Lightfoot Knives. **Mark:** Shark with Lightfoot Knives below.

LIKARICH, STEVE, 26075 Green Acres Rd., Colfax, CA, 95713/530-346-8480
Specialties: Fancy working knives; art knives of his design. **Patterns:** Hunters, fighters and art knives of his design. **Technical:** Grinds ATS-34, 154CM and 440C; likes high polishes and filework. **Prices:** $200 to $2,000; some higher. **Remarks:** Full-time maker; first knife sold in 1987. **Mark:** Name.

LILE, MARILYN (JIMMY), Lile Handmade Knives Corp, 2721 S Arkansas Ave, Russellville, AR, 72801/501-968-2011
Specialties: Fancy working knives. **Patterns:** Bowies, full line of straight knives, button-lock folders. **Technical:** Grinds D2 and 440C. **Prices:** $125 to $800; some higher. **Remarks:** Full-time maker; first knife sold in 1944. Creator of the original *First Blood* and *Rambo* survival knives. **Mark:** Last name with a dot between the I and L.

LINCOLN, JAMES, 5359 Blue Ridge Pkwy., Bartlett, TN, 38134/901-372-5577
Specialties: Fancy and embellished automatics with unusual/hidden releases, in standard patterns. **Patterns:** locking folders and automatics. **Technical:** Grinds ATS-34, RWL & Damasteel. Filework on most knives. Most blades and bolsters hand-finished and polished. Prefers pearl and ivory for handle material, occasionally uses precious stones and gold. Offers engraving. **Prices:** $400 to $1,000; some to $1500. **Remarks:** Part-time maker; first knife sold in 1994. Doing business as JBL Knives. **Mark:** Handmade by J.B. Lincoln.

LINDSAY, CHRIS A., 1324 N.E. Locksley Dr., Bend, OR, 97701/541-389-3875
Specialties: Working knives in standard patterns. **Patterns:** Hunters and camp knives. **Technical:** Hollow- and flat-grinds 440C and ATS-34; offers brushed finishes, tapered tangs. **Prices:** $75 to $160; knife kits $60 to $80. **Remarks:** Part-time maker; first knife sold in 1980. **Mark:** Last name, town and state in oval.

LINKLATER, STEVE, 8 Cossar Drive, Aurora, Ont., CANADA, L4G 3N8/905-727-8929
Specialties: Traditional working/using straight knives and folders of his design. **Patterns:** Fighters, hunters and locking folders. **Technical:** Grinds ATS-34, 440V and D2. **Prices:** $125 to $350; some to $600. **Remarks:** Part-time maker; first knife sold in 1987. Doing business as Links Knives. **Mark:** LINKS, year and Ontario, Canada.

LISTER JR., WELDON E., 9140 Sailfish Dr., Boerne, TX, 78006/210-981-2210
Specialties: One-of-a-kind fancy and embellished folders. **Patterns:** Locking and slip-joint folders. **Technical:** Commercial Damascus and O1. All knives embellished. Engraves, inlays, carves and scrimshaws. **Prices:** Upscale. **Remarks:** Spare-time maker; first knife sold in 1991. **Mark:** Last name.

LITTLE, JIMMY L., P.O. Box 871052, Wasilla, AK, 99687/907-373-7831
Specialties: Working straight knives; fancy period pieces. **Patterns:** Bowies, bush swords and camp knives. **Technical:** Grinds 440C, 154CM and ATS-34. **Prices:** $100 to $1,000. **Remarks:** Full-time maker; first knife sold in 1984. **Mark:** First and middle initials, last name.

LITTLE, GARY M., HC84 Box 10301, P.O. Box 156, Broadbent, OR, 97414/503-572-2656
Specialties: Fancy working knives. **Patterns:** Hunters, tantos, Bowies, axes and buckskinners; locking folders and interframes. **Technical:** Forges and grinds O1, L6, 1095; makes his own Damascus; bronze fittings. **Prices:** $85 to $300; some to $2,500. **Remarks:** Full-time maker; first knife sold in 1979. Doing business as Conklin Meadows Forge. **Mark:** Name, city and state.

LIVELY, TIM AND MARIAN, P.O. Box 8784 CRB, Tucson, AZ, 85738/
Specialties: Multi-cultural primitive knives of their design on speculation. **Patterns:** Neo-tribal one of a kinds. **Technical:** Hand forges using ancient techniques; hammer finish. **Prices:** Moderate. **Remarks:** Full-time makers; first knife sold in 1974. **Mark:** Last name.

LIVINGSTON, ROBERT C., P.O. Box 6, Murphy, NC, 28906/704-837-4155
Specialties: Art letter openers to working straight knives. **Patterns:** Minis to machetes. **Technical:** Forges and grinds most steels. **Prices:** Start at $20. **Remarks:** Full-time maker; first knife sold in 1988. Doing business as Mystik Knifeworks. **Mark:** MYSTIK.

LOCKE, KEITH, PO Box 48363, Ft Worth, TX, 76148/817-514-7272
Technical: Forges carbon steel and handcrafts sheaths for his knives. **Remarks:** Sold first knife in 1996.

LOCKETT, LOWELL C., 116 South Mill Creek Ct., Woodstock, GA, 30188/770-926-2998
Specialties: Traditional and working/using knives. **Patterns:** Bowies, hunters and utility/camp knives. **Technical:** Forges 5160, 1098, L6 and high-carbon. Makes his own guards; sewn or riveted sheaths. **Prices:** Start at $100. **Remarks:** Full-time maker; first knife sold in 1994. **Mark:** Script initials. ABS Journeyman Smith.

LOCKETT, STERLING, 527 E. Amherst Dr., Burbank, CA, 91504/818-846-5799
Specialties: Working straight knives and folders to customer specs. **Patterns:** Hunters and fighters. **Technical:** Grinds. **Prices:** Moderate. **Remarks:** Spare-time maker. **Mark:** Name, city with hearts.

LOERCHNER, WOLFGANG, P.O. Box 255, Bayfield, Ont., CANADA, N0M 1G0/519-565-2196
Specialties: Traditional straight knives, mostly ornate. **Patterns:** Small swords, daggers and stilettos; locking folders and miniatures. **Technical:** Grinds D2, 440C and 154CM; all knives hand-filed and flat-ground. **Prices:** $300 to $5,000; some to $10,000. **Remarks:** Part-time maker; first knife sold in 1983. Doing business as Wolfe Fine Knives. **Mark:** WOLFE.

LONEWOLF, J. AGUIRRE, 481 Hwy 105, Demorest, GA, 30535/706-754-4660
Specialties: High-art working and using straight knives of his design. **Patterns:** Bowies, hunters, utility/camp knives and fint steel blades. **Technical:** Forges Damascus and hig-carbon steel. Most knives have hand-carved moose antler handles. **Prices:** $55 to $500; some to $2000. **Remarks:** Full-time maker; first knife sold in 1980. Doing business as Lonewolf Trading Post. **Mark:** Stamp.

LONG, GLENN A., 10090 SW 186th Ave, Dunnellon, FL, 34432/352-489-4272
Specialties: Classic working and using straight knives of his design and to customer specs. **Patterns:** Hunters, Bowies, utility. **Technical:** Grinds 440C D2 and 440V. **Prices:** $85 to $300; some to $800. **Remarks:** Part-time maker; first knife sold in 1990. **Mark:** Last name inside diamond.

LONGWORTH, DAVE, 1811 SR 774, Hamersville, OH, 45130/513-876-3637
Specialties: High-tech working knives. **Patterns:** Locking folders, hunters, fighters and elaborate daggers. **Technical:** Grinds O1, ATS-34, 440C; buys Damascus. **Prices:** $125 to $600; some higher. **Remarks:** Part-time maker; first knife sold in 1980. **Mark:** Last name.

LOOS, HENRY C., 210 Ingraham, New Hyde Park, NY, 11040/516-354-1943
Specialties: Miniature fancy knives and period pieces of his design. **Patterns:** Bowies, daggers and swords. **Technical:** Grinds O1 and 440C. Uses sterling, 18K, rubies and emeralds. All knives come with handmade hardwood cases. **Prices:** $90 to $195; some to $250. **Remarks:** Spare-time maker; first knife sold in 1990. **Mark:** Script last initial.

LORO, GENE, 2457 State Route 93 NE, Crooksville, OH, 43731/740-982-4521
Specialties: Hand forged knives. **Patterns:** Damascus - random and ladder. **Prices:** $100 and up. **Remarks:** I do not make folders. **Mark:** Loro.

LOVELESS, R.W., P.O. Box 7836, Riverside, CA, 92503/909-689-7800
Specialties: Working knives, fighters and hunters of his design. **Patterns:** Contemporary hunters, fighters and boots. **Technical:** Grinds 154CM and ATS-34. **Prices:** $850 to $4,950. **Remarks:** Full-time maker since 1969. **Mark:** Name in logo.

LOVESTRAND, SCHUYLER, 1136 19th St SW, Vero Beach, FL, 32962/561-778-0282
Specialties: Fancy working straight knives of his design and to customer specs; unusual fossil ivories. **Patterns:** Hunters, fighters, Bowies and fishing knives. **Technical:** Grinds ATS-34. **Prices:** $150 to $1,095; some higher. **Remarks:** Part-time maker; first knife sold in 1982. **Mark:** Name in logo.

LOZIER, DON, 5394 SE 168th Ave., Ocklawaha, FL, 32179/352-625-3576
Specialties: Fancy and working straight knives of his design and in standard patterns. **Patterns:** Daggers, fighters, boot knives, and hunters. **Technical:** Grinds ATS-34, 440C & damascus. Most Pieces are highly embellished by notable artisans. Taking limited number of orders per annum. **Prices:** Start at $250; most are $1,250 to $3,000; some to $12,000. **Remarks:** Full-time maker. **Mark:** Name.

LUBRICH, MARK, P.O. Box 122, Matthews, NC, 28106-0122/704-567-7692
Specialties: Traditional working and using straight knives of his design and to customer specs. **Patterns:** Hunters and utility/camp knives. Some woodcarving sets. **Technical:** Forges O1, 5160 and 1095; using some cable, brass and silver inlaid handles. Differentially heat-treats; makes sheaths; hardwood/stag or leather/stag handles. **Prices:** $250 to $700; some to $500. **Remarks:** Part-time maker; first knife sold in 1980. Doing business as Handmade Knives by Mark Lubrich. **Mark:** Etched last name on stock removal; stamped logo on forged blades.

LUCHAK, BOB, 15705 Woodforest Blvd., Channelview, TX, 77530/281-452-1779
Specialties: Presentation knives; start of The Survivor series. **Patterns:** Skinners, Bowies, camp axes, steak knife sets and fillet knives. **Technical:** Grinds 440C. Offers electronic etching; filework. **Prices:** $50 to $1,500. **Remarks:** Full-time maker; first knife sold in 1983. Doing business as Teddybear Knives. **Mark:** Full name, city and state with Teddybear logo.

LUCIE, JAMES R., 4191 E. Fruitport Rd., Fruitport, MI, 49415/616-865-6390
Specialties: Hand-forges William Scagel-style knives. **Patterns:** Authentic scagel-style knives and miniatures. **Technical:** Forges 5160. **Prices:** Start at $550. **Remarks:** Full-time maker; first knife sold in 1975. Believes in sole authorship of his work. **Mark:** Scagel Kris with maker's name and address.

LUCKETT, BILL, 108 Amantes Ln., Weatherford, TX, 76088/817-613-9412
Specialties: Uniquely patterned robust straight knives. **Patterns:** Fighters, Bowies, hunters. **Technical:** Grinds 440C and commercial Damascus; makes heavy knives with deep grinding. **Prices:** $275 to $1,000; some to $2,000. **Remarks:** Part-time maker; first knife sold in 1975. **Mark:** Last name over Bowie logo.

LUDWIG, RICHARD O., 57-63 65 St., Maspeth, NY, 11378/
Specialties: Traditional working/using knives. **Patterns:** Boots, hunters and utility/camp knives. Technical Grinds 440C, ATS-34 and 154CM. File work on guards and handles; silver spacers. Offers scrimshaw. **Prices:** $240 to $400: some to $600. **Remarks:** Full-time maker. **Mark:** Stamped first initial, last name, state.

LUI, RONALD M., 4042 Harding Ave., Honolulu, HI, 96816/808-734-7746
Specialties: Working straight knives and folders in standard patterns. **Patterns:** Hunters, boots and liner locks. **Technical:** Grinds 440C and ATS-34. **Prices:** $100 to $700. **Remarks:** Spare-time maker; first knife sold in 1988. **Mark:** Initials connected.

LUM, ROBERT W., 901 Travis Ave., Eugene, OR, 97404/541-688-2737
Specialties: High-art working knives of his design. **Patterns:** Hunters, fighters, tantos and folders. **Technical:** Grinds 440C, 154CM and ATS-34; plans to forge soon. **Prices:** $175 to $500; some to $800. **Remarks:** Full-time maker; first knife sold in 1976. **Mark:** Chop with last name underneath.

LUNDSTROM, JAN-AKE, Mastmostigen 8, 66010 Dals-Langed, SWEDEN, /0531-40270
Specialties: Viking swords, axes and knives in cooperation with handle-makers. **Patterns:** All traditional styles, especially swords and inlaid blades. **Technical:** Forges his own Damascus and laminated steel.

Prices: $200 to $1,000. **Remarks:** Full-time maker; first knife sold in 1985; collaborates with museums. **Mark:** Runic.

LUNN, LARRY A., 3432 State Route 580, #312, Safety Harbor, FL, 34695/813-796-2386
Specialties: Art knives of his design, collector folders and straight knives. **Patterns:** Folders, straight knives and swords. **Technical:** Grinds stainless steel and forges own Damascus; makes own mokume. Offers filework; uses exotic handle materials. **Prices:** Start at $300. **Remarks:** Part-time maker; first knife sold in 1989. **Mark:** Name in script and small samurai helmet in a circle.

LUTZ, GREG, 149 Effie Dr., Greenwood, SC, 29649/864-229-7340
Specialties: Working and using knives and period pieces of his design and to customer specs. **Patterns:** Fighters, hunters and swords. **Technical:** Forges 1095 and O1; grinds ATS-34. Differentially heat-treats forged blades; uses cryogenic treatment on ATS-34. **Prices:** $50 to $350; some to $1,200. **Remarks:** Part-time maker; first knife sold in 1986. Doing business as Scorpion Forge. **Mark:** First initial, last name.

LYLE III, ERNEST L., 4501 Meadowbrook Ave., Orlando, FL, 32808/407-299-7227
Specialties: Fancy period pieces; one of a kind and limited editions. **Patterns:** Arabian/Persian influenced fighters, military knives, Bowies and Roman short swords; several styles of hunters. **Technical:** Grinds 440C, D2 and 154 CM. Engraves. **Prices:** Upscale. **Remarks:** Full-time maker; first knife sold in 1972. Doesn't accept orders. **Mark:** Last name in capital letters.

LYONS, RANDY, Rt. 3 Box 677A, Lumberton, TX, 77656/409-755-3860
Specialties: Working straight knives and folders. **Patterns:** Bowies, hunters, locking folders and utility/camp knives. **Technical:** Grinds ATS-34, 440C and D2. **Prices:** $60 to $300; some to $600. **Remarks:** Full-time maker; first knife sold in 1989. Doing business as The Lyons Den. **Mark:** First and middle initials, last name, city and state.

LYTTLE, BRIAN, Box 5697, High River, AB, CANADA, T1V 1M7/403-558-3638
Specialties: Fancy working straight knives and folders; art knives. **Patterns:** Hunters, Bowies, daggers, stilettos, fighters and miniatures. **Technical:** Forges his own Damascus, cable and motorcycle chain; offers scrimshaw and forged jewelry to Damascus bits and spurs. **Prices:** $350 to $800; some to $5,000. **Remarks:** Full-time maker; first knife sold in 1983. **Mark:** Last name, country.

m

MACBAIN, KENNETH C., 30 Briarwood Ave., Norwood, NJ, 07648/201-768-0652
Specialties: Fantasy straight knives and folders, some high-tech. **Patterns:** Swords, knife-rings, push daggers and some miniatures. **Technical:** Forges and grinds A2, W2 and O1. **Prices:** $200 to $500; some to $2,500. **Remarks:** Part-time maker; first knife sold in 1986. **Mark:** Initials.

MACDONALD, JOHN, 9 David Drive, Raymond, NH, 03077/603-895-0918
Specialties: Working/using straight knives of his design and to customer specs. **Patterns:** Japanese cutlery, bowies, hunters and working knives. **Technical:** Grinds O1, L6 and ATS-34. Swords have matching handles and scabbards with Japanese flair. **Prices:** $70 to $250; some to $500. **Remarks:** Part-time maker; first knife sold in 1988. Wood/glass-topped custom cases. Doing business as Mac the Knife. **Mark:** Initials.

MACKRILL, STEPHEN, P.O. Box 1580, Pinegowrie 2123, Johannesburg, SOUTH AFRICA, /27-11-886-2893
Specialties: Fancy and working knives. **Patterns:** Fighters, hunters and utility/camp knives. **Technical:** N690, K110, 12C27. Silver and gold inlay on handles; wooden sheaths. **Prices:** $98 to $700; some to $1,800. **Remarks:** Full-time maker; first knife sold in 1978. **Mark:** First initial, last name.

MADISON II, BILLY D., 2295 Tyler Rd., Remlap, AL, 35133/205-680-6722
Specialties: Traditional working and using straight knives and folders of his design. **Patterns:** Hunters, Locking folders, utility/camp knives, and fighters. **Technical:** Grinds 440C, ATS-34, D2 & BG-42; forges some high carbons. Prefers natural handle material. Ivory, bone, exotic woods & horns. **Prices:** $100 to $400; some to $1,000. **Remarks:** Part-time

custom knifemakers

maker; first knife sold in 1978. **Mark:** Last name and year. Offers sheaths.

MAE, TAKAO, 1-6-38, Kinrakuji-cho, Amagasaki City HYOGO, JAPAN, /06-6481-1627
Distinctial sytlish in art-forged blades, with lacquered ergonomic handles.

MAESTRI, PETER A., S11251 Fairview Rd., Spring Green, WI, 53588/ 608-546-4481
Specialties: Working straight knives in standard patterns. **Patterns:** Camp and fishing knives, utility green-river styled. **Technical:** Grinds 440C, 154CM and 440A. **Prices:** $15 to $45; some to $150. **Remarks:** Full-time maker; first knife sold in 1981. Privides professional cutler service to professional cutters. **Mark:** CARISOLO, MAESTRI BROS., or signature.

MAIENKNECHT, STANLEY, 38648 S.R. 800, Sardis, OH, 43946/

MAINES, JAY, SUNRISE RIVER CUSTOM KNIVES, 5584 266th St, Wyoming, MN, 55092/651-462-5301
Specialties: Heavy duty working, classic and traditional fixed blades. Some high-tech and fancy embellished knives available. **Patterns:** Hunters, skinners, Bowies, Tantos, fillet, fighters, daggers, boot and cutlery sets. **Technical:** Hollow ground, stock removal blades of 440C, ATS34 and CPM T 440-V. Prefers natural handle materials, exotic hard woods, and stag, rams and buffalo horns. Offers dovetailed bolsters in brass, stainless steel and nickel silver. Custom sheaths from matching wood or hand-stitched from heavy duty water buffalo hide. **Prices:** Moderate to up-scale. **Remarks:** Part-time maker; first knife sold in 1992. Doing business as Sunrise River Custom Knives. **Mark:** Full name under a Rising Sun logo.

MAISEY, ALAN, PO Box 197, Vincentia 2540, NSW AUSTRALIA, /2-44437997
Specialties: Daggers, especially krisses; period pieces. **Technical:** Offers knives and finished blades in Damascus and nickel Damascus. **Prices:** $75 to $2,000; some higher. **Remarks:** Part-time maker; provides complete restoration service for krisses. Trained by a Javanese kris smith. **Mark:** None, triangle in a box, or three peaks.

MALLOY, JOE, P.O. Box 156, 1039 Schwabe St., Freeland, PA, 18224/ 570-636-2781
Specialties: Working straight knives and lock back folders-plain and fancy-of his design. **Patterns:** Hunters, utility, Bowie, survival knives, folders. **Technical:** Grinds ATS-34, 440C, D2 and A2 and Damascus. Makes own leather and kyder sheaths. **Prices:** $100 to $1,800. **Remarks:** Part-time maker; first knife sold in 1982. **Mark:** First and middle initials, last name, city and state.

MANABE, MICHAEL K., 3659 Tomahawk Lane, San Diego, CA, 92117/ 619-483-2416
Specialties: Classic and high-art straight knives of his design or to customer specs. **Patterns:** Bowies, fighters, hunters, utility/camp knives; all knives one of a kind. **Technical:** Forges and grinds 52100, 5160 and 1095. does multiple quenching for distinctive temper lines. Each blade triple-tempered. **Prices:** Start at $200. **Remarks:** part-time maker; first knife sold in 1994. Mark First and middle initials, last name and J.S. on other side.

MANEKER, KENNETH, RR 2, Galiano Island, B.C., CANADA, V0N 1P0/604-539-2084
Specialties: Working straight knives; period pieces. **Patterns:** Camp knives and hunters; French chef knives. **Technical:** Grinds 440C, 154CM and Vascowear. **Prices:** $50 to $200; some to $300. **Remarks:** Part-time maker; first knife sold in 1981. Doing business as Water Mountain Knives. **Mark:** Japanese Kanji of initials, plus glyph.

MARAGNI, DAN, R.D. 1, Box 106, Georgetown, NY, 13072/315-662-7490
Specialties: Heavy-duty working knives, some investor class. **Patterns:** Hunters, fighters and camp knives, some Scottish types. **Technical:** Forges W2 and his own Damascus; toughness and edge-holding a high priority. **Prices:** $125 to $500; some to $1,000. **Remarks:** Full-time maker; first knife sold in 1975. **Mark:** Celtic initials in circle.

MARKLEY, KEN, 7651 Cabin Creek Lane, Sparta, IL, 62286/618-443-5284
Specialties: Traditional working and using knives of his design and to customer specs. **Patterns:** Fighters, hunters and utility/camp knives. **Technical:** Forges 5160, 1095 and L6; makes his own Damascus; does

filework. **Prices:** $150 to $800; some to $2,000. **Remarks:** Part-time maker; first knife sold in 1991. Doing business as Cabin Creek Forge. **Mark:** Last name, JS.

MARKS, CHRIS, 1061 Sherwood Dr., Breaux Bridge, LA, 70517/318-332-3930
Specialties: Traditional straight knives of his design; period pieces. **Patterns:** Bowies, hunters and utility/camp knives. **Technical:** Forges W2, 5160 and his own Damascus. **Prices:** NA. **Mark:** Name in anvil logo and Master Smith, ABS.

MARLOWE, DONALD, 2554 Oakland Rd., Dover, PA, 17315/717-764-6055
Specialties: Working straight knives in standard patterns. **Patterns:** Bowies, fighters, boots and utility knives. **Technical:** Grinds D2 and 440C. **Prices:** $120 to $525. **Remarks:** Spare-time maker; first knife sold in 1977. **Mark:** Last name.

MARSHALL, GLENN, P.O. Box 1099, 1117 Hofmann St, Mason, TX, 76856/915-347-6207
Specialties: Working knives and period pieces. **Patterns:** Straight and folding hunters, fighters and camp knives. **Technical:** Steel used 440C, D2, CPM & 440V. **Prices:** $90 to $450 according to options. **Remarks:** Full-time maker; first knife sold in 1932. **Mark:** First initial, last name, city and state with anvil logo.

MARTIN, BRUCE E., Rt. 6, Box 164-B, Prescott, AR, 71857/501-887-2023
Specialties: Fancy working straight knives of his design. **Patterns:** Bowies, camp knives, skinners and fighters. **Technical:** Forges 5160, 1095 and his own Damascus. Uses natural handle materials; filework available. **Prices:** $75 to $350; some to $500. **Remarks:** Full-time maker; first knife sold in 1979. **Mark:** Name in arch.

MARTIN, GENE, P.O. Box 396, Williams, OR, 97544/541-846-6755
Specialties: Straight knives and folders. **Patterns:** Fighters, hunters, skinners, boot knives, spring back and lock back folders. **Technical:** Grinds ATS-34, 440C, Damascus and 154CM. Forges; makes own Damascus; scrimshaws. **Prices:** $100 TO $1,200, some higher. **Remarks:** Full-time maker; first knife sold in 1993. Doing business as Provision Forge. **Mark:** Name and/or crossed staff and sword.

MARTIN, JIM, 1120 S. Cadiz Ct., Oxnard, CA, 93035/805-985-9849
Specialties: Fancy and working/using folders of his design. **Patterns:** Automatics, locking folders and miniatures. **Technical:** Grinds 440C, AEB-L, 304SS and Damascus. **Prices:** $350 to $700; some to $1,500. **Remarks:** Full-time maker; first knife sold in 1992. Doing business as Jim Martin Custom Knives.

MARTIN, MICHAEL W., Box 572, Jefferson St., Beckville, TX, 75631/ 903-678-2161
Specialties: Classic working/using straight knives of his design and in standard patterns. **Patterns:** Hunters. **Technical:** Grinds ATS-34, 440C, O1 and A2. Bead blasted, Parkerized, high polish and satin finishes. Sheaths are handmade. Also hand forges cable Damascus. **Prices:** $145 to $230. **Remarks:** Part-time maker; first knife sold in 1995. Doing business as Michael W. Martin Knives. **Mark:** Name and city, state in arch.

MARTIN, PETER, 28220 N. Lake Dr., Waterford, WI, 53185/414-662-3629
Specialties: Fancy, fantasy and working straight knives and folders of his design and in standard patterns. **Patterns:** Bowies, fighters, hunters, locking folders and liner locks. **Technical:** Grinds ATS-34, 440C, A2 and D2; forges 1095, 5160, W1, 4340 and his own Damascus. Prefers natural handle material; offers filework and carved handles. **Prices:** $100 to $500; some to $2,000. **Remarks:** Part-time maker; first knife sold in 1988. Doing business as Martin Custom Products. **Mark:** Martin Knives, city and state.

MARTIN, RANDALL J., 1477 Country Club Rd., Middletown, CT, 06457/860-347-1161
Specialties: High-performance using knives. **Patterns:** Neck knives, tactical liner locks, survival, utility and Japanese knives. **Technical:** Grinds BG42, CPMM4, D2 and A2; aerospace composite materials; carbon fiber sheaths. **Prices:** Start at $150. **Remarks:** Part-time maker; first knife sold in 1976. Doing business as Martinsite Knives. **Mark:** First and middle initials, last name.

MARTIN, ROBB, 7 Victoria St., Elmira, Ontario, CANADA, N3B 1R9/

MARTRILDONNO, PAUL, 140 Debary Dr., Debary, FL, 32713-3460/ **Specialties:** One of a kind fantasy knives. **Patterns:** "Knifelace,"--necklace with push dagger, knuckle knives, fantasy tantos, etc. **Technical:** Grinds 440C and 154CM. Reforges commercial Damascus. **Prices:** $400 to $1,500; some to $5,000. **Remarks:** Full-time maker; first knife sold in 1982. **Mark:** PAULIE, or signature.

MARZITELLI, PETER, 19929 35A Ave., Langley, BC, CANADA, V3A 2R1/604-532-8899 **Specialties:** Specializes in natural handle materials; bone, antler, prehistoric ivory, gemstones and shells. **Patterns:** Daggers, Bowies, tantos, hunters, folders and art knives. **Technical:** Grinds ATS-34, 440C, D2 and 12C27. **Prices:** $100 to $1,000. **Remarks:** Full-time maker; first knife sold in 1984. **Mark:** "Marz."

MASON, BILL, 1114 St. Louis, #33, Excelsior Springs, MO, 64024/816-637-7335 **Specialties:** Combat knives; some folders. **Patterns:** Fighters to match knife types in book *Cold Steel*. **Technical:** Grinds O1, 440C and ATS-34. **Prices:** $115 to $250; some to $350. **Remarks:** Spare-time maker; first knife sold in 1979. **Mark:** Initials connected.

MASSEY, AL, Box 14, Site 15, RR#2, Mount Uniacke, Nova Scotia, CANADA, B0N 1Z0/902-866-4754 **Specialties:** Working knives and period pieces. **Patterns:** Swords and daggers of celtic to medieval design, bowies. **Technical:** Forges sigo, 1084 and 1095. Makes own Damascus. **Prices:** $100.00 to $350.00, some to $500.00. **Remarks:** Part-time maker, first blade sold in 1988. **Mark:** Initials and JS on Ricasso.

MASSEY, ROGER, RR 19, Box 3300, Texarkana, AR, 71854/870-779-1018 **Specialties:** Traditional and working straight knives and folders of his design and to customer specs. **Patterns:** Bowies, hunters, daggers and utility knives. **Technical:** Forges 1084 & 52100, makes his own Damascus. Offers filework and silver wire inlay in handles. **Prices:** $200 to $1500; some to $2500. **Remarks:** Part-time maker; first knife sold in 1991. **Mark:** Last name, M.S.

MASSEY, RON, 61638 El Reposo St., Joshua Tree, CA, 92252/760-366-9239 after 5 p.m. **Specialties:** Classic, traditional, fancy/embellished, high art, period pieces, working/using knives, straight knives, folders, and automatics. Your design, customer specs, about 175 standard patterns. **Patterns:** Automatics, hunters and fighters. All my folders are side locking folder. Unless requested as lock books slip joint I specialize or custom design. **Technical:** ATS-34, 440C, D-2 upon request. Engraving, filework, scrimshaw, most of the exotic handle materials. All aspects are performed by me - inlay work in pearls or stone, hand made Pem' work. **Prices:** $110 to $2,500; some to $6,000. **Remarks:** Part-time maker; first knife sold in 1976.

MATTIS, JAMES K., 500 N. Central Ave., Suite 740, Glendale, CA, 91203/818-247-3400 **Specialties:** Working straight knives in standard patterns. **Patterns:** Hunters, kitchen knives and small utility or specialty patterns. **Technical:** Offers ATS-34, 440C and carbon; hand-rubbed finishes, hardwood and Micarta handles; mosaic pins. **Prices:** $75 to $250. **Remarks:** Sparetime maker; first knife sold in 1990. Usually uses blades by Bob Engnath. **Mark:** Last name plus Hebrew word for "life."

MAXFIELD, LYNN, 382 Colonial Ave., Layton, UT, 84041/801-544-4176 **Specialties:** Sporting knives, some fancy. **Patterns:** Hunters, survival and fishing knives; some locking folders. **Technical:** Grinds 440C, ATS-34, 154CM, D2, 440V and Damascus. **Prices:** $125 to $400; some to $900. **Remarks:** Part-time maker; first knife sold in 1979. **Mark:** Name, city and state.

MAXWELL, DON, 3164 N. Marks, Suite 122, Fresno, CA, 93722/209-497-8441 **Specialties:** Fancy working and using straight knives of his design. **Patterns:** Hunters, fighters, utility/camp knives, liner lock folders and fantasy knives. **Technical:** Grinds 440C, ATS-34, D2 and commercial Damascus. **Prices:** $100 to $500; some to $2,000. **Remarks:** Full-time maker; first knife sold in 1987. **Mark:** Last name, city, state or last name only.

MAYNARD, LARRY JOE, P.O. Box 493, Crab Orchard, WV, 25827/ **Specialties:** Fancy and fantasy straight knives. **Patterns:** Big knives; a Bowie with a full false edge; fighting knives. **Technical:** Grinds standard steels. **Prices:** $350 to $500; some to $1,000. **Remarks:** Full-time maker; first knife sold in 1986. **Mark:** Middle and last initials.

MAYNARD, WILLIAM N., 2677 John Smith Rd., Fayetteville, NC, 28306/910-425-1615 **Specialties:** Traditional and working straight knives of all designs. **Patterns:** Bowies, fighters, hunters and utility knives. **Technical:** Grinds 440C, ATS-34 and commercial Damascus. Offers fancy filework; handmade sheaths. **Prices:** $100 to $300; some to $500. **Remarks:** Part-time maker; first knife sold in 1988. **Mark:** Last name.

MAYO JR., TOM, 67-420 Alahaka St., Waialua, HI, 96791/808-637-6560 **Specialties:** Presentation grade working knives. **Patterns:** Combat knives, hunters, Bowies and folders. **Technical:** Uses BG-42 & 440V (ATS-34 and 440C upon reques). **Prices:** Start at $250. **Remarks:** Part-time maker; first knife sold in 1983. **Mark:** Volcano logo with name and state.

MAYVILLE, OSCAR L., 2130 E. County Rd. 910S., Marengo, IN, 47140/812-338-3103 **Specialties:** Working straight knives; period pieces. **Patterns:** Kitchen cutlery, Bowies, camp knives and hunters. **Technical:** Grinds A2, O1 and 440C. **Prices:** $50 to $350; some to $500. **Remarks:** Full-time maker; first knife sold in 1984. **Mark:** Initials over knife logo.

McABEE, WILLIAM, 27275 Norton Grade, Colfax, CA, 95713/530-389-8163 **Specialties:** Working/using knives. **Patterns:** Fighters, Bowies, Hunters. **Technical:** Grinds ATS-34. **Prices:** $75 to $200; some to $350. **Remarks:** Part-time maker; first knife sold in 1990. **Mark:** Stylized WM stamped.

McBURNETTE, HARVEY, P.O. Box 227, Eagle Nest, NM, 87718/505-377-6254 **Specialties:** Fancy working folders; some to customer specs. **Patterns:** Front-locking folders. **Technical:** Grinds D2, 440C and 154CM; engraves. **Prices:** $450 to $3,000. **Remarks:** Full-time maker; first knife sold in 1972. **Mark:** Last name, city and state.

McCARLEY, JOHN, 4165 Harney Rd, Taneytown, MD, 21787/ **Specialties:** Working straight knives; period pieces. **Patterns:** Hunters, Bowies, camp knives, miniatures, throwing knives. **Technical:** Forges W2, O1 and his own Damascus. **Prices:** $150 to $300; some to $1,000. **Remarks:** Part-time maker; first knife sold in 1977. **Mark:** Initials in script.

McCARTY, HARRY, 1121 Brough Ave., Hamilton, OH, 45015/ **Specialties:** Period pieces. **Patterns:** 18th & 19th Century trade knives, bowies and belt knives.. **Technical:** Grinds & forges high carbon steel. **Prices:** $125 to $650; some higher. **Remarks:** Part-time maker; first knife sold in 1977. **Mark:** Stylized initials inside shamrock.

McCARTY, ZOLLAN, 1011 Ave. E, Thomaston, GA, 30286/404-647-6869 **Specialties:** Working knives; period pieces. **Patterns:** Straight knives and folders; Scagel replicas; gut hook hatchets. **Technical:** Forges and grinds 440C, 154CM and ATS-34. **Prices:** $110 to $600. **Remarks:** Full-time maker; first knife sold in 1971. Doing business as Z Custom Knives. **Mark:** First initial, last name.

McCLURE, LEONARD, 212 S.W. Ave. I, Seminole, TX, 79360/915-758-3929 **Specialties:** Traditional working/using straight knives of his design or in standard patterns. **Patterns:** Bowies, hunters and utility/camp knives. **Technical:** Grinds O1, D2 and ATS-34. **Prices:** $50 to $150; some to $500. **Remarks:** Spare-time maker; first knife sold in 1970. Doing business as Shamrock Knives. **Mark:** A shamrock.

McCLURE, MICHAEL, 803-17th Ave., Menlo Park, CA, 94025/650-323-2596 **Specialties:** Working/using straight knives of his design and to customer specs. **Patterns:** Bowies, hunters, skinners, utility/camp, tantos, fillets and boot knives. **Technical:** Grinds ATS-34, 440C, D2, and commerical Damascus. Makes sheaths. **Prices:** Start at $100. **Remarks:** Part-time maker; first knife sold in 1991. **Mark:** Full name.

custom knifemakers

McCONNELL, CHARLES R., 158 Genteel Ridge, Wellsburg, WV, 26070/304-737-2015
Specialties: Working straight knives. **Patterns:** Hunters, Bowies, daggers, minis and push knives. **Technical:** Grinds 440C and 154CM; likes full tangs. **Prices:** $65 to $325; some to $800. **Remarks:** Part-time maker; first knife sold in 1977. **Mark:** Name.

McCONNELL JR., LOYD A., 1710 Rosewood, Odessa, TX, 79761/915-363-8344
Specialties: Working straight knives and folders, some fancy. **Patterns:** Hunters, boots, Bowies, locking folders and slip-joints. **Technical:** Grinds CPM Steels, ATS-34 and BG-42 and commercial Damascus. **Prices:** $175 to $900; some to $10,000. **Remarks:** Full-time maker; first knife sold in 1975. Doing business as Cactus Custom Knives. **Mark:** Name, city and state in cactus logo.

McCOUN, MARK, 14212 Pine Dr., DeWitt, VA, 23840/804-469-7631
Specialties: Working/using straight knives of his design and in standard patterns; custom miniatures. **Patterns:** Hunters and tantos. **Technical:** Grinds ATS-34 and 440C. **Prices:** $70 to $150. **Remarks:** Part-time maker; first knife sold in 1989. **Mark:** Name, city and state.

McCRACKIN AND SON, V.J., 3720 Hess Rd., House Springs, MO, 63051/314-677-6066
Specialties: Working straight knives in standard patterns. **Patterns:** Hunters, Bowies and camp knives. **Technical:** Forges L6, 5160, his own Damascus, cable Damascus. **Prices:** $125 to $700; some to $1,500. **Remarks:** Part-time maker; first knife sold in 1983. Son Kevin helps make the knives. **Mark:** Last name, M.S.

McCULLOUGH, JERRY, RR #3, Box 413-L, Georgiana, AL, 36033/
Specialties: Standard patterns or custom designs. **Technical:** Forge and grind scrap-tool and Damascus steels. Use natural handle materials & turquoise trim on some. Filework on others. **Prices:** $65 to $250 and up. **Remarks:** Part-time maker. **Mark:** Initials.

McDEARMONT, DAVE, 1618 Parkside Trail, Lewisville, TX, 75067/214-436-4335
Specialties: Collector-grade knives. **Patterns:** Hunters, fighters, boots and folders. **Technical:** Grinds ATS-34; likes full tangs, mirror finishes. **Prices:** $200 to $1,000. **Remarks:** Part-time maker; first knife sold in 1981. **Mark:** Name.

McDONALD, RICH, 4590 Kirk Rd., Columbiana, OH, 44408/330-482-0007
Specialties: Traditional working/using and art knives of his design. **Patterns:** Bowies, hunters, folders, primitives and tomahawks. **Technical:** Forges 5160, 1084, 1095, 52100 and his own Damascus. Fancy filework. **Prices:** $200 to $1,500. **Remarks:** Full-time maker; first knife sold in 1994. **Mark:** First and last initials connected.

McDONALD, ROBERT J., 14730 61 Court N., Loxahatchee, FL, 33470/561-790-1470
Specialties: Traditional working straight knives to customer specs. **Patterns:** Fighters, swords and folders. **Technical:** Grinds 440C, ATS-34 and forges own Damascus. **Prices:** $150 to $1,000. **Remarks:** Part-time maker; first knife sold in 1988. **Mark:** Electro-etched name.

McDONALD, W.J. "JERRY", 7173 Wickshire Cove E., Germantown, TN, 38138/901-756-9924
Specialties: Classic and working/using straight knives of his design and in standard patterns. **Patterns:** Bowies, hunters and kitchen knives. **Technical:** Grinds ATS-34, D2 and 440C. **Prices:** $125 to $1,000. **Remarks:** Full-time maker; first knife sold in 1989. **Mark:** First and middle initials, last name, maker, city and state. Some of my knives are stamped McDonald in script.

McELHANNON, MARCUS, 310 Darby Trails, Sugar Land, TX, 77479/713-494-1345
Specialties: Working straight knives and folders of his design and to customer specs. **Patterns:** Fighters, hunters and locking folders. **Technical:** Grinds ATS-34, 440C and 440V. **Prices:** $125 to $300; some to $1,500. **Remarks:** Spare-time maker; first knife sold in 1988. **Mark:** First name.

McFALL, KEN, P.O. Box 458, Lakeside, AZ, 85929/602-537-2026
Specialties: Fancy working straight knives and some folders. **Patterns:** Daggers, boots, tantos, Bowies; some miniatures. **Technical:** Grinds D2, ATS-34 and 440C. **Prices:** $175 to $900. **Remarks:** Part-time maker; first knife sold in 1984. **Mark:** Name, city and state.

McFARLIN, ERIC E., P.O. Box 2188, Kodiak, AK, 99615/907-486-4799
Specialties: Working knives of his design. **Patterns:** Bowies, skinners, camp knives and hunters. **Technical:** Flat and convex grinds 440C, A2 and AEB-L. **Prices:** Start at $200. **Remarks:** Part-time maker; first knife sold in 1989. **Mark:** Name and city in rectangular logo.

McFARLIN, J.W., 3331 Pocohantas Dr., Lake Havasu City, AZ, 86404/520-855-8095
Technical: Flat grinds, D2, ATS-34, 440C, Thomas & Peterson Damascus. **Remarks:** From working knives to investment. Customer designs always welcome. **Prices:** $150 to $3,000.

McGILL, JOHN, P.O. Box 302, Blairsville, GA, 30512/404-745-4686
Specialties: Working knives. **Patterns:** Traditional patterns; camp knives. **Technical:** Forges L6 and 9260; makes Damascus. **Prices:** $50 to $250; some to $500. **Remarks:** Full-time maker; first knife sold in 1982. **Mark:** XYLO.

McGOVERN, JIM, 31 Scenic Dr., Oak Ridge, NJ, 07438/201-697-4558
Specialties: Working straight knives and folders. **Patterns:** Hunters and boots. **Technical:** Hollow-grinds 440C, ATS-34; prefers full tapered tangs. Offers filework. **Prices:** Straight knives, $165 to $250; folders start at $325. **Remarks:** Full-time maker; first knife sold in 1985. **Mark:** Name.

McGOWAN, FRANK E., 12629 Howard Lodge Dr., Sykesville, MD, 21784/410-489-4323
Specialties: Fancy working knives & folders to customer specs. **Patterns:** Survivor knives, fighters, fishing knives, folders and hunters. **Technical:** Grinds and forges O1, 440C, 5160 and ATS-34. **Prices:** $75 to $500; some to $600. **Remarks:** Full-time maker; first knife sold in 1986. **Mark:** Last name.

McGRODER, PATRICK J., 5725 Chapin Rd., Madison, OH, 44057/216-298-3405
Specialties: Traditional working/using knives of his design. **Patterns:** Bowies, hunters and utility/camp knives. **Technical:** Grinds ATS-34, D2 and customer requests. Does reverse etching; heat-treats; prefers natural handle materials; custom made sheath with each knife. **Prices:** $125 to $250. **Remarks:** Part-time maker. **Mark:** First and middle initials, last name, maker, city and state.

McGUANE IV, THOMAS F., 410 South 3rd Ave., Bozeman, MT, 59715/406-522-9739
Specialties: Traditional straight knives and folders of his design. **Patterns:** Tantos, swords and locking folders. **Technical:** Forges 1095 and L6; hand-smelted Japanese style steel. Silk and same handles. **Prices:** $375 to $850; some to $3,000. **Remarks:** Full-time maker; first knife sold in 1988. **Mark:** Last name, city, state.

McHENRY, WILLIAM JAMES, Box 67, Wyoming, RI, 02898/401-539-8353
Specialties: Fancy high-tech folders of his design. **Patterns:** Locking folders with various mechanisms. **Technical:** Forges and grinds commercial Damascus and his Damascus. Most pieces disassemble and feature top-shelf materials including gold, silver and gems. **Prices:** Upscale. **Remarks:** Full-time maker; first knife sold in 1988. **Mark:** Last name or first and last initials.

McINTOSH, DAVID L., P.O. Box 948, Haines, AK, 99827/907-766-3673
Specialties: Working straight knives and folders of all designs. **Patterns:** All styles, except swords. **Technical:** Grinds ATS-34 and top name maker Damascus. Engraves; offers tooling on sheaths. Uses fossil ivory. **Prices:** $60 to $800; soclme to $2,000. **Remarks:** Full-time maker; first knife sold in 1984. **Mark:** Last name, serial number, steel type, city and state.

McLUIN, TOM, 36 Fourth St., Dracut, MA, 01826/978-957-4899
Specialties: Working straight knives and folders of his design. **Patterns:** Boots, hunters and folders. **Technical:** Grinds ATS-34, 440C, O1 and Damascus; makes his own mokume. **Prices:** $100 to $400; some to $700. **Remarks:** Full-time maker; first knife sold in 1991. **Mark:** Last name.

McMAHON, JOHN P., 44871 Santa Anita #A, Palm Desert, CA, 92260/619-341-4238
Specialties: Classic working and using straight knives of his design or to customer specs. **Patterns:** Hunters, Bowies and fighters. **Technical:** Grinds 5160 spring steel for large knives and O1 tool steel for small ones. Differentially tempers. **Prices:** $45 to $300; some to $1,000. **Remarks:**

Full-time maker; first knife sold in 1989. Doing business as J.P.M. Knives. **Mark:** Initials.

McMANUS, DANNY, 413 Fairhaven Drive., Taylors, SC, 29687/864-268-9849
Specialties: High-tech and traditional working/using straight knives of his design, to customer specs and in standard patterns. **Patterns:** Boots, Bowies, fighters, hunters and utility/camp knives. **Technical:** Forges stainless steel Damascus; grinds ATS-34. Offers engraving and scrimshaw. **Prices:** $300 to $2,000; some to $3,000. **Remarks:** Full-time maker; first knife sold in 1997. Doing business as Stamascus KnifeWorks Corp. **Mark:** Stamascus N/V.

McNABB, TOMMY, 4015 Brownsboro rd, Winston-Salem, NC, 27106/336-759-0640
Specialties: Working and using straight knives of his design. **Patterns:** Hunters, fighters and utility/camp knives. **Technical:** Forges his own Damascus; grinds ATS-34. **Prices:** $100 to $1250; some to $2,500. **Remarks:** Full-time maker; first knife sold in 1979. **Mark:** Carolina Custom Knives.

McNEIL, JIMMY, 1175 Mt. Moriah Rd., Memphis, TN, 38117/901-544-0710 or 901-683-8133
Specialties: Fancy high-art straight knives of his design. **Patterns:** Bowies, daggers and swords. **Technical:** Grinds O1 and Damascus. Engraves, carves and inlays. **Prices:** $50 to $300; some to $2,000. **Remarks:** Spare-time maker; first knife sold in 1993. Doing business as McNeil's Minerals and Knives. **Mark:** Crossed mining picks and serial number.

McRAE, J MICHAEL, 7750 Matthews-Mint Hill Rd, McRae, Mint Hill, NC, 28227/704-545-2929
Specialties: Scottish dirks and sgian dubhs. **Patterns:** Traditional blade styles with traditional and slightly non-traditional handle treatments. **Technical:** Forges 1084,5160 and re-forges commercial Damascus. Prefers Stag and exotic hardwoods for handles, some intricately carved. **Prices:** $100 to $450, some much higher. **Remarks:** Part-time maker, first knife sold in 1982. Doing business as Scotia Metalwork. **Mark:** Last name underlined with a claymore.

McWILLIAMS, SEAN, Venture Edge, 311 Gem Lane, Bayfield, CO, 81122/970-884-9854
Specialties: Fixed blade combat, survival, sports and utility knives. High-tech Kydex-nylon sheaths and carry systems. Forges only; CPM 440V, BG42. **Prices:** Hand forged blades $400 to $800; Venture Edge production forged blades in BG42, $80 to $250. **Remarks:** Full-time maker; first knife sold in 1979. **Mark:** Stylized bear paw. **Other:** Specializes in forged stainless.

MEIER, DARYL, 75 Forge Rd., Carbondale, IL, 62901/618-549-3234
Specialties: One-of-a-kind knives and swords. **Patterns:** Collaborates on blades. **Technical:** Forges his own Damascus, W1 and A203E, 440C, 431, nickel 200 and clad steel. **Prices:** $250 to $450; some to $6,000. **Remarks:** Full-time smith and researcher since 1974; first knife sold in 1974. **Mark:** Name or circle/arrow symbol or SHAWNEE.

MEIQUISEDEC R, BOSCOLI, (no address available)
Specialites: Small and medium size fighters in modern styles or based on WWII and Viet Nam War period knives. **Technical:** Grinds 440C, exclusively. Likes leather washer handles. Does heat treating. Makes sheaths. Part-time maker. Makes knives since 1990. Former partner of Flàvio Ikoma at IMK knives. **Prices:** start from $150. Stamp: M. R. Boxcoli - Hand Made

MELLO, JACINTO, R. Macolò, 388, Parà de Minas MG 35.660, BRAZIL, /55-37-2323934
Specialties: bowies and hunters with natural materials. **Technical:** grinds D6 steel and forges 52100, Stainless fittings and filework are his trademarks. Uses only natural materials for handles. Does his own heat treating. Full-time knifemaker and gunsmith. **Prices:** start from $150. Stamp: M. Knives exclusively sold through his agent, Ivan Campos.

MELOY, SEAN, 7148 Rosemary Lane, Lemon Grove, CA, 91945-2105/619-465-7173
Specialties: Traditional working straight knives of his design. **Patterns:** Bowies, fighters and utility/camp knives. **Technical:** Grinds 440C, ATS-34 and D2. **Prices:** $125 to $300. **Remarks:** Part-time maker; first knife sold in 1985. **Mark:** Broz Knives.

MENSCH, LARRY, RD #3, Box 1444, Milton, PA, 17847/717-742-9554
Specialties: Fancy and embellished working/using straight knives in standard patterns, of his design and to customer specs. **Patterns:** Bowies, daggers, hunters, tantos, short swords and miniatures. **Technical:** Grinds ATS-34, carbon and stainless steel Damascus; blade grinds hollow, flat and slack. Filework; bending guards and fluting handles with finger grooves. Offers engraving and scrimshaw. **Prices:** $100 to $300; some to $1,000. **Remarks:** Part-time maker; first knife sold in 1993. Doing business as Larry's Knife Shop. **Mark:** Connected capital "L" and small "m" in script.

MERCER, MIKE, 149 N. Waynesville Rd., Lebanon, OH, 45036/513-932-2837
Specialties: Jeweled gold and ivory daggers; multi-blade folders. **Patterns:** 1-1/4" folders, hunters, axes, replicas. **Technical:** Uses O1 Damascus and mokume. **Prices:** $150 to $1,500. **Remarks:** Full-time maker since 1991. **Mark:** Last name in script.

MERCHANT, TED, 7 Old Garrett Ct., White Hall, MD, 21161/410-343-0380
Specialties: Traditional and classic working knives. **Patterns:** Bowies, hunters, camp knives, fighters, daggers and skinners. **Technical:** Forges W2 and 5160; makes own Damascus. Makes handles with wood, stag, horn, silver and gem stone inlay; fancy filework. **Prices:** $125 to $600; some to $1,500. **Remarks:** Full-time maker; first knife sold in 1985. **Mark:** Last name.

MERZ III, ROBERT L., 20219 Prince Creek Dr., Katy, TX, 77450/281-492-7337
Specialties: Working straight knives and folders, some fancy, of his design. **Patterns:** Hunters, skinners, fighters and camp knives. **Technical:** Flat-grinds 440C, 154CM, ATS-34, 440V and commercial Damascus. **Prices:** $150 to $450; some to $600. **Remarks:** Part-time maker; first knife sold in 1974. **Mark:** MERZ KNIVES, city and state, or last name in oval.

MESHEJIAN, MARDI, 33 Elm Dr., E. Northport, NY, 11731/516-757-4541
Specialties: One of a kind fantasy and high-art straight knives of his design. **Patterns:** Swords, daggers, finger knives and other edged weapons. **Technical:** Hand-forged chainsaw and timing chain Damascus. **Prices:** $150 to $2,500; some to $3,000. **Remarks:** Part-time maker; first knife sold in 1996. Doing business as Tooth and Nail Metalworks. **Mark:** Etched stylized "M".

MESSER, DAVID T., 134 S. Torrence St., Dayton, OH, 45403-2044/513-228-6561
Specialties: Fantasy period pieces, straight and folding, of his design. **Patterns:** Bowies, daggers and swords. **Technical:** Grinds 440C, O1, 06 and commercial Damascus. Likes fancy guards and exotic handle materials. **Prices:** $100 to $225; some to $375. **Remarks:** Spare-time maker; first knife sold in 1991. **Mark:** Name stamp.

METHENY, H.A. "WHITEY", 7750 Waterford Dr., Spotsylvania, VA, 22553/703-582-3228
Specialties: Working and using straight knives of his design and to customer specs. **Patterns:** Hunters and kitchen knives. **Technical:** Grinds 440C and ATS-34. Offers filework; tooled custom sheaths. **Prices:** $150 to $350. **Remarks:** Spare-time maker; first knife sold in 1990. **Mark:** Initials/full name football logo.

METTLER, J. BANJO, 129 S. Second St., North Baltimore, OH, 45872/419-257-2210
Specialties: Fancy folders of his design. **Patterns:** Locking folders, interframes, "A-5" automatic and "L-3" lockbacks of his design, deer-foot-style lockbacks 1-inch closed. **Technical:** Grinds ATS-34, D2 and O1. **Prices:** Start at $100. **Remarks:** Part-time maker; first knife sold in 1988. **Mark:** Deer foot underlined with profile of knife.

MICHINAKA, TOSHIAKI, I-679 Koyamacho-nishi, Totton-shi, Tottori 680-0947, JAPAN, /0857-28-5911

MIDDLETON, KEN, , Citrus Heights, CA, 95621/916-966-6070
Specialties: Traditional and fantasy straight knives and folders of his design. **Patterns:** Hunters, Bowies and daggers. **Technical:** Grinds 440C, ATS-34 and D2. Likes natural handle materials. **Prices:** $150 to $800; some to $3,500. **Remarks:** Spare-time maker; first knife sold in 1986. **Mark:** Last name or Middleton Custom.

custom knifemakers

MILFORD, BRIAN A., RD 2 Box 294, Knox, PA, 16232/814-797-2595 **Specialties:** Traditional and working/using straight knives of his design or to customer specs. **Patterns:** Fighters, hunters and utility/camp knives. **Technical:** Forges Damascus and 52100; grinds 440C. **Prices:** $50 to $300; some to $750. **Remarks:** Part-time maker; first knife sold in 1991. Doing business as BAM Forge. **Mark:** Full name or initials.

MILITANO, TOM, Custom Knives, 77 Jason Rd, Jacksonville, AL, 36265-6655/256-436-7132 **Specialties:** Fixed blade, one of a kind knives. **Patterns:** Bowies, fighters, hunters and tactical knives. **Technical:** Grinds 440C, ATS-34, A2, and Damascus. Hollow grinds, flat grinds, and decorative filework. **Prices:** $150.00 plus. **Remarks:** Part-time maker. **Mark:** Name, city and state in oval with maker in the center. Sold first knives in the mid to late 1980's.

MILLARD, FRED G., 5317 N. Wayne, Chicago, IL, 60640/773-769-5160 **Specialties:** Working/using straight knives of his design or to customer specs. **Patterns:** Bowies, hunters, utility/camp knives, kitchen/steak knives. **Technical:** Grinds ATS-34, O1, D2 and 440C. Makes sheaths. **Prices:** $80 to $250. **Remarks:** Full-time maker; first knife sold in 1993. Doing business as Millard Knives. **Mark:** Mallard duck in flight with serial number.

MILLER, RICK, RD 3 Box 273, Rockwood, PA, 15557/814-926-2059 **Specialties:** Working/using straight knives of his design and in standard patterns. **Patterns:** Bowies, daggers, hunters and friction folders. **Technical:** Grinds L6. Forges 5160, L6 and Damascus. Patterns for Damascus are random, twist, rose or ladder. **Prices:** $75 to $250; some to $400. **Remarks:** Part-time maker; first knife sold in 1982. **Mark:** Initials.

MILLER, MICHAEL E., R #3 Box 234-1, Stroud, OK, 74079/918-968-0102 **Specialties:** Traditional working/using knives of his design. **Patterns:** Bowies, hunters and kitchen knives. **Technical:** Grinds ATS-34, CPM 440V; forges Damascus and cable Damascus and 52100.. Prefers scrimshaw, fancy pins, basket weave and embellished sheaths. **Prices:** $60 to $175; some to $500. **Remarks:** Part-time maker; first knife sold in 1984. Doing business as Miller Custom Knives. **Mark:** First and middle initials, last name, maker, city and state.

MILLER, L. MAURICE, P.O. Box 3064, Missoula, MT, 59806-3064/406-549-3276 **Specialties:** Personally designed knives. **Patterns:** Fighters, folders and skinners. **Technical:** Grinds Damascus and 440C, fileart standard. All knives sold with sheath or displayed on walnut base. **Prices:** Damascus $850 to $1,400; 440C $250 to $600; folders $85 to $400. **Remarks:** Professional/artist maker; first knife sold in 1980. **Mark:** Buffalo skull with last name.

MILLER, M.A., 8979 Pearl St., Apt. 2005, Thornton, CO, 80229/303-427-8756 **Specialties:** Using knives for hunting. 3-1/2"-4" Loveless drop-point. Made to customer specs. **Patterns:** Skinners and camp knives. **Technical:** Grinds 440C, D2, O1 and ATS-34 Damascus miniatures. **Prices:** $225 to $275; miniatures $75. **Remarks:** Part-time maker; first knife sold in 1988. **Mark:** Last name stamped in block letters or first and middle initials, last name, maker, city and state with triangles on either side etched.

MILLER, HANFORD J., Box 97, Cowdrey, CO, 80434/070 723 4708 **Specialties:** Working knives in Moran style; period pieces. **Patterns:** Bowies, fighters, camp knives and other large straight knives. **Technical:** Forges W2, 1095, 5160 and his own Damascus; differential tempers; offers wire inlay. **Prices:** $300 to $800; some to $2,000. **Remarks:** Full-time maker; first knife sold in 1968. **Mark:** Initials or name within Bowie logo.

MILLER, DON, 1604 Harrodsburg Rd., Lexington, KY, 40503/606-276-3299

MILLER, JAMES P., 9024 Goeller Rd., RR 2, Box 28, Fairbank, IA, 50629/319-635-2294 **Specialties:** All tool steel Damascus; working knives and period pieces. **Patterns:** Hunters, Bowies, camp knives and daggers. **Technical:** Forges and grinds 1095, 52100, 440C and his own Damascus. **Prices:** $100 to $350; some to $1,500. **Remarks:** Full-time maker; first knife sold in 1970. **Mark:** First and middle initials, last name with knife logo.

MILLER, R.D., 10526 Estate Lane, Dallas, TX, 75238/214-348-3496 **Specialties:** One-of-a-kind collector-grade knives. **Patterns:** Boots, hunters, Bowies, camp and utility knives, fishing and bird knives, miniatures. **Technical:** Grinds a variety of steels to include O1, D2, 440C, 154CM and 1095. **Prices:** $65 to $300; some to $900. **Remarks:** Full-time maker; first knife sold in 1984. **Mark:** R.D. Custom Knives with date or bow and arrow logo.

MILLER, MICHAEL K., 28510 Santiam Hwy., Sweet Home, OR, 97386/541-367-4927 **Specialties:** Specializes in kitchen cutlery of his design or made to customer specs. **Patterns:** Hunters, utility/camp knives and kitchen cutlery. **Technical:** Grinds ATS-34, AEBL & 440-C. Wife does scrimshaw as well. Makes custom sheaths and holsters. **Prices:** $200. **Remarks:** Full-time maker; first knife sold in 1989. **Mark:** M&M Kustom Krafts.

MILLER, TED, P.O. Box 6328, Santa Fe, NM, 87502/505-984-0338 **Specialties:** Carved antler display knives of his design. **Patterns:** Hunters, swords and miniatures. **Technical:** Grinds 440C. **Prices:** $110 to $350; some average $900. **Remarks:** Full-time maker; first knife sold in 1971. **Mark:** Initials and serial number.

MILLER, RONALD T., 12922 127th Ave. N., Largo, FL, 34644/813-595-0378 (after 5 p.m.) **Specialties:** Working straight knives in standard patterns. **Patterns:** Combat knives, camp knives, kitchen cutlery, fillet knives, locking folders and butterflies. **Technical:** Grinds D2, 440C and ATS-34; offers brass inlays and scrimshaw. **Prices:** $45 to $325; some to $750. **Remarks:** Part-time maker; first knife sold in 1984. **Mark:** Name, city and state in palm tree logo.

MILLER, ROBERT, , Ormond Beach, FL, 32175/904-676-1193 **Specialties:** Working straight knives, some fancy, of his design or to customer specs. **Patterns:** Large Bowies, hunters, miniatures, boot knives, daggers. **Technical:** Grinds O1, D2 and 440C. Offers inlay and fancy filework; inlaid military insignias. **Prices:** $75 to $750. **Remarks:** Full-time maker; first knife sold in 1986. Doing business as Holly Knives. **Mark:** Holly.

MILLER, BOB, 7659 Fine Oaks Pl., Oakville, MO, 63129/314-846-3851 **Specialties:** Mosaic Damascus; collector using straight knives and folders. **Patterns:** Hunters, Bowies, utility/camp knives, daggers. **Technical:** Forges own Damascus, mosaic-Damascus and 52100. **Prices:** $125 to $500. **Remarks:** Part-time maker; first knife sold in 1983. **Mark:** First and middle initials and last name, or initials.

MILLS, LOUIS G., 9450 Waters Rd., Ann Arbor, MI, 48103/313-668-1839 **Specialties:** High-art Japanese-style period pieces. **Patterns:** Traditional tantos, daggers and swords. **Technical:** Makes steel from iron; makes his own Damascus by traditional Japanese techniques. **Prices:** $900 to $2,000; some to $8,000. **Remarks:** Spare-time maker in partnership with Jim Kelso. **Mark:** Yasutomo in Japanese Kanji.

MILLS, ANDY, 414 E. Schubert, Fredericksburg, TX, 78624/512-997-8167 **Specialties:** Working straight knives and folders. **Patterns:** Hunters. **Technical:** Grinds 440C, D2, A2 and 154CM. Offers leatherwork, fabrication, heat-treating. **Prices:** Moderate. **Remarks:** Full-time maker; first knife sold in 1980. **Mark:** Name.

MINK, DAN, P.O. Box 861, 196 Sage Circle, Crystal Beach, FL, 34681/813-786-5408 **Specialties:** Traditional and working knives of his design. **Patterns:** Bowies, fighters, folders and hunters. **Technical:** Grinds ATS-34, 440C and D2. Blades and tanges embellished with fancy filework. Uses natural and rare handle materials. **Prices:** $125 to $450. **Remarks:** Part-time maker; first knife sold in 1985. **Mark:** Name and star encircled by custom made, city, state.

MINNICK, JIM, 144 North 7th St., Middletown, IN, 47356/317-354-4108 **Specialties:** Traditional working and using straight knives and folders; classic high-art and fancy/embellished knives of his design or to customer specs. **Patterns:** Hunters, Bowies, daggers, fighters, boots, art knives, locking folders and slip-joint folders. **Technical:** Grinds 440C and 154CM. **Prices:** $185 to $225; some to $1,800. **Remarks:** Part-time maker; first knife sold in 1976. **Mark:** Last name.

MITCHELL, R.W. "MITCH", 24530 Bundy Canyon Road, Wildomar, CA, 92595-8732/909-244-4953
Specialties: Working straight knives with Indian influence. **Patterns:** Bowies, fighters, hunters with horseshoe guards, etc. **Technical:** Grinds 440C and ATS-34; prefers natural handle materials; heat-treats. **Prices:** $125 to $750. **Remarks:** Part-time maker; first knife sold in 1988. **Mark:** Mitch with arrow logo.

MITCHELL, JAMES A., P.O. Box 4646, Columbus, GA, 31904/404-322-8582
Specialties: Fancy working knives. **Patterns:** Hunters, fighters, Bowies and locking folders. **Technical:** Grinds D2, 440C and commercial Damascus. **Prices:** $100 to $400; some to $900. **Remarks:** Part-time maker; first knife sold in 1976. Sells knives in sets. **Mark:** Signature and city.

MITCHELL, WM. DEAN & PATRICIA, 8438 Cty Rd 1, Lamar, CO, 81052/719-336-8807
Specialties: Classic, period and high-art knives in standard patterns. **Patterns:** Bowies, hunters, daggers and swords. **Technical:** Forges 52100, 1095, 5160; makes pattern, composite and mosiac Damascus; offers filework and electroplating. Makes wooden display cases. **Prices:** Mid to upper scale. **Remarks:** Part-time maker; first knife sold in 1986. Doing business as Pioneer Forge & Woodshop. **Mark:** Full name or initials, MS. Other: Husband/wife team.

MITCHELL, MAX, DEAN AND BEN, 3803 V.F.W. Rd., Leesville, LA, 71440/318-239-6416
Specialties: Hatchet and knive sets with folder & belt & holster all match. **Patterns:** Hunters, 200 L6 steel. **Technical:** L6 steel; soft back, hand edge. **Prices:** $300 to $500. **Remarks:** Part-time makers; first knife sold in 1965. Custom orders only; no stock. **Mark:** First names.

MOMCILOVIC, GUNNAR, Nordlysv, 16, N-30055 Krokstadelva, NORWAY, /0111-47-3287-3586

MONK, NATHAN P., 1304 4th Ave. SE, Cullman, AL, 35055/205-737-0463
Specialties: Traditional working and using straight knives of his design and to customer specs; fancy knives. **Patterns:** Bowies, daggers, fighters, hunters, utility/camp knives, bird knives and one of a kinds. **Technical:** Grinds ATS-34, 440C and A2. **Prices:** $50 to $175. **Remarks:** Spare-time maker; first knife sold in 1990. **Mark:** First and middle initials, last name, city, state.

MONTANO, GUS A, 11217 WESTONHILL DR, SAN DIEGO, CA, 92126-1447/619-273-5357
Specialties: Traditional working/using straight knives of his design. **Patterns:** Boots, Bowies and fighters. **Technical:** Grinds 1095 and 5160; grinds and forges cable. Double or triple hardened and triple drawn; hand rubbed finish. Prefers natural handle materials. **Prices:** $200 to $400; some to $600. **Remarks:** Spare-time maker; first knife sold in 1997. **Mark:** First initial and last name.

MONTEIRO, VICTOR, Maleves Ste Marie, 1360 Perwez, BELGIUM, / 010 88 0441
Specialties: Working and fancy straight knives, folders and integrals of his design. **Patterns:** Bowies, fighters and hunters. **Technical:** Grinds ATS-34, 440C and commercial Damascus. Offers heat-treating, embellishment, filework and domed pins. **Prices:** $300 to $1000, some higher. **Remarks:** Part-time maker; first knife sold in 1989. Doing business as Monteiro Knives S.C. **Mark:** Logo with initials connected.

MONTJOY, CLAUDE, 706 Indian Creek Rd, Clinton, SC, 29325/864-697-6160
Specialties: Fancy working knives. **Patterns:** Hunters, boots, fighters, some art knives and folders. **Technical:** Grinds ATS-34 and 440C. Offers inlaid handle scales. **Prices:** $100 to $500. **Remarks:** Part-time maker; first knife sold in 1982. **Mark:** Last name.

MOORE, JAMES B., 1707 N. Gillis, Ft. Stockton, TX, 79735/915-336-2113
Specialties: Classic working straight knives and folders of his design. **Patterns:** Hunters, Bowies, daggers, fighters, boots, utility/camp knives, locking folders and slip-joint folders. **Technical:** Grinds 440C, ATS-34, D2, L6, CPM and commercial Damascus. **Prices:** $85 to $700; exceptional knives to $1,500. **Remarks:** Full-time maker; first knife sold in 1972. **Mark:** Name, city and state.

MOORE, BILL, 806 Community Ave., Albany, GA, 31705/912-438-5529
Specialties: Working and using folders of his design and to customer specs. **Patterns:** Bowies, hunters and locking folders. **Technical:** Grinds ATS-34, forges 5168 and cable Damascus. Filework. **Prices:** $100 to $400. **Remarks:** Part-time maker; first knife sold in 1988. **Mark:** Moore Knives.

MOORE, TED, 340 E Willlow St, Elizabethtown, PA, 17022-1946/717-367-3939
Specialties: Folders, locking liner, lock back & slip joint, anodized titanium. **Patterns:** Gents, tactical, hunters & fancy. **Technical:** Grinds ATS34-Damascus. **Prices:** $200 to $600; some to $1,200. **Remarks:** Part-time maker; first knife sold 1993. **Mark:** Last name and U.S.A.

MORAN JR., WM. F., P.O. Box 68, Braddock Heights, MD, 21714/301-371-7543
Specialties: High-art working knives of his design. **Patterns:** Fighters, camp knives, Bowies, daggers, axes, tomahawks, push knives and miniatures. **Technical:** Forges W2, 5160 and his own Damascus; puts silver wire inlay on most handles; uses only natural handle materials. **Prices:** $400 to $7,500; some to $9,000. **Remarks:** Full-time maker. **Mark:** First and middle initials, last name, M.S.

MORGAN, JEFF, 9200 Arnaz Way, Santee, CA, 92071/619-448-8430
Specialties: Fancy working straight knives. **Patterns:** Hunters, fighters, boots, miniatures. **Technical:** Grinds D2, 440C and ATS-34; likes exotic handles. **Prices:** $65 to $140; some to $500. **Remarks:** Full-time maker; first knife sold in 1977. **Mark:** Initials connected.

MORGAN, TOM, 14689 Ellett Rd., Beloit, OH, 44609/330-537-2023
Specialties: Working straight knives and period pieces. **Patterns:** Hunters, boots and presentation tomahawks. **Technical:** Grinds O1, 440C and 154CM. **Prices:** Knives, $65 to $200; tomahawks, $100 to $325. **Remarks:** Full-time maker; first knife sold in 1977. **Mark:** Last name and type of steel used.

MORRIS, ERIC, 306 Ewart Ave., Beckley, WV, 25801/304-255-3951

MORRIS, DARRELL PRICE, 92 Union, St. Plymouth, Devon, ENGLAND, PL1 3EZ/0752 223546
Specialties: Traditional Japanese knives, Bowies and high-art knives. **Technical:** Nickel Damascus and mokume. **Prices:** $1,000 to $4,000. **Remarks:** Part-time maker; first knife sold in 1990. **Mark:** Initials and Japanese name--Kuni Shigae.

MORRIS, C.H., 1590 Old Salem Rd., Frisco City, AL, 36445/334-575-7425
Specialties: Liner lock folders. **Patterns:** Interframe liner locks. **Technical:** Grinds 440C and ATS-34. **Prices:** Start at $350. **Remarks:** Full-time maker; first knife sold in 1973. Doing business as Custom Knives. **Mark:** First and middle initials, last name.

MORTENSON, ED, 2742 Hwy. 93 N, Darby, MT, 59829/406-821-3146
Specialties: Period pieces and working/using straight knives of his design, to customer specs and in standard patterns. **Patterns:** Bowies, hunters and kitchen knives. **Technical:** Grinds ATS-34, 5160 and 1095. Sheath combinations - flashlite/knife, hatchet/knife, etc. **Prices:** $60 to $140; some to $300. **Remarks:** Full-time maker; first knife sold in 1993. Doing business as The Blade Lair. **Mark:** M with attached O.

MOSSER, GARY E., 11827 NE 102nd Place, Kirkland, WA, 98033-5170/206-827-2279
Specialties: Working knives. **Patterns:** Hunters, skinners, camp knives, some art knives. **Technical:** Stock removal method; prefers ATS-34. **Prices:** $100 to $250; special orders and art knives are higher. **Remarks:** Part-time maker; first knife sold in 1976. **Mark:** Name.

MOULTON, DUSTY, 135 Hillview Lane, Loudon, TN, 37774/
Specialties: Fancy and working straight knives. **Patterns:** Hunters, fighters, fantasy and miniatures. **Technical:** Grinds exclusively ATS-34. **Prices:** $160 to $600; some to $1,500. **Remarks:** Full-time maker; first knife sold in 1991. **Mark:** Last name. Other: Also does scrimshaw on own knives or other makers knives.

MOUNT, DON, 4574 Little Finch Ln., Las Vegas, NV, 89115/702-531-2925
Specialties: High-tech working and using straight knives of his design. **Patterns:** Bowies, fighters and utility/camp knives. **Technical:** Uses 440C and ATS-34. **Prices:** $150 to $300; some to $1,000. **Remarks:** Part-time maker; first knife sold in 1985. **Mark:** Name below a woodpecker.

custom knifemakers

MOUNTAIN HOME KNIVES, P.O. Box 167, Jamul, CA, 91935/619-669-0833
Specialties: High-quality working straight knives. **Patterns:** Hunters, fighters, skinners, tantos, utility and fillet knives, Bowies and *san-mai* Damascus Bowies. **Technical:** Hollow-grind 440C by hand. Feature linen Micarta handles, nickel-silver handle bolts and handmade sheaths. **Prices:** $65 to $270. **Remarks:** Company owned by Jim English. **Mark:** Mountain Home Knives.

MOYER, RUSS, HC 36 Box 57C, Havre, MT, 59501/406-395-4423
Specialties: Working knives to customer specs. **Patterns:** Hunters, Bowies and survival knives. **Technical:** Forges W2. **Prices:** $150 to $350. **Remarks:** Part-time maker; first knife sold in 1976. **Mark:** Initials in logo.

MULLIN, STEVE, 500 Snowberry Lane, Sandpoint, ID, 83864/208-263-7492
Specialties: Damascus period pieces and folders. **Patterns:** Full range of folders, hunters and Bowies. **Technical:** Forges and grinds O1, D2, 154CM and his own Damascus. Engraves. **Prices:** $100 to $2,000. **Remarks:** Full-time maker; first knife sold in 1975. Sells line of using knives under Pack River Knife Co. **Mark:** Full name, city and state.

MURPHY, DAVE, P.O. Box 256, Gresham, OR, 97030/503-665-8634
Specialties: Working knives of his design; small kitchen knives. **Patterns:** Hunters, fighters and boots. **Technical:** Grinds 440C, ATS-34 and L6; likes narrow tangs, composite handles. **Prices:** $44 to $12,500. **Remarks:** Full-time maker; first knife sold in 1940. **Mark:** Name, city and state with likeness of face on blade.

MURSKI, RAY, 12129 Captiva Ct., Reston, VA, 22091-1204/703-264-1102
Specialties: Fancy working/using folders of his design. **Patterns:** Hunters, slip-joint folders and utility/camp knives. **Technical:** Grinds 440C, O1 and D2. **Prices:** $125-$500. **Remarks:** Spare-time maker; first knife sold in 1996. **Mark:** Etched name with serial number under name.

MYERS, PAUL, 614 W. Airwood Dr., E. Alton, IL, 62024/
Specialties: Fancy working straight knives and folders. **Patterns:** Full range of folders, straight hunters and Bowies; tie tacks; knife and fork sets. **Technical:** Grinds D2, 440C, ATS-34 and 154CM. **Prices:** $100 to $350; some to $3,000. **Remarks:** Full-time maker; first knife sold in 1974. **Mark:** Initials with setting sun on front; name and number on back.

MYERS, MEL, 611 Elmwood Drive, Spencer, IA, 51301/712-262-3383
Specialties: Working knives. **Patterns:** Hunters and small utilitarian knives. **Technical:** Uses 440C and no power tools except polisher. **Prices:** $75 to $150. **Remarks:** Spare-time maker; first knife sold in 1982. **Mark:** Signature.

n

NATEN, GREG, 1916 16th St. #B, Bakersfield, CA, 93301-5005/805-861-0845
Specialties: Fancy and working/using folders of his design. **Patterns:** Fighters, hunters and locking folders. **Technical:** Grinds 440C, ATS-34 and CPM440V. Heat-treats; prefers desert ironwood, stag and mother of pearl. Designs and sews leather sheaths for straight knives. **Prices:** $175 to $600; some to $950. **Remarks:** Spare-time maker; first knife sold in 1992. **Mark:** Last name above battle-ax, handmade.

NEALEY, IVAN F. (FRANK), Anderson Dam Rd., Box 65, HC #87, Mt. Home, ID, 83647/208-587-4060
Specialties: Working straight knives in standard patterns. **Patterns:** Hunters, skinners and utility knives. **Technical:** Grinds D2, 440C and 154CM. **Prices:** $90 to $135; some higher. **Remarks:** Part-time maker; first knife sold in 1975. **Mark:** Name.

NEALY, BUD, 1439 Poplar Valley Rd, Stroudsburg, PA, 18360/570-992-8020
Specialties: Original design concealment knives with designer multi-concealment sheath system. **Patterns:** Concealment knives, boots, combat and collector pieces. **Technical:** Grinds ATS-34; uses Damascus. **Prices:** $175 to $1,200. **Remarks:** Full-time maker; first knife sold in 1980. **Mark:** Name, city, state or signature.

NEDVED, DAN, 206 Park Dr., Kalispell, MT, 59901/406-752-5060
Specialties: Slip joint folders, liner locks, straight knives. **Patterns:** Mostly traditional or modern blend with traditional lines. **Technical:** Grinds ATS34, 440C, 1095 and uses other makers Damascus. **Prices:** $95 and up. Mostly in the $150 to $200 range. **Remarks:** Part-time maker, averages 2 a month. **Mark:** Dan Nedved or Nedved with serial # on opposite side.

NEELEY, VAUGHN, 666 Grand Ave., Mancos, CO, 81328/303-533-7982
Specialties: High-tech working straight knives and folders. **Patterns:** High-tech approaches; locking folders and interframes. **Technical:** Grinds 440C, D2 and 154CM. **Prices:** Upscale. **Remarks:** Full-time maker; first knife sold in 1982. **Mark:** Name.

NEELY, GREG, 9605 Radio Rd., Houston, TX, 77075-2238/713-991-2677
Specialties: Traditional patterns and his own patterns for work and/or collecting. **Patterns:** Hunters, Bowies and utility/camp knives. **Technical:** Forges own Damascus, 1084, 5160 and some tool steels. Differentially tempers. **Prices:** $225 to $5,000. **Remarks:** Part-time maker; first knife sold in 1987. **Mark:** Last name or interlocked initials, MS.

NELSON, KEN, 2219 S Kinnickinnic Ave #2, Milwaukee, WI, 53207/414-481-8276
Specialties: Working straight knives, period pieces. **Patterns:** Utility, hunters, dirks, daggers, throwers, hawks, axes, swords, and polearms. **Technical:** Forges 5160, 52100, W2, 10xx, L6, and own Damascus. Multiple and differential heat treating. **Prices:** $50 to $350, some to $3000. **Remarks:** Part-time maker. First knife sold in 1995. Doing business as Iron Wolf Forge. **Mark:** Stylized wolf paw print.

NETO JR., NELSON AND DE CARVALHO, HENRIQUE M., R. Joao Margarido, No. 20-V, Guerra, Braganca Paulista, SP-12900-000, BRAZIL, /011-7843-6889
Specialties: Straight knives and folders. **Patterns:** Bowies, katanas, jambyias and others. **Technical:** Forges hig carbon steels. **Prices:** $70 to $3000. **Remarks:** Full-time makers; first knife sold in 1990. **Mark:** H&N.

NEUHAEUSLER, ERWIN, Heiligenangerstrasse 15, 86179 Augsburg, GERMANY, /0821-814997
Specialties: Traditional working/using straight knives of his design. **Patterns:** Boots, hunters and Japanese style knives. **Technical:** Grinds ATS-34, Damascus and RWL-34. **Prices:** $250 to $750. **Remarks:** Spare-time maker; first knife sold in 1991. **Mark:** Etched logo, last name and city.

NEWCOMB, CORBIN, 628 Woodland Ave., Moberly, MO, 65270/660-263-4639
Specialties: Working straight knives and folders; period pieces. **Patterns:** Hunters, axes, Bowies, folders, buckskinner blades and boots. **Technical:** Hollow-grinds D2, 440C and 154CM; prefers natural handle materials. Makes own Damascus; offers cable Damascus. **Prices:** $100 to $500. **Remarks:** Full-time maker; first knife sold in 1982. Doing business as Corbin Knives. **Mark:** First name and serial number.

NEWTON, LARRY, 1758 Pronghorn Ct., Jacksonville, FL, 32225/904-221-2340
Specialties: Traditional and slender high grade gentlemen's folders, locking liner type tacticals, and working straight knives. **Patterns:** Front release locking folders, interframes, hunters, and skinners. **Technical:** Grinds Damascus, ATS-34, 440C and D2. **Prices:** Folders start at $275, straights start at $150. **Remarks:** Spare-time maker; first knife sold in 1989. **Mark:** Last name.

NICHOLSON, R. KENT, P.O. Box 204, Phoenix, MD, 21131/410-323-6925
Specialties: Large using knives. **Patterns:** Bowies and camp knives in the Moran style. **Technical:** Forges W2, 9260, 5160; makes Damascus. **Prices:** $150 to $995. **Remarks:** Part-time maker; first knife sold in 1984. **Mark:** Name.

NIELSON, JEFF V., PO Box 365, Monroe, UT, 84754/801-527-4242
Specialties: Classic folders of his design and to customer specs. **Patterns:** Fighters, hunters, locking folders; miniatures. **Technical:** Grinds 440C stainless & Damascus. **Prices:** $80 to $500. **Remarks:** Part-time maker; first knife sold in 1991. **Mark:** Name, location.

NIEMUTH, TROY, 3143 North Ave., Sheboygan, WI, 53083/414-452-2927
Specialties: Period pieces and working/using straight knives of his design and to customer specs. **Patterns:** Hunters and utility/camp

knives. **Technical:** Grinds 440C, 1095 and A2. **Prices:** $85 to $350; some to $500. **Remarks:** Full-time maker; first knife sold in 1995. **Mark:** Etched last name.

NISHIUCHI, MELVIN S., 6121 Forest Park Dr., Las Vegas, NV, 89115/702-438-2327
Specialties: Working knives; collector pieces. **Patterns:** Hunters, fighters, locking liner folders, and some fancy personal knives. **Technical:** Grinds ATS-34; prefers exotic wood and/or semi-precious stone handle materials. **Prices:** $250 to $2,000. **Remarks:** Part-time maker; first knife sold in 1985. **Mark:** Circle with a line above it.

NOLEN, R.D. AND STEVE, 1110 Lakeshore Dr., Estes Park, CO, 80517-7113/970-586-5814
Specialties: Working knives; display pieces. **Patterns:** Wide variety of straight knives, butterflies and buckles. **Technical:** Grind D2, 440C and 154CM. Offer filework; make exotic handles. **Prices:** $150 to $800; some higher. **Remarks:** Full-time makers; first knife sold in 1968. **Mark:** NK in oval logo.

NOLFI, TIM, P.O. Box P, Chapel Hill Rd., Dawson, PA, 15428/412-529-2439
Specialties: High-art straight knives and folders of his design; working and using knives. **Patterns:** Hunters, Bowies, fighters and some locking folders. **Technical:** Forges and grinds his own Damascus, O1 and 1095. Also works with wrought iron and 200 nickel. **Prices:** $125 to $1,500; some to $4,000. **Remarks:** Full-time maker; first knife sold in 1988. **Mark:** Nolfi Forge or last name alone.

NORDELL, INGEMAR, Skarpå 2103, 82041 Färila, SWEDEN, /0651-23347
Specialties: Classic working and using straight knives. **Patterns:** Hunters, Bowies and fighters. **Technical:** Forges and grinds ATS-34, D2 and Sandvik. **Prices:** $120 to $1,500. **Remarks:** Part-time maker; first knife sold in 1985. **Mark:** Initials or name.

NORFLEET, ROSS W., 3947 Tanbark Rd., Richmond, VA, 23235/804-276-4169
Specialties: Classic, traditional and working/using knives of his design or in standard patterns. **Patterns:** Hunters and folders. **Technical:** Hollow-grinds 440C and ATS-34. **Prices:** $150 to $550. **Remarks:** Part-time maker; first knife sold in 1993. **Mark:** Last name.

NORRIS, DON, 4711 N. Paseo Sonoyta, Tucson, AZ, 85750/520-299-6531
Specialties: Classic and traditional working/using straight knives of his design, to customer specs and in standard patterns. **Patterns:** Bowies, daggers, fighters, hunters and utility/camp knives. **Technical:** Grinds and forges Damascus; grinds ATS-34 and 440C. Cast sterling guards and bolsters on Bowies. **Prices:** $350 to $2,000, some to $3500. **Remarks:** Full-time maker; first knife sold in 1990. Doing business as Norris Custom Knives. **Mark:** Last name.

NORTH, DAVID AND PRATER, MIKE, 105 Sharp, Chickamauga, GA, 30707/706-931-2396
Specialties: Variety of horn- and stag-handled belt knives. **Patterns:** Standard patterns in large and small narrow-tang construction. **Technical:** Grind O1, D2 and Damascus. **Prices:** $165 to $10,000. **Remarks:** First knife sold in 1980. **Mark:** Names, date, serial number.

NORTON, DON, 7517 Mountain Quail Dr, Las Vegas, NV, 89146/703-642-5036
Specialties: Fancy and plain straight knives. **Patterns:** Hunters, small Bowies, tantos, boot knives, fillets. **Technical:** Prefers 440C, Micarta, exotic woods and other natural handle materials. Hollow-grinds all knives except fillet knives. **Prices:** $165 to $1,500; average is $200. **Remarks:** Full-time maker; first knife sold in 1980. **Mark:** Full name, Hsi Shuai, city, state.

NORTON, DENNIS, 5334 Ashland Dr., Ft. Wayne, IN, 46835/219-486-3851
Specialties: Traditional working and using knives of his design; martial arts weapons. **Patterns:** Bowies, fighters and utility/camp knives. **Technical:** Grinds 440C, D2 and O1. Most knives have filework and exotic hardwood handles. **Prices:** $60 to $300; some to $750. **Remarks:** Part-time maker; first knife sold in 1985. **Mark:** Initials and last name.

NOTT, RON P., P.O. Box 281, Summerdale, PA, 17093/717-732-2763
Specialties: High-art folders and some straight knives. **Patterns:** Scale release folders. **Technical:** Grinds ATS-34, 416 and nickel-silver.

Engraves, inlays gold. **Prices:** $250 to $3,000. **Remarks:** Full-time maker; first knife sold in 1993. Doing business as Knives By Nott, customer engraving. **Mark:** First initial, last name and serial number.

NOWLAND, RICK, 3677 E Bonnie Rd., Waltonville, IL, 62894/618-279-3170
Specialties: Fancy single blade slip joints & trappers using Damascus & Mokume. **Patterns:** Uses several Remington patterns and also his own designs. **Technical:** Uses ATS-34, 440C; forges his own Damascus; makes mokume. **Prices:** Start at $200. **Remarks:** Part-time maker; first knife sold in 1986. **Mark:** Last name.

NUNN, GREGORY, CVSR Box 2107, Moab, UT, 84532/801-259-8607
Specialties: High-art working and using knives of his design; new edition Emperor's Choice knife with purple sheen obsidian handle; new edition knife with handle made from agatetized dinosaur bone - first ever made. **Patterns:** Flaked stone knives. **Technical:** Uses gem-quality agates, jaspers and obsidians for blades. **Prices:** $125 to $600; some to $1,000. **Remarks:** Full-time maker; first knife sold in 1989. **Mark:** Name, knife and edition numbers, year made.

O

O'CEILAGHAN, MICHAEL, 1623 Benhill Rd., Baltimore, MD, 21226/410-355-1660
Specialties: High-art and traditional straight knives of his design and to customer specs. **Patterns:** Fighters, hunters and utility/camp knives. **Technical:** Forges 5160, O6, 1045 and railroad spikes. Blades are "Hamon" tempered and drawn; handles are either horn or hand-carved wood. **Prices:** $100 to $325; some to $750. **Remarks:** First knife sold in 1992. Doing business as Howling Wolf Forge. **Mark:** Howling Wolf Forge, signed signature, date forged.

OCHS, CHARLES F., 124 Emerald Lane, Largo, FL, 33771/727-536-3827
Specialties: Working knives; period pieces. **Patterns:** Hunters, fighters, Bowies, buckskinners and folders. **Technical:** Forges 52100, 5160 and his own Damascus. **Prices:** $150 to $1,800; some to $2,500. **Remarks:** Full-time maker; first knife sold in 1978. **Mark:** OX Forge.

ODA, KUZAN, 629 W. 15th Ave., Anchorage, AK, 99501-5005/907-746-3018
Specialties: High-tech Japanese-style knives; contemporary working knives. **Patterns:** Swords, fighters, hunters and folders. **Technical:** Forges and grinds BG42, 154CM, tamahagane and his own Damascus; offers traditional and authentic Japanese sword-smithing and polishing. **Prices:** $200 to $600; some to $8,000. **Remarks:** Full-time maker; first knife sold in 1957. Waiting list only. **Mark:** First name.

OGLETREE JR., BEN R., 2815 Israel Rd., Livingston, TX, 77351/409-327-8315
Specialties: Working/using straight knives of his design. **Patterns:** Hunters, kitchen and utility/camp knives. **Technical:** Grinds ATS-34, W1 and 1075; heat-treats. **Prices:** $200 to $400. **Remarks:** Part-time maker; first knife sold in 1955. **Mark:** Last name, city and state in oval with a tree on either side.

OKAYSU, KAZOU, 12-2 1 Chome Higashi Veno, Taito-Ku, Tokyo 110, JAPAN, /

OLIVER, ANTHONY CRAIG, 1504 Elaine Pl., Ft. Worth, TX, 76106/817-625-0825
Specialties: Fancy and embellished traditional straight knives of his design. **Patterns:** Hunters, full-size folders, Bowies, daggers and miniatures in stainless and nickel Damascus with tempered blades. **Technical:** Grinds 440C and ATS-34. **Prices:** $40 to $500. **Remarks:** Part-time maker; first knife sold in 1988. **Mark:** Initials and last name.

OLSON, WAYNE C., 11655 W. 35th Ave., Wheat Ridge, CO, 80033/303-420-3415
Specialties: High-tech working knives. **Patterns:** Hunters to folding lockers; some integral designs. **Technical:** Grinds 440C, 154CM and ATS-34; likes hand-finishes; precision-fits stainless steel fittings--no solder, no nickel silver. **Prices:** $275 to $600; some to $3,000. **Remarks:** Part-time maker; first knife sold in 1979. **Mark:** Name, maker.

custom knifemakers

OLSON, ROD, Box 5973, High River, AB, CANADA, T1V 1P6/403-652-2744
Specialties: Traditional and working/using folders of his design; period pieces. **Patterns:** Locking folders. **Technical:** Grinds ATS-34. Offers filework, sculptured steel frames. **Prices:** $300 to $750. **Remarks:** Part-time maker; first knife sold in 1979. Doing business as Olson Pocket Knives. Mark Last name on blade; country, serial number inside frame.

OLSON, DARROLD E., P.O. Box 1539, Springfield, OR, 97477/541-726-8300
Specialties: Straight knives and folders of his design and to customer specs. **Patterns:** Hunters, liner locks and locking folders. **Technical:** Grinds 440C, ATS-34 and 154CM. Uses anodized titanium; sheaths wet-moulded. **Prices:** $150 to $350. **Remarks:** Part-time maker; first knife sold in 1989. **Mark:** Initials and last name.

ONION, KENNETH J., 91-990 Oaniani St., Kapolei, HI, 96707/808-674-1300
Specialties: Straight knives and folders. **Patterns:** Bowies, daggers, tantos, fighters, boots, hunters, utility knives and art knives. **Technical:** ATS-34, 440C, Damascus, 5160, D2. **Prices:** $135 to $1,500. **Remarks:** Part-time maker; first knife sold in 1991. All knives fully guaranteed. Call for availability. **Mark:** Name and state.

ORTON, RICHARD, P.O. Box 7002, La Verne, CA, 91750/909-596-8344
Specialties: Classic and traditional working and using straight knives of his design, to customer specs and in standard patterns and collectible bowies. **Patterns:** concealment, necklace with Kydex sheaths, boots, daggers, and hunters. **Technical:** Grinds ATS-34, 440C and file steel. Filework on blades and handle backs. Handles of exotic hardwoods, stag and mother-of-pearl with gemstones and silver inlay. Hand-stitched leather sheaths, some with tooling. **Prices:** $150 to $350; some to $750. **Remarks:** Full-time maker; first knife sold in 1992. Doing business as Orton Knife Works. **Mark:** Last name, city and state.

OSBORNE, MICHAEL, 585 Timber Ridge Dr., New Braunfels, TX, 78132/210-609-0118
Specialties: Traditional and working/using straight knives of his design. **Patterns:** Bowies, fighters and hunters. **Technical:** Forges 5160, 52100 and 10. Tempers all blades. Some filework. Embellishes with silver wire inlay. **Prices:** $125 to $500; some to $1,000. **Remarks:** Part-time maker; first knife sold in 1988. **Mark:** Engraved signature and year.

OSBORNE, WARREN, 215 Edgefield, Waxahachie, TX, 75165/972-935-0899
Specialties: Investment grade collectible, interframes, one of a kinds; unique locking mechanisms. **Patterns:** Folders; bolsters and interframes; conventional lockers, frontlockers and backlockers; some slip-joints; some high-art pieces; fighters. **Technical:** Grinds ATS-34, 440 and 154; some Damascus and CPM400V. **Prices:** $400 to $2,000; some to $4,000. Interframes $650 to $1,500. **Remarks:** Full-time maker; first knife sold in 1980. **Mark:** Last name in boomerang logo.

OSTERMAN, DANIEL E., 1644 W. 10th, Junction City, OR, 97448/541-998-1503
Specialties: One-third scale copies of period pieces, museum class miniatures. **Patterns:** Antique Bowies. **Technical:** Grinds all cutlery grade steels, engraves, etches, inlays and overlays. **Prices:** Start at $2,500. **Remarks:** Full-time maker; first miniature knife sold in 1975. **Mark:** Initials.

OUTLAW, ANTHONY L., 4115 Gaines St., Panama City, FL, 32404/904-769-7754
Specialties: Traditional working straight knives. **Patterns:** Tantos, Bowies, camp knives, etc. **Technical:** Grinds A2, W2, O1, L6, 1095 and stainless steels to mirror finish. **Prices:** $85 to $175; some to $300. **Remarks:** Part-time maker; first knife sold in 1984. **Mark:** Last name.

OVEREYNDER, T.R., 1800 S. Davis Dr., Arlington, TX, 76013/817-277-4812
Specialties: Highly finished collector-grade knives. **Patterns:** Fighters, Bowies, daggers, locking folders, slip-joints and 90 percent collector-grade interframe folders. **Technical:** Grinds D2, 440C and 154CM. Has been making titanium-frame folders since 1977. **Prices:** $500 to $1,500; some to $7,000. **Remarks:** Part-time maker; first knife sold in 1977. Doing business as TRO Knives. **Mark:** T.R. OVEREYNDER KNIVES, city and state.

OWENS, JOHN, 6513 E. Lookout Dr., Parker, CO, 80138/
Specialties: Contemporary working straight knives; period pieces. **Patterns:** Hunters, Bowies and camp knives. **Technical:** Grinds and forges 440C, 154CM, ATS-34 and O1. **Prices:** $175 to $600. **Remarks:** Spare-time maker. **Mark:** Last name.

OWNBY, JOHN C., 1716 Hastings Ct., Plano, TX, 75023-5027/
Specialties: Traditional working and using straight knives and folders of his design. **Patterns:** Hunters, locking folders and utility/camp knives. **Technical:** Grinds 440C, 1095, and ATS-34. Blades are flat ground. Prefers natural materials for handles--exotic woods, horn and antler. **Prices:** $125 to $250; some to $500. **Remarks:** Part-time maker; first knife sold in 1993. Doing business as John C. Ownby Handmade Knives. **Mark:** Name, city, state.

OYSTER, LOWELL R., 543 Grant Road, Corinth, ME, 04427/207-884-8663
Specialties: Traditional and original designed multi-blade slip-joint folders. **Patterns:** Hunters, minis, camp and fishing knives. **Technical:** Grinds O1; heat-treats. **Prices:** $55 to $450; some to $750. **Remarks:** Full-time maker; first knife sold in 1981. **Mark:** A scallop shell.

p

PACHI, MIRELLA, Via Pometta, 1, 17046 Sassello (SV) ITALY, /019 720086
Specialties: Fancy and working knives. **Patterns:** Hunters, and skinners. **Technical:** Grinds ATS-34 and Damascus. **Prices:** $400 to $2,500. **Remarks:** Full-time maker; first knife sold in 1991. **Mark:** Logo with last name.

PACHI, FRANCESCO, Via Pometta, 1, 17046 Sassello (SV), ITALY, /019 720086
Specialties: Fancy and working knives. **Patterns:** Hunters, and skinners. **Technical:** Grinds ATS-34 and Damascus. **Prices:** $400 to $2,500. **Remarks:** Full-time maker; first knife sold in 1991. **Mark:** Logo with last name.

PACKARD, BOB, P.O. Box 311, Elverta, CA, 95626/916-991-5218
Specialties: Traditional working/using straight knives of his design and to customer specs. **Patterns:** Hunters, fishing knives, utility/camp knives. **Technical:** Grinds ATS-34, 440C; Forges 52100, 5168 and cable Damascus. **Prices:** $75 to $225. **Mark:** Engraved name and year.

PADGETT JR., EDWIN L., 845 Bank St., New London, CT, 06320/860-443-2938
Specialties: Skinners and working knives of any design. **Patterns:** Straight and folding knives. **Technical:** Grinds ATS-34 or any tool steel upon request. **Prices:** $50 to $300. **Mark:** Name.

PADILLA, GARY, P.O. Box 741, Weimar, CA, 95736/916-637-5182
Specialties: Native American influenced working and using straight knives of his design. **Patterns:** Hunters, kitchen knives, utility/camp knives and obsidian ceremonial knives. **Technical:** Grinds 440C, ATS-34, O1 and Damascus. **Prices:** $65 to $195; some to $500. **Remarks:** Part-time maker; first knife sold in 1977. Doing business as Bighorn Knifeworks. **Mark:** Stylized initials or name over company name.

PAGE, REGINALD, 6587 Groveland Hill Rd., Groveland, NY, 14462/716-243-1643
Specialties: High-art straight knives and one-of-a-kind folders of his design. **Patterns:** Hunters, locking folders and slip-joint folders. **Technical:** Forges O1, 5160 and his own Damascus. Prefers natural handle materials but will work with Micarta. **Remarks:** Spare-time maker; first knife sold in 1985. **Mark:** First initial, last name.

PAGE, LARRY, 165 Rolling Rock Rd., Aiken, SC, 29803/803-648-0001
Specialties: Working knives of his design; period pieces. **Patterns:** Hunters, boots and fighters. **Technical:** Grinds 154CM and ATS-34. **Prices:** Start at $85. **Remarks:** Part-time maker; first knife sold in 1983. **Mark:** Name, city and state in oval.

PANKIEWICZ, PHILIP R., RFD #1, Waterman Rd., Lebanon, CT, 06249/
Specialties: Working straight knives. **Patterns:** Hunters, daggers, minis and fishing knives. **Technical:** Grinds D2, 440C and 154CM. **Prices:** $60 to $125; some to $250. **Remarks:** Spare-time maker; first knife sold in 1975. **Mark:** First initial in star.

PAPP, ROBERT, P.O. Box 29596, Parma, OH, 44129/216-888-9299
Specialties: Swords--broad and fantasy; variety of display knives. **Patterns:** Integral-designed hunters, fighters, minis and boots. **Technical:** Grinds D2, 440C, 154CM, ATS-34, CPM108 and CPM440C. **Prices:** $95 to $10,000; some higher. **Remarks:** Full-time maker; first knife sold in 1964. **Mark:** Full name, city and state.

PARDUE, MELVIN M., Rt. 1, Box 130, Repton, AL, 36475/205-248-2686
Specialties: Fancy straight knives and folders. **Patterns:** Locking and push-button folders, tantos, krisses, liner locks, fighters and boots. **Technical:** Grinds D2, 440C, 154CM and UHB-A-EBL; uses anodized titanium. Likes coffin handles. **Prices:** $140 to $350. **Remarks:** Full-time maker; first knife sold in 1974. **Mark:** Last name.

PARKER, J.E., 1300 E. Main, Clarion, PA, 16214/814-226-4837
Specialties: Fancy/embellished, traditional and working straight knives of his design and to customer specs. **Patterns:** Bowies and hunters. **Technical:** Grinds 440C, 440V, ATS-34 and nickel Damascus. Prefers mastadon, oosik, amber and malachite handle material. **Prices:** $90 to $550; some to $750. **Remarks:** Part-time maker; first knife sold in 1991. Doing business as Custom Knife. **Mark:** Name and city with knife stamped in blade.

PARKER, ROBERT NELSON, 5223 Wilhelm Rd. N.W., Rapid City, MI, 49676/
Specialties: Traditional working and using straight knives of his design. **Patterns:** Hunters, fighters, utility/camp knives; some Bowies. **Technical:** Grinds ATS-34; hollow and flat grinds, full and hidden tangs. Hand-stitched leather sheaths. **Prices:** $225 to $500; some to $1,000. **Remarks:** Part-time maker; first knife sold in 1986. **Mark:** Full name.

PARKS, JOHN, 3539 Galilee Church Rd., Jefferson, GA, 30549/706-367-4916
Specialties: Traditional working and using straight knives of his design. **Patterns:** Trout knives, hunters and integral bolsters. **Technical:** Forges 1095 and 5168. **Prices:** $100 to $250; some to $600. **Remarks:** Part-time maker; first knife sold in 1989. **Mark:** Initials in script.

PARKS, BLANE C., 15908 Crest Dr., Woodbridge, VA, 22191/703-221-4680
Specialties: Knives of his design. **Patterns:** Boots, Bowies, daggers, fighters, hunters, kitchen knives, locking and slip-joint folders, utility/camp knives, letter openers and friction folders. **Technical:** Grinds ATS-34, 440C, D2 and other carbon steels. Offers filework, silver wire inlay and wooden sheaths. **Prices:** Start at $250 & up. **Remarks:** Part-time maker; first knife sold in 1993. Doing business as B.C. Parks Knives. **Mark:** First and middle initials, last name.

PARRISH, ROBERT, 271 Allman Hill Rd., Weaverville, NC, 28787/704-645-2864
Specialties: Heavy-duty working knives of his design or to customer specs. **Patterns:** Survival and duty knives; hunters and fighters. **Technical:** Grinds 440C, D2, O1 and commercial Damascus. **Prices:** $200 to $300; some to $6,000. **Remarks:** Full-time maker; first knife sold in 1970. **Mark:** Initials connected, sometimes with city and state.

PARRISH III, GORDON A., 940 Lakloey Dr., North Pole, AK, 99705/907-488-0357
Specialties: Classic and high-art straight knives of his design and to customer specs; working and using knives. **Patterns:** Bowies and hunters. **Technical:** Grinds tool steel and ATS-34. Uses mostly Alaskan handle materials. **Prices:** $125 to $750. **Remarks:** Spare-time maker; first knife sold in 1980. **Mark:** Last name, state.

PARSONS, MICHAEL R., McKee Knives, 1600 S. 11th St, Terre Haute, IN, 47802-1722/812-234-1679
Specialties: Fancy straight knives. **Patterns:** Railroad spike knives and variety of one of a kinds including files. **Technical:** Forges and hand-files scrap steel. Etches, carves, wire inlays and offers leatherwork. **Prices:**

$150 to $1,500. **Remarks:** Full-time maker; first knife sold in 1965. **Mark:** Mc with key logo.

PATE, LLOYD D., 219 Cottontail Ln., Georgetown, TX, 78626/512-863-7805
Specialties: Traditional working straight knives. **Patterns:** Hunters, fighters and Bowies. **Technical:** Hollow-grinds D2, 440C and ATS-34; likes mirror-finishes. **Prices:** $75 to $350; some to $500. **Remarks:** Part-time maker; first knife sold in 1983. **Mark:** Last name.

PATRICK, CHUCK, P.O. Box 127, Brasstown, NC, 28902/704-837-7627
Specialties: Period pieces. **Patterns:** Hunters, daggers, tomahawks, pre-Civil War folders. **Technical:** Forges all hardware, 5160, his own cable and Damascus, available in fancy pattern and mosaic. **Prices:** $150 to $1,000; some higher. **Remarks:** Full-time maker; first knife sold in 1980. **Mark:** Hand-engraved name, date or flying owl.

PATRICK, PEGGY, P.O. Box 127, Brasstown, NC, 28902/828-837-7627
Specialties: Authentic period and Indian sheath. Beads and quillwork.

PATRICK, WILLARD C., P.O. Box 5716, Helena, MT, 59604/406-458-6552
Specialties: Working straight knives and one-of-a-kind art knives of his design or to customer specs. **Patterns:** Hunters, Bowies, fish, patch and kitchen knives. **Technical:** Grinds ATS-34, 1095, O1, A2 and Damascus. **Prices:** $85 to $350; some to $600. **Remarks:** Full-time maker; first knife sold in 1989. Doing business as Wil-A-Mar Cutlery. **Mark:** Shield with last name and a dagger.

PATRICK, BOB, 12642 24A Ave., S. Surrey, B.C., CANADA, V4A 8H9/604-538-6214
Specialties: Field grade to presentation grade traditional straight knives and period pieces of his design. **Patterns:** Bowies, Pierce-Arrow throwing knives, daggers and more. **Technical:** Prefers D2, 5160 and Damascus by Devon or Daryl. **Prices:** $160 for a set of P.A. throwers and up. **Remarks:** Full-time maker; first knife sold in 1987. Doing business as Crescent Knife Works. **Mark:** Logo with name and province or Crescent Knife Works.

PATTAY, RUDY, 510 E. Harrison St., Long Beach, NY, 11561/516-431-0847
Specialties: Fancy and working straight knives of his design. **Patterns:** Bowies, hunters, utility/camp knives. **Technical:** Hollow-grinds ATS-34, 440C, O1. Offers commercial Demascus, stainless steel soldered guards; fabricates guard and buttcap on lathe and milling machine. Heat-treats. Prefers synthetic handle materials. Offers hand-sewn sheaths. **Prices:** $100 to $350; some to $500. **Remarks:** Part-time maker; first knife sold in 1990. **Mark:** First initial, last name in sorcerer logo.

PATTERSON, KARL, 8 Madison Ave., Silver Creek, NY, 14136/716-934-2578
Specialties: Working and using straight knives of his design or to customer specs. **Patterns:** Drop-point hunters, utility/camp knives and skinners. **Technical:** Grinds 440C, ATS-34 and O1. Prefers natural wood but will use Micarta, etc., for strength. **Prices:** Start at $75. **Remarks:** Spare-time maker; first knife sold in 1990. **Mark:** First name.

PATTERSON, ALAN W., Rt. 3, Box 131, Hayesville, NC, 28904/704-389-9103
Specialties: Working straight knives and folders of his design or to customer specs; period pieces. **Patterns:** Forged knives, swords, tomahawks and folders. **Technical:** Damascus, cable and tool steels. Some custom leatherwork; wife offers scrimshaw. **Prices:** $125 to $5,000. **Remarks:** Full-time maker; first knife sold in 1990. **Mark:** Patterson Forge.

PATTON, DICK & ROB, 206F W. 38th St., Garden City, ID, 83714/208-395-0896

PAULO R, FERNANDES, R Raposo Tavares, 213, Lengois Paulista, SP, 18680, BRAZIL, /014-2634892
Specialties: An aprentice of Josè Alberto Paschoarelli, his designs are heavily besed on the later designs. **Technical:** Grinds tool steels and stainless steels. Part-time knifemakers for one year now. **Prices:** Start from $100. **Stamp:** P.R.F.

custom knifemakers

PAVACK, DON, Elk Meadow Ranch, Leo Rt., Hanna, WY, 82327/307-325-9245
Specialties: Working straight knives. Will work with customer designs. **Patterns:** Hunters and fillet knives; folders. **Technical:** Grinds ATS-34, 440C, 154CM and Damascus steel. Prefers natural handle materials; uses Micarta and diamond wood. **Prices:** $95 to $2,000. **Mark:** Signature and initials.

PEAGLER, RUSS, P.O. Box 1314, Moncks Corner, SC, 29461/803-761-1008
Specialties: Traditional working straight knives of his design and to customer specs. **Patterns:** Hunters, fighters, boots. **Technical:** Hollow-grinds 440C, ATS-34 and O1; uses Damascus steel. Prefers bone handles. **Prices:** $85 to $300; some to $500. **Remarks:** Spare-time maker; first knife sold in 1983. **Mark:** Initials.

PEASE, W.D., Rt. 2 Box 37AA, Ewing, KY, 41039/606-845-0387
Specialties: Display-quality working straight knives and folders. **Patterns:** Fighters, tantos and boots; locking folders and interframes. **Technical:** Grinds 440C, ATS-34 and commercial Damascus; has own side-release lock system. **Prices:** $300 to $500; some to $1,500. **Remarks:** Full-time maker; first knife sold in 1970. **Mark:** First and middle initials, last name.

PEELE, BRYAN, 219 Ferry St., P.O. Box 1363, Thompson Falls, MT, 59873/406-827-4633
Specialties: Fancy working and using knives of his design. **Patterns:** Hunters, Bowies and fighters. **Technical:** Grinds 440C, ATS-34, D2, O1 and commerical Damascus. **Prices:** $110 to $300; some to $900. **Remarks:** Part-time maker; first knife sold in 1985. **Mark:** The Elk Rack, full name, city, state.

PENDLETON, LLOYD, 24581 Shake Ridge Rd., Volcano, CA, 95689/209-296-3353
Specialties: Contemporary working knives in standard patterns. **Patterns:** Hunters, fighters and boots. **Technical:** Grinds 154CM and ATS-34; mirror finishes. **Prices:** $300 to $700; some to $2,000. **Remarks:** Full-time maker; first knife sold in 1973. **Mark:** First initial, last name logo, city and state.

PENDRAY, ALFRED H., 13950 NE 20th St, Williston, FL, 32696/352-528-6124
Specialties: Working straight knives and folders; period pieces. **Patterns:** Fighters and hunters, axes, camp knives and tomahawks. **Technical:** Forges Wootz steel; makes his own Damascus; makes traditional knives from old files and rasps. **Prices:** $125 to $1,000; some to $3,500. **Remarks:** Part-time maker; first knife sold in 1954. **Mark:** Last intial in horseshoe logo.

PENNINGTON, C.A., 137 Riverlea Estate Dr., Stewarts Gully, Christchurch 9, NEW ZEALAND, /0064 33237292
Specialties: Classic working and collectors knives. Folders a specialty. **Patterns:** Classical styling for hunters and collectors. **Technical:** Forges his own all tool steel Damascus. Grinds 02 when requested. **Prices:** $240 to $2,000. **Remarks:** Full-time maker; first knife sold in 1988. **Mark:** Name, country. **Other:** color brochure $3.

PEPIOT, STEPHAN, 73 Cornwall Blvd., Winnipeg, Man., CANADA, R3J-1E9/204-888-1499
Specialties: Working straight knives in standard patterns. **Patterns:** Hunters and camp knives. **Technical:** Grinds 440C and Industrial hacksaw blades. **Prices:** $75 to $125. **Remarks:** Spare-time maker; first knife sold in 1982. Not currently taking orders. **Mark:** PEP.

PERRY, CHRIS, 1654 W. Birch, Fresno, CA, 93711/209-498-2342
Specialties: Traditional working/using straight knives of his design. **Patterns:** Boots, hunters and utility/camp knives. **Technical:** Grinds ATS-34 and 416 ss fittings. **Prices:** $190 to $225. **Remarks:** Spare-time maker. **Mark:** Name above city and state.

PERRY, JOHN, 9 South Harrell Rd., Mayflower, AR, 72106/501-470-3043
Specialties: Investment grade and working folders; some straight knives. **Patterns:** Front and rear lock folders, liner locks and hunters. **Technical:** Grinds CPM440V, D2 and Damascus. Offers filework. **Prices:** $250 to $750; some to $950. **Remarks:** Part-time maker; first knife sold in 1990. Doing business as Perry Custom Knives. **Mark:** Initials or last name in high relief set in a diamond shape.

PERSSON, CONNY, PL 605, 820 50 Loos, SWEDEN, /+46 657 10305
Mosaic Damascus.

PETEAN, FRANCISCO AND MAURICIO, R. Dr.Carlos de Carvalho Rosa, 52, Centro, Birigui, SP-16200-000, BRAZIL, /0186-424786
Specialties: Classic knives to customer specs. **Patterns:** Bowies, boots, fighters, hunters and utility knives. **Technical:** Grinds D6, 440C and high carbon steels. Prefers natural handle material. **Prices:** $70 to $500. **Remarks:** Full-time maker; first knife sold in 1985. **Mark:** Last name, hand made.

PETERSEN, DAN L., 3015 SW Clark Ct., Topeka, KS, 66604/
Specialties: Period pieces and forged integral hilts on hunters and fighters. **Patterns:** Texas style Bowies, boots and hunters in high carbon and Damascus steel. **Technical:** Austempers forged high-carbon blades. **Prices:** $200 to $3,000. **Remarks:** First knife sold in 1978. **Mark:** Stylized initials, MS.

PETERSON, ELDON G., 260 Haugen Heights Rd., Whitefish, MT, 59937/406-862-2204
Specialties: Fancy and working folders, any size. **Patterns:** Lockback interframes, integral bolster folders, liner locks, and two-bladers. **Technical:** Grinds 440C and ATS-34. Offers gold inlay work, gem stone inlays and engraving. **Prices:** $285 to $5,000. **Remarks:** Full-time maker; first knife sold in 1974. **Mark:** Name, city and state.

PETERSON, CHRIS, Box 143, 2175 W. Rockyford, Salina, UT, 84654/801-529-7194
Specialties: Working straight knives of his design. **Patterns:** Large fighters, boots, hunters and some display pieces. **Technical:** Forges O1 and meteor. Makes and sells his own Damascus. Engraves, scrimshaws and inlays. **Prices:** $150 to $600; some to $1,500. **Remarks:** Full-time maker; first knife sold in 1986. **Mark:** A drop in a circle with a line through it.

PHILIPPE, D A, 295 Holmes Rd, Pittsfield, MA, 01201/413-448-2226
Specialties: Traditional working straight knives. **Patterns:** Hunters, trout & bird, camp knives etc. **Technical:** Grinds ATS-34, 440c, A-2, Damascus, flat and hollow ground. Exotic woods and antler handles. Brass, nickel, silver and stainless components. **Prices:** $95 - $500. **Remarks:** Part-time maker, first knife sold in 1984. **Mark:** First initial, last name over city & state.

PHILLIPS, SCOTT C, 671 California Rd, Gouverneur, NY, 13642/315-287-1280
Specialties: Fixed blade hunters, boot knives, Bowies, buck skinners (hand forged & stock removal). **Technical:** 440C, 01, W2, 5160, 1095 & 52100. **Prices:** Start at $100. **Remarks:** Part-time maker; first knife sold in 1993. **Mark:** First & middle initials, last name, year made.

PHILLIPS, RANDY, 759 E. Francis St., Ontario, CA, 91761/909-923-4381
Specialties: Hunters, collector-grade liner locks and high-art daggers. **Technical:** Grinds D2, 440C and 154CM; embellishes. **Prices:** Start at $200. **Remarks:** Part-time maker; first knife sold in 1981. Not currently taking orders. **Mark:** Name, city and state in eagle head.

PICKENS, SELBERT, Rt. 1, Box 216, Liberty, WV, 25124/304-586-2190
Specialties: Using knives. **Patterns:** Standard sporting knives. **Technical:** Stainless steels; stock removal method. **Prices:** Moderate. **Remarks:** Part-time maker. **Mark:** Name.

PIENAAR, CONRAD, 19A Milner Rd., Bloemfontein 9300, SOUTH AFRICA, /051 436 4180
Specialties: Fancy working and using straight knives and folders of his design, to customer specs and in standard patterns. **Patterns:** Hunters, locking folders, cleavers, kitchen and utility/camp knives. **Technical:** Grinds 12C27, D2 and ATS-34. Uses some Damascus. Scrimshaws; inlays gold. Knives come with wooden box and custom-made leather sheath. **Prices:** $300 to $1,000. **Remarks:** Part-time maker; first knife sold in 1981. Doing business as C.P. Knifemaker. **Mark:** Initials and serial number.

PIERCE, HAROLD L., 106 Lyndon Lane, Louisville, KY, 40222/502-429-5136
Specialties: Working straight knives, some fancy. **Patterns:** Big fighters and Bowies. **Technical:** Grinds D2, 440C, 154CM; likes sub-hilts. **Prices:** $150 to $450; some to $1,200. **Remarks:** Full-time maker; first knife sold in 1982. **Mark:** Last name with knife through the last initial.

PIERGALLINI, DANIEL E., 4011 N. Forbes Rd., Plant City, FL, 33565/813-754-3908
Specialties: Traditional and fancy straight knives and folders of my design or to customer's specs. **Patterns:** Hunters, fighters, three-fingered skinners, fillet, working and camp knives. **Technical:** Grinds 440C, O1, D2, ATS-34, some Damascus, and usually natural handle material; forges his own mokume. Uses natural handle material. **Prices:** $150 to $500; some to $1,200. **Remarks:** Part-time maker; sold first knife in 1994. **Mark:** Last name, city, state or last name in script.

PIESNER, DEAN, 30 King St., St. Jacobs, Ont., CANADA, N0B 2N0/519-664-3622
Specialties: Classic and period pieces of his design and to customer specs. **Patterns:** Bowies, skinners, fighters and swords. **Technical:** Forges 5160, 52100, steel Damascus and nickel-steel Damascus. Makes own mokume gane with copper, brass and nickel silver. Silver wire inlays in wood. **Prices:** Start at $125. **Remarks:** Full-time maker; first knife sold in 1990. **Mark:** First initial, last name, JS.

PIOREK, JAMES S., P.O. Box 733, Lakeside, MT, 59922/406-844-2620
Specialties: Custom tailored and (SCP) semi custom production, advanced concealment blades; sheaths and total body harness systems. **Patterns:** Tactical/personal defense fighters, swords, utility and custom patterns. **Technical:** Grinds A2; heat-treats. Sheaths: Kydex or Kydex-lined leather laminated. Exotic materials available. **Prices:** $275 to $10,000. **Remarks:** Full-time maker. Doing business as Blade Rigger. **Mark:** Initials with abstract cutting edge.

PITT, DAVID F., P.O. Box 1564, Pleasanton, CA, 94566/415-846-9751
Specialties: Working straight knives. **Patterns:** Knives for deer and elk hunters, including hatchets and cleavers; small gut hook hunters and capers. **Technical:** Grinds A2, 440C and 154CM. **Prices:** $100 to $200; some to $450. **Remarks:** Full-time maker; first knife sold in 1972. **Mark:** Bear paw with name.

PLUNKETT, RICHARD, 29 Kirk Rd., West Cornwall, CT, 06796/860-672-3419; Toll free: 888-KNIVES-8
Specialties: Traditional, fancy folders and straight knives of his design. **Patterns:** Slip-joint folders and small straight knives. **Technical:** Grinds O1 and stainless steel. Offers many different file patterns. **Prices:** $150 to $450. **Remarks:** Full-time maker; first knife sold in 1994. **Mark:** Signature and date under handle scales.

POAG, JAMES, RR 1, Box 212A, Grayville, IL, 62844/618-375-7106
Specialties: Working straight knives and folders; period pieces; of his design or to customer specs. **Patterns:** Bowies and camp knives, lockers and slip-joints. **Technical:** Forges and grinds stainless steels and others; provides serious leather; offers embellishments; scrimshaws, engraves and does leather work for other makers. **Prices:** $65 to $1,200. **Remarks:** Full-time maker; first knife sold in 1967. **Mark:** Name.

POGREBA, LARRY, Box 861, Lyons, CO, 80540/303-823-6691
Specialties: Steel and Damascus lightweight hunters; kitchen knives. **Technical:** Forges, grinds, Damascus since 1978. **Prices:** $40 to $1,000. **Remarks:** Part-time maker; first knife sold in 1976. Doing business as Cadillac Blacksmithing. **Mark:** Initials.

POLK, CLIFTON, 4625 Webber Creek Rd., Van Buren, AR, 72956/501-474-3828
Specialties: Fancy working straight knives and folders. **Patterns:** Locking folders, slip-joints, two-blades, straight knives. **Technical:** Offers 440C, D2 ATS-34 and Damascus. **Prices:** $150 to $3,000. **Remarks:** Full-time maker. **Mark:** Last name.

POLKOWSKI, AL, 8 Cathy Ct., Chester, NJ, 07930/908-879-6030
Specialties: High-tech straight knives and folders for adventurers and professionals. **Patterns:** Fighters, side-lock folders, boots and concealment knives. **Technical:** Grinds D2 and ATS-34; features satin and bead-blast finishes; Kydex sheaths. **Prices:** Start at $100. **Remarks:** Full-time maker; first knife sold in 1985. **Mark:** Full name, Handmade.

POLZIEN, DON, 1912 Inler Suite-L, Lubbock, TX, 79407/806-791-0766
Specialties: Traditional Japanese-style blades; restores antique Japanese swords, scabbards and fittings. **Patterns:** Hunters, fighters, one-of-a-kind art knives. **Technical:** 1045-1050 carbon steels, 440C, D2, ATS-34, standard and cable Damascus. **Prices:** $150 to $2,500. **Remarks:** Full-time maker. First knife sold in 1990. **Mark:** Oriental characters inside square border.

PONZIO, DOUG, 3212 93rd St., Kenosha, WI, 53142/414-694-3188

POOLE, MARVIN O., P.O. Box 5234, Anderson, SC, 29623/803-225-5970
Specialties: Traditional working/using straight knives and folders of his design and in standard patterns. **Patterns:** Bowies, fighters, hunters, locking folders, bird and trout knives. **Technical:** Grinds 440C, D2, ATS-34. **Prices:** $50 to $150; some to $750. **Remarks:** Part-time maker; first knife sold in 1980. **Mark:** First initial, last name, year, serial number.

POOLE, STEVE L., 200 Flintlock Trail, Stockbridge, GA, 30281/770-474-9154
Specialties: Traditional working and using straight knives and folders of his design, to customer specs and in standard patterns. **Patterns:** Bowies, fighters, hunters, utility and locking folders. **Technical:** Grinds ATS-34 and 440V; buys Damascus. Heat-treats; offers leatherwork. **Prices:** $85 to $350; some to $800. **Remarks:** Spare-time maker; first knife sold in 1991. **Mark:** Stylized first and last initials.

POPLIN, JAMES L., 103 Oak St., Washington, GA, 30673/404-678-2729
Specialties: Contemporary hunters. **Patterns:** Hunters and boots. **Technical:** Hollow-grinds. **Prices:** Reasonable. **Mark:** POP.

POPP SR., STEVE, 6573 Winthrop Dr., Fayetteville, NC, 28311/910-822-3151
Specialties: Working straight knives. **Patterns:** Hunters, Bowies and fighters. **Technical:** Forges and grinds his own Damascus, O1, L6 and spring steel. **Prices:** $75 to $600; some to $1,000. **Remarks:** Full-time maker; first knife sold in 1984. **Mark:** Initials and last name.

POSKOCIL, HELMUT, Oskar Czeijastrasse 2, A-3340 Waidhofen/Ybbs, AUSTRIA, /0043-7442-54519
Specialties: High-art and classic straight knives and folders of his design. **Patterns:** Bowies, daggers, hunters and locking folders. **Technical:** Grinds ATS-34 and stainless and carbon Damascus. Hardwoods, fossil ivory, horn and amber for handle material; silver wire and gold inlays; silver butt caps. Offers engraving and scrimshaw. **Prices:** $350 to $850; some to $3,500. **Remarks:** Part-time maker; first knife sold in 1991. **Mark:** Name.

POSNER, BARRY E., 12501 Chandler Blvd., Suite 104, N. Hollywood, CA, 91607/818-752-8005
Specialties: Working/using straight knives. **Patterns:** Hunters, kitchen and utility/camp knives. **Technical:** Grinds ATS-34; forges 1095 and nickel. **Prices:** $95 to $400. **Remarks:** Part-time maker; first knife sold in 1987. Doing business as Posner Knives. Supplier of finished mosaic handle pin stock. **Mark:** First and middle initials, last name.

POSTON, ALVIN, 1197 Bass Rd., Pamplico, SC, 29583/803-493-0066
Specialties: Working straight knives. **Patterns:** Hunters, Bowies and fishing knives; some miniatures. **Technical:** Grinds 154CM and ATS-34. **Prices:** Start at $100. **Remarks:** Part-time maker; first knife sold in 1979. **Mark:** Last name.

POTIER, TIMOTHY F., P.O. Box 711, Oberlin, LA, 70655/318-639-2229
Specialties: Classic working and using straight knives to customer specs; some collectible. **Patterns:** Hunters, Bowies, utility/camp knives and belt axes. **Technical:** Forges carbon steel and his own Damascus; offers filework. **Prices:** $300 to $1,800; some to $4,000. **Remarks:** Part-time maker; first knife sold in 1981. **Mark:** Last name, MS.

POTOCKI, ROGER, Route 1, Box 333A, Goreville, IL, 62939/618-995-9502

POTTER, FRANK, 25 Renfrew Ave, Middletown, RI, 02842/401-846-5352
Specialties: Collector-grade folders with unique mechanisms. **Patterns:** Locking folders with my own lock design. **Technical:** Grinds Damascus, handle material, ivory & pearl. **Prices:** $1,000 to $3,000. **Remarks:** Full-time maker, first knife sold 1996. **Mark:** Frank Potter

POYTHRESS, JOHN, P.O. Box 585, 625 Freedom St., Swainsboro, GA, 30401/912-237-9233
Specialties: Traditional working and using straight knives of his design or to customer specs. **Patterns:** Hunters. **Technical:** Uses 440C, ATS-34 and D2. **Prices:** $75 to $250; some to $400. **Remarks:** Spare-time maker; first knife sold in 1983. **Mark:** J.W. Poythress Handcrafted, serial number.

custom knifemakers

PRESSBURGER, RAMON, 59 Driftway Rd., Howell, NJ, 07731/908-363-0816
Specialties: Traditional working knives to customer specs. **Patterns:** Hunters, skinners and utility/camp knives. **Technical:** Uses ATS-34, D2 and BG 42 and high-carbon steels. **Prices:** $70 to $500. **Remarks:** Full-time maker; first knife sold in 1970. **Mark:** NA.

PRICE, STEVE, 899 Ida Lane, Kamloops, BC, CANADA, V2B 6V2/604-579-8932
Specialties: Working knives and fantasy pieces of his design or to customer specs. **Patterns:** Hunters, axes, tantos, survival knives, locking folders and some miniatures. **Technical:** Grinds D2, 440C and ATS-34; buys Damascus. **Prices:** $90 to $350; some to $1200. **Remarks:** Full-time maker; first knife sold in 1982. **Mark:** First initial, last name.

PRICE, JOEL HIRAM, RR1, Box 18GG, Interlochen, FL, 32148-9709/
Specialties: Working straight knives to customer specs. **Patterns:** Variety of straight knives. **Technical:** Forges and grinds W2, O1, D2 and 440C--customer choice; buys Damascus. All knives have filework. **Prices:** $50 to $250; some $750 and higher. **Remarks:** Full-time maker; first knife sold in 1984. **Mark:** Hiram Knives in script.

PRICE, TIMMY, P.O.Box 906, Blairsville, GA, 30514/706-745-5111

PRITCHARD, RON, 613 Crawford Ave., Dixon, IL, 61021/815-284-6005
Specialties: Plain and fancy working knives. **Patterns:** Variety of straight knives, locking folders, interframes and miniatures. **Technical:** Grinds 440C, 154CM and commercial Damascus. **Prices:** $100 to $200; some to $1,500. **Remarks:** Part-time maker; first knife sold in 1979. **Mark:** Name and city.

PROVENZANO, JOSEPH D., 3024 Ivy Place, Chalmette, LA, 70043/504-279-3154
Specialties: Working straight knives and folders in standard patterns. **Patterns:** Hunters, Bowies, folders, camp and fishing knives. **Technical:** Grinds ATS-34, 440C, 154CM, CPM 4400, CPM420W and Damascus. Hollow-grinds hunters. **Prices:** $90 to $300; some to $600. **Remarks:** Part-time maker; first knife sold in 1980. **Mark:** Joe-Pro.

PUGH, JIM, P.O. Box 711, Azle, TX, 76020/817-444-2679
Specialties: Fancy/embellished limited editions by request. **Patterns:** 5- to 7-inch Bowies, wildlife art pieces, hunters, daggers and fighters; some commemoratives. **Technical:** Multi color transplanting in solid 18K gold, fine gems; grinds 440C and ATS-34. Offers engraving, fancy file etching and leather sheaths for wildlife art pieces. Ivory and cocobolo handle material on limited editions. Designs animal head buttcaps and paws or bear claw guards; sterling silver heads and guards. **Prices:** $60,000 to $80,000 each in the Big Five 2000 edition.. **Remarks:** Full-time maker; first knife sold in 1970. **Mark:** Pugh (old English).

PULIS, VLADIMIR, Horna Ves 43/B/25, 96701 Kremnica, SLOVAKIA, /421-857-6757-x214
Specialties: Fancy and high-art straight knives of his design. **Patterns:** Daggers and hunters. **Technical:** Forges Damast steel. All work done by hand. **Prices:** $250 to $3,000; some to $10,000. **Remarks:** Full-time maker; first knife sold in 1990. **Mark:** Initials in octagon.

PULLEN, MARTIN, 1701 Broken Bow Rd., Granbury, TX, 76049/817-573-1784
Specialties: Working straight knives; period pieces. **Patterns:** Fighters, Bowies and daggers; locking folders. **Technical:** Grinds D2, 440C, ATS-34 and 154CM. **Prices:** Start at $150. **Remarks:** Full-time maker; first knife sold in 1978. **Mark:** Last name.

PULLIAM, MORRIS C., 560 Jeptha Knob Rd., Shelbyville, KY, 40065/502-633-2261
Specialties: Working knives; classic Bowies. **Patterns:** Bowies, hunters, Fort Meigs axes and tomahawks. **Technical:** Forges L6, W2, 1095, Damascus and nickel-sheet and bar 320 TO 640 layer Damascus. **Prices:** $165 to $1,200. **Remarks:** Full-time maker; first knife sold in 1974. Makes knives for Native American festivals. Doing business as Knob Hill Forge. **Mark:** Last name or last initial.

PURSLEY, AARON, BOX 1037, Big Sandy, MT, 59520/406-378-3200
Specialties: Fancy working knives. **Patterns:** Locking folders, straight hunters and daggers, personal wedding knives and letter openers. **Technical:** Grinds O1 and 440C; engraves. **Prices:** $300 to $600; some to $1,500. **Remarks:** Full-time maker; first knife sold in 1975. **Mark:** Initials connected with year.

PUTNAM, DONALD S., 590 Wolcott Hill Rd., Wethersfield, CT, 06109/203-563-9718
Specialties: Working knives for the hunter and fisherman. **Patterns:** His design or to customer specs. **Technical:** Uses stock removal method, O1, W2, D2, ATS-34, 154CM, 440C and CPM REX 20; stainless steel Damascus on request. **Prices:** NA. **Remarks:** Full-time maker; first knife sold in 1985. **Mark:** Last name with a knife outline.

q

QUARTON, BARR, P.O. Box 4335, McCall, ID, 83638/208-634-3641
Specialties: Plain and fancy working knives; period pieces. **Patterns:** Hunters, tantos and swords. **Technical:** Forges and grinds 154CM, ATS-34 and his own Damascus. **Prices:** $180 to $450; some to $4,500. **Remarks:** Part-time maker; first knife sold in 1978. Doing business as Barr Custom Knives. **Mark:** First name with bear logo.

QUATTLEBAUM, CRAIG, 2 Ridgewood Ln., Searcy, AR, 72143/
Specialties: Traditional straight knives and one-of-a-kind knives of his design; period pieces. **Patterns:** Bowies and fighters. **Technical:** Forges 5168, 52100 and own Damascus. **Prices:** $100 to $1,200. **Remarks:** Part-time maker; first knife sold in 1988. **Mark:** Stylized initials.

QUICK, MIKE, 23 Locust Ave., Kearny, NJ, 07032/201-991-6580
Specialties: Traditional working/using straight knives. **Patterns:** Bowies. **Technical:** 440C and ATS-34 for blades; Micarta, wood and stag for handles.

r

RACHLIN, LESLIE S., 1200 W. Church St., Elmira, NY, 14905/607-733-6889
Specialties: Classic and working/using straight knives and folders of his design. **Patterns:** Hunters, locking folders and utility/camp knives. **Technical:** Grinds 440C and Damascus. **Prices:** $110 to $200; some to $450. **Remarks:** Spare-time maker; first knife sold in 1989. Doing business as Tinkermade Knives. **Mark:** Stamped initials or Tinkermade, city and state.

RADOS, JERRY F., 7523 E 5000 N Rd., Grant Park, IL, 60940/815-472-3350
Specialties: Deluxe period pieces. **Patterns:** Hunters, fighters, locking folders, daggers and camp knives. **Technical:** Forges and grinds his own Damascus which he sells commercially; makes pattern-welded Turkish Damascus. **Prices:** Start at $900. **Remarks:** Full-time maker; first knife sold in 1981. **Mark:** Last name.

RAGSDALE, JAMES D., 3002 Arabian Woods Dr., Lithonia, GA, 30038/770-482-6739
Specialties: Fancy and embellished working knives of his design or to customer specs. **Patterns:** Hunters, folders and fighters. **Technical:** Grinds 440C, ATS-34 and A2. **Prices:** $100 to $350; some to $800. **Remarks:** Full-time maker; first knife sold in 1984. **Mark:** Fish symbol with name above, town below.

RAINVILLE, RICHARD, 126 Cockle Hill Rd., Salem, CT, 06420/860-859-2776
Specialties: Traditional working straight knives. **Patterns:** Outdoor knives, including fishing knives. **Technical:** L6, 400C, ATS-34. **Prices:** $100 to $800. **Remarks:** Full-time maker; first knife sold in 1982. **Mark:** Name, city, state in oval logo.

RALPH, DARREL, 4185 S St Rt 605, Galena, OH, 43021/740-965-9970
Specialties: Fancy, high-art, high-tech, collectible straight knives and folders of his design and to customer specs; unique mechanisms, some disassemble. **Patterns:** Daggers, fighters and swords. **Technical:** Forges his own Damascus, nickel and high carbon. Uses mokume and Damascus; mosaics and special patterns. Engraves and heat-treats. Prefers pearl, ivory and abolone handle material; uses stones and jewels. **Prices:** $250 to six figures. **Remarks:** Full-time maker; first knife sold in 1987. Doing business as Briar Knives. **Mark:** DDR.

RAMEY, MARSHALL F., P.O. Box 2589, West Helena, AR, 72390/501-572-7436
Specialties: Traditional working knives. **Patterns:** Designs military combat knives; makes butterfly folders, camp knives and miniatures. **Technical:** Grinds D2 and 440C. **Prices:** $100 to $500. **Remarks:** Full-time maker; first knife sold in 1978. **Mark:** Name with ram's head.

RANDALL, BILL, 765 W. Limberlost #30, Tucson, AZ, 85705/502-887-9776
Specialties: High-art and period pieces of his design. **Patterns:** Fighters, hunters and neo-tribal. **Technical:** Forges A6 and carbon steel; forges and grinds Damascus. Hammer-finish on neo-tribal style knives. Uses natural handle material; makes own sheaths. **Prices:** $85 to $250; some to $500. **Remarks:** Part-time maker; first knife sold in 1995. Doing business as Bill Randall Knives. **Mark:** Last name.

RANDALL MADE KNIVES, P.O. Box 1988, Orlando, FL, 32802/407-855-8075
Specialties: Working straight knives. **Patterns:** Hunters, fighters and Bowies. **Technical:** Forges and grinds O1 and 440B. **Prices:** $65 to $250; some to $450. **Remarks:** Full-time maker; first knife sold in 1937. **Mark:** Randall, city and state in scimitar logo.

RANKL, CHRISTIAN, Possenhofenerstr. 33, 81476 Munchen, GERMANY, /0171-3662679
Specialties: Tail-lock knives. **Patterns:** Fighters, hunters and locking folders. **Technical:** Grinds ATS-34, 4034 and stainless Damascus by F. Schneider. **Prices:** $450 to $950; some to $2,000. **Remarks:** Full-time maker; first knife sold in 1989. **Mark:** Electrochemical etching on blade.

RAPP, STEVEN J., 7479 S. Ramanee Dr., Midvale, UT, 84047/801-567-9553
Specialties: Gold quartz,; mosaic handles. **Patterns:** Daggers, Bowies, fighters and San Francisco knives. **Technical:** Hollow- and flat-grinds 440C and Damascus. **Prices:** Start at $500. **Remarks:** Full-time maker; first knife sold in 1981. **Mark:** Name and state.

RAPPAZZO, RICHARD, 142 Dunsbach Ferry Rd., Cohoes, NY, 12047/518-783-6843
Specialties: Damascus locking folders and straight knives. **Patterns:** Folders, dirks, fighters and tantos in original and traditional designs. **Technical:** Hand-forges all blades; specializes in Damascus; uses only natural handle materials. **Prices:** $400 to $1,500. **Remarks:** Part-time maker; first knife sold in 1985. **Mark:** Name, date, serial number.

RARDON, ARCHIE F., 1589 SE Price Dr, Polo, MO, 64671/660-354-2330
Specialties: Working knives. **Patterns:** Hunters, Bowies and miniatures. **Technical:** Grinds O1, D2, 440C, ATS-34, cable and Damascus. **Prices:** $50 to $500. **Remarks:** Part-time maker. **Mark:** Boar hog.

RARDON, A.D., 1589 S.E. Price Dr., Polo, MO, 64671/660-354-2330
Specialties: Folders, miniatures. **Patterns:** Hunters, buckskinners, Bowies, miniatures and daggers. **Technical:** Grinds O1, D2, 440C and ATS-34. **Prices:** $150 to $2,000; some higher. **Remarks:** Full-time maker; first knife sold in 1954. **Mark:** Fox logo.

RAY, ALAN W., P.O. Box 479, Lovelady, TX, 75851/409-636-2350
Specialties: Working straight knives of his design. **Patterns:** Hunters, camp knives, steak knives and carving sets. **Technical:** Forges L6 and 5160 for straight knives; grinds D2 and 440C for folders and kitchen cutlery. **Prices:** $200 to $500. **Remarks:** Full-time maker; first knife sold in 1979. **Mark:** Stylized initials.

RECE, CHARLES V., P.O. Box 868, Paw Creek, NC, 28130/704-391-0209
Specialties: Traditional straight knives and presentation knives. **Patterns:** Bowies, hunters and presentation knives. **Technical:** Grinds ATS-34, D2 and 440C. Scrimshawed handles are standard. **Prices:** $150 to $400. **Remarks:** Limited-production maker; first knife sold in 1986. Doing business as Uwharrie Rattler Knives and Wildwood Art. **Mark:** Engraved timber rattler.

RED, VERNON, 2020 Benton Cove, Conway, AR, 72032/501-450-7284
Specialties: Traditional straight knives and folders of my design and special orders. Most are one of a kind. **Patterns:** Hunters, fighters, Bowies, fillet, folders & lock-blades. **Technical:** Hollow Grind 90%; use 440C, D-2, ATS-34 and Damascus. Uses natural woods, pakka, pearl, horn, stag, ivory & bone. **Prices:** $125 and up. **Remarks:** Part-time maker; first knife sold in 1992. Do scrimshaw on ivory & micarta. **Mark:** Last name. Other: aka Custom Made Knives by Vernon Red.

REDDIEX, BILL, 27 Galway Ave., Palmerston North, NEW ZEALAND, /06-357-0383
Specialties: Collector-grade working straight knives. **Patterns:** Traditional-style Bowies and drop-point hunters. **Technical:** Grinds 440C, D2 and O1; offers variety of grinds and finishes. **Prices:** $130 to $750. **Remarks:** Full-time maker; first knife sold in 1980. **Mark:** Last name around kiwi bird logo.

REED, DAVE, Box 132, Brimfield, MA, 01010/413-245-3661
Specialties: Traditional styles. Makes knives from chains, rasps, gears, etc. **Patterns:** Bush swords, hunters, working minis, camp and utility knives. **Technical:** Forges 1075 and his own Damascus. **Prices:** Start at $50. **Remarks:** Part-time maker; first knife sold in 1970. **Mark:** Initials.

REED, DEL, 13765 SW Parkway, Beaverton, OR, 97005/
Specialties: Unusual configurations. **Patterns:** Swing-blade knives. **Technical:** Grinds stainless steel. **Prices:** $100 to $125. **Remarks:** First knife sold in 1988. **Mark:** ORION.

REEVE, CHRIS, 11624 W. President Dr., Ste. B, Boise, ID, 83713/208-375-0367
Specialties: Originator and designer of the One Piece range of fixed blade utility knives and of the Sebenza Integral Lock folding knives made by Chris Reeve Knives. Currently makes only one or two pieces per year himself. **Patterns:** Working and art folders; variety of fixed-blade shapes in one-piece design. **Technical:** Grinds BG-42, Damascus and other materials to his own design. **Prices:** $1000 and upwards. **Remarks:** Full-time in knife business; first knife sold in 1982. **Mark:** Signature and date.

REEVES, WINFRED M., P.O. Box 300, West Union, SC, 29696/803-638-6121
Specialties: Working straight knives; some elaborate pieces. **Patterns:** Hunters, tantos and fishing knives. **Technical:** Grinds D2, 440C and ATS-34. Does not solder joints; does not use buffer unless requested. **Prices:** $75 to $150; some to $300. **Remarks:** Part-time maker; first knife sold in 1975. **Mark:** Last name, Walhalla, state.

REGGIO JR., SIDNEY J., P.O. Box 851, Sun, LA, 70463/504-886-5886
Specialties: Miniature classic and fancy straight knives of his design or in standard patterns. **Patterns:** Fighters, hunters and utility/camp knives. **Technical:** Grinds 440C, ATS-34 and commercial Damascus. Engraves; scrimshaws; offers filework. Hollow grinds most blades. Prefers natural handle material. Offers handmade sheaths. **Prices:** $85 to $250; some to $500. **Remarks:** Part-time maker; first knife sold in 1988. Doing business as Sterling Workshop. **Mark:** Initials.

REH, BILL, 2061 Tomlinson Rd., Caro, MI, 48723/517-673-1195
Specialties: Traditional and working/using straight knives of his design and to customer specs. **Patterns:** Boots, hunters and Bowies. **Technical:** Stock removal; uses all kinds of steel. **Prices:** $100 to $180. **Remarks:** Spare-time maker; first knife sold in 1981. Doing business as Reh Custom Knives. **Mark:** Last name in sun-ray logo.

REMINGTON, DAVID W., 12928 Morrow Rd, Gentry, AR, 72734-9781/501-846-3526
Specialties: Fancy and traditional straight knives of his design and to customer specs. **Patterns:** Bowies, daggers and hunters. **Technical:** Grinds ATS-34, A2 and D2. Makes own twist and random-pattern Damascus. Wholesale D2, A2, stag and ossic sheephorn. Rope and thorn pattern filework; tapered tangs; heat treats. **Prices:** $65 to $250; some to $1,000. **Remarks:** Part-time maker; first knife sold in 1991. **Mark:** First and last name, Custom.

REPKE, MIKE, 4191 N. Euclid Ave., Bay City, MI, 48706/517-684-3111
Specialties: Traditional working and using straight knives of their design or to customer specs; classic knives; display knives. **Patterns:** Hunters, Bowies, skinners, fighters boots, axes and swords. **Technical:** Grind 440C. Offer variety of handle materials. **Prices:** $99 to $1,500. **Remarks:** Full-time makers. Doing business as Black Forest Blades. **Mark:** Knife logo.

custom knifemakers

REVERDY, PIERRE, 5 rue de l'egalite', 26100 Romans, FRANCE, /334 75 05 10 15
Specialties: Art knives; legend pieces. **Patterns:** Daggers, Bowies, hunters and other large patterns. **Technical:** Forges his Damascus and "poetique Damascus"; works with his own EDM machine to create any kind of pattern inside the steel with his own touch. **Prices:** $2000 and up. **Remarks:** Full-time maker; first knife sold in 1986. Nicole (wife) collaborates with enamels. **Mark:** Initials connected.

REVISHVILI, ZAZA, 2102 Linden Ave, Madison, WI, 53704 5303/
Specialties: Fancy/embellished and high-art straight knives and folders of his design. **Patterns:** Daggers, swords and locking folders. **Technical:** Uses Damascus; silver filigree inlay in wood; enameling. **Prices:** $1,000 to $9,000; some to $15,000. **Remarks:** Full-time maker; first knife sold in 1987. **Mark:** Initials, city.

REVISHVILI, ZAZA, P.O. Box 29, 125438 Moscow, RUSSIA, /718-628-91-98

REXROAT, KIRK, 527 Sweetwater Circle, Box 224, Wright, WY, 82732/307-464-0166
Specialties: Using and collectible straight knives and folders of his design or to customer specs. **Patterns:** Bowies, hunters, folders. **Technical:** Forges damascus patterns, mosaic and 42100. **Prices:** $400 and up. **Remarks:** Part-time maker, journeymansmith in the ABS; first knife sold in 1984. Doing business as Rexroat Knives. **Mark:** Last name.

REYNOLDS, JOHN C., #2 Andover, HC77, Gillette, WY, 82716/307-682-6076
Specialties: Working knives, some fancy. **Patterns:** Hunters, Bowies, tomahawks and buckskinners; some folders. **Technical:** Grinds D2, ATS34, 440C and I forge my own Damascus and Knifes now. Scrimshaws. **Prices:** $200 to $3,000. **Remarks:** Spare-time maker; first knife sold in 1969. **Mark:** On ground blades JC Reynolds Gillette,Wy, On forged blades, my initials make my mark-JCR.

REYNOLDS, DAVE, Rt. 2, Box 36, Harrisville, WV, 26362/304-643-2889
Specialties: Working straight knives of his design. **Patterns:** Bowies, kitchen and utility knives. **Technical:** Grinds and forges L6, 1095 and 440C. Heat-treats. **Prices:** $50 to $85; some to $175. **Remarks:** Full-time maker; first knife sold in 1980. Doing business as Terra-Gladius Knives. **Mark:** Mark on special orders only; serial number on all knives.

RHEA, DAVID, Rt. 1, Box 272, Lynnville, TN, 38472/615-363-5993
Specialties: High-art fantasy knives. **Patterns:** Fighters, Bowies, survival knives and locking folders. **Technical:** Grinds D2, 440C, 154CM and Damascus. Embellishes; offers precious stones, metals and ivory. **Prices:** $300 to $2,000 and higher. **Remarks:** Part-time maker; first knife sold in 1982. **Mark:** Last name.

RHO, NESTOR LORENZO, Primera Junta 589, (6000) Junin, Buenos Aires, ARGENTINA, /(0362) 32247
Specialties: Classic and fancy straight knives of his design. **Patterns:** Bowies, fighters and hunters. **Technical:** Grinds 420C, 440C and 1050. Offers semi-precious stones on handles, acid etching on blades and blade engraving. **Prices:** $60 to $300 some to $1,200. **Remarks:** Full-time maker; first knife sold in 1975. **Mark:** Name.

RHODES, JAMES D., 205 Woodpoint Ave., Hagerstown, MD, 21740/301-739-2657
Specialties: Traditional working and using straight knives of his design. **Patterns:** Bowies, fighters, hunters and kitchen knives. **Technical:** Forges 5160, 1085, and 9260; makes own Damascus. Hard edges, soft backs, dead soft tangs. Heat-treats. **Prices:** $150 to $350. **Remarks:** Part-time maker. **Mark:** Last name, JS.

RIAL, DOUGLAS, Rt. 2, Box 117A, Greenfield, TN, 38230/901-235-3994
Specialties: Working knives to customer specs; period pieces. **Patterns:** Hunters, fighters, boots, locking folders, slip-joints and miniatures. **Technical:** Grinds D2, 440C and 154CM. **Prices:** $60 to $100; some to $250. **Remarks:** Spare-time maker; first knife sold in 1978. **Mark:** Name and city.

RICARDO ROMANO, BERNARDES, R Cel Rennò, 1261, Itajuba MG 37500/55-31-6222524
Specialties: likes loveless styled knives. **Technical:** Grinds blades of most stainless and tools steels. Will work with any material the customer desires or supplies. **Prices:** $200. **Stamp:** Ramono over fencing sword.

RICE, ADRIENNE, P.O. Box 252, Lopez Island, WA, 98261/
Specialties: Folders and straight knives of her own and traditional designs; marine-oriented knives. **Patterns:** Traditional and neo-traditional folders; fillet and rigging knives; primitive inspired pieces. **Technical:** Grinds ATS-34, D2 and O1; forges old steel and Damascus. Uses natural handle materials. **Prices:** $150 to $750. **Remarks:** Full-time maker; first knife sold in 1981. Formerly Madrona Knives. **Mark:** Logo, name, handmade.

RICHARD, RON, 4875 Calaveras Ave., Fremont, CA, 94538/510-796-9767
Specialties: High-tech working straight knives of his design. **Patterns:** Bowies, swords and locking folders. **Technical:** Forges and grinds ATS-34, 154CM and 440V. All folders have dead-bolt button locks. **Prices:** $650 to $850; some to $1400. **Remarks:** Full-time maker; first knife sold in 1968. **Mark:** Full name.

RICHARDSON JR., PERCY, P.O. Box 973, Hemphill, TX, 75948/409-787-2279
Specialties: Traditional and working straight knives and folders in standard patterns and to customer specs. **Patterns:** Bowies, daggers, hunters, automatics, locking folders, slip-joints and utility/camp knives. **Technical:** Grinds ATS-34, 440C and D2. **Prices:** $125 to $600; some to $1,800. **Remarks:** Full-time maker; first knife sold in 1990. Doing business as Lone Star Custom Knives. **Mark:** Lone Star with last name across it.

RICHTER, JOHN C., 932 Bowling Green Trail, Chesapeake, VA, 23320/
Specialties: Hand-forged knives in original patterns. **Patterns:** Hunters, fighters, utility knives and other belt knives, folders, swords. **Technical:** Hand-forges high carbon and his own Damascus; makes mokume-gane. **Prices:** $75 to $1,500. **Remarks:** Part-time maker. **Mark:** Richter Forge.

RICHTER, SCOTT, 516 E. 2nd St., S. Boston, MA, 02127/617-269-4855
Specialties: Traditional working/using folders. **Patterns:** Locking folders, swords and kitchen knives. **Technical:** Grinds ATS-34, 5160 and A2. High-tech materials. **Prices:** $150 to $650; some to $1,500. **Remarks:** Full-time maker; first knife sold in 1991. Doing business as Richter Made. **Mark:** Last name, Made.

RICKE, DAVE, 1209 Adams, West Bend, WI, 53095/414-334-5739
Specialties: Working knives; period pieces. **Patterns:** Hunters, boots, Bowies; locking folders and slip-joints. **Technical:** Grinds ATS-34, A2, 440C and 154CM. **Prices:** $75 to $260; some to $1,200. **Remarks:** Part-time maker; first knife sold in 1976. **Mark:** Last name.

RIETVELD, BERTIE, P.O. Box 53, Magaliesburg 1791, SOUTH AFRICA, /27145-771294
Specialties: Damascus, Persian, art daggers, button-lock folders. **Patterns:** Mostly one-ofs. **Technical:** Work only in own stainless Damascus and other exotics. **Prices:** $350 to $3,000. **Remarks:** First knife made 1980, Chairman of SA Knifemakers Guild. **Mark:** Elephant with last name.

RIGNEY JR., WILLIE, 191 Colson Dr., Bronston, KY, 42518/606-679-4227
Specialties: High-tech period pieces and fancy working knives. **Patterns:** Fighters, boots, daggers and push knives. **Technical:** Grinds 440C and 154CM; buys Damascus. Most knives are embellished. **Prices:** $150 to $1,500; some to $10,000. **Remarks:** Full-time maker; first knife sold in 1970. **Mark:** First initial, last name.

RINKES, SIEGFRIED, Am Sportpl 2, D 91459, Markterlbach, GERMANY, /

RIZZI, RUSSELL J., 6 King Arthur's Ct., E. Setauket, NY, 11733/516-689-2698
Specialties: Fancy working and using straight knives and folders of his design or to customer specs. **Patterns:** Hunters, locking folders and fighters. **Technical:** Grinds 440C, D2 and commercial Damascus. **Prices:** $150 to $750; some to $2,500. **Remarks:** Part-time maker; first knife sold in 1990. **Mark:** Last name, Long Island, NY.

ROATH, DEAN, 3050 Winnipeg Dr., Baton Rouge, LA, 70819/504-272-5562
Specialties: Classic working knives; specifically turkey hunting knives. **Patterns:** Hunters, boating/sailing and trail knives. **Technical:** Grinds 440C and ATS-34. **Prices:** $200 to $500; some to $1,500. **Remarks:** Part-time maker; first knife sold in 1978. **Mark:** Name, city and state.

ROBBINS, HOWARD P., 1407 S. 217th Ave., Elkhorn, NE, 68022/402-289-4121
Specialties: High-tech working knives with clean designs, some fancy. **Patterns:** Folders, hunters and camp knives. **Technical:** Grinds 440C and ATS-34. Heat-treats; likes mirror finishes. Offers leatherwork. **Prices:** $100 to $500; some to $1,000. **Remarks:** Full-time maker; first knife sold in 1982. **Mark:** Name, city and state.

ROBERTS, MICHAEL, 601 Oakwood Dr., Clinton, MS, 39056/601-924-3154; Pager 601-978-8180
Specialties: Working and using knives in standard patterns and to customer specs. **Patterns:** Hunters, Bowies, tomahawks and fighters. **Technical:** Forges 5160, O1, 1095 and his own Damascus. Uses only natural handle materials. **Prices:** $145 to $500; some to $1,100. **Remarks:** Part-time maker; first knife sold in 1988. **Mark:** Last name or first and last name in Celtic script.

ROBERTS, CHUCK, 5004 W. 92nd Ave., #207, Westminster, CO, 80030/303-650-4563
Specialties: Traditional straight knives. **Patterns:** Bowies, hunters and California knives. **Technical:** Grinds 440C, 5160, Damascus and ATS-34. Handles made of stag, ivory or mother-of-pearl. **Prices:** Start at $350. **Remarks:** Full-time maker. **Mark:** Last initial or last name.

ROBERTS, GEORGE A., 93 Lewes Blvd., Apt. 207B, Whitehorse, Yukon Territories, CANADA, Y1A 3J4/403-667-7099
Specialties: Hunters, liner lockers and fancy fillet knives. **Patterns:** Bowies, hunters, liner lockers, fillet knives and ivory handled letter openers. **Technical:** Grinds ATS-34, 440C, Boye Dendritic, O1, mild Damascus and 440V. Liner lock liners are titanium. Etches, engraves and offers fancy filework on blades; scrimshaws and carves handles; makes leather sheaths. Uses fossilized mastodon ivory. **Prices:** $80 to $2,500. **Remarks:** Full-time maker; first knife sold in 1986. Doing business as Bandit Blades. **Mark:** Bandit.

ROBINSON, ROBERT W., 1569 N. Finley Pt., Polson, MT, 59860/406-887-2259
Specialties: High-art straight knives, folders and automatics of his design. **Patterns:** Hunters and locking folders. **Technical:** Grinds ATS-34, 154CM and 440V. Inlays pearl and gold; engraves sheep horn and ivory. **Prices:** $150 to $500; some to $2,000. **Remarks:** Full-time maker; first knife sold in 1983. Doing business as Robbie Knife. **Mark:** Name on left side of blade.

ROBINSON, CHUCK, Sea Robin Forge, 1423 Third Ave, Picayune, MS, 39466/601-798-0060
Specialities: Deluxe period pieces and working / using knives of his design and to customer specs. **Patterns:** Bowies, fighters, hunters, folders, utility knives and original designs. **Technical:** Forges own Damascus, 52100, 01, L6 and 1070 thru 1095. **Prices:** Start At $225. **Remarks:** First knife 1958. Recently transitioned to full-time maker. **Mark:** Fish logo, anchor and initials C.R. **Specialties:** Deluxe period pieces and working/using knives of his design and to customer specs. **Patterns:** Bowies, fighters, hunters, folders, utility knives and original designs. **Technical:** Forges own Damascus, 52100, 01, L6, and 1070 thru 1095. **Prices:** Start at $225. **Remarks:** First knive 1958. Recently transitioned to full-time maker. **Mark:** FISH LOGO, Anchor and initials C.R.

ROBINSON, CHARLES (DICKIE), P.O. Box 221, Vega, TX, 79092/806-267-2629
Specialties: Classic and working/using knives. **Patterns:** Bowies, daggers, fighters, hunters and camp knives. **Technical:** Forges O1, 5160, 52100 and his own Damascus. **Prices:** $125 to $850; some to $2,500. **Remarks:** Part-time maker; first knife sold in 1988. Doing business as Robinson Knives. **Mark:** Last name, JS.

ROBINSON III, REX R., 10531 Poe St., Leesburg, FL, 34788/352-787-4587
Specialties: One-of-a-kind high-art automatics of his design. **Patterns:** Automatics, liner locks and lock back folders. **Technical:** Uses tool steel and stainless Damascus and mokume; flat grinds. Hand carves folders. **Prices:** $1,000 to $2,600; some to $3,500. **Remarks:** First knife sold in 1988. **Mark:** First name inside oval.

ROCHFORD, MICHAEL R., P.O. Box 577, Dresser, WI, 54009/715-755-3520
Specialties: Working straight knives and folders. Classic Bowies and Moran traditional. **Patterns:** Bowies, fighters, hunters: slip-joint, locking and liner locking folders. **Technical:** Grinds ATS-34, 440C, 154CM and D-2; forges W2, 5160, and his own Damascus. Offers metal & metal and leather sheaths. Filework and wire inlay. **Prices:** $150 to $1,000; some to $2,000. **Remarks:** Full-time maker; first knife sold in 1984. **Mark:** Name.

RODKEY, DAN, 18336 Ozark Dr., Hudson, FL, 34667/727-863-8264
Specialties: Traditional straight knives of his design and in standard patterns. **Patterns:** Boots, fighters and hunters. **Technical:** Grinds 440C, D2 and ATS-34. **Prices:** Start at $200. **Remarks:** Full-time maker; first knife sold in 1985. Doing business as Rodkey Knives. **Mark:** Etched logo on blade.

ROE JR., FRED D., 4005 Granada Dr., Huntsville, AL, 35802/205-881-6847
Specialties: Highly finished working knives of his design; period pieces. **Patterns:** Hunters, fighters and survival knives; locking folders; specialty designs like divers' knives. **Technical:** Grinds 154CM, ATS-34 and Damascus. Field-tests all blades. **Prices:** $125 to $250; some to $2,000. **Remarks:** Part-time maker; first knife sold in 1980. **Mark:** Last name.

ROGERS, R S, PO Box 769, Magdalena, NM, 87825/505-854-2567
Specialties: Multi-blade folders, one-of-a-kind fixed blades. **Patterns:** Folders: sowbelly stockman, sowbelly trapper, serpentine stockman, toothpick, gent's knife. Fixed blades: bowies, daggers, hunters, utility knives. **Technical:** Use various steels, like natural handle materials. **Prices:** $135 to $1000. **Mark:** Last name.

ROGERS, RODNEY, 602 Osceola St., Wildwood, FL, 34785/352-748-6114
Specialties: Traditional straight knives and folders. **Patterns:** Fighters, hunters, skinners. **Technical:** Flat-grinds ATS-34 and Damascus. Prefers natural materials. **Prices:** $150 to $1,400. **Remarks:** Full-time maker; first knife sold in 1986. **Mark:** Last name, Handmade.

ROGERS JR., ROBERT P., 3979 South Main St., Acworth, GA, 30101/404-974-9982
Specialties: Traditional working knives. **Patterns:** Hunters, 4-inch trailing-points. **Technical:** Grinds D2, 154CM and ATS-34; likes ironwood and ivory Micarta. **Prices:** $125 to $175. **Remarks:** Spare-time maker; first knife sold in 1975. **Mark:** Name.

ROGHMANS, MARK, 607 Virginia Ave., LaGrange, GA, 30240/706-885-1273
Specialties: Classic and traditional knives of his design. **Patterns:** Bowies, daggers and fighters. **Technical:** Grinds ATS-34, D2 and 440C. **Prices:** $250 to $500. **Remarks:** Part-time maker; first knife sold in 1984. Doing business as LaGrange Knife. **Mark:** Last name and/or LaGrange Knife.

ROHN, FRED, W7615 Clemetson Rd., CRoeur d'Alene, ID, 83814/208-667-0774
Specialties: Working straight knives, some unusual. **Patterns:** Hunters, fighters, a unique Bowie design and locking folders. **Technical:** Grinds 440C and 154CM; stainless steel pins, bolsters and guards on all knives. **Prices:** $65 to $200; some to $450 and higher. **Remarks:** Part-time maker. **Mark:** Name in logo and serial number.

ROLAND, DAN, 1966 W. 13th Lane, Yuma, AZ, 85364/520-343-2818

ROLLERT, STEVE, P.O. Box 65, Keenesburg, CO, 80643-0065/303-732-4858
Specialties: Highly finished working knives. **Patterns:** Variety of straight knives; locking folders and slip-joints. **Technical:** Forges and grinds W2, 1095, ATS-34 and his pattern-welded, cable Damascus and nickel Damascus. **Prices:** $300 to $1,000; some to $3,000. **Remarks:** Full-time maker; first knife sold in 1980. Doing business as Dove Knives. **Mark:** Last name in script.

ROSA, PEDRO GULLHERME TELES, R. das Magnolias, 45 CECAP Presidente Prudente, SP-19065-410, BRAZIL, /0182-271769
Specialties: Using straight knives and folders to customer specs; some high-art. **Patterns:** Fighters, Bowies and daggers. **Technical:** Grinds and forges D6, 440C, high carbon steels and Damascus. **Prices:** $60 to $400. **Remarks:** Full-time maker; first knife sold in 1991. **Mark:** A hammer over "Hammer."

custom knifemakers

ROSENFELD, BOB, 955 Freeman Johnson Road, Hoschton, GA, 30548/770-867-2647
Specialties: Fancy and embellished working/using straight knives of his design and in standard patterns. **Patterns:** Daggers, hunters and utility/camp knives. **Technical:** Forges 52100, A203E, 1095 and L6 Damascus. Offers engraving. **Prices:** $125 to $650; some to $1,000. **Remarks:** Full-time maker; first knife sold in 1984. Also makes folders. **Mark:** Last name or full name, Knifemaker.

ROSS, GREGG, 4556 Wenhart Rd., Lake Worth, FL, 33463/407-439-4681
Specialties: Working/using straight knives. **Patterns:** Bowies, hunters and utility/camp knives. **Technical:** Forges and grinds ATS-34, Damascus and cable Damascus. Uses decorative pins. **Prices:** $125 to $250; some to $400. **Remarks:** Part-time maker; first knife sold in 1992. **Mark:** Name, city and state.

ROSS, STEPHEN, 534 Remington Dr., Evanston, WY, 82930/307-789-7104
Specialties: One-of-a-kind collector-grade classic and contemporary straight knives and folders of his design and to customer specs; some fantasy pieces. **Patterns:** Combat and survival knives, hunters, boots and folders. **Technical:** Grinds stainless; forges spring and tool steel. Engraves, scrimshaws. Makes leather sheaths. **Prices:** $160 to $3,000. **Remarks:** Partl-time maker; first knife sold in 1971. **Mark:** Last name in modified Roman; sometimes in script.

ROSS, TIM, 3239 Oliver Rd., RR #17, Thunder Bay, ONT, CANADA, P7B 6C2/807-935-2667
Specialties: Fancy working knives of his design. **Patterns:** Fishing and hunting knives, Bowies, daggers and miniatures. **Technical:** Uses D2, Stellite 6K and 440C; forges 52100 and Damascus. Makes antler handles and sheaths; has supply of whale teeth and moose antlers for trade. Prefers natural materials only. Wife Katherine scrimshaws. **Prices:** $100 to $350; some to $2,100. **Remarks:** Part-time maker; first knife sold in 1975. **Mark:** Last name stamped on tang.

ROSS, D.L., 27 Kinsman St., Dunedin, NEW ZEALAND, /64 3 464 0239
Specialties: Working straight knives of his design. **Patterns:** Hunters, various others. **Technical:** Grinds 440C. **Prices:** $100 to $450; some to $700 NZ dollars. **Remarks:** Part-time maker; first knife sold in 1988. **Mark:** Dave Ross, Maker, city and country.

ROTELLA, RICHARD A., 643--75th St., Niagara Falls, NY, 14304/
Specialties: Working knives of his design. **Patterns:** Various fishing, hunting and utility knives; folders. **Technical:** Grinds ATS-34. Prefers hand-rubbed finishes. **Prices:** $65 to $450; some to $900. **Remarks:** Spare-time maker; first knife sold in 1977. Not taking orders at this time; only sells locally. **Mark:** Name and city in stylized waterfall logo.

ROULIN, CHARLES, 113 B Rt. de Soral, 1233 Geneva, SWITZERLAND, /022-757-4479
Specialties: Fancy high-art straight knives and folders of his design. **Patterns:** Bowies, locking folders, slip-joint folders and miniatures. **Technical:** Grinds 440C, ATS-34 and D2. Engraves; carves nature scenes and detailed animals in steel, ivory, on handles and blades. **Prices:** $500 to $3,000; some to $10,000. **Remarks:** Full-time maker; first knife sold in 1988. **Mark:** Symbol of fish with name or name engraved.

ROWE, STEWART G., 8-18 Coreen Court, Mt. Crosby, Brisbane 4306, AUSTRALIA, /Ph: 073-201-0906
Specialties: Designer knives, reproduction of ancient weaponry, traditional Japanese tantos and edged tools. **Patterns:** "Shark"--blade range. **Technical:** Forges W1, W2, D2; creates own Tamahagne steel and composite pattern-welded billets. Gold, silver and ivory fittings available. **Prices:** $300 to $11,000. **Remarks:** Full-time maker; first knife sold in 1981. Doing business as Stewart Rowe Productions Pty Ltd .

RUA, GARY (WOLF), 329 Snell St, Fall River, MA, 02721/508-677-2664
Specialties: Working knives of his design; 18th and 19th century period pieces. **Patterns:** Bowies, hunters, fighters, buckskinners and patch knives. **Technical:** Forges 5160, 1095, old files; uses only natural handle materials. **Prices:** $100 to $500; some to $1,000. **Remarks:** Part-time maker. Doing business as Harvest Moon Forge. **Mark:** Last name.

RUANA KNIFE WORKS, Box 520, Bonner, MT, 59823/406-258-5368
Specialties: Working knives and period pieces. **Patterns:** Variety of straight knives. **Technical:** Forges 5160 chrome alloy for Bowies and

1095. **Prices:** $70 and up. **Remarks:** Full-time maker; first knife sold in 1938. **Mark:** Name.

RUBLEY, JAMES A., 5765 N. 500 W., Angola, IN, 46703/219-833-1255
Specialties: Working American knives and collectibles for hunters, buckskinners and re-enactment groups from Pre-Revolutionary War through the Civil War. **Patterns:** Anything authentic, barring folders. **Technical:** Iron fittings, natural materials; forges files. **Prices:** $175 to $2,500. **Remarks:** Museum consultant and blacksmith for two decades. **Mark:** Lightning bolt.

RUPERT, BOB, 301 Harshaville Rd., Clinton, PA, 15026/724-573-4569
Specialties: Wrought period pieces with natural elements. **Patterns:** Elegant straight blades - friction folders. **Technical:** Forges colonial 7; 1095; 5160; diffuse mokume-gane and form Damascus. **Prices:** $150 to $1500; some higher. **Remarks:** Part-time maker; first knife sold in 1980. Evening hours studio since 1980. **Mark:** R etched in Old English. **Other:** Likes simplicity that disassembles.

RUPLE, WILLIAM H., P.O. Box 370, Charlotte, TX, 78011/830-277-1371
Specialties: Multi blade folders, slip joints, some lock backs. **Patterns:** Like to reproduce old patterns. **Technical:** Grinds 440C, ATS-34, D2 and commercial Damascus. Offers filework on back springs and liners. **Prices:** $300 to $500; some to $1,000. **Remarks:** Full-time maker; first knife sold in 1988. **Mark:** Ruple.

RUSS, RON, 5351 NE 160th Ave., Williston, FL, 32696/352-528-2603
Specialties: Damascus and Mokume. **Patterns:** Ladder, rain drop and butterfly. **Technical:** Most knives, including Damascus, are forged from 52100-E. **Prices:** $65 to $2,500. **Mark:** Russ.

RUSSELL, TOM, 6500 New Liberty Rd., Jacksonville, AL, 36265/205-492-7866
Specialties: Straight working knives of his design or to customer specs. **Patterns:** Hunters, folders, fighters, skinners, Bowies and utility knives. **Technical:** Grinds D2, 440C and ATS-34; offers filework. **Prices:** $75 to $225. **Remarks:** Part-time maker; first knife sold in 1987. Full-time tool and die maker. **Mark:** Last name with tulip stamp.

RUSSELL, MICK, 4 Rossini Rd., Pari Park, Port Elizabeth 6070, SOUTH AFRICA, /
Specialties: Art knives. **Patterns:** Working and collectible bird, trout and hunting knives, defense knives and folders. **Technical:** Grinds D2, 440C, ATS-34 and Damascus. Offers mirror or satin finishes. Uses nickel-silver, 303 stainless and titanium fittings and wide variety of African hardwoods; ivory, buffalo and antelope horn and bone handle materials. **Prices:** Start at $100. **Remarks:** Full-time maker; first knife sold in 1986. **Mark:** Stylized rhino incorporating initials.

RUSSELL, A.G., 1705 Hwy. 71 N., Springdale, AR, 72764/501-751-7341
Specialties: Morseth knives; contemporary working knives. **Patterns:** Hunters and Bowies; personal utility knives in Morseth line, drop-points and boots in Russell line. **Technical:** Laminated blades in Morseth line; modern stainless steel in Russell line; classic shapes. **Prices:** Moderate. **Remarks:** Old name still at work. Doing business as Morseth Sports Equip. Co. **Mark:** Morseth or first and middle initials, last name.

RYAN, J.C., Rt. 5 Box 183-A, Lexington, VA, 24450/703-348-5014

RYAN, C.O., 902-A Old Wormley Creek Rd., Yorktown, VA, 23692/757-898-7797
Specialties: Working/using knives. **Patterns:** Hunters, kitchen knives, locking folders. **Technical:** Grinds 440C and ATS-34. **Prices:** $45 to $130; some to $450. **Remarks:** Part-time maker; first knife sold in 1980. **Mark:** Name.

RYBAR JR., RAYMOND B., 277 Stone Church Road, Finleyville, PA, 15332/412-348-4841
Specialties: Fancy/embellished, high-art and traditional working using straight knives and folders of his design and in standard patterns; period pieces. **Patterns:** Daggers, fighters and swords. **Technical:** Forges Damascus. All blades have etched biblical scripture or biblical significance. **Prices:** $120 to $1,200; some to $4,500. **Remarks:** Full-time maker; first knife sold in 1972. Doing business as Stone Church Forge. **Mark:** Last name or business name.

RYBERG, GOTE, Faltgatan 2, S-562 00 Norrahammar, SWEDEN, / 4636-61678

RYDER, BEN M., P.O. Box 133, Copperhill, TN, 37317/615-496-2750 **Specialties:** Working/using straight knives of his design and to customer specs. **Patterns:** Fighters, hunters, utility/camp knives. **Technical:** Grinds 440C, ATS-34, D2, commercial Damascus. **Prices:** $75 to $400. **Remarks:** Part-time maker; first knife sold in 1992. **Mark:** Full name in double butterfly logo.

S

SAINDON, R. BILL, 11 Highland View Rd., Claremont, NH, 03743/603-542-9418 **Specialties:** Collector-quality folders of his design or to customer specs. **Patterns:** Latch release, liner lock and lockback folders. **Technical:** Offers limited amount of own Damascus; also uses Damas makers steel. Prefers natural handle material, gold and gems. **Prices:** $500 to $4,000. **Remarks:** Full-time maker; first knife sold in 1981. Doing business as Daynia Forge. **Mark:** Sun logo or engraved surname.

SAKAKIBARA, MASAKI, 20-8 Sakuragaoka, 2-Chome Setagaya-ku, Tokyo 156, JAPAN, /03-420-0375

SAKMAR, MIKE, 1670 Morley, Rochester, MI, 48307/248-852-6775 **Specialties:** Fancy and working straight knives of his design and to customer specs. **Patterns:** Bowies, fighters, hunters and integrals. **Technical:** Ginds ATS-34, Damascus and high-carbon tool steels. Uses mostly natural handle materials--elephant ivory, walrus, ivory stag, wildwood, oosic, etc. Makes mokume for resale. **Prices:** $150 to $2,500; some to $4,000. **Remarks:** Part-time maker; first knife sold in 1990. **Mark:** Last name.

SALLEY, JOHN D., 3965 Frederick-Ginghamsburg Rd., Tipp City, OH, 45371/513-698-4588 **Specialties:** Fancy working knives and art pieces. **Patterns:** Hunters, fighters, daggers and some swords. **Technical:** Grinds ATS-34, 12C27 and W2; buys Damascus. **Prices:** $85 to $1,000; some to $6,000. **Remarks:** Part-time maker; first knife sold in 1979. **Mark:** First initial, last name.

SAMPSON, LYNN, 381 Deakins Rd., Jonesborough, TN, 37659/423-348-8373 **Specialties:** Highly finished working knives, mostly folders. **Patterns:** Locking folders, slip-joints, interframes and two-blades. **Technical:** Grinds D2, 440C and ATS-34; offers extensive filework. **Prices:** Start at $300. **Remarks:** Full-time maker; first knife sold in 1982. **Mark:** Name and city in logo.

SANDERS, BILL, 335 Bauer Ave., P.O. Box 957, Mancos, CO, 81328/970-533-7223 **Specialties:** Working straight knives, some fancy and some fantasy, of his design. **Patterns:** Hunters, boots, utility knives, using belt knives. **Technical:** Grinds 440C, ATS-34 and commercial Damascus. Provides wide variety of handle materials. **Prices:** $170 to $350; some to $800. **Remarks:** Full-time maker. **Mark:** Name, city and state.

SANDERS, MICHAEL M., P.O. Box 1106, Ponchatoula, LA, 70454/225-294-3601 **Specialties:** Working straight knives and folders, some deluxe. **Patterns:** Hunters, fighters, Bowies, daggers, large folders and deluxe Damascus miniatures. **Technical:** Grinds O1, D2, 440C, ATS-34 and Damascus. **Prices:** $75 to $650; some higher. **Remarks:** Full-time maker; first knife sold in 1967. **Mark:** Name and state.

SANDERS, A.A., 3850 72 Ave. NE, Norman, OK, 73071/405-364-8660 **Specialties:** Working straight knives and folders. **Patterns:** Hunters, fighters, daggers and Bowies. **Technical:** Forges his own Damascus; offers stock removal with ATS-34, 440C, A2, D2, O1, 5160 and 1095. **Prices:** $85 to $1,500. **Remarks:** Full-time maker; first knife sold in 1985. Formerly known as Athern Forge. **Mark:** Name.

SANDERSON, RAY, 4403 Uplands Way, Yakima, WA, 98908/509-965-0128 **Specialties:** One-of-a-kind Buck knives; traditional working straight knives and folders of his design. **Patterns:** Bowies, hunters and fighters. **Technical:** Grinds 440C and ATS-34. **Prices:** $200 to $750. **Remarks:** Part-time maker; first knife sold in 1984. **Mark:** Sanderson Knives in shape of Bowie.

SANDLIN, LARRY, 4580 Sunday Dr., Adamsville, AL, 35005/205-674-1816 **Specialties:** High-art straight knives of his design. **Patterns:** Boots, daggers, hunters and fighters. **Technical:** Forges 1095, L6, O1, carbon steel and Damascus. **Prices:** $200 to $1,500; some to $5,000. **Remarks:** Part-time maker; first knife sold in 1990. **Mark:** Chiseled last name in Japanese.

SASSER, JIM, 926 Jackson, Pueblo, CO, 81004/ **Specialties:** Working straight knives and folders of his design. **Patterns:** Makes elk hunters' tools, axes, camp knives, a variety of folders and limited editions. **Technical:** Grinds ATS-34. **Prices:** $75 to $300; some to $800. **Remarks:** Full-time maker; first knife sold in 1970. **Mark:** Last name or full name in circle.

SAWBY, SCOTT, 480 Snowberry Ln, Sandpoint, ID, 83864/208-263-4171 **Specialties:** Folders, working and fancy. **Patterns:** Locking folders, patent locking systems and interframes. **Technical:** Grinds D2, 440C, 154CM, CPM-T-440V and ATS-34. **Prices:** $400 to $1,000. **Remarks:** Full-time maker; first knife sold in 1974. **Mark:** Last name, city and state.

SAYEN, MURAD, P.O. Box 127, Bryant Pond, ME, 04219/207-665-2224 **Specialties:** Carved handles. **Patterns:** Fighters, boots, Bowies, daggers and fantasy knives. **Technical:** Forges carbon and Damascus steel only. Handles carved and inlaid, some with stones. **Prices:** $750 to $5,000. **Remarks:** Full-time maker; first knife sold in 1977. Doing business as Kemal. **Mark:** Last name with date.

SCARROW, WIL, c/o L&W Mail Service, 16236 Chicago Ave., Bellflower, CA, 90706/562-866-6384 **Specialties:** Carving knives, also working straight knives in standard patterns or to customer specs. **Patterns:** Carving, fishing, hunting, skinning, utility, swords & bowies. **Technical:** Forges and grinds: A2, L6, W1, D2, 5160, 1095, 440C, AEB-L, ATS-34 and others on request. Offers some filework. **Prices:** $65 to $850; some higher. Prices include sheath (carver's $40 and up). **Remarks:** Spare-time maker; first knife sold in 1983. Two to eight month construction time on custom orders. Doing business as Scarrow's Custom Stuff and Gold Hill Knifeworks (in Oregon). **Mark:** SC with arrow and date/year made.

SCHALLER, ANTHONY BRETT, 5609 Flint Ct. NW, Albuquerque, NM, 87120/505-899-0155 **Specialties:** Traditional working/using straight knives of his design and in standard patterns. **Patterns:** Boots, fighters and utility knives; some folders. **Technical:** Grinds ATS-34 and Damascus. Offers filework, mirror finishes and full and narrow tangs. Prefers exotic woods or Micarta for handle materials. **Prices:** $60 to $195; some to $450. **Remarks:** Part-time maker; first knife sold in 1990. **Mark:** Last name.

SCHEID, MAGGIE, 124 Van Stallen St., Rochester, NY, 14621-3557/ **Specialties:** Simple working straight knives. **Patterns:** Kitchen and utility knives; some miniatures. **Technical:** Forges 5160 high-carbon steel. **Prices:** $100 to $200. **Remarks:** Part-time maker; first knife sold in 1986. **Mark:** Full name.

SCHELL, CLYDE M., 4735 NE Elliott Circle, Corvallis, OR, 97330/503-752-0235

SCHEMPP, MARTIN, P.O. Box 1181, 5430 Baird Springs Rd. N.W., Ephrata, WA, 98823/509-754-2963 **Specialties:** Fantasy and traditional straight knives of his design, to customer specs and in standard patterns; Paleolithic styles. **Patterns:** Fighters and Paleolithic designs. **Technical:** Uses opal, Mexican rainbow and obsidian. Offers scrimshaw. **Prices:** $15 to $100; some to $250. **Remarks:** Spare-time maker; first knife sold in 1995. **Mark:** Initials and date.

SCHEMPP, ED, P.O. Box 1181, Ephrata, WA, 98823/509-754-2963 **Specialties:** High-tech working/using straight knives; integral Damascus knives and tomahawks. **Patterns:** Fighters, hunters and utility/camp knives. **Technical:** Grinds CPM440V; forges 52100 and Damascus. Makes sheaths. **Prices:** $100 to $400; some to $2,000. **Remarks:** Part-time maker; first knife sold in 1991. Doing business as Ed Schempp Knives. **Mark:** Ed Schempp Knives over five heads of wheat, city and state.

custom knifemakers

SCHEPERS, GEORGE B., Box 83, Chapman, NE, 68827/308-986-2444 **Specialties:** Fancy period pieces of his design. **Patterns:** Bowies, swords, tomahawks; locking folders and miniatures. **Technical:** Grinds W1, W2 and his own Damascus; etches. **Prices:** $125 to $600; some higher. **Remarks:** Full-time maker; first knife sold in 1981. **Mark:** Schep.

SCHEURER, ALFREDO E. FAES, Av. Rincon de los Arcos 104, Col. Bosque Res. del Sur, C.P. 16010, MEXICO, /5676 47 63 **Specialties:** Fancy and fantasy knives of his design. **Patterns:** Daggers. **Technical:** Grinds stainless steel; casts and grinds silver. Sets stones in silver. **Prices:** $2,000 to $3,000. **Remarks:** Spare-time maker; first knife sold in 1989. **Mark:** Symbol.

SCHIRMER, MIKE, 28 Biltmore Rd., P.O. Box 534, Twin Bridges, MT, 59754/406-684-5868 **Specialties:** Working straight knives of his design or to customer specs; mostly hunters and personal knives. **Patterns:** Hunters, camp, kitchen, bowies and fighters. **Technical:** Grinds O1, D2, A2 and Damascus and Talonoite. **Prices:** Start at $150. **Remarks:** Full-time maker; first knife sold in 1992. Doing business as Ruby Mountain Knives. **Mark:** Name or name & location.

SCHLOMER, JAMES E., 991 Hickory Ct., Kissimmee, FL, 34743/407-348-8044 **Specialties:** Working and show straight knives. **Patterns:** Hunters, Bowies and skinners. **Technical:** Stock removal method, 440C and L6. Scrimshaws; carves sambar stag handles. Works on corean and Micarta. **Prices:** $75 to $500. **Remarks:** Full-time maker. **Mark:** Name and steel number.

SCHMIDT, RICK, P.O. Box 1318, Whitefish, MT, 59937/406-862-6471 **Specialties:** Traditional working and using straight knives and folders of his design and to customer specs. **Patterns:** Fighters, hunters, cutlery and utility knives. **Technical:** Flat-grinds D2 and ATS-34. Custom leather sheaths. **Prices:** $120 to $250; some to $1,900. **Remarks:** Full-time maker; first knife sold in 1975. **Mark:** Stylized initials.

SCHMIDT, JAMES A., 1167 Eastern Ave., Ballston Lake, NY, 12019/518-882-9322 **Specialties:** High-art Damascus folders and collector-quality period pieces. **Patterns:** Schmidt patterns in folders; variety of investor-class straight knives. **Technical:** Forges W2 and his own Damascus; offers elaborate filework and etching; uses exotic handle materials. **Prices:** $900 to $2,200; some to $5,000. **Remarks:** Full-time maker; first knife sold in 1975. **Mark:** Last name.

SCHNEIDER, KARL A., 209 N. Brownleaf Rd., Newark, DE, 19713/302-737-0277 **Specialties:** Traditional working and using straight knives of his design. **Patterns:** Hunters, kitchen and fillet knives. **Technical:** Grinds ATS-34. Shapes handles to fit hands; uses Micarta, Pakkawood and exotic woods. Makes hand-stitched leather cases. **Prices:** $95 to $225. **Remarks:** Part-time maker; first knife sold in 1984-85. **Mark:** Name, address; also name in shape of fish.

SCHNEIDER, HERMAN J., 10 Sun Hala Dr., Pittsburg, TX, 75686-9318/903-856-9802 **Specialties:** Investor-class straight knives and fantasy pieces of his design. **Patterns:** Fully finished hunters, daggers, fighters and push knives. **Technical:** Forges and grinds 154CM, ATS-34 and his Damascus. Exotic materials are a specialty. **Prices:** Start at $800 for hunters. **Remarks:** Full-time maker; first knife sold in 1972. **Mark:** First and middle initials, last name.

SCHNEIDER, CRAIG M., 285 County Rd. 1400 N., Seymour, IL, 61875/217-687-2651 **Specialties:** Traditional working straight knives of his design or to customer specs. **Patterns:** Hunters, fighters, Bowies and utility/camp knives. **Technical:** Grinds 440C, 440V, ATS-34, D2 and O1; uses various animal horns, antlers, bones, jawbones, gold, silver, precious stones, minerals and fossil ivory for handle materials. **Prices:** $50 to $3,000. **Remarks:** Part-time maker; first knife sold in 1985. **Mark:** Stylized initials.

SCHOEMAN, CORRIE, Box 573, Bloemfontein 9300, SOUTH AFRICA, /051-4383528 Cell: 082-3750789 **Specialties:** High-tech folders of his design or to customer's specs. **Patterns:** Liner lock folders. **Technical:** ATS-34 or Damascus blades with titanium frames; Prefers exotic materials for handles. **Prices:** $300 to $500. **Remarks:** Part-time maker; first knife sold in 1984. **Mark:** Etched name logo in knife shape.

SCHOENFELD, MATTHEW A., RR #1, Galiano Island, B.C., CANADA, V0N 1P0/250-539-2806 **Specialties:** Working knives of his design. **Patterns:** Kitchen cutlery, camp knives, hunters, swords. **Technical:** Grinds 440C buys Damascus. **Prices:** $85 to $500. **Remarks:** Part-time maker; first knife sold in 1978. **Mark:** Signature, Galiano Is. B.C., and date.

SCHOLL, TIM, 1389 Langdon Rd., Angier, NC, 27501/910-897-2051 **Specialties:** Fancy and working/using straight knives and folders of his design and to customer specs. **Patterns:** tomahawks, swords, tantos and fantasy knives. **Technical:** Grinds ATS-34; forges carbon and tool steel and Damascus. Offers filework, engraving and scrimshaw. **Prices:** $100 to $650; some to $1,500. **Remarks:** Full-time maker; first knife sold in 1990. Doing business as Tim Scholl Custom Knives. **Mark:** Last name or last initial with arrow.

SCHRAP, ROBERT G., 7024 W. Wells St., Wauwatosa, WI, 53213/414-771-6472 **Specialties:** Leatherwork.

SCHROEN, KARL, 4042 Bones Rd., Sebastopol, CA, 95472/707-823-4057 **Specialties:** Using knives made to fit. **Patterns:** Sgian dubhs, carving sets, wood-carving knives, fishing knives, kitchen knives and new cleaver design. **Technical:** Forges A2, ATS-34 and D2. **Prices:** $100 to $800. **Remarks:** Full-time maker; first knife sold in 1968. Author of *The Hand Forged Knife.* **Mark:** Last name.

SCHULTZ, RICHARD A., 22971 Triton Way Ste C, Laguna Hills, CA, 92653-1229/714-661-3879 **Specialties:** Traditional working and using straight knives of his design, to customer specs and in standard patterns. **Patterns:** Fighters, hunters, Specwar and survival knives. **Technical:** Grinds 440C, ATS-34, tool steels and titanium. **Prices:** Start at $200. **Remarks:** Part-time maker; first knife sold in 1991. Manufactures specialized knives in titanium to U.S. Government Specwar teams as Mission Knives & Tools, Inc. **Mark:** First initial, last name, year.

SCHWARZER, STEPHEN, P.O. Box 4, Pomona Park, FL, 32181/904-649-5026 **Specialties:** Mosaic Damascus. **Patterns:** Hunters, fighters, locking folders, axes and buckskinners. **Technical:** Forges W2, O1, Wootz steel and his own Damascus; all knives have carving or filework. **Prices:** $150 to $500; some to $5,000. **Remarks:** Full-time maker; first knife sold in 1976. **Mark:** Name over anvil; folders marked inside liner.

SCHWARZER, JAMES, P.O. Box 4, Pomona Park, FL, 32181/904-649-5026 **Specialties:** Working straight knives of his design. **Patterns:** Capers and small hunters. **Technical:** Forges high-carbon steel and Damascus. **Prices:** $50 to $300. **Remarks:** Twelve-year-old part-time maker; first knife sold in 1989. Sells only at shows. **Mark:** Last name with anvil and first name underneath.

SCOFIELD, EVERETT, 2873 Glass Mill Rd., Chickamauga, GA, 30707/706-375-2790 **Specialties:** Historic and fantasy miniatures. **Patterns:** All patterns. **Technical:** Uses only the finest tool steels and other materials. Uses only natural, precious and semi precious materials. **Prices:** $100 to $1,500. **Remarks:** Full-time maker; first knife sold in 1971. Doing business as Three Crowns Cutlery. **Mark:** Three Crowns logo.

SCORDIA, PAOLO, Via Terralba 143Secondario 23, 00550 Torrimpietra, ROMA, ITALY, /06-61697231 **Specialties:** Plain working knives. **Patterns:** Skinners, hunters, utility and boot knives, fighters, daggers, bush swords, kitchen knives and liner lock folders. **Technical:** Grinds 420C, 440C, ATS-34; uses hardwoods and Micarta for handles, brass and nickel-silver for fittings. Makes sheaths. **Prices:** $80 to $500. **Remarks:** Part-time maker; first knife sold in 1988. **Mark:** Initials with sun and moon logo.

SCOTT, WINSTON, Rt. 2, Box 62, Huddleston, VA, 24104/703-297-6130 **Specialties:** Working knives. **Patterns:** Hunting and fishing knives. **Technical:** Grinds ATS-34, 440C and 154CM; likes full and narrow tangs, natural materials, sterling silver guards. **Prices:** $100 to $200;

some to $400. **Remarks:** Part-time maker; first knife sold in 1984. **Mark:** Last name.

SCOTT, AL, HC63 Box 802, Harper, TX, 78631/830-864-4182
Specialties: High-art straight knives of his design. **Patterns:** Daggers, swords, early European, Middle East and Japanese knives. **Technical:** Uses ATS-34, 440C and Damascus. Hand engraves; does file work cuts filigree in the blade; offers ivory carving and precious metal inlay. **Remarks:** Full-time maker; first knife sold in 1994. Doing business as Al Scott Maker of Fine Blade Art. **Mark:** Name engraved in old English, sometime inlaid in 24K gold.

SEARS, MICK, 1697 Peach Orchard Rd. #302, Sumter, SC, 29154/803-499-5074
Specialties: Scots and confederate reproductions; Bowies and fighters. **Patterns:** Bowies, fighters. **Technical:** Grinds 440C and 1095. **Prices:** $50 to $150; some to $300. **Remarks:** Part-time maker; first knife sold in 1975. Doing business as Mick's Custom Knives. **Mark:** First name.

SELENT, CHUCK, P.O. Box 1207, Bonners Ferry, ID, 83805-1207/208-267-5807
Specialties: Period, art and fantasy miniatures; exotics; one-of-a-kinds. **Patterns:** Swords, daggers and others. **Technical:** Works in Damascus, meteorite, 440C and tool steel. Offers scrimshaw. Offers his own casting and leatherwork; uses jewelry techniques. Makes display cases for miniatures. **Prices:** $75 to $400. **Remarks:** Part-time maker; first knife sold in 1990. **Mark:** Last name and bear paw print logo scrimshawed on handles or leatherwork.

SELF, ERNIE, 950 O'Neill Ranch Rd., Dripping Springs, TX, 78620-9760/512-858-7133
Specialties: Traditional and working straight knives and folders of his design and in standard patterns. **Patterns:** Hunters, locking folders and slip-joints. **Technical:** Grinds 440C, D2, 440V, ATS-34 and Damascus. Offers fancy filework. **Prices:** $125 to $500; some to $1,500. **Remarks:** Full-time maker; first knife sold in 1982. **Mark:** Initials brand. Other: I also customize Buck 110's and 112's folding hunters.

SELLEVOLD, HARALD, S.Kleivesmau:2, PO Box 4134, N5834 Bergen, NORWAY, /55-310682
Specialties: Norwegian styles; collaborates with other Norse craftsmen. **Patterns:** Distinctive ferrules and other mild modifications of traditional patterns; Bowies and friction folders. **Technical:** Buys Damascus blades; blacksmiths his own blades. Semi-gemstones used in handles; gemstone inlay. **Prices:** $350 to $2,000. **Remarks:** Full-time maker; first knife sold in 1980. **Mark:** Horseshoe last initial.

SELVIDRO, RALPH, PO Box 248, Wyoming, RI, 02898/401-397-9768

SENTZ, MARK C., 4084 Baptist Rd., Taneytown, MD, 21787/410-756-2018
Specialties: Fancy straight working knives of his design. **Patterns:** Hunters, fighters, folders and utility/camp knives. **Technical:** Forges 1085, 1095, 5160, 5155 and his Damascus. Most knives come with wood-lined leather sheath or wooden presentation sheath. **Prices:** Start at $275. **Remarks:** Full-time maker; first knife sold in 1989. Doing business as M. Charles Sentz Gunsmithing, Inc. **Mark:** Last name.

SERAFEN, STEVEN E., 24 Genesee St., New Berlin, NY, 13411/607-847-6903
Specialties: Traditional working/using straight knives of his design and to customer specs. **Patterns:** Bowies, fighters, hunters. **Technical:** Grinds ATS-34, 440C, high-carbon steel. **Prices:** $175 to $600; some to $1,200. **Remarks:** Part-time maker; first knife sold in 1990. **Mark:** First and middle initial, last name in script.

SERVEN, JIM, P.O. Box 1, Fostoria, MI, 48435/517-795-2255
Specialties: Highly finished unique folders. **Patterns:** Fancy working folders, axes, miniatures and razors; some straight knives. **Technical:** Grinds 440C; forges his own Damascus. **Prices:** $150 to $800; some to $1,500. **Remarks:** Full-time maker; first knife sold in 1971. **Mark:** Name in map logo.

SHADLEY, EUGENE W., 26315 Norway Dr., Bovey, MN, 55709/218-245-3820
Specialties: Classic multi-blade folders. **Patterns:** Stockman, sowbelly, congress, trapper, etc. **Technical:** Grinds ATS-34, 416 frames. **Prices:** Start at $300. **Remarks:** Full-time maker; first knife sold in 1985. Doing business as Shadley Knives. **Mark:** Last name.

SHARRIGAN, MUDD, 111 Bradford Rd, Wiscasset, ME, 04578-4457/207-882-9820
Specialties: Wood carvers knives, custom designs, seaman's knives; repair straight knives, handles and blades on heirloom pieces; custom leather sheaths. **Patterns:** Daggers, fighters, hunters, buckskinner, Indian crooked knives and seamen working knives; traditional Scandinavian styles. **Technical:** Forges 1095, O1. Laminates 1095 and mild steel. **Prices:** $50 to $325; some to $1,200. **Remarks:** Full-time maker; first knife sold in 1982. **Mark:** First name and swallow tail carving.

SHELTON, PAUL S., 1406 Holloway, Rolla, MO, 65401/314-364-3151
Specialties: Fancy working straight knives of his design or to customer specs. **Patterns:** All types from camp knives to miniatures, except folders. **Technical:** Grinds ATS-34 and commercial Damascus. Offers filework, texturing, natural handle materials and exotic leather sheaths. **Prices:** Start at $100. **Remarks:** Part-time maker; first knife sold in 1984. **Mark:** Last name and serial number.

SHIKAYAMA, TOSHIAKI, 259-2 Suka Yoshikawa City, Saitama 342-0057, JAPAN, /04-89-81-6605
Specialties: Folders in standard patterns. **Patterns:** Locking and multi-blade folders. **Technical:** Grinds ATS, carbon steel, high speed steel. **Prices:** $400 to $2,500; some to $8,000. **Remarks:** Full-time maker; first knife sold in 1952. **Mark:** First initial, last name.

SHINOSKY, ANDY, 3117 Meanderwood Dr, Canfield, OH, 44515/330-793-9810
Specialties: Collectible fancy folders and interframes. **Patterns:** Drop points, trailing points and daggers. **Technical:** Grinds ATS-34 and Damascus. Prefers natural handle materials. **Prices:** Start at $450. **Remarks:** Part-time maker; first knife sold in 1992. **Mark:** Name or bent folder logo.

SHOEBOTHAM, HEATHER, HEATHER'S BLACKSMITH SHOP, PRIVATE BAG 1890, GOLD REEF CITY 2159 JOHANNESBURG, S AFRICA, /+27 11 496 1600
Specialties: All steel hand forged knives of my own design. **Patterns:** Traditional African weapons, friction folders and by-gone forged styles. **Technical:** Own Damascus, specializing in drive chain and steel wire rope, Meteorite, 420 & Mokume. Also using forged brass, copper and titanium fittings. All work hand-forged using a traditional coal fire. Differential heat-treatment used. **Prices:** $150 to $3,000. **Remarks:** Full-time practicing blacksmith and farrier and part-time bladesmith. First Damascus sold in 1995. First knife sold in 1998. **Mark:** Knives: Rearing unicorn in horseshoe surround with first name. Damascus: Sold under "Damsel Damascus".

SHOEMAKER, SCOTT, 316 S. Main St., Miamisburg, OH, 45342/513-859-1935
Specialties: Twisted, wire-wrapped handles on swords, fighters and fantasy blades; new line of seven models with quick-draw, multi-carry Kydex sheaths. **Patterns:** Bowies, boots and one of a kinds in his design or to customer specs. **Technical:** Grinds A6 and ATS-34; buys Damascus. Hand satin finish is standard. **Prices:** $100 to $1,500; swords to $8,000. **Remarks:** Part-time maker; first knife sold in 1984. **Mark:** Angel wings with last initial, or last name.

SHOEMAKER, CARROLL, 380 Yellowtown Rd., Northup, OH, 45658/740-446-6695
Specialties: Working/using straight knives of his design. **Patterns:** Hunters, utility/camp and early American backwoodsmen knives. **Technical:** Grinds ATS-34; forges old files, O1 and 1095. Uses some Damascus; offers scrimshaw and engraving. **Prices:** $100 to $175; some to $350. **Remarks:** Spare-time maker; first knife sold in 1977. **Mark:** Name and city or connected initials.

SHOGER, MARK O., 14780 SW Osprey Dr., Suite 345, Beaverton, OR, 97007/503-579-2495
Specialties: Working and using straight knives and folders of his design; fancy and embellished knives. **Patterns:** Hunters, Bowies, daggers and locking folders. **Technical:** Forges O1, W2 and his own pattern-welded Damascus. **Remarks:** Spare-time maker. **Mark:** Last name or stamped last initial over anvil.

SHOSTLE, BEN, 1121 Burlington, Muncie, IN, 47302/765-282-9073
Specialties: Fancy high-art straight knives of his design. **Patterns:** Bowies, daggers and fighters. **Technical:** Uses 440C, ATS-34 and commerical Damascus. All knives and engraved. **Prices:** $900 to $3,200; some to

custom knifemakers

$4,000. **Remarks:** Full-time maker; first knife sold in 1987. Doing business as The Gun Room (T.G.R.). **Mark:** Last name.

SHUFORD, RICK, Rt. 8, Box 256A, Statesville, NC, 28677/704-873-0633
Specialties: Fancy working knives to customer specs. **Patterns:** Hunters, buckskinners, camp and fishing knives and miniatures. **Technical:** Forges and grinds O1, D2 and 440C. **Prices:** $125 to $250; some to $450. **Remarks:** Part-time maker; first knife sold in 1981. **Mark:** Last name and three dots.

SIBRIAN, AARON, 4308 Dean Dr., Ventura, CA, 93003/805-642-6950
Specialties: Tough working knives of his design and in standard patterns. **Patterns:** Makes a "Viper utility"--a kukri derivative and a variety of straight using knives. **Technical:** Grinds 440C and ATS-34. Offers traditional Japanese blades; soft backs, hard edges, temper lines. **Prices:** $60 to $100; some to $250. **Remarks:** Spare-time maker; first knife sold in 1989. **Mark:** Initials in diagonal line.

SIGMAN, CORBET R., Rt. 1, Box 212-A, Liberty, WV, 25124/304-586-9131
Specialties: Collectible working straight knives and folders. **Patterns:** Hunters, fighters, boots, camp knives and exotics such as sgian dubhs--distinctly Sigman lines; folders. **Technical:** Grinds D2, 154CM, plain carbon tool steel and ATS-34. **Prices:** $60 to $800; some to $4,000. **Remarks:** Full-time maker; first knife sold in 1970. **Mark:** Name or initials.

SIGMAN, JAMES P., 52474 Johnson Rd., Three Rivers, MI, 49093/616-279-2508
Specialties: High-tech working knives of his design. **Patterns:** Daggers, hunters, fighters and folders. **Technical:** Forges and grinds L6, O1, W2 and his Damascus. **Prices:** $150 to $750. **Remarks:** Part-time maker; first knife sold in 1982. **Mark:** First initial, last name or SIG.

SIMMONS, H.R., 1100 Bay City Road, Aurora, NC, 27806/252-322-5969
Specialties: Working/using straight knives of his design. **Patterns:** Fighters, hunters and utility/camp knives. **Technical:** Forges and grinds Damascus and L6; grinds ATS-34. **Prices:** $150 to $250; some to $400. **Remarks:** Part-time maker; first knife sold in 1987. Doing business as HRS Custom Knives, Royal Forge & Trading Company. **Mark:** Initials.

SIMONELLA, GIANLUIGI, 15, via Rosa Brustolo, 33085, Maniago, ITALY/01139-427-730350
Specialties: Traditional and classic folding and working/using knives of his design and to customer specs. **Patterns:** Bowies, fighters, hunters, utility/camp knives. **Technical:** Forges ATS-34, D2, 440C. **Prices:** $250 to $400; some to $1,000. **Remarks:** Full-time maker; first knife sold in 1988. **Mark:** Wilson.

SIMONICH, ROB, P.O. Box 278, Clancy, MT, 59634/406-933-8274
Specialties: Working knives in standard patterns. **Patterns:** Hunters, combat knives, Bowies and small fancy knives. **Technical:** Grinds D2, ATS-34 and 440C; forges own cable Damascus. Offers filework on most knives. **Prices:** $75 to $300; some to $1,000. **Remarks:** Spare-time maker; first knife sold in 1984. Not currently taking orders. **Mark:** Last name in buffalo logo.

SIMONS, BILL, 6217 Michael Ln., Lakeland, FL, 33811/941-646-3783
Specialties: Working folders. **Patterns:** Locking folders, liner locks, hunters, clip joints most patterns; como straight oamp knivoo. **Toohnioal:** Grinds D2, ATS-34 and O1. **Prices:** Start at $100. **Remarks:** Full-time maker; first knife sold in 1970. **Mark:** Last name.

SIMS, BOB, P.O. Box 772, Meridian, TX, 76665/254-435-6240
Specialties: Traditional working straight knives and folders in standard patterns; banana/sheepfoot blade combinations in trapper patterns. **Patterns:** Locking folders, slip-joint folders and hunters. **Technical:** Grinds D2, ATS-34 and O1. Offers filework on some knives. **Prices:** $150 to $275; some to $600. **Remarks:** Part-time maker; first knife sold in 1975. **Mark:** The division sign.

SINCLAIR, J.E., 520 Francis Rd., Pittsburgh, PA, 15239/412-793-5778
Specialties: Fancy hunters & Fighters. **Patterns:** Boots, daggers, fighters and hunters. **Technical:** Flat-grinds & hollow grind, prefers hand rubbed satin finsh. Uses natural handle materials; prefers mirror finishes. **Prices:** $185 to $800. **Remarks:** Part-time maker; first knife sold in 1995. **Mark:** First and middle initials, last name and maker.

SINYARD, CLESTON S., 27522 Burkhardt Dr., Elberta, AL, 36530/334-987-1361
Specialties: Working straight knives and folders of his design. **Patterns:** Hunters, buckskinners, Bowies, daggers, fighters and all-Damascus folders. **Technical:** Makes Damascus from 440C, stainless steels, D2 and regular high-carbon steel; forges "forefinger pad" into hunters and skinners. **Prices:** In Damascus $450 to $1,500; some $2,500. **Remarks:** Full-time maker; first knife sold in 1980. Doing business as Nimo Forge. **Mark:** Last name, U.S.A. in anvil.

SISKA, JIM, 6 Highland Ave., Westfield, MA, 01085/413-568-9787
Specialties: Traditional working straight knives and folders. **Patterns:** Hunters, fighters, Bowies and one of a kinds; folders. **Technical:** Grinds D2 and ATS-34; buys Damascus. Likes exotic woods. **Prices:** $195 to $2,500. **Remarks:** Part-time maker; first knife sold in 1983. **Mark:** Last name in Old English.

SJOSTRAND, KEVIN, 1541 S. Cain St., Visalia, CA, 93292/209-625-5254
Specialties: Traditional and working/using straight knives and folders of his design or to customer specs. **Patterns:** Bowies, hunters, utility/camp knives, lockback, springback and liner lock folders. **Technical:** Grinds ATS-34, 440C and 1095. Prefers high polished blades and full tang. Natural and stabilized hardwoods, Micarta and stag handle material. **Prices:** $75 to $300. **Remarks:** Part-time maker; first knife sold in 1992. Doing business as Black Oak Blades. **Mark:** Oak tree, Black Oak Blades, name, or just last name.

SKELLERN, DR. M.J., P.O. Munster 4278, , SOUTH AFRICA, /03930-92537
Specialties: Fancy high-tech folders of his design. **Patterns:** Locking and slip-joint folders. **Technical:** Grinds ATS-34 and Sandvick 12C27; uses Damascus. Inlays his stainless steel integral handles; offers rare African handle materials. **Prices:** $200 to $500; some to $700. **Remarks:** Part-time maker; first knife sold in 1986. **Mark:** Last name.

SLEE, FRED, 9 John St., Morganville, NJ, 07751/908-591-9047
Specialties: Working straight knives, some fancy, to customer specs. **Patterns:** Hunters, fighters, boots, fancy daggers and folders. **Technical:** Grinds D2, 440C and ATS-34. **Prices:** $125 to $550. **Remarks:** Part-time maker; first knife sold in 1980. **Mark:** Last name in old English.

SLOAN, SHANE, Rt. 1, Box 17, Newcastle, TX, 76372/817-846-3290
Specialties: Collector-grade straight knives and folders. **Patterns:** Bowies, lockers, slip-joints, fancy folders, fighters and period pieces. **Technical:** Grinds D2 and ATS-34. Uses hand-rubbed satin finish. Prefers rare natural handle materials. **Prices:** $250 to $1,600. **Remarks:** Full-time maker; first knife sold in 1985. **Mark:** Name and city.

SLOBODIAN, SCOTT, 4101 River Ridge Dr., P.O. Box 1498, San Andreas, CA, 95249/209-286-1980
Specialties: Japanese-style knives and swords, period pieces, fantasy pieces and miniatures. **Patterns:** Small kweikens, tantos, wakazashis, katanas, traditional samurai swords. **Technical:** Flat-grinds 1050, commercial Damascus. **Prices:** $800 to $3,500; some to $7,500. **Remarks:** Full-time maker; first knife sold in 1987. **Mark:** Blade signed in Japanese characters and various scripts.

SMALL, ED, Rt. 1, Box 178-A, Keyser, WV, 26726/304-298-4254
Specialties: Working knives of his design; period pieces. **Patterns:** Hunters, daggers, buckskinners and camp knives; likes one of a kinds. **Technical:** Forges and grinds W2, L6 and his own Damascus. **Prices:** $150 to $1,500. **Remarks:** Full-time maker; first knife sold in 1978. Doing business as Iron Mountain Forge Works. **Mark:** Script initials connected.

SMART, STEATEN, 15815 Acorn Circle, Tavares, FL, 32778/352-343-8423

SMART, STEVE, 1 Meadowbrook Cir., Melissa, TX, 75454/214-837-4216
Specialties: Working/using straight knives and folders of his design, to customer specs and in standard patterns. **Patterns:** Bowies, hunters, kitchen knives, locking folders, utility/camp, fishing and bird knives. **Technical:** Grinds ATS-34, D2, 440C and O1. Prefers mirror polish or satin finish; hollow-grinds all blades. All knives come with sheath. Offers some filework. **Prices:** $95 to $225; some to $500. **Remarks:** Spare-time maker; first knife sold in 1983. **Mark:** Name, Custom, city and state in oval.

SMIT, CORN, P.O. Box 31, Darwendale, Zimbabwe, /110-263-69-3107
Specialties: Working/using knives, custom made collectors knives. Your design and customer specs. **Patterns:** Daggers, Bowies, hunters, and exclusive one off designs. **Technical:** Grind 440C stainless and D-2. We photo etch animals, names, logos, etc. on the blades. We do gold plating of etches and scrimshaw on handles. Guards can be brass or sterling or horn. Handles indigenous wood or horns. **Prices:** $150 to $1,000; some to $5,000. **Remarks:** Full-time maker; first knife sold in 1984. We give a limited lifetime guarantee. **Mark:** Blacksmith - Zimbabwe with SMIT underneath.

SMIT, GLENN, 627 Cindy Ct., Aberdeen, MD, 21001/410-272-2959
Specialties: Working and using straight and folding knives of his design or to customer specs. Customizes and repairs all types of cutlery. **Patterns:** Hunters, Bowies, daggers, fighters, utility/camp, folders, kitchen knives and miniatures. **Technical:** Grinds 440C, ATS-34, O1 and A2; reforges commercial Damascus and makes own Damascus. **Prices:** Miniatures start at $20; full-size knives start at $40. **Remarks:** Spare-time maker; first knife sold in 1986. Doing business as Wolf's Knives. **Mark:** G.P. SMIT, with year on reverse side.

SMITH, JOHN W., 1416 Cow Branch Rd., West Liberty, KY, 41472/606-743-3599
Specialties: Fancy and working locking folders of his design or to customer specs. **Patterns:** Interframes, traditional and daggers. **Technical:** Grinds ATS-34, 440C and commercial Damascus. Offers gold inlay, engraving with gold inlay, hand-fitted mosaic pearl inlay and filework. Prefers hand-rubbed finish. Pearl and ivory available. **Prices:** $650 to $1,500; some higher. **Remarks:** Full-time maker. **Mark:** Initials engraved inside diamond.

SMITH, BOBBIE D., 802 W. Hwy. 90., Bonifay, FL, 32425/904-547-5935
Specialties: Working straight knives and folders. **Patterns:** Bowies, hunters and slip-joints. **Technical:** Grinds 440C and ATS-34; custom sheaths for each knife. **Prices:** $75 to $250. **Remarks:** Part-time maker. **Mark:** NA.

SMITH, D. NOEL, P.O. Box 1363, Canon City, CO, 81215-1363/719-275-2574
Specialties: Fantasy art knives of his own design or to standard patterns. **Patterns:** Daggers, hunters and art knives. **Technical:** Grinds O1, D2, 440C stainless and Damascus. Offers natural and synthetic carved handles, engraved and acid etched blades, sculptured guards, buttcaps and bases. **Prices:** Start at $250. **Remarks:** Full-time maker; first knife sold in 1990. Doing business as Minds' Eye Metalmaster. **Mark:** Signature.

SMITH, GREGORY H., 8607 Coddington Ct., Louisville, KY, 40299/502-491-7439
Specialties: Traditional working straight knives and fantasy knives to customer specs. **Patterns:** Fighters and modified Bowies; camp knives and swords. **Technical:** Grinds O1, 440C and commercial Damascus bars. **Prices:** $55 to $300. **Remarks:** Part-time maker; first knife sold in 1985. **Mark:** JAGED, plus signature.

SMITH, J.D., 516 E. Second St., No. 38, S. Boston, MA, 02127/617-269-1699
Specialties: Classic working and using straight knives and folders; period pieces mainly from his design. **Patterns:** Bowies, fighters and locking folders. **Technical:** Forges and grinds ATS-34, his Damascus, O1, 1095 and wootz-pattern hammer steel. **Prices:** $200 to $800; some to $1,500. **Remarks:** Full-time maker; first knife sold in 1987. Doing business as Hammersmith. **Mark:** Last initial alone or in cartouche.

SMITH, JOHN M., 3450 E Beguelin Rd, Centralia, IL, 62801/618-249-6444
Specialties: Art knives and some work knives. **Patterns:** Daggers, Bowies, fighters, boots, and folders. **Technical:** Forges Damascus. **Prices:** $700 to $3,000. **Remarks:** Full-time maker; first knife sold in 1980. **Mark:** Etched signature or logo.

SMITH, JOSH, Box 64, Lincoln, MT, 59639/406-362-4485
Specialties: Working/using and hunting knives. **Patterns:** Hunters and skinners. **Technical:** Hand-forges 5160; stock removal 1095. **Prices:** Start at $100. **Remarks:** Part-time maker; first knife sold in 1992. **Mark:** First and last name and Custom Knives.

SMITH, NEWMAN L., 676 Glades Rd., Shop #3, Gatlinburg, TN, 37738/423-436-3322
Specialties: Collector-grade and working knives. **Patterns:** Hunters, slip-joint and lock-back folders, some miniatures. **Technical:** Grinds O1 and ATS-34; makes fancy sheaths. **Prices:** $110 to $450; some to $1,000. **Remarks:** Full-time maker; first knife sold in 1984. Partners part-time to handle Damascus blades by Jeff Hurst; marks these with SH connected. **Mark:** First and middle initials, last name.

SMITH, RALPH L., 522 Hendrix Road, Greer, SC, 29651-7950/864-848-1247
Specialties: Working knives. **Patterns:** Hunters, folders, fighters and boots. **Technical:** Grinds ATS-34 and D2. **Prices:** $140 to $600. **Remarks:** Part-time maker; first knife sold in 1971. **Mark:** Last name, handcrafted knives, in state map logo.

SMITH, RAYMOND L., Box 370, Breesport, NY, 14816/607-739-3126
Specialties: Working/using straight knives and folders to customer specs and in standard patterns; period pieces. **Patterns:** Bowies, hunters, slip-joints. **Technical:** Forges 5160, 52100, 1018 Damascus and wire cable Damascus. Filework. **Prices:** $55 to $225; some to $500. **Remarks:** Part-time maker; first knife sold in 1991. Doing business as The Anvils Edge. **Mark:** Initials in script.

SMITH, W.M., 802 W. Hwy. 90, Bonifay, FL, 32425/904-547-5935

SMITH, MICHAEL J., 11507 Ola Ave N, TAMPA, FL, 33612/813-933-9395
Specialties: Fancy and high-tech folders folders of his design. **Patterns:** Locking folders. **Technical:** Grinds ATS-34 and commercial Damascus. Hand-rubbed satin finish. Prefers ivory and pearl materials. Liners are GAL4V titanium. **Prices:** $500 to $3,000. **Remarks:** Full-time maker; first knife sold in 1989. **Mark:** Name, city, state.

SMITH JR., JAMES B. "RED", Rt. 2, Box 1525, Morven, GA, 31638/912-775-2844
Specialties: Folders. **Patterns:** Rotating rear-lock folders. **Technical:** Grinds ATS-34, D2 and Vascomax 350. **Prices:** Start at $350. **Remarks:** Full-time maker; first knife sold in 1985. **Mark:** GA RED in cowboy hat.

SMOKER, RAY, 113 Church Rd., Searcy, AR, 72143/501-796-2712
Specialties: Working/using fixed blades of his design only. **Patterns:** Hunters, skinners, utility/camp and flat-ground knives. **Technical:** Forges his own Damascus and 52100; makes sheaths. Uses improved multiple edge quench he developed. **Prices:** $140 to $200; price includes sheath. **Remarks:** Full-time maker; first knife sold in 1992. **Mark:** Last name.

SMYTHE, KEN, Box 494, Underberg 4590, SOUTH AFRICA, /033-7011542
Specialties: Working and using straight knives of his design and to customer specs. **Patterns:** Fighters and hunters. **Technical:** Grinds 12C27 and 440C. Scrimshaws. **Prices:** $150 to $480. **Remarks:** Part-time maker; first knife sold in 1982. **Mark:** Sword lying on Bible.

SNARE, MICHAEL, 3352 E. Mescal St., Phoenix, AZ, 85028/

SNELL, JERRY L., 235 Woodsong Dr., Fayetteville, GA, 30214/770-461-0586
Specialties: Working straight knives of his design and in standard patterns. **Patterns:** Hunters, boots, fighters, daggers and a few folders. **Technical:** Grinds 440C, ATS-34; buys Damascus. **Prices:** $175 to $1,000. **Remarks:** Part-time maker. **Mark:** Last name, or name, city and state.

SNOW, BILL, 4824 18th Ave., Columbus, GA, 31904/706-576-4390
Specialties: Traditional working/using straight knives and folders of his design and to customer specs. Offers engraving and scrimshaw. **Patterns:** Bowies, fighters, hunters and folders. **Technical:** Grinds ATS-34, 440V, 440C, 420V, CPM350, BG42, A2, D2, 5160, 52100 and O1; forges if needed. Cryogenically quenches all steels; inlaid handles; some integrals; leather or Kydex sheaths. **prices:** $125 to $700; some to $3,500. **Remarks:** Full-time maker; first knife sold in 1958. Doing business as Tipi Knifeworks. **Mark:** Old English scroll "S" inside a tipi.

SOLOMON, MARVIN, 23750 Cold Springs Rd., Ferndale, AR, 72122/501-821-3170
Specialties: Traditional working and using straight knives of his design and to customer specs. **Patterns:** Bowies, hunters and utility/camp knives. **Technical:** Forges 5160, 1095, O1 and random Damascus. **Prices:** $100 to $500. **Remarks:** Part-time maker; first knife sold in 1990. Doing business as Cold Springs Forge. **Mark:** Last name.

custom knifemakers

SONTHEIMER, G. DOUGLAS, 12604 Bridgeton Dr., Potomac, MD, 20854/301-963-3855
Specialties: Working straight knives of his design. **Patterns:** Fighters, backpackers, claws and straight edges. **Technical:** Grinds. Price: $275 to $900; some to $1,500. **Remarks:** Spare-time maker; first knife sold in 1976. **Mark:** LORD.

SOPPERA, ARTHUR, Morgenstalstr. 37, P.O. Box 708, CH-8038 Zurich, SWITZERLAND, /1-482 86 12
Specialties: High-art, high-tech knives of his design. **Patterns:** Mostly locking folders, some straight knives. **Technical:** Grinds ATS-34 and commercial Damascus. Folders have button lock of his own design; some are fancy folders in jeweler's fashion. Also makes jewelry with integrated small knives. **Prices:** $200 to $1,000; some $2,000 and higher. **Remarks:** Full-time maker; first knife sold in 1986. **Mark:** Stylized initials, name, country.

SORNBERGER, JIM, 25126 Overland Dr., Volcano, CA, 95689/209-295-7819
Specialties: Collectible straight knives. **Patterns:** Fighters, daggers, Bowies; miniatures; hunters, custom canes, liner locks folders. **Technical:** Grinds 440C, 154CM and ATS-34; engraves, carves and embellishes. **Prices:** $500 to $7,500 & up. **Remarks:** Full-time maker; first knife sold in 1970. **Mark:** First initial, last name, city and state.

SPANO, DOMINICK, 2726 Rice Ave., San Angelo, TX, 76904/915-944-9630
Specialties: Working/using straight knives of his design and to customer specs. **Patterns:** Boots, hunters, slip-joints and lockbacks. **Technical:** Grinds ATS-34. Heat-treats. Makes sheaths. **Prices:** $145 to $300. **Remarks:** Part-time maker; first knife sold in 1989. Doing business as Spano Knives. **Mark:** Last name in script.

SPECK, DOUG, 483 Nairn Ave., Toronto, ONT., CANADA, M6E 4J2/
Specialties: Fixed and filding blades. **Patterns:** Hunters, utility, camping, folding knives. **Technical:** Forge, grind and heat-treat carbon steels 01 & 5160 stainless on special order. **Prices:** Fixed blades from $85, folding knives from $200. **Remarks:** Will work with customers on knife patterns, knife come with sheaths. **Mark:** Doug Speck, Maker, Toronto, ON.

SPENCER, JOHN E., HC63 Box 267, Harper, TX, 78631/512-864-4216
Specialties: Working straight knives. **Patterns:** Hunters, fighters and survival knives; locking folders; axes. **Technical:** Grinds O1, D2 and 440C; commercial Damascus. **Prices:** $60 to $300; some to $500. **Remarks:** Full-time maker; first knife sold in 1982. **Mark:** Last name.

SPINALE, RICHARD, 4021 Canterbury Ct., Lorain, OH, 44053/216-282-1565
Specialties: High-art working knives of his design. **Patterns:** Hunters, fighters, daggers and locking folders. **Technical:** Grinds 440C, ATS-34 and 07; engraves. Offers gold bolsters and other deluxe treatments. **Prices:** $300 to $1,000; some to $3,000. **Remarks:** Spare-time maker; first knife sold in 1976. **Mark:** Name, address, year and model number.

SPIVEY, JEFFERSON, 9244 W. Wilshire, Yukon, OK, 73099/405-721-4442
Specialties: The Sabertooth: a combination hatchet, saw and knife. **Patterns:** Built for the wilderness, all are one of a kind. **Technical:** Grinds chromemoly steel. The sawtooth spine curves with a double row of biangular teeth. **Prices:** Start at $300. **Remarks:** First knife sold in 1977. **Mark:** Name and serial number.

SPRAGG, WAYNE E., P.O. Box 508, 1314 3675 East Rd., Ashton, ID, 83420/
Specialties: Working straight knives, some fancy. **Patterns:** Hunters, skinners, kitchen knives, Bowies and miniatures. **Technical:** Grinds ATS-34, 440C, D2, O1 and commercial Damascus. Likes filework and fancy handlework. All blades heat-treated by Paul Bos. **Prices:** $110 to $400; some higher. **Remarks:** Spare-time maker; first knife sold in 1989. **Mark:** Name, city and state with bucking horse logo.

SPROUSE, TERRY, 1633 Newfound Rd., Asheville, NC, 28806/704-683-3400
Specialties: Traditional and working straight knives of his design. **Patterns:** Bowies and hunters. **Technical:** Grinds ATS-34, 440C and D2. Makes sheaths. **Prices:** $85 to $125; some to $225. **Remarks:** Part-time maker; first knife sold in 1989. **Mark:** NA.

STAFFORD, RICHARD, 104 Marcia Ct., Warner Robins, GA, 31088/912-923-6372
Specialties: High-tech straight knives and some folders. **Patterns:** Hunters in several patterns, fighters, boots, camp knives, combat knives and period pieces. **Technical:** Grinds ATS-34 and 440C; satin finish is standard. **Prices:** Starting at $75. **Remarks:** Part-time maker; first knife sold in 1983. **Mark:** Last name.

STALTER, HARRY L., 2509 N. Trivoli Rd., Trivoli, IL, 61569/309-362-2306
Specialties: Fancy working knives of his design and in standard patterns; period pieces. **Patterns:** Hunters, fighters and Bowies; fancy daggers, miniatures-fancy swords, daggers, fantasy knives. **Technical:** Stock removal; 440C, D2, 154 CM and Damascus. Currently makes 60 styles of miniatures with 440C, Damascus. **Prices:** $110 to $2000. **Remarks:** Full-time maker; first knife sold in 1980. **Mark:** Last name.

STAPEL, CRAIG, Box 1617, Glendale, CA, 91209/213-668-2669
Specialties: Working knives. **Patterns:** Hunters, tantos and fishing knives. **Technical:** Grinds 440C and AEB-L. **Prices:** $80 to $150. **Remarks:** Spare-time maker; first knife sold in 1981. **Mark:** First and middle initials, last name.

STAPEL, CHUCK, Box 1617, Glendale, CA, 91209/213-66-KNIFE
Specialties: Working knives of his design. **Patterns:** Variety of straight knives tantos, hunters, folders and utility knives. **Technical:** Grinds D2, 440C and AEB-L. **Prices:** $185 to $3,000. **Remarks:** Full-time maker; first knife sold in 1974. **Mark:** Last name or last name, U.S.A.

STEEL MASTER, , , /847-473-9987
Specialties: Working and using straight knives to customer specs; period pieces. **Patterns:** Boots, Bowies, skinners, fighters and utility/camp knives. **Technical:** Forges Damascus and O1; grinds D2 and 440. **Prices:** $100 to $400. **Remarks:** Full-time maker; first knife sold in 1976. **Mark:** None.

STEGALL, KEITH, 2101 W. 32nd, Anchorage, AK, 99517/907-276-6002
Specialties: Traditional working straight knives. **Patterns:** Most patterns. **Technical:** Grinds 440C and 154CM. **Prices:** $100 to $300. **Remarks:** Spare-time maker; first knife sold in 1987. **Mark:** Name and state with anchor.

STEGNER, WILBUR G., 9242 173rd Ave. SW, Rochester, WA, 98579/360-273-0937
Specialties: Working/using straight knives and folders of his design. **Patterns:** Hunters and locking folders. **Technical:** Grinds ATS-34 and other tool steels. Quenches, tempers and hardness tests each blade. **Prices:** $80 to $400; some to $3,000. **Remarks:** Full-time maker; first knife sold in 1979. **Mark:** First and middle initials, last name in bar over shield logo.

STEIGER, MONTE L., Box 186, Genesee, ID, 83832/208-285-1769
Specialties: Traditional working/using straight knives of all designs. **Patterns:** Hunters, utility/camp knives. **Technical:** Grinds 1095, O1, 440C, ATS-34. Handles of stacked leather, natural wood, Micarta or Pakkawood. Each knife comes with right- or left-handed sheath. **Prices:** $70 to $220. **Remarks:** Spare-time maker; first knife sold in 1988. **Mark:** First initial, last name, city and state.

STEIGERWALT, KEN, P.O. Box 172, Orangeville, PA, 17859/717-683-5156
Specialties: Fancy classic folders of his design. **Patterns:** Folders, button locks and rear locks. **Technical:** Grinds ATS-34, 440C and commercial Damascus. Experiments with unique filework. **Prices:** $200 to $600; some to $1,500. **Remarks:** Full-time maker; first knife sold in 1981. **Mark:** Initials.

STEINAU, JURGEN, Julius-Hart Strasse 44, Berlin 0-1162, GERMANY, /372-6452512
Specialties: Fantasy and high-art straight knives of his design. **Patterns:** Boots, daggers and switch-blade folders. **Technical:** Grinds 440B, 2379 and X90 Cr.Mo.V. 78. **Prices:** $1,500 to $2,500; some to $3,500. **Remarks:** Full-time maker; first knife sold in 1984. **Mark:** Symbol, plus year, month day and serial number.

STEINBERG, AL, 2499 Trenton Dr., San Bruno, CA, 94066/415-583-8281
Specialties: Fancy working straight knives to customer specs. **Patterns:** Hunters, Bowies, fishing, camp knives, push knives and high end kitchen knives. **Technical:** Grinds O1, 440C and 154CM. **Prices:** $60 to $2,500.

Remarks: Full-time maker; first knife sold in 1972. **Mark:** Signature, city and state.

STEKETEE, CRAIG A., 871 N. Hwy. 60, Billings, MO, 65610/417-744-2770
Specialties: Classic and working straight knives and swords of his design. **Patterns:** Bowies, Japanese style swords and hunters. **Technical:** Forges his own Damascus; bronze and silver cast fittings. Engraves; offers filework. Prefers exotic and natural handle materials. **Prices:** $125 to $4,000. **Remarks:** Full-time maker. **Mark:** STEK.

STEPHAN, DANIEL, 2201 S. Miller Rd., Valrico, FL, 33594/813-684-2781

STERLING, MURRAY, 523 Round Peak Church Rd., Mount Airy, NC, 27030/336-352-5110
Specialties: Single & dual blade folders. Interframes & integral dovetail frames. **Technical:** Grinds ATS-34 or Damascus by Mike Norris and/or Devin Thomas. **Prices:** $300 & up. **Remarks:** Full-time maker; first knife sold in 1991. **Mark:** Last name stamped.

STEVENS, BARRY B., 901 Amherst, Cridersville, OH, 45806/419-221-2446
Specialties: Small fancy folders of his design and to customer specs; mini-hunters and fighters. **Patterns:** Fighters, hunters, liner locks, lockback and bolster release folders. **Technical:** Grinds ATS-34, 440C, Damascus and SS Damascus. Prefers hand-rubbed finishes and natural handle materials-horn, ivory, pearls, exotic woods. **Prices:** $300 to $1,000; some to $2,500. **Remarks:** Part-time maker; first knife sold in 1991. Doing business as Bare Knives. **Mark:** First and middle initials, last name.

STICE, DOUGLAS W, 446 W 6th St, Haysville, KS, 67060 1622/
Specialties: Working straight knives. **Patterns:** Hunters, bowies, fighters, tantos and ifshing knives. **Technical:** Grinds 440C, ATS-34 and D2. **Prices:** $50 to $150; some to $225. **Remarks:** Part-time maker; first knife sold in 1985. **Mark:** Name.

STIPES, DWIGHT, 8089 SE Country Estates Way, Jupiter, FL, 33458/407-743-0550
Specialties: Traditional and working straight knives in standard patterns. **Patterns:** Boots, Bowies, daggers, hunters and fighters. **Technical:** Grinds 440C, D2 and D3 tool steel. Handles of natural materials, animal, bone or horn. **Prices:** $75 to $150. **Remarks:** Full-time maker; first knife sold in 1972. **Mark:** Last name.

STODDARD'S, INC., COPLEY PLACE, 100 Huntington Ave, Boston, MA, 02116/617-536-8688
Specialties: Cutlery (kitchen, pocket knives, Randall-made Knives, custom knives, scissors, & manicure tools) Binoculars, low vision aids, personal care items (hair brushes, manicure sets, mirrors.)

STODDART, W.B. BILL, 917 Smiley, Forest Park, OH, 45240/513-851-1543
Specialties: Sportsmen's working knives and multi-blade folders. **Patterns:** Hunters, camp and fish knives; multi-blade reproductions of old standards. **Technical:** Grinds A2, 440C and ATS-34; makes sheaths to match handle materials. **Prices:** $80 to $300; some to $850. **Remarks:** Part-time maker; first knife sold in 1976. **Mark:** Name, Cincinnati, state.

STOKES, ED, 22614 Cardinal Dr., Hockley, TX, 77447/713-351-1319
Specialties: Working straight knives and folders of all designs. **Patterns:** Boots, Bowies, daggers, fighters, hunters and miniatures. **Technical:** Grinds ATS-34, 440C and D2. Offers decorative buttcaps, tapered spacers on handles and finger grooves, nickel-silver inlays, hand-made sheaths. **Prices:** $185 to $290; some to $350. **Remarks:** Full-time maker; first knife sold in 1973. **Mark:** First and last name, Custom Knives with Apache logo.

STONE, JERRY, P.O. Box 1027, Lytle, TX, 78052/512-772-4502
Specialties: Traditional working and using folders of his design and to customer specs; fancy knives. **Patterns:** Fighters, hunters, locking folders and slip-joints. **Technical:** Grinds 440C and ATS-34. Offers filework. **Prices:** $125 to $375; some to $700. **Remarks:** Full-time maker; first knife sold in 1973. **Mark:** Initials.

STORCH, ED, R.R. 4 Mannville, Alberta T0B 2W0, CANADA, /403-763-2214
Specialties: Working knives, fancy fighting knives, kitchen cutlery and art knives. **Patterns:** Working patterns, bowies and folders. **Technical:** Forges his own damascus and carbon steel. Grinds ATS-34. Builds Tita-

nium folders. **Prices:** $45 to $750 (US). **Remarks:** Part-time maker; first knife sold in 1984. **Mark:** Last Name.

STOUT, JOHNNY, 1205 Forest Trail, New Braunfels, TX, 78132/830-629-1011
Specialties: Working knives, some fancy. **Patterns:** Hunters, tactical, Bowies, automatics, liner locks and slip-joints. **Technical:** Grinds stainless and carbon steels; forges own Damascus. **Prices:** $450 to $895; some to $3,500. **Remarks:** Full-time maker; first knife sold in 1983. **Mark:** Name and city in logo with serial number.

STOVER, TERRY "LEE", 1809 N. 300 E., Kokomo, IN, 46901/765-452-3928
Specialties: Damascus folders with filework; Damascus Bowies of his design or to customer specs. **Patterns:** Lockback folders and Sheffield-style Bowies. **Technical:** Forges 1095, Damascus using O2, 203E or O2, pure nickel. Makes mokume. Uses only natural handle material. **Prices:** $300 to $1,700; some to $2,000. **Remarks:** Part-time maker; first knife sold in 1984. **Mark:** First and middle initials, last name in knife logo; Damascus blades marked in Old English.

STRAIGHT, DON, P.O. Box 12, Points, WV, 25437/304-492-5471
Specialties: Traditional working straight knives of his design. **Patterns:** Hunters, Bowies and fighters. **Technical:** Grinds 440C, ATS-34 and D2. **Prices:** $75 to $125; some to $225. **Remarks:** Spare-time maker; first knife sold in 1978. **Mark:** Last name.

STRANDE, POUL, Soster Svenstrup Byvej 16, Dastrup 4130 Viby Sj., DENMARK, /46 19 43 05
Specialties: Classic fantasy working knives. **Patterns:** Bowies, daggers, fighters, hunters and swords. **Technical:** Uses carbon steel and 15C20 steel. **Prices:** NA. **Remarks:** Full-time maker; first knife sold in 1985. **Mark:** First and last initials.

STRAUSS, LEVI, 5979 N. West 151st St., Miami Lakes, FL, 33014/
Specialties: Fancy working knives of his design. **Patterns:** Hunters, fighters and camp knives; locking folders. **Technical:** Grinds D2, 440C and ATS-34. **Prices:** $75 to $250; some to $700. **Remarks:** Part-time maker; first knife sold in 1983. **Mark:** Name.

STRICKLAND, DALE, 1440 E. Thompson View, Monroe, UT, 84754/435-896-8362
Specialties: Traditional and working straight knives and folders of his design and to customer specs. **Patterns:** Hunters, folders, miniatures and utility knives. **Technical:** Grinds Damascus and 440C. **Prices:** $120 to $350; some to $500. **Remarks:** Part-time maker; first knife sold in 1991. **Mark:** Oval stamp of name, Maker.

STRONG, SCOTT, 2138 Oxmoor Dr., Beavercreek, OH, 45431/937-426-9290
Specialties: Working knives, some deluxe. **Patterns:** Hunters, fighters, survival and military-style knives, art knives. **Technical:** Forges and grinds O1, A2, D2, 440C and ATS-34. Uses no solder; most knives disassemble. **Prices:** $75 to $450; some to $1,500. **Remarks:** Spare-time maker; first knife sold in 1983. **Mark:** Strong Knives.

STROYAN, ERIC, Box 218, Dalton, PA, 18414/717-563-2603
Specialties: Classic and working/using straight knives and folders of his design. **Patterns:** Hunters, locking folders, slip-joints. **Technical:** Forges Damascus; grinds ATS-34, D2. **Prices:** $200 to $600; some to $2,000. **Remarks:** Part-time maker; first knife sold in 1968. **Mark:** Signature or initials stamp.

STUART, STEVE, Box 168, Gores Landing, Ont., CANADA, K0K 2E0/905-342-5617
specialties: Straight knives. **Patterns:** Tantos, fighters, skinners, file and rasp knives. **Technical:** Uses 440C, files, Micarta and natural handle materials. **Prices:** $60 to $400. **Remarks:** Part-time maker. **Mark:** Interlocking SS with last name.

SUEDMEIER, HARLAN, RFD 2, Box 299D, Nebraska City, NE, 68410/402-873-4372
Specialties: Working straight knives. **Patterns:** Hunters, fighters and Bowies. **Technical:** Grinds ATS-34 and 440C; forges 52100. **Prices:** Start at $75. **Remarks:** Part-time maker; first knife sold in 1982. Not currently taking orders. **Mark:** First initial, last name.

SUGIHARA, KEIDOH, 4-16-1 Kamori-Cho, Kishiwada City, Osaka, F596-0042, JAPAN, /
Specialties: High-tech working straight knives and folders of his design. **Patterns:** Bowies, hunters, fighters, fishing, boots, some pocket knives

custom knifemakers

and liner lock folders. **Technical:** Grinds ATS-34, COS-25, buys Damascus and high carbon steels. Prices $40 to $2000. **Remarks:** Full-time maker; first knife sold in 1980. **Mark:** Initial logo with fish design.

SUMMERS, DENNIS K., 827 E. Cecil St., Springfield, OH, 45503/513-324-0624
Specialties: Working/using knives. **Patterns:** Fighters and personal knives. **Technical:** Grinds 440C, A2 and D2. Makes drop and clip point. **Prices:** $75 to $200. **Remarks:** Part-time maker; first knife sold in 1995. **Mark:** First and middle initials, last name, serial number.

SUMMERS, ARTHUR L., 8700 Brigner Rd., Mechanicsburg, OH, 43044/937-834-3776
Specialties: Collector-grade knives in drop points, clip points or straight blades. **Patterns:** Fighters, hunters, Bowies and personal knives. **Technical:** Grinds 440C, ATS-34, D2 and Damascus. **Prices:** $150 to $650; some to $2,000. **Remarks:** Part-time maker; first knife sold in 1987. **Mark:** Last name and serial number.

SUMMERS, DAN, 2675 NY Rt. 11, Whitney Pt., NY, 13862/

SUNDERLAND, RICHARD, Box 248, Quathiaski Cove, BC, CANADA, V0P 1N0/250-285-3038
Specialties: Personal and hunting knives with carved handles in oosic and ivory. **Patterns:** Hunters, Bowies, daggers, camp and personal knives. **Technical:** Grinds 440C, ATS 34 and O1. Handle materials of rosewoods, fossil mammoth ivory and oosic. **Prices:** $150 to $1,000. **Remarks:** Full-time maker; first knife sold in 1983. Doing business as Sun Knife Co. **Mark:** SUN.

SUTHERLAND, GREG, P.O. Box 23516, Flagstaff, AZ, 86002-3516/520-774-6050
Specialties: Classic working/using straight knives of his design and in standard patterns. **Patterns:** Bowies, hunters, fighters, boots, kitchen, duty and utility/camp knives. **Technical:** Grinds ATS-34, O1. Offers occasional filework and some bronze guards and bolsters. Likes desert ironwood. Hunting and utility knives come with leather or Kydex sheath. **Prices:** $100 to $1,000. **Remarks:** Full-time maker; first knife sold in 1989. Doing business as Sutherland Knives Outdoors West. **Mark:** Last name, city, state.

SUTTON, S. RUSSELL, 4900 Cypress Shores Dr., New Bern, NC, 28562/252-637-3963
Specialties: Straight knives and folders to customer specs and in standard patterns. **Patterns:** Boots, hunters and locking folders. **Technical:** Grinds ATS-34 and 440C. Makes own sheaths. **Prices:** $145 to $450; some to $625. **Remarks:** Part-time maker; first knife sold in 1992. **Mark:** Etched last name.

SWAIN, ROD, 1020 Avon Pl., South Pasadena, CA, 91030/818-799-7666
Specialties: Working straight knives, some fancy, of his design and to customer specs. **Patterns:** Outdoor patterns, Bowies and push knives, utility drop-points. **Technical:** Grinds O1, 440C, AEB-L. **Prices:** $75 to $250; some to $450. **Remarks:** Part-time maker; first knife sold in 1981. **Mark:** Last name in logo.

SWYHART, ART, 509 Main St., P.O. Box 267, Klickitat, WA, 98628/509-369-3451
Specialties: Traditional working and using knives of his design. **Patterns:** Bowies, hunters and utility/camp knives. **Technical:** Forges 52100, 5160 and Damascus 1084 mixed with either 15N20 or O186. Blades differentially heat-treated with visible temper line. **Prices:** $75 to $250; some to $350. **Remarks:** Part-time maker; first knife sold in 1983. **Mark:** First name, last initial in script.

SYSLO, CHUCK, 3418 South 116 Ave., Omaha, NE, 68144/402-333-0647
Specialties: High-tech working straight knives. **Patterns:** Hunters, daggers and survival knives; locking folders. **Technical:** Flat-grinds D2, 440C and 154CM; hand polishes only. **Prices:** $175 to $500; some to $3,000. **Remarks:** Part-time maker; first knife sold in 1978. **Mark:** CISCO in logo.

SZILASKI, JOSEPH, 29 Carroll Dr., Wappingers Falls, NY, 12590/914-297-5397
Specialties: Straight knives, folders and tomahawks of his design, to customer specs and in standard patterns. Many pieces are one of a kind. **Patterns:** Bowies, daggers, fighters, hunters, art knives and early American styles. **Technical:** Forges A2, D2, O1 and Damascus. **Prices:** $350 to $1250; some to $7,000. **Remarks:** Full-time maker; first knife sold in 1990. **Mark:** Snake logo.

t

TAGLIENTI, ANTONIO J., 164 Rhodes Dr., Beaver Falls, PA, 15010-1438/
Specialties: Working straight knives in standard patterns. **Patterns:** Hunters--likes forefinger radius; Bowies, tantos and camp knives. **Technical:** Grinds D2, 440C and 154CM. Emphasizes full tangs; offers filework. **Prices:** $85 to $200; some to $350. **Remarks:** Part-time maker; first knife sold in 1985. **Mark:** Last name.

TAKAHASHI, MASAO, 39-3 Sekine-cho, Maebashi-shi, Gunma 371, JAPAN, /0272-34-2223

TALLY, GRANT C., 14618 Cicotte, Allen Park, MI, 48101/313-381-0100
Specialties: Straight knives and folders of his design. **Patterns:** Bowies, daggers, fighters. **Technical:** Grinds ATS-34, 440C and D2. Offers filework. **Prices:** $250 to $1000. **Remarks:** Part-time maker; first knife sold in 1985. Doing business as GT Knives. **Mark:** G.

TAMBOLI, MICHAEL, 12447 N. 49 Ave., Glendale, AZ, 85304/602-978-4308
Specialties: Miniatures, some full size. **Patterns:** Miniature hunting knives to fantasy art knives. **Technical:** Grinds 440C, 154CM and Damascus. **Prices:** $75 to $500; some to $1,000. **Remarks:** Part-time maker; first knife sold in 1978. **Mark:** Initials or last name, city and state.

TASAKI, SEICHI, 24 Shizuwa, Shimotsuga-Gun, Tochigi, JAPAN, /0482-55-6066
Specialties: High-tech traditional straight knives and folders. **Patterns:** Variety of hunters, miniatures, interframe folders and more. **Technical:** Forges and grinds 440C and carbon steel. **Prices:** $230 to $850; some to $5,000. **Remarks:** Full-time maker; first knife sold in 1984. **Mark:** Initials connected.

TAY, LARRY C-G, Siglap P.O. Box 315, Singapore 9145, SINGAPORE, /65-2419421
Specialties: Working and using straight knives and folders of his design; Marble's Safety Knife with stained or albino Asian buffalo horn and bone or rosewood handles. **Patterns:** Fighters, locking folders and utility/camp knives. **Technical:** Forges and grinds 440C; uses Damascus USA billets, truck leaf springs. **Prices:** $50 to $200; some to $500. **Remarks:** Spare-time maker; first knife sold in 1957. **Mark:** LDA/LAKELL

TAYLOR, SHANE, 18 Broken Bow Ln., Miles City, MT, 59301/406-232-7175
Specialties: One-of-a-kind fancy Damascus straight knives and folders. **Patterns:** Bowies, folders and fighters. **Technical:** Forges own mosaic and pattern welded Damascus. **Prices:** $200 and up. **Remarks:** Full-time maker; first knife sold in 1982. **Mark:** First name.

TAYLOR, C. GRAY, 137 Lana View Dr., Kingsport, TN, 37664/423-288-5969
Specialties: High-art display knives; period pieces. **Patterns:** Fighters, Bowies, daggers, locking folders and interframes. **Technical:** Grinds 440C, 154CM and ATS-34. **Prices:** $200 to $3,000; some to $7,000. **Remarks:** Part-time maker; first knife sold in 1975. **Mark:** Name, city and state.

TAYLOR, BILLY, 10 Temple Rd., Petal, MS, 39465/601-544-0041
Specialties: Straight knives of his design. **Patterns:** Bowies, skinners, hunters and utility knives. **Technical:** Flat-grinds 440C, ATS-34 and 154CM. **Prices:** $60 to $300. **Remarks:** Part-time maker; first knife sold in 1991. **Mark:** Full name, city and state.

TERAUCHI, TOSHIYUKI, 7649-13 219-11 Yoshida, Fujita-Cho Gobo-Shi, JAPAN, /

TERRILL, STEPHEN, 21363 Rd. 196, Lindsay, CA, 93247/209-562-4395
Specialties: Deluxe working straight knives and folders. **Patterns:** Fighters, tantos, boots, locking folders and axes; traditional oriental patterns. **Technical:** Forges 440C, 1084 and his Damascus. **Prices:** Moderate. **Remarks:** Part-time maker; first knife sold in 1972. **Mark:** Name, city, state in logo.

TERZUOLA, ROBERT, 3933 Agua Fria St, Santa Fe, NM, 87501/505-473-1002
Specialties: Working folders of his design; period pieces. **Patterns:** High-tech utility, defense and gentleman's folders. **Technical:** Grinds ATS-34. Offers titanium and G10 composite for side-lock folders & tactical folders. **Prices:** $350 to $425, carbon fibre. **Remarks:** Full-time maker; first knife sold in 1980. **Mark:** Mayan dragon head, name and motto meaning "second to none".

THAYER, DANNY, 4504 W. 660 S., Lafayette, IN, 47905/765-538-3105
Specialties: Traditional working and using straight knives in standard patterns and to customer specs. **Patterns:** Hunters, Bowies, daggers, utility/camp and kitchen knives. **Technical:** Forges O1, W2, 1095 and 5160. **Prices:** $150 to $1,000. **Remarks:** Spare-time maker; first knife sold in 1988. **Mark:** Last name.

THEIS, TERRY, HC 63, Box 213, Harper, TX, 78631/830-864-4438

THILL, JIM, 10242 Bear Run, Missoula, MT, 59803/406-251-5475
Specialties: Traditional and working/using knives of his design. **Patterns:** Fighters, hunters and utility/camp knives. **Technical:** Grinds D2 and ATS-34; forges 10-95-85, 52100, 5160, 10 series, reg. damascus-mosaic. Offers hand cut sheaths with rawhide lace. **Prices:** $145 to $350; some to $1,250. **Remarks:** Full-time maker; first knife sold in 1962. **Mark:** Running bear in triangle.

THOMAS, ROCKY, 204 Columbia Dr., Ladson, SC, 29456/803-553-6843
Specialties: Traditional working and using straight knives in standard patterns. **Patterns:** Hunters and utility/camp knives. **Technical:** Grinds 440C, ATS-34 and commercial Damascus. **Prices:** $75 to $125. **Remarks:** Spare-time maker; first knife sold in 1986. **Mark:** First name in script.

THOMAS, KIM, P.O. Box 13, Brunswick, OH, 44212/330-483-3416
Specialties: Fancy and traditional straight knives of his design and to customer specs; period pieces. **Patterns:** Boots, daggers, fighters, swords. **Technical:** Forges own Damascus from 5160, 1010 and nickel. **Prices:** $135 to $1,500; some to $3,000. **Remarks:** Part-time maker; first knife sold in 1986. Doing business as Thomas Iron Works. **Mark:** Initials.

THOMAS, DANIEL, 1017 Rollins Dr. SW, Leesburg, VA, 22075/703-442-6877
Specialties: Traditional working and using straight knives and folders of his design. **Patterns:** Hunters, slip-joint and locking folders. **Technical:** Grinds ATS-34, D2 and commercial Damascus. Offers fixed blade and folder repair and rebuilding. **Prices:** $125 to $200; some to $350. **Remarks:** Spare-time maker; first knife sold in 1983. **Mark:** Last name, Handcrafted.

THOMAS, DEVIN, 90 N. 5th St., Panaca, NV, 89042/702-728-4363
Specialties: Traditional straight knives and folders in standard patterns. **Patterns:** Bowies, fighters, hunters. **Technical:** Forges stainless Damascus, nickel and 1095. Uses, makes and sells Mokume with brass, copper and nickel-silver. **Prices:** $300 to $1,200. **Remarks:** Full-time maker; first knife sold in 1979. **Mark:** First and last name, city and state with anvil, or first name only.

THOMPSON, KENNETH, 4887 Glenwhite Dr., Duluth, GA, 30136/770-446-6730
Specialties: Traditional working and using knives of his design. **Patterns:** Hunters, Bowies and utility/camp knives. **Technical:** Forges 5168, O1, 1095 and 52100. **Prices:** $75 to $1,500; some to $2,500. **Remarks:** Part-time maker; first knife sold in 1990. **Mark:** P/W; or name, P/W, city and state.

THOMPSON, TOMMY, 4015 NE Hassalo, Portland, OR, 97232-2607/503-235-5762
Specialties: Fancy and working knives; mostly liner lock folders. **Patterns:** Fighters, hunters and liner locks. **Technical:** Grinds D2, ATS-34, CPM440V and T15. Handles are either hardwood inlaid with wood banding and stone or shell, or made of agate, jasper, petrified woods, etc. **Prices:** $75 to $500; some to $1,000. **Remarks:** Part-time maker; first knife sold in 1987. Doing business as Stone Birds. **Mark:** First and last name, city and state. Other: Knifemaking temporarily stopped due to family obligations.

THOMPSON, LEON, 1735 Leon Drive, Forest Grove, OR, 97116/503-357-2573
Specialties: Working knives. **Patterns:** Locking folders, slip-joints and liner locks. **Technical:** Grinds ATS-34, D2 and 440C. **Prices:** $200 to $600. **Remarks:** Full-time maker; first knife sold in 1976. **Mark:** First and middle initials, last name, city and state.

THOMPSON, LLOYD, P.O. Box 1664, Pagosa Springs, CO, 81147/970-264-5837
Specialties: Working and collectible straight knives and folders of his design. **Patterns:** Hunter drop-points, lockbacks and hawkbills. **Technical:** Hollow-grinds ATS-34, D2 and O1. Uses sambar stag and exotic woods. **Prices:** $125 to $400. **Remarks:** Full-time maker; first knife sold in 1985. Doing business as Trapper Creek Knife Co. **Mark:** Name.

THOMSEN, LOYD W., HCR-46, Box 19, Oelrichs, SD, 57763/605-535-6162
Specialties: High-art and traditional working/using straight knives and folders of his design and to customer specs; period pieces. **Patterns:** Bowies, hunters, locking folders and utility/camp knives. **Technical:** Forges and grinds 1095HC, 440C stainless steel, nickel 200; special restoration process on period pieces. Makes sheaths. Uses natural materials for handles. **Prices:** $350 to $1,000. **Remarks:** Full-time maker; first knife sold in 1995. Doing business as Horsehead Creek Knives. **Mark:** Initials and last name over a horse's head.

THOUROT, MICHAEL W., T-814 Co. Road 11, Napoleon, OH, 43545/419-533-6832
Specialties: Working straight knives to customer specs. Designed two-handled skinning ax and limited edition engraved knife and art print set. **Patterns:** Fishing and fillet knives, Bowies, tantos and hunters. **Technical:** Grinds O1, D2, 440C and Damascus. **Prices:** $200 to $5,000. **Remarks:** Part-time maker; first knife sold in 1968. **Mark:** Initials.

THUESEN, KEVIN, 10649 Haddington, Suite 180, Houston, TX, 77043/713-461-8632
Specialties: Working straight knives. **Pattersn** Hunters, including upswept skinners, and custom walking sticks. **Technical:** Grinds D2, 440C, 154CM and ATS-34. **Prices:** $85 to $125; some to $200. **Remarks:** Part-time maker; first knife sold in 1985. **Mark:** Initials on slant.

THUESEN, ED, P.O. Box 86, Needville, TX, 77461-0086/409-793-3973 or 409-793-7733
Specialties: Working straight knives. **Patterns:** Hunters, fighters and survival knives. **Technical:** Grinds D2, 440C, ATS-34 and Vascowear. **Prices:** $85 to $250; some to $600. **Remarks:** Part-time maker; first knife sold in 1979. Runs knifemaker supply business. **Mark:** Last name.

TICHBOURNE, GEORGE, 7035 Maxwell Rd. #5, Mississauga, Ont., CANADA, L5S 1R5/905-670-0200
Specialties: Traditional working and using straight knives of his design. **Patterns:** Bowies, hunters, outdoor, kitchen & occasional artpieces. **Technical:** 440C stock removal. Does filework and scrimshaw. **Prices:** $80 to $350; some to $500. **Remarks:** Full-time maker; first knife sold in 1990. **Mark:** Full name over maple leaf.

TIGHE, BRIAN, RR 1, Ridgeville, Ont, CANADA, L0S 1M0/905-892-2734
Specialties: High tech tactical folders. **Patterns:** Boots, daggers, locking and slip-joint folders. **Technical:** Grinds 440C, ATS-34, BG-42 and Damascus. Prefers natural handle material inlay; hand finishes. **Prices:** $2000; some higher. **Remarks:** Part-time maker; first knife sold in 1989. **Mark:** Etched signature.

TILL, CALVIN E. AND RUTH, 619 Mears St., Chadron, NE, 69337/
Specialties: Fantasy and traditional straight knives of his design and to customer specs. **Patterns:** Bowies, hunters and locking folders. **Technical:** Grinds spring steel only. Full or threaded tangs. Prefers mirror polishes. **Prices:** $80 to $120; some to $250. **Remarks:** Part-time maker; first knife sold in 1986. **Mark:** RC Till

TODD, ED, 9 Woodlawn Rd., Putnam Valley, NY, 10579/

TOICH, NEVIO, Via Pisacane 9, Rettorgole di Caldogna, Vincenza, ITALY, 36030/0444-985065
Specialties: Working/using straight knives of his design or to customer specs. **Patterns:** Bowies, hunters, skinners and utility/camp knives. **Technical:** Grinds 440C, D2 and ATS-34. Hollow-grinds all blades and uses mirror polish. Offers hand-sewn sheaths. Uses wood and horn.

custom knifemakers

Prices: $120 to $300; some to $450. **Remarks:** Spare-time maker; first knife sold in 1989. Doing business as Custom Toich. **Mark:** Initials and model number punched.

TOKAR, DANIEL, Box 1776, Shepherdstown, WV, 25443/
Specialties: Working knives; period pieces. **Patterns:** Hunters, camp knives, buckskinners, axes, swords and battle gear. **Technical:** Forges L6, 1095 and his Damascus; makes mokume, Japanese alloys and bronze daggers; restores old edged weapons. **Prices:** $25 to $800; some to $3,000. **Remarks:** Part-time maker; first knife sold in 1979. Doing business as The Willow Forge. **Mark:** Arrow over rune and date.

TOLLEFSON, BARRY A., 177 Blackfoot Trail, Gunnison, CO, 81230-9720/970-641-0752
Specialties: Working straight knives, some fancy. **Patterns:** Hunters, skinners, fighters and camp knives. **Technical:** Grinds 440C, ATS-34 and D2. Likes mirror-finishes; offers some fancy filework. Handles made from elk, deer and exotic hardwoods. **Prices:** $75 to $300; some higher. **Remarks:** Part-time maker; first knife sold in 1990. **Mark:** Stylized initials.

TOMES, P.J., 2061 Harvard St., Middleburg, FL, 32068/904-282-7095
Specialties: Scagel reproductions. **Patterns:** Front lock folders. **Technical:** Forges 52100. **Prices:** $150 to $750. **Mark:** Last name, USA, MS, stamped in forged blades.

TOMES, ANTHONY S., 8190 Loch Seaforth Ct., Jacksonville, FL, 32244/
Specialties: Working knives and period pieces. **Patterns:** Hunters, daggers, folders and liner locks. **Technical:** Grinds D2 and ATS-34. **Prices:** $50 to $500. **Remarks:** Part-time maker. **Mark:** Initials.

TOMPKINS, DAN, P.O. Box 398, Peotone, IL, 60468/708-258-3620
Specialties: Working knives, some deluxe, some folders. **Patterns:** Hunters, boots, daggers and push knives. **Technical:** Grinds D2, 440C, ATS-34 and 154CM. **Prices:** $85 to $150; some to $400. **Remarks:** Part-time maker; first knife sold in 1975. **Mark:** Last name, city, state.

TONER, ROGER, 531 Lightfoot Place, Pickering, Ont., CANADA, L1V 5Z8/905-420-5555
Specialties: Exotic Sword canes. **Patterns:** Bowies, daggers and fighters. **Technical:** Grinds 440C, D2 and Damascus. Scrimshaws and engraves. Silvercast pommels and guards in animal shapes; twisted silver wire inlays. Uses semi-precious stones. **Prices:** $200 to $2000; some to $3000. **Remarks:** Part-time maker; first knife sold in 1982. **Mark:** Last name.

TOPLISS, M.W. "IKE", 1668 Hermosa Ct., Montrose, CO, 81401/970-249-4703
Specialties: Working/using straight knives of his design and to customer specs. **Patterns:** Boots, hunters, utility/camp knives. **Technical:** {refers ATS-34. Other steels available on request. Likes stabilized wood, natural hardwoods, antler and Micarta. **Prices:** $175 to $300; some to $800. **Remarks:** Part-time maker; first knife sold in 1984. **Mark:** Name, city, state.

TOWELL, DWIGHT L., 2375 Towell Rd., Midvale, ID, 83645/208-355-2419
Specialties: Solid, elegant working knives; art knives. **Patterns:** Hunters, Bowies, daggers; folders in several weights. **Technical:** Grinds 154CM; some engraving. **Prices:** $250 to $800; some $3,500 and higher. **Remarks:** Part-time maker; first knife sold in 1970. **Mark:** Last name.

TOWNSEND, J.W., PO Box 756, Watson, LA, 70786-0756/225-665-5779
Specialties: One of a kinds. **Patterns:** Fantasy knives and fighters. **Technical:** Grinds 440C, O1, commercial Damascus and ATS-34. **Prices:** $250 to $2,500; some higher. **Remarks:** Full-time maker; first knife sold in 1985. **Mark:** First and middle initials and last name, or stylized last name.

TRABBIC, R.W., 4550 N. Haven, Toledo, OH, 43612/419-478-9578
Specialties: Working knives. **Patterns:** Hunters, Bowies, locking hunters and springbacks in standard patterns. **Technical:** Grinds D2, 440C and 154CM. **Prices:** $80 to $250. **Remarks:** Part-time maker; first knife sold in 1973. **Mark:** First and middle initials, last name.

TRACY, BUD, 15500 Fawn Ln., Reno, NV, 89511/

TREIBER, LEON, P.O. Box 342, Ingram, TX, 78025/830-367-2246
Specialties: Folders of his design and to customer specs. **Patterns:** Locking folders. **Technical:** Grinds CPM-T-440V, D2, 440C, dAMASCUS, 420v & ats34. **Prices:** $250 to $1,500. **Remarks:** Part-time maker; first knife sold in 1992. Doing business as Treiber Knives. **Mark:** First initial, last name, city, state.

TREML, GLENN, RR #14, Site 11-10, Thunder Bay, Ont., CANADA, P7B 5E5/807-767-1977
Specialties: working straight knives of his design and to customer specs. **Patterns:** Hunters, kitchen knives and double-edged survival knives. Technical Grinds 440C, ATS-34 and O1; stock removal method. Uses various woods and Micarta for handle material. **Prices:** $60 to $400; some higher. **Mark:** Stamped last name.

TRINDLE, BARRY, 1660 Ironwood Trail, Earlham, IA, 50072-8611/515-462-1237
Specialties: Engraved folders. **Patterns:** Mostly small folders, classical styles and pocket knives. **Technical:** 440 only. Engraves. Handles of wood or mineral material. **Prices:** Start at $750. **Mark:** Name on tang.

TRITZ, JEAN JOSE, Schopstrasse 23, 20255 Hamburg, GERMANY, / 040-49 78 21
Specialties: Scandinavian knives, Japanese kitchen knives, friction folders, swords. **Patterns:** Puukkos, Tollekniven, Hocho, friction folders, swords. **Technical:** Forges tool steels, carbon steels, 52100 Damascus Mokume, San Maj. **Prices:** $200 to $2,000; some higher. **Remarks:** Full-time maker; first knife sold in 1989. **Mark:** Initials in monogram. Other: Does own leatherwork, prefers natural materials. Sole authorship. Speaks French, German, English, Norwegian.

TRUDEL, PAUL, 525 Braydon Ave, Ottawa ON CANADA, K1G 0W7/

TRUJILLO, MIRANDA, 3001 Tanglewood Dr., Anchorage, AK, 99517/907-243-6093
Specialties: Working/using straight knives of her design. **Patterns:** Hunters and utility/camp knives. **Technical:** Grinds ATS-34 and 440C. Sheaths are water resistant. **Prices:** $145 to $400; some to $600. **Remarks:** Spare-time maker; first knife sold in 1989. Doing business as Alaska Knife & Service Co. **Mark:** NA.

TRUJILLO, ADAM, 3001 Tanglewood Dr., Anchorage, AK, 99517/907-243-6093
Specialties: Working/using straight knives of his design. **Patterns:** Hunters and utility/camp knives. **Technical:** Grinds 440C, ATS-34 and O1; ice tempers blades. Sheaths are dipped in wax and oil base. **Prices:** $200 to $500; some to $1,000. **Remarks:** Spare-time maker; first knife sold in 1995. Doing business as Alaska Knife & Service Co. **Mark:** NA.

TRUJILLO, THOMAS A., 3001 Tanglewood Dr., Anchorage, AK, 99517/907-243-6093
Specialties: High-end art knives. **Patterns:** Hunters, Bowies, daggers and locking folders. **Technical:** Grinds to customer choice, including rock and commercial Damascus. Inlays jewels and carves handles. **Prices:** $150 to $900; some to $6,000. **Remarks:** Full-time maker; first knife sold in 1976. Doing business as Alaska Knife & Service Co. **Mark:** Alaska Knife and/or Thomas Anthony.

TSCHAGER, REINHARD, Piazza Parrocchia 7, I-39100 Bolzano, ITALY, /0471-970642
Specialties: Classic, high-art, collector-grade straight knives of his design. **Patterns:** Hunters. **Technical:** Grinds ATS-34, D2 and Damascus. Oval pins. Gold inlay. Offers engraving. **Prices:** $500 to $1,200; some to $4,000. **Remarks:** Spare-time maker; first knife sold in 1979. **Mark:** Gold inlay stamped with initials.

TURCOTTE, LARRY, 1707 Evergreen, Pampa, TX, 79065/806-665-9369, 806-669-0435
Specialties: Fancy and working/using knives of his design and to customer specs. **Patterns:** Hunters, kitchen knives, utility/camp knives. **Technical:** Grinds 440C, D2, ATS-34. Engraves, scrimshaws, silver inlays. **Prices:** $150 to $350; some to $1,000. **Remarks:** Part-time maker; first knife sold in 1977. Doing business as Knives by Turcotte. **Mark:** Last name.

TURECEK, JIM, P.O. Box 882, Derby, CT, 06418/203-734-8406 **Specialties:** Exotic folders, art knives and some miniatures. **Patterns:** Trout and bird knives with split bamboo handles and one-of-a-kind folders. **Technical:** Grinds and forges stainless and carbon Damascus. **Prices:** $750 to $1,500; some to $3,000. **Remarks:** Full-time maker; first knife sold in 1983. **Mark:** Last initial in script, or last name.

TURNBULL, RALPH A., 5722 Newburg Rd., Rockford, IL, 61108/815-398-3799 **Specialties:** Plain or fancy working knives. **Patterns:** Hunters, fighters, boots, folders and Bowies. **Technical:** Grinds ATS-34, 440C, 154CM, CPM and other's Damascus. Makes wood inlay handles. **Prices:** $100 to $300; some to $2,000. **Remarks:** Full-time maker; first knife sold in 1973. **Mark:** Signature or initials.

TURNER, KEVIN, 17 Hunt Ave., Montrose, NY, 10548/914-739-0535 **Specialties:** Working straight knives of his design and to customer specs; period pieces. **Patterns:** Daggers, fighters and utility knives. **Technical:** Forges 5160 and 52100. **Prices:** $90 to $500. **Remarks:** Part-time maker; first knife sold in 1991. **Mark:** Acid-etched signed last name and year.

TYCER, ART, 23820 N Cold Springs Rd, paron, AR, 72122/501-821-4487 **Specialties:** Fancy working/using straight knives of his design, to customer specs and standard patterns. **Patterns:** Boots, Bowies, daggers, fighters, hunters, kitchen and utility knives. **Technical:** Grinds ATS-34, 440C, D2 and A2. Uses exotic woods with spacer material, stag and water buffalo. Offers filework. **Prices:** $100 to $600. **Remarks:** Part-time maker; first knife sold in 1990. Now starting to use Damascus steel. **Mark:** Flying "T" over first initial.

TYSER, ROSS, 1015 Hardee Court, Spartanburg, SC, 29303/864-585-7616 **Specialties:** Traditional working and using straight knives and folders of his design and in standard patterns. **Patterns:** Bowies, hunters and slip-joint folders. **Technical:** Grinds 440C and commercial Damascus. Mosaic pins; stone inlay. Does filework and scrimshaw. Offers engraving and cut-work and some inlay on sheaths. **Prices:** $45 to $125; some to $400. **Remarks:** Part-time maker; first knife sold in 1995. Doing business as RT Custom Knives. **Mark:** Stylized initials.

u

UEKAMA, NOBUYUKI, 3-2-8-302 Ochiai, Tama City, Tokyo, JAPAN, /

UNIVERSAL AGENCIES INC, 330 Hannaford Dr, Roswell, GA, 30075-3271/770-640-9330 **Specialties:** Suppliers of India Stag, Buffalo Horn, Mother of Pearl, Damascus, Damascus Blades & Knife Kits.

v

VACHON, YVON, 98 Lehoux St., Robertsonville, Que., CANADA, G0N 1L0/418-338-6601 **Specialties:** Functional miniatures and micro straight knives in standard patterns, and full size knives. **Patterns:** Automatics, daggers, folders, locking folders, swords and knife pistols. **Technical:** Grinds ATS34, 316 and Damascus. Uses gold, exotic wood, malachite, buffalo horn, mother-of-pearl and abalone. **Prices:** $100 to $10,000. **Remarks:** Full-time maker; first knife sold in1982. Doing business as Creations Yvon Vachon. **Mark:** Initials punched.

VAGNINO, MICHAEL, P.O. Box 67, Visalia, CA, 93279/559-528-2800 **Specialties:** Working & using straight knives & folders of his design and to customer specs. **Patterns:** Hunters, bird & trout, camp, Bowie, boot & kitchen knives and linerlock folders. **Technical:** Forges Damascus, 5160, 52100, AZ & grinds ATS-34. **Prices:** $150 to $500; some to $1,000. **Remarks:** Full-time maker; first knife sold in 1995. **Mark:** Logo and name.

VALLOTTON, SHAWN, 621 Fawn Ridge Dr., Oakland, OR, 97462/503-459-2216 **Specialties:** Left-hand knives. **Patterns:** All styles. **Technical:** Grinds 440C, ATS-34 and Damascus. Uses titanuim. Prefers bead-blasted or

anodized finishes. **Prices:** $250 to $1,400. **Remarks:** Full-time maker. **Mark:** Name and specialty.

VALLOTTON, RAINY D., 1295 Wolf Valley Dr, Umpqua, OR, 97486/541-459-0465 **Specialties:** Folders, one-handed openers and art pieces. **Patterns:** All patterns. **Technical:** Stock removal all steels; uses titanium liners and bolsters; uses all finishes. **Prices:** $350 to $3500. **Remarks:** Full-time maker. **Mark:** Name.

VALLOTTON, THOMAS, 621 Fawn Ridge Dr, Oakland, OR, 97462/541-459-2216 **Specialties:** Custom autos. **Patterns:** Tactical, fancy. **Technical:** File work, uses Damascus, uses Spectrum Metal. **Prices:** From $350 to $700. **Remarks:** Full-time maker. **Mark:** T and a V mingled. **Other:** Maker of Protégé 3 canoe.

VALLOTTON, BUTCH AND AREY, 621 Fawn Ridge Dr., Oakland, OR, 97462/541-459-2216 **Specialties:** Quick opening knives w/complicated mechanisms. **Patterns:** Tactical, fancy, working, and some art knives. **Technical:** Grinds all steels, uses others Damascus. Uses Spectrum Metal. **Prices:** From $350 to $4,500. **Remarks:** Full-time maker since 1984; first knife sold in 1981. **Mark:** Name w/viper head in the "V". **Other:** Co/designer, Appelgate Fairbarn folding w/Bill Harsey

VALOIS, A. DANIEL, 3552 W. Lizard Ck. Rd., Lehighton, PA, 18235/717-386-3636 **Specialties:** Big working knives; various sized lock-back folders with new safety releases. **Patterns:** Fighters in survival packs, sturdy working knives, belt buckle knives, military-style knives, swords. **Technical:** Forges and grinds A2, O1 and 440C; likes full tangs. **Prices:** $65 to $240; some to $600. **Remarks:** Full-time maker; first knife sold in 1969. **Mark:** Anvil logo with last name inside.

VAN DE MANAKKER, THIJS, Koolweg 34, 5759 px Helenaveen, HOLLAND, /0493539369 **Specialties:** Classic high-art knives. **Patterns:** Swords, utitity/camp knives and period pieces. **Technical:** Forges soft iron, carbon steel and Bloomery Iron. Makes own Damascus, Bloomery Iron and patterns. **Prices:** $20 to $2,000; some higher. **Remarks:** Full-time maker; first knife sold in 1969. **Mark:** Stylized "V".

VAN DEN ELSEN, GERT, Purcelldreef 83, 5012 AJ Tilburg, NETHERLANDS, /013-4563200 **Specialties:** Fancy, working/using, miniatures and integral straight knives of the maker's design or to customer specs. **Patterns:** Bowies, fighters and hunters. **Technical:** Grinds ATS-34 and 440C; forges Damascus. Offers filework, differentially tempered blades and some mokume-gane fittings. **Prices:** $350 to $1000; some to $4000. **Remarks:** Part-time maker; first knife sold in 1982. Doing business as G-E Knives. **Mark:** Initials GE in lozenge shape.

VAN ELDIK, FRANS, Ho Flaan 3, 3632BT Loenen, NETHERLANDS, /0031 294 233 095 **Specialties:** Fancy collector-grade straight knives and folders of his design. **Patterns:** Hunters, fighters, boots and folders. **Technical:** Forges and grinds D2, 154CM, ATS-34 and stainless Damascus. **Prices:** Start at $225. **Remarks:** Spare-time maker; first knife sold in 1979. **Mark:** Lion with name and Amsterdam.

VAN HOY, ED & TANYA, 1826 McCallum Road, Candor, NC, 27229/+31 10 4742952 **Specialties:** Traditional and working/using straight knives of his design, make folders. **Patterns:** Fighters, straight knives, folders, hunters and art knives. **Technical:** Grinds ATS-34 and 440V; forges D2. Offers filework, engraves, acid etching, mosaic pins, decorative bolsters and custom fitted English bridle leather sheaths. **Prices:** $250 to $3,000. **Remarks:** Full-time maker; first knife sold in 1977. Wife also engraves. Doing business as Van Hoy Custom Knives. **Mark:** Acid etched last name.

VAN RIJSWIJK, AAD, AvR Knives, Arij Koplaan 16B, 3132 AA Vlaardingen, THE NETHERLANDS, /0181-640334 **Specialties:** High-art interframe folders of his design and in standard patterns. **Patterns:** Hunters and locking folders. **Technical:** ATS-34 and stainless Damascus. Uses semi-precious stones. Handle materials include ivory, mammoth ivory, iron wood. Offers hand-made sheaths. **Prices:** $550 to $2,200; some to $2,000. **Remarks:** Full-time maker; first knife sold in 1993. **Mark:** NA.

custom knifemakers

VAN SCHAIK, BASTIAAN, Post Box 75269, 1070 AG, Amsterdam, NETHERLANDS, /31-20-633-80-25
Specialties: Working/using straight knives and axes of his design. **Patterns:** Daggers, fighters, push daggers and battle axes. **Technical:** Grinds ATS-34 and 440C; forges high-carbon steel. Uses Damascus and high-tech coatings. **Prices:** $400 to $1,500; some to $2,000. **Remarks:** Full-time maker; first knife sold in 1993. Doing business as Licorne Edged Creations. **Mark:** Unicorn head.

VANDERFORD, CARL G., Rt. 9, Box 238B, Columbia, TN, 38401/615-381-1488
Specialties: Traditional working straight knives and folders of his design. **Patterns:** Hunters, Bowies and locking folders. **Technical:** Forges and grinds 440C, O1 and wire Damascus. **Prices:** $60 to $125. **Remarks:** Part-time maker; first knife sold in 1987. **Mark:** Last name.

VEATCH, RICHARD, 2580 N. 35th Pl., Springfield, OR, 97477/541-747-3910
Specialties: Traditional working and using straight knives of his design and in standard patterns; period pieces. **Patterns:** Daggers, hunters, swords, utility/camp knives and minis. **Technical:** Forges and grinds his own Damascus; uses L6 and O1. Prefers natural handle materials; offers leatherwork. **Prices:** $50 to $300; some to $500. **Remarks:** Full-time maker; first knife sold in 1991. **Mark:** Stylized initials.

VEIT, MICHAEL, 3289 E. Fifth Rd., LaSalle, IL, 61301/815-223-3538
Specialties: Fancy straight knives and Damascus folders. **Technical:** Forges his own Turkish Damascus. Engraves. **Prices:** $1,500 to $2,500. **Remarks:** Part-time maker; first knife sold in 1985. **Mark:** Name in script.

VELARDE, RICARDO, 746 E. 200 N., Provo, UT, 84606/801-375-0519
Specialties: Working and using straight knives of his design and in standard patterns. **Patterns:** Boots, fighters and hunters; flat or hollow grind. **Technical:** Grinds ATS-34, 440C and D2. **Prices:** Start at $250. **Remarks:** First knife sold in 1992. **Mark:** First initial, last name on blade; city, state, U.S.A. at bottom of tang.

VENSILD, HENRIK, Gl Estrup, Randersvei 4, DK-8963 Auning, DENMARK, /+45 86 48 44 48
Specialties: Classic and traditional working and using knives of his design; Scandinavian influence. **Patterns:** hunters and using knives. **Technical:** Forges Damascus. Hand makes handles, sheaths and blades. **Prices:** $350 to $1,000. **Remarks:** Part-time maker; first knife sold in 1967. **Mark:** Initials.

VIALLON, HENRI, Les Belins, 63300 Thiers, FRANCE, /04-73-80-24-03
Specialties: Traditional straight knives and folders, of his design. **Patterns:** Hunters, folders, boots and utility knives. **Technical:** Forges and grinds 12C27, D2, 440C ATS-34 and his own Damascus; mosaic Damascus. **Prices:** $175 to $375; some to $1,500. **Remarks:** Full-time maker; first knife sold in 1985. **Mark:** First initial, last name.

VIELE, H.J., 88 Lexington Ave., Westwood, NJ, 07675/201-666-2906
Specialties: Folding knives of distinctive shapes. **Patterns:** High-tech folders. **Technical:** Grinds 440C and ATS-34. **Prices:** Start at $475. **Remarks:** Full-time maker; first knife sold in 1973. **Mark:** Last name with stylized throwing star.

VILLA, LUIZ, R. Com. Miguel Calfat, 398 Itaim Bibi, Sao Paulo, SP-04537-081, BRAZIL, /011-8290649
Specialties: One-of-a-kind straight knives and jewel knives of all designs. **Patterns:** Bowies, hunters, utility/camp knives and jewel knives. **Technical:** Grinds D6, Damascus and 440C; forges 5160. Prefers natural handle material. **Prices:** $70 to $200. **Remarks:** Part-time maker; first knife sold in 1991. **Mark:** Last name and serial number.

VILLAR, RICARDO, Al. dos Jasmins, 243, Mairipora, S.P. 07600-000, BRAZIL, /011-4851649
Specialties: Straight working knives to customer specs. **Patterns:** Bowies, fighters and utility/camp knives. **Technical:** Grinds D6, ATS-34 and 440C stainless. **Prices:** $80 to $200. **Remarks:** Part-time maker; first knife sold in 1993. **Mark:** Percor over sword and circle.

VISTNES, TOR, N-6930 Svelgen, , NORWAY, /047-57795572
Specialties: Traditional and working knives of his design. **Patterns:** Hunters and utility knives. **Technical:** Grinds Uddeholm Elmax. Handles made of rear burls of different Nordic stabilized woods. **Prices:** $300 to $1100. **Remarks:** Part-time maker; first knife sold in 1988. **Mark:** Etched name and deer head.

VOSS, BEN, 362 Clark St., Galesburg, IL, 61401/309-342-6994
Specialties: Fancy working knives of his design. **Patterns:** Bowies, fighters, hunters, boots and folders. **Technical:** Grinds 440C, ATS-34 and D2. **Prices:** $35 to $1,200. **Remarks:** Part-time maker; first knife sold in 1986. **Mark:** Name, city and state.

VOTAW, DAVID P., Box 327, Pioneer, OH, 43554/419-737-2774
Specialties: Working knives; period pieces. **Patterns:** Hunters, Bowies, camp knives, buckskinners and tomahawks. **Technical:** Grinds O1 and D2. **Prices:** $100 to $200; some to $500. **Remarks:** Part-time maker; took over for the late W.K. Kneubuhler. Doing business as W-K Knives. **Mark:** WK with V inside anvil.

VUNK, ROBERT, 4408 Buckeye Ct., Orlando, FL, 32804/407-628-3970
Specialties: Working knives, some fancy; period pieces. **Patterns:** Variety of tantos, fillet knives, kitchen knives, camp knives and folders. **Technical:** Grinds O1, 440C and ATS-34; provides mountings, cases, stands. **Prices:** $55 to $1,300. **Remarks:** Part-time maker; first knife sold in 1985. Doing business as RV Knives. **Mark:** Initials.

W

WADA, YASUTAKA, Fujinokidai 2-6-22, Nara City, Nara prefect 631-0044, JAPAN, /0742 46-0689
Specialties: Fancy and embellished one-of-a-kind straight knives of his design. **Patterns:** Bowies, daggers and hunters. **Technical:** Grinds ATS-34, Cowry X and Cowry X L-30 laminate. **Prices:** $400 to $2,500. **Remarks:** Part-time maker; first knife sold in 1990. **Mark:** Owl eyes with initial and last name underneath.

WAGAMAN, JOHN K., 903 Arsenal Ave., Fayetteville, NC, 28305/910-485-7860
Specialties: Fancy working knives. **Patterns:** Bowies, miniatures, hunters, fighters and boots. **Technical:** Grinds D2, 440C, 154CM and commercial Damascus; inlays mother-of-pearl. **Prices:** $110 to $2,000. **Remarks:** Part-time maker; first knife sold in 1975. **Mark:** Last name.

WAGNER, DAN, 112 Delaware St., New Castle, DE, 19720-4814/
Specialties: Fantasy and working/using straight knives of his design and to customer specs. **Patterns:** Daggers, fighters, hunters. **Technical:** Grinds ATS-34, 52100, CPM440V. Offers full or tapered tangs, fancy filework. Uses expensive burls and exotic woods for handles. Offers custom leather work. **Prices:** $75 to $250; some to $650. **Remarks:** Part-time maker; first knife sold in 1991. **Mark:** Oaktree Forge or acorn.

WAHLSTER, MARK DAVID, 1404 N. Second St., Silverton, OR, 97381/503-873-3775
Specialties: Automatics, antique and high tech folders in standard patterns and to customer specs. **Patterns:** Hunters, fillets and combat knives. **Technical:** Flat grinds 440C, ATS-34, D2 and Damascus. Uses titanium in folders. **Prices:** $100 to $1,000. **Remarks:** Full-time maker; first knife sold in 1981. **Mark:** Name, city and state or last name.

WALDROP, MARK, 14562 SE 1st Ave. Rd., Summerfield, FL, 34491/352-347-9034
Specialties: Period pieces. **Patterns:** Bowies and daggers. **Technical:** Uses stock removal. Engraves. **Prices:** Moderate to upscale. **Remarks:** Part-time maker; first knife sold in 1978. **Mark:** Last name.

WALKER, GEORGE A., Star Route, Alpine, WY, 83128/307-883-2372
Specialties: Deluxe working knives. **Patterns:** Hunters, boots, fighters, Bowies and folders. **Technical:** Forges his own Damascus and cable; engraves, carves, scrimshaws. Makes sheaths. **Prices:** $125 to $750; some to $1,000. **Remarks:** Full-time maker; first knife sold in 1979. Partners with wife. **Mark:** Name, city and state.

WALKER, JIM, 22 Walker Lane, Morrilton, AR, 72110/501-354-3175
Specialties: Period pieces and working/using knives of his design and to customer specs. **Patterns:** Bowies, fighters, hunters, camp knives. **Technical:** Forges 5160, O1, L6, 52100, 1084, 1095. **Prices:** Start at $225. **Remarks:** Part-time maker; first knife sold in 1993. **Mark:** Three arrows with last name/MS.

WALKER, JOHN W., 10620 Moss Branch Rd., Bon Aqua, TN, 37025/931-670-4754
Specialties: Straight knives, daggers and folders; sterling rings, 14K gold wire wrap; some stone setting. **Patterns:** Hunters, boot knives, others. **Technical:** Grinds 440C, ATS-34, L6, etc. Buys Damascus. **Prices:**

$150 to $500; some to $1000. **Remarks:** Part-time maker; first knife sold in 1982. **Mark:** Hohenzollern Eagle with name, or last name.

WALKER, MICHAEL L., P.O. Box 1924, Taos, NM, 87571/505-757-3086
Specialties: Innovative knife designs and locking systems; Titanium and SS furniture and art. **Patterns:** Folders from utility grade to museum quality art; others upon request. **Technical:** State-of-the-art materials…titanium, stainless Damascus, gold, etc. **Prices:** $3500 and above. **Remarks:** Designer/MetalCrafts; Full-time professional knifemaker since 1980; Four U.S. Patents; Invented LinerLock® and was awarded Registered U.S. Trademark No. 1,585,333. **Mark:** Early mark MW, Walker's Lockers by M.L. Walker; current M.L. Walker or Michael Walker.

WALLACE, ROGER L., 4902 Collins Lane, Tampa, FL, 33603/813-239-3261
Specialties: Working straight knives, Bowies and camp knives to customer specs. **Patterns:** Hunters, skinners and utility knives. **Technical:** Forges high-carbon steel. **Prices:** Start at $75. **Remarks:** Part-time maker; first knife sold in 1985. **Mark:** First initial, last name.

WALTERS, A.F., P.O. Box 523, 275 Crawley Rd., TyTy, GA, 31795/912-528-6207
Specialties: Working knives, some to customer specs. **Patterns:** Locking folders, straight hunters, fishing and survival knives. **Technical:** Grinds D2, 154CM and 13C26. **Prices:** Start at $150. **Remarks:** Part-time maker. Label: "The jewel knife" **Mark:** "J" in diamond and knife logo.

WARD, W.C., 817 Glenn St., Clinton, TN, 37716/615-457-3568
Specialties: Working straight knives; period pieces. **Patterns:** Hunters, Bowies, swords and kitchen cutlery. **Technical:** Grinds O1. **Prices:** $85 to $150; some to $500. **Remarks:** Part-time maker; first knife sold in 1969. He styled the Tennessee Knife Maker. **Mark:** TKM.

WARD, CHUCK, 1010 E. North St., Benton, AR, 72015/501-778-4329
Specialties: Traditional working and using straight knives and folders of his design. **Technical:** Grinds 440C, D2, A2 and O1; uses natural and composite handle materials. **Prices:** $90 to $400, some higher. **Remarks:** Full-time maker; first knife sold in 1990. **Mark:** First initial, last name.

WARD, J.J., 7501 S.R. 220, Waverly, OH, 45690/614-947-5328
Specialties: Traditional and working/using straight knives and folders of his design. **Patterns:** Hunters and locking folders. **Technical:** Grinds ATS-34, 440C and Damascus. Offers handmade sheaths. **Prices:** $125 to $250; some to $500. **Remarks:** Spare-time maker; first knife sold in 1980. **Mark:** Etched name.

WARD, KEN, 5122 Lake Shastina Blvd, Weed, CA, 96094/530-938-9720
Specialties: Working knives, some to customer specs. **Patterns:** Straight and folding hunters, axes, Bowies, buckskinners and miniatures. **Technical:** Grinds ATS-34, Damascus and Stellite 6K. **Prices:** $100 to $700. **Remarks:** Part-time maker; first knife sold in 1977. **Mark:** Name.

WARD, RON, 409 Arrowhead Trails, Loveland, OH, 45140/513-683-8729
Specialties: Classic working and using straight knives, fantasy knives. **Patterns:** Bowies, hunters, fighters, nad utility/camp knives. **Technical:** Grinds 440C, 154CM, ATS-34 uses composite nad natural handle materials, makes sheaths. **Prices:** $65 to $150, some to $500. **Remarks:** Part-time maker; first knife sold in 1992. Doing business as Ron Ward Blades. **Mark:** Ron Ward Blades, Loveland OH.

WARDELL, MICK, 85 Coneybury, Bletchingley, Surrey RH1 4PR, ENGLAND, /01883742918
Specialties: Folders of his design. **Patterns:** Locking and slip-joint folder, hunters and Bowies. **Technical:** Grinds CPM-T-440V, D2 and Damascus. Heat-treats. **Prices:** £85 to £500; some to £700. **Remarks:** Full-time maker; first knife sold in 1986. **Mark:** Last name or initials.

WARDEN, ROY A., 275 Tanglewood Rd., Union, MO, 63084/314-583-8813
Specialties: Complex mosaic designs of "EDM wired figures" and "Stack up" patterns and "Lazer Cut" and "Torch cut" and "Sawed" patterns combined. **Patterns:** Mostly "all mosaic" folders, automatics, fixed blades. **Technical:** Mosaic Damascus with all tool steel edges. **Prices:** $500 to $2000 and up. **Remarks:** Part-time maker; first knife sold in 1987. **Mark:** WARDEN stamped or initials connected.

WARDIAN, PAUL G., 460 SW Halsey Loop, Troutdale, OR, 97060/503-661-4324
Specialties: Fancy straight knives and miniatures. **Patterns:** Bowies, daggers, fighters and miniatures. **Technical:** Grinds 5160, tool steel and Damascus. Carves antler and wood, sculpts blades, engraves and scrimshaws. **Prices:** $55; some to $3500. **Remarks:** Part-time maker; first knife sold in 1988. Doing business as One Of A Kind Knives. **Mark:** Engraved initials in logo.

WARE, TOMMY, P.O. Box 488, Datil, NM, 87821/505-772-5817
Specialties: Traditional working and using straight knives, folders and automatics of his design and to customer specs. **Patterns:** Hunters, automatics and locking folders. **Technical:** Grinds ATS-34, 440C and D2. Offers engraving and scrimshaw. **Prices:** $225 to $575; some to $1,000. **Remarks:** Full-time maker; first knife sold in 1990. Doing business as Wano Knives. **Mark:** Last name inside oval, business name above, city and state below, year on side.

WARENSKI, BUSTER, P.O. Box 214, Richfield, UT, 84701/801-896-5319
Specialties: Investor-class straight knives. **Patterns:** Daggers, swords, fighters and Bowies. **Technical:** Grinds, engraves and inlays; offers surface treatments. **Prices:** Upscale. **Remarks:** Full-time maker. Not currently taking orders. **Mark:** First or last name.

WARREN, DANIEL, 571 Love Jay Rd, Canton, NC, 28716/828-645-7351
Five finish in using-size blades in contemporary patterns. **Mark:** Warren.

WARREN, AL, 1423 Sante Fe Circle, Roseville, CA, 95678/916-784-3217
Specialties: Working straight knives and folders, some fancy. **Patterns:** Hunters, Bowies, daggers, short swords, fillets and kitchen knives. **Technical:** Grinds D2, ATS-34 and 440C. **Prices:** $110 to $950. **Remarks:** Part-time maker; first knife sold in 1978. **Mark:** First and middle initials, last name.

WARREN, DELLANA (SEE DELLANA)

WARTHER, DALE, 331 Karl Ave., Dover, OH, 44622/216-343-7513
Specialties: Working knives; period pieces. **Patterns:** Kitchen cutlery, daggers, hunters and some folders. **Technical:** Forges and grinds O1, D2 and 440C. **Prices:** $250 to $7,000. **Remarks:** Full-time maker; first knife sold in 1967. Takes orders only at shows or by personal interviews at his shop. **Mark:** Warther Originals.

WATANABE, WAYNE, P.O. Box 3563, Montebello, CA, 90640/323-728-6867
Specialties: Straight knives in Japanese styles. One of a kind designs; welcomes customer designs. **Patterns:** Tantos to katanas, Bowies. **Technical:** Flat grinds A2, O1 and ATS-34. Offers hand-rubbed finishes and wrapped handles. **Prices:** Start at $200. **Remarks:** Part-time maker. **Mark:** Name in characters with flower.

WATSON, BERT, P.O. Box 26, Westminster, CO, 80030-0026/303-426-7577
Specialties: Working/using straight knives of his design and to customer specs. **Patterns:** Fighters, hunters, utility/camp knives. **Technical:** Grinds O1, ATS-34, 440C, D2, A2 and others. **Prices:** $50 to $250. **Remarks:** Full-time maker; first knife sold in 1974. Doing business as Game Trail Knives. **Mark:** GTK stamped or etched, sometimes with first or last name.

WATSON, TOM, 1103 Brenau Terrace, Panama City, FL, 32405/850-785-9209
Specialties: Folders with G10 handles. **Patterns:** Folding drop-point hunters, folding boot knives, fixed blade hunters, boots and small fighters. **Technical:** Flat-grinds ATS-34 & Damascus. Heat-treats with multiple tempering and hardness testing. Prefers satin finishes. **Prices:** Starting at $150. **Remarks:** Part-time maker; first knife sold in 1978. **Mark:** Name and city.

WATSON, PETER, 66 Kielblock St., La Hoff 2570, SOUTH AFRICA, /018-84942
Specialties: Traditional working and using straight knives and folders of his design. **Patterns:** Hunters, locking folders and utility/camp knives. **Technical:** Sandvik and 440C. **Prices:** $120 to $250; some to $1500. **Remarks:** Part-time maker; first knife sold in 1989. **Mark:** Buffalo head with name.

custom knifemakers

WATSON, BILLY, 440 Forge Rd., Deatsville, AL, 36022/334-365-1482
Specialties: Working and using straight knives and folders of his design; period pieces. **Patterns:** Hunters, Bowies and utility/camp knives. **Technical:** Forges and grinds his own Damascus, 1095, 5160 and 52100. **Prices:** $25 to $1500. **Remarks:** Full-time maker; first knife sold in 1970. Doing business as Billy's Blacksmith Shop. **Mark:** Last name.

WATSON, DANIEL, 350 Jennifer Ln., Driftwood, TX, 78619/512-847-9679
Specialties: One-of-a-kind knives and swords. **Patterns:** Hunters, daggers, swords and miniatures. **Technical:** Hand-purify and carbonize his own high-carbon steel, pattern-welded Damascus, cable and carbon-induced crystalline Damascus. European and Japanese tempering. **Prices:** $90 to $4,000; swords to $25,000. **Remarks:** Full-time maker; first knife sold in 1979. **Mark:** "Angel Sword" on forged pieces; "Bright Knight" for stock removal.

WATT III, FREDDIE, P.O. Box 1372, Big Spring, TX, 79721/915-263-6629
Specialties: Working straight knives, some fancy. **Patterns:** Hunters, fighters and Bowies. **Technical:** Grinds A2, D2, 440C and ATS-34; prefers mirror finishes. **Prices:** $150 to $350; some to $750. **Remarks:** Full-time maker; first knife sold in 1979. **Mark:** Last name, city and state.

WATTELET, MICHAEL A., P.O. Box 649, 125 Front, Minocqua, WI, 54548/715-356-3069
Specialties: Working and using straight knives of his design and to customer specs; fantasy knives. **Patterns:** Daggers, fighters and swords. **Technical:** Grinds 440C and L6; forges and grinds O1. Silversmith. **Prices:** $75 to $1,000; some to $5,000. **Remarks:** Full-time maker; first knife sold in 1966. Doing business as M & N Arts Ltd. **Mark:** First initial, last name.

WATTS, MIKE, Rt. 1 Box 81, Gatesville, TX, 76528/

WATTS, WALLY, 9560 S. Hwy. 36, Gatesville, TX, 76528/254-487-2866
Specialties: Unique traditional folders of his design. **Patterns:** One- to five-blade folders and single-blade gents in various blade shapes. **Technical:** Grinds ATS-34; D2 and 440C on request. **Prices:** $150 to $250; some to $500. **Remarks:** Full-time maker; first knife sold in 1986. **Mark:** Last name.

WEBER, FRED E., 517 Tappan St., Forked River, NJ, 08731/609-693-0452
Specialties: Working knives in standard patterns. **Patterns:** Hunters, slip-joint and lock-back folders, Bowies and various-sized fillets. **Technical:** Grinds D2, 440V and ATS-34. **Prices:** $125 to $250; some to $500. **Remarks:** Full-time maker; first knife sold in 1973. **Mark:** First and middle initials, last name.

WEDDLE JR., DEL, 2703 Green Valley Rd., St. Joseph, MO, 64505/816-364-1981
Specialties: Working knives; some period pieces. **Patterns:** Hunters, fighters, locking folders, push knives. **Technical:** Grinds D2 and 440C; can provide precious metals and set gems. Offers his own forged wire-cable Damascus in his finished knives. **Prices:** $80 to $250; some to $2,000. **Remarks:** Full-time maker; first knife sold in 1972. **Mark:** Signature with last name and date.

WEHNER, RUDY, 297 William Warren Rd, Collins, MS, 39428/601-765-4997
Specialties: Reproduction antique Bowies and contemporary Bowies in full and miniature. **Patterns:** Skinners, camp knives, fighters, axes and Bowies. **Technical:** Grinds 440C, ATS-34, 154CM and Damascus. **Prices:** $100 to $500; some to $850. **Remarks:** Full-time maker; first knife sold in 1975. **Mark:** Last name on Bowies and antiques; full name, city and state on skinners.

WEILAND JR., J. REESE, 612 Superior Ave., Tampa, FL, 33606/813-971-5378(7:30-5:00 pm); 813-671-0661 (after 6 pm)
Specialties: Traditional working straight knives and folders; liner locks and Hawk bills. **Patterns:** Hunters, tantos, Bowies, fantasy knives, spears and some swords. **Technical:** Grinds ATS-34 and Damascus

bars. Offers titanium hardware on his liner locks and button locks. Distinctive bird-shaped handle on some models. **Prices:** $100 to $4,000. **Remarks:** Full-time maker; first knife sold in 1983. **Mark:** RW slant.

WEILER, DONALD E., P.O. Box 1576, Yuma, AZ, 85366-9576/520-782-1159
Specialties: Working straight knives; period pieces. **Patterns:** Strong springback folders, blade & spring ATS-34. **Technical:** Forges O1, W2, 5160, ATS-34, D2 and cable Damascus. Makes his own high-carbon steel Damascus. **Prices:** $80 to $1,000. **Remarks:** Full-time maker; first knife sold in 1952. **Mark:** Last name, city.

WEINAND, GEROME M., 14440 Harpers Bridge Rd., Missoula, MT, 59802/406-543-0845
Specialties: Working straight knives. **Patterns:** Bowies, fishing and camp knives, large special hunters. **Technical:** Grinds O1, 440C, ATS-34, 1084 and L6; makes all-tool steel Damascus; Dendritic D2 from powdered steel. Heat-treats. **Prices:** $30 to $100; some to $500. **Remarks:** Full-time maker; first knife sold in 1982. **Mark:** Last name.

WEINSTOCK, ROBERT, Box 39, 520 Frederick St., San Francisco, CA, 94117/415-731-5968
Specialties: Fancy and high-art straight knives of his design. **Patterns:** Daggers, folders, poignards and miniatures. **Technical:** Grinds A2, O1 and 440C. Chased and hand-carved blades and handles. **Prices:** $1,000 to 5,000+. **Remarks:** Full-time maker; first knife sold in1994. **Mark:** Last name carved.

WEISS, CHARLES L., 18847 N. 13th Ave., Phoenix, AZ, 85027/623-582-6147
Specialties: High-art straight knives and folders; deluxe period pieces. **Patterns:** Daggers, fighters, boots, push knives and miniatures. **Technical:** Grinds 440C, 154CM and ATS-34. **Prices:** $300 to $1,200; some to $2,000. **Remarks:** Full-time maker; first knife sold in 1975. **Mark:** Name and city.

WELCH, WILLIAM H., 8232 W. Red Snapper Dr., Kimmell, IN, 46760/219-856-3577
Specialties: Working knives; deluxe period pieces. **Patterns:** Hunters, tantos, Bowies. **Technical:** Grinds ATS-34, D2 and 440C. **Prices:** $100 to $600. **Remarks:** Part-time maker; first knife sold in 1976. **Mark:** Last name.

WERNER JR., WILLIAM A., 336 Lands Mill, Marietta, GA, 30067/404-988-0074
Specialties: Fantasy and working/using straight knives. **Patterns:** Bowies, daggers, fighters. **Technical:** Grinds 440C stainless, 10 series carbon and Damascus. **Prices:** $150 to $400; some to $750. **Remarks:** Part-time maker. Doing business as Werner Knives. **Mark:** Last name.

WERTH, GEORGE W., 5223 Woodstock Rd., Poplar Grove, IL, 61065/815-544-4408
Specialties: Period pieces, some fancy. **Patterns:** Straight fighters, daggers and Bowies. **Technical:** Forges and grinds O1, 1095 and his Damascus, including mosaic patterns. **Prices:** $200 to $650; some higher. **Remarks:** Full-time maker. Doing business as Fox Valley Forge. **Mark:** Name in logo or initials connected.

WESCOTT, CODY, 5330 White Wing Rd., Las Cruces, NM, 88012/505-382-5008
Specialties: Fancy and presentation-grade working knives. **Patterns:** Hunters, locking folders and Bowies. **Technical:** Hollow-grinds D2 and ATS-34; all knives fileworked. Offers some engraving. Makes sheaths. **Prices:** $80 to $300; some to $950. **Remarks:** Full-time maker; first knife sold in 1982. **Mark:** First initial, last name.

WEST, CHARLES A., 1315 S. Pine St., Centralia, IL, 62801/618-532-2777
Specialties: Classic, fancy, high tech, period pieces, traditional and working/using straight knives and folders. **Patterns:** Bowies, fighters and locking folders. **Technical:** Grinds ATS-34, O1 and Damascus. Prefers hot blued finishes. **Prices:** $100 to $1,000; some to $2,000. **Remarks:** Full-time maker; first knife sold in 1963. Doing business as West Custom Knives. **Mark:** Name or name, city and state.

custom knifemakers

WEST, PAT, P.O. Box 9, Charlotte, TX, 78011/830-277-1290 **Specialties:** Classic working and using straight knives and folders. **Patterns:** Hunters, kitchen knives, slip-joint folders. **Technical:** Grinds ATS-34, D2 and Vascowear. Offers filework and decorates liners on folders. **Prices:** $300 to $600. **Remarks:** Spare-time maker; first knife sold in 1984. **Mark:** Name.

WESTBERG, LARRY, 305 S. Western Hills Dr., Algona, IA, 50511/515-295-9276 **Specialties:** Traditional and working straight knives of his design and in standard patterns. **Patterns:** Bowies, hunters, utility knives and miniatures. **Technical:** Grinds 440C, D2 and 1095. Heat-treats. Uses natural handle materials. **Prices:** $85 to $600; some to $1,000. **Remarks:** Part-time maker; first knife sold in 1987. **Mark:** Last name.

WHIPPLE, WESLEY A., P.O. Box 47, Thermopolis, WY, 82443/307-864-2255 **Specialties:** Working straight knives, some fancy. **Patterns:** Hunters, Bowies, camp knives, fighters. **Technical:** Forges high carbon steels, Damascus, offers relief carving & silver wire inlay. **Prices:** $125 to $450; some higher. **Remarks:** Part-time maker; first knife sold in 1989. **Mark:** Last name.

WHITE, BRYCE, 1415 W Col. Glenn Rd, Little Rock, AR, 72210/501-821-2956 Hunting & fishing - grinds & forges. Makes Damascus. Main steels L-6-10-75-01. Handle materials-wood & bone-stags my favorite. **Prices:** $100 to $250. I make a lot of spike knives and do a lot of file work. Diamond and vine patterns. Sold first knife in 1995. **Mark:** Last name. Part-time maker.

WHITE, GENE E., 6620 Briarleigh Way, Alexandria, VA, 22315/703-924-1268 **Specialties:** Small utility/gents knives. **Patterns:** Eight standard hunters; most other patterns on commission basis. Currently no swords, axes and fantasy knives. **Technical:** Stock removal 440C and D2; others on request. Mostly hollow grinds; some flat grinds. Prefers natural handle materials. Makes own sheaths. **Prices:** Start at $85. **Remarks:** Part-time maker; first knife sold in 1971. **Mark:** First and middle intials, last name.

WHITE, ROBERT J., RR 1, 641 Knox Rd. 900 N., Gilson, IL, 61436/309-289-4487 **Specialties:** Working knives, some deluxe. **Patterns:** Bird and trout knives, hunters, survival knives and locking folders. **Technical:** Grinds A2, D2 and 440C; commercial Damascus. Heat-treats. **Prices:** $125 to $250; some to $600. **Remarks:** Full-time maker; first knife sold in 1976. **Mark:** Last name in script.

WHITE, SCOTTIE H., Rt. 2, Box 556G, Pecks Mill, WV, 25547/304-752-0239 **Specialties:** Working and using straight knives of his design and to customer specs. **Patterns:** Daggers, fighters and hunters. **Technical:** Grinds ATS-34 and 440C. Offers engraving. **Prices:** $175 to $1,200. **Remarks:** Full-time maker; first knife sold in 1986. Doing business as S.H. White Custom Knives. **Mark:** First and middle initials, and last name.

WHITE JR., ROBERT J. BUTCH, RR 1, Gilson, IL, 61436/309-289-4487 **Specialties:** Folders of all sizes. **Patterns:** Hunters, fighters, boots and folders. **Technical:** Forges Damascus; grinds tool and stainless steels. **Prices:** $500 to $1,800. **Remarks:** Full-time maker; first knife sold in 1980. **Mark:** Last name in block letters.

WHITEHEAD, JAMES D., 1231 W. 20th St., Florence, OR, 97439/541-902-8837 **Specialties:** Miniature straight & folding knives. Larger folders to 3". **Technical:** Forges and grinds O1 and commercial Damascus. **Prices:** $400 to $5000. **Remarks:** Part-time maker; first knife sold in 1985. **Mark:** Initials.

WHITENECT, JODY, Elderbank, Halifax County, Nova Scotia, CANADA, B0N 1K0/902-384-2511 **Specialties:** Fancy and embellished working/using straight knives of his design and to customer specs. **Patterns:** Bowies, fighters and hunters. **Technical:** Forges 1095 and O1; forges and grinds ATS-34. Various filework on blades and bolsters. **Prices:** $200 to $400; some to $800.

Remarks: Part-time maker; first knife sold in 1996. **Mark:** Longhorn stamp or engraved.

WHITLEY, WAYNE, 210 E. 7th St., Washington, NC, 27889/919-946-5648 **Specialties:** Working/using straight knives of his design and to customer specs. **Patterns:** Bowies, hunters, utility/camp knives. **Technical:** Grinds ATS-34, D2, 440C; forges own Damascus and cable and high-carbon tool steels. **Prices:** $65 to $650; some to $1,500. **Remarks:** Part-time maker; first knife sold in 1990. Doing business as WW Custom Knives. **Mark:** Name, city, state or stylized initials.

WHITLEY, WELDON G., 6316 Jebel Way, El Paso, TX, 79912/915-584-2274 **Specialties:** Working knives of his design or to customer specs. **Patterns:** Hunters, folders and various double-edged knives. **Technical:** Grinds 440C, 154CM and ATS 34. **Prices:** $150 to $1250. **Mark:** Name, address, road-runner logo.

WHITMAN, JIM, 21044 Salem St., Chugiak, AK, 99567/907-688-4575 **Specialties:** Working straight knives and folders; some art pieces. **Patterns:** Hunters, skinners, Bowies, camp knives, working fighters, swords and hatchets. **Technical:** Grinds AEB-L Swedish, 440C, ATS-34, commercial Damascus in full convex. Prefers exotic hardwoods, natural and native handle materials--whale bone, antler, ivory and horn. **Prices:** Start at $150. **Remarks:** Full-time maker; first knife sold in 1983. **Mark:** Name, city, state.

WHITMIRE, EARL T., 725 Colonial Dr., Rock Hill, SC, 29730/803-324-8384 **Specialties:** Working straight knives, some to customer specs; some fantasy pieces. **Patterns:** Hunters, fighters and fishing knives. **Technical:** Grinds D2, 440C and 154CM. **Prices:** $40 to $200; some to $250. **Remarks:** Full-time maker; first knife sold in 1967. **Mark:** Name, city, state in oval logo.

WHITTAKER, WAYNE, 2900 Woodland Ct., Metamore, MI, 48455/810-797-5315 **Specialties:** High-art working/using straight knives of his design. **Patterns:** Bowies, daggers and hunters. **Technical:** Grinds O1 tool steel. **Prices:** $150 to $250; some to $2,000. **Remarks:** Spare-time maker; first knife sold in 1985. **Mark:** Initials, year on other side.

WHITTAKER, ROBERT E., P.O. Box 204, Mill Creek, PA, 17060/ **Specialties:** Using straight knives. Has a line of knives for buckskinners. **Patterns:** Hunters, skinners and Bowies. **Technical:** Grinds O1, A2 and D2. Offers filework. **Prices:** $35 to $100. **Remarks:** Part-time maker; first knife sold in 1980. **Mark:** Last initial or full initials.

WHITWORTH, KEN J., 41667 Tetley Ave., Sterling Heights, MI, 48078/313-739-5720 **Specialties:** Working straight knives and folders. **Patterns:** Locking folders, slip-joints and boot knives. **Technical:** Grinds 440C, 154CM and D2. **Prices:** $100 to $225; some to $450. **Remarks:** Part-time maker; first knife sold in 1976. **Mark:** Last name.

WICKER, DONNIE R., 2544 E. 40th Ct., Panama City, FL, 32405/904-785-9158 **Specialties:** Traditional working and using straight knives of his design or to customer specs. **Patterns:** Hunters, fighters and slip-joint folders. **Technical:** Grinds 440C, ATS-34, D2 and 154CM. Heat-treats and does hardness testing. **Prices:** $90 to $200; some to $400. **Remarks:** Part-time maker; first knife sold in 1975. **Mark:** First and middle initials, last name.

WIGGINS, HORACE, 203 Herndon, Box 152, Mansfield, LA, 71502/318-872-4471 **Specialties:** Fancy working knives. **Patterns:** Straight and folding hunters. **Technical:** Grinds O1, D2 and 440C. **Prices:** $90 to $275. **Remarks:** Part-time maker; first knife sold in 1970. **Mark:** Name, city and state in diamond logo.

WILCHER, WENDELL L., RR 6 Box 6573, Palestine, TX, 75801/903-549-2530 **Specialties:** Fantasy, miniatures and working/using straight knives and folders of his design and to customer specs. **Patterns:** Fighters, hunters, locking folders. **Technical:** Hand works (hand file and hand sand knives), not grind. **Prices:** $75 to $250; some to $600. **Remarks:** Part-time maker; first knife sold in 1987. **Mark:** Initials, year, serial number.

custom knifemakers

WILLEY, W.G., R.D. 1, Box 235-B, Greenwood, DE, 19950/302-349-4070
Specialties: Fancy working straight knives. **Patterns:** Small game knives, Bowies and throwing knives. **Technical:** Grinds 440C and 154CM. **Prices:** $225 to $600; some to $1,500. **Remarks:** Part-time maker; first knife sold in 1975. Owns retail store. **Mark:** Last name inside map logo.

WILLIAM E, STAPLETON, BUFFALO 'B' FORGE, 5425 COUNTRY LN, MERRITT ISLAND, FL, 32953/
Specialties: Classic and traditional knives of my design and customer spec. **Patterns:** Hunters and using knives. **Technical:** Forges, 01 and L-6 Damascus, cable Damascus and 5160; stock removal on request. **Prices:** $150 to $1,000. **Remarks:** Part-time maker, first knive sold 1990. Doing business as Buffalo "B" Forge. **Mark:** Anvil with S initial in center of anvil.

WILLIAMS, JASON L., P.O. Box 67, Wyoming, RI, 02898/401-539-8353
Specialties: Fancy & high tech folders of his design, co-inventor of the Axis Lock. **Patterns:** Fighters, locking folders, automatics and fancy pocketknives. **Technical:** Forges Damascus and other steels by request. Uses exotic handle materials and precious metals. Offers inlaid spines and gemstone thumb knobs. **Prices:** $1,000 and up. **Remarks:** Full-time maker; first knife sold in 1989. **Mark:** First and last initials on pivot.

WILLIAMS, MICHAEL L., Rt. 4, P.O. Box 64-1, Broken Bow, OK, 74728/405-494-6326
Specialties: Plain to fancy working and dress knives. **Patterns:** Hunters, Bowies, camp knives and others. **Technical:** Forges 5160, L6, 52100, cable and pattern-welded steel. **Prices:** Start at $140. **Remarks:** Part-time maker; first knife sold in 1989. **Mark:** Last name.

WILLIAMS JR., RICHARD, 1440 Nancy Circle, Morristown, TN, 37814/615-581-0059
Specialties: Working and using straight knives of his design or to customer specs. **Patterns:** Hunters, dirks and utility/camp knives. **Technical:** Forges 5160 and uses file steel. Hand-finish is standard; offers filework. **Prices:** $80 to $180; some to $250. **Remarks:** Spare-time maker; first knife sold in 1985. **Mark:** Last initial or full intials.

WILLIAMSON, TONY, Rt. 3, Box 503, Siler City, NC, 27344/919-663-3551
Specialties: Flint knapping--knives made of obsidian flakes and flint with wood, antler or bone for handles. **Patterns:** Skinners, daggers and flake knives. **Technical:** Blades have width/thickness ratio of at least 4 to 1. Hafts with methods available to prehistoric man. **Prices:** $58 to $160. **Remarks:** Student of Errett Callahan. **Mark:** Initials and number code to identify year and number of knives made.

WILLSON, HARLAN M., P.O. Box 2113, Lompoc, CA, 93436/805-735-0085
Specialties: Working, fantasy and art straight knives of his design and to customer specs. **Patterns:** Various styles. **Technical:** Grinds ATS-34, 440C, 1095 and O1. Prefers bone and natural handle materials; some exotic woods. Carves custom handle designs. **Prices:** $200 to $500; some to $1,000. **Remarks:** Full-time maker; first knife sold in 1990. Doing business as Harlan Willson Custom Cutlery. **Mark:** Initials and last name or heart within bear paw.

WILSON, JAMES G., P.O. Box 4024, Estes Park, CO, 80517/303-586-3944
Specialties: Bronze Age knives; Medieval and Scottish styles; tomahawks. **Patterns:** Bronze knives, daggers, swords, spears and battle axes; 12-inch steel Misericorde daggers, sgian dubhs, "his and her" skinners, bird and fish knives, capers, boots and daggers. **Technical:** Casts bronze; grinds D2, 440C and ATS-34. **Prices:** $49 to $400; some to $1,300. **Remarks:** Part-time maker; first knife sold in 1975. **Mark:** WilsonHawk.

WILSON, JAMES R., Rt. 2 Box 175HC, Seminole, OK, 74868/405-382-7230
Specialties: Traditional working knives. **Patterns:** Bowies, hunters, skinners, fighters and camp knives. **Technical:** Forges 5160, 1095, O1 and his Damascus. **Prices:** Start at $125. **Remarks:** Part-time maker; first knife sold in 1994. **Mark:** First initial, last name.

WILSON, JON J., 1826 Ruby St., Johnstown, PA, 15902/814-266-6410
Specialties: Miniatures only. **Patterns:** Bowies, daggers and hunters. **Technical:** Grinds Damascus, 440C and O1. Scrimshaws and carves. **Prices:** $65 to $175; some to $250. **Remarks:** Full-time maker; first knife sold in 1988. **Mark:** First and middle initials, last name.

WILSON, MIKE, 2619 Fork Creek Ln., Bowman, GA, 30624/706-245-0823
Specialties: Fancy working and using straight knives of his design or to customer specs. **Patterns:** Hunters, Bowies, utility knives, gut hooks, skinners, fighters and miniatures. **Technical:** Hollow-grinds 440C, ATS-34 and D2. Mirror finishes are standard. Offers filework. **Prices:** $70 to $300. **Remarks:** Full-time maker; first knife sold in 1985. **Mark:** Last name.

WILSON, PHILIP C., 1064 Lomitas Ave., Livermore, CA, 94550/925-455-9475
Specialties: Working knives; emphasis on salt water fillet knives and utility hunters of his design. **Patterns:** Fishing knives, hunters, kitchen knives. **Technical:** Grinds CPM420V and 154CM. Heat-treats and Rockwell tests all blades. **Prices:** Start at $240. **Remarks:** First knife sold in 1985. Doing business as Sea-Mount Knife Works. **Mark:** Signature.

WILSON, RON, 2289 Falcon Ridge Ln., Los Osos, CA, 93402/805-528-5645
Specialties: Classic and fantasy straight knives of his design. **Patterns:** Daggers, fighters, swords and axes--mostly all miniatures. **Technical:** Forges and grinds Damascus and various tool steels; grinds meteorite. Uses gold, precious stones and exotic woods. **Prices:** Vary. **Remarks:** Part-time maker; first knife sold in 1995. **Mark:** Stamped first and last initials.

WILSON, R.W., P.O. Box 2012, Weirton, WV, 26062/304-723-2771
Specialties: Working straight knives; period pieces. **Patterns:** Bowies, tomahawks and patch knives. **Prices:** $85 to $175; some to $1,000. **Technical:** Grinds 440C; scrimshaws. **Remarks:** Part-time maker; first knife sold in 1966. Knifemaker supplier. Offers free knifemaking lessons. **Mark:** Name in tomahawk.

WILSON (SEE SIMONELLA, GIANLUIGI)

WIMPFF, CHRISTIAN, P.O. Box 700526, 70574 Stuttgart 70, GERMANY, /7131 4854 06
Specialties: High-tech folders of his design. **Patterns:** Boots, locking folders and liners locks. **Technical:** Grinds CPM-T-440V, ATS-34 and Schneider stainless Damascus. Offers meteorite bolsters and blades. **Prices:** $1,000 to $2,800; some to $4,000. **Remarks:** Full-time maker; first knife sold in 1984. **Mark:** First initial, last name.

WINE, MICHAEL, 265 S. Atlantic Ave., Cocoa Beach, FL, 32931/407-784-2187
Specialties: Traditional working straight knives. **Patterns:** Fishing, hunting and kitchen knives. **Technical:** Grinds carbon, high-chrome tool steels, Stellite; casts 440C. **Prices:** Start at $145. **Remarks:** Spare-time maker; first knife sold in 1971. **Mark:** First initial, last name with palm tree.

WINGO, GARY, 8438 Cty Rd 1, Lamar, CO, 81052/719-336-4241
Specialties: Folder specialist. Steel 44DC, D2, others on request. Handle bone-stag, others on request. **Patterns:** Trapper-three blade stockman, 4 blade congress, single and 2 blade barlows. **Prices:** 150 to $400. **Mark:** First knife sold 1994. Steer head with Wingo Knives or Straight line Wingo Knives.

WINGO, PERRY, 22 55th St., Gulfport, MS, 39507/228-863-3193
Specialties: Traditional working straight knives. **Patterns:** Hunters, skinners, Bowies and fishing knives. **Technical:** Grinds 440C. **Prices:** $75 to $1,000. **Remarks:** Full-time maker; first knife sold in 1988. **Mark:** Last name.

WINKLER, DANIEL, P.O. Box 2166, Blowing Rock, NC, 28605/704-295-9156
Specialties: Period pieces, some made to look old; buckskinner working knives. **Patterns:** Buckskinners, axes, tomahawks, patch knives, daggers, folders, skinners and fighters. **Technical:** Forges and grinds 52100, L6, O1, old files and his Damascus. **Prices:** $200 to $2,500. **Remarks:** Full-time maker; first knife sold in 1984. **Mark:** Initials connected.

WINN, TRAVIS A., 558 E. 3065 S., Salt Lake City, UT, 84106/801-467-5957
Specialties: Fancy working knives and knives to customer specs. **Patterns:** Hunters, fighters, boots, Bowies and fancy daggers, some miniatures, tantos and fantasy knives. **Technical:** Grinds D2 and 440C. Embellishes. **Prices:** $125 to $500; some higher. **Remarks:** Part-time maker; first knife sold in 1976. **Mark:** TRAV stylized.

WINSTON, DAVID, 1671 Red Holly St., Starkville, MS, 39759/601-323-1028
Specialties: Fancy and traditional knives of his design and to customer specs. **Patterns:** Bowies, daggers, hunters, boot knives and folders. **Technical:** Grinds 440C, ATS-34 and D2. Offers filework; heat-treats. **Prices:** $40 to $750; some higher. **Remarks:** Part-time maker; first knife sold in 1984. Offers lifetime sharpening for original owner. **Mark:** Last name.

WISE, DONALD, 304 Bexhill Rd., St. Leonardo-On-Sea, East Sussex, TN3 8AL, ENGLAND, /
Specialties: Fancy and embellished working straight knives to customer specs. **Patterns:** Hunters, Bowies and daggers. **Technical:** Grinds Sandvik 12C27, D2 D3 and O1. Scrimshaws. **Prices:** $110 to $300; some to $500. **Remarks:** Full-time maker; first knife sold in 1983. **Mark:** KNIFECRAFT.

WISE, JOHN, P.O. Box 994, Winchester, OR, 97495/
Specialties: Classic high-art straight knives and folders to customer specs. **Patterns:** Daggers, fighters, locking folders, miniatures. **Technical:** Grinds 440C, ATS-34, commercial Damascus. **Prices:** $150 to $350; some to $1,000. **Remarks:** Part-time maker; first knife sold in 1989. **Mark:** Stylized name.

WITSAMAN, EARL, 3957 Redwing Circle, Stow, OH, 44224/330-688-4208
Specialties: Straight and fantasy miniatures. **Patterns:** Wide variety--Randalls to D-guard Bowies. **Technical:** Grinds O1, 440C and 300 stainless; buys Damascus; highly detailed work. **Prices:** $70 to $200. **Remarks:** Part-time maker; first knife sold in1974. **Mark:** Initials.

WOLF, BILL, 4618 N. 79th Ave., Phoenix, AZ, 85033/602-846-3585
Specialties: Investor-grade folders and straight knives. **Patterns:** Lockback, slip joint and sidelock interframes. **Technical:** Grinds ATS-34 and 440C. **Prices:** $650 to $12,000. **Remarks:** Full-time maker; first knife sold in 1989. **Mark:** Name.

WOOD, WEBSTER, 22041 Shelton Trail, Atlanta, MI, 49709/517-785-2996
Specialties: Fancy working knives. **Patterns:** Hunters, survival knives, locking folders and slip-joints. **Technical:** Grinds O1, 440C and 154CM; engraves and scrimshaws. **Prices:** $100 to $500; some to $3,000. **Remarks:** Full-time maker; first knife sold in 1980. **Mark:** Initials inside shield and name.

WOOD, ALAN, Greenfield Villa, Greenhead, Carlisle, CA6 7HH, ENGLAND, /016977-47303
Specialties: High-tech working straight knives of his design. **Patterns:** Hunters, utility/camp and woodcraft knives. **Technical:** Grinds Sandvik 12C27, D2 and O1. Blades are cryogenic treated. **Prices:** $150 to $400; some to $750. **Remarks:** Full-time maker; first knife sold in 1979. **Mark:** First initial, last name and country.

WOOD, BARRY B. AND IRIE MICHAEL L., dba Wood, Irie & Co, 3002 E Gunnison St, Colorado Springs, CO, 80909/719-578-9226
Specialties: Fixed blade knives and high-tech working folders in a variety of styles, materials and techniques. **Patterns:** Thirty-four variations of five designs. **Technical:** Blades are ATS-34, BG-42, 440C, with some outside Damascus. Handles for folders are milled from 17-4 pH, Beryllium Copper, 6AL4V Titanium, etc. **Prices:** Fixed blades $125 and up; folders $350 and up. **Remarks:** Wood is a full-time maker since 1970, Irie since 1991. **Mark:** Two sets of initials in script within linked triangles of arcs.

WOOD, LARRY B., 6945 Fishburg Rd., Huber Heights, OH, 45424/513-233-6751
Specialties: Fancy working knives of his design. **Patterns:** Hunters, buckskinners, Bowies, tomahawks, locking folders and Damascus miniatures. **Technical:** Forges 1095, file steel and his own Damascus. **Prices:**

$125 to $500; some to $2,000. **Remarks:** Full-time maker; first knife sold in 1974. Doing business as Wood's Metal Studios. **Mark:** Variations of last name, sometimes with blacksmith logo.

WOOD, LEONARD J., 36 SUNRISE HILL RD, FISHKILL, NY, 12524/914-896-4657
Specialties: Traditional working/using straight knives of all designs. **Patterns:** Linerlock folders. **Technical:** Grinds ATS-34, 440C, commercial Damascus. **Prices:** $85 to $375; some to $450. **Remarks:** Spare-time maker; first knife sold in 1993. Doing business as Wood's Custom Knives. **Mark:** Last initial with wings.

WOOD, OWEN DALE, P.O. Box 515, Honeydew 2040 (Transvaal), SOUTH AFRICA, /011-958-1789
Specialties: Fancy working knives. **Patterns:** Hunters and fighters; variety of big knives; sword canes. **Technical:** Forges and grinds 440C, 154CM and his own Damascus. Uses rare African handle materials. **Prices:** $280 to $450; some to $3,000. **Remarks:** Full-time maker; first knife sold in 1976. **Mark:** Initials.

WOOD, WILLIAM W., P.O. Box 606, Seymour, TX, 76380/817-888-5832
Specialties: Exotic working knives with Middle-East flavor. **Patterns:** Fighters, boots and some utility knives. **Technical:** Grinds D2 and 440C; buys Damascus. Prefers hand-rubbed satin finishes; uses only natural handle materials. **Prices:** $300 to $600; some to $2,000. **Remarks:** Full-time maker; first knife sold in 1977. **Mark:** Name, city and state.

WOODARD, WILEY, 4527 Jim Mitchell W., Colleyville, TX, 76034/
Specialties: Straight knives, Damascus carbon and stainless, all natural material.

WOODCOCK, DENNIS "WOODY", PO Box 416, Nehalem, OR, 97131/503-368-7511
Specialties: Working knives. **Patterns:** Hunters, Bowies, skinners, hunters. **Technical:** Grinds ATS-34, D2, 440C, 440V. Offers filework; makes sheaths. **Prices:** $50 to $500. **Remarks:** Full-time maker; first knife sold in 1982. Doing business as Woody's Custom Knives. **Mark:** Nickname, last name, city, state.

WORKMAN JR., HUBERT L., Tyree Rd., Williamsburg, WV, 24991/304-645-4815
Specialties: Working knives of his design and to customer specs; period pieces. **Patterns:** Daggers, fighters and hunters. **Technical:** Uses obsidian, flint and chert; prefers natural materials. **Prices:** $25 to $150; some to $250. **Remarks:** Part-time maker; first knife sold in 1989. **Mark:** NA.

WORRELL, MORRIS C., 308 Collage Ave., Brownsburg, IN, 46112/317-852-7337
Specialties: Fancy period pieces and working knives to customer specs or my own pattern. **Patterns:** Bowies, fighters, tantos, daggers. **Technical:** Forges 5160, 1095, and his own Damascus, prefers fossil ivory for handles. **Prices:** $150 to $1,000 some higher. **Remarks:** Part-time maker, first knife sold in 1980. **Mark:** WORRELL MAKER.

WRIGHT, KEVIN, 671 Leland Valley Rd. W, Quilcene, WA, 98376-9517/360-765-3589
Specialties: Fancy working or collector knives to customer specs. **Patterns:** Hunters, boots, buckskinners, miniatures. **Technical:** Forges and grinds L6, 1095, 440C and his own Damascus. **Prices:** $75 to $500; some to $2,000. **Remarks:** Part-time maker; first knife sold in 1978. **Mark:** Last initial in anvil.

WRIGHT, TIMOTHY, P.O. Box 3746, Sedona, AZ, 86340/520-282-4180
Specialties: High-tech folders and working knives. **Patterns:** Interframe locking folders, non-inlaid folders, straight hunters and kitchen knives. **Technical:** Grinds BG-42, AEB-L, K190 and Cowry X; works with new steels. All folders can disassemble and are furnished with tools. **Prices:** $150 to $1,800; some to $3,000. **Remarks:** Full-time maker; first knife sold in 1975. **Mark:** Last name and type of steel used.

WYATT, WILLIAM R., Box 237, Rainelle, WV, 25962/304-438-5494
Specialties: Classic and working knives of all designs. **Patterns:** Hunters and utility knives. **Technical:** Forges and grinds saw blades, files and rasps. Prefers stag handles. **Prices:** $45 to $95; some to $350. **Remarks:** Part-time maker; first knife sold in 1990. **Mark:** Last name in star with knife logo.

custom knifemakers

y

YEATES, JOE A., 730 Saddlewood Circle, Spring, TX, 77381/281-367-2765
Specialties: Bowies and period pieces. **Patterns:** Bowies, toothpicks and combat knives. **Technical:** Grinds 440C, D2 and ATS-34. **Prices:** $400 to $2,000; some to $2,500. **Remarks:** Full-time maker; first knife sold in 1975. **Mark:** Last initial within outline of Texas; or last initial.

YORK, DAVID C., PO Box 3166, Chino Valley, AZ, 86323/520-636-1709
Specialties: Working straight knives and folders. **Patterns:** Prefers small hunters and skinners; locking folders. **Technical:** Grinds D2 and 440C; buys Damascus. **Prices:** $75 to $300; some to $600. **Remarks:** Full-time maker; first knife sold in 1975. **Mark:** Last name.

YOUNG, GEORGE, 713 Pinoak Dr., Kokomo, IN, 46901/765-457-8893
Specialties: Fancy/embellished and traditional straight knives and folders of his design and to customer specs. **Patterns:** Hunters, fillet/camp knives and locking folders. **Technical:** Grinds 440C, CPM440V, and Stellite 6K. Fancy ivory, black pearl and stag for handles. Filework--all Stellite construction (6K and 25 alloys). Offers engraving. **Prices:** $350 to $750; some $1,500 to $3,000. **Remarks:** Full-time maker; first knife sold in 1954. Doing business as Young's Knives. **Mark:** Last name integral inside Bowie.

YOUNG, PAUL A., 168 Elk Ridge Rd., Boone, NC, 28607/704-264-7048
Specialties: Working straight knives and folders of his design or to customer specs; some art knives. **Patterns:** Small boot knives, skinners, 18th century period pieces and folders. **Technical:** Forges O1 and file steels. Full-time embellisher--engraves and scrimshaws. Prefers floral designs; any design accepted. Does not engrave hardened metals. **Prices:** Determined by type and design. **Remarks:** Full-time maker; first knife sold in 1978. **Mark:** Initials in logo.

YOUNG, ERROL, 4826 Storey Land, Alton, IL, 62002/618-466-4707
Specialties: Traditional working straight knives and folders. **Patterns:** Wide range, including tantos, Bowies, miniatures and multi-blade folders. **Technical:** Grinds D2, 440C and ATS-34. **Prices:** $75 to $650; some to $800. **Remarks:** Part-time maker; first knife sold in 1987. **Mark:** Last name with arrow.

YOUNG, BUD, Box 336, Port Hardy, BC, CANADA, V0N 2P0/250-949-6478
Specialties: Fixed blade, working knives, some fancy. **Patterns:** Drop-points to skinners. **Technical:** Hollow or flat grind, 5160, 440-C, mostly ATS-34, satin finish. **Prices:** $150 to $500 CDN. **Remarks:** Spare-time maker; making knives since 1962; first knife sold in 1985. **Mark:** Name. Other: Not taking orders at this time, sell as produced.

YOUNG, CLIFF, Fuente De La Cibeles No. 5, Atascadero, San Miguel De Allende, GTO., MEXICO, /37700
Specialties: Working knives. **Patterns:** Hunters, fighters and fishing knives. **Technical:** Grinds all; offers D2, 440C and 154CM. **Prices:** Start at $250. **Remarks:** Part-time maker; first knife sold in 1980. **Mark:** Name.

YUNES, YAMIL R., P.O. Box 573, Roma, TX, 78584/512-849-1001
Specialties: Traditional straight knives and folders. **Patterns:** Locking folders, slip-joints, hunters, fighters and utility knives. **Technical:** Grinds 440C, O1 and D2. Has patented cocking design for folders. **Prices:** $45 to $140; some to $300. **Remarks:** Part-time maker; first knife sold in 1975. **Mark:** Last name.

YURCO, MIKE, P.O. Box 712, Canfield, OH, 44406/330-533-4928
Specialties: Working straight knives. **Patterns:** Hunters, utility knives, Bowies and fighters, push knives, claws and other hideouts. **Technical:** Grinds 440C, ATS-34 and 154CM; likes mirror and satin finishes. **Prices:** $20 to $500. **Remarks:** Part-time maker; first knife sold in 1983. **Mark:** Name, steel, serial number.

z

ZACCAGNINO JR., DON, 2256 Bacom Point Rd, Pahokee, FL, 33476-2622/407-924-7844
Specialties: Working knives and some period pieces of their designs. **Patterns:** Heavy-duty hunters, axes and Bowies; a line of light-weight hunters, fillets and personal knives. **Technical:** Grinds 440C and 17-4 PH--highly finished in complex handle and blade treatments. **Prices:** $165 to $500; some to $2,500. **Remarks:** Part-time maker; first knife sold in 1969 by Don Zaccagnino Sr. **Mark:** ZACK, city and state inside oval.

ZAHM, KURT, 488 Rio Casa, Indialantic, FL, 32903/407-777-4860
Specialties: Working straight knives of his design or to customer specs. **Patterns:** Daggers, fancy fighters, Bowies, hunters and utility knives. **Technical:** Grinds D2, 440C; likes filework. **Prices:** $75 to $1,000. **Remarks:** Part-time maker; first knife sold in 1985. **Mark:** Last name.

ZAKABI, CARL S., P.O. Box 893161, Mililani Town, HI, 96789-0161/808-626-2181
Specialties: Working and using straight knives of his design. **Patterns:** Fighters, hunters and utility/camp knives. **Technical:** Grinds 440C and ATS-34. **Prices:** $55 to $200. **Remarks:** Spare-time maker; first knife sold in 1988. Doing business as Zakabi's Knifeworks. **Mark:** Last name and state.

ZAKHAROV, CARLOS, R. Sergipe 68, Rio Comprido Jacarel, SP-12300-000, BRAZIL, /0123-515192
Specialties: Using straight knives of his design. **Patterns:** Hunters, kitchen and utility/camp knives. **Technical:** Grinds his own "secret steel." **Prices:** $60 to $200. **Remarks:** Full-time maker. **Mark:** Archip.

ZEMBKO III, JOHN, 140 Wilks Pond Rd., Berlin, CT, 06037/860-828-3503
Specialties: Working knives of his design or to customer specs. **Patterns:** Variety of working straight knives. **Technical:** Grinds ATS-34, A2 and O1; forges O1. **Prices:** $50 to $400; some higher. **Remarks:** First knife sold in 1987. **Mark:** Name.

ZEMITIS, JOE, 14 Currawong Rd., Cardiff Hts., 2285 Newcastle, AUSTRALIA, /0249549907
Specialties: Traditional working straight knives. **Patterns:** Hunters, Bowies, tantos, fighters and camp knives. **Technical:** Grinds O1, D2, W2 and 440C; makes his own Damascus. Embellishes; offers engraving and scrimshaw. **Prices:** $150 to $3,000. **Remarks:** Full-time maker; first knife sold in 1983. **Mark:** First initial, last name and country, or last name.

ZIMA, MICHAEL F., 732 State St., Ft. Morgan, CO, 80701/970-867-6078
Specialties: Working straight knives and folders. **Patterns:** Hunters; utility, locking and slip-joint folders. **Technical:** Grinds D2, 440C and ATS-34. **Prices:** $150 to $300; some higher. **Remarks:** Full-time maker; first knife sold in 1982. **Mark:** Last name.

ZINSMEISTER, PAUL D., HC 63, Box 53B, Harper, TX, 78631/830-864-4574
Specialties: Traditional working and using straight knives and folders of his design. Also custom made leather products. **Patterns:** Automatics, hunters, locking folders, slip-joint folders, daggers, Bowies and miniatures. **Technical:** Uses 440C and ATS-34 stainless steel. **Prices:** $85 to $250; some to $1,500. **Remarks:** Full-time maker; first knife sold in 1982. **Mark:** Handmade with stylized last initial.

ZIRBES, RICHARD, Neustrasse 15, D-54526 Niederkail, GERMANY, /06575 13 71
Specialties: Fancy/embellished, classic and traditional working and using straight and jack knives of my design. **Patterns:** Boots, fighters, jack-knife and hunters folders. **Technical:** Grinds ATS-34, CPM-T-440V, 440 and D2; forges and grinds Damascus. **Prices:** $250 to $650; some to $1,600. **Remarks:** Part-time maker; first knife sold in 1991.

ZOWADA, TIM, 4509 E. Bear River Rd., Boyne Falls, MI, 49713/616-348-5416
Specialties: Working knives, some fancy. **Patterns:** Hunters, camp knives, boots, swords, fighters, tantos and locking folders. **Technical:** Forges O2, L6, W2 and his own Damascus. **Prices:** $150 to $1,000; some to $5,000. **Remarks:** Full-time maker; first knife sold in 1980. **Mark:** Lower case gothic letters for initials.

ZSCHERNY, MICHAEL, 2512 " N" Ave. NW, Cedar Rapids, IA, 52405/319-396-3659
Specialties: Folders and daggers. **Patterns:** Slip-joints, lock-back folders, fancy daggers. **Technical:** Grinds 440C and 154CM; prefers natural handle materials. **Prices:** $150 to $1,000; some to $1,700. **Remarks:** Part-time maker. Not currently taking orders. **Mark:** Last name.

alabama

Andress, Ronnie	Satsuma
Batson, James	Madison
Coffman, Danny	Jacksonville
Conn JR., C.T.	Attalla
Connell, Steve	Adamsville
Cutchin, Roy D.	Seale
Daniels, Alex	Town Creek
Di Marzo, Richard	Birmingham
Fikes, Jimmy L.	Jasper
Fogg, Don	Jasper
Gilbreath, Randall	Dora
Gilpin, David	Alabaster
Hammond, Jim	Arab
Hodge, J.B.	Huntsville
Howard, Durvyn M.	Hokes Bluff
Howell, Len	Opelika
Howell, Ted	Wetumpka
Hulsey, Hoyt	Steele
Madison II, Billy D.	Remlap
McCullough, Jerry	Georgiana
Militano, Tom	Jacksonville
Monk, Nathan P.	Cullman
Morris, C.H.	Frisco City
Pardue, Melvin M.	Repton
Roe Jr., Fred D.	Huntsville
Russell, Tom	Jacksonville
Sandlin, Larry	Adamsville
Sinyard, Cleston S.	Elberta
Watson, Billy	Deatsville

alaska

Amoureux, A.W.	Anchorage
Barrett, R.W.	Madison
Brennan, Judson	Delta Junction
Breuer, Lonnie	Wasilla
Broome, Thomas A.	Kenai
Bucholz, Mark A.	Eagle River
Bullard, Bill	Andalusia
Cannon, Raymond W.	Homer
Chamberlin, John A.	Anchorage
Dempsy, Gordon S.	N. Kenai
Dufour, Arthur J.	Anchorage
England, Virgil	Anchorage
Gouker, Gary B.	Sitka
Grebe, Gordon S.	Anchor Point
Hibben, Westley G.	Anchorage
Kommer, Russ	Anchorage
Lance, Bill	Eagle River
Little, Jimmy L.	Wasilla
McFarlin, Eric E.	Kodiak
McIntosh, David L.	Haines
Oda, Kuzan	Anchorage
Parrish III, Gordon A.	North Pole
Stegall, Keith	Anchorage
Trujillo, Adam	Anchorage
Trujillo, Miranda	Anchorage
Whitman, Jim	Chugiak

arizona

Anders, David	Center Ridge
Knife Source	Phoenix
Beaver, D. "Butch" and "Judy"	Phoenix
Boye, David	Dolan Springs
Brown, Jim	Little Rock
Burnett, Max	Paris
Cheatham, Bill	Laveen
Choate, Milton	Somerton
Conable, Matt	Chino Valley
Cook, James R.	Nashville
Craft III, John M.	Williams
Crawford, Pat	West Memphis
Crowell, James L.	Mtn. View
Dozier, Bob	Springdale

Dunge, Lawrence	Little Rock
Duvall, Fred	Benton
Edge, Tommy	Cash
Evans, Vincent K. & Grace	Show Low
Ferguson, Lee	Hindsville
Fisk, Jerry	Lockesburg
Flournoy, Joe	El Dorado
Frizzell, Ted	West Fork
Gaston, Bert	North Little Rock
Goo, Tai	Tucson
Grigsby, Ben	Mt. View
Guignard, Gib	Quartzsite
Gundersen, D.F. "Doc"	Tempe
Hancock, Tim	Scottsdale
Hoel, Steve	Pine
Holder, D'Alton	Peoria
Hull, Michael J.	Cottonwood
Karp, Bob	Phoenix
Kopp, Todd M.	Apache Jct.
Lampson, Frank G.	Rimrock
Lane, Ben	North Little Rock
Lawrence, Alton	De Queen
Lee, Randy	St. Johns
Lile, Marilyn (Jimmy)	Russellville
Lively, Tim and Marian	Tucson
Martin, Bruce E.	Prescott
Massey, Roger	Texarkana
McFall, Ken	Lakeside
McFarlin, J.W.	Lake Havasu City
Norris, Don	Tucson
Perry, John	Mayflower
Polk, Clifton	Van Buren
Quattlebaum, Craig	Searcy
Ramey, Marshall F.	West Helena
Randall, Bill	Tucson
Red, Vernon	Conway
Remington, David W.	Gentry
Roland, Dan	Yuma
Smoker, Ray	Searcy
Snare, Michael	Phoenix
Solomon, Marvin	Ferndale
Sutherland, Greg	Flagstaff
Tamboli, Michael	Glendale
Tycer, Art	Paron
Ward, Chuck	Benton
Weiler, Donald E.	Yuma
Weiss, Charles L.	Phoenix
White, Bryce	Little Rock
Wolf, Bill	Phoenix
Wright, Timothy	Sedona
York, David C.	Chino Valley
Walker, Jim	Morrilton

arkansas

Johnson, David L.	Talkeetna
Russell, A.G.	Springdale

california

Abernathy, Paul J.	Eureka
Barron, Brian	San Mateo
Benson, Don	Escalon
Berger, Max A.	Carmichael
Biggers, Gary	Ventura
Blum, Chuck	Brea
Boyd, Francis	Berkeley
Brack, Douglas D.	Camirillo
Breshears, Clint	Manhatten Beach
Brown, Ted	Downey
Brunetta, David	Laguna Beach
Chelquist, Cliff	Arroyo Grande
Clark, W.R.	Santa Fe Springs
Cohen, Terry A.	Laytonville
Collins, A.J.	Arleta
Connolly, James	Oroville
Davis, Charlie	Santee
Dillon, Earl E.	Arleta

Dion, Greg	Oxnard
Dixon Jr., Ira E.	Ventura
Donovan, Patrick	San Jose
Doolittle, Mike	Novato
Driscoll, Mark	La Mesa
Eaton, Al	Clayton
Ellis, David	San Diego
Ellis, William Dean	Fresno
Emerson, Ernest R.	Redondo Beach
English, Jim	Jamul
Essegian, Richard	Fresno
Ferguson, Jim	Temecula
Fisher, Theo (Ted)	Montague
Fox, Jack L.	Citrus Heights
Fraley, Derek	Dixon
Francis, Vance	Alpine
Fred, Reed Wyle	Sacramento
Freer, Ralph	Seal Beach
Fulton, Mickey	Willows
Gamble, Frank	Fremont
George, Tom	Magalia
Gofourth, Jim	Santa Paula
Golding, Robin	Lathrop
Hardy, Scott	Placerville
Harris, Jay	Redwood City
Hartsfield, Phill	Newport Beach
Hayes, Dolores	Los Angeles
Helton, Roy	Bakersfield
Hermes, Dana E.	Fremont
Herndon, WM. R. "Bill"	Acton
Hink III, Les	Stockton
Hogstrom, Anders T.	Belmont
Hoy, Ken	North Fork
Hume, Don	Sherman Oaks
Humenick, Roy	Rescue
Jacks, Jim	Covina
Johnson, Randy	Turlock
Jones, Curtis J.	Palmdale
Kruse, Martin	Reseda
Larson, Richard	Turlock
Leland, Steve	Fairfax
Lewis, Mike	Tracy
Likarich, Steve	Colfax
Lockett, Sterling	Burbank
Loveless, R.W.	Riverside
Manabe, Michael K.	San Diego
Martin, Jim	Oxnard
Massey, Ron	Joshua Tree
Mattis, James K.	Glendale
Maxwell, Don	Fresno
McBee, Williams	Colfax
McClure, Michael	Menlo Park
McMahon, John P.	Palm Desert
Melroy, Sean	Lemon Grove
Middleton, Ken	Citrus Heights
Mitchell, R.W. "Mitch"	Wildomar
Montano, Gus A.	San Diego
Morgan, Jeff	Santee
Mountain Home Knives	Jamul
Naten, Greg	Bakersfield
Orton, Richard	La Verne
Packard, Bob	Elverta
Padilla, Gary	Weimar
Pendleton, Lloyd	Volcano
Perry, Chris	Fresno
Phillips, Randy	Ontario
Pitt, David F.	Pleasanton
Posner, Barry E.	N. Hollywood
Richard, Ron	Fremont
Scarrow, Wil	Bellflower
Schroen, Karl	Sebastopol
Schultz, Richard A.	Laguna Hills
Sibrian, Aaron	Ventura
Sjostrand, Kevin	Visalia
Slobodian, Scott	San Andreas
Sornberger, Jim	Volcano
Stapel, Craig	Glendale
Steinberg, Al	San Bruno
Swain, Rod	South Pasadena

directory

Terrill, Stephen	Lindsay
Tinker, Carolyn D.	Whittier
Vagnino, Michael	Visalia
Ward, Ken	Weed
Warren, Al	Roseville
Watanabe, Wayne	Montebello
Weinstock, Robert	San Francisco
Willson, Harlan M.	Lompoc
Wilson, Philip C.	Livermore
Wilson, Ron	Los Osos

colorado

Anderson, Mel	Cedaredge
Appleton, Ray	Byers
Barrett, Cecil Terry	Colorado Springs
Booco, Gordon	Hayden 186
Brock, Kenneth L.	Allenspark
Campbell, Dick	Conifer
Coughlin, Michael M.	Denver
Davis, Don	Loveland
Dawson, Barry	Durango
DeLong, Dick	Aurora
Dennehy, Dan	Del Norte
Dennehy, John D.	Wellington
DeYong, Clarence	Fort Collins
Dill, Robert	Loveland
Eckerson, Charley	Pueblo
Genge, Roy E.	Eastlake
High, Tom	Alamosa
Hockensmith, Dan	Drake
Hodgson, Richard J.	Boulder
Hughes, Ed	Grand Junction
Leck, Dal	Hayden
Letcher, Billy	Fort Collins
Lewis, Steve	Woodland Park
McWilliams, Sean	Bayfield
Miller, Hanford J.	Cowdrey
Miller, M.A.	Thornton
Mitchell, Wm. Dean & Patricia	Lamar
Neeley, Vaughn	Mancos
Nolen, R.D. and Steve	Estes Park
Olson, Wayne C.	Wheat Ridge
Owens, John	Parker
Pogreba, Larry	Lyons
Roberts, Chuck	Westminster
Rollert, Steve	Keenesburg
Sanders, Bill	Mancos
Sasser, Jim	Pueblo
Smith, D. Noel	Canon City
Thompson, Lloyd	Pagosa Springs
Tollefson, Barry A.	Colorado
Topliss, M.W. "Ike"	Montrose
Watson, Bert	Westminster
Wilson, James G.	Estes Park
Wingo, Gary	Lamar
Wood, Barry B. and Irie Michael	
	Colorado Springs
Zima, Michael F.	Ft. Morgan

connecticut

Buebendorf, Robert E.	Monroe
Chapo, William G.	Wilton
Hubbard, Arthur J.	Monroe
Jean, Gerry	Manchester
Lepore, Michael J.	Bethany
Martin, Randall J.	Middletown
Padgett Jr., Edwin L.	New London
Pankiewicz, Phillip R.	Lebanon
Plunkett, Richard	West Cornwall
Putnam, Donald S.	Wethersfield
Rainville, Richard	Salem
Turecek, Jim	Derby
Zembko III, John	Berlin

delaware

Antonio Jr., William J.	Newark
Schneider, Karl A.	Newark
Wagner, Dan	New Castle
Willey, W.G.	Greenwood

district of columbia

Cumming, R.J.	Washington

florida

Adams, Les	Hialeah
Atkinson, Dick	Wausau
Barry III, James J.	West Palm Beach
Bartrug, Hugh E.	St. Petersburg
Beers, Ray	Lake Wales
Benjamin Jr., George	Kissimmee
Blackton, Andrew E.	Bayonet Point
Bosworth, Dean	Key Largo
Bradley, John	Pomona Park
Bray Jr., W. Lowell	New Port Richey
Brown, Harold E.	Arcadia
Chase, Alex	DeLand
Cobb, Lowell D.	Daytona Beach
Cross, John M.	Bryceville
Davenport, Jack	Dade City
DeGraeve, Richard	Sebastian
Dietzel, Bill	Middleburg
Dotson, Tracy	Baker
Ek, Gary Whitney	North Miami
Ellerbe, W.B.	Geneva
Embry, Brad	Plant City
Enos III, Thomas M.	Orlando
Farris, Cal	Altoona
Ferrara, Thomas	Naples
Fowler, Charles R.	Ft. McCoy
Gamble, Roger	St. Petersburg
Garcia, Tony	West Palm Beach
Garner Jr., William O.	Pensacola
Gibson, James Hoot	Bunnell
Goers, Bruce	Lakeland
Griffin Jr., Howard A.	Davie
Harris, Ralph Dewey	Brandon
Heitler, Henry	Tampa
Hennon, Robert	Ft. Walton Beach
Hill, Steven E.	Orlando
Hodge III, John	Palatka
Hoffman, Kevin L.	Winter Park
Hughes, Dan	West Palm Beach
Humphreys, Joel	Bowling Green
Hytovick, Joe "Hy"	Dunnellon
Jernigan, Steve	Milton
Johnson, Durrell Carmon	Sparr
Kelly, Lance	Edgewater
Krapp, Denny	Apopka
Lazo, Robert T.	Miami
Levengood, Bill	Tampa
Leverett, Ken	Lithia
Long, Glenn A.	Dunnellon
Lovestrand, Schuyler	Vero Beach
Lozier, Don	Ocklawaha
Lunn, Larry A.	Safety Harbor
Lyle III, Ernest L.	Orlando
Martrildonno, Paul	Debary
McDonald, Robert J.	Loxahatchee
Miller, Robert	Ormond Beach
Miller, Ronald T.	Largo
Mink, Dan	Crystal Beach
Newton, Larry	Jacksonville
Ochs, Charles F.	Largo
Outlaw, Anthony L.	Panama City
Pendray, Alfred H.	Williston
Piergallini, Daniel E.	Plant City
Price, Joel Hiram	Interlochen
Randall Made Knives	Orlando

Robinson III, Red R.	Leesburg
Rodkey, Dan	Hudson
Rogers, Rodney	Wildwood
Ross, Gregg	Lake Worth
Russ, Ron	Williston
Schlomer, James E.	Florida
Schwarzer, James	Pomona Park
Schwarzer, Stephen	Pomona Park
Simons, Bill	Lakeland
Smart, Steve	Tavares
Smith, Bobbie D.	Bonifay
Smith, Michael J.	Tampa
Smith, W.M.	Bonifay
Stephan, Daniel	Valrico
Stipes, Dwight	Jupiter
Strauss, Levi	Miami Lakes
Tomes, Anthony S.	Jacksonville
Tomes, P.J.	Middleburg
Vunk, Robert	Orlando
Waldrop, Mark	Summerfield
Wallace, Roger L.	Tampa
Watson, Tom	Panama City
Weiland Jr., J. Reese	Tampa
Wicker, Donnie R.	Panama City
William E, Stapleton	Merritt Island
Wine, Michael	Cocoa Beach
Zaccagnino Jr., Don	Pahokee
Zahm, Kurt	Indialantic

georgia

Arrowood, Dale	Sharpsburg
Ashworth, Boyd	Powder Springs
Barker, Robert G.	Bishop
Black, Scott	Covington
Bradley, Dennis	Blairsville
Buckner, Jimmie H.	Putney
Carey Jr., Charles W.	Griffin
Chamblin, Joel	Concord
Cofer, Ron	Loganville
Cole, Welborn L.	Atlanta
Cosby, E. Blanton	Columbus
Crockford, Jack	Chamblee
Davis, Steve	Powder Springs
Dunn, Charles K.	Shiloh
Ford, Allen	Smyrna
Fuller, John W.	Douglasville
Greene, David	Covington
Halligan, Ed	Sharpsburg
Harmon, Jay	Woodstock
Hawkins, Rade	Fayetteville
Haynie, Charles	Toccoa
Hegwood, Joel	Summerville
Hensley, Wayne	Conyers
Hinson and Son, R.	Columbus
Holland, John H.	Calhoun
Hyde, Jimmy	Ellenwood
Johnson, Harold "Harry" C.	Trion
Jones, Franklin (Frank) W.	Columbus
Landers, John	Newnan
Lockett, Lowell C.	Woodstock
Lonewolf, J. Aguirre	Demorest
McCarty, Zollan	Thomaston
McGill, John	Blairsville
Mitchell, James A.	Columbus
Moore, Bill	Albany
North, David and Prater, Mike	Chickamauga
Parks, John	Jefferson
Poole, Steve L.	Stockbridge
Poplin, James L.	Washington
Poythress, John	Swainsboro
Price, Timmy	Blairsville
Ragsdale, James D.	Lithonia
Rogers Jr., Robert P.	Acworth
Rosenfeld, Bob	Hoschton
Scofield, Everett	Chickamauga
Smith Jr., James B. "Red"	Morven
Snell, Jerry L.	Fayetteville
Snow, Bill	Columbus

Stafford, Richard	Warner Robins
Thompson, Kenneth	Duluth
Universal Agencies Inc.	Roswell
Walters, A.F.	TyTy
Werner Jr., William A.	Marietta
Wilson, Jon J.	Johnstown
Wilson, Mike	Bowman
Roghams, Mark	LaGrange

hawaii

Dolan, Robert L.	Kula
Fujisaka, Stanley	Kaneohe
Luci, Ronald M.	Honolulu
Mayo Jr., Tom	Waialua
Onion, Kenneth J.	Kapolei
Zakabi, Carl S.	Mililani Town

idaho

Steiger, Monte L.	Genesee
Alderman, Robert	Sagle
Andrews, Don	Coeur d'Alene
Hatch, Ken	Kooskia
Hawk, Gavin	Idaho City
Hawk, Grant	Idaho City
Horton, Scot	Buhl
Kranning, Terry L.	Pocatello
Ledbetter, Randy R.	Payette
Mullin, Steve	Snowberry Lane
Nealy, Ivan F. (Frank)	Mt. Home
Patton, Dick & Rob	Garden City
Quarton, Barr	McCall
Reeve, Chris	Boise
Rohn, Fred	Coeur d'Alene
Sawby, Scott	Sandpoint
Selent, Chuck	Bonners Ferry
Spragg, Wayne E.	Ashton
Towell, Dwight L.	Midvale

illinois

Abbott, William M.	Chandlerville
Bloomer, Alan T.	Maquon
Brandsey, Edward P.	Woodstock
Brignardello, E.D.	Crete
Caudell, Richard M.	Lawrenceville
Cook, Louise	Ozark
Cook, Mike	Ozark
Detmer, Phillip	Breese
Eaker, Allen L.	Paris
Guth, Kenneth	Chicago
Hill, Rick	Maryville
James, Peter	Hoffman Estates
Knuth, Joseph E.	Rockford
Kovar, Eugene	Evergreen Park
Lang, Kurt	McHenry
Markley,Ken	Sparta
Meier, Daryl	Carbondale
Meyers, Paul	E. Alton
Millard, Fred G.	Chicago
Nowland, Rick	Waltonville
Poag, James	Grayville
Potocki, Roger	Goreville
Pritchard, Ron	Dixon
Rados, Jerry F.	Grant Park
Schneider, Craig M.	Seymour
Smith, John M.	Centralia
Stalter, Harry L.	Trivoli
Tompkins, Dan	Peotone
Turnbull, Ralph A.	Rockford
Veit, Michael	LaSalle
Voss, Ben	Galesburg
Werth, George W.	Poplar Grove
West Charles A.	Centralia
White Jr., Robert J. Butch	Gilson
White, Robert J.	Gilson
Young, Errol	Alton

indiana

Allen, Joe	Princeton
Ball, Ken	Mooresville
Bose, Reese	Lewis
Bose, Tony	Shelburn
Broughton, Don R.	Floyd Knobs
Chaffee, Jeff L.	Morris
Claiborne, Jeff	Franklin
Damlovac, Sava	Indianapolis
Darby, Jed	Greensburg
Fitzgerald, Dennis M.	Fort Wayne
Flynn, Bruce	Knightstown
Imel, Billy Mace	New Castle
Johnson, C.E. Gene	Portage
Keeslar, Steven C.	Hamilton
Keeton, William L.	Laconia
Ledford, Bracy R.	Indianapolis
Mayville, Oscar L.	Marengo
Minnick, Jim	Middletown
Norton, Dennis	Ft. Wayne
Parsons, Michael R.	Terre Haute
Rubley, James A.	Angola
Shostle, Ben	Muncie
Stover, Terry "Lee"	Kokomo
Thayer, Danny	Lafayette
Welch, William H.	Kimmell
Worrell, Morris C.	Brownsburg
Young, George	Kokomo

iowa

Brooker, Dennis	Derby
Brower, Max	Boone
Clark, Howard F.	Runnells
Lainson, Tony	Council Bluffs
Miller, James P.	Fairbank
Myers, Mel	Spencer
Trindel, Barry	Earlham
Westberg, Larry	Algona
Zscherny, Michael	Cedar Rapids

kansas

Ames, Mickey L.	Ft. Scott
Battle Axe, The	Wichita
Bradburn, Gary	Wichita
Chard, Gordon R.	Iola
Courtney, Eldon	Wichita
Craig, Roger L.	Topeka
Culver, Gloria	Valley Falls
Culver, Steve	Valley Falls
Dawkins, Dudley L.	Topeka
Dugger, Dave	Westwood
Dunn, Melvin T.	Rossville
George, Les	Wichita
Hegwald, J.L.	Humboldt
Herman, Tim	Overland Park
Kennelley, J.C.	Arkansas City
Kraft, Steve	Abilene
Petersen, Dan L.	Topeka
Stice, Douglas W.	Haysville

kentucky

Barr, A.T.	Nicholasville
Baskett, Lee Gene	Eastview
Bodner, Gereald "Jerry"	Louisville
Bybee, Barry J.	Cadiz
Carson, Harold J. "Kit"	Vine Grove
Clay, J.D.	Greenup
Coil, Jimmie J.	Owensboro
Corbit, Gerald E.	Elizabethtown
Downing, Larry	Bremen
Dunn, Steve	Smiths Grove
Fannin, David A.	Lexington

Finch, Ricky D.	West Liberty
Fister, Jim	Simpsonville
France, Dan	Cawood
Gevedon, Hanners (Hank)	Crab Orchard
Greco, John & Sherry	Greensburg
Hemphill, Jesse	Berea
Hibben, Daryl	LaGrange
Hibben, Gil	LaGrange
Hibben, Joleen	LaGrange
Hoke, Thomas M.	LaGrange
Holbrook, H.L.	Olive Hill
Howser, John C.	Frankfort
Keeslar, Joseph F.	Almo
Miller, Don	Lexington
Pease, W.D.	Ewing
Pierce, Harold L.	Louisville
Pulliam, Morris C.	Shelbyville
Rigney Jr., Willie	Bronston
Smith, Gregory H.	Louisville
Smith, John W.	West Liberty

louisiana

Townsend, J.W.	Watson
Blaum, Roy	Covington
Caldwell, Bill	West Monroe
Camp, Jeff	Dubach
Capdepon, Randy	Carencro
Capdepon, Robert	Carencro
Chauvin, John	Scott
Culpepper, John	Monroe
Dake, C.M.	New Orleans
Durio, Fred	Opelousas
Elkins, R. Van	Bonita
Faucheaux, Howard J.	Loreauville
Forstall, Al	Pearl River
Gorenflo, James T. (JT)	Baton Rouge
Graffeo, Anthony L.	Chalmette
Holmes, Robert	Baton Rouge
Laurent, Kermit	LaPlace
Marks, Chris	Breaux Bridge
Mitchell, Max, Dean and Ben	Leesville
Potier, Timothy F.	Oberlin
Provenzano, Joseph D.	Chalmette
Reggio Jr., Sidney	Sun
Roath, Dean	Baton Rouge
Sanders, Michael M.	Ponchatoula
Wiggins, Horace	Mansfield

maine

Bohrmann, Bruce	Yarmouth
Coombs JR., Lamont	Bucksport
Courtois, Bryan	Saco
Fuegen, Larry	Wiscasset
Gray, Daniel	Brownville
Hillman, Charles	Friendship
Kravitt, Chris	Ellsworth
Lawler, Tim	Grand Ledge
Leavitt Jr., Earl F.	E. Boothbay
Oyster, Lowell R.	Corinth
Sayen, Murad	Bryant Pond
Sharrigan, Mudd	Wiscasset

maryland

Barnes, Aubrey G.	Hagerstown
Barnes, Gary L.	New Windsor
Beers, Ray	Monkton
Bouse, D. Michael	Waldorf
Cohen, N.J. (Norm)	Baltimore
Freiling, Albert J.	Finksburg
Fuller, Jack A.	New Market
Hart, Bill	Pasadena
Hendrickson, E. Jay	Frederick
Hudson, C. Robbin	Rock Hall
Hurt, William R.	Frederick

directory

Kremzner, Raymond L.	Stevenson
Kretsinger Jr., Phillip W.	Boonsboro
McCarley, John	Taneytown
McGowan, Frankie E.	Sykesville
Merchant, Ted	White Hall
Moran Jr. Wm. F.	Braddock Heights
Nicholson, R. Kent	Phoenix
O'Ceilaghan, Michael	Baltimore
Rhodes, James D.	Hagerstown
Sentz, Mark C.	Taneytown
Smit, Glenn	Aberdeen
Sontheimer, G. Douglas	Potomac

massachusetts

Smith, J.D.	Boston
Aoun, Charles	Wakefield
Daconceicao, John M.	Rehoboth
Dahl, Chris W.	Lake Geneva
Dailey, G.E.	Seekonk
Gaudette, Linden L.	Wilbraham
Grossman, Stewart	Clinton
Gwozdz, Bob	Attleboro
Jarvis, Paul M.	Cambridge
Kubasek, John A.	East Hampton
Lapen, Charles	Brookfield
McLuin, Tom	Dracut
Philippe, D A,	Pittsfield
Richter, Scott	S. Boston
Rua, Gary (Wolf)	Fall River
Stoddard's, Inc., Copley Place	Boston
Reed, Dave	Brimfield
Siska, Jim	Westfield

mexico

Scheurer, Alfredo E. Faes	C.P. 16010
Young, Cliff	San Miguel De Allende

michigan

Andrews, Eric	Grand Ledge
Behnke, William	Lake City
Bethke, Lora Sue	Grand Haven
Booth, Philip W.	Ithaca
Buckbee, Donald M.	Grayling
Carlisle, Frank	Detroit
Cashen, Kevin R.	Hubbardston
Cook, Mike A.	Portland
Corwin, Don	Saline
Cousino, George	Onsted
Cowles, Don	Royal Oak
Dilluvio, Frank J.	Warren
Enders, Robert	Cement City
Erickson, Walter E.	Warren
Garbe, Bob	Fraser
Gottage, Dante	Clinton Twp.
Gottage, Judy	Clinton Twp.
Hartman, Arlan (Lanny)	N. Muskegon
Hughes, Daryle	Nunica 214
Kalfayan, Edward N.	Ferndale
Krause, Roy W.	St. Clair Shores
Lankton, Scott	Ann Arbor
Leach, Mike J.	Swartz Creek
Lucie, James R.	Fruitport
Mills, Louis G.	Ann Arbor
Parker, Robert Nelson	Rapid City
Reh, Bill	Caro
Repke, Mike	Bay City
Sakmar, Mike	Rochester
Serven, Jim	Fostoria
Sigman, James P.	Three Rivers
Tally, Grant C.	Allen Park
Whittaker, Wayne	Metamore
Whitworth, Ken J.	Sterling Heights
Wood, Webster	Atlanta
Zowada, Tim	Boyne Falls

minnesota

Dingman, Scott	Bemidji
Dube, Paul	Chaska
Fiorini, Bill	Dakota
Goltz, Warren L.	Ada
Hagen, Philip L.	Pelican Rapids
Janiga, Matthew A.	Andover
Johnson, R.B.	Clearwater
Lange, Donald G.	Pelican Rapids
Maines, Jay	Wyoming
Ransen, Robert	Cambridge
Shadley, Eugene W.	Bovey

mississippi

Boleware. David	Carson
Craft, Richard C.	Jackson
Winston, David	Starkville
Fowler, Ricky	Richton 203
Hand M.D., James E.	Gloster
Landru, Leonard "Len"	Lumberton
Lebatard, Paul M.	Vancleave
Roberts, Michael	Clinton
Robinson, Chuck	Picayune
Taylor, Billy	Petal
Wehner, Rudy	Collins
Wingo, Perry	Gulfport

missouri

Bolton, Charles B.	Jonesburg
Cover, Raymond A.	Mineral Point
Cox, Colin J.	Raymore
Davis, Jesse W.	Sarah
Davis, W.C.	Raymore
Dearing, John	DeSoto
Dees, Jay	Collins
Dippold, A.W.	Perryville
Driskill, Beryl	Braggadocio
Duvall, Larry E.	Gallatin
Engle, William	Boonville
Glaser, Ken	Purdy
Mason, Bill	Excelsior Springs
McCrackin and Son, V.J.	House Springs
Miller, Bob	Oakville
Newcomb, Corbin	Moberly
Rardon, A.D.	Polo
Rardon, Archie F.	Polo
Shelton, Paul S.	Rolla
Steketee, Craig	Billings
Warden, Roy A.	Union
Weddle Jr., Del	St. Joseph

montana

Barnes, Jack	Whitefish
Beam, John R.	Kalispell
Brooks, Steve	Big Timber
Burrows, Stephen R.	Kansas City
Caffrey, Edwards J.	Great Falls
Colter, Wade	Colstrip
Conklin, George L.	Benton
Crowder, Robert	Thompson Falls
Des Jardins, Dennis	Plains
Dunkerley, Rick	Lincoln
Eaton, Rick	Shepherd
Ellefson, Joel	Manhattan
Fassio, Melvin G	Bonner
Forthofer, Pete	Whitefish
Gallagher, Barry	Lewistown
Griffin, Thomas J.	Windom
Harkins, J.A.	Conner
Hill, Howard E.	Polson
Hintz, Gerald M.	Helena
Hollar, Bob	Great Falls

Hulett, Steve	Yellowstone
Kauffman, Dave	Montana City
Kraft, Elmer	Big Arm
McGuane IV, Thomas F.	Bozeman
Miller, L. Maurice	Missoula
Mortenson, Ed	Darby
Moyer, Russ	Havre
Nedved, Dan	Kalispell
Patrick, Willard C.	Helena
Peele, Bryan	Thompson Falls
Peterson, Eldon G.	Whitefish
Piorek, James S.	Lakeside
Pursley, Aaron	Big Sandy
Robinson, Robert W.	Polson
Ruana Knife Works	Bonner
Schirmer, Mike	Twin Bridges
Schmidt, Rick	Whitefish
Simonich, Rob	Clancy
Smith, Josh	Lincoln
Taylor, Shane	Miles City
Thill, Jim	Missoula
Weinand, Gerome M.	Missoula

nebraska

Hielscher, Guy	Alliance
Jensen Jr., Carl A.	Blair
Jokerst, Charles	Omaha
Robbins, Howard P.	Elkhorn
Schepers, George B.	Chapman
Suedmeier, Harlan	Nebraska City
Syslo, Chuck	Omaha
Till, Calvin E. and Ruth	Chadron

nevada

Blanchard, G.R. (Gary)	Las Vegas
Cameron, Ron G.	Logandale
Defeo, Robert A.	Henderson
Duff, Bill	Virginia City
Hrisoulas, Jim	Las Vegas
Mount, Don	Las Vegas
Nishiuchi, Melvin S.	Las Vegas
Norton, Don	Las Vegas
Thomas, Devin	Panaca
Tracy, Bud	Reno

new hampshire

Classic Cutlery	Hopkinton
Gunn, Nelson L.	Epping
Hitchmough, Howard	Peterborough
MacDonald, John	Raymond
Saidon, R. Bill	Claremont

new jersey

D'Andrea, John	Wayne
Foley, Barney	Somerset
Grussenmeyer, Paul G.	Lindenwold
MacBain, Kenneth C.	Norwood
McGovern, Jim	Oak Ridge
Polkowski, Al	Chester
Pressburger, Ramon	Howel
Quick, Mike	Kearny
Slee, Fred	Morganville
Viele, H.J.	Westwood
Weber, Fred	Forked River

new mexico

Beckett, Norman L.	Farmington
Black, Tom	Albuquerque
Coleman, Keith E.	Albuquerque
Cordova, Joseph G.	Peralla

Digange, Joseph M.	Santa Cruz
Duran, Jerry T.	Albuquerque
Dyess, Eddie	Roswell
Fisher, Jay	Magdalena
Goode, Bear	Navajo Dam
Gunter, Brad	Tijeras
Hethcoat, Don	Clovis
Hurst, Gerard	Albuquerque
Jones, Bob	Albuquerque
Lewis, Tom R.	Carlsbad
McBurnette, Harvey	Eagle Nest
Miller, Ted	Santa Fe
Rogers, R S.	Nagdalena
Schaller, Anthony Brett	Albuquerque
Terzuola, Robert	Santa Fe
Walker, Michael L.	Taos
Ware, Tommy	Datil
Wescott, Cody	Las Cruces

new york

Anderson, Edwin	Glen Cove
Baker, Wild Bill	Boiceville
Champagne, Paul	Mechanicville
Cute, Thomas	Cortland
Davis, Barry L.	Castleton
Eneboe, James	Schenectady
Farr, Dan	Rochester
Faust, Dick	Rochester
Isgro, Jeffery	West Babylon
Levin, Jack	Brooklyn
Licata, Steven	Mineola
Loos, Henry C.	New Hyde Park
Ludwig, Richard O.	Maspeth
Maragni, Dan	Georgetown
Meshejian, Mardi	E. Northport
Page, Reginald	Groveland
Pattay, Rudy	Long Beach
Patterson, Karl	Silver Creek
Phillips, Scott C.	Gouverneur
Rachlin, Leslie S.	Elmira
Rappazzo, Richard	Cohoes
Rizzi, Russell J.	E. Setauket
Rotella, Richard A.	Niagra Falls
Scheid, Maggie	Rochester
Schmidt, James A.	Ballston Lake
Serafen, Steven E.	New Berlin
Smith, Raymond L.	Breesport
Summers, Dan	Whitney Pt.
Szilaski, Joseph	Wappingers Falls
Todd, Ed	Putnam Valley
Turner, Kevin	Montrose
Wood, Leonard J.	Fishkill

north carolina

Baker, Herb	Eden
Bauchop, Peter	Cary
Britton, Tim	Kinston
Busfield, John	Roanoke Rapids
Chastain, Wade	Horse Shoe
Clark, Dave	Andrews
Daniel, Travis E.	Winston-Salem
Edwards, Fain E.	Topton
Fox, Paul	Claremont
Gaddy, Gary Lee	Washington
Goguen, Scott	Newport
Greene, Chris	Shelby
Gross, W.W.	High Point
Gurganus, Carol	Colerain
Gurganus, Melvin H.	Colerain
Guthrie, George B.	Bassemer City
Harless, Walt	Stoneville
Livingston, Robert C.	Murphy
Lubrich, Mark	Matthews
Maynard, William N.	Fayetteville
McNabb, Tommy	Winston-Salem
McRae, J. Michael	Mint Hill

Parrish, Robert	Weaverville
Patrick, Chuck	Brasstown
Patrick, Peggy	Brasstown
Patterson, Alan W.	Hayesville
Popp Sr., Steve	Fayetteville
Rece, Charles V.	Paw Creek
Scholl, Tim	Angier
Shuford, Rick	Statesville
Simmons, H.R.	Aurora
Sprouse, Terry	Asheville
Sterling, Murray	Mount Airy
Sutton, S. Russell	New Bern
Van Hoy, Ed & Tanya	Candor
Wagaman, John K.	Fayetteville
Warren, Daniel	Canton
Whitley, Wayne	Washington
Williamson, Tony	Siler City
Winkler, Daniel	Blowing Rock
Young, Paul A.	Boone

north dakota

Keidel, Gene W. and Scott J.	Dickinson

ohio

Babcock, Raymond G.	Vincent
Bailey, Ryan	Galena
Busse, Jerry	Wauseon
Click, Joe	Liberty Center
Collins, Harold	West Union
Collins, Lynn M.	Elyria
Cottrill, James L.	Columbus
Darby, Rick	Youngstown
Downing, Tom	Cortland
Downs, James F.	Londonderry
Etzler, John	Grafton
Foster, R.L. (Bob)	Mansfield
Franklin, Mike	Aberdeen
Geisler, Gary R.	Clarksville
Glover, Ron	Mason
Greiner, Richard	Green Springs
Grubb, Richard E.	Columbus
Guess, Raymond L.	Mechanicstown
Hietmanski, Thomas S.	Mansfield
Hinderer, Rick	Wooster
Imboden II, Howard L.	Dayton
Koutsopoulos, George	LaGrange
Koval, Michael T.	New Albany
Kubaiko, Hank	Winesburg
Longworth, Dave	Hamersville
Loro, Gene	Crooksville
Maienknecht, Stanley	Sardis
McCarty, Harry	Hamilton
McDonald, Rich	Columbiana
McGroder, Patrick J.	Madison
Mercer, Mike	Lebanon
Messer, David T.	Dayton
Mettler, J. Banjo	North Baltimore
Morgan, Tom	Beloit
Papp, Robert	Parma
Ralph, Darrel	Galena
Salley, John D.	Tipp City
Shinosky, Andy	Canfield
Shoemaker, Carroll	Miamisburg
Shoemaker, Carroll	Northup
Spinale, Richard	Lorain
Stevens, Barry B.	Cridersville
Stoddart, W.B. Bill	Forest Park
Strong, Scott	Beavercreek
Summers, Arthur L.	Mechanicsburg
Summers, Dennis K.	Springfield
Thomas, Kim	Brunswick
Thourot, Michael W.	Napoleon
Trabbic, R.W.	Toledo
Votaw, David P.	Pioneer
Ward, J.J.	Waverly
Ward, Ron	Loveland

Warther, Dale	Dover
Witsaman, Earl	Stow
Wood, Larry B.	Huber Heights
Yurco, Mike	Canfield

oklahoma

Baker, Ray	Sapulpa
Barngrover, Jerry	Afton
Brown, Troy L.	Park Hill
Burke, Dan	Edmond
Crenshaw, Al	Eufaula
Dill, Dave	Bethany
Englebretson, George	Oklahoma City
Geoner, Don	Norman
Johns, Rob	Enid
Kennedy Jr., Bill	Yukon
Miller, Michael E.	Stroud
Sanders, A.A.	Norman
Spivey, Jefferson	Yukon
Williams, Michael L.	Broken Bow
Wilson, James R.	Seminole
Alverson, Tim (R.V.)	Klamath Falls

oregon

Bell, Michael	Coquille
Bochman, Bruce	Grants Pass
Buchman, Bill	Bend
Buchner, Bill	Idleyld Park
Coats, Eldon	Bonanza
Coon, Raymond C.	Gresham
Corrado, Jim	Glide
Davis, Terry	Sumpter
Dowell, T.M.	Bend
Eck, Larry A.	Terrebonne
Ferdinand, Don	Shady Cove
Fox, Wendell	Springfield
Frank, Heinrich H.	Seal Rock
Goddard, Wayne	Eugene
Griesi, Christian	Springfield
Harsey, William H.	Creswell
Hergert, Bob	Port Orford
Hilker, Thomas N.	Williams
Horn, Jess	Florence
Huey, Steve	Eugene
Kelley, Gary	Aloha
Lake, Ron	Eugene
Lindsay, Chris A.	Bend
Little, Gary M.	Broadbent
Lum, Robert W.	Eugene
Martin, Gene	Williams
Miller, Michael K.	Sweet Home
Murphy, Dave	Gresham
Olson, Darrold E.	Springfield
Osterman, Daniel E.	Junction City
Reed, Del	Beaverton
Schell, Clyde M.	Corvallis
Shoger, Mark O.	Beaverton
Thompson, Leon	Forest Grove
Thompson, Tommy	Portland
Vallotton, Butch and Arey	Oakland
Vallotton, Rainy D.	Umpqua
Vallotton, Shawn	Oakland
Vallotton, Thomas	Oakland
Veatch, Richard	Springfield
Wahlster, Mark David	Silverton
Wardian, Paul G.	Troutdale
Whitehead, James D.	Florence
Wise, John	Winchester
Woodcock, Dennis "Woody"	Nehalem

pennsylvania

Amor JR., Miguel	Lancaster
Anderson, Gary D.	Spring Grove
Anderson, Tom	Manchester

directory

Besedick, Frank E.	Ruffsdale
Candrella, Joe	Warminister
Clark, D.E. (Lucky)	Mineral Point
Frey Jr., W. Frederick	Milton
Goldberg, David	Blue Bell
Goldberg, Metalsmith, David	Blue Bell
Gottschalk, Gregory J.	Carnegie
Malloy, Joe	Freeland
Marlowe, Donald	Dover
Mensch, Larry	Milton
Milford, Brian A.	Knox
Miller, Rick	Rockwood
Moore, Ted	Elizabethtown
Nealy, Bud	Stroudsburg
Nolfi, Tim	Dawson
Nott, Ron P.	Summerdale
Parker, J.E.	Clarion
Rupert, Bob	Clinton
Rybar Jr., Raymond B.	Finleyville
Sinclair, J.E.	Pittsburgh
Steigerwalt, Ken	Orangeville
Stroyan, Eric	Dalton
Taglienti, Antonio J.	Beaver Falls
Valois, A. Daniel	Lehighton
Whittaker, Robert E.	Mill Creek

rhode island

Bardsley, Norman P.	Pawtucket
Burak, Chet	E Providence
Dickison, Scott S.	Narragansett
Jensen, John Lewis	Providence
Lambert, Ronald S.	Johnston
McHenry, Williams James	Wyoming
Potter, Frank	Middletown
Selvidro, Ralph	Wyoming
Williams, Jason L.	Wyoming

south carolina

Barefoot, Joe W.	Liberty
Beatty, Gordon H.	Seneca
Branton, Robert	Awendaw
Brend, Walter J.	Walterboro
Bridewell, Richard A.	Taylors
Cannady, Daniel L.	Allendale
Cox, Sam	Gaffney
Davis, Dixie	Clinton
Defreest, William G.	Barnwell
Easler Jr., Russell O.	Woodruff
Easler, Paula	Woodruff
Fecas, Stephen J.	Anderson
Gainey, Hal	Greenwood
Gaston, Ron	Woodruff
George, Harry	Aiken
Gregory, Michael	Belton
Hendrix, Wayne	Allendale
Herron, George	Springfield
Kaufman, Scott	Anderson
Kay, J. Wallace	Liberty
Langley, Gene H.	Florence
Lee, Tommy	Taylors
Lewis, K.J.	Lugoff
Lutz, Greg	Greenwood
McManus, Danny	Taylors
Montjoy, Claude	Clinton
Page, Larry	Aiken
Peagler, Russ	Moncks Corner
Poole, Marvin	Anderson
Poston, Alvin	Pamplico
Reeves, Winfred M.	West Union
Sears, Mick	Sumter
Smith, Ralph L.	Greer
Thomas, Rocky	Ladson
Tyser, Ross	Spartanburg
Whitmire, Earl T.	Rock Hill

south dakota

Thomsen, Lloyd W.	Oelrichs

tennessee

Bailey, Joseph D.	Nashville
Baker, Vance	Riceville
Bartlow, John	Norris
Canter, Ronald E.	Jackson
Cargill, Bob	Ocoee
Casteel, Dianna	Monteagle
Casteel, Douglas	Monteagle
Centofante, Frank and Tony	Madisonville
Claiborne, Ron	Knox
Clay, Wayne	Pelham
Conley, Bob	Jonesboro
Coogan, Robert	Smithville
Copeland, George Steve	Alpine
Corby, Harold	Johnson City
Harley, Larry W.	Bristol
Hurst, Jeff	Rutledge
Johnson, Ryan M.	Hixson
Langston, Bennie E.	Memphis
Levine, Bob	Tullahoma
Lincoln, James	Bartlett
McDonald, W.J. "Jerry"	Germantown
McNeil, Jimmy	Memphis
Moulton, Dusty	Loudon
Rhea, David	Lynnville
Rial, Douglas	Greenfield
Ryder, Ben M.	Copperhill
Sampson, Lynn	Jonesborough
Smith, Newman L.	Gatlinburg
Taylor, C. Gray	Kingsport
Vanderford, Carl G.	Columbia
Walker, John W.	Bon Aqua
Ward, W.C.	Clinton
Williams Jr., Richard	Morristown

texas

Adams, William D.	Houston
Allen, Mike "Whiskers"	Malakoff
Allred, Elvan	Wichita Falls
Ashby, Douglas	Dallas
Bailey, Kirby C.	Lytle
Barbee, Jim	Stockton
Barnes, Jim	San Angelo
Batts, Keith	Hooks
Blasingame, Robert	Kilgore
Blum, Kenneth	Brenham
Boatright, Basel	New Braunfels
Brayton, Jim	Burkburnett
Brightwell, Mark	Leander
Broadwell, David	Wichita Falls
Brooks, Michael	Lubbock
Bullard, Randall	Canyon
Bullard, Tom	Comfort
Burden, James	Burkburnett
Callahan, F. Terry	Boerne
Carter, Fred	Wichita Falls
Champion, Robert	Amarillo
Chase, John E.	Aledo
Churchman, T.W.	San Antonio
Clark, Roger	Rockdale
Connor, Michael	Winters
Cosgrove, Charles G.	Amarillo
Costa, Scott	Spicewood
Crain, Jack W.	Granbury
Davis, Vernon M.	Waco
Dean, Harvey J.	Rockdale
Dietz, Howard	New Braunfels
Dominy, Chuck	Colleyville
Edwards, Lynn	Columbia
Eldridge, Allan	Ft. Worth
Elishewitz, Allen	Dallas

Eriksen, James Thorlief	Garland
Ferguson, Jim	San Angelo
Fischer, Clyde E.	Nixon
Fortune Products, Inc.	Marble Falls
Foster, Al	Magnolia
Fowler, Jerry	Hutto
Fritz, Jesse	Slaton
Fuller, Bruce A.	Baytown
Gardner, Rob	Port Aransas
Gault, Clay	Lexington
Green, Bill	Garland
Green, Roger M.	Joshua
Griffin, Rendon and Mark	Houston
Hajovsky, Robert J.	Scotland
Hamlet JR., Johnny	Clute
Hand, Bill	Spearman
Hays, Mark	Carrollton
Hesser, David	Dripping Springs
Howell, Robert L.	Kilgore
Hudson, Robert	Humble
Hughes, Lawrence	Plainview
Jetton, Cay	Winnsboro
Johnson, Gorden W.	Houston
Johnson, Ruffin	Houston
Kennedy, Kelly S.	Odessa
Ladd, Jim S.	Deer Park
Ladd, Jimmie Lee	Deer Park
Lambert, Jarrell D.	Granado
Laplante, Brett	McKinney
Laughlin, Don	Vidor
Lay, L.J.	Burkburnett
Leblanc, John	Winnsboro
Lister Jr., Weldon E.	Boerne
Locke, Keith	Ft. Worth
Luchak, Bob	Channelview
Luckett, Bill	Weatherford
Lyons, Randy	Lumberton
Marshall, Glenn	Mason
Martin, Michael W.	Beckville
McClure, Leonard	Seminole
McConnell Jr., Loyd A.	Odessa
McDearmont, Dave	Lewisville
McElhannon, Marcus	Sugar Land
Merz III, Robert L.	Katy
Miller, R.D.	Dallas
Mills, Andy	Fredericksburg
Moore, James B.	Ft. Stockton
Neely, Greg	Houston
Ogletree Jr., Ben R.	Livingston
Oliver, Anthony Craig	Ft. Worth
Osborne, Michael	New Braunfels
Osborne, Warren	Waxahachie
Overeynder, T.R.	Arlington
Ownby, John C.	Plano
Pate, Lloyd D.,	Georgetown
Polzien, Don	Lubbock
Pugh, Jim	Azle
Pullen, Martin	Granbury
Ray, Alan W.	Lovelady
Richardson Jr., Percy	Hemphill
Robinson, Charles (Dickie)	Vega
Ruple, William H.	Charlotte
Schneider, Herman J.	Pittsburg
Scott, Al	Harper
Self, Ernie	Dripping Springs
Sims, Bob	Meridian
Sloan, Shane	Newcastle
Smart, Steve	Melissa
Spano, Dominick	San Angelo
Spencer, John E.	Harper
Stokes, Ed	Hockley
Stone, Jerry	Lytle
Stout, Johnny	New Braunfels
Theis, Terry	Harper
Thuesen, Ed	Needville
Thuesen, Kevin	Houston
Treiber, Leon	Ingram
Turcotte, Larry	Pampa
Watson, Daniel	Driftwood

Watt III, Freddie	Big Spring
Watts, Mike	Gatesville
Watts, Wally	Gatesville
Whitley, Weldon G.	El Paso
Wilcher, Wendell L.	Palestine
Wood, Williams W.	Seymour
Woodard, Wiley	Colleyville
Yeates, Joe A.	Spring
Yunes, Yamil R.	Roma
Zinsmeister, Paul D.	Harper

utah

Black, Earl	Salt Lake City
Davis, Greg	Fillmore
Ence, Jim	Richfield
Erickson, Curt	Ogden
Erickson, L.M.	Liberty
Hunter, Hyrum	Aurora
Johnson, Steven R.	Manti
Maxfield, Lynn	Layton
Nielson, Jeff V.	Monroe
Nunn, Gregory	Moab
Peterson, Chris	Salina
Rapp, Steven J.	Midvale
Stickland, Dale	Monroe
Velarde, Ricardo	Provo
Warenski, Buster	Richfield

vermont

Haggerty, George S.	Jacksonville
Kelso, Jim	Worcester

virginia

Ballew, Dale	Bowling Green
Barber, Robert E.	Charlottesville
Batson, Richard G.	Rixeyville
Beverly II, Larry H.	Spotsylvania
Callahan, Erret	Lynchburg
Catoe, David R.	Norfolk
Chamberlain, Charles R.	Barren Springs
Compton, William E.	Sterling
Conkey, Tom	Nokesville
Davidson, Edmund	Goshen
Douglas, John J.	Lynch Station
Fielder, William V.	Richmond
Frazier, Ron	Powhatan
Hawk, Jack L.	Ceres
Hawk, Joe	Ceres
Hawk, Joey K.	Ceres
Hedrick, Don	Newport News
Hendricks, Samuel J.	Maurertown
Holloway, Paul	Norfolk
Jones, Barry M. and Phillip G	Danville
Jones, Enoch	Warrenton
Kellogg, Brian R.	New Market
McCoun, Mark	DeWitt
Metheny, H.A. "Whitey"	Spotslyvnia
Murski, Ray	Reston
Norfleet, Ross W.	Richmond
Parks, Blane C.	Woodbridge
Richter, John C.	Chesapeake
Ryan, C.O.	Yorktown
Ryan, J.C.	Lexington
Scott, Winston	Huddleston
Thomas, Daniel	Leesburg
White, Gene E.	Alexandria

washington

Baldwin, Phillip	Snohomish
Ball, Robert	Port Angeles
Ber, Dave	San Juan Island
Blomberg, Gregg	Lopez

Boguszewski, Phil	Tacoma
Boyer, Mark	Bothell
Brothers, Robert L.	Colville
Brunckhorst, Lyle	Bothell
Chamberlain, John B.	Wenatchee
Chamberlain, Jon A.	Wenatchee
Conti, Jeffrey D.	Port Orchard
Crain, Frank	Spokane
D'Angelo, Laurence	Vancouver
Davis, John	Selah
Davis, K.M. Twig	Monroe
Goertz, Paul S.	Renton
Gray, Bob	Spokane
Greenfield, G.O.	Everett
Huddleston, Joe D.	Yelm
Hurst, Cole	Wenatchee
Kramer, Bob	Seattle
Leet, Larry W.	Burien
Mosser, Gary E.	Kirkland
Rice, Adrienne	Lopez Island
Sanderson, Ray	Yakima
Schempp, Martin	Ephrata
Schempp,Ed	Ephrata
Stegner, Wilbur G.	Rochester
Swyhart, Art	Klickitat
Wright, Kevin	Quilcene

west virgina

Barnett, Van	Saint Albans
Bowen, Tilton	Baker
Dellana	St. Albans
Derr, Herbert	Clendenin
Drost, Jason D.	French Creek
Drost, Michael B.	French Creek
Elliott, J.P.	Charleston
Jeffries, Robert W.	Red House
Liegey, Kenneth R.	Millwood
Maynard, Larry Joe	Crab Orchard
McConnell, Charles R.	Wellsburg
Morris, Eric	Beckley
Pickens, Selbert	Liberty
Reynolds, Dave	Harrisville
Sigman, Corbet R.	Liberty
Small, Ed	Keyser
Straight, Don	Points
Tokar, Daniel	Shepherdstown
White, Scottie H.	Pecks Mill
Wilson, R.W.	Weirton
Workman Jr., Hubert L.	Williamsburg
Wyatt, William R.	Rainelle

wisconsin

Boyes, Tom	Menomonee Falls
Genske, Jay	Fond du Lac
Hanson, Travis	Mosinee
Johnson, Kenneth	Mindoro
Kohls, Jerry	Princeton
Kolitz, Robert	Beaver Dam
Lary, Ed	Mosinee
Lerch, Matthew	Sussex
Maestri, Peter A.	Spring Green
Martin, Peter	Waterford
Nelson, Ken	Milwaukee
Niemuth, Troy	Sheboygan
Ponzio, Doug	Kenosha
Revishvili, Zaza	Madison
Ricke, Dave	West Bend
Rochford, Michael R.	Dresser
Schrap, Robert G.	Wauwatosa
Wattelet, Michael A.	Minocqua

wyoming

Alexander, Darrel	Ten Sleep
Ankrom, W.E.	Cody

Archer, Ray	Medicine Bow
Banks, David I.	Riverton
Bridges, Justin W.	Dubois
Draper, Audra	Riverton
Draper, Mike	Riverton
Fowler, Ed A.	Riverton
Friedly, Dennis E.	Cody
Pavack, Don	Hanna
Rexroat, Kirk	Wright
Reynolds, John C.	Gillette
Ross, Stephen	Evanston
Walker, George A.	Alpine
Whipple, Wesley A.	Thermopolis

foreign countries

africa

Burger, Pon Woodlands,	
	Bulawayo, Zimbabwe

argentina

Ayarragaray, Cristian L.	
	(3100) ParanaEntre Rios
Kehiayan, Alfredo	CP 1623 Buenos Aires
Rho, Nestor Lorenzo	Buenos Aires

austrailia

Bennett, Peter	Engadine N.S.W. 2233
Brown, Peter	Emerald Beach
Crawley, Bruce R.	Victoria
Cross, Robert	NSW
Del Raso, Peter	Victoria 3149
Gerus, Gerry	G.P.O. Cairns, Qtd.
Giljevic, Branko	Queanbeyan 2620, N.S.W.
Green, William (Bill)	View Bank
Husiak, Myron	Altona 3018, Victoria
Jones, John	QLD 4179
K B S. Knives	Vic 3450
Kerley, Tasman	Victoria
Maisey, Alan	Vincentia 2540
Rowe, Stewart G.	Brisbane 4306
Zemitis, Joe	2285 Newcastle

austria

Poskocil, Helmut	A-3340 Waidhofen/Ybbs

belgium

Monteiro, Victor	1360 Perwez

brazil

Barbosa, R Rui	Prudente-sp
Bodolay, Antal	
	Belo Horizonte MG-31730-700
Gaeta. Angelo	SP-17201-310
Garcia, Mario Eiras	Sao-Paulo SP-05516-070
Ikoma, Flavio Yuji, R. Manoel R	
	Teixeira, 108SP-19031-220
Lala, Paulo Ricardo P. and Lala, Roberto P.	
	SP-19031-260
Mello, Jacinto	Para de Minas MG 35.660
Neto Jr., Nelson and De Carvalho, Henrique M.	
	SP-12900-000
Paulo R, Fernandes	SP, 18680
Petean, Francisco and Mauricio	SP-16200-000
Ricardo Romano, Bernardes	1261, Itajuba MG
Rosa, Pedro Gullherme Teles	SP-19065-410
Villa, Luiz	SP-04537-081
Villar, Ricardo	S.P. 07600-000
Zakharov, Carlos	SP-12300-000

canada

Arnold, Joe	London, Ont.
Beauchamp, Gaetan	Stoneham, PQ
Bell, Donald	Bedford, Nova Scotia
Bold, Stu	Sarnia, Ont.
Boos, Ralph	Edmonton, Alberta
Bourbeau, Jean Yveslle	Perrot, Quebec
Debraga, Jose C.	Quebec
Deringer, Christoph	Sherbrooke, Quebec
Doussot, Laurent	Montreal, Quebec

Downie, James T. — Port Franks, Ont.
Dublin, Dennis — Enderby, BC
Fraser, Grant — Foresters Falls, Ont.
Freeman, John — Cambridge, Ont.
Gilbert, Chantal — St. Romuald, Quebec
Graham, Randal — Medicine Hat, AB, T1A 1C1
Grenier, Roger — Saint Jovite, Que.
Harildstad, Matt — Edmonton, Ab, T5T 2M8
Hartmann, Bruce James — Ontario
Hayes, Wally — St. Orleans, Ont.
Haynes, Chap — Tatamagouche, NS
Hoffmann, UWE H. — Vancouver, BC
Kaczor, Tom — London, Ont.
Lay, R.J. (Bob) — Vanderhoof, B.C.
Leber, Heinz — BC
Lemaire, Denis — Boucherville P.Q.
Lightfoot, Greg — AB
Linklater, Steve — Aurora, Ont.
Loerchner, Wolfgang — Bayfield, Ont.
Lyttle, Brian — High River, AB
Maneker, Kenneth — B.C.,
Martin, Robb — Ontario
Marzitelli, Peter — Langley, BC
Massey, Al — Nova Scotia
Olson, Rod — AB
Patrick, Bob — B.C.
Pepiot, Stephan — Man.
Piesner, Dean — Ont.
Price, Steve — BC
Roberts, George A. — Yukon Territories
Ross, Tim — Ont.
Schoenfeld, Matthew A. — Galiano Island, B.C.
Speck, Doug — Toronto, Ont.
Storch, Ed — Alberta T0B 2W0
Stuart, Steve — Ont.
Sunderland, Richard — BC
Tichbourne, George — Ont.
Tighe, Brian — Ridgeville, Ont.
Toner, Roger — Pickering, Ont.
Treml, Glenn — Thunder Bay, Ont.
Trudel, Paul — Ottawa On
Vachon, Yvon — Robertsville Que.
Whitenect, Jody — Nova Scotia
Young, Bud — Port Hardy, BC

denmark

Andersen, Henrik Lefolii — 3480, Fredensborg
Anso, Jens — DK 8220 Brabrand
Carlsson, Marc Bjorn — 1112 Copenhagen K
Dyrnoe, Per — Tulstrup, DK 3400 Hilleroed
Henriksen, Hans J. — DK 3200 Helsinge
Strande, Poul — Dastrup 4130 Viby Sj.
Vensild, Henrik — DK-8963 Auning 254

england

Boden, Harry — Derbyshire DE4 2AJ
Farid, 8 Sidney Close — Kent
Hague, Geoff — Wilton Marlborough
Henry & Son, Peter — Wokingham, Berkshire
Jackson, Jim — Berkshire SL4 5EP
Jones, Charles Anthony — No. Devon E31 4AL
Lamprey, Mike — Devon EX38 7BX
Morris, Darrell Price — Devon
Wardell, Mick — Surrey RH1 4PR
Wise, Donald — St. Leonardo-On-Sea
Wood, Alan — Carlisle, CA6 7HH

france

Bertholus, Bernard — 06600 Antibes
Doursin, Gerard — F 84210, Pernes les Fontaines
Ganster, Jean-Pierre — F-67000 Strasbourg
Graveline, Pascal And Isabelle — 29350 Moelan-sur-Mer
Reverdy, Pierre — 26100 Romans
Viallon, Henri — 63300 Thiers

germany

Balbach, Markus
Becker, Franz — 84533, Marktl/Inn
Boehlke, Guenter — Grossholbach
Borger, Wolf — Graben-Neudorf
Bürger, Günter — Castrop-Rauxel
Dell, Wolfgang — D-73277 Owen-Teck
Faust, Dick — 95497 Goldkronach
Fruhmann, Ludwig — 84489 Burghausen
Greisse, Jockl — 73252, Gutenberg
Hehn, Richard Karl — 55444 Dorrebach
Herbst, Peter — 91207 Lauf a.d. Pegn
Joehnk, Bernd — Kiel
Kaluza, Werner — Nurnberg
Kressler, D.F. — Odetzhausen
Neuhaeusler, Erwin — 86179 Augsburg
Rankl, Christian — 81476 Muchen
Rinkes, Siegfried — Markterlbach
Steinau, Jurgen — Berlin 0-1162
Tritz, Jean Jose — 20255 Hamburg
Wimpff, Christian — 70574 Stuttgart 70
Zirbes, Richard — D-54526 Niederkail

great britain

Elliott, Marcus Great Orme, — Llandudno Gwynedd

holland

Van De Manakker, Thijs — 5759 px Helenaween

italy

Albericci, Emilio — 24100, Bergamo
Ameri, Mauro — 16121 Genova
Ballestra, Santino — 18039 Ventimiglia (IM)
Bertuzzi, Ettore — 24068 Seriate (Bergamo)
Bonassi, Franco — Pordenone 33170
Fogarizzu, Boiteddu — 07016 Pattada
Giagu, Salvatore and Deroma Maria Rosaria — 07016 Pattada (SS)
Pachi, Francesco — 17046 Sassello (SV)
Pachi, Mirella — 17046 Sassello (SV)
Scordia, Paola — Roma
Simonella, Gianluigi — Maniago
Toich, Nevio — Vincenza
Tschager, Reinhard — Bolzano

japan

Aida. Yoshihito — Itabashi-ku, Tokyo 175
Carter, Murray M. — Uek Kamoto, Kumamoto
Fujikawa, Shun — Osaka 597
Fukuta, Tak — Seki-City, Gifu-Pref
Hara, Kouji — Gifu-Pref, 501-32
Hirayama, Harumi — Saitama Pref.
Ishihara, Hank — Sakura City, Chiba Pref.
Kagawa, Koichi — Kanagawa
Kanda, Michio — Yamaguchi 746
Kato, Kiyoshi — Tokyo 152
Kawasaki, Akihisa — Kobe
Koyama, Captain Bunshichi — Nagoya City
Mae, Takao — Amagasaki City HYOGO
Michinaka, Toshiaki — Tottori
Okaysu, Kazou — Tokyo
Sakakibara, Masaki — Tokyo 156
Shikayama, Toshiaki — Saitama 342-0057
Sugihara, Keidoh — Kishiwada City
Takahashi, Masao — Gunma 371
Tasaki, Seichi — Tochigi
Terrill, Stephen — Fujita-Cho Goboshi
Uekama, Nobuyuki — Tokyo
Wada, Yasutaka — Nara prefect 631-0044

n. wales u.k.

Heasman, H.G. — Llandudno

netherlands

Van Eldik, Frans — 3632BT Loenen
Van Rijswijk, Aad — 3132 AA Vlaardingen
Van Schaik, Bastiaan — Amsterdam
Van Den Elsen, Gert — 5012 AJ Tilburg

new zealand

Pennington, C.A., — Christchurch 9
Reddiex, Bill — Palmerton North
Ross, D.L. — Dunedin

norway

Bache-Wiig, Tom — Eivindvik
Holum, Morten — Oslo
Jorgensen, Gerd — N-3262 Larvik
Momcilovic, Gunnar — N-30055 Krokstadelva
Sellevold, Harald — N5834 Bergen
Vistnes, Tor — Swelgen,

russia

Revishvili, Zaza — Moscow

s.p. brazil

Bossaerts, Carl — 14051-110, Ribeirao Preto, SP
Gaeta, Roberto — 05351 Sao Paulo

singapore

Tay, Larry C-G — Singapore 9145

slovakia

Bojtos, Árpád — 98403 Lucenec
Pulis, Vladimir — 96701 Kremnica

south africa

Bauchop, Robert — Munster, Kwazulu-Natal, 4278
Beukes, Tinus — Vereeniging 1939
Bezuidenhout, Buzz — Malvern, Queensburgh, Natal 4093
Boardman, Guy — New Germany 3619
Brown, Rob E. — Emerald Hill 6011, Port Elizabeth
Burger, Fred — Munster 4278, Kwa-zulu Natal
De Villiers, Andre & Kirsten — Pietermantzburg 3206
Dickerson, Gavin — Petit 1512
Frankland, Andrew — Wilderness 6560
Grey, Piet — Silverton 0127
Harvey, Kevin — Johannesburg
Kojetin, W. — Germiston 1401
La Grange, Fanie — Bellville 7530
LaGrange, Fannie — Table View 7441
Lancaster, C.G. — Par 45 Free State
Liebenberg, Andre — Bordeauxrandburg 2196
Mackrill, Stephen — Johannesburg
Pienaar, Conrad — Bloemfontein 9300
Rietveld, Bertie — Magaliesburg 1791
Russell, Mick — Port Elizabeth 6070
Schoeman, Corrie — Bloemfontein 9300
Shoebotham, Heather — Gold Reef City 2159 Johannesburg
Skellern, Dr. M.J. — Munster 4278
Smythe, Ken — Underberg 4590
Watson, Peter — La Hoff 2570
Wood, Owen Dale — Honeydew

sweden

Bergh, Roger — 83070 NRA
Eklund, Maihkel — S-82041 Frila
Embretsen, Kaj — S-82821 Edsbyn
Johansson, Anders — Västerås
Lundstom, Jan-Ake — 66010 Dals-Langed
Nordell, Ingemar — Farila
Persson, Conny — 820 50 Loos

switzerland

Roulin, Charles — Geneva
Soppera, Arthur — Zurich

uruguay

Gonzalez, Leonardo Williams — CP 20000

western australia

Harvey, Max — Perth 6155

zimbabwe

Smit, Corn — Darwendale

knifemakers membership lists

Not all knifemakers are organization-types, but those listed here are in good standing with these organizations.

knifemakers guild

2000 voting membership

a Les Adams, Yoshihito Aida, Mike "Whiskers" Allen, R.V. Alverson, Michael Anderson, W.E. Ankrom, Joe Arnold, Boyd Ashworth, Dick Atkinson.

b Joseph D. Bailey, Norman Bardsley, A.T. Barr, Van Barnett, James Barry III, John Bartlow, Gene Baskett, James Batson, Gaetan Beauchamp, Raymond Beers, Charlie Bennica, Tom Black, Andrew Blackton, Gary Blanchard, Alan Bloomer, Arpad Bojtos, Philip Boguszewski, Wolf Borger, Tony Bose, Dennis Bradley, Edward Brandsey, W. Lowell Bray Jr., Judson Brennan, Clint Breshears, Tim Britton, David Broadwell, David Brown, Harold Brown, Rick Browne, John Busfield.

c Bill Caldwell, Errett Callahan, Daniel Cannady, Ronald Canter, Harold J. "Kit" Carson, Fred Carter, Dianna Casteel, Douglas Casteel, Frank Centofante, Joel Chamblin, William Chapo, Alex Chase, William Cheatham, Howard F. Clark, Wayne Clay, Lowell Cobb, Keith Coleman, Vernon Coleman, Alex Collins, Blackie Collins, Bob Conley, Harold Corby, Joe Cordova, Gerald Corbit, Jim Corrado, George Cousino, Raymond Cover, Colin Cox, John Craft III, Pat Crawford, John M. Cross, Bob Crowder, James Crowell, Dan Cruze, Roy Cutchin.

d George Dailey, Charles M. Dake, Alex Daniels, Jack Davenport, Edmund Davidson, Barry Davis, Terry Davis, Vernon M. Davis, W.C. Davis, Harvey Dean, Robert DeFeo, Bill DeFreest, Dan Dennehy, William Dietzel, Robert Dill, Frank Dilluvio, Charles Dintruff, Allen Dippold, T.M. Dowell, Larry Downing, Tom Downing, Bob Dozier, Bill Duff, Melvin Dunn, Steve Dunn, Jerry Duran.

e Russell & Paula K. Easler, Al Eaton, Rick Eaton, Fain Edwards, Allen Elishewitz, Joel Ellefson, Jim Elliott, David Ellis, Kaj Embretsen, Brad Embry, Ernest Emerson, Jim Ence, Virgil England, William Engle, James T. Eriksen.

f Stephen Fecas, Lee Ferguson, Thomas M. Ferrara, Bill Fiorini, Jay Fisher, Jerry Fisk, Joe Flournoy, Pete Forthofer, Ricky Flowler, Paul Fox, Henry Frank, Michael H. Franklin, Ron Frazier, Ralph Freer, Dennis Friedly, Larry Fuegen, Shun Fujikawa, Stanley Fujisaka, Tak Fukuta, Shiro Furukawa.

g Frank Gamble, Roger Gamble, Robert Garbe, William Garner, Ronald Gaston, Clay Gault, Harry George, James "Hoot" Gibson Sr., Bruce Goers, David Goldberg, Warren Goltz, Greg Gottschalk, Roger M. Green, Jockl Greiss, Carol Gurganus, Melvin Gurganus, Kenneth Guth.

h Philip L. "Doc" Hagen, Ed Halligan & Son, Jim Hammond, Tim Hancock, James E. Hand, M.D., Travis Hanson, Kouji Hara, Jeffrey Harkins, Walt Harless, Larry Harley, Jay Harmon, Ralph Harris, Rade Hawkins, Richard Hehn, Henry Heitler, Earl Jay Hendrickson, Wayne Hendrix, Wayne Hensley, Peter Herbst, Tim Herman, George Herron, Don Hethcoat, Thomas S. Hetmanski, Gil Hibben, Howard Hill, Steven Hill, R. Hinson & Son, Harumi Hirayama, Howard Hitchmough, Steve Hoel, Kevin Hoffman, D'Alton Holder,

Jess Horn, Durvyn Howard, Arthur Hubbard, Rob Hudson, Daryle Hughes, Joel Humphreys, Joseph Hytovick.

i Billy Mace Imel.

j Jim Jacks, Paul Jarvis, Steve Jernigan, Tom Johanning, Brad Johnson, Ronald Johnson, Ruffin Johnson, Steve Johnson, W.C. Johnson, Enoch D. Jones, Robert Jones.

k Edward N. Kalfayan, Dave Kauffman, William Keeton, Bill Kennedy Jr., Jot Khalsa, Keith Kilby, Bill King, Joe Kious, Russell Klingbeil, Terry Knipschield, R.C. Knipstein, Michael Koval, Dennis G. Krapp, Roy Krause, D.F. Kressler.

l Ron Lake, Jarrell Lambert, Frank Lampson, Edward Lary, Kermit Laurent, Mike Leach, Randy Lee, Tommy Lee, William Letcher, Bill Levengood, Bob Levine, Yakov Levin, Steve Linklater, Wolfgang Loerchner, Juan A. Lonewolf, R.W. Loveless, Schuyler Lovestrand, Don Lozier, Bob Luchak, Robert Lum, Ernest Lyle, Brian Lyttle.

m Joe Malloy, Dan Maragni, Peter Martin, Randall J. Martin, Zollan McCarty, Charles McConnell, Loyd McConnell, Robert J. McDonald, W. J. McDonald, Ken McFall, Frank McGowan, W.J. McHenry, David McIntosh, Tommy McNabb, Mike Mercer, Ted Merchant, Robert Merz III, James Miller, Steve Miller, Louis Mills, Dan Mink, Jim Minnick, Gunnar Momcilovic, James B. Moore, Jeff Morgan, C.H. Morris, Dusty Moulton, Paul Myers.

n Bud Nealy, Corbin Newcomb, Larry Newton, R.D. & George Nolen, Ross Norfleet, Don Norton.

o Charles Ochs, Ben R. Ogletree Jr., Warren Osborne, T.R. Overeynder, John Owens.

p Larry Page, Robert Papp, Melvin Pardue, Bob Patrick, W.D. Pease, Alfred Pendray, John L. Perry, Eldon Peterson, Kenneth Pfeiffer, David Pitt, Leon Pittman, Clifton Polk, Al Polkowski, Joe Prince, Jim Pugh, Martin Pullen, Morris Pulliam.

r Jerry Rados, James D. Ragsdale, Steven Rapp, A.D. Rardon, Chris Reeve, John Reynolds, Ron Richard, David Ricke, Bertie Rietveld, Willie Rigney, Dean Roath, Howard Robbins, Rex Robinson III, Robert Robinson, Fred Roe, Rodney Rogers, Charles Roulin, Ronald Russ, A.G. Russell, Gote Ryberg.

s Bill Saindon, Masaki Sakakibara, Mike Sakmar, Hiroyuki Sakurai, John Salley, Scott Sawby, Michael Schirmer, James Schmidt, Herman Schneider, Maurice & Alan Schrock, Steve Schwarzer, Al Scott, Mark C. Sentz, Eugene W. Shadley, Ben Shostle, Bill Simons, R.J. Sims, Cleston Sinyard, Jim Siska, Fred Slee, Scott Slobodian, J.D. Smith, John Smith, John W. Smith, Michael J. Smith, Ralph Smith, Jerry Snell, Marvin Solomon, Arthur Soppera, Jim Sornberger, Harry Stalter, Ken Steigerwalt, Jurgen Steinau, Daniel Stephan, Murray Sterling, Barry Stevens, Johnny Lee Stout, Keidoh Sugihara, Arthur

Summers, Greg Sutherland, S. Russell Sutton, Charles Syslo, Joseph Szilaski.

t Grant Tally, David A. Taylor, Gray Taylor, Robert Terzuola, Leon Thompson, Brian Tighe, P.J. Tomes, Dan Tompkins, John Toner, Dwight Towell, Leon Treiber, Barry Trindle, Reinhard Tschager, Jim Turecek, Ralph Turnbull.

v Yvon Vachon, Frans Van Eldik, Edward T. Van Hoy, Aad Van Rijswijk, Michael Veit, Howard Viele.

w John W. Walker, George Walker, Michael Walker, Charles Ward, Tommy Ware, Buster Warenski, Dellana Warren, Dale Warther, Thomas J. Watson, Charles Weeber, Reese Weiland, Robert Weinstock, Charles Weiss, Wayne Whittaker, Weldon Whitley, Donnie R. Wicker, Jason Williams, Gordon Wilson, R.W. Wilson, Daniel Winkler, Earl B. Witsaman, Frank Wojtinowski, William Wolf, Owen Wood, Wood, Irie & Company, Webster Wood, Tim Wright.

y Joe Yeates, Yoshindo Yoshihara, George Young, Mike Yurco.

z Brad Zinker, Tim Zowada

american bladesmith society(MS) = Master Smith

a Robin Eileen Ackerson, Bill Adams, Richard L. Adkins, Eugene Alexander, Mickey L. Ames, David Anders (MS), Autumn D. Anderson, Brian Anderson, Gary D. Anderson (MS), Ronnie A. Andress, Sr., Alan H. Arrington M.D., Doug, Asay, Boyd Ashworth

b Vance L. Baker, Robert Ball, Romas Banaitis, David L. Banks, C. David Barker, R.G. Barker, Aubrey G. Barnes (MS), Eric Barnes, Gary Barnes (MS), Marlen R. Barnes, Richard Barney, Almon T. Barton, Hugh E. Bartrug (MS), James L. Batson (MS), Robert K. Batts, Geneo Beasley, James S. Beaty III, Robert B. Beaty, William H. Behnke, George Benjamin, Jr., C.L. (Larry) Bentley, Lara Sue Bethke, Hal Bish, Scott Black, William A. Black, R. Gordon Bloomquist, Kenneth Blum, Geoffrey W. Boos, John P. Boots, Raymond A. Boysen, Garrick A. Bradford, John C. Bradley, Robert Branton, W. Lowell Bray, Jr., Don Broughton (MS), John T. Brown, Troy L. Brown, Thomas L. Browning, Lisa Broyles, Jimmie Buckner (MS), John F. Buffington, Bill Bullard, Jay Burger, Paul E. Burke, Stephan R. Burrows, Owen John C. Bush, John Butler, Dee Button-Inman, Sue G. Button.

c Michael Cabbage, Buddy Cabe, Edward J. Caffrey, Terry F. Callahan, Robert W. Calvert, Jeff Camp, Courtenay M. Campbell, Robert D. Carignan, Ron Carpenter, Murray M. Carter, Kevin R. Cashen (MS), Chris Cawthorne, Tom S. Cellum, Frank Cherry, Ron Clairborne, Peter John Clapp, Howard F. Clark (MS), James R. Coker, Harold A. Collins, Wade Colter, Larry D. Coltrain, Roger Comar, Roger Combs, John W. Conner, Michael L. Connor (MS), James R. Cook (MS), George S. Cook, Louise Cook, J. Michael Cook, Rachel Cook, Raymond C. Coon, Todd A. Cooper Joseph G. Cordova (MS), James H. Corry, Mike Corvin, Dr. Timothy L. Costello, Billy W. Cothran Sr., Houston L. Cotton, Monty L. Crain, Dawnavan M. Crawford, John M. Cross (MS), James L. Crowell (MS), William M. Culnon, Steven M. Culver.

d Mary H. Dake, Benjamin M. Daland, Sava Damlovac, Barry Davis, Don Davis, Dudley L. Dawkins, Harvey J. Dean, Jr. (MS), Marco A.M. de Castro, Anthony Del Giorno, John C. Delavan, Larry Russell Dement, Mike de Punte, Christoph Deringer (MS), Herbert Derr, Dennis E. DesJardins, John Thomas Devardo, Steven Deweese, Gordon S. Dickerson, William J. Dietzel, A.W. Dippold, Audra L. Draper, Mike Draper, Joseph D. Drouin, Paul Dube, Philip F. Duffy, Brad M. Dugan, Rick Dunkerley, Steve Dunn (MS), Kenneth Durham, Fred Durio, Oliver H. Durrell.

e Robert A. Ebersole, Roger Echols, Hugh E. Eddy, Lynn Edwards, Mitch Edwards, Perry B. Elder Jr., Ronald V. Elkins, Terry W. Ellerbee, Dave Ellis, Kaj Embretsen, James Eneboe, David Etchieson, Ronald B. Evans, Vincent K. Evans, Wyman Ewing.

f James A. Fagan, George Fant Jr., Jack S. Feder, Gregory K. Ferrier, Ioannis-Minas Filippou, Edward Finn, William R. Fiorini, Clyde E. Fischer, Don Fisher, Jerry Fisk (MS), Jim Fister (MS), John S. Fitch, Joe Flournoy(MS), Don Fogg, Gerald J. Fontenot, Norvell C. Foster, Ronnie E. Foster, Charles Ronald Fowler, Ed A. Fowler (MS), Jerry B. Fowler, Ricky Fowler, Wendell Fox, Walter P. Framski, Daniel Frank, Ralph Freer, Larry Friedrich, Daniel Fronefield, DeWayne Frost, Larry Fuegen (MS), Bruce A. Fuller (MS), Jack A. Fuller (MS).

g Peter Gagstaher, Yvon Gagueche, Barry Gallagher, Sean Gallagher, Timothy P. Garrity, Bert Gaston (MS), Leslie George, Thomas Gerner, Richard Gerson, Bruymimx Gert, John Glasscock, Sherwood M. Glotfelty, Jim Gofourth, Wayne L. Goddard (MS), Scott K. Goguen, David Goldberg, Robert Golden, Phillipe Gontier, Gabe Gorenflo, James T. Gorenflo, Greg Gottschalk, Gordon Graham, Walter M. Graves, Bob Gray, Don Greenaway, Chris L. Greene, David Greene, Richard F. Greiner, D.F. Gundersen, Ralph Gutekunst.

h Philip L. Hagen, Ed Halligan (MS), N.P. Pete Hamilton, Phil Hammond, Timothy J. Hancock (MS), Bill Hand, Scott Hardy, Larry Harley, Paul W. Harm, R.L. Harper, Cass Harris, Jeffrey A. Harris, Tom Harrison, Rade Hawkins, Scotty Hayes, Wally Hayes (MS), Charles E. Haynes (MS), Mary Margaret Haynes, Bob Dale Hays, John Heinz, Earl J. Hendrickson (MS), Shawn E. Hendrickson, Carl E. Henkle, A.J. Hermann, Bill Herndon, Jay Heselschwerdt, Don Hethcoat (MS), Jerry Hewitt, B.W. Hicks, Kent Hicks, Gene R. Hobart, Dan Hockensmith, Thomas R. Hogan, Bob Hollar, Robert A. Howes, C. Robbin Hudson (MS), Bill R. Hughes, Daryle Hughes, Lawrence H. Hulett, Richard D. Hunter, William Hurt, Joe Hytovick.

i Paul R. Inman III, Carole Ivie.

j Charlton R. (Jack) Jackson, Jim L. Jackson, John R. Johnson, Randy Johnson, Robert Johnston, Enoch (Nick) Jones, Franklin W. Jones, Andrew S. Jordan.

k Al J. Kajin, J. Michael Keeney II, Michael Keeney, Joseph F. Keeslar (MS), John C. Keller, Jerry Kennedy, Kelly S. Kennedy, R.W. Kern, Hyman S. Kessler, Shiva Ki, Keith Kilby (MS), Richard L. Kimberley, Fred King, Todd Kinnikin, Ray Kirk, Russell K. Klingbeil, Hank Knickmeyer(MS), Kurt Knickmeyer, Charles Ray Knowles, Bob Kramer, Lefty Kreh, Raymond Kremzner, Phillip W. Kretsinger (MS), Danny L. Kyle.

l Cliff Lacey, Christian Laferriere, Curtis J. Lamb, Jarrell D. Lambert, Leonard Landrum, Bud Lang, Donald G. Lange (MS), Kermit J. Laurent, Charles A. Lawless, Alton Lawrence, Dal Leck, Rick Leeson, Nick Leone III, Bernard Levine, H. Stephen Lewis, Jack Lewis, Peter Lin, Wayne B. Lindsey, Guy A. Little, Lowell C. Lockett, J.A. Lonewolf, Aldo Lorenzi, Eugene F. Loro, Mark Lubrich, James R. Lucie, Gerard P. Lukaszevicz, Larry A. Lunn, Greg Lutz, William R. Lyons.

m Clent Mackay, Robert Mackay, Raymond J. Malaby, Michael K. Manabe, Ken Mankel, James Maples, Dan Maragni (MS), Ken Markley, Chris Marks (MS), Stephen R. Marshall, Bruce E. Martin, Gene Martin, John Alexander Martin, Peter Martin, Bill Mason, Alan Robert Massey, Roger D. Massey (MS), Frederick L. McCoy, Kevin McCrackin, Victor J. McCrackin (MS), Richard McDonald, Robert J. McDonald, Frank McGowan, David Brian McKenzie, Tommy McNabb, Mardi Meshecian, James L. Meyers, Bob Miller, Hanford J. Miller (MS), Kent Miller, Richard Miller, Delbert Mills, Stephen J. Mischke, W. Dean Mitchell (MS), Gustav Moertensson, Michael Steven Moncus, Gus A. Montano, Billy R. Moore, Marve Moore, William F. Moran, Jr. (MS), Dennis L. Morris, Franklin D. Morris, Jan Muchnikoff, Dawn Mulbery, Jack W. Muse.

n Angelo Navagato, Gregory T. Neely (MS), Carl Nelson, Robert M. Newhouse, Ron Newton, Tim Nolfi.

o Winston Oakes, Charles F. Ochs III (MS), Clyde O'Dell, Vic Odom, Randy W. Ogden, Michael E. Olive, Ben M. Ortega, Dr. Michael R. Osborne, Stephen H. Overstreet, Donald Owens.

p Jeff Pacelt, Beuford M. Pardue, John Parks, Thomas O. Parler, Chuck Patrick, Michael D. Pemberton, Alfred H. Pendray (MS), Frederic Perrin, Jim Perry, Johnny Perry, Dan L. Peterson (MS), Lloyd C. Peterson, Clay C. Peyton, Edward W. Phillips, James M. Phillips, Dean Piesner, David Pitman, Dietmar Pohl, James P. Poling, Douglas Ponzio, James E. Porter (MS), Timothy F. Potier (MS), Karlis A. Povisils, James Powell, Houston Price, Terry Primos, Jonathan K. Purviance.

q Thomas C. Quakenbush, Craig Quattlebaum.

r R. Wayne Raley, Darrel Ralph, Richard A. Ramsey, Gary Randall, Ralph Randow, Robert Renkoski, Kirk Rexroat, James D. Rhodes, Douglas R. Rice, Stephen E. Rice, Alvin C. Richards, Jr., David M. Rider, E. Ray Roberts, Michael Roberts, Charles R. Robinson, Michael R. Rochford, Walter D. Rollick, Jerry Romig, Bob Rosenfeld, Robert N. Rossdeutscher Jr., Charles Roulin, Kenny Rowe, Gary Rua, J. Ken Rudder Jr., Al Runyon, Bob Rupert, Ronald S. Russ, Raymond B. Rybar Jr., Gerald Rzewnicki.

s Bill Saindon, Reisuke Saitoh, Ed Schempp, Tom Schilling, James S. Schippnick, James A. Schmidt (MS), Raymond E. Schmitz, Randy Schmoker, Tim Scholl, Charles E. Schultz, Robert W. Schultz, Steven C. Schwarzer (MS), Barry Scott, James A. Scroggs, Robert J. Scroggs, W.P. Semon Jr., Mark C. Sentz (MS), Steve Shackleford, William B. Shackleford, Thomas J. Sheehy, Steven Sheets, Tom Siess, James P. Sigman, Harland R. Simmons, S. Ted Sketos, Wayne Smallwood, J.D. Smith, John M. Smith, Joshua J. Smith, Lenerd C. Smith, Raymond L. Smith, Timothy E. Smock, Marvin Solomon, Gregory Noble Spickler, Thomas K. St. Clair, H. Red St. Cyr, Chuck Stancer, Udo Stegemann, Craig Steketee, Edward L. Stewart, Gary Kenneth Stine, Marc Stokeld, Johnnie L. Stout, Howard Stover, James K. Stover, Terry Lee Stover, Kenneth J. Straight, Frank Stratton III, Terry Stults, Harlan Suedmeier, Cynthia Ann Summers, Daniel L. Summers, Mike Sweany, Arthur Swyhart, Daniel L. Syrcle, Mark G. Szarek, Joseph Szilaski, Joseph G. Szopa.

t Scott Taylor, Shane Taylor, Jimmy D. Tharp, Danny Thayer, Jean-Paul Thevenot, Devin Thomas, Kenneth Thompson, P.J. Tomes (MS), Samuel L. Torgeson, Kenneth W. Trisler, Kevin Turner, Randall W. Turner, Jerry L. Tyer.

v Wayne Valachovic, (MS), James N. Van Riper, Jonny David Vasquez, Jan Vaughan, Arthur V. Velasco, Patrik Vogt, Lew Von Lossberg, Bruce Voyles.

w Bill Walker, Don Walker, James L. Walker (MS), John Wade Walker III, Roger L. Wallace, Charles W. Wallingford, Wellington Tu Wang, Charles B. Ward, Michael B. Ward, Ken Warner, Dellana Warren, Robert Lee Washburn Jr., Herman Harold Waters, Lu Waters, Billy Watson, Daniel Watson, Haines R. (Dick) Wendell, Jim Weyer, Robert R. Wheeler, Wesley Whipple, Richard T. White, Stephen Whitham, Lenwood W. Whitley, Randy Whittaker, A.L. Williams, Larry D. Williams, Michael L. Williams, Richard T. Williams, Wayne Willson, Jesse Allen Wilmer, George H. Wilson, James R. Wilson, Dan Winkler (MS), George Winter, Donald Witzler, Jim Woods, Randy Wootton, Bill Worthen, Travis Wuertz.

y Yasuhiro Yamanaka, Todd Yelverton, Yoshindo Yoshihara.

z William H. Zeanon.

miniature knifemaker's society

Paul Abernathy, Mel Anderson, Mary W. Bailey, Paul Charles Basch, Jesse J. Bass, Ray Beers, John Biggers, Blade Magazine, Dennis Blaine, Gerald Bodner, Gary F. Bradburn, Mary Bray, Brock Custom Knives, David Bullard, Dan Carlson, Fred Carter, Eddie Contreras, Kenneth W. Corey, Thomas A. Counts, Damascus USA, Gary Demns, Diana Duff, Paula K. Easler, Albert Eaton, Jay Eisenberg, Allan Eldridge, Gwen Flournoy, Jean Pierre Ganster, Les George, Wayne Goddard, Donald Gossens, Art Grossman, Tommie F. Guinn, Melvin and Carol Gurganus, Ralph Dewey Harris, Terry Ann Hayes, Richard Heise, Bob Hergert, Tom Hetmanski, Albert Izuka, Roger Jones, Wallace J. Kay, Gary Kelley, Shiva Ki, R.F. Koebbeman, Terry Kranning, Gary Ladd, Bernard Levine, Les Levinson, Jack Lewis, Kenneth R. Liegey, Henry C. Loos, Jim Martin, Marlene Marton, Ken McFall, McMullen & Yee Publishing, M.C. "Mal" Mele, Mike Mercer, Paul Meyers, Wayne Morrison, Rateep Mosrie, Allen R. Olsen, Charles Ostendorf, Daniel E. Osterman, Houston Price, Jim Pugh, John Rakusan, Sidney Reggio, Stephan Ricketts, Cindy Rogers, Mark Rogers, David J. Schwan, Al Sears, Paul C. Sheffield, Glen Paul Smit, Sporting Blades, Harry Stalter, Wilson Streeter, Mike Tamboli, Jim Turacek, Yvon Vachon, Rudy Wehner, Jim Weyer, James D. Whitehead, Michael Whittingham, Will Wickliffe, Ron Wilson, Dennis Windmiller, Earl Witsaman, Errol & Mary Young.

professional knifemaker's association

Darrel D. Alexander, Melvin Anderson, Jerry J. Barngrover, Cecil T. Barrett, Justin W. Bridges, David P. Brodziak, Tom W. Bullard, Stephen R. Burrows, C. H. Camper, James L. Chaffee, Terrence C. Collins, Del Corsi, Sava Damlovac, Jed Darby, Don Davis, Dan Dennehy, Emmet E. Dickie, Audra Drader, Melvin T. Dunn, Dwayne Dushane, Charley Eckerson, Ray W. Ennis, James T. Eriksen, Jack S. Feder, Norvell C. Foster, Ricky B. Fowler, Bentley Fuller, Barry C. Gallagher, Robert A. Garbe, Larry J. Golczewski, Sal Glesser, Lyn Griffen, Robert J. Hajovsky, James E. Hand, Ronald J. Hansen, Marge Hartman, Charles W. Hawes, Wayne Hendrix, Kenneth Henschel, David W. Hesser, Scot Horton, Steve Hulett, Michael J. Hull, Robert J. Hunter, Mike P. Igo, Michael L. Irie, Jason W. Jacks, Steven R. Johnson, Donald Jones, Harvey G. King, James R. Largent, Jim L. Lemcke, Randy W. Lyons, James T. Magee, Mike L. Mann, James W. Martin, Ken McFall, David McIntosh, Errol W. Meredith, Tom Militano, Clayton Miller, J. P. Moss, Ronald K. Newton, Henry K. Parker, Robert K. Patrick, Willard C. Patrick, Robert R. Patton, Clifton E. Polk, James L. Poplin, Roger W. Potocki, Martin J. Pullen, Lee Reeves, Percy Richardson, Steve Rollert, Derrick Rothermel, Clinton D. Sampson, Tim L. Scholl Michael J. Schirmer, Ernie Self, Richard Self, James Sigg, Randy Simon, Gary R. Shaw, Craig Steketee, Johnny L. Stout, Larry L. Turcotte, Bill E. Waldrup, Gerome M. Weinand, Jacque Weir, George W. Werth, Charles A. West, Barry B. Wood, W. W. Wood, and Mike F. Zima

state/regional association

alaska knifemakers association (1996 data)
A.W. Amoureux, John Arnold, Bud Aufdermauer, Robert Ball, J.D. Biggs, Lonnie Breuer, Tom Broome, Mark Bucholz, Irvin Campbell, Virgil Campbell, Raymond Cannon, Christopher Cawthorne, John Chamberlin, Bill Chatwood, George Cubic, Bob Cunningham, Gordon S. Dempsey, J.L. Devoll, James Dick, Art Dufour, Alan Eaker, Norm Grant, Gordon Grebe, Dave Highers, Alex Hunt, Dwight Jenkins, Hank Kubaiko, Bill Lance, Bob Levine, Michael Miller, John Palowski, Gordon Parrish, Mark W. Phillips, Frank Pratt, Guy Recknagle, Ron Robertson, Steve Robertson, Red Rowell, Dave Smith, Roger E. Smith, Gary R. Stafford, Keith Stegall, Wilbur Stegner, Norm Story, Robert D. Shaw, Thomas Trujillo, Ulys Whalen, Jim Whitman, Bob Willis.

arizona knifemakers association (1996 data)
D. "Butch" Beaver, Bill Cheatham, Dan Dagget, Tom Edwards, Anthony Goddard, Steve Hoel, Ken McFall, Milford Oliver, Jerry Poletis, Merle Poteet, Mike Quinn, Elmer Sams, Jim Sornberger, Glen Stockton, Bruce Thompson, Sandy Tudor, Charles Weiss.

arkansas knifemakers association (1996 data)
David Anders, Auston Baggs, Reggie Barker, Marlen R. Barnes, Paul Charles Basch, Lora Sue Bethke, James Black, R.P. Black, Davie Boultinghouse, Joel Bradford, Gary Braswell, Paul Brown, Shawn Brown, Troy L. Brown, Jim Butler, Buddy Cabe, Roy A. Cline, Larry Connelley, James Cook, Gary L. Crowder, Jim Crowell, Ben Daland, Lewis M. Deen, Michael Deming, Steve Dunn, Fred Duvall, Rodger Echols, David Etchieson, Lee Ferguson, Jerry Fisk, John Fitch, Joe & Gwen Flournoy, John C. Ford, Muller Forge, Dewayne Forrester, John Fortenbury, Ronnie Foster, Tim Foster, Dewayne Funderburg, Larry Garner, Ed Gentis, Ed Gentis, Paul Giller, James T. Gilmore, Terry Glassco, John Glasscock, D.R. (Rick) Gregg, Lynn Griffith, Arthur J. Gunn, Jr., Morris Herring, Don "Possum" Hicks, David Highers, Mark D. Hoffmann, H. Steven Holliman, B. R. Hughes, Newton O. Hughes, Terry Johnson, Ray Kirk, Douglas Knight, Lile Handmade Knives, Tom Krien, Jerry Lairson Sr., Claude Lambert, Alton Lawrence, Michael H. Lewis, Willard Long, Dr. Jim Lucie, Roger D. Massey, Douglas Mays, Howard McCallen Jr., Charles McCorkle, John McKeehan, Joe McVay, Bart Messina, Thomas V. Militano, Jim Moore, Robert Morales, Greg Neely, Ron Newton, Clyde O'Dell, Keith Page, Henry Parker, John Perry, Pete Peterson, Cliff Polk, Terry Primos, Paul E. Pyle Jr., Ted Quandt, Vernon Red, Tim Richardson, Dennis Riley, Charles R. Robinson, Scott Robson, Kenny Rowe, Pat Ryan, Terry Shurtleff, Roy Slaughter, Joe D. Smith, Marvin Solomon, James W. Spears, Larry Spurlin, Mark Stephens, Charles Stout, Jack Thomas, Bud Tilbury, Mark Townsend, Arthur Tycer, Ross Tyser, James Walker, Chuck Ward, Herman Waters, Bryce White, Mike Williams, Rick Wilson, Ray Young.

australian knifemakers guild inc.
Tim Anson, Peter Bald, Wayne Barrett, Alf Bennett, Peter Bennett, Wayne Bennett, Wally Bidgood, Peter Binns, David Brodziak, Stuart Burdett, Mike Carroll, Neil Charity, Bruce Crawley, John Creedy, Mark Crowley, Les Curry, Lance Davison, Steve Dawson, Malcolm Day, Jim Deering, Peter Del Raso, Robert Di Martino, Glen Duncan, Chris Erickson, Marcus Everett, Michael Fechner, Thomas Gerner, Branko Giljevic, Eric Gillard, Russ Gillard, Peter Gordon, Stephen Gregory-Jones, Frank Harbottle, Lloyd Harding, Rod Harris, Max Harvey, Glen Henke, Barry Hosking, Michael Hunt, Myron Husiak, Raymond Jenkins, Ross Johnston, John Jones, Jason Jonker, Simeon Jurkijevic, Wolf Kahrau, Peter Kandavnieks, Peter Kenney, Tasman Kerley, John Kilby, Mitchell Lowe, Greg Lyell, Paul Maffi, Maurice McCarthy, Ray Mende, Dave Myhill, Adam Parker, John Pattison, Chris Pennington, Mike Petersen, Greg Reader, Peter Reardon, David Ross, Murray Shanaughan, Gary Siemer, Kurt Simmonds, Jim Steele, Rod Stines, David Strickland, Kelvin Thomas, Doug Timbs, Len Van Dongen, Robert Venturin, David Walford, Hardy Wangemann, Brendon Ware, Glen Waters, Bob Wilhelm, Angleo Xepapas, Ross Yeats, Joe Zemitis, David Zerbe.

california knifemakers association
Arnie Abegg, George J Antinarelli, Elmer Art, Gregory Barnes, Mary Michael Barnes, Hunter Baskins, Gary Biggers, Roger Bost, Clint Breshears, Buzz Brooks, Steven E. Bunyea, Peter Carey, Joe Caswell, Frank Clay, Richard Clow, T.C. Collins, Richard Corbaley, Stephanie Engnath, Alex Felix, Jim Ferguson, Dave Flowers, Logwood Gion, Peter Gion, Joseph Girtner, Tony Gonzales, Russ Green, Tony Guarnera, Bruce Guidry, Dolores Hayes, Bill Herndon, Neal A. Hodges, Richard Hull, Jim Jacks, Lawrence Johnson, David Kazsuk, James P. Kelley, Richard D. Keyes, Michael P. Klein, Steven Koster, John Kray, Bud Lang, Tomas N. Lewis, R.W. Loveless, John Mackie, Thomas Markey, James K. Mattis, Toni S. Mattis, Patrick T. McGrath, Larry McLean, Jim Merritt, Greg Miller, Walt Modest, Russ Moody, Emil Morgan, Gerald Morgan, Mike Murphy, Thomas Orth, Tom Paar, Daniel Pearlman, Mel Peters, Barry Evan Posner, John Radovich, James L. Rodebaugh, Clark D. Rozas, Ron

Ruppe, Brian Saffran, Red St. Cyr, James Stankovich, Bill Stroman, Tony Swatton, Gary Tamms, James P. Tarozon, Scott Taylor, Tru-Grit Inc., Tommy Voss, Jessie C. Ward, Wayne Watanabe, Charles Weiss, Steven A. Williams, Harlan M. Willson, Steve Wolf, Barry B. Wood.

knifemakers' guild of southern africa

George Baartman, Francois Basson, Peter Bauchop, Arno Bernard, Gert Bezuidenhout, Wolf Borger, Peet Bronkhorst, Rob Brown, Fred Burger, William Burger, Jacobus De Wet Coetzee, Z. André De Beer, André De Villiers, Gavin Dickerson, Roy H. Dunseith, Charl Du Plooy, J.M. Du Plooy, Dries Esterhuizen, Leigh Fogarty, Andrew Frankland, Ettoré Gianferrari, John Grey, Piet Grey, J.C. Greyling, Kevin Harvey, Howard Hitchmough, Des Horn, Ben Kleynhans, Willibald Kojetin, Mark Kretschmer, Fanie LaGrange, Garry Lombard, Steve Lombard, Theo Martins, Francois Massyn, Edward G. Mitchell, Willie Paulsen, Conrad Pienaar, David Schalk Pienaar, Jan Potgieter, Neels Pretorius, Hilton Purvis, Derek Rausch, Chris Reeve, Bertie Rietveld, Dean Riley, John Robertson, Mick Russel, Corrie Schoeman, Elke Schönert, Michael J. Skellern, Toi Skellern, Carel Smith, Ken Smythe, Brent E. Sandow, Graham Sparks, J.H. Stander, André E. Thorburn, Fanie Van Der Linde, Marius Van Der Vyver, Boekoe Van Rensburg, Marlene Van Schalkwyk, Sias Van Schalkwyk, Danie Van Wyk, Shalk Van Wyk, Ben Venter, Willie Venter, Gert Vermaak, René Vermeulen, Tony Victor, Peter Watson, Ted Whitfield, John Wilmot, Armin Winkler, Wollie Wolfaardt, Owen Wood.

midwest knifemakers association

E.R. Andrews III, Frank Berlin, Charles Bolton, Tony Cates, Mike Chesterman, Ron Duncan, Larry Duvall, Bobby Eades, Jackie Emanuel, James Haynes, John Jones, Mickey Koval, Ron Lichlyter, George Martoncik, Gene Millard, William Miller, Corbin Newcomb, Chris Owen, A.D. Rardon, Archie Rardon, Max Smith, Ed Stewart, Charles Syslo, Melvin Williams.

montana knifemaker's association

Angelique Adamson, Mike Alber, Robert Alderman, Darrel Alexander, Bruce Althoff, Mel Anderson, Doug and Connie Asay, Donald Babcock, Lyle Bainbridge, Jack Barnes, Wendell Barnes, Steve Becker, Robert Bizzell, Allen Blade, Gene Bland, R.J. (Ric) Bosshardt, Mark Boyer, Chuck Bragg, Paul Bray, Peter Bromley, Glenn Brown, Lyle Brunckhorst, Ed Caffrey, Jeff Carlisle, Alex Chase, Michael Clancy, Jake Clouse, Foy Cochran, Wade Colter, Jack Cory, Bob Crowder, Gary Debrock, Dennis DesJardins, Frank Dobesh, Elizabeth Dolbare, Audra Draper, Rick Dunkerley, Hugh Eddy M.D., Joel Ellefson, Joel Ellefson, Bruce Emery, Ray Ennis, Melvin Fassio, Gary Flohr, Wendell Fox, Barry Gallagher, Frank Gamble, Wayne Goddard, Jack Gohn, Bob Gray, James Hand, Barry Hands, Jeff Harkins, Scott Higginbotham, Howard Hill, Bob Hollar, Ken Hoy, Steve Hulett, Randy Janisko, Travis Johnson, Al Kajin, Dave Kauffman, George Kirtley, James Largent, Einar Larsen, Randy Livingston, Mel Long, Mike Mann, Turning Bear Mason, David McGonagle, Thomas McGuane, Larry Miller, Jim Minnick, Ed Mortenson, Louis Morton, Russell Moyer, Dick Murphy, David Neagle, Dan Nedved, Vaughn Oligny, Willard Patrick, Brian Peele, Eldon

Peterson, Tony Piondexter, Joe Rapier, Raymond Rasmussen, Bill Reh, Kirk Rexroat, Jim Riddle, Lori Ristinen, Wayne Robbins, Gary Rodewald, Ed Schempp, Bob Schopp, Dean Schroeder, Randy Simon, Harry Smith, Josh Smith, Alfred St. Pierre, Art Swyhart, Shane Taylor, Jim Thill, Leon Thompson, Jack Todd, J.W. Townsend, Frank Towsley, Butch Vollotton, Bill Waldrup, Jim Walker, Ken Ward, Gerome Weinand, Daniel Winkler.

new england bladesmiths guild (1996 data)

Phillip Baldwin, Gary Barnes, Paul Champagne, Jimmy Fikes, Don Fogg, Larry Fuegen, Rob Hudson, Midk Langley, Louis Mills, Dan Maragni, Jim Schmidt, Wayne Valachovic and Tim Zowada.

north carolina custom knifemakers' guild (1996 data)

Herbert M. Baker, Ronnie Banks, Dr. James Batson, Sam Beale, Jack L. Brewer, Tim Britton, Richard Brown, Doug Burns, John (Jack) H. Busfield, Max M. Butcher, Erret Callahan, Ray Clontz, Joe Corbin, Travis Daniel, Don Fogg, Alan Folts, Jeff A. Fox, Norman A. Gervais, Scott Goguen, Mark Gottesman, Anthony Griffin, Carol & Melvin Gurganus, Ed Halligan, Ken Heafner, George Herron, Daniel Hildenberg, Jesse Houser, Jack Hyer, Tommy Johnson, Barry & Phillip Jones, David Jump, Tony Kelly, Robert Knight, Bill Maynard, Tom McArdle, Andrew McLurkin, Tommy McNabb, John McPearson Jr., J. Michael McRae, Claude Montjoy, Hassonjee Nayger, Bill Moran, Bill Pate, Howear Peacock, James Poplin, Michael L. Powell, John W. Poythress, Joan Poythress, Darrel Ralph, Bob Rosenfeld, Henry Clay Runion, Bruce M. Ryan, Ellis Sawyer, Tim & Kathy Scholl, Danks Seel, J. Wayne Short, HR Simmons, Chuck Staples, Philip Starkley, Murray Sterling, Mark Stone, Russ Sutton, Bruce Turner, Daniel Warren, Scottie H. White, Wayne Whitley, James A. Williams, Daniel Winkler.

ohio knifemakers association (1996 data)

Raymond Babcock, Van Barnett, Harold A. Collins, Larry Detty, Tom Downing, Jim Downs, Patty Ferrier, Jeff Flannery, James Fray, Bob Foster, Raymond Guess, Scott Hamrie, Rick Hinderer, Curtis Hurley, Ed Kalfayan, Michael Koval, Judy Koval, Larry Lunn, Stanley Maienknecht, Dave Marlott, Mike Mercer, David Morton, Patrick McGroder, Charles Pratt, Darrel Ralph, Roy Roddy, Carroll Shoemaker, John Smith, Clifton Smith, Art Summers, Jan Summers, Donald Tess, Dale Warther, John Wallingford, Earl Witsaman, Joanne Yurco, Mike Yurco.

south carolina association of knifemakers (1996 data)

Ritchie Batchelor, Bobby Branton, Dan Cannady, Wayne Childress, John Conn, Charles S. Cox, William DeFreest, Geno Denning, Charlie Douan, Hal Gainey, Harry George, Wayne Hendrix, George Herron, T.J. Hucks, Johnny Johnson, Ralph Kessler, Col. Thomas D. Kreger, Gene Langley, David Manley, Claude Montjoy, Larry Page, Russ Peagler, Timothy O. Peake, Joe Prince, Ralph Smith, S. David Stroud, Rocky Thomas, Woodrow W. Walker, Charlie Webb.

tennessee knifemakers association (1996 data)

John Bartlow, Doug Casteel, Harold Crisp, Larry Harley, John W. Walker, Harold Woodward, Harold Wright.

knife photo index

knives 2000

Revishvili, Zaza: 96, 99, 100, 102, 147
Rexroat, Kirk: 146
Richard Knife Co.: 170
Roberts, Michael: 72
Robinson, Rex: 96
Rowe, Kenny: 148, 149
Ruana Knife Works: 132
Rue, Gary (Wolf): 71
Rupert, Bob: 109
Rybar Jr., Ramond B.: 100
Sahlin, Viveca: 152, 153, 154
Sanders, Michael M.: 63
Schempp, Ed: 80
Schrap, Robert G.: 148, 150
Schwarzer, Steve: 124, 135, 146, 161
Scordia, Paolo: 82, 141
Scrap, Robert G.: 150
Sears, Mick: 103
Sellevold, Harald: 87
Selvidio, Ralph: 126, 127
Sentz, Mark C.: 109

Shadley, Eugene W.: 77
Shaw, Bruce: 156
Simmonds, Kurt B.: 115
Simonich, Robert N.: 135
Simons, Bill: 75, 76
Sloan, Shane: 75
Slobodian, Scott: 91, 104
Smith, John W.: 60
Snow, Bill: 73
Solomon, Marvin: 86
Sorenberger, Jim: 129, 159
St. Cyr, Red: 72
Stahl, John: 153, 154
Stephan, Dan: 141
Stephan, Daniel: 89
Stuart, Stephen: 152
Sugihara, Keidoh: 120
Sutton, S. Russell: 84
Szilaski, Joseph: 88, 93, 130, 161
Tamboli, Mike: 80
Taylor, Shane: 146
Terzuola's, Bob: 59

Thorlief, James: 110
Tichbourne, George: 111
Tighe, Brian: 116
Tomes, P.J.: 76
Tomlin, Lisa: 159
Tschager, Reinhard: 119
Turner, P.J.: 177
Vagnino, Michael: 115
Vagnino, Mike: 60
Valloton, Rainy: 83
Valloton, Rainy D.: 124
Van Den Elsen, Gert: 119
Van Hoy, Tanya: 158
Van Rijswijk, Aad: 117
Velarde, Ricardo: 108, 110
Viallon, Henri: 146
Viele, Howard: 43
W.R. Case & Sons: 178
Wada, Yasutaka: 149
Walker, Jim: 70
Warenski, Buster: 98
Warenski, Julie: 157
Warren, Dellana: 95

Watanabe, Wayne: 104
Water, Glenn: 94
Waters, Glenn: 100, 118, 132
Watson, Tom: 62
Wegner, Tim: 170, 171
Weiland: 96, 147
Weiland Jr., J. Reese: 147
Weinstock, Bob: 112
Weiss, Charles A.: 128
Weiss, Charles L.: 70
West, Charles: 99
Whitehead, James D.: 130
Wilson, Ron: 130
Wingo, Gary: 77
Winkler, Daniel: 93
Witsaman, Earl: 129
Worrell, Morris C.: 67, 85
Wright, Richard S.: 127
Young, George: 138, 139
Yurco, Mike: 85
Zakabi, Carl: 61
Zakabi, Carl S.: 85

engravers

Adlam, Tim: 159
Bates, Billy: 156
Bell, Don: 157, 158
Blair, Jim: 156
Davidson, Jere: 122, 159
Eaton, Rick: 159

Forthofer, Pete: 157
George, Tim & Christy: 97
Lyttle, Brian: 157
Lytton, Simon: 158
Meyer, Chris: 157
Meyer, Christian: 73

Minnick, Joyce: 97
Morton, David: 158
Nott, Ron P.: 156
Peterson, E.G.: 158
Shaw, Bruce: 156
Sornberger, Jim: 159

Tomlin, Lisa: 159
Van Hoy, Tanya: 158
Warenski, Julie: 157

scrimshanders

Beauchamp, Gaetan: 155
Bellet, Connie: 154
Benade, Lynn: 152

Dietrich, Roni: 153, 154, 155
Eklund, Maihkel: 155
High, Tom: 153, 154

Karst, Linda: 129, 153, 155
Moulton, Dusty: 155
Sahlin, Viveca: 152, 153, 154

Stahl, John: 153, 154
Stuart, Stephen: 152

leatherworkers/sheathmakers

Ciaramitaro, Phil: 150
Foley, Barney: 151
Fowler, Susan: 150, 151
Headrick, Gary P.: 148

Hurst, Gerry: 150, 151
Imboden, Howard: 151
Kranz, Judy: 150
Kravitts, Chris: 148, 149

Larsen, Richard: 149
Patrick, Peggy: 149, 151
Rowe, Kenny: 148, 149
Schrap, Robert G.: 148, 150

Shook, Karen: 93
Wada, Yasutaka: 149

etchers/carvers

de Braga: 116

knife photo index

knives '95-'99

The Knife Photo Index includes only the last five editions of photos.

a

Adams, Les: *K'99*:62, 142
Adams, William D.: *K'97*:145
Alda, Yoshihito: *K'95*:216
Alden Jr., Kenneth E.: *K'95*:83, 128
Alderman, Robert: *K'96*:63
Alexander, Robert: *K'99*:86
Allen, Joe: *K'97*:123
Allred, Elvan: *K'95*:140, 216; *K'96*:76
Alverson, Tim: *K'95*:217
Ameri, Mauro: *K'95*:117
Ames, Mickey L: *K'95*:99; *K'96*:61, 103
Anders, David: *K'95*:93, 95, 217; *K'96*:94; *K'98*:69, 145; *K'99*:132, 137
Anderson, Edwin: *K'97*:94, 128
Anderson, Gary D.: *K'97*:137; *K'98*:72
Anderson, Mel: *K'97*:90, 135; *K'98*:99, 125, 159
Anderson, Michael D.: *K'95*:87, 155
Andress, Ronnie: *K'96*:63, 145
Ankrom, W.E.: *K'95*:127; *K'99*:151
Aoun, Charles: *K'97*:107; *K'98*:136, 138, 169
Appleton, Ray: *K'99*:112
Appleton, Ron: *K'99*:112
Archer, Harry and Ken Warner: *K'97*:33
Archer, Harry: *K'97*:33
Arnold, Joe: *K'95*:216
Arrowood, Dale: *K'95*:217
Ashworth, Boyd: *K'99*:88
Atkinson, Dick: *K'99*:58
Auon, Charles: *K'97*:148
Ayarragaray, Cristian L.: *K'95*:116

b

Bache-Wilg, Tom: *K'96*:91
Bailey, Joseph D.: *K'97*:154
Bailey, Kirby C.: *K'95*:133; *K'96*:97
Baker, Vance: *K'95*:217
Baker, Wild Bill: *K'95*:155; *K'97*:116; *K'99*:96
Baldwin, Phillip: *K'95*:92; *K'98*:171
Ballew, Dale: *K'96*:116, 118
Banaitis, Romas: *K'97*:130, 136; *K'98*:88; *K'99*:110
Barber, Robert E.: *K'96*:94; *K'97
Bardsley, Norman P.: *K'98*:148
Barndt, Kristen: *K'99*:155
Barnes, A.G.: *K'99*:116
Barnes, Aubrey G.: *K'96*:65; *K'97*:Cover, 113, 124
Barnes, Gary L.: *K'95*:134
Barnett, Van: *K'99*:88, 90, 91
Barnett, V.H.: *K'99*:55
Barr, A.T.: *K'95*:83, 108, 139; *K'96*:74, 77, 80, 104; *K'97*:97, 157
Barrett, Cecil Terry: *K'98*:115
Barrett, Rick: *K'99*:83
Barrett, R.W.: *K'95*:162
Barrett-Smythe: *K'99*:56, 57
Barron, Brian: *K'96*:106
Barton, Al: *K'99*:127
Bartrug, Hugh E.: *K'97*:159
Baskett, Lee Gene: *K'95*:146, 163; *K'96*:138

Batson, James: *K'95*:78, 94, 103; *K'96*:92, 93; *K'97*:113, 115, 116, 128; *K'98*:43, 58
Batson, Richard G.: *K'95*:96
Batts, Keith: *K'95*:93; *K'96*:61
Beauchamp, Gaetan: *K'95*:164; *K'96*:139; *K'98*:66; *K'99*:106, 107, 125, 161
Beaver, Judy: *K'99*:153
Becker, Franz: *K'96*:112
Beckett, Norman L.: *K'98*:54; *K'99*:128
Beers, Ray: *K'97*:121
Behnke, Bill: *K'99*:98
Behnke, William: *K'95*:104, 122; *K'96*:102; *K'98*:123
Bell, Donald: *K'95*:156, 157, 216; *K'97*:146
Bell, Michael: *K'96*:57; *K'98*:64, 82
Benetti, Stephen: *K'99*:86
Bennett, Peter: *K'95*:142
Bennica, Charles: *K'99*:72, 73
Berger, Max A.: *K'98*:106; *K'99*:106, 107, 112
Bertholus, Bernard: *K'99*:97, 98
Bertuzzi, Ettore: *K'96*:89; *K'97*:74; *K'98*:105
Beverly II, Larry H.: *K'95*:144
Bill, Donald: *K'99*:105
Black, Tom: *K'96*:96, 149; *K'97*:79; *K'98*:155, 156; *K'99*:83
Blaine, Dennis: *K'97*:145
Blair, Jim: *K'99*:150
Blanchard, G.R. (Gary): *K'97*:104, 152
Blasingame, Robert: *K'96*:76, 145
Bloomer, Alan T.: *K'96*:73
Blum, Michael: *K'96*:84
Blum, Roy: *K'96*:83, 126
Boatwright, Basel: *K'98*:138
Bodner, Jerry: *K'99*:94
Boehlke, Guenter: *K'97*:77, 143; *K'98*:59, 80
Bogachov, Anatoly: *K'95*:103
Boguszewski, Phil: *K'95*:81, 101, 129; *K'96*:74, 81; *K'98*:91; *K'99*:59, 70, 145
Bojtos, Arpad: *K'96*:84; *K'97*:76; *K'98*:159
Bold, Stu: *K'97*:86, 127; *K'98*:123
Boleware, David: *K'97*:127
Bonaitis, Romas: *K'99*:137
Bonassi, Franco: *K'96*:90
Booco, Gordon: *K'99*:119, 138
Boos, Ralph: *K'97*:93; *K'98*:79
Booth, Phillip W.: *K'96*:71, 98; *K'98*:114, 115, 116, 139; *K'99*:79, 80
Bose, Reese: *K'98*:117
Bose, Tony: *K'96*:71, 72; *K'99*:68
Bourbeau, Jean-Yves: *K'96*:84; *K'98*:85
Boye, David: *K'95*:217; *K'97*:89, 160; *K'99*:174
Brack, Douglas D.: *K'95*:65
Brady: *K'99*:77
Brady, Sandra: *K'99*:Cover; *K'99*:154, 155, 156, 157, 161
Brag, Lowell: *K'99*:120
Brandsey, Edward P.: *K'95*:107
Brandsey, Ed: *K'99*:99
Branton, Bobby: *K'99*:63
Branton, Robert: *K'96*:61, 108
Brend, Walter J.: *K'95*:161
Brennan, Judson: *K'95*:78; *K'98*:54, 161
Brillard, Tom: *K'99*:164
Britton, Tim: *K'95*:216; *K'98*:102, 119
Broadwell, David: *K'96*:131, 140; *K'97*:145; *K'98*:146; *K'99*:163

Brock, Kenneth N.: *K'99*:118
Bronkhorst, Peet: *K'99*:77
Brooks, Steve R.: *K'95*:145, 216; *K'96*:145; *K'97*:129
Broughton, Don: *K'99*:96, 98, 99, 125, 132
Broughton, Don R.: *K'95*:91; *K'96*:65, 126; *K'97*:114, 115, 125, 137; *K'98*:52
Brown, Harold: *K'99*:170
Brown, Harold E.: *K'98*:113
Brown, Jim: *K'96*:103
Brown, Rob E.: *K'95*:217
Browne, Rick: *K'98*:70, 110
Brunetta, David: *K'97*:146; *K'99*:127
Buchner, Bill: *K'99*:110
Buffoni, Gianpaolo: *K'99*:74, 76
Bullard, Bill: *K'95*:90
Burger, Gunter: *K'98*:145
Burger, Pon: *K'97*:154
Burger, Sharon: *K'99*:158
Burke, Dan: *K'98*:114, 115, 117; *K'99*:69, 70, 71
Burrows, Stephen R.: *K'95*:167; *K'97*:137; *K'98*:84, 99; *K'99*:84, 141
Busfield, John: *K'96*:70, 122; *K'97*:150; *K'98*:62, 92, 113, 114
Busse, Jerry: *K'96*:79
Butler: *K'99*:140
Byrd, Don E.: *K'95*:110, 119

c

Cabona, G.: *K'99*:93
Caffey, Bill: *K'99*:104
Caffrey, Ed: *K'99*:101
Caldwell, Bill: *K'95*:119
Callahan, Errett: *K'95*:111, 219; *K'96*:132, 159; *K'97*:132, 133
Callahan, Everett: *K'99*:107, 134, 171
Callahan, F. Terry: *K'95*:91, 120; *K'98*:167
Candrella, Joe: *K'97*:101
Cannady, Daniel L. (Slim): *K'95*:108, 219; *K'96*:82; *K'99*:120
Cannon, Raymond W.: *K'97*:137
Cannon, Wes: *K'95*:166; *K'99*:121
Capdepon, Randy: *K'96*:105
Carey Jr., Charles W.: *K'95*:218; *K'96*:118
Carlsson, Marc Bjorn: *K'95*:117, 126; *K'96*:88, 91, 140; *K'97*:68
Carson, Harold J. "Kit": *K'95*:Cover, 135, 146; *K'96*:80, 150, 153, 155
Carter, Fred: *K'95*:163; *K'96*:127; *K'97*:68, 69, 92, 121; *K'99*:63, 91, 138
Carter, Murray: *K'99*:86, 148
Cashen, Kevin R.: *K'97*:128, 131; *K'98*:65, 67; *K'99*:83, 85, 86
Casteel, Dianna: *K'97*:130
Casteel, Doug: *K'99*:111
Casteel, Douglas: *K'95*:78, 96; *K'96*:54, 98; *K'97*:121, 130; *K'98*:74
Casteel, Douglas and Diana: *K'98*:107
Caudell, Richard M.: *K'97*:69, 90; *K'98*:172
Centofante, Frank and Tony: *K'95*:127, 137, 162, 164; *K'96*:152, 153
Chaffee, Jeff: *K'99*:140
Chaffee, Jeff L.: *K'96*:111; *K'97*:89, 90, 157

Chamblin, Joel: *K'95*:129; *K'99*:102
Chapo, William G.: *K'95*:219; *K'96*:142
Chard, Gordon: *K'99*:64
Chard, Gordon R.: *K'95*:92; *K'97*:68, 87, 100; *K'98*:87, 95
Chase, Alex: *K'98*:62
Chase, John E.: *K'95*:219
Chavar, Ed: *K'99*:144
Cheatham, Bill: *K'95*:131; *K'99*:172
Choate, Milton: *K'98*:119, 141; *K'99*:117, 118
Clark, Dave: *K'97*:66; *K'98*:155
Clark, Howard F.: *K'96*:63, 66; *K'97*:71, 96; *K'98*:88
Clark, Roger: *K'95*:93
Clark, W.R.: *K'98*:101
Clay, J.D.: *K'95*:83, 125; *K'98*:29
Clay, Wayne: *K'96*:68, 150; *K'97*:110, 148
Click, Joe: *K'98*:112
Cobb, Lowell D.: *K'95*:69
Coffman, Danny: *K'95*:137
Cole: *K'99*:121
Coleman, Keith E.: *K'96*:74, 81
Colter, Wade: *K'98*:112; *K'99*:93, 146
Conable, Matt: *K'97*:160; *K'99*:63
Conable, Matthew: *K'99*:138
Conley, Bob: *K'98*:91
Conroy, Frank: *K'99*:135
Cook, James R.: *K'98*:66
Cook, James Ray: *K'96*:129
Cook, Louise: *K'96*:108
Cook, Mike A.: *K'97*:133
Cook, Scott: *K'97*:84
Coombs, Jr., Lamont: *K'96*:160
Copeland, George "Steve": *K'98*:96
Corbit, Gerald E.: *K'96*:111; *K'98*:Cover
Corbit, Gerald E. and Philip E.: *K'96*:153, 155; *K'98*:93
Corbit, Jerry: *K'99*:80, 81, 160
Corby, Harold: *K'95*:147; *K'96*:Cover; *K'98*:166; *K'99*:62, 78
Cordova, Joseph G.: *K'95*:105; *K'96*:144; *K'97*:140; *K'98*:76, 171
Corrado, Jim: *K'97*:92, 98
Cosby, E. Blanton: *K'95*:133
Cote, Yves: *K'95*:87
Cousino: *K'96*:107
Cousino, George: *K'98*:123
Cover, Ray: *K'99*:162
Cover, Jr., Raymond A.: *K'98*:146
Cowles, Don: *K'98*:57, 58
Cox, Collin J.: *K'95*:218; *K'98*:109, 110
Crain, Frank: *K'98*:161
Crain, Jack W.: *K'97*:135
Crawford, Pat: *K'96*:80; *K'98*:59, 68, 141; *K'99*:Cover; 62, 145
Crenshaw, Al: *K'98*:116
Cross, John M.: *K'95*:94; *K'96*:103
Crowley, Michael: *K'99*:87
Cubic, George: *K'99*:169
Cutchin, Roy D.: *K'95*:126; *K'96*:Cover, 129; *K'97*:95; *K'99*:170

d

Dake, C.M.: *K'99*:79
D'Andrea, John: *K'98*:126, 164, 169
Daconceicao, John M.: *K'97*:147

engravers

scrimshanders

Pankova-Clark, Inna: *K'98*:155
Pitt, Chris: *K'99*:158
Rece, Charles V.: *K'96*:153, 154; *K'98*:154
Rodkey, Sheryl: *K'99*:159

Sahlin, Viveca: *K'98*:153, 154, 156
Sahlir, Viveca: *K'99*:160
Scholl, Tim: *K'98*:152
Stahl, John: *K'99*:158, 159, 160
Stuart, Stephen: *K'96*:153

Vancura, Vladimir: *K'98*:146
Walker, Karen: *K'98*:156
Warren, Al: *K'99*:160

Williams, Gary: *K'95*:Inside Cover, 76, 146, 163; *K'96*:116, 138, 153, 155
Williams, Gary (Garbo): *K'98*:157
Zemitis, Jolanta: *K'95*:165

etchers/carvers

Anderson, Mel: *K'98*:159
Bojtos, Arpad: *K'98*:159
Bourbeau: *K'95*:166
Bullard, Tom: *K'96*:158
Burrows, Stephen R.: *K'95*:167
Casteel, Doug: *K'95*:166
Clark, Howard F.: *K'96*:158
Crain, Frank: *K'98*:161
DeBraga, Jose C.: *K'95*:167
Damlovac, Sava: *K'97*:158
DiMarzo, Richard: *K'95*:167; *K'97*:158, 160; *K'98*:160
Doussot, Laurent: *K'98*:160

Ellefson, Joe: *K'95*:167
Fisk, Jerry: *K'97*:160
Greco, John: *K'95*:166
Grussenmeyer, Paul: *K'95*:166, 167; *K'96*:158, 159; *K'97*:73, 134, 158, 159
Grussenmeyer, Paul G.: *K'98*:159
Hergert, Bob: *K'96*:115
Hume, Don: *K'96*:159
Imboden II, Howard L.: *K'97*:159
Kelso, Jim: *K'95*:166
Kinnikin, Todd: *K'96*:158
Kondria, Denise: *K'96*:159

Krogman, Pam: *K'98*:160
Lee, Ray: *K'98*:159, 161
Lonewolf, J. Aguirre: *K'95*:167
Lott, Sherry: *K'96*:95, 158
Marlatt, David: *K'97*:158
Martin, Francine: *K'97*:160
Maxfield, Lynn: *K'96*:159
McHenry, William James: *K'98*:161
Olsen, Geoff: *K'95*:166
Poskocil, Helmut: *K'98*:160
Pulis, Vladimir: *K'97*:159
Roulin, Charles: *K'98*:158

Rua, Gary (Wolf): *K'96*:158
Schlomer, James E.: *K'98*:158
Schlott, Harald: *K'98*:15
Skiles, Kirsten: *K'98*:161
Soppera, Arthur: *K'98*:161
Sornberger, Jim: *K'95*:167
Steigerwalt, Ken: *K'96*:158
Stephan, Daniel: *K'98*:160
Stratton: *K'99*:70
Sunderland, Richard: *K'97*:158
Szilaski, Joseph: *K'97*:158
Turecek, Jim: *K'96*:159
Viallon, Henri: *K'96*:159

leatherwork/sheathmakers

Ameri, Mauro: *K'98*:163
Anderson, Gary D.: *K'97*:163
Aoun, Charles: *K'98*:169
Behnke, William: *K'97*:162
Callahan, F. Terry: *K'98*:169
Cashen, Kevin R.: *K'95*:170; *K'97*:165
Congdon, David: *K'98*:162
Cook, James Ray: *K'96*:164
Cooper, Harold: *K'96*:164
Corby, Harold: *K'98*:166
Cubic, George: *K'97*:161; *K'98*:163, 164, 165; *K'99*:169
D'Andrea, John: *K'98*:164, 169
Davidson, Hal: *K'95*:149
Dawkins, Dudley: *K'95*:168
Defeo, Robert A.: *K'95*:170
Dell, Wolfgang: *K'98*:166
Dennehy, John D.: *K'98*:162, 167
DesJardins, Dennis: *K'98*:165
Downing, Larry: *K'98*:167
Dunn, Melvin T.: *K'95*:169
Fisher, Jay: *K'98*:162
Fister, Jim: *K'95*:169; *K'96*:164; *K'97*:163

Foley, Barney: *K'95*:168, 170; *K'96*:163; *K'97*:161; *K'99*:168, 169
Fowler, Susan: *K'99*:166
Fox, Wendell: *K'98*:166
Frey, Jim: *K'95*:111
Genske, Jay: *K'97*:162; *K'98*:162
Goldberg, Robin: *K'98*:168
Graves, Dave: *K'96*:161
Green, Roger M.: *K'96*:162, 164
Halligan, Ed: *K'95*:168
Hancock, Tim: *K'96*:162
Hartman, Bruce James: *K'97*:164
Hawkins, Rade: *K'98*:167; *K'99*:169
Hendrickson, E. Jay: *K'96*:162; *K'97*:162; *K'99*:166, 167
Hendryx, Scott: *K'97*:165; *K'98*:168
Hoffmann, Uwe H.: *K'98*:163
Hughes, Ed: *K'96*:163
Imboden II, Howard L.: *K'98*:166
Jackson, Jim: *K'98*:163; *K'99*:166
Kennedy, Kelly S.: *K'96*:162

Kommer, Russ: *K'98*:165
Koutsopoulos, George: *K'97*:163
Kravitt, Chris: *K'96*:160, 161, 162, 163; *K'98*:57, 169
Lee, Sonja: *K'95*:169; *K'96*:160; *K'97*:164; *K'99*:168
Leland, Steve: *K'99*:167
Lile, Jimmy: *K'95*:169
Lozler, Don: *K'95*:170
Malloy, Joe: *K'97*:161; *K'99*:166
Martin, Peter: *K'98*:169
Maynard, William N.: *K'97*:162
McGowan, Liz: *K'96*:163
McLuin, Tom: *K'96*:163
Moran, Jr., Wm. F.: *K'98*:166
Morrissey, Martin: *K'98*:165
Nealy, Bud: *K'96*:160; *K'99*:167
Osborne, Michael: *K'97*:163
Patrick, Bob: *K'99*:167, 168
Patrick, Peggy: *K'99*:167
Pennington, C.A.: *K'96*:160
Piorek, James S.: *K'97*:165; *K'98*:168
Polkowski, Al: *K'95*:169, 170
Rardon, A.D.: *K'99*:169

Reeve, Chris: *K'95*:168
Rho, Nestor-Lorenzo: *K'98*:164
Rowe, Kenny: *K'95*:93, 96, 170; *K'96*:160, 163; *K'97*:161, 164; *K'98*:119, 164, 165, 167, 169; *K'99*:37, 141
Schirmer, Mike: *K'96*:164
Schrap, Robert G.: *K'95*:170; *K'96*:161; *K'98*:163, 169; *K'99*:168, 169
Scordia, Paolo: *K'98*:168
Self, Ernie: *K'97*:162
Sharrigan, Mudd: *K'97*:164
Shook, Karen: *K'95*:112; *K'96*:162; *K'97*:114, 116, 165; *K'98*:162; *K'99*:96, 136
Shouk, Karen: *K'99*:97
Simonella, Gianluigi: *K'97*:164
Stout, Johnny: *K'96*:160
Tree Stump Leather: *K'97*:163
Tritz, Jean Jose: *K'97*:163
Tyler, Ross: *K'99*:168
Weiler, Donald E.: *K'97*:162
Zembko III, John: *K'97*:161

handle artisans

Davidson, Hal: *K'95*:148, 149
Minnick, Joyce: *K'96*:127

Revishvilli, Zaza: *K'97*:136; *K'98*:74

Schlott, Harald: *K'98*:159
Terzuola, Bob: *K'99*:122

Winkler, Daniel: *K'97*:67

sporting cutlers

The firms listed here are special in the sense that they make or market special kinds of knives made in facilities they own or control either in the U.S. or overseas. Or they are special because they make knives of unique design or function.

ACE OF BLADES
P.O. Box 1778
Herndon, VA 22070-1778
Phone: 703-904-8629
Specialties: Discreet personal defense cutlery by John Mitchell, owner and designer.

ALCAS COMPANY
1125 E. State St.
Olean, NY 14780
Phone: 718-372-3111
Specialties: Owns cutco, a direct marketer of specialty household knives and KA-Bar Knives, now launched once again.

ALPEC-TEAM INC
201 Rickenbaker Circle
Livermore CA 94550
Phone: 925-606-8245
Specialties: Maker of Tekna knives.

B&D TRADING CO.
3935 Fair Hill Rd.
Fair Oaks, CA 95628
Phone: 916-967-9366;800-334-3790
FAX: 916-967-4873
Specialties: Carries the full line of Executive Edge- Brazil's locking folders.

BARTEAUX MACHETES, INC.
1916 S.E. 50th St.
Portland, OR 97215
Phone: 503-233-5880
FAX: 503-233-5838
Specialties: Machetes of high-carbon and stainless steel. Line greatly expanded of late.

BAY KNIFE COMPANY
37780 Hills Tech Drive
Farmington Hills, MI 48331
Phone: 810-848-0590
FAX: 810-848-6883
Specialties: Camping and survival knives; "The Cobra"

BEAR MGC CUTLERY
1111 Bear Blvd. SW
Jacksonville, AL 36265
Phone: 205-435-2227
FAX: 205-435-9348
Specialties: General line of traditional folders and belt knives-wide range of patterns.

BENCHMADE KNIFE CO. INC.
300 Beaver Creek Rd.
Oregon City, OR 97045
Phone: 503-655-6004
FAX: 503-655-6223
Specialties: Tactical patterns in folders, automatics, U.S. made.

BENCHMARK KNIVES
936 N. Manetta St.
Gastonia NC 28054
Specialties: Hunting knives again - rolexes included.

BERETTA U.S.A. CORP.
17601 Beretta Dr.
Accokeek, MD 20607
Phone: 301-283-2191
Specialties: A variety of Beretta-only designs, including folding tactical knives.

BIG COUNTRY KNIVES
(SEE KNIFEWARE INC.)

BLACKJACK
(SEE KNIVEWARE INC.)

BLUE MOUNTAIN TURQUOISE
State Rte 32 MM
Quemado MN 87829
Specialties: Turquoise handles or specialty knives.

BROWNING
Rt. 1
Morgan, UT 84050
Phone: 800-333-3288
Specialties: Has its own name on sports knives of all kinds, all in Browning finish.

BRUNTON/LAKOTA U.S.A.
620 E. Monroe Ave.
Riverton, WY 82501
Phone: 307-856-6559
FAX: 307-856-8282
Specialites: Heavy-duty sports knives, straight and folding, on a distinctive design theme.

BULLFROG BRAND
(SEE LAKE & WALKER)

BUSSE COMBAT KNIFE CO.
19203 12th
Wauseon, OH 43567
Phone; 419-923-6471
Specialites: Simple and very strong straight knife designs for tactical and expedition use.

COLD STEEL, INC.
2128-D Knoll Dr.
Ventura, CA 93003
Phone: 800-255-4716
FAX: 805-642-9727
Specialties: Variety of urban survival instruments-big in tantos, Bowie's and hunter's; several new and exclusive specialty designs.

COLONIAL KNIFE CO., INC.
Agens At Magnolia ST.
Providence, RI 02909
Phone: 800-558-7824
Fax: 401-421-2047
Specialties: Commercial Pocketknives for competitive pricing: some belt knives.

CTECH PLASTICS ENGINEERING
Shaun Cavanaugh
266 Calle Pintoresco
San Clemente, CA 92672-7504
Specialties: Knives in thermosets and thermoplastics. Custom injection molding, prototype tooling and engineering services.

EDGE DESIGN INC.
Suite 1950
1034 S. Brentwood Blvd.
St. Louis, MO 63117
Specialties: Tactical folders in Michael Collins designer.

EMERSON KNIVES, INC.
P.O. Box 4325
Redondo Beach, CA 90278
Phone: 310-542-3050
Specialties: Production versions of original tactical bladeware from a top designer of such.

FISKARS
(SEE GERBER LEGENDARY BLADES)

GATCO (GREAT AMERICAN TOOL CO., INC.)
P.O. Box 600
Getzville, NY 14068
Phone: 716-877-2200
Specialties: Besides their sharpeners, they now own and market Timberline knives and other Neely designs.

GENUINE ISSUE INC.
949 Middle Country Rd.
Selden, NY 11784
Phone: 516-696-3802
FAX: 516-696-3802

GERBER LEGENDARY BLADES
14200 SW 72nd Ave.
Portland OR 97223
Phone: 503-639-6161
Fax: 503-884-7008
Specialties: Well-known sports and dining cutlery line, plus Fiskars cutlery.

GIESSER MESSERFABRIK GMBH, JOHANNES
(SEE IMPORTERS & FOREIGN CUTLERS)

GIGAND USA
701 Penhoun Ave
Secsucus NJ 07094
Phone: 201-583-5968
Specialties: Imports designed by Fred Carter.

GT KNIVES
7716 Anjos Dr.
San Diego, CA 92126
Phone: 619-566-1511
FAX: 619-530-0734
WEB: http://www.coherent data.com/GTknives
Specialties: High-tech machined folders.

H&B FORGE CO.
235 Geisinger Rd.
Shiloh, OH 44878
Phone: 419-895-1856
Specialties: Tomahawks and throwing knives.

HONEYCUTT MARKETING, INC., DAN
3165 A-2 So. Campbell
St. Louis, MO 65807
Phone: 417-886-2888
FAX: 417-886-5664
Specialties: Manufacturer of the Honeycomb.

IMPERIAL SCHRADE CORP.
7 Schrade Ct..
Ellenville, NY 12428
Phone: 914-647-7601
FAX: 914-647-8701
Specialties: Probably the biggest; Owns Imperial and Schrade. Sells many labels in several brands, U.S. made and imported.

IRON MOUNTAIN KNIFE CO.
1270 Greg St.
Sparks, NV 89431-6005
Phone: 702-356-3632
FAX: 702-356-3640
Specialties: Line of fixed-blade hunters based on special patented handle shape.

KATZ KNIVES, INC.
P.O. Box 730
Chandler, AZ 85224-0730

Phone: 602-786-9334
FAX: 602-786-9338

KELLAM KNIVES CO.
3422 Old Capitol Trail, Suite 831
Wilmington, DE 19808
Phone: 302-996-3386
FAX: 516-232-1747
Specialties: Makers of Lapp folders; extensive selection of hand-made Finnish knives.

KERSHAW KNIVES
25300 SW Parkway
Wilsonville, OR 97070
Phone: 503-682-1966; 800-325-2891
FAX: 503-682-7168
WEB: http://www.kershawknives.com
Specialties: Former Gerber designer's heavy-duty sports knives made overseas; also smaller "pocket jewelry"; handsome scrimshaw; new designs in using knives and pocket tools.

KNIFEWARE INC.
P.O. Box 3
Greenville WV 24945
Phone: 304-832-6636
Specialties: Big Country knives - fresh designs in trail blades; Blackjack knives in new designs, sold only at knifeware@inetone.com

KNIVES OF ALASKA, INC.
715 N. Tone
Denison, TX 75020 (Southern office)
P.O. Box 675
Cordova, AK 99574 (Northern office)
Phone: 800-572-0980
FAX: 903-463-7165
Specialties: Husky edged tools for big game hunting and fishing.

KUTMASTER
820 Noyles St.
Utica NY 13503
Phone: 315-733-4663
Specialties: Mini-master pocket tool, multi-master tools, folding and fixed blade knives, much else. (Formerly Litica Cutlery)

LAKE & WALKER
P.O. Box 1210
Veneta, OR 97487-1210
Phone: 541-935-1635
FAX: 541-465-8973
Specialties: Bullfrog brand.

LAKOTA U.S.A.
(SEE BRUNTON/LAKOTA U.S.A.)

LEATHERMAN TOOL GROUP, INC.
P.O. Box 20595
Portland, OR 97294
Phone: 503-253-7826
FAX: 503-253-7830
Specialties: All-in-one pocket tool in lots sizes.

MAR KNIVES, INC., AL
5755 SW Jean Rd., Suite 101
Lake Oswego, OR 97035
Phone: 503-635-9229
FAX: 503-223-0467
Specialties: Founded by the late Al Mar, a designer, the company continues to market Mar's designs under the direction of Ann Mar.

MARBLE ARMS
420 Industrial Park
Gladstone, MI 49837
Phone: 906-428-3710
Specialties: The grand old Marble's knives again from the grand old U.P. stan

MASTER OF DEFENSE
1941 Comp Branch Rd
Waynesville NC 28788
Phone: 828-452-4158
Specialties: Tactical user knives, designers for MOD exclusively.

MEYERCO USA
4481 Exchange Service Dr
Dallas, TX 75235
Phone: 214-461-8949
Specialties: Blackie coltins designs in folders, like the Strut 'N' cut.

MICRO TECHNOLOGY
932 36th Ct. SW
Vero Beach, FL 32968
Phone: 561-569-3058
Specialties: High-tech folders in their own works; some double-action liner locks.

MISSION KNIVES & TOOLS, INC.
P.O. Box 1616
San Juan Capistrano, CA 92693
Phone: 714-951-3879
Specialties: Titanium blade knives and all titanium folders. Currently supplying certified non-magnetic SPECWAR knives to the U.S. Navy SEALS and EOD teams.

MORTY THE KNIFE MAN, INC.
P.O. Box 630007
Little Neck, NY 11363-0007
Phone: 516-491-5764/800-247-2511
Specialties: Everything for the fish trade; own and make both U.S. and import brands; includes many working knives not easily found, as well as chain mesh protection gloves and aprons.

MYERCHIN MARINE CLASSICS
850 W. Randall Ave.
P.O. Box 911
Rialto, CA 92377
Phone: 909-875-3592
FAX: 909-874-6058
E-MAIL: myerchin@aol.com
Specialties: The Myerchin Offshore System-a quality cutlery package for the yachtsman or deep water sailor; supplier to the U.S. Navy and Coast Guard.

ONTARIO KNIFE CO.
P.O. Box 145
Franklinville, NY 14737
Phone: 716-676-5527
Fax: 716-676-5535
Specialties: Some pocketknives; a new Bowie line; many military styles; many styles of utility knives for hosuehold and restaurant use.

OUTDOOR EDGE CUTLERY CORP.
2888 Bluff St., Suite 130
Boulder, CO 80301
Phone: 303-652-8212
FAX: 303-652-8238
Specialties: Rapidly adding more outdoors designs and tactical folders to basic line of hunter's cutlery kits.

PARAGON CUTLERY CO.
2015 Asheville Hwy.
Hendersonville, NC 28791
Phone: 704-697-8833
Specialties: Now selling automatic folders through appropriate channels; has other sports designs.

PILTDOWN PRODUCTIONS
Errett Callahan
2 Fredonia Ave.
Lynchburg, VA 24503

Phone: 804-528-3444
Specialties: Makes obsidian scalpels and knives; replicates Stone Age tools and weapons-all types-for museums and academia. $3 for catalog.

QUEEN CUTLERY
P.O. Box 500
Franklinville, NY 14737
Phone: 716-676-5527
Fax: 716-676-5535
Specialties: Old name. The line is growing, moving toward collector appeal; makes Schatt & Morgan folders.

REMINGTON ARMS CO., INC.
870 Remington Drive
P.O. Box 700
Madison, NC 27025
Phone: 800-243-9700
Specialties: Old and new patterns in the Remington style and more to come.

RICKARD KNIFE CO. LLC
10950 Horseback Ridge Rd.
Missoula MT 59804
Phone: 406-728-2550
Specialties: Reversible blade doubles cutting life in patented design.

ROUND EYE KNIFE & TOOL LLC
P.O. Box 818
Sagle ID 83660
Phone: 208-265-8858
Specialties: Rolling lock folders, Hobbit warrior, other quality whimsy.

SANTA FE STONEWORKS
3790 Cerrillos Rd.
Santa Fe, NM 87505
Phone: 505-471-3953
FAX: 505-471-0036
Specialties: Embellished personal and gift cutlery and desk accessories.

SCHRADE CUTLERY CORP.
(SEE IMPERIAL SCHRADE CORP.)

SEBERTECH
2438 Cades Way
Vista CA 92083
Phone: 760-598-8888
Specialties: Key ring tool set, the essence of small.

SKYLINE TECHNOLOGY INC.
2 Pennsylvania Ave.
Malvern, PA 19355
Phone: 610-296-7501
Specialties: The current source for the swell old Woodsman's Pal.

SOG SPECIALTY KNIVES & TOOLS, INC.
6521 212th St. S.W.
Lynwood, WA 98036
Phone: 206-771-6230
FAX: 206-771-7689
Specialties: High-quality folding and combat knives, and a multi-tool, as well.

SPYDERCO, INC.
P.O. Box 800
Golden, CO 80402-0800
Phone: 303-279-8383; 800-525-7770
FAX: 303-278-2229
Specialties: Clipit folding knives; sharpening gear. Has kitchen and diving knives and new stuff every year. Sells Moki knives.

SWISS ARMY BRANDS LTD.
(SEE IMPORTERS & FOREIGN CUTLERS)

SWISS-TECH
5613 East Ave.
Mentor, OH 44060
Phone: 800-414-8799
Specialties: The pantented pocket tools, of
course.

TIKNIVES
1725 Smith Rd.
Fortson, GA 31808
Phone: 888-537-9991
Specialties: Tactical and Fighters folders and
straight knives - Exoctically high-tech.

TRU-BALANCE KNIFE CO.
P.O. Box 140555
Grand Rapids, MI 49514
Phone: 616-453-3679
Specialties: The late Harry McEvoy's full line of
throwers-a design for any throwing job. Can
provide custom-made throwing knives.

Catalog and throwing instructions can be had
with a SASE.

TURNER, P.J., KNIFE MFG., INC.
P.O. Box 1549
Afton, WY 83110
Phone: 307-886-3423
Specialties: A fold-up pick axe for elk hunters
and other deep-woods travellers.

UNITED CUTLERY BRANDS
1425 United Blvd.
Sevierville TN 83110
Phone: 423-428-2532
Specialties: Names like Cole, Rigid, United,
Harley-Davidson, Gil Hibben and David
Yellowhorse. 'Nuff said.

UTICA CUTLERY CO.
820 Noyes St.
Utica NY 13503
Phone: Outside NY 800-888-4223; 315-733-
4563
Fax: 315-733-6802

Specialties: Nice line of pocketknives,
including Barlows and hunters and working
pattern knives, Brands: Kutmaster, Walco.

WESTERN CUTLERY
(SEE CAMILLUS CUTLERY CO.)

W.R. CASE & SONS CUTLERY CO.
Owens Way
Bradford, PA 16701
Phone: 800-523-6350
Specialties: At the same old stand producing
the good base patterns, and widely advertised
these days.

WYOMING KNIFE CORP.
101 Commerce Dr.
Ft. Collins, CO 80524
Phone: 303-224-3454
Specialties: A tool for dealing with game
animals-gutting and skinning. Also makes a
short folding saw, and the Powder River
folders.

importers & foreign cutlers

Knives are imported by almost every sort of commercial cutler, but the names here are those whose specialty is
importing, whether it be their brand, famous overseas brands, or special knives for special purposes best made
overseas. Every effort is made to keep the list updated, but importing is sometimes an uncertain endeavor.

ADAMS INTERNATIONAL KNIFEWORKS
8710 Rosewood Hills
Edwardsville, IL 62025
Phone: 618-656-9868
FAX: 618-656-9868
Specialties: Antique or current automatic
knives designed for law enforcement, military
and collectors. Largest dealer of Linder-
Solingen, Germany knives; offers Muela, Cold
Steel, SOG, Kershaw, Ka-Bar-Boker and
Henckels to name a few.

AITOR-CUCHILLERIA DEL NORTE, S.A.
P.O. Box No. 1
48260 Ermua (Vizcaya)
SPAIN
Phone: 34-43-17 00 01
Specialties: Full range of Aitor products from
jungle knives to folding pocketknives.

ATLANTA CUTLERY CORP.
2143 Gees Mill Rd.
Box 839XZ
Conyers, GA 30207
Phone: 404-922-3700
Specialties: Carefully chosen inventory from all
over the world; selected Indian, Pakistani,
Spanish, Japanese, German, English and
Italian knives; often new ideas-a principal
source for kukris.

BAILEY'S
P.O. Box 550
Laytonville, CA 95454
Specialties: Importers of Tuatahi brand axes
from New Zealand.

BOKER USA, INC.
1550 Balsam St.
Lakewood, CO 80215-3117
Phone: 303-462-0662
FAX: 303-462-0668
Specialties: Tree Brand knives and a host of
new knives in the Boker USA label.

CAMPOS, IVAN DE ALMEIDA
Custom and Old Knives Trader
R. Stelio M. Loureiro, 206
Centro, Tatui, BRAZIL
Phone: 0152-512102 or 51-6952
FAX: 0152-514896
Specialties: Knives of all Brazilian makers.

C.A.S. IBERIA, INC./MUELA KNIVES
650 Industrial Blvd.
Sale Creek, TN 37373
Phone: 423-332-4700
FAX: 423-332-7248
Specialties: Knives made in Spain by people
with an eye on U.S. custom makers.

CLASSIC INDUSTRIES
1325 Howard Ave., Suite 408
Burlingame, CA 94010
Phone: 415-343-7196
FAX: 415-401-6061
Specialties: Hunting, sportsmen, pocket and
kitchen knives and leather sheaths,
manufactured in Pakistan factory.

COAST CUTLERY CO.
2045 SE Ankeny St.
Portland, OR 97214
Phone: 503-234-4545
FAX: 503-234-4422
Specialties: Long-time large wholesaler now
national Puma reps; exclusive Puma importer.

COLUMBIA PRODUCTS CO.
P.O. Box 1333
Sialkot 51310, PAKISTAN
Phone: 011-92-432-86921
FAX: 011-92-432-558417
Specialties: See Columbia Products Int'l.

COLUMBIA PRODUCTS INT'L
P.O. Box 8243
New York, NY 10116-8243
Phone: 201-854-8504
FAX: 201-854-7058

Specialties: Lockblade and slip-joint folders in
old and new U.S.-style patterns; heavy-duty
belt knives; low prices.

COMPASS INDUSTRIES, INC.
104 E. 25th St.
New York, NY 10010
Phone: 212-473-2614; 800-221-9904
FAX: 212-353-0826
Specialties: Imports for dealer trade from all
over at many price and quality levels; two hot
brands are Silver Falcon and Sportster.

CONFEDERATE STATES ARMORY
2143 Gees Mill Rd.
Box 839XZ
Conyers, GA 30207
Phone: 800-241-3664
Specialties: Replicas of Confederate arms of
the Civil War.

CONSOLIDATED CUTLERY CO., INC.
696 NW Sharpe St.
Port St. Lucie, FL 34983
Phone: 407-878-6139/800-288-6288
Specialties: Hunting knives, wood-carving
tools, stag- handled steak/carving sets,
camping axes, knife sharpening steels.

CRAZY CROW TRADING POST
P.O. Box H-K96
Pottsboro, TX 75020
Phone: 903-463-1366
FAX: 903-463-7734
Specialties: Mountain man cutlery and fixings.
Knife blades, books, knifemaking supplies; $3
for catalog.

DAMCO/MESSERMEISTER
418 Bryant CR "A"
Ojal, CA 93023
Phone: 805-640-0051
Specialties: many German and one Japanese
live of professional food preparation cutlery.

DER FLEISSIGEN BEAVER
(THE BUSY BEAVER)
Harvey Silk
P.O. Box 1166
64343 Griesheim, GERMANY
Phone: 06155-2232
FAX: +49-6155-2433
Specialties: Specialized importer/wholesaler of American custom-made knives; displays at 40 German antique knife and fine arts exhibitions each year.

EKA
(SEE NICHOLS CO.)

EMPIRE CUTLERY CORP.
12 Kruger Ct.
Clifton, NJ 07013
Phone: 201-472-5155; 800-325-6433
FAX: 201-779-0759
Specialties: Imports Frost knives from Mora in Sweden, including the new Swedish soldier's knives. Knives are priced to sell.

EXECUTIVE EDGE
(SEE B&D TRADING CO.)

FALLKNIVEN AB
Box 204
S-961 23 Boden, SWEDEN
Phone: Int. 011-46-921-54422
FAX: 011-46-921-54433
Specialties: Folders and hunting knives.

FIGHT'N ROOSTER
PO Box 936
Lebanon TN 37087
Phone: 615-444-8070
Specialties: Frank Buster's eminent line of German - made collectible folders.

FORSCHNER GROUP, INC, THE
(SEE SWISS ARMY BRANDS LTD.)

FREDIANI COLTELLI FINLANDESI
Via Lago Maggiore 41
I-21038 Leggiuno, ITALY
Phone: 0039 332 647 362
Specialties: Purveyors from Italy of the Finnish knives, some with Italian decorative touches.

FROSTS KNIFE MANUFACTURING
(MORA, SWEDEN)
(SEE SCANDIA INTERNATIONAL)
GIESSER MESSERFABRIK GMBH, JOHANNES
P.O. Box 168; Waiblingerstr. 5+7
D-71349 Winnenden, GERMANY
Phone: 0049-7195-1808-0
FAX: 0049-7195-64466
Specialties: Manufacturer of fine professional and kitchen cutlery. See Illinois Cutlery and Markuse Corp.

GROHMANN KNIVES LTD.
116 Water St.
Pictou Nova Scotia CANADA
B0K 1H0
Phone: 902-484-4224
Specialties: Canadian made knives, especially Russell designs.

HENCKELS ZWILLINGSWORK, INC., J.A.
171 Saw Mill River Road
Hawthorne, NY 10532
Phone: 914-747-0300
FAX: 914-747-1850
Specialties: U.S. office of world-famous Solingen cutlers-high-quality pocket and sportsman's knives with the "twin" logo.

HIMALAYAN IMPORTS
225 W. Moana Ln., Suite 226
Reno, NV 89509
Specialties: Just one: Nepalese-made kukris, which they spell khukuri, hand-forged in that mountain kingdom.

ILLINOIS CUTLERY
P.O. Box 607
Barrington, IL 60011-0607
Phone: 847-426-5002
FAX: 847-426-4942
Specialties: Illinois Cutlery knives.

JOY ENTERPRISES
1104 53rd Court South
Mangonia Park, FL 33407
Phone: 561-863-3205
FAX: 561-863-3277
Specialties: Sporting and combat-style cutlery under the Fury label-full range. Folders and swords. Wholesale only.

JUNGLEE KNIVES
(SEE GUTMANN CUTLERY)

KA-BAR KNIVES, COLLECTOR'S DIVISION
(SEE ALCAS COMPANY)

KELLAM KNIVES CO.
3422 Old Capitol Trail, Suite 831
Wilmington, DE 19808
Phone: 302-996-3386
FAX: 516-232-1747
Specialties: Largest selection of Finnish knives; over 300 models from over 30 makers, everyday use to fancy collectibles.

KLÖTZLI
(SEE MESSER KLÖTZLI)

KNIFE COLLECTORS ASSN.-JAPAN
(SEE MURAKAMI, ICHIRO)

KNIFE IMPORTERS, INC.
P.O. Box 1000
Manchaca, TX 78652
Phone: 512-282-6860
FAX: 512-282-7504
Specialties: Eye Brand cutlery.

KOPROMED, USA
1701 Broadway, Suite 282
Vancouver, WA 98663
Phone: 360-695-8864
FAX: 360-690-8576
Specialties: U.S. distributor for Kopromed forged 440C hunting knives and table cutlery from Poland.

KRIS CUTLERY
P.O. Box 133 KN
Pincie, CA 94584
Phone: 510-758-9912
Fax: 510-223-8968
Specialties: Medieval swords and daggers, Indonesian and Moro kriases, Damascus bailsongs.

LEISURE PRODUCTS CORP.
P.O. Box 1171
Sialkot-51310, PAKISTAN
Phone: 92-432-86921/592009
FAX: 92-432-588417/591030
Specialties: A wide range of lockblade and slip-joint folders in old and new U.S.-style patterns; heavy-duty belt knives; low prices.

LINDER, CARL NACHF.
Erholungstr. 10

42699 Solingen, GERMANY
Phone: 0212-330856
FAX: 0212-337104
Specialties: German brands in German style - old line company.

MACKRILL CUSTOM KNIVES
PO Box 1580
Pinegowne, Johannesburg
SOUTH AFRICA 2123
Phone: 0027-11-334-3729
Specialties: Family business creating exotic knife styling with exotic materials.

MARKUSE CORP., THE
10 Wheeling Ave.
Woburn, MA 01801
Phone: 617-932-9444
FAX: 617-933-1930
Specialties: U.S. agent for Johannes Giesser Messerfabrik GmbH's "Creative Collection" range of knives.

MARTTIINI KNIVES
P.O. Box 44 (Marttiinintie 3)
96101 Rovaniemi, FINLAND
Phone: 358-60-330330
FAX: 358-60-3303399
Specialties: Finnish knives straight from Finland's biggest cutler. Includes fancy Finn-type hunters.

MATTHEWS CUTLERY
4401 Sentry Dr., Suite K
Tucker, GA 30084
Phone: 404-939-6915
Specialties: Wholesalers only. Carries all major brands which include over 2,800 patterns. Has U.S. distribution;OEM manufacturing.

MORTY THE KNIFE MAN, INC.
(SEE SPECIALTY CUTLERS)

MUELA
(SEE C.A.S. IBERIA, INC./MUELA)

MURAKAMI, ICHIRO
Knife Collectors Assn. Japan
Tokuda Nishi 4 chome, 76 banchi, Ginancho Hashimagun, Gifu, JAPAN
Phone: 81 58 274 1960
FAX: 81 58 273 7369
Specialties: Buys collector-grade and commercial U.S. knives for sale in Japan.

MUSEUM REPLICAS LIMITED
2143 Gees Mill Rd., Box 839 XZ
Conyers, GA 30207
Phone: 404-922-3703
Specialties: Battle-ready hand-forged edged weapons. Carry swords, daggers, halberds, dirks and axes. Catalog $2.

NICHOLS CO.
P.O. Box 473, #5 The Green
Woodstock, VT 05091
Phone: 802-457-3970
FAX: 802-457-2051
Specialties: Importer/distributor of precision-engineered EKA pocketknives from Sweden; also fixed- blade knives from Norway and Finland.

NORMARK CORP.
Craig Weber
10395 Yellow Circle Drive
Minnetonka, MN 55343
Phone: 612-933-7060
FAX: 612-933-0046

Specialties: Scandinavian-made sturdy knives for fishermen; puuko-style belt knives for hunters, fillet knives. Good stainless steel.

OKAPI KNIVES
58/60 Green St.
Isithebe
Kwa Zulu-Natal
Republic of Africa
Phone: 27 32 4592883
Fax: 032 459234
Specialties: Way down-market sturdy carbon-steel working knives for back-country working people world wide.

PRECISE INTERNATIONAL
15 Corporate Dr.
Orangeburg, NY 10962
Phone: 800-431-2996
FAX: 914-425-4700
Specialties: Wenger Swiss Army knives.

PUUKKO CUTLERY
P.O. Box 303
Wolf Lake, MN 56593
Phone: 218-538-6633
FAX: 218-538-6633
Specialties: A full and complete Finnish cutlery line, including the Puukko cutlery line, all custom/hand- forged. Offers Scandinavian or Nordic expertise on makers and knife values.

PUMA CUTLERY
(SEE COAST CUTLERY)

REFLECTIONS OF EUROPE
Peter Ward
151 Rochelle Ave.
Rochelle Park, NJ 07662
Phone: 201-845-8120
FAX: 201-843-8419

Specialties: Importer for Eberhard Schaaf kitchen cutlery and professional chef knives.

RUSSELL CO., A.G.
1705 Highway 71 North
Springdale, AR 72764
Phone: 501-751-7341
Specialties: Morseth knives; Russell-marked special designs-"Woods Walker," Sting, CIA letter opener, Russell One-Hand knives, lots more every year.

SCANDIA INTERNATIONAL, INC.
118 English Neighborhood Rd., P.O. Box 218
East Woodstock, CT 06244-0218
Phone: 860-928-9525
FAX: 860-928-1779
Specialties: U.S. importer of Frosts Knife Manufacturing AB of Mora, Sweden-over 800 models.

STAR SALES CO., INC.
1803 N. Central St., P.O. Box 1503
Knoxville, TN 37901
Phone: 615-524-0771
FAX: 615-524-4889
Specialties: New collector pocketknives; imports Star knives and Kissing Crane knives.

SUOMI SHOP
(SEE PUUKKO CUTLERY)

SVORD KNIVES
Smith Rd., RD 2
Waiuku, South Auckland, NEW ZEALAND
Phone: +64 9 235 8846
FAX: +64 9 298 7670
Specialties: New Zealand private cutler makes belt knives and commercial knives.

SWISS ARMY BRANDS LTD.
The Forschner Group, Inc.
One Research Drive
Shelton, CT 06484
Phone: 800-243-4032
FAX: 800-243-4006
Specialties: This is the Victorinox headquarters in the U.S.; all current production comes through here; manages service center also. Group also manages flow of excellent Forschner commercial and household cutlery.

TAYLOR CUTLERY
P.O. Box 1638
1736 N. Eastman Rd.
Kingsport, TN 37662
Phone: 423-247-2406, 800-251-0254
FAX: 423-247-5371
Specialties: Taylor-Seto folders and straight knives, a line of scrimshaw knives, stag handles and many other imports; mfg. Smith & Wesson knives.

VALOR CORP.
5555 N.W. 36th Ave.
Miami, FL 33142
Phone: 305-633-0127
FAX: 305-634-4536
Specialties: Emphasizes lockback folders from overseas in popular styles. Over 100 knife models imported.

ZEST INTERNATIONAL
1500 NE Jackson St.
Minneapolis, MN 55413
Phone: 800-453-8937/612-781-5036
FAX: 612-781-1452
Specialties: Full line of sports cutlery-dozens of models-with Zest trademark in 440A steel.

ZWILLINGSWORK
(SEE HENCKELS, J.A.)

knifemaking supplies

The firms listed here specialize in furnishing knifemaking supplies in small amounts. Professional knifemakers have their own sources for much of what they use, but often patronize some of these firms. All the companies listed below have catalogs of their products, some available for a charge. For information about obtaining one, send a self-addressed and stamped envelope to the company. Firms are listed here by their request. New firms may be included by sending a catalog or the like to our editorial offices. We cannot guarantee any company's performance.

AFRICAN IMPORT CO.
Alan Zanotti
20 Braunecker Rd.
Plymouth, MA 02360
Phone: 508-746-8552
Specialties: Exotic African handle materials such as elephant and fossil ivory; exotic skins and leathers.

ALASKAN ANTLERCRAFT & IVORY
Roland and Kathy Quimby
Apr. to Oct.: P.O. Box 350
Ester, AK 99725
Nov. to Mar.: Box 3175-RB
Casa Grande, AZ 85222
Phone: Summer: 907-479-9335; Winter: 520-723-5827
Specialties: Mammoth and fossil walrus ivory, oosick and antler.

AMERICAN SIEPMANN CORP.
65 Pixley Industrial Parkway
Rochester, NY 14624
Phone: 716-247-1640
Specialties: Manufactures Siepmann grinders.

ART JEWEL ENTERPRISES, LTD.
460 Randy Rd.
Carol Stream, IL 60188
Phone: 708-260-0400
FAX: 708-260-0486
Specialties: Handles-stag, ivory, pearl, horn, rosewood, ebony.

ATLANTA CUTLERY CORP.
2143 Gees Mill Rd., Box 839XE
Conyers, GA 30207
Phone: 800-241-3595

BATAVIA ENGINEERING
P.O. Box 53
Magaliesburg, 2805, SOUTH AFRICA
Phone: +27142-771294
E-MAIL: batavia@www.caseynet.co.za
Specialties: Belt grinders (Cutlermatic and Mini Cutlermatic); Discmatic disc grinder; contact wheels. Damascus steel in various blends and patterns and stainless steel Damascus. Price sheet.

BILL'S CUSTOM CASES
P.O. Box 2
Dunsmuir, CA 96025
Phone: 916-235-0177 or 235-2455

FAX: 916-235-4959
Specialties: Soft knife cases made of Cordura, Propex, pig suede and leather.

BLADEMASTER GRINDERS
P.O. Box 812
Crowley, TX 76036
Phone: 817-473-1081
Specialties: Manufactures knifemaking machine called "Blademaster." Wholesale and retail.

BLADES "N" STUFF
1019 E. Palmer Ave.
Glendale, CA 91205
Phone: 818-956-5110
FAX: 818-956-5120
Specialties: Full line of supplies and equipment, including excellent selection of tropical woods. Does big business in custom-ground heat-treated blades in dozens of shapes. Catalog $5.

BOONE TRADING CO., INC.
Box BB
Brinnon, WA 98320
Phone: 206-796-4330

Specialties: Exotic handle materials including elephant, fossil walrus, mastodon, warthog and hippopotamus ivory. Also sambar stag, oosic, impala and sheephorn.

BORGER, WOLF
Benzstrasse 8
76676 Graben-Neudorf
GERMANY
Phone: 07255-8314
FAX: 07255-6921
Specialties: Supplies European knifemakers, and others. German text catalog-write for details.

BOYE KNIVES
P.O. Box 1238
Dolan Springs, AZ 86441
Phone: 520-767-4273
FAX: 520-767-3030
Specialties: Casts dendritic blades and bar stock for knifemaking. Information $1.

BRIAR KNIVES
Darrel Ralph
7032 E. Livingston Ave.
Renoldsburg, OH 43068
Phone: 614-577-1040, 614-241-9793 (pager)
Specialties: Sells commercial Damascus, titanium and carbon fiber.

BRONK'S KNIFEWORKS
C. Lyle Brunckhorst
23716 Bothell-Everett Hwy.
Country Village, Suite B
Bothell, WA 98021
Phone: 206-402-3484
WEB: http://www.net-tech.com/bronks/bronks.htm
Specialties: Knifemaking school, supplies, blades and kits; professional sharpening and heat treating.

CHARLTON, LTD.
(SEE DAMASCUS-USA)

CHRISTOPHER MFG., E.
P.O. Box 685
Union City, TN 38281
Phone: 901-885-0374
FAX: 901-885-0440
Specialties: Knife supplies for buckskinners; much early American hardware; blades; catalog $5 (outside U.S. $6). Also has knives made overseas, including Bowie replicas.

CUSTOM FURNACES
P.O. Box 353
Randvaal, 1873, SOUTH AFRICA
Phone: +27 16 365 5723
FAX: +27 16 365 5738
E-MAIL: jj300155@cls.co.za
Specialties: Hardening and tempering furnaces.

CUSTOM KNIFEMAKER'S SUPPLY
Bob Schrimsher
P.O. Box 308
Emory, TX 75440
Phone: 903-473-3330
FAX: 903-743-2235
Specialties: Big catalog full of virtually everything for knifemaking. Many years in business.

CUSTOM KRAFT
14919 Nebraska Ave.
Tampa, FL 33613
Phone: 813-972-5336
Specialties: Knifemakers Ron Miller and Reese Weiland make up Custom Kraft; they specialize in hard-to-find knifemaking supplies like titanium naltex, safety gear, mills, taps,

Fuller brand files, and Allen/ spline drive screws, to name a few. Catalog $1.

CUTLERY SPECIALTIES
Dennis Blaine
22 Morris Ln.
Great Neck, NY 11024-1707
Phone: 516-829-5899
FAX: 516-773-8076
E-MAIL: dennis13@aol.com
Specialties: Sole agent for "Renaissance" wax/polish and other restoration and preservation materials. Also buy, sell and trade antique to custom made knives. Price list.

DAMASCUS-USA
149 Deans Farm Rd.
Tyner, NC 27980-9718
Phone: 919-221-2010
FAX: 919-221-2009
Specialties: Manufactures carbon and stainless Damascus bar stocks and blanks, sells complete knives as specialty purveyor.

DAN'S WHETSTONE CO., INC.
130 Timbs Place
Hot Springs, AR 71913
Phone: 501-767-1616
FAX: 501-767-9598
Specialties: Traditional sharpening materials and abrasive products.

DIAMOND MACHINING TECHNOLOGY, INC.
85 Hayes Memorial Dr.
Marlborough, MA 01752
Phone: 508-481-5944
FAX: 508-485-3924
Specialties: Quality diamond sharpening tools to hone all knife edges, including a unique serrated knife sharpener for all serration sizes.

EDGECRAFT CORP.
825 Southwood Rd.
Avondale PA 19311
Phone: 800-342-3255
Specialties: Chef's Choice powered and manual sharpeners.

EKLUND
P.O. Box 483
Nome, AK 99762-0483
Phone: NA
Specialties: Exotic handle materials like fossil walrus ivory, fossil whale and mammoth bone, mammoth ivory, oosic horn and antler. Eskimo artifacts and trophy tusks; price sheet $1.

EZE-LAP DIAMOND PRODUCTS
3572 Arrowhead Dr.
Carson City, NV 89706
Phone: 800-843-4815, 702-888-9500
FAX: 702-888-9555
Specialties: Diamond-coated sharpening instruments, various sizes.

FIELDS, RICK B.
26401 Sandwich Pl.
Mt. Plymouth, FL 32776
Phone: 352-383-6270
FAX: 352-383-6270
Specialties: Fossil walrus, mammoth ivory and ancient bone. Price list.

FLITZ INTERNATIONAL, LTD.
821 Mohr Ave.
Waterford, WI 53185
Phone: 800-558-8611
FAX: 414-534-2991
Specialties: General line of polishers.

FORTUNE PRODUCTS, INC.
HC 04, Box 303

Hwy. 1431 E. (Smithwick)
Marble Falls, TX 78654
Phone: 210-693-6111
FAX: 210-693-6394
Specialties: "Accu-sharp" sharpeners.

GILMER CO.
2211 NW St. Helens Rd.
Portland, OR 97210
Phone: 503-274-1271
FAX: 503-274-9839
Specialties: Knife-sharpening systems and Timberline Knives.

GILMER WOOD CO.
2211 NW St. Helena Rd.
Portland, OR 97210
Phone: 503-274-1271
Fax: 503-274-9839
Specialties: They list 112 varieties of natural woods.

GOLDEN AGE ARMS CO.
115 E. High St.
P.O. Box 366
Ashley, OH 43003
Phone: 614-747-2488
Specialties: Many types of blades; stag for handles; cast items-much for the buckskinner. Catalog $4.

GRS CORP.
Don Glaser
P.O. Box 1153
900 Overlander St.
Emporia, KS 66801
Phone: 316-343-1084 (Kansas); 800-835-3519
FAX: 316-343-9640
Specialties: Engraving products such as the Gravermeister and the Gravermax.

HALPERN TITANIUM
Leslie Halpern
14 Maxwell Road
Monson, MA 01057
Phone: 888-23-8627
FAX: 888-283-8627
Specialties: Full line of titanium sheet and rod; G-10 and carbon fiber sheet; titanium pocket clip blanks; Kydex sheet. Call or fax for free brochure and price list.

HARMON, JOE T.
8014 Fisher Drive
Jonesboro, GA 30236
Phone: 770-471-0024
Specialties: Maker of mini mills, surface grinders, pin routers.

HAWKINS CUSTOM KNIVES & SUPPLIES
110 Buckeye Rd.
Fayetteville, GA 30214
Phone: 770-964-1177
FAX: 770-306-2877
Specialties: Various size steel blanks, belts, buffing compounds and wheels; stag and drill bits.

HAYDU, THOMAS G.
2507 Bimini Lane
Ft. Lauderdale, FL 33312
Phone: 305-792-0185
Specialties: Deluxe boxes for knives that stay at home- some from Tomway Corp. have tambour covers.

HILTARY INDUSTRIES
7117 Third Ave.
Scottsdale, AZ 85251
Phone: 602-994-5752
FAX: 602-994-3680

Specialties: Gemstones, Damascus, meteorite and exotic steels.

**HOUSE OF MUZZLE LOADING, THE
(SEE BLADES "N" STUFF)**

HOUSE OF TOOLS LTD.
#136, 8228 MacLeod Tr. S.E.
Calgary, AB T2H 2B8, CANADA
Phone: 403-258-0005
FAX: 403-252-0149
Specialties: 440C and ATS34 handle and bolster material, sand belts, buff wheels and a large selection of tools.

HOV KNIVES & SUPPLIES
Box 8005
S-700 08 Orebro, SWEDEN
Phone: 46-19-187466
FAX: 46-19-100685
Specialties: Blades, exotic woods, stabilized woods, Amber, MoP, Abalone, horn, recon, stone and steel. Catalog $3.

INDIAN JEWELERS SUPPLY CO.
Mlg: P.O. Box 1774
Gallup, NM 87305-1774
Shpg: 601 East Coal Ave.
Gallup, NM 87301-6005
Phone: 505-722-4451
FAX: 505-722-4172
Specialties: Native American jewelry stones, castings and findings at the professional level; jeweler tools and supplies; catalogs.

**INDIAN RIDGE TRADERS
(SEE KOVAL KNIVES, INC.)**

INTERAMCO INC.
5210 Exchange Dr.
Flint, MI 48507
Phone:810-732-8181
Specialties: Manufacturers Berger grinding machines.

JANTZ SUPPLY
P.O. Box 584-GD
Davis, OK 73030-0584
Phone: 405-369-2316
FAX: 405-369-3082
E-MAIL: jantz@brightok.net
WEB: http://www.jantzsupply.com
Specialties: Polishing and finishing supplies, engraving tools, abrasives and bluing equipment. Price list.

JOHNSON, R.B.
I.B.S. Int'l. Folder Supplies
Box 11
Clearwater, MN 55320
Phone: 320-558-6128
Specialties: Folder supplies, threaded pivot pins, stainless and black oxide screws, taps and compasses.

JOHNSON WOOD PRODUCTS
34968 Crystal Rd.
Strawberry Point, IA 52076
Phone: 319-933-4930 or 933-6504
Specialties: Fancy domestic and imported knife handle woods. Price list.

K&G FINISHING SUPPLIES
P.O. Box 980
Lakeside, AZ 85929
Phone: 800-972-1192
Specialties: Belts, buffers, compounds, grinders, knife blanks, steel, sharpeners, handle material.

KNIFE & CUTLERY PRODUCTS, INC.
4122 N. Troost Ave.
Kansas City, MO 64116
Phone: 816-454-9879
Specialties: Offers 14 pages of knifemaking supplies such as exotic woods, wheels, bar stock and blades in a variety of shapes. Catalog $2; list of pocketknives $1.

KNIFE AND GUN FINISHING SUPPLIES
P.O. Box 458
Lakeside, AZ 85929
Phone: 520-537-8877
FAX: 520-537-8066
Specialties: Complete line of machine and materials for knifemaking and metal finishing. Custom ground blades and lots of factory blades to choose from. Specializing in rare and exotic handle materials-oosic, ivory, rare hardwoods, horn, stag and stabilized woods. Catalog $2.

KNIVES, ETC.
2522 N. Meridian
Oklahoma City, OK 73107
Phone: 405-943-9221
FAX: 405-943-4924
Specialties: Exotic woods; variety of blade steels; stag.

KOVAL KNIVES, INC.
5819 Zarley St.
New Albany, OH 43054
Phone: 614-855-0777
FAX: 614-855-0945
Specialties: Full range of Micarta and other materials for handles; brass, nickel silver, steels; machines and supplies for all knifemaking; some knife kits; catalog.

KWIK-SHARP
350 N. Wheeler St.
Ft. Gibson, OK 74434
Phone: 918-478-2443
Specialties: Ceramic rod knife sharpeners.

LANSKY SHARPENERS
P.O. Box 800
Buffalo NY 14231-0800
Phone: 716-677-7511
Specialties: Knife sharpeing systems, Including Crock-Stick.

LINDER-SOLINGEN KNIFE PARTS
4401 Sentry Dr., Suite K
Tucker, GA 30084
Phone: 404-939-6915
Specialties: German-made knifemaking parts and blades. Wholesale catalog-send $2.

LITTLE GIANT POWER HAMMER
420 4th Corso
Nebraska City, NE 68410
Phone: 402-873-6602
Specialties: Little Giant Power Hammer parts and service; rebuilt power hammers.

LOGISTICAL SOLUTION
P.O. Box 211961
Augusta, GA 30917
Phone: 650-0252
FAX: 706-860-1623
Specialties: Modular component knife carry/storage systems.

LOHMAN CO., FRED
3405 N.E. Broadway
Portland, OR 97232
Phone: 503-282-4567
FAX: 503-288-3533
Specialties: Sword polishing and handle wrapping service, quality replacement parts,

for the restoration of Japanese-style swords, both new and old. Catalog $5.

MARKING METHODS, INC.
Laura Jimenez
301 S. Raymond Ave.
Alhambra, CA 91803-1531
Phone: 818-282-8823
FAX: 818-576-7564
Specialties: Manufacturer of electro-chemical etching equipment and supplies for the knifemaking trade- power units & kits, long life photo stencils, and accessories.

MASECRAFT SUPPLY CO.
170 Research Pkwy #3
P.O. Box 423
170 Research Pkwy. #3
Meriden, CT 06450
Phone: 800-682-5489, 203-238-3049
FAX: 203-238-2373
Specialties: Handle materials.

MCGOWAN MFG. CO.
25 Michigan St.
Hutchinson MN 55350
Phone: 320-587-2222
Specialties: Sharpeing atones and systems.

MEIER STEEL
Daryl Meier
75 Forge Rd.
Carbondale, IL 62901
Phone: 618-549-3234
FAX: 618-549-6239
Specialties: Supplier and creator of "Meier Steel." Price sheet.

MOTHER OF PEARL CO.
D.A. Culpepper
P.O. Box 445, 401 Old GA Rd.
Franklin, NC 28734
Phone: 704-524-6842;
FAX: 704-369-7809
Specialties: Pearl, black pearl, abalone, pink pearl, sheephorn, bone, buffalo horn, stingray skin, exotic leathers, snake skin.

NICHOLAS EQUIPMENT CO.
730 E. Washington St.
Sandusky, OH 44870
Phone: 419-626-6342
Specialties: Manufactures commercial grinding machines.

NORTHWEST KNIFE SUPPLY
525-L S.W. Calapooia Ave.
Sutherlin, OR 97479
Phone: 541-459-2216
FAX: 541-459-4460
Specialties: Coote grinders, Klingspor abrasives, exotic woods, Micarta, stag, other supplies. Catalog $2; foreign $4.

NORTON COMPANY
1 New Bond St.
Worcester MA 01606
Phone: 508-795-2041
Specialties: Leading abraisers manufacturer - really wide variety.

OREGON ABRASIVE & MFG. CO.
11303 NE 207th Ave.
Brush Prairie, WA 98606
Phone: 206-254-5400
FAX: 206-892-3025
Specialties: Sharpening stones made under their own roof, and sharpening systems based on those.

OZARK KNIFE
3165 S. Campbell

directory

Springfield, MO 65807
Phone: 417-886-3888
FAX: 417-886-5664
Specialties: Offers list of custom knives for sale, plus general cutlery collectibles; Randall knives, Shining Wave Damascus and mokume.

PAPAI, ABE
5013 N. 800 E.
New Carlisle, IN 46552
Specialties: Knife sharpeners.

PARAGON INDUSTRIES, INC.
2011 South Town East Blvd.
Mesquite, TX 75149-1122
Phone: 800-876-4328; 972-288-7557
FAX: 972-222-0646
Specialties: Manufacturer of knifemak

PARAGON INDUSTRIES, INC.
2011 South Town East Blvd.
Mesquite, TX 75149-1122
Phone: 800-876-4328; 972-288-7557
FAX: 972-222-0646
Specialties: Manufacturer of knifemaker's heat-treating furnaces in five available sizes.

POPLIN, JAMES/POP KNIVES & SUPPLIES
103 Oak St.
Washington, GA 30673
Phone: 404-678-2729
Specialties: Sanding belts, handle screws, buffing wheels and compound woods for knife handles, etc.

PUGH, JIM
Mlg: P.O. Box 711
Azle, TX 76098
Shpg: 917 Carpenter St.
Azle, TX 76020
Phone: 817-444-2679
FAX: 817-444-5455
Specialties: Kydex sheath material; limited.

RADOS, JERRY
P.O. Box 531
7523E 5000 N. Rd.
Grant Park, IL 60940
Phone: 815-472-3350
FAX: 815-472-3944
Specialties: Offers many distinct patterns of Damascus in forged-to-shape blades or customer designs.

REACTIVE METALS STUDIO, INC.
P.O. Box 890
Clarkdale, AZ 86324
Phone: 520-634-3434
FAX: 520-634-6734
E-MAIL: reactive@sedona.net
Specialties: Phil Baldwin heads up another business and this is a source for titanium and like exotic metals plus the equipment for coloring or anodizing them.

REAL WOOD
36 Fourth St.
Dracut, MA 01826
Phone: 508-957-4899
Specialties: Exotic wood for knife handles; carry over 60 different species and are always adding more; catalog $1.

REPRODUCTION BLADES
17485 SW Pheasant Ln.
Beaverton, OR 97006
Phone: 503-848-9313
Specialties: Custom cast blades.

RIVERSIDE KNIFE & FORGE SUPPLY
205 W. Stillwell
DeQueen, AR 71832
Phone: 501-642-7643
FAX: 501-642-4023
Specialties: Grinders, belts, wood, steel, blade stamps, Riverside Stampmaster, trip hammer repair, parts and sales.

ROCKY MOUNTAIN KNIVES
George L. Conklin
P.O. Box 902, 615 Franklin
Ft. Benton, MT 59442
Phone: 406-622-3268
FAX: 406-622-5670
Specialties: Knife sharpening; supplies.

SANDPAPER, INC. OF ILLINOIS
270 Eisenhower Ln. N., Unit 5B
Lombard, IL 60148
Phone: 630-629-3320
FAX: 630-629-3324
Specialties: Coated abrasives in belts, sheets, rolls, discs or any coated abrasive specialty.

SCHELL, CLYDE M.
4735 N.E. Elliott Circle
Corvallis, OR 97330
Phone: 503-752-0235
Specialties: Knife and exotic wood material.

SCHEP'S FORGE
Box 83
Chapman, NE 68827
Phone: 308-986-2444
Specialties: Damascus steel made in Nebraska.

SHEFFIELD KNIFEMAKERS SUPPLY, INC.
P.O. Box 741107
Orange City, FL 32774-1107
Phone: 904-775-6453
FAX: 904-774-5754
Specialties: Full line of knifemaking materials and machinery. Includes large inventory of steels, handle materials, N.S., brass, copper, aluminum, abrasives and much more. Catalog $5.

SHINING WAVE METALS
P.O. Box 563
Snohomish, WA 98290-0563
Phone: 425-334-5569
FAX: 425-334-5569
Specialties: Phil Baldwin makes and sells mokume, Damascus and a variety of Japanese alloys (for knife furniture, not blades) to order or from stock. Wholesale only.

SMEDEFIRMA
(SEE STRANDE, POUL)

SMITH WHETSTONE, INC.
1700 Sleepy Valley Rd.
Hot Springs, AR 71901
Phone: 501-321-2244
FAX: 501-321-9232
Specialties: Sharpeners of every kind, ceramic sharpeners, oils, kits and polishing creams.

SMOLEN FORGE, INC.
Nick Smolen
Rt. 2, Box 191A
Westby, WA 54667
Phone: 608-634-3569
FAX: 608-634-3569
Specialties: Makes custom Damascus steel. Various patterns and steel combinations and mokume available. Makes jigs, fixtures and hydraulic presses.

STRANDE, POUL
Soster Svenstrup Byvej 16
Dastrup 4130 Viby Sj
DENMARK
Phone: 01-45-46194305
FAX: 01-45-46195319
Specialties: Blades and Damascus blade stock.

SUEDMEIER, HARLAN "SID"
(SEE LITTLE GIANT POWER HAMMER)

TEXAS KNIFEMAKERS SUPPLY
10649 Haddington, Suite 180
Houston, TX 77043
Phone: 713-461-8632
FAX: 713-461-8221
Specialties: Bar stock, factory blades, much handle material; offers heat-treating; catalog $3.

TRIPLE GRIT
(SEE OREGON ABRASIVE & MFG. CO.)

TRU-GRIT, INC.
760 E. Francis St. #N
Ontario, CA 91761
Phone: 909-923-4116, 800-532-3336
Specialties: Complete selection of 3M, Norton, Klingspor and Hermes belts for grinding and polishing, also Burr-King and Square Wheel grinders, Baldor buffers and an excellent line of machines for knifemakers; ATS-34 and 440C steel.

WASHITA MOUNTAIN WHETSTONE CO.
P.O. Box 378
Lake Hamilton, AR 71951
Phone: 501-525-3914
Specialties: Knife sharpeners.

WILD WOODS
Jim Fray
P.O. Box 104
Monclova, OH 43542
Phone: 419-866-0435
FAX: 419-867-0656
Specialties: Stabilized woods in a variety of colors in four grades.

WILSON, R.W.
113 Kent Way
Weirton, WV 26062
Phone: 304-723-2771
Specialties: Full range of supplies, but sells nothing he doesn't use himself.

WOOD CARVERS SUPPLY, INC.
P.O. Box 7500-K
Englewood, FL 34295-7500
Phone: 941-698-0123
Specialties: Carving tools, etc.

WYVERN INDUSTRIES
P.O. Box 1564
Shady Cove, OR 97539-1564
Phone: NA
E-MAIL: dufiron1@aol.com
Specialties: Purveyors of the hard-to-get for those who use anvils in their work.

ZOWADA CUSTOM KNIVES
Tim Zowada
4509 E. Bear River Rd.
Boyne Falls, MI 49713
Phone: 616-348-5416
FAX: 616-348-5416
E-MAIL: tzowada@freeway.net
Specialties: Damascus bars and billets, mokume and gas forge kits.

mail order sales

AMERICAN TARGET KNIVES
1030 Brownwood NW
Grand Rapids, MI 49504
Phone: 616-453-1998
Specialties: Throwing knives

ARIZONA CUSTOM KNIVES
Jay and Karen Sadow
8617 E. Clydesdale
Scottsdale, AZ 85258
Phone: 602-951-0699
Specialties: Custom and factory made knives,
tactical and/or investment grade. Color catalog
of wide selection, always available: $3 US/$5
INT'L. Buy, sell, trade, consign.

ARTHUR, GARY B.
Rt. 7 Box 215
Forest, VA 24551
Phone: 804-525-8315
FAX: 804-525-8364
Specialties: Sells, buys and trades custom-
made, investment-grade knives.

ATLANTA CUTLERY CORP.
2143 Gees Mill Rd., Box 839XZ
Conyers, GA 30207
Phone: 404-922-3700
Specialties: Catalog on request; wide selection
of knives; aims to provide working-quality
knives and give good value; showroom.
Catalog $2.

**ATLANTIC BLADESMITHS/PETER
STEBBINS**
32 Bradford St.
Concord, MA 01742
Phone: 508-369-3608
Specialties: Factory and custom-made knives,
over 100 in stock at all times, for immediate
sale. List $3.

BALLARD CUTLERY
1495 Brummel Ave.
Elk Grove Village, IL 60007
Phone: 708-228-0070
FAX: 708-228-0077
Specialties: Special-purchase knives, all
types. Tries for good buys.

BARRETT-SMYTHE, LTD.
30E 81st Grd Floor
New York, NY 10028
Phone: 212-249-5500
FAX: 212-249-5550
Specialties: One-of-a-kind folding knives on
sale in uptown Manhattan at prices suitable for
their station.

BECK'S CUTLERY SPECIALTIES
748F East Chatham St.
Cary, NC 27511
Phone: 919-460-0203
FAX: 919-460-1684
Specialties: South African Peter Bauchop's
tactical designs; other U.S. big-ticket tactical
names.

BELL SR., R.T. "BOB"
P.O. Box 690147
Orlando, FL 32869
Phone: 407-352-1082
Specialties: Wide range of quality knives.

BLAIRS BLADES & ACCESSORIES
531 Main St., Suite 651
El Segundo, CA 90245
Phone: 310-322-1063
FAX: 310-322-3112
Specialties: Sales reps for Anza File Knives.

BLUE RIDGE KNIVES
Rt. 6, Box 185
Marion, VA 24354-9351
Phone: 540-783-6143
FAX: 540-783-9298
Specialties: Wholesale only; top brand knives.

BOONE TRADING CO., INC.
P.O. Box BB
Brinnon, WA 98320
Phone: 206-796-4330
Specialties: Ivory; catalog features
scrimshawed and carved ivory-handled
knives.

CARMEL CUTLERY
Dolores & 6th; P.O. Box 1346
Carmel, CA 93921
Phone: 408-624-6699
FAX: 408-624-6780
Specialties: Knife retailer; factory and custom
knives.

CLASSIC CUTLERY
39 Roosevelt Ave.
Hudson, NH 03051-2828
Phone: 603-883-1199
FAX: 603-883-1199
Specialties: Factory knives and accessories,
all discounted. Also custom, rare and
discontinued knives. Genuine stone handle
materials, jigged bone and mother-of-pearl;
from the common to the unusual. Huge catalog
$5 (refundable).

COHEN & NEAL CUSTOM KNIVES
P.O. Box 831
Cockeysville, MD 21030
Phone: 410-628-6262

CORRADO CUTLERY
Otto Pomper
26 N. Clark St.
Chicago, IL 60602
Phone: 312-368-8450
FAX: 312-368-8451
WEB: http://www.otto-corrado.com
E-MAIL: info@otto-corrado.com
Specialties: Premier fine cutlery, gifts and
gadgets.

CREATIVE SALES & MFG.
Box 550
Whitefish, MT 59937
Phone: 406-862-5533
FAX: 406-862-6229
Specialties: Patent knife sharpeners.

CUTLERY SHOPPE
P.O. Box 610
Meridian, ID 83680-0610
Phone: 800-231-1272; 208-884-7575
Specialties: Discounts; custom and unusual
balisongs; tactical knives in a wide range;
catalog $1.

DENTON, J.W.
102 N. Main St., Box 429
Hiawassee, GA 30546

Phone: 706-896-2292
FAX: 706-896-1212
Specialties: Buys and sells Loveless knives—
has lists.

EDGE CO. KNIVES
P.O. Box 826
Brattleboro, VT 05302
Phone: 800-732-9976
FAX: 802-257-1967
Specialties: A variety of opportunity knives.

FAZALARE, ROY
P.O. Box 1335
Agoura Hills, CA 91376
Phone: 818-879-6161
Specialties: Specializing in custom handmade
multi- blade folders.

GENUINE ISSUE, INC.
949 Middle Country Rd.
Selden, NY 11784
Phone: 516-696-3802
FAX: 516-696-3803
Specialties: Representing the Digby line.

GODWIN, INC., G. GEDNEY
2139 Welsh Valley Rd.
Valley Forge, PA 19481
Phone: 610-783-0670
Specialties: Reenactment gear—18th and
19th century complete.

HAWTHORN GALLERIES, INC.
P.O. Box 6071
Branson, MO 65616
Phone: 417-335-2170
FAX: 417-335-2011
Specialties: Buys, sells and trades collector-
grade knives by mail and at major shows.

HERITAGE ANTIQUE KNIVES
Bruce Voyles
P.O. Box 22171
Chattanooga, TN 37422
Phone: 423-894-8319
Specialties: Deals in old knives, mostly U.S.
and English and mostly folders; some Bowies.
List.

HUNTER SERVICES
Fred Hunter
P.O. Box 14241
Parkville, MD 64152
Phone: 816-587-9959
FAX: 816-746-5680
E-MAIL: fhunter@kcnet.net
Specialties: Quality antique pocketknives and
related items. Select custom and military
cutlery. Lists.

IRONSTONE DISTINCTIVE BLADEWARE
16350 S. Golden Rd.
Golden, CO 80401
Phone: 800-828-1925
FAX: 303-278-2057
Specialties: Carry full line of Spyderco
products, others.

JENCO SALES, INC.
P.O. Box 1000
Manchaca, TX 78652
Phone: 512-282-6860
FAX: 512-282-7504
Specialties: Full line of domestic and imported
knives and accessories.

**KENEFICK, DOUG
(SEE COHEN & NEAL)**

KNIFE-AHOLICS UNANIMOUS
P.O. Box 831
Cockeysville, MD 21030
Phone: 410-628-6262
Specialties: David Cohen—purveyor of custom knives.

KNIFE & CUTLERY PRODUCTS, INC.
P.O. Box 12480
North Kansas City, MO 64116
Phone: 816-454-9879
Specialties: Sells brand-name commercial cutlery, some collectibles; 14-page list $2

KNIFEMASTERS CUSTOM KNIVES/J&S FEDER
P.O. Box 2419
Westport, CT 06880
Phone: 203-226-5211
FAX: 203-226-5312
Specialties: Dealers in fine investment grade custom knives.

LDC CUSTOM KNIVES
P.O. Box 211961
Augusta, GA 30917
Phone: 706-650-0252
FAX: 706-860-1623
Specialties: Specializing in collectible custom combat knives.

LES COUTEAUX CHOISSIS DE ROBERTS
Ron Roberts
P.O. Box 273
Mifflin, PA 17058
Phone: 717-436-5010
FAX: 717-436-9691
Specialties: Handles all types of manufacturers knives and related items for collectors and users.

LONDON, RICK
P.O. Box 21303
Oakland, CA 94620
Phone: 510-482-2775
Specialties: Purveyor of collectible knives. A special eye for fine crafted folders.

**LOVELESS KNIVES
(SEE DENTON, J.W.)**

MORTY THE KNIFE MAN, INC.
4 Manorhaven Blvd.
Port Washington, NY 11050
Phone: 516-767-2357

FAX: 516-767-7058
Specialties: The world's fish knives—all of them.

MUSEUM REPLICAS LTD.
2143 Gees Mill Rd., Box 840XZ
Conyers, GA 30207
Phone: 404-922-3703
Specialties: Authentic edged weapons of the ages, battle-ready—over 50 models; subsidiary of Atlanta Cutlery; catalog $2.

NASHOBA VALLEY KNIFEWORKS
373 Langen Rd., Box 35
Lancaster, MA 01523
Phone: 508-365-6593
FAX: 508-368-4171
Specialties: Custom sales, emphasis on Guild members knives, plus Randall and Ruana. Large inventory; 6 lists a year. List $2.

NORDIC KNIVES
1634CZ Copenhagen Dr.
Solvang, CA 93463
Phone: 805-688-3612
Specialties: Custom and Randall knives; custom catalog $3; Randall catalog $2; both catalogs $4.

PARKER'S KNIFE COLLECTOR SERVICE
6715 Heritage Business court
Chattanooga, TN 37422
Phone: 423-892-0448
Specialties: Highly specialized into limited run Case folders for modern collectors.

PEN AND THE SWORD LTD., THE
1833 E. 12th St.
Brooklyn, NY 11229
Phone: 718-382-4847
FAX: 718-376-5745
Specialties: Custom knives in a wide price range.

PLAZA CUTLERY, INC.
3333 S. Bristol St., South Coast Plaza
Costa Mesa, CA 92626
Phone: 714-549-3932
Specialties: List of custom knives for collectors, many top names every time; $1.

RAMSHEAD ARMOURY, INC.
P.O. Box 85
Maryville, IL 62062-0085
Phone: 888-ARMOURY
FAX: 888-ARMOURY
Specialties: Stocks swords, daggers and such for the Renaissance dragon-slaying-tournament trade. Catalog $2.

ROBERTSON'S CUSTOM CUTLERY
P.O. Box 211961
Augusta, GA 30917
Phone: 706-650-0252
FAX: 706-860-1623
Specialties: Combat cutlery, investment grade knives and one-of-a-kind pieces. Catalog $5 US/$10 INTL.

ROBINSON, ROBERT W.
1569 N. Finley Pt.
Polson, MT 59860
Phone: 406-887-2259
FAX: 406-887-2259
Specialties: Investment grade modern, ancient, fixed and folding.

RUSSELL CO., A.G.
1705 Highway 71 North
Springdale, AR 72764
Phone: 501-751-7341; 800-255-9034
Specialties: Regularly lists custom knives by all makers; sold on consignment; also commemoratives, Russell and Morseth knives.

SHAW, GARY
24 Central Ave.
Ridgefield Park, NJ 07660
Phone: 201-641-8801
Specialties: Investment-grade knives of all kinds.

SMOKY MOUNTAIN KNIFE WORKS
P.O. Box 4430
Sevierville, TN 37864
Phone: 800-251-9306
Specialties: Retail and wholesale sales of all kinds of knives and supplies.

STIDHAM'S KNIVES
P.O. Box 570
Roseland, FL 32957-0570
Phone: 561-589-0618
FAX: 561-589-3162
Specialties: Purveyors of fine custom knives—antique knives, military knives. Founders of Randall Knife Collectors Society.

STODDARD'S, INC.
Copley Place
100 Huntington Ave.
Boston, MA 02116
Phone: 617-536-8688
FAX: 617-357-8263
Specialties: Oldest cutlery retailer in the country; handmade and Randall knives, other fine production knives—Spyderco and Al Mar knives, etc. Manager: Steven Weingrad. Two additional stores in MA area.

knife services

engravers

Adlam, Tim, 1705 Witzel Ave., Oshkosh, WI 54902 / 920-235-4589; Fax: 920-235-4589

Alfano, Sam, 36180 Henry Gaines Rd., Pearl River, LA 70452

Allard, Gary, 2395 Battlefield Rd., Fishers Hill, VA 22626

Allred, Scott, 2403 Lansing Blvd., Wichita Falls, TX

Alpen, Ralph, 7 Bentley Rd., West Grove, PA 19390

Baron Technology Inc., David, David Baron, 62 Spring Hill Rd., Trumbull, CT 06611 / 203-452-0515

Bates, Billy, 2302 Winthrop Dr. SW, Decatur, AL 35603

Beaver, Judy, 48835 N. 25 Ave., Phoenix, AZ 85027

Becker, Franz, Am Kreuzberg 2, 84533 Marktl/Inn, GERMANY

Bettenhausen, Merle L., 17358 Ottawa, Tinley Park, IL 60477

Blair, Jim, P.O. Box 64, 59 Mesa Verde, Glenrock, WY 82637 / 307463-8115

Bleile, C. Roger, 5040 Ralph Ave., Cincinnati, OH 45238

Bonshire, Benita, 1121 Burlington, Muncie, IN 47302

Boster, A.D., 3744 Pleasant Hill Dr., Gainesville, GA 30504

Bratcher, Dan, 311 Belle Aire Pl., Carthage, MO 64836

Brooker, Dennis B., Rt. 1 Box 12A, Derby, IA 50068

Churchill, Winston G., RFD Box 29B, Proctorsville, VT 05153

Collins, Michael, Rt. 3075, Batesville Rd., Woodstock, GA 30188

Collins, David, Rt. 2 Box 425, Monroe, VA 24574

Cupp, Alana, P.O. Box 207, Annabella, UT 84711

Dashwood, Jim, 255 Barkham Rd., Wokingham, Berkshire RG11 4BY, ENGLAND

Davidson, Jere, 104 Fox Creek Dr, Goode, VA 24556 / 540-586-5150

Dean, Bruce, 13 Tressider Ave., Haberfield, N.S.W. 2045, AUSTRALIA

DeLorge, Ed, 6734 W Main St, Houma, LA 70360 / 504-223-0206

Dickson, John W., P.O. Box 49914, Sarasota, FL 34230

Dolbare, Elizabeth, P.O. Box 222, Sunburst, MT 59482

Downing, Jim, P.O. Box 4224, Springfield, MO 65808 / 417-865-5953

Drain, Mark, SE 3211 Kamilche Pt. Rd., Shelton, WA 98584

Duarte, Carlos, 108 Church St., Rossville, CA 95678

Dubben, Michael, 414 S. Fares Ave., Evansville, IN 47714

Dubber, Michael W., 8205 Heather Pl, Evansville, IN 47710-4919

Eklund, Maihkel, Föne 1155, S-82041 Färila, SWEDEN

Eldridge, Allan, 1424 Kansas Lane, Gallatin, TN 37066

Engel, Terry (Flowers), P.O. Box 96, Midland, OR 97634

Eyster, Ken, 6441 Bishop Rd., Centerburg, OH 43011

Fisher, Jay, 104 S. Main St., P.O. Box 267, Magdela, NM 87825

Flannery Engraving Co., Jeff, 11034 Riddles Run Rd., Union, KY 41091

Foster Enterprises, Norvell Foster, P.O. Box 200343, San Antonio, TX 78220

Fountain Products, 492 Prospect Ave., West Springfield, MA 01089

French, James Ronald, 1745 Caddo Dr, Irving, TX 75060-5837

George, Tim and Christy, Rt. 1, Box 45, Evington, VA 24550

Gipe, Sandi, Rt. 2, Box 1090A, Kendrick, ID 83537

Glimm, Jerome C., 19 S. Maryland, Conrad, MT 59425

Gournet, Geoffroy, 820 Paxinosa Ave., Easton, PA 18042 / 610-559-0710

Hands, Barry Lee, 26192 E. Shore Rte., Bigfork, MT 59911

Harrington, Fred A., Winter: 3725 Citrus, St. James City, FL 33956

Henderson, Fred D., 569 Santa Barbara Dr., Forest Park, GA 30297 / 770-968-4866

Hendricks, Frank, HC03, Box 434, Dripping Springs, TX 78620

Holder, Pat, 7148 W. Country Gables Dr., Peoria, AZ 85381

Hudson, Tommy, P.O. Box 2046, Monroe, NC 28110

Ingle, Ralph W., 112 Manchester Ct., Centerville, GA 31028

Jiantonio, Robert, P.O. Box 986, Venice, FL 34284

Johns, Bill, 7927 Ranch Rd. 965, Fredericksburg, TX 78624 / 830-997-6795

Kelly, Lance, 1723 Willow Oak Dr., Edgewater, FL 32132

Kelso, Jim, RD 1, Box 5300, Worcester, VT 05682

Koevenig, Eugene and Eve, Rabbit Gulch, Box 55, Hill City, SD 57745-0055

Kostelnik, Joe and Patty, RD #4, Box 323, Greensburg, PA 15601

Kraft, Brenda, Box 1143, Polson, MT 59860

Kudlas, John M., HC 66 Box 22680, Barnes, WI 54873 / 715-795-2031

Lee, Ray, 209 Jefferson Dr., Lynchburg, VA 24502

Limings Jr., Harry, 959 County Rd. 170, Marengo, OH 43334-9625

Lindsay, Steve, 3714 West Cedar Hills Drive, Kearney, NE 68847

Lyttle, Brian, Box 5697, High River AB CANADA, T1V 1M7

Lytton, Simon M., 19 Pinewood Gardens, Hemel Hempstead, Herts. HP1 1TN, ENGLAND

McCombs, Leo, 1862 White Cemetery Rd., Patriot, OH 45658

McDonald, Dennis, 8359 Brady St., Peosta, IA 52068

directory

McKenzie, Lynton, 6940 N. Alvernon Way, Tucson, AZ 85718

Meyer, Chris, 39 Bergen Ave., Wantage, NJ 07461 / 973-875-6299

Miller, James K. and Vicky, American Etching, 22500 Hwy. 72 W., Tuscumbia, AL 35674

Montgomery, Charles, 4517 Summer Ave., Memphis, TN 38122

Morgan, Tandie, P.O. Box 693, 30700 Hwy. 97, Nucla, CO 81424

Morton, David A., 1110 W. 21st St., Lorain, OH 44052

Moschetti, Mitch, 1435 S. Elizabeth, Denver, CO 80210

Nelida, Toniutti, via G. Pasconi 29/c, Maniago 33085 (PN), ITALY

Norton, Jeff, 2009 65th St., Lubbock, TX 79412

Nott, Ron, Box 281, Summerdale, PA 17093

Parsons, Michael R., McKee Knives, 1600 S. 11th St., Terre Haute, IN 47802-1722 / 812-234-1679

Patterson, W.H., P.O. Drawer DK, College Station, TX 77841

Perdue, David L., Rt. 1 Box 657, Gladys, VA 24554

Peri, Valerio, Via Meucci 12, Gardone V.T. 25063, ITALY

Pilkington Jr., Scott, P.O. Box 97, Monteagle, TN 37356

Poag, James, RR1, Box 212A, Grayville, IL 62844

Potts, Wayne, 912 Poplar St., Denver, CO 80220

Rabeno, Martin, Spook Hollow Trading Co., 92 Spook Hole Rd., Ellenville, NY 12428

Raftis, Andrew, 2743 N. Sheffield, Chicago, IL 60614

Roberts, J.J., 7808 Lake Dr., Manassas, VA 22111

Robidoux, Roland J., DMR Fine Engraving, 25 N. Federal Hwy. Studio 5, Dania, FL 33004

Robyn, Jon, Ground Floor, 30 E. 81st St., New York, NY 10028

Rosser, Bob, Hand Engraving, 1824 29th Ave. South, Suite 214, Birmingham, AL 35209

Rudolph, Gil, 386 Mariposa Dr., Ventura, CA 93001

Rundell, Joe, 6198 W. Frances Rd., Clio, MI 48420

Schickl, L., Ottingweg 497, A-5580 Tamsweg, AUSTRIA/ 0043 6474 8583

Schlott, Harald, Zingster Str. 26, 13051 Berlin, GERMANY

Schönert, Elke, 18 Lansdowne Pl., Central, Port Elizabeth, SOUTH AFRICA

Shaw, Bruce, P.O. Box 545, Pacific Grove, CA 93950 / 831-646-1937; Fax: 831-644-0941

Sherwood, George, 46 North River Dr., Roseburg, OR 97470

Shostle, Ben, 1121 Burlington, Muncie, IN 47302

Sinclair, W.P., 3, The Pippins, Warminster, Wiltshire BA12 8TH, ENGLAND

Smith, Jerry, 7029 East Holmes Rd., Memphis, TN 38125

Smith, Ron, 5869 Straley, Ft. Worth, TX 76114

Smitty's Engraving, 800 N. Anderson Rd., Choctaw, OK 73020

Spode, Peter, Tresaith Newland, Malvern, Worcestershire WR13 5AY, ENGLAND

Steduto, Giovanni, Gardone, V.T., ITALY

Swartley, Robert D., 2800 Pine St., Napa, CA 94558

Takeuchi, Shigetoshi, 21-14-1-Chome kamimuneoka Shiki shi, 353 Saitama, JAPAN

Thierry, Ivan, 15 Côte de Villancé, 28350 Saint-Lubin-des-Joncherets, FRANCE

Valade, Robert B., 931 3rd Ave., Seaside, OR 97138

Waldrop, Mark, 14562 SE 1st Ave. Rd., Summerfield, FL 34491

Wallace, Terry, 385 San Marino, Vallejo, CA 94589

Warenski, Julie, 590 East 500 N., Richfield, UT 84701

Warren, Kenneth W., P.O. Box 2842, Wenatchee, WA 98807-2842 / 509-663-6123; Fax: 509-663-6123

Watson, Silvia, 350 Jennifer Lane, Driftwood, TX 78619

Whitehead, James D., 204 Cappucino Way, Sacramento, CA 95838

Whitmore, Jerry, 1740 Churchill Dr., Oakland, OR 97462

Williams, Gary, 221 Autumn Way, Elizabeth, KY 42701

Winn, Travis A., 558 E. 3065 S., Salt Lake City, UT 84106

Wood, Mel, P.O. Box 1255, Sierra Vista, AZ 85636

Zietz, Dennis, 5906 40th Ave., Kenosha, WI 53144

heat-treaters

Aoun, Charles, Galeb Knives, 69 Nahant St, Wakefield, MA 01880 / 781-224-3353; Fax: 781-224-3353

Barbee, Jim, RR1 Box B, Fort Stockton, TX 79735-8507

Bay State Metal Treating Co., 6 Jefferson Ave., Woburn, MA 01801

Bos Heat Treating, Paul, Shop: 1900 Weld Blvd., El Cajon, CA 92020

El Monte Steel, 355 SE End Ave., Pomona, CA 91766

Hauni Richmond Inc., 2800 Charles City Rd., Richmond, VA 23231

Holt, B.R., 1238 Birchwood Drive, Sunnyvale, CA 94089

Lamprey, Mike, 32 Pathfield, Great Torrington, Devon EX38 TBX, ENGLAND

Metal Treating Bodycote Inc, 710 Burns St., Cincinnati, OH 45204

O&W Heat Treat Inc., One Bidwell Rd., South Windsor, CT 06074 / 860-528-9239; Fax: 860-291-9939

Texas Heat Treating Inc., 303 Texas Ave., Round Rock, TX 78664

Texas Knifemakers Supply, 10649 Haddington, Suite 180, Houston, TX 77043

The Tinker Shop, 1120 Helen, Deer Park, TX 77536

Valley Metal Treating Inc., 355 S. East End Ave., Pomona, CA 91766

Wilson, R.W., P.O. Box 2012, Weirton, WV 26062

Leatherworker

Anonymous Leather & Mfg., Vary Ltd., 519 Castro St., #M38, San Francisco, CA 94114

Baker, Don and Kay, 5950 Foxfire Dr., Zanesville, OH 43701

Cheramie, Grant, 4260 West Main, Rt. 3, Box 940, Cut Off, LA 70345

Clements' Custom Leathercraft, Chas, 1741 Dallas St., Aurora, CO 80010-2018

Congdon, David, 1063 Whitchurch Ct., Wheaton, IL 60187

Cooper, Harold, 136 Winding Way, Frankfort, KY 40601

Cooper, Jim, 2148 Cook Pl., Ramona, CA 92065-3214

Cow Catcher Leatherworks, 3006 Industrial Dr, Raleigh, NC 27609

Cubic, George, GC Custom Leather Co., 10561 E. Deerfield Pl., Tucson, AZ 85749 / 520-760-5988

Dawkins, Dudley, 221 N. Broadmoor, Topeka, KS 66606-1254

Evans, Scott V, Edge Works Mfg, 1171 Halltown Rd, Jacksonville, NC 28546 / 910-455-9834; Fax: 910-346-5660

Fannin, David A., 2050 Idle Hour Center #191, Lexington, KY 40502

Foley, Barney, 3M Reler Lane, Somerset, NJ 08873

Genske, Jay, 2621/2 Elm St., Fond du Lac, WI 54935

Harris, Tom, 519 S. 1st St., Mount Vernon, WA 98273

Hawk, Ken, Rt. 1, Box 770, Ceres, VA 24318-9630

Hendryx Design, Scott, 5997 Smokey Way, Boise, ID 83714 / 208-377-8044; Fax: 208-377-2601

Homyk, David N., 8047 Carriage Ln., Wichita Falls, TX 76306

John-D Custom Leatherworks and Handmade Knives, John D. Dennehy, P.O. Box 431, Wellington, CO 80549-0431

K&J Leatherworks, P.O. Box 609, Watford, ON N0M 2S0 CANADA

Kravitt, Chris, HC 31 Box 6484, Rt 200, Ellsworth, ME 04605-9805 / 207-584-3000

Larson, Richard, 549 E. Hawkeye, Turlock, CA 95380

Lay, Judy M., Box 2781, Vanderhoof, BC V0J 3A0 CANADA/ 250-567-3856

Layton, Jim, 2710 Gilbert Avenue, Portsmouth, OH 45662

Lee, Randy, P.O. Box 1873, St. Johns, AZ 85936 / 520-337-5002; Fax: 520-337-2594

Mason, Arne, 125 Wimer St., Ashland, OR 97520

McGowan, Liz, 12629 Howard Lodge Dr., Sykesville, MD 21784

Metheny, H.A. Whitey, 7750 Waterford Dr., Spotsylvania, VA 22553

Miller, Michael K., 28510 Santiam Highway, Sweet Home, OR 97386

Mobley, Martha, 240 Alapaha River Road, Chula, GA 31733

Morrissey, Martin, 4578 Stephens Rd., Blairsville, GA 30512

Niedenthal, John Andre, Beadwork & Buckskin, Studio 3955 NW 103 Dr., Coral Springs, FL 33065-1551

Poag, James H., RR #1 Box 212A, Grayville, IL 62844

Ravon Industries, P.O. Box 670, Denton, TX 76202

Red's Custom Leather, Ed Todd, 9 Woodlawn Rd., Putnam Valley, NY 80121

Riney, Norm, 6212 S. Marion Way, Littleton, CO 71801

Rowe, Kenny, 1406 W. Ave. C, Hope, AR 91204 / 870-777-8216; Fax: 870-777-2974

Ruiz Industries Inc., 1513 Gardena Ave., Glendale, CA 53213-3717

Schrap, Robert G., 7024 W. Wells St., Wauwatosa, WI 53213 /Fax: 414-784-2996

Spragg, Wayne E., P.O. Box 508, Ashton, ID 26241

Strahin, Robert, 401 Center Ave., Elkins, WV

Stuart, V. Pat, Rt. 1, Box 447-S, Greenville, VA 24440

Stumpf, John R., 523 S. Liberty St., Blairsville, PA 15717

Tierney, Mike, 447 Rivercrest Dr., Woodstock ON CANADA, N4S 5W5

Turner, Kevin, 17 Hunt Ave., Montrose, NY 10548

Velasquez, Gil, 7120 Madera Dr., Goleta, CA 93117

Walker, John, 17 Laber Circle, Little Rock, AR 72209

Watson, Bill, #1 Presidio, Wimberly, TX 78676

Wegner, Tim, 8818-158th St. E., Puyallup, WA 98373

Whinnery, Walt, 1947 Meadow Creek Dr., Louisville, KY 40218

Williams, Sherman A., 1709 Wallace St., Simi Valley, CA 93065

photographers

Alfano, Sam, 36180 Henery Gaines Rd., Pearl River, LA 70452

Allen, John, Studio One, 3823 Pleasant Valley Blvd., Rockford, IL 61114

Berchtold, Robert, 820 Greenbriar Circle Suite #26, Chesapeake, VA 23320

Berisford, Bob, 505 West Adams St., Jacksonville, FL 32202

Bilal, Mustafa, Turk's Head Productions, 908 NW 50th St., Seattle, WA 98107-3634 / 206-782-4164; Fax: 206-783-5677

Bittner, Rodman, 3444 North Apache Circle, Chandler, AZ 85224

Bloomer, Peter L., Horizons West, 427 S. San Francisco St., Flagstaff, AZ 86001

Bogaerts, Jan, Regenweg 14, 5757 Pl., Liessel, HOLLAND

Box Photography, Doug, 1804 W Main St, Brenham, TX 77833-3420

Brown, Tom, 6048 Grants Ferry Rd., Brandon, MS 39042-8136

Buffaloe, Edwin, 104 W. Applegate, Austin, TX 78753

Burdette, Roger W., 1516 E. 19th St., Des Moines, IA 50316-2708

Burger, Gunter, Horststr. 55, 44581 Castrop-Rauseel, GERMANY

Butman, Steve, P.O. Box 5106, Abilene, TX 79608

Calidonna, Greg, 205 Helmwood Dr., Elizabethtown, KY 42701

Campbell, Jim, 7935 Ranch Rd., Port Richey, FL 34668

Catalano, John D., 56 Kingston Ave., Hicksville, NY 11801

Chan, Stanley B., 550 Weddell Dr. #7, Sunnyvale, CA 94089

Chastain, Christopher, B&W Labs, 1462 E. Michigan St., Orlando, FL 32806

Clark, Ryerson, P.O. Box 1193, Dartmouth NS CANADA, B2Y 4B8

Clark, John W., 604 Cherry St., Des Moines, IA 50309

Cotton, William A., 749 S. Lemay Ave. A3-211, Fort Collins, CO 80524

Courtice, Bill, P.O. Box 1776, Duarte, CA 91010-4776

Crosby, Doug, RFD 1, Box 1111, Stockton Springs, ME 04981

Danko, Michael, 3030 Jane Street, Pittsburgh, PA 15203

Davis, Marshall B., P.O. Box 3048, Austin, TX 78764

Dikeman, Lawrence, 2169 Arbor Ave., Muskegon, MI 49441

Durant, Ross, 316 E. 1st Ave., Vancouver BC CANADA, V5T 1A9

Earley, Don, 1241 Ft. Bragg Rd., Fayetteville, NC 28305

Eggly, Eric R., 810 Seneca St., Toledo, OH 43608

Ehrlich, Linn M., 2643 N. Clybourn Ave., Chicago, IL 60614

Ellison, Troy, P.O. Box 94393, Lubbock, TX 79493

Etzler, John, 11200 N. Island Rd., Grafton, OH 44044

Fahrner, Dave, 1623 Arnold St., Pittsburgh, PA 15205

Faul, Jan W., 903 Girard St. NE, Rr. Washington, DC 20017

Fedorak, Allan, 28 W. Nicola St., Amloops BC CANADA, V2C 1J6

Fisher, Jay, P.O. Box 267, Magdalena, NM 87825

Fitzgerald, Dan, P.O. Box 198, Beverly Hills, CA 90213

Forster, Jenny, 1112 N. McAree, Waukegan, IL 60085

Fox, Daniel, Lumina Studios, 6773 Industrial Parkway, Cleveland, OH 44070 / 440-734-2118; Fax: 440-734-3542

Gardner, Chuck, 116 Quincy Ave., Oak Ridge, TN 37830

Gawryla, Don, 1105 Greenlawn Dr., Pittsburgh, PA 15220

Godby, Ronald E., 204 Seven Hollys Dr., Yorktown, VA 23692

Goffe Photographic Associates, 3108 Monte Vista Blvd., NE, Albuquerque, NM 87106

Graham, James, 7434 E Northwest Hwy, Dallas, TX 75231

Graley, Gary W., RR2 Box 556, Gillett, PA 16925

Gray, Corey, 760 Warehouse Rd. Suite D, Toledo, OH 43615

Griggs, Dennis, 118 Pleasant Pt Rd, Topsham, ME 04086 / 207-725-5689

Hanusin, John, 3306 Commercial, Northbrook, IL 60062

Hardy, Scott, 639 Myrtle Ave., Placerville, CA 95667

Hodge, Tom, 7175 S US Hwy 1 Lot 36, Titusville, FL 32780-8172

Holter, Wayne V., 125 Lakin Ave., Boonsboro, MD 21713

Kelley, Gary, 17485 SW Pheasant Lane, Aloha, OR 97006

Kerns, Bob, 18723 Birdseye Dr., Germantown, MD 20874

LaFleur, Gordon, 111 Hirst, Box 1209, Parksville BC CANADA, V0R 270

Landis, George E., 16 Prospect Hill Rd., Cromwell, CT 06416

Lautman, Andy, 4906 41st N.W., Washington, DC 20016

Lear, Dale, 6450 Cora Mill Rd, Gallipolis, OH 45631 / 740-245-5499

LeBlanc, Paul, No. 3 Meadowbrook Cir., Melissa, TX 75454

Lenz Photography, 939 S. 48th St., Suite 206, Tempe, AZ 85281

Lester, Dean, 2801 Junipero Ave Suite 212, Long Beach, CA 90806-2140

Leviton, David A., A Studio on the Move, P.O. Box 2871, Silverdale, WA 98383 / 360-697-3452

Long, Gary W., 3556 Miller's Crossroad Rd., Hillsboro, TN 37342

Long, Jerry, 402 E. Gladden Dr., Farmington, NM 87401

Lum, Billy, 16307 Evening Star Ct., Crosby, TX 77532

McCollum, Tom, P.O. Box 933, Lilburn, GA 30226

Moake, Jim, 18 Council Ave., Aurora, IL 60504

Moya Inc., 4212 S. Dixie Hwy., West Palm Beach, FL 33405

Newton, Thomas D., 136 1/2 W. 2nd St., Reno, NV 89501

Norman's Studio, 322 S. 2nd St., Vivian, LA 71082

Owens, William T., Box 99, Williamsburg, WV 24991

Palmer Studio, 2008 Airport Blvd., Mobile, AL 36606

Parker, T.C., 1720 Pacific, Las Vegas, NV 89104

Parsons, 15 South Mission, Suite 3, Wenatchee, WA 98801

Payne, Robert G., P.O. Box 141471, Austin, TX 78714

Peterson Photography, Kent, 230 Polk St., Eugene, OR 97402

Pigott, John, 231 Heidelberg Drive, Loveland, OH 45140 / 513-683-4875

Rasmussen, Eric L., 1121 Eliason, Brigham City, UT 84302

Reinders, Rick, 1707 Spring Place, Racine, WI 53404

Rhoades, Cynthia J., Box 195, Clearmont, WY 82835

Rice, Tim, 310 Wisconsin Ave., Whitefish, MT 59937

Richardson, Kerry, 2520 Mimosa St., Santa Rosa, CA 95405 / 707-575-1875

Robertson, Kathy, Impress by Design, PO Box 211961, Augusta, GA 30917 / 706-650-0982; Fax: 706-860-1623

Ross, Bill, 28364 S. Western Ave. Suite 464, Rancho Palos Verdes, CA 90275

Rubicam, Stephen, 14 Atlantic Ave., Boothbay Harbor, ME 04538-1202

Ruby, Tom, Holiday Inn University, 11200 E. Goodman Rd., Olive Branch, MS 38654

Rush, John D., 2313 Maysel, Bloomington, IL 61701

Schreiber, Roger, 429 Boren Ave. N., Seattle, WA 98109

Semmer, Charles, 7885 Cyd Dr., Denver, CO 80221

Silver Images Photography, 21 E. Aspen Ave., Flagstaff, AZ 86001

Sims Photography, 461 Breezy Dr., Marietta, GA 30064

Slobodian, Scott, 4101 River Ridge Dr., P.O. Box 1498, San Andreas, CA 95249 / 209-286-1980; Fax: 209-286-1982

Smith, Randall, 1720 Oneco Ave., Winter Park, FL 32789

Smith, Earl W., 5121 Southminster Rd., Columbus, OH 43221

Stenzel Photography, P.O. Box 1504, Bozeman, MT 59771

Storm Photo, 334 Wall St., Kingston, NY 12401

Surles, Mark, P.O. Box 147, Falcon, NC 28342

Tardiolo, 9381 Wagon Wheel, Yuma, AZ 85365

Third Eye Photos, 140 E. Sixth Ave., Helena, MT 59601

Thurber, David, P.O. Box 1006, Visalia, CA 93279

Tighe, Brian, RR 1, Ridgeville ON CANADA, L0S 1M0/ 905-892-2734

Towell, Steven L., 3720 N.W. 32nd Ave., Camas, WA 98607

Troutman, Harry, 107 Oxford Dr., Lititz, PA 17543

Valley Photo, 2100 Arizona Ave., Yuma, AZ 85364

Vara, Lauren, 4412 Waples Rd., Granbury, TX 76049

Verhoeven, Jon, 106 San Jose Dr., Springdale, AR 72764-2538

Verno Studio, Jay, 3030 Jane Street, Pittsburgh, PA 15203

Wells, Carlene L., 1060 S. Main Sp. 52, Colville, WA 99114

Weyer International, 2740 Nebraska Ave., Toledo, OH 43607 / 800-448-8424; Fax: 419-534-2697

Wise, Harriet, 242 Dill Ave., Frederick, MD 21701

Worley, Holly, 6360 W David Dr, Littleton, CO 80128-5708

scrimshanders

Adlam, Tim, 1705 Witzel Ave., Oshkosh, WI 54902 / 920-235-4589; Fax: 920-234-4589

Anderson, Terry Jack, 10076 Birnamwoods Way, Riverton, UT 84065-9073

Bailey, Mary W., 3213 Jonesboro Dr., Nashville, TN 37214

Baker, Duane, 2145 Alum Creek Dr., Cambridge Park Apt. #10, Columbus, OH 43207

Barndt, Kristen A., RR3, Box 72, Kunkletown, PA 18058

Barrows, Miles, 524 Parsons Ave., Chillicothe, OH 45601

Beauchamp, Gaetan, 125 de la Riviere, Stoneham, PQ G0A 4P0 CANADA/ 418-848-1914; Fax: 418-848-6859

Beaver, Judy, 48835 N. 25 Ave., Phoenix, AZ 85027

Bellet, Connie, PO Box 347, Unity, ME 04988 / 207-948-6107

Bonshire, Benita, 1121 Burlington Dr., Muncie, IN 47302

Boone Trading Co. Inc., P.O. Box BB, Brinnon, WA 98320

Bowles, Rick, 1416 Debbs Rd., Chesapeake, VA 23320

Brady, Sandra, P.O. Box 104, Monclova, OH 43542 / 419-866-0435; Fax: 419-867-0656

Bruce, Lisa, c/o Joe Arnold, 47 Patience Cres., London ON CANADA, N6E 2K7

Bryan, Bob, 1120 Oak Hill Rd., Carthage, MO 64836

Byrne, Mary Gregg, 1018 15th St., Bellingham, WA 98225-6604

Cable, Jerry, 332 Main St., Mt. Pleasant, PA 15666

Caudill, Lyle, 7626 Lyons Rd., Georgetown, OH 45121

Collins, Michael, Rt. 3075, Batesville Rd., Woodstock, GA 30188

Conover, Juanita Rae, P.O. Box 70442, Eugene, OR 97401 / 541-747-1726 or 543-4851

Courtnage, Elaine, Box 473, Big Sandy, MT 59520

Cover Jr., Raymond A., Rt. 1, Box 194, Mineral Point, MO 63660

Cox, J. Andy, 116 Robin Hood Lane, Gaffney, SC 29340

Davenport, Susan, 36842 Center Ave., Dade City, FL 33525

DeYoung, Brian, 1448 Glen Haven Dr, Ft. Collins, CO 80526-2408

Dietrich, Roni, Wild Horse Studio, 1257 Cottage Dr, Harrisburg, PA 17112 / 717-469-0587

DiMarzo, Richard, 2357 Center Place, Birmingham, AL 35205

Dolbare, Elizabeth, P.O. Box 222, Sunburst, MT 59482

Eklund, Maihkel, Föne 1111, S-82041 Färila, SWEDEN/ +46 6512 4192

Eldridge, Allan, 1424 Kansas Lane, Gallatin, TN 37066

Eubank, Mary Ann, Rt. 1, Box 196, Pottsboro, TX 75076

Evans, Rick M., 2717 Arrowhead Dr., Abilene, TX 79606

Fields, Rick B., 26401 Sandwich Pl., Mt. Plymouth, FL 32776 / 352-383-6270; Fax: 352-383-6270

Fisk, Dale, Box 252, Council, ID 83612

Foster Enterprises, Norvell Foster, P.O. Box 200343, San Antonio, TX 78220

Fountain Products, 492 Prospect Ave., West Springfield, MA 01089

Garbe, Sandra, 1246 W. Webb, DeWitt, MI 48820

Gill, Scott, 925 N. Armstrong St., Kokomo, IN 46901

Halligan, Ed, 14 Meadow Way, Sharpsburg, GA 30277

Hands, Barry Lee, 26192 East Shore Route, Bigfork, MT 59911

Hargraves Sr., Charles, RR 3 Bancroft, Ontario CANADA, K0L 1C0

Harless, Star, c/o Arrow Forge, P.O. Box 845, Stoneville, NC 27048-0845

Harrington, Fred A., Summer: 2107 W Frances Rd, Mt Morris MI 48458 8215 Winter: 3725 Citrus, St. James City, FL 33956 / Winter 941-283-0721; Fax: Summer 810-686-3008

Henry, Michael K., Rte. 2, Box 161-J, Robbinsville, NC 28771

Hielscher, Vickie, 655C Otoe Rd, P.O. Box 992, Alliance, NE 69301

High, Tom, 5474 S. 112.8 Rd., Alamosa, CO 81101

Himmelheber, David R., 11289 40th St. N., Royal Palm Beach, FL 33411

Holland, Dennis K., 4908-17th Place, Lubbock, TX 79416

Hoover, Harvey, 5750 Pearl Dr., Paradise, CA 95969-4829

Houser, Jesse, P.O. Box 993, Biscoe, NC 27209

Imboden II, Howard L., 620 Deauville Dr., Dayton, OH 45429 / 937-439-1536

Johnson, Corinne, W3565 Lockington, Mindora, WI 54644

Johnston, Kathy, W. 1134 Providence, Spokane, WA 99205

Karst, Linda K., 402 Hwy. 27 E., Ingram, TX 78025

Kelso, Jim, RD 1, Box 5300, Worcester, VT 05682

Kirk, Susan B., 1340 Freeland Rd., Merrill, MI 48637

Koevenig, Eugene and Eve, Koevenig's Engraving Service, Rabbit Gulch, Box 55, Hill City, SD 57745-0055

Kostelnik, Joe and Patty, RD #4, Box 323, Greensburg, PA 15601

Kudlas, John M., HC 66 Box 22680, Barnes, WI 54873 / 715-795-2031

Land, John W., P.O. Box 917, Wadesboro, NC 28170

Lemen, Pam, 3434 N. Iroquois Ave., Tucson, AZ 85705

Letschnig, Franz, RR1, Martintown ON, CANADA

Martin, Diane, 28220 N. Lake Dr., Waterford, WI 53185

McDonald, René Cosimini-, 14730 61 Court N., Loxahatchee, FL 33470

McFadden, Berni, 2547 E Dalton Ave. Dalton Gardens, ID 83815-9631

McGowan, Frank, 12629 Howard Lodge Dr., Sykesville, MD 21784

McGrath, Gayle, 12641 Panasoffkee, N Ft. Myers, FL 33903

McLaran, Lou, 603 Powers St., Waco, TX 76705

McWilliams, Carole, P.O. Box 693, Bayfield, CO 81122

Mead, Faustina L., 2550 E. Mercury St., Inverness, FL 34453-0514 / 352-344-4751

Minnick, Joyce, 144 N. 7th St., Middletown, IN 47356

Mitchell, James, 1026 7th Ave., Columbus, GA 31901

Moore, James B., 1707 N. Gillis, Stockton, TX 79735

Ochonicky, Michelle Mike, 31 High Trail, Eureka, MO 63025

Ochs, Belle, 124 Emerald Lane, Largo, FL 33771 / 727-530-3826

Pachi, Mirella, Via Pometta 1, 17046 Sassello (SV), ITALY/ 019 720086

Pankova-Clark, Inna, P.O. Box 597, Andrews, NC 28901

Parish, Vaughn, 103 Cross St., Monaca, PA 15061

Peck, Larry H., 4021 Overhill Rd., Hannibal, MO 63401

Peterson, Lou, 514 S. Jackson St., Gardner, IL 60424

Poag, James H., RR #1 Box 212A, Grayville, IL 62844

Polk, Trena, 4625 Webber Creek Rd., Van Buren, AR 72956

Purvis, Hilton, P.O. Box 371, Noordhoek, 7985, REP. OF SOUTH AFRICA

Ramsey, Richard, 8525 Trout Farm Rd, Neosho, MO 64850

Raoux, Serge, 22 rue de Nohanent, 63100 Clermont-FD, FRANCE

Rece, Charles V., P.O. Box 868, Paw Creek, NC 28130

Riffe, Glen, 4430 See Saw Cir., Colorado Springs, CO 80917

Ristinen, Lori, P.O. Box 41, Wolf Lake, MN 56593

Roberts, J.J., 7808 Lake Dr., Manassas, VA 22111

Rodkey, Sheryl, 18336 Ozark Dr., Hudson, FL 34667

Rundell, Joe, 6198 W. Frances Rd., Clio, MI 48420

Saggio, Joe, 1450 Broadview Ave. #12, Columbus, OH 43212

Sahlin, Viveca, Lövhagsgatan 39, S-724 71 Västerås, SWEDEN

Satre, Robert, 518 3rd Ave. NW, Weyburn SK CANADA, S4H 1R1

Schlott, Harald, Zingster Str. 26, 13051 Berlin, 929 33 46, GERMANY

Schulenburg, E.W., 25 North Hill St., Carrollton, GA 30117

Schwallie, Patricia, 4614 Old Spartanburg Rd. Apt. 47, Taylors, SC 29687

Selent, Chuck, P.O. Box 1207, Bonners Ferry, ID 83805

Semich, Alice, 10037 Roanoke Dr., Murfreesboro, TN 37129

Sherwood, George, 46 N. River Dr., Roseburg, OR 97470

Shostle, Ben, 1121 Burlington, Muncie, IN 47302

Sinclair, W.P., 3, The Pippins, Warminster, Wiltshire BA12 8TH, ENGLAND

Smith, Peggy, 676 Glades Rd., #3, Gatlinburg, TN 37738

Smith, Ron, 5869 Straley, Ft. Worth, TX 76114

Smith, Jerry, 7029 East Holmes Rd., Memphis, TN 38125

Stahl, John, Images In Ivory, 2049 Windsor Rd., Baldwin, NY 11510 / 516-223-5007

Steigerwalt, Jim, RD#3 Sunbury, , PA 17801

Stuart, Stephen, 15815 Acorn Circle, Tavares, FL 32778 / 352-343-8423; Fax: 352-343-8916

Talley, Mary Austin, 2499 Countrywood Parkway, Cordova, TN 38018

Thompson, Larry D., 23040 Ave. 197, Strathmore, CA 93267

Tong, Jill, P.O. Box 572, Tombstone, AZ 85638

Toniutti, Nelida, Via G. Pascoli, 33085 Maniago-PN, ITALY

Tucker, Steve, 3518 W. Linwood, Turlock, CA 95380

Tyser, Ross, 1015 Hardee Court, Spartanburg, SC 29303

Veenstra, Gerry, 420 Wellington St., Apt. 206, St. Thomas, Ont. N5R 5P4, CANADA

Velasquez, Gil, Art of Scrimshaw, 7120 Madera Dr., Goleta, CA 93117

Walker, Karen, Star Route, Alpine, WY 83128

Warren, Al, 1423 Santa Fe Circle, Roseville, CA 95678

Williams, Gary, (Garbo), 221 Autumn Way, Elizabethtown, KY 42701

Winn, Travis A., 558 E. 3065 S., Salt Lake City, UT 84106

Young, Mary, 4826 Storeyland Dr., Alton, IL 62002

Zima, Russell, 7291 Ruth Way, Denver, CO 80221

miscellaneous

custom grinders

Forosisky, Nicholas, 1414 Solomon St., Johnstown, PA 15902-4203

High, Tom, Rocky Mountain Scrimshaw & Arts, 5474 S. 112.8 Rd., Alamosa, CO 81101

McGowan Manufacturing Company, 25 Michigan St., Hutchinson, MN 55350 / 800-342-4810; Fax: 320-587-7966

McLuin, Tom, 36 Fourth St., Dracut, MA 01826 / 978-957-4899

Peele, Bryan, The Elk Rack, 215 Ferry St. P.O. Box 1363, Thompson Falls, MT 59873

Wilson, R.W., P.O. Box 2012, Weirton, WV 26062

custom handle artisans

Cooper, Jim, 2148 Cook Pl., Ramona, CA 92065-3214 / 760-789-1097; Fax: 760-788-7992

Eccentric Endeavors, Michel Santos and Peggy Quinn, P.O. Box 97, Douglas Flat, CA 95229

Grussenmeyer, Paul G., 101 S. White Horse Pike, Linden-wold, NJ 08021-2304 / 856-435-1500; Fax: 856-435-3786

High, Tom, Rocky Mountain Scrimshaw & Arts, 5474 S. 112.8 Rd., Alamosa, CO 81101

Holden, Larry, PO Box 2017, Ridgecrest, CA 93556-2017

Holland, Dennis K., 4908-17th Pl., Lubbock, TX 79416

Imboden II, Howard L., hi II Originals, 620 Deauville Dr., Dayton, OH 45429

Kelso, Jim, 577 Collar Hill Rd, Worcester, VT 05682 / 802-229-4254; Fax: 802-223-0595

Knack, Gary, 309 Wightman, Ashland, OR 97520

Krogman, Pam, 838 Merlarkkey St., Winnemucca, NV 89445

Lee, Ray, 209 Jefferson Dr., Lynchburg, VA 24502

Lott, Sherry, 100 Mattie Jones Rd., Greensburg, KY 42743 / 270-932-3335

Marlatt, David, 67622 Oldham Rd., Cambridge, OH 43725 / 740-432-7549

Mead, Dennis, 2250 E. Mercury St., Inverness, FL 34453-0514

Miller, Robert, 216 Seminole Ave., Ormond Beach, FL 32176

Myers, Ron, 6202 Marglenn Ave., Baltimore, MD 21206 / 410-866-6914

Sayen, Murad, P.O. Box 127, Bryant Pond, ME 04219

Smith, D. Noel, P.O. Box 1363, Canon City, CO 81215-1363

Smith, Glen, 1307 Custer Ave., Billings, MT 59102

Snell, Barry A., 4801 96th St. N., St. Petersburg, FL 33708-3740

Vallotton, A., 621 Fawn Ridge Dr., Oakland, OR 97462

Watson, Silvia, 350 Jennifer Lane, Driftwood, TX 78619

Williams, Gary, (GARBO), 221 Autumn Way, Elizabethtown, KY 42701

Willson, Harlan M., P.O. Box 2113, Lompoc, CA 93438

display cases and boxes

American Display Company, 55 Cromwell St., Providence, RI 02904

Bill's Custom Cases, P.O. Box 2, Dunsmuir, CA 96025 / 530-235-0177; Fax: 530-235-4959

Brooker, Dennis, Rt. 1, Box 12A, Derby, IA 50068

Chas Clements' Custom Leathercraft, Chas, 1741 Dallas St., Aurora, CO 80010-2018 / 303-364-0403

Dennehy, John D., John-D Custom Leatherworks and Handmade Knives, P.O. Box 431 3926 Hayes Ave., Wellington, CO 80549-0431

Gimbert, Nelson, P.O. Box 787, Clemmons, NC 27012

Haydu, Thomas G., Tomway Products, 750 E Sahara Ave, Las Vegas, NV 89104 / 8884 Tomway; Fax: 702-366-0626

Mesa Case, Arne Mason, 125 Wimer St., Ashland, OR 97520 / 541-482-2260; Fax: 541-482-7785

directory

Miller, Robert, P.O. Box 2722, Ormond Beach, FL 32176

Miller, Michael K., M&M Kustom Krafts, 28510 Santiam Highway, Sweet Home, OR 97386

Retichek, Joseph L., W9377 Co. TK. D, Beaver Dam, WI 53916

Robbins, Wayne, 11520 Inverway, Belvidere, IL 61008

S&D Enterprises, 20 East Seventh St., Manchester, OH 45144 / 937-549-2602; Fax: 937-549-2602 or 2603

etchers

Baron Technology Inc., David Baron, 62 Spring Hill Rd., Trumbull, CT 06611

Eubank, Mary Ann, Rt. 1, Box 196, Pottsboro, TX 75076

Fountain Products, 492 Prospect Ave., West Springfield, MA 01089

Hayes, Dolores, P.O. Box 41405, Los Angeles, CA 90041

Holland, Dennis, 4908 17th Pl., Lubbock, TX 79416

Kelso, Jim, RD1, Box 5300, Worcester, VT 05682

Larstein, Francine, David Boye Knives Gallery, 111-B Marine View, Davenport, CA 95017 / 800-557-1525; Fax: 831-426-6048

Lefaucheux, Jean-Victor, Saint-Denis-Le-Ferment, 27140 Gisors, FRANCE

Leibowitz, Leonard, 1025 Murrayhill Ave., Pittsburgh, PA 15217

MacBain, Kenneth C., 30 Briarwood Ave., Norwood, NJ 07648

Miller, James K. and Vicky, American Etching, 22500 Hwy. 72, Tuscumbia, AL 35674

Myers, Ron, 6202 Marglenn Ave., Baltimore, MD 21206

Sayen, Murad, P.O. Box 127, Bryant Pond, ME 04219

Smith, Glen, 1307 Custer Ave., Billings, MT 59102

Vallotton, A., Northwest Knife Supply, 621 Fawn Ridge Dr., Oakland, OR 97462

Watson, Silvia, 350 Jennifer Lane, Driftwood, TX 78619

knife appraisers

Levine, Bernard, P.O. Box 2404, Eugene, OR 97402 / 541-484-0294

Russell, A.G., 1705 Hwy. 71 North, Springdale, AR 72764

Vallini, Massimo, Via Dello Scalo 2/3, 40131 Bologna, ITALY

organizations & publications

organizations

AMERICAN BLADESMITH SOCIETY
c/o Joseph G. Cordova, P.O. Box 977, Peralta, NM 87042/ 505-869-3912

If you're interested in the forged blade, you are welcome here. The Society has a teaching program, East and West, and awards stamps to Journeymen and Master smiths after they pass tests—tough tests at a hot forge. You don't have to make knives to belong. A list of knifemaker members appears on page 270.

AMERICAN KNIFE THROWERS ALLIANCE
c/o Bobby Branton, 4976 Seewee Rd., Awendaw, SC 29429

ART KNIFE COLLECTOR'S ASSOCIATION
c/o Mitch Weiss, Pres., 2211 Lee Road, Suite 104, Winter Park, FL 32789/407-740-8778; FAX: 407-649-7273; http://www.artknife.com; E-MAIL: mitch@artknife.com

The high-grade knife on the Internet with Web sites for everyone interested—makers and collectors.

AUSTRALIAN KNIFEMAKERS GUILD INC.
P.O. Box 659, Belgrave 3160, Victoria, Australia

The guild was formed by a group of dedicated custom knifemakers in 1984, with the express purpose of fostering the design, manufacture, sale and use of Australian made custom knives. A list of members appears on page 272.

CALIFORNIA KNIFEMAKERS GUILD
c/o Barry Evan Posner, Mbrshp. Chairman., 5222 Beeman Ave., N. Hollywood, CA 91607/818-980-7689. A list of members appears on page 272.

CANADIAN KNIFEMAKERS GUILD
c/o John Freeman, Sec./Treas., 160 Concession St., Cambridge, Ont. N1R 2H7 Canada/519-740-2767. Newly formed group—1994.

JAPANESE SWORD SOCIETY OF THE U.S.
P.O. Box 712, Breckenridge, TX 76424

They publish a newsletter bi-monthly and a bulletin once a year.

KNIFEMAKERS GUILD
c/o Billy Mace Imel, Sec./Treas., 1616 Bundy Ave., New Castle, IN 47362/765-529-1651; FAX: 765-521-8696

This continues to be the big one. The Guild has prospered, as have its members. It screens prospects to ensure they are serious craftsmen; and it runs a big show in New Orleans in July through year 2000, where over 250 Guild members show their best work, all in one room. Not all good knifemakers belong; some joined and later left for their own reasons; the Guild drops some for cause now and again. The Knifemakers Guild is an organization with a function. A list of Guild members appears on page 269.

KNIFEMAKERS GUILD OF SOUTHERN AFRICA, THE
c/o Bertie Rietveld, Chairman, P.O. Box 53, Magaliesburg, South Africa/+27142-771294.

MIDWEST KNIFEMAKERS ASSOCIATION
c/o Corbin Newcomb, Pres., 628 Woodland Ave., Moberly, MO 65270/816-263-4639

The MKA currently has a membership of 49 makers from 10 states in the Midwest. A list appears on page 273

MINIATURE KNIFEMAKERS' SOCIETY
c/o Gary F. Bradburn, Sec., 1714 Park Pl., Wichita, KS 67203/316-269-4273

The MKS is dedicated to improving the quality of custom miniature knives. The MKS welcomes miniature makers and collectors as members, publishes a bi-monthly newsletter, and awards miniature collectors who publicly show their collections. Send $1 for a list of members and an application. A list of knifemaker members appears on page 271.

THE MONTANA KNIFEMAKERS' ASSOCIATION
2608 Central Ave. West, Great Falls, MT 59404/406-727-9102. A list of members appears on page 273.

NORTH CAROLINA CUSTOM KNIFEMAKERS GUILD
c/o Tommy McNabb, Pres., 4015 Brownsboro Rd., Winston-Salem, NC 27106/910-759-0640. A list of members appears on page 273.

PROFESSIONAL KNIFEMAKERS ASSOCIATION
2905 N. Montana Ave., Ste. 30027, Helena, MT 59601/406-458-6552; E-MAIL: don-davis@csn.net; WEB: www.web2.com/pka. A list of members appears on page 272.

NEO-TRIBAL METALSMITHS
P.O. Box 44095, Tucson, AZ 85773-4095

The Neo-Tribal approach to metalsmithing combines ancient and modern tools, materials and techniques. It relies heavily on salvaged and recycled materials and the efficient use of both. The emphasis is on high quality and traditional hand craftsmanship.

REGIONAL ASSOCIATIONS
There are a number of state and regional associations with goals possibly more directly related to promotion of their members' sales than the Guild and the ABS. Among those known to us are the Arizona Knifemakers Association; the Arkansas Knifemakers Association; the South Carolina Association of Knifemakers; the New England Bladesmiths Guild; Ohio Knifemakers Association; and the Association of Southern Knifemakers. List of members of most of these may be found on page 272.

UNITED KINGDOM BLADE ASSOCIATION (UKBA)
P.O. Box 1, Brampton, CA67GD, England

Promotes the study of knives as a sensible and fascinating pastime.

publications

BLADE MAGAZINE

Krause Publications, 700 E. State St., Iola, WI 54990/800-272-5233

Editor: Steve Shackleford. Monthly. Official magazine of the knifemakers Guild. $3.25 on newsstand; $19.95 per year. Also publishes *Edges*, a quarterly ($12.95 for six issues); *Blade Trade*, a cutlery trade magazine; and knife books.

DBI BOOKS, a division of Krause Publications, Inc.

700 E. State St., Iola, WI 54990/715-445-2214; FAX: 715-445-4087

In addition to this *Knives* annual, DBI publishes *Gun Digest book of Knives*, by Jack Lewis and Roger Combs; *Knifemaking*, also by Lewis and combs; and *Levine's Guide to Knives* and Their Values, by Bernard Levine.

KNIFE WORLD

P.O. Box 3395, Knoxville, TN 37927/800-828-7751

Editor: Mark Zalesky. Monthly. Tabloid size on newsprint. Covers custom knives, knifemakers, collecting, old factory knives, etc. General coverage for the knife enthusiast. Subscription $15 year.

KNIVES ILLUSTRATED

265 S. Anita Dr., Ste. 120, Orange, CA 92868/714-939-9991

Editor; Bud Lang. $3.50 on newsstands; $14.95 for six issues. Plenty of four-color, all on cutlery; concentrates on handmade knives.

NATIONAL KNIFE MAGAZINE

P.O. Box 21070, Chattanooga, TN 37424/423-899-9456

For members of the National Knife Collectors Association. Emphasis on pocketknife collecting, of course, together with association show news. Membership $25 year; $28 for new members.

RESOURCE GUIDE AND NEWSLETTER / AUTOMATIC KNIVES

2269 Chestnut St., Suite 212, San Francisco, CA 94123/ 415-731-0210

Editor: Sheldon Levy. In its eighth year as a quarterly. Deep coverage of automatic folders. $30 year by mail.

TACTICAL KNIVES

Harris Publications, 1115 Broadway, New York, NY 10010/212-807-7100; FAX: 212-627-4678

Editor: Steve Dick. Aimed at emergency-service knife designs and users, this new publication has made a great start. Price $4.95; $14.95 for six issues. On newsstands.

TRIBAL NOW!

Neo-Tribal Metalsmiths, P.O. Box 44095, Tucson, AZ 85733-4095

Editor: Bill Randall. (See Neo-Tribal Metalsmith under Organizations.) Price: $10 per year for four issues with two- to four- page supplements sent out on a regular basis.

UK BLADE

United Kingdom Blade Associations, P.O. Box 1, Brampton CA67GD England

On a base of UK knifemakers, the UKBA, seeks to sweep the knife fancy of Britain all into one tent. Membership dues: Ordinary £16 year; husband and wife (one magazine) £20 year; trade £30 year. And they have no phone yet.

WEYER INTERNATIONAL BOOK DIVISION

2740 Nebraska Ave., Toledo, OH 43607, 419-534-2020, 419-534-2697

Publishers of the *Knives: Points of Interest* series. Sells knife-related books at attractive prices; has other knife-publishing projects in work.

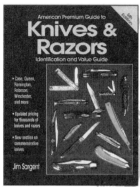

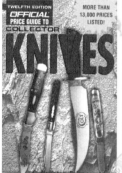
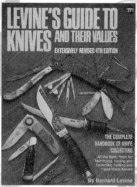

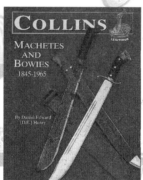

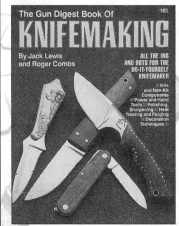
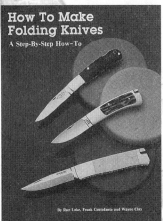
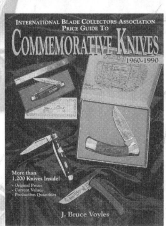
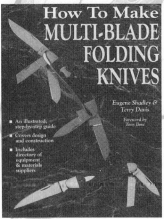
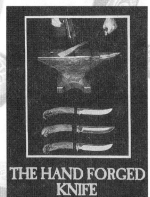